The Good Life Guide To Sydney

Tessa Mountstephens

HARK! PUBLICATIONS

The Good Life Guide To Sydney
1st Edition
ISBN 0 646 26645 4

Written and Photographed by Tessa Mountstephens
Architectural Notes Written by Kate Mountstephens
Designed by Bradley Seymour

First Published in 1996 by HARK! Publications
10 Torokina Avenue St Ives Sydney NSW 2075

Printed by Rotary Offset Press in Australia

HARK! Publications and the authors have made every effort to ensure the accuracy of all the information in *The Good Life Guide To Sydney*. However, they can accept no responsibility for any loss, injury or inconvenience sustained by any person using this book as a result of reliance on information or advice contained in this book. Reference in this book to any property does not imply a right of entry by the public or a right to encroach on the privacy of its owners or occupiers. All prices are in Australian dollars.

Many of you will come across some new and great establishments, and some old ones which have changed for the worse. Please let us know of any suggestions or corrections for inclusion in the next edition by writing to: HARK! Publications PO Box 211 St Ives NSW 2075. All enquiries regarding the publication should also be sent to this address.

Special Sales
The Good Life Guide To Sydney is available to companies and organisations for use as gifts. For more information, please contact HARK! Publications at the above address, or by telephone on (02) 449 4460.

National Library of Australia Cataloguing-in-Publication

Mountstephens, Tessa
The good life guide to Sydney.

Includes index.
ISBN 0 646 26645 4.

1. Sydney (N.S.W.) - Guidebooks.
2. Sydney (N.S.W.) - Description and travel. I. Title.

919.4410463

CONTENTS

READ THIS FIRST:

HOW TO USE THIS GUIDE

The Good Life Guide To Sydney is designed to give you the most out of Sydney in a straightforward way.

The chapters The Sydney Year, Sights To See, Sydney Icons and Sydney By Area are intended to give an introductory overview to the star attractions, precincts and activities of the city. Museums and galleries are listed in their own chapter. The chapters Walks Around Sydney and Tours Around Sydney detail various ways to discover the city, whether independently or as part of an organised tour. The chapters Shopping, Markets, Cafes, Food and Pubs contain specific listings in all major areas of the city, and are also listed in the Area By Area Directories. The city's open air lifestyle is covered in three chapters: Open Air Sydney, Bushwalks and Sports. Individual features on Children, Students, Disabled Visitors and Gay Sydney follow. Several Day Trips Out Of Sydney make up the next chapter, while, finally, practical advice and information is contained in the chapters A~Z Practical Basics, Transport and Accommodation, to help you find your way around the workings of the city. Finally,

How do you put it all together when you have only a vague idea of what to see and where it is?

If you follow the simple system below, the secrets of Sydney will be laid bare at you feet.

1. Read the History chapter, so that the historical references throughout the guide make sense. There is no point reading about the First Fleet if you think it's a car rental company. Scan the Sydney Year to see what is happening around the time you will be in Sydney. Examine the map, and get a feel for the lie of the land.

2. Read Sights To See, Sydney Icons and Sydney By Area to find what interests you and to get a feel for the city. Follow up the cross-references to find other ways of seeing the sight or area. Pay particular attention to relevant Walks and Tours.

3. Turn to Transport and consult the How To Get To The Sights & Suburbs By Public Transport.

4. Once there, check the relevant area's Directory for the names of nearby cafes, restaurants and pubs.

6. Find full details and descriptions of each in the Cafes, Food and Pubs chapters.

Remember that each entry in the guide is cross-referenced to other entries elsewhere in the guide regarding the same subject or attraction. However, if all else fails, try the index.

How To Read The Entries

The entries in the guide follow two patterns. These are as the following examples from the Sights To See and Food chapters show.

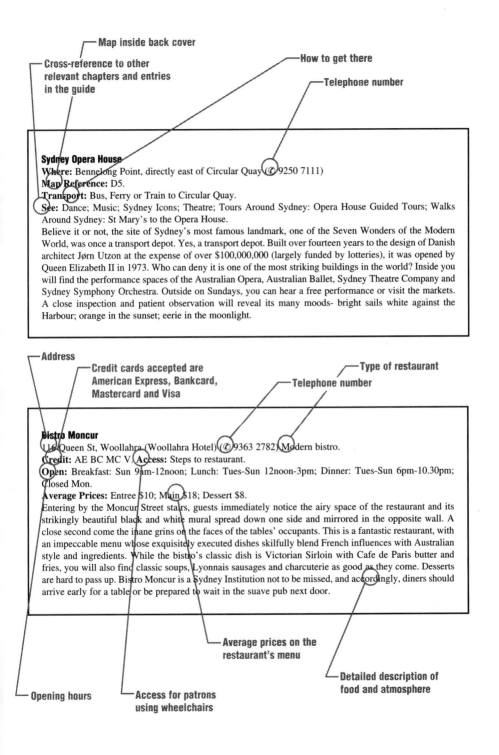

Map inside back cover

Cross-reference to other relevant chapters and entries in the guide

How to get there

Telephone number

Sydney Opera House
Where: Bennelong Point, directly east of Circular Quay (✆ 9250 7111)
Map Reference: D5.
Transport: Bus, Ferry or Train to Circular Quay.
See: Dance; Music; Sydney Icons; Theatre; Tours Around Sydney: Opera House Guided Tours; Walks Around Sydney: St Mary's to the Opera House.
Believe it or not, the site of Sydney's most famous landmark, one of the Seven Wonders of the Modern World, was once a transport depot. Yes, a transport depot. Built over fourteen years to the design of Danish architect Jørn Utzon at the expense of over $100,000,000 (largely funded by lotteries), it was opened by Queen Elizabeth II in 1973. Who can deny it is one of the most striking buildings in the world? Inside you will find the performance spaces of the Australian Opera, Australian Ballet, Sydney Theatre Company and Sydney Symphony Orchestra. Outside on Sundays, you can hear a free performance or visit the markets. A close inspection and patient observation will reveal its many moods- bright sails white against the Harbour; orange in the sunset; eerie in the moonlight.

Address

Credit cards accepted are American Express, Bankcard, Mastercard and Visa

Type of restaurant

Telephone number

Bistro Moncur
116 Queen St, Woollahra (Woollahra Hotel) (✆ 9363 2782) Modern bistro.
Credit: AE BC MC V. **Access:** Steps to restaurant.
Open: Breakfast: Sun 9am-12noon; Lunch: Tues-Sun 12noon-3pm; Dinner: Tues-Sun 6pm-10.30pm; Closed Mon.
Average Prices: Entree $10; Main $18; Dessert $8.
Entering by the Moncur Street stairs, guests immediately notice the airy space of the restaurant and its strikingly beautiful black and white mural spread down one side and mirrored in the opposite wall. A close second come the inane grins on the faces of the tables' occupants. This is a fantastic restaurant, with an impeccable menu whose exquisitely executed dishes skilfully blend French influences with Australian style and ingredients. While the bistro's classic dish is Victorian Sirloin with Cafe de Paris butter and fries, you will also find classic soups, Lyonnais sausages and charcuterie as good as they come. Desserts are hard to pass up. Bistro Moncur is a Sydney Institution not to be missed, and accordingly, diners should arrive early for a table or be prepared to wait in the suave pub next door.

Average prices on the restaurant's menu

Detailed description of food and atmosphere

Opening hours

Access for patrons using wheelchairs

A HISTORY OF SYDNEY

Imagine how they must have felt. Evicted from England in convict transport ships, six months of squalid conditions, disease and uncertainty on board, journeying to a land where there was not one single sign of familiar western life. No houses. No lights. Just a vast, seemingly untouched continent. However, the continent was already inhabited, and tragically, many of the faces which watched from amongst the trees as the strange white men arrived were to become casualties of British Imperialism. Still, from the moment the British flag was planted on Australian soil on 26 January 1788, Sydney began to grow from an accidental and unwilling group of less than a thousand convicts, sailors, troops, settlers and animals to become Australia's biggest and (arguably) best city, a cosmopolitan, gastronomic, sophisticated metropolis of over three million people.

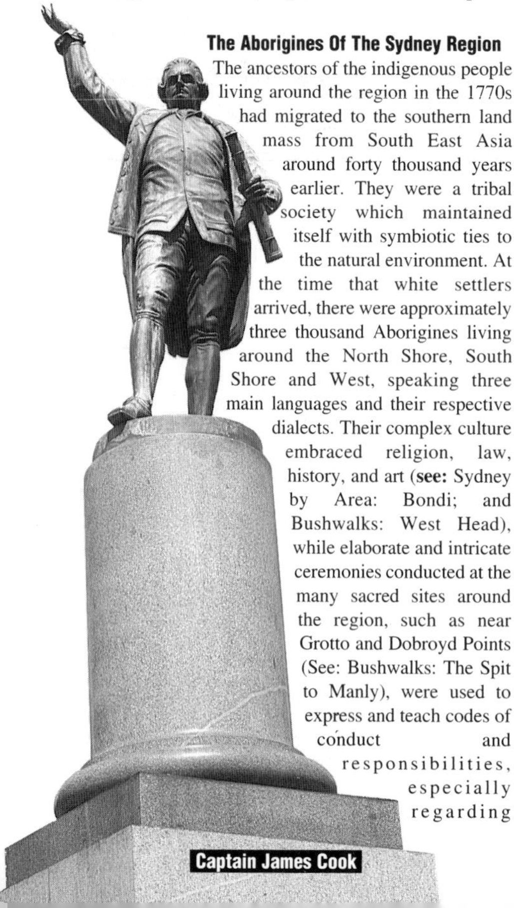

Captain James Cook

The Aborigines Of The Sydney Region

The ancestors of the indigenous people living around the region in the 1770s had migrated to the southern land mass from South East Asia around forty thousand years earlier. They were a tribal society which maintained itself with symbiotic ties to the natural environment. At the time that white settlers arrived, there were approximately three thousand Aborigines living around the North Shore, South Shore and West, speaking three main languages and their respective dialects. Their complex culture embraced religion, law, history, and art (**see:** Sydney by Area: Bondi; and Bushwalks: West Head), while elaborate and intricate ceremonies conducted at the many sacred sites around the region, such as near Grotto and Dobroyd Points (See: Bushwalks: The Spit to Manly), were used to express and teach codes of conduct and responsibilities, especially regarding the land and its bounty. It was this developed and sophisticated culture which the British negated when they invaded and declared that the continent was Terra Nullius: there was no system of law in operation and no owners of the land, and therefore, English law could be and was pronounced to be in force in its entirety. (For a wonderfully poetic representation of the Sydney region's Aboriginal heritage, See: Museums & Galleries: Museum of Sydney).

European Invasion and Settlement

Despite the common belief that the British discovered Australia, it was in fact the Dutch who were the first Europeans to see the Australian continent (1606, near Cape York Peninsula). Over the following decades, a number of Dutch navigators explored the west coast, among them Dirck Hartog, who placed a pewter plate on a tree in 1616. This is the oldest record of European contact with Australia, and is to be found in the Dutch National Museum in Amsterdam. Others filled in the puzzle of the continent's coastline until Abel Tasman sighted the east coast in 1642. As trading possibilities failed to materialise, the Dutch lost interest in the land they referred to as New Holland.

When Captain James Cook left England in 1768 to observe an eclipse in the Pacific, he was secretly instructed to search for the southern continent, map as much as possible of its coast, and claim "convenient situations" for Britain. He anchored in Botany Bay in April 1770, and continue northwards, nearly completing the mapping of the continent. (See: Statue of Cook in Hyde Park, City.)

The harsh criminal law of eighteenth century England had two extreme forms of punishment at its disposal:

death and transportation. However, while felons were continually being sentenced to transportation, American Independence (1783) had ruled out that country as a possible dumping ground for 'undesirables'. England's prisons were drastically overcrowded and bloated prison hulks floated in the country's waterways. Understandably, the verdant and sheltered bay on the great, 'uninhabited' southern continent presented an attractive prospect.

In 1787, seven hundred and fifty convicts, two hundred and eleven marines and officers, twenty-seven officers' wives, thirty-two children, Captain Arthur Phillip (See: statue in Botanic Gardens, City) and his staff of nine prepared to sail for Botany Bay. Their eleven ships sailed to Teneriffe, Rio de Janeiro and the Cape of Good Hope, bringing with them plants thought likely to grow in New South Wales such as coffee, cocoa, cotton, banana, orange and lemon, around five hundred animals and enough supplies to last two years. All contact with friends and families was cut off.

The Aborigines had no idea of what was about to hit them; the settlers, on the other hand, were expecting to find what Cook had enthusiastically described as lush pastures, meadows and a fine harbour, rather than the lacklustre, exposed, shallow bay which greeted them.

Such was their disappointment that Phillip left with three boats to look for a more suitable place to set up camp. On travelling north a short distance, he found hidden behind tall headlands what struck him as the finest harbour in the world, and chose the land surrounding a freshwater spring as the place to establish the settlement. It was only this cove which he honoured with the name of the Secretary of the Home Office, Lord Sydney; the settlement's planned name was Albion. Having moved the fleet to Sydney Cove, he stepped ashore into the thick wood on 26 January 1788 and hoisted the flag. The Australian continent became part of the British Empire, the flotsam of which was about to be unloaded onto its shores. (A replica of the flag that was hoisted by Phillip can be seen approximately in its original position in Loftus Street, City beside the Customs House opposite Circular Quay. See also: Museums: Museum of Sydney: installation facing Bridge Street.)

They soon began to set up camp on either side of the Tank Stream, which now debouches by the western most quay of Circular Quay, with the officers on the east and the convicts on the west. Orders that the Aborigines were to be treated with respect, care and friendship were given, a somewhat ironic command considering they had just dispossessed them of their land.

Europeanisation

As the Europeans came to terms with their new environment, it must have been a staggering realisation that aside from their tiny scrap of settlement, there was nothing but darkness on the entire continent. The isolation fostered a general sense of doom and destitution when coupled with the hunger and deprivation wrought by failed crops, low supplies, and a total absence of communication with the civilised world. Meanwhile, the Aborigines were appalled by the white people's apparent intention to stay and began a campaign of resistance. In response, Phillip set about convincing them of the supposedly great benefits European civilisation would bring.

Captain Arthur Phillip

Governor Phillip also formulated a plan to create a colony worthy of membership of the British Empire: free settlers, officers and worthy emancipists must be assigned land and enough convicts to work it. However, he would have to overcome water shortage, wretched living conditions, rationing, drought, drunkenness and loose morals in order to succeed, and the battle broke his health and spirit. He returned to England in 1792, leaving Major Grose in charge.

Rum & Growth (1792 - 1810)

To ensure his support, Major Grose installed the military into all important official functions and allocated many land grants in an attempt to increase food production. Yet most of the land under cultivation rested in the hands of a privileged few who used convicts as their slaves. As ships arrived in port, officers would audaciously take what they wanted and soon operated a trade monopoly. The New South Wales Corps was quickly dubbed *The Rum Corps*, and the spirit became the colony's universal barter. With land, power and money in their hands, the Rum Corps effectively held

Sydney in a stranglehold, overpowering Governors Hunter and King who followed, and even arresting Governor Bligh in the Rum Rebellion of 1808.

Meanwhile, the inevitable battle for social standing and economic power was raging between officers and convicts, Catholics and Protestants, wealthy traders and wealthy pastoralists. Free settlers such as John Macarthur, a successful pioneer of merino flocks and founder of Australia's wool industry, made it clear that the colony offered great opportunities, and with encouraged by offers of free passage, large land grants and convicts to work it, the population began to grow.

There were also possibilities for ex-convicts, once reformed. If granted a ticket of leave, they were released and could be engaged in any lawful occupation for their own advantage. Particularly worthy cases, often political transportees, were often awarded a conditional or absolute pardon and could apply for a land grant if they chose to stay. Many went on to become wealthy, which outraged those with fixed ideas of social status and hierarchy.

However, of greatest concern to the British was the power of the Rum Corps, and so Lachlan Macquarie was dispatched with his own regiment to take control as Governor. Once in Sydney, he crushed the Rum Corps' stranglehold and set about instigating social reform, converting the temporary penal settlement to a grand town in the process.

The Age Of Governor Macquarie (1810-1821)

Macquarie turned the concept of the rum monopoly to Sydney's advantage by transferring it to three contractors who were to build Sydney a hospital using the profits. During his eleven year governorship, the population grew rapidly; land under cultivation grew fourfold; heads of sheep and cattle rocketed; the Bank of New South Wales (now Westpac) was formed, as was a police force; roads and bridges were constructed; horse racing and cart registration were introduced; and convicts were forced to attend church. With architect Francis Greenway (transported in 1814 for forging a signature following a business collapse), he set about giving Sydney many of its most beautiful buildings, such as the Hyde Park Barracks and St James Church (See: Walks Around Sydney: Macquarie Street).

However, Macquarie's grand vision was perceived as reckless extravagance by the British who disapproved greatly of the construction of ornamental and expensive buildings in the convict settlement. Macquarie was roundly castigated by the Bigge Report, condemnation which was supported by those opposed to his programs of emancipation and liberalisation, especially those who wished still to have large land grants and convict labour at their disposal. So it was that despite the great progress made during his governorship, Macquarie was replaced and left Sydney, later dying in poverty in London (1824), feeling he had not received recognition for his work. He is greatly appreciated today, as are his ideas which are visible throughout the city.

1820s to 1850s: A Growing Spirit.

Governor Lachlan Macquari

In the following years, further advances and improvements were made by the Europeans: a Legislative Council was appointed (1824); a turf club was established in 1825, as were a subscription library and public library (1826); and cricket began to be played regularly, a vast improvement on Sydney's pre-existing leisure pursuits such as cow racing in Hyde Park, bare knuckle fights, cock fighting and ratting. There was large scale shipping activity in the Harbour, drinking activity in the town's one hundred and ninety-seven pubs and illegal drinking dens, and the Rocks became a 'badlands' of vice. Dubious as it was, this activity fostered a spirit of independence. *The Sydney Morning Herald* was first published in April 1831, the colony's first free press; transportation ended in 1840, helped by the efforts of anti-transportation campaigners; and in 1842, *An Act to declare the Town of Sydney to be a City and to incorporate the Inhabitants thereof* was passed. People started moving out to the 'suburbs' of Double Bay, St Leonards and Elizabeth Bay as the population grew towards fifty thousand. The first elections for the Legislative Council took place in 1843, and it finally seemed that Sydney had become something more than a collection of outcasts living in exile. They were beginning to forge their own destiny.

The Gold Rush of the 1850s.

The large quantities of gold found near Bathurst in 1851 drew people from all over the world to Sydney. However, as most of the larger finds were in Victoria, Melbourne boomed to become the largest city in Australia, and remained so until the depression of the 1890s. Sydney could not keep up despite a high level of energy in the city: the Stock Exchange appeared; trading increased; the first train ran between Sydney and Parramatta in 1855; the University of Sydney was built. In short, Sydney was transformed, and social changes came too.

This frenetic activity continued into the next three decades, as steam trams were introduced; omnibuses criss-crossed the city; cultural pursuits such as theatres and art galleries appeared; and the enormous International Exhibition was held. Yet, as the century drew to a close, two sour tastes appeared: a distrust of the sizeable Chinese community, and economic depression. Calls for the separate colonies to federate began to get louder. Under the cries of "One People, One Nation, One Destiny", Australians considered the advantages that federation could bring.

The Turn of the 20th Century

New Year's Day 1901 saw the inauguration of the Commonwealth of Australia, and with it the colony of New South Wales became a State of the new Australian nation, and Sydney its capital. In a curious contrast, an outbreak of Bubonic Plague, traced to the docks below The Rocks, instigated widespread quarantining, cleaning, rat catching and the demolition of many buildings. Yet, development went on: a reservoir was constructed, electric light replaced gaslight, and women got the vote in 1903. Meanwhile, agitation for an alternative way to cross the Harbour was increasing, and the planning and discussion of bridge possibilities continued over the next twenty years.

English social restrictions were gradually being thrown off, as women rode horses in trousers, and daylight bathing became accepted. Despite increasing independence from England, a national sense of loyalty and a desire to show Australia's maturity as a nation dictated that Australian troops would fight the allied cause in the First World War. But more than anything, the war was a catalyst for the emergence of a strong Australian identity, in turn allowing the emergence of political identities.

Between The Wars

Expansion and development continued until the Great Depression brought widespread unemployment and poverty; however, work continued on the most conspicuous public project of the period: the Harbour Bridge. The realisation of John Job Crew Bradfield's design was one of the most expensive and impressive engineering feats of the period, and a sense of anticipation grew as the two massive arches approached each other in the centre and finally met on 19 August 1930. The Coat Hanger was finally opened in August 1932. However, the depression had caused political tension, and the social conscience of the city had been shocked.

Second World War

The impression of Sydney's remoteness finally dissipated as Australian troops went off to fight in the Pacific: Sydney suddenly realised it was not alone in the region and felt vulnerable, and a boom and net barrier was erected across the Harbour entrance between Camp Cove and the North Shore to protect the city and the United States fleet base. Nevertheless, 1942 saw two attempted attacks on Sydney by Japanese midget submarines and their parent ship. Yet, one of the most intense lasting effects of the war on Sydney was the attack on Australian social norms brought about by the strong American presence in the city. Sydney became cosmopolitan.

Post War

The city spread rapidly as immigrants swelled the population. However, as the post war decades continued to be dominated by an Americanised way of life and increased American political influence, it was not surprising that the Australian government committed troops to the Vietnam war in the 1960s. As the conflict dragged on, the use of conscription to amass troops provoked major civil unrest which saw Sydney's streets blocked with demonstrators on several occasions.

Meanwhile, the City's sedate, old buildings were gradually shrinking into dwarfs amongst the multiplying high rises. The evolution of the Opera House over the 1960s and 1970s into one of the world's great buildings took place as the pulse of the city's life quickened. Simultaneously, the degree of internationalisation evident in the city increased as the members of all the various cultural groups continued to contribute their own cultural elements into the mixing pot. As an indirect result of this multicultural society, the 1980s and 1990s fostered the development of a particularly Australian style of food, incorporating the flavours and influences of many different cuisines. In the current decade, Sydney has become a food lover's paradise, the main exponent of the Modern Australian cuisine. Over these past decades, steps towards reconciliation with the Aborigines were begun and necessarily still continue, yet it is shameful that it was not until 1992 that the fundamentally flawed presumption of Terra Nullius was finally overturned by the High Court of Australia in the famous Mabo decision.

Today, Sydney sees itself as the brightest, most colourful, most confident, most modern, most brashly commercial, most sophisticated, most vibrant and most diverse city in Australia, an opinion held not entirely without basis.

Throughout the course of this tumultuous change, the Harbour has been the stage on and around which all these events have taken place; the beaches, once undefiled and unadulterated, now form the centre of an energetic and brassy culture; the intensity of nature's colours now faces stiff competition from the neon and glitz. As a symbol of Western impact on the landscape of Sydney, the Harbour Bridge and Opera House are more than appropriate. On one hand, they appear incongruous, overpowering the Harbour with their giant scale; yet on the other hand, they suit the confident brashness of the city and the craziness of its people, and bestows the dazzling harbour with a worthy focus.

Thomas Mort

A CHRONOLOGY

c. 40,000 BC Aborigines moved to land mass from South East Asia; recorded history on the continent begins.

1760 George III succeeds his grandfather, George II, as King of Great Britain and her colonies.

1770 Captain James Cook sails past a wide bay on the eastern coast of the largely unmapped great southern continent and claims it for England. Botany Bay is named for the variety of unknown species recorded there by Joseph Banks.

1783 Treaty of Paris finalises American Independence; English convicts can no longer be sent to that country.

1787 736 convicts, 211 officers, 27 officers' wives and 32 children leave England in 11 ships under the command of Captain Arthur Phillip "bound for Botany Bay" and known as the First Fleet.

1788 The First Fleet arrives at Botany Bay but quickly abandons it in favour of Sydney Cove where they set up camp to establish a penal colony which was to be called Albion. The British Flag is raised on 26 January near Circular Quay and the colony of New South Wales is established, dispossessing Aborigines of their land.

1793 After surviving desperation and starvation, the original settlers and convicts are joined on the empty continent by small numbers of free settlers. By this stage, the name Sydney has been adopted in practice and rum has become the currency of the colony.

1810 Despite numerous setbacks and the unlikelihood of survival, the population has climbed to 10,000. Governor Lachlan Macquarie has begun curbing the power of the Rum Corps and making his grand vision of Sydney a reality. Over the next decade, many of Sydney's elegant colonial buildings are constructed.

1811 George IV commences rule of Great Britain as Prince Regent during his father's supposed derangement.

1813 Explorers Blaxland, Wentworth and Lawson finally find a way across the Blue Mountains, west of Sydney, and desperately needed farming land is made available.

1817 Governor Macquarie proposes that the continent, then known as New Holland, should be renamed Australia, as suggested by ex-convicts and emancipists.

1819 Population reaches 26,000.

1820 The Prince Regent succeeds his father as King and becomes known as George IV.

1830 King William IV ascends the throne on the death of his brother, George IV.

1831 British government assistance of settlers begins, a program which helps and encourages over 70,000 free settlers to move to Sydney in the course of the next decade. The independent *Sydney Morning Herald* is first published.

1837 On the death of her uncle, William IV, Queen Victoria commences rule of Great Britain and its colonies.

1840 Transportation of convicts to Australia ends as a result of vigorous campaigning by anti-transportation groups.

1842 Sydney becomes a city under *An Act to declare the Town of Sydney to be a City and to incorporate the Inhabitants thereof*. The following year, the first elections for the Legislative Council of New South Wales are held.

1861-1891 Population reaches 96,000 and climbs steeply in the next thirty years to 383,283, on the back of the Gold Rush, before Depression sets in.

1901 The six colonies of the continent are united as The Commonwealth of Australia, a federation of States. Soon after, an outbreak of Bubonic Plague in The Rocks causes widespread demolition and clearing of the area.
Queen Victoria dies and her eldest son, Edward VII, takes the throne after a sixty year apprenticeship as Prince of Wales.

1902 Daylight bathing at beaches is finally allowed, and the first Surf Bathers' Life Saving Club is formed four years later at Bondi.

1910 George V becomes King on the death of his father, Edward VII.

1923 Construction of the Harbour Bridge begins, designed by John Job Crew Bradfield.

1925 Sydney becomes a metropolis with the population reaching 1,000,000.

19 August 1930 The two arcs of the Harbour Bridge meet in the middle.

1932 The biggest public work of the period, the Harbour Bridge, is completed and opened in August amid great celebration.

1936 Edward VIII takes the throne but abdicates in December when his younger brother, George VI, becomes King.

1939-1949 The war period brings ends Australia's isolation

A CHRONOLOGY

and brings American culture and lifestyle to Sydney. Immigrants from all over Europe arrive, and begin the process of cultural interaction. Sydney begins to lose its predominantly Anglo-Saxon culture, and becomes cosmopolitan. Steaming espresso machines herald the arrival of the Italians.

1952 George VI dies and the current Queen, Elizabeth II, takes the throne.

1962 The Federal Parliament of Australia gives Aborigines the right to vote, 174 years after they had been dispossessed of their land.

1963 Sydney's population reaches 2,000,000.

1973 The Opera House, designed by Danish architect Jørn Utzon, is officially opened after years of construction and controversy. Here to open the building, Queen Elizabeth II becomes the first reigning English monarch to visit the country.

1988 Bicentenary of European settlement celebrated widely, with the Harbour and a re-enactment of the First Fleet's arrival (or invasion) forming the centre of celebrations and arguments about Aboriginal Land Rights.

1993 Sydney erupts into a giant, spontaneous party after win ning the right to host the 2000 Olympic Games.

1995 Population reaches 3,700,000. Pyrmont Bridge is opened in December. Sydney continues its preparations for the 2000 Olympics.

Explorer, WC Wentworth

THE SYDNEY YEAR

The climate in Sydney is so consistently mild that the theatres and cultural activities must compete with the open air lifestyle every month of the year for the locals' attentions. Apart from the following listings, you will find symphony concerts and theatre performances taking place year round. However, when the temperature rises, the city's pace goes into overdrive. Summer (December to February) is the busiest time for festivals and visitors, although those who cannot bear heat and humidity should plan their trip in Spring or Autumn. This chapter includes brief listings of the annual events comprising the social, cultural and sporting life of the city. Full details can be found as indicated in other chapters of the guide. To be sure of exact dates, contact the New South Wales Travel Centre (19 Castlereagh St, City; ✆ 13 20 77), which produces an annual calender.

SPRING

Spring weather can be very variable and unreliable in Sydney, as the city shakes off its winter mantle and prepares for the big time heat of the summer. Cool days may be shocked by the occasional hot spell, and the warming sun begins to clear the rains of winter. Sydney's European trees become vibrantly green, contrasting with the evergreen brown-green of the Australian native vegetation. As the weather improves, a few optimistic souls begin to appear on the beaches.

September

The Botanic Gardens Spring Festival (all month) celebrates the coming of Spring with four weeks of events (**See:** Open Air Sydney).

The Festival of the Winds (second weekend) sees Bondi Beach erupt into airborne colour in all shapes and sizes (**See:** Open Air Sydney).

Rugby League and Rugby Union competitions culminate (all month) in gladiatorial finals and grand finals at the Football Stadium (**See:** Sports).

The **Australian Opera's winter season** continues at the Opera House.

October

The Manly Jazz Festival (first weekend) makes the Labour Day long weekend one of the busiest of the year for the seaside suburb (**See:** Music).

Over the Harbour, the **Sydney Opera House** holds its annual Open Day and Pageant.

The winter season of the **Australian Opera** finishes.

November

The **Melbourne Cup** (first Tuesday) is the horse race of the year, even though it is in Melbourne.

The Uncle Toby's **Iron Man competition** takes place on one of Sydney's many beaches, with swimming, paddling, running and board riding selecting the ultimate endurance athlete.

The sporty flavour of November continues with the opening of the **cricket test** season at the Sydney Cricket Ground (**See:** Sports).

SUMMER

With the heat and humidity peaking in January, Sydney rediscovers its love affair with the beach. With five public holidays in December and January, vacations are on everybody's mind, and the city gets over its Festive Season hang over by cranking up the partying again as the Sydney Festival rolls into town. Open air concerts in balmy evenings complete the picture of this, Sydney's most enjoyable season.

December

The **Australian Ballet** has a short summer season at the Opera House (**See:** Dance).

Cricket fever continues as the **world series** one day matches get under way at the Sydney Cricket Ground (**See:** Sports).

Carols By Candlelight (second week) draws thousands to The Domain for a giant open air Christmas celebration (**See:** Music).

The **Sydney to Hobart Yacht Race** (26 January) leaves from the Harbour in a flurry of colour and spectators (**See:** Sports).

January

Australia Day (26 January) is celebrated all over the city, but especially on the Harbour, to commemorate the landing of the First Fleet in 1788 (**See:** History).

The **Sydney Festival** (all month) sees theatrical and musical performances and events attract great crowds throughout the city (**See:** Music; Theatre).

The summer season of the **Australian Opera** begins at the Opera House and continues until mid March (**See:** Music).

The **NSW Tennis Open** attracts international and local stars to White City in the lead up to the Australian Open in Melbourne (**See:** Sport).

Meanwhile, **cricket finals** wrap up the season at the Sydney **Cricket** Ground (**See:** Sports).

The more informal **Sydney Fringe Festival** (Information © 9365 7271) hosts a variety of dance, theatre, music, film and visual arts events, such as the open air Flickerfest, a series of short films from around the world.

Opera in the Park, Jazz in the Park and Symphony under the Stars (all month) are the biggest open air concerts of the year, all held in the Domain and all completely free (**See:** Music).

February

Chinese New Year (variable) is celebrated with dragon parades and celebrations in Chinatown and Darling Harbour (**See:** Sydney By Area).

The Sydney Gay and Lesbian **Mardi Gras Festival** (all month) kicks off with a host of events centred around Darlinghurst (**See:** Gay Sydney).

Over in Darlinghurst, the **Tropicana Short Film Festival** (usually middle Sunday) sees a day of intense creativity (**See:** Film).

The **Australian Opera** continues its summer season at the Opera House (**See:** Music).

AUTUMN

As the humidity begins slowly to dissipate, the air cools and the weather settles into a very pleasant and (usually) stable pattern, although summer sometimes makes a last stand to scare the cooler weather away. The Mardi Gras festival culminates in the world famous parade, and the theatrical and musical activity of the city's cultural institutions quickens.

March

The Gay & Lesbian **Mardi Gras Parade** (first weekend) is an international draw card of great exuberance (**See:** Gay Sydney).

The **Sydney Comedy Festival** (all month) sees many comedy acts spread over a number of pubs and theatres.

As the **Opera** summer season finishes, **Musica Viva's** concert series begins (**See:** Music) and the **Australian Ballet** commences its winter season and continues until May (**See:** Dance).

ANNUAL PUBLIC HOLIDAYS:

New Year's Day (1 January)
Australia Day Holiday (1st Monday after 26 January)
Good Friday (Friday before Easter)
Easter Monday (Monday after Easter)
Anzac Day (25 April)
Queen's Birthday Holiday long weekend (usually 2nd Monday in June)
Bank Holiday (1st Monday in June; banks closed)
Labour Day (Monday after 1st weekend in October)
Christmas Day (25 December)
Boxing Day (26 December)

The annual fundraiser, **Walk Against Want** (fourth week) gets thousands out on the streets.

At the Art Gallery of New South Wales, the **Archibald, Wynne and Sulman prizes** are judged, awarded and displayed (**See:** Museums & Galleries).

St Patrick's Day (17 March) is celebrated with free-flowing consumption of Guinness in The Rocks (**See:** Pubs) and a parade through the City.

The **Easter Show** (otherwise known as the Sydney Royal Agricultural Show) (third week to April) begins, with animals and agricultural produce on show, and hair-raising rides.

Horse fiends head for the Autumn Carnival **Golden Slipper** Horse Racing festival at Randwick and Canterbury Park (**See:** Sports).

April

Heritage Week (mid month) sees the National Trust leading many tours and walks around historic houses and properties (**See:** Tours Around Sydney).

Petrol heads flock to the **Australian Motor Cycle Grand Prix** at Eastern Creek.

Anzac Day (25 April) is the annual commemoration of Australian soldiers of all wars, and is marked by parades, ceremonies and a public holiday.

Horse Racing continues all month with the glamorous **Autumn Carnival.**

The **Australian Ballet** and **Musica Viva** continue at the Opera House.

May

As Sydney slips into winter, sport takes over as the city's main activity, and the **State of Origin** rugby series begins (all month).

The **Sydney Half Marathon** (mid May) dashes between The Rocks, Farm Cove and Darling Harbour.

The **Australian Ballet** wraps up its winter season at the Opera House (**See:** Dance).

WINTER

Those not interested in football have plenty of other things to occupy them through the cold months, and as the weather luckily does not get uncomfortably cold, open air activities can continue. However, there is plenty of competition for Sydneysiders' attention indoors.

June

The **Sydney Film Festival** (usually second and third weeks) brings bleary-eyed film addicts to the State Theatre for almost continuous features and documentaries (**See:** Film).

Every even year sees the Australian Arts **Biennale** take place (all month), with exhibitions centred around the Art Gallery Of New South Wales (**See:** Museums and Galleries).

The winter season of the **Australian Opera** commences at the Opera House and continues until October (**See:** Music).

Out on the water, Sail Cancer's **Three Island Race** around Scotland, Dangar and Lion Islands on Pittwater

CLIMATE

Sydney's climate is generally pleasant all year round, with a temperate Autumn (March to May); a mild winter (June to August); a warm, dry Spring (September to November); and a hot, humid Summer (December to February). However, don't think of Sydney as a permanent tropical paradise. Averages can belie the extremes of temperature which often besiege Sydney in summer, when the city can swelter under 35° (or higher) heat, and in winter, when the city shivers at 6°C. Spring and Autumn days can see-saw unexpectedly between hot and cool.

Rain

It rarely drizzles in Sydney: when it does rain, it pours. Despite the high rainfall levels, the result is many sunny days and an enjoyable climate. Spring is the driest season (229mm), followed by Summer (301mm), then comes Winter (312mm), and Autumn (382mm) is the wettest. The summer months of November to February are the most active for thunderstorms. Don't forget to bring a small umbrella.

Sun

Ultra-violet radiation from the sun is often extreme in the months between November and March, when a hat and SPF 15+ sun screen should be worn outside. During mid-summer, the beach (and sun in general) should be avoided between 11.30am and 3pm.

What clothing is comfortable in this climate?

For all seasons, a lightweight rain and wind jacket will be useful.

Spring: cotton and wool sweaters; heavy cotton clothing;

Summer: lightweight cotton or fine wool clothing; cotton sweater; light shirts and t-shirts;

Autumn: cotton and wool sweater; waterproof shoes; heavy cotton clothing;

Winter: waterproof shoes; wool sweaters; a mid-weight jacket; wool and heavy cotton clothing.

Month	°C Min & Max Temp	°F Conversion	Rain Days	Rain (mm)	Daily Sunshine Hours
Jan	19-26	69-82	13	103	7.5
Feb	19-26	69-82	13	118	7.3
Mar	18-25	66-80	14	134	7
Apr	15-23	61-76	13	128	6.6
May	12-20	55-71	13	120	5.8
Jun	10-18	51-67	12	131	6.1
Jul	8-17	48-65	11	100	6.5
Aug	8-17	50-67	11	81	7.8
Sept	11-20	53-71	11	69	7.9
Oct	14-22	59-75	12	78	8.1
Nov	16-24	62-77	12	82	8.2
Dec	18-25	67-80	12	80	7.2

takes place (**See:** Sports).

Skiers start thinking about organising the annual pilgrimage to the Snowy Mountains, beginning with the **Opening of the Ski Season** at the region's resorts.

Bandemonium (from the Queen's Birthday Holiday long weekend) sees Darling Harbour erupt into a festival of jazz, rock, folk, country and world music, continuing until mid July.

July

The **Australian Opera's** winter season continues at the Opera House (**See:** Music).

Paddington celebrates with the **Paddington Festival of Arts & Heritage.**

Festival fever continues with the **Sydney Quilt Festival** (!) at Darling Harbour (Usually mid July).

Darling Harbour hosts the Sydney International Boat Show and Dive Tourism Expo at the Sydney Exhibition Centre.

Yuletide or **Christmas in July** celebrations heat up the Blue Mountains.

The **Sydney International Piano Competition** (mid July) sees some of the world's most promising pianists in town.

The **Rugby League season** continues all over Sydney, as do 'Aussie Rules' matches.

August

The **City to Surf** (second Sunday) is the biggest community sporting event in Australia, in which over forty thousand participants run, walk or are carried fourteen kilometres from Hyde Park to Bondi Beach.

The **Australian Opera** winter season continues at the Opera House.

Footy fever continues to dominate the city's sporting arenas.

The seasons of the **Sydney Symphony Orchestra** and **Australian Chamber Orchestra** continue, mainly at the Opera House.

Performances by the **Sydney Theatre Company** continue at The Wharf and the Opera House.

SYDNEY ICONS

There are certain things which at once embody and create the essence and character of Sydney. Many of them are distinctly odd. To find full details of the following icons, turn to the chapters referred to below, or the index.

The Beach

See: Open Air Sydney: Beaches; Sights To See: Bondi Beach; Sydney By Area; Tours Around Sydney: Bondi & Bay Explorer, Northern Beaches & Pittwater; Walks Around Sydney: Bronte-Bondi Cliff Walk.

With over thirty kilometres of Sydney's coast dripping with broad stretches of golden sand, it is to be expected that the beach plays a major part in the life of the city. In fact, there is an entire beach culture. Daylight bathing was not permitted here until 1902, and propriety was maintained at all other times by the inclusion in men's neck-to-knee swimming costumes of the riotously named skirt, the "modesty panel". The famous Speedos first appeared in the late 1920s, although male torsos were not legally bared until the 1930s; bashfulness was overcome by the 1950s when the little 'spray on' briefs which now grace our sand became regulation garb. For all, the beach should involve the "Slip Slop Slap" ritual of applying SPF 15+ blockout, donning a hat, sunglasses and a shirt, and avoiding the beach between from 11am to 3pm in summer. Once on the sand, the ritual involves marking out a territory with a towel; obtaining an ice cream; watching that ice cream melt down the hand and arm of the eater; coating the creamy mess with sand; going for a swim (while avoiding rips and dumpers) to wash it off; and finally, lying down on the towel to dry, enjoying the colourful scene all around.

Bondi Beach And The Icebergs

See: Sights To See: Bondi Beach; Sydney By Area: Bondi Beach; Tours Around Sydney: Bondi & Bay Explorer; Walks Around Sydney: Bronte-Bondi Cliff Walk.

If only the tip of an iceberg is visible above the surface, what lies beneath? In the case of this mysteriously exclusive winter swimming club, established in 1929 at the southern end of Australia's most famous beach, images of a secret society qualified by tortuous ice rituals and eccentric patterns of behaviour come to mind. Each year, the season is opened by the club president sitting on a throne of ice, challenging intending members to brave the initiation ritual of swimming four consecutive winter weekends out of five. Apart from that, the club is really quite normal. The pool itself is open to the public, although the secretive members only area upstairs is not accessible. It is probably just as well: while the average age of members is said to be under forty, a lot of the older men enjoy nude sunbaking (perfecting the colour of deeply tanned leather) on the private verandah, sheltered from public view.

Cafe Society

See: Cafes; Sydney By Area: Darlinghurst, Paddington.

The amounts of coffee consumed in Sydney are staggering, but it was not always so. Tea was almost exclusively Australia's favourite hot beverage until the waves of European immigrants brought the espresso to Sydney in the 1950s. The spread of the steam pressure espresso machine became a demographic and cultural indicator of the city's changing population. Gradually, Sydneysiders became more relaxed about the concept of the cafe as ambience and recreation, and today represents a very important part of Sydney's social culture, while specialist cafes attract fidelities similar to those of the most die-hard beer connoisseurs. Take a caffeine dependent Sydneysider out of this cafe heaven, and chances are that desperate searches for a glimpse of an espresso machine or the sound of steam swirling through milk will be appeased only by free-flowing consumption. Hail Bo Ema, Gaggia, Rancillio!

The Gap

See: Open Air Sydney: Picnics; Sydney By Area: Watsons Bay; Tours Around Sydney: Bondi & Bay Explorer.

It was the wrecking of *The Dunbar* in 1857, leaving just one survivor from over one hundred passengers, which first earned South Head its macabre reputation. As P.R. Stephensen wrote in his book, *The History of Sydney Harbour*, it was enhanced by its popularity with those seeking a solution to their problems in the wave-lashed rocks far below the cliffs. During the 1930s depression, many Sydneysiders spent their last few pence on a one-way tram fare to The Gap, while others took the cheaper option of "going over the bridge", although why they bothered to save money at that point is a mystery. The alarmingly high number of suicides at the Gap not only caused concern, it caused logistical difficulties: how to get down the cliffs safely to recover the bodies? The Cliff Rescue Unit was formed in 1942 and gradually mutated into the Police Rescue Squad with much wider rescue duties, and today the subject of an internationally screened television series. The Gap, macabre as it is, today has a special place in Sydney's psyche!

Gowings & their $5 haircut

See: Shopping; Walks Around Sydney.

"Walk through, no-one asked to buy" reads the sign on the awning of this Sydney Icon on the corner of Market and George Streets, City. Gowings' success in supplying Sydney blokes and boys with shorts, socks, shirts, ties, hats and other 'gear' spans over one hundred and twenty-five years, and no doubt reflects the perverse pleasure to be had in rummaging around this independent and specialised department store. The phrase "Gone to Gowings" was introduced as a publicity slogan during the second world war, and immediately entered the vernacular: when notorious criminal Darcy Dugan escaped from jail in 1940, he simply scribbled "Gone to Gowings" on the wall of his cell! However, much of the mystique comes from the barber's shop on the first floor, where the amazing still happens: a no gimmicks men's haircut for only $5.

The Harbour

See: Bushwalks: Bradleys Head to Chowder Bay, The Spit to Manly; Open Air Sydney: Beaches, Boat Hire, Picnics; Sports: Swimming, Boating; Sydney By Area: The Harbour; Tours Around Sydney: Cruises, Harbour Islands; Walks Around Sydney: Cremorne Point, St Mary's to the Opera House.

Few cities are fortunate enough to have such a beautiful, glistening blue centrepiece as Port Jackson. Although the demographic centre is roughly fourteen kilometres west of the City, the Harbour remains Sydney's focus and greatest icon. With densely wooded hills reaching down in voluptuous curves to the water's edge, leafy parkland, naval installations and a spectacular Opera House, it hosts an entire culture of walking tracks, beaches, boating, picnic spots and of course, that other Sydney Icon, the Harbour Bridge. Sitting in a quiet spot and watching the lapping water dapple the sunlight on the surface is one of the many eminently pleasurable ways to enjoy its charms; cruising the bays on a yacht, picnicking on a beach or island, exploring a shoreline walking track, or strolling through a harbourside suburb rank close behind.

Harry's Cafe de Wheels

See: Tours Around Sydney: Sydney Explorer; Walks Around Sydney: Kings Cross & Elizabeth Bay.

One of the city's most enduringly popular eateries does not have an architect designed interior, does not have expertly trained waiters and sommeliers, and amazingly, does not serve Modern Australian cuisine. Harry's Cafe de Wheels started in the 1940s as a little cart (now in the Powerhouse Museum) dishing out *the* pie floaters: meat pies surrounded by mushy peas. The cart may have been replaced with a caravan and may have moved one hundred metres along the road, and the caravan's wheels may have been replaced with solid piles of bricks, but the world's most famous vendor of the meat pie floater remains one of the best known icons of Sydney foodlore.

Jacarandas

See: Sydney By Area: The Eastern Suburbs.

Every November appears the "chalky lavender smudge" of which Ruth Park so evocatively wrote in her book, *The Companion Guide to Sydney*: the blooming of thousands of Jacaranda trees. Although their generous green foliage and vibrantly coloured flowers are to be found all over Sydney, the tree is not a native, but an acclimatised Brazilian immigrant. A certain Michael Guilfoyle emigrated to Australia to take up the post of gardener for local entrepreneur Thomas Mort, and went on to open his own large exotic plants nursery in the 1850s at the corner of Ocean Avenue, Double Bay. Such was the success of the introduction and the popularity of these charming trees, that they today are an important part of Sydney's spring character. One even graces the University of Sydney's historic quadrangle, assuming the role of university mascot and study guide: legend has it that if the Jacaranda has started blooming before you have started studying for the exams, it is too late.

Multiculturalism

See: Cafes; Food; History; Sydney By Area.

Walking around the streets of Sydney, it becomes apparent that there are many diverse cultural groups whose peoples mass together to form the city's population. Until the late 1940s, Sydney was predominantly populated by Anglo-Saxons following the Catholic and Protestant faiths. Many European and Jewish settlers began to arrive at the conclusion of the war, and were soon followed by further waves of Europeans during the 1960s, attracted to the country by the promise of the good life, free passage and financial incentives: Sydney discovered good coffee and tasty food. The second half of the 1970s saw an ideological move towards Asia as refugees and immigrants from Vietnam and Cambodia entered the country. While there has been a very large Chinese community in the country since the Gold Rush of the 1850s, the most recent influx of immigrants has been of Chinese nationals opposed to their country's politics and economics. It is not invalid to see Australia as a kind of refuge island to which manifold waves of settlers have come over the past two centuries, and it is perhaps due to this that each new wave is accepted as a new facet of the mixed bunch that is already here.

Paddington Chocolates

See: Cafes; Shopping; Walks Around Sydney: Paddington.

Sydney's oldest surviving chocolate confectionery was started by Russian immigrant Wladyslaw Pulkownik during the 1930s depression, a time when Paddington was a strongly working class suburb slipping into slum. As his business thrived, the confectioner, known affectionately as Walter, would hand out free chocolates over the counter to a whole generation of Paddington's children suffering under the effects of their parents' newfound poverty. Although the company has grown and moved to larger premises in Camperdown, the chocolates are still made to Mr Pulkownik's original recipes. They have rapture-inducingly smooth centres such as the evocatively named Natasha Marzipan, grand marnier, creme de menthe and cointreau, all smothered in rich, dark chocolate, wrapped in silver paper and twisted into a square of coloured cellophane. The hallowed ground of the original shop and factory is well honoured and preserved as the Chocolate Factory Cafe (8 Elizabeth St, Paddington), where the chocolates are available individually or in bulk.

(Former) Skippy's Former Residence: Waratah Park

See: Tours Around Sydney: Northern Beaches & Pittwater.
Information: Waratah Park (Off Mona Vale Rd, Duffy's Forest; ✆ 9450 2377).

One of Sydney's most famous residents is said still to live to the north of the City at Waratah Park. "Skippy the bush kangaroo, Skippy a friend ever true", the world's most famous, most highly skilled kangaroo: driver of cars, operator of two-way radios, saviour of humans vexed by crime and disaster, single-pawed administrator of the National Park Headquarters, communicator and star of her own show. And all this can be yours... almost. Enter the sandstone Ranger's Headquarters, and behold the radio and the office of Park Ranger Matt Hammond, left much as it was when filming stopped. One almost expects Sonny, Matt, Tony, or even the great star herself to appear. However, the kangaroos here seem sadly unable to accomplish any of the above feats: there's not one kangaroo in sight that can drive a car . It seems all that's left of Skippy is a bunch of disappointing distant relatives. They are extremely friendly, though, and can be patted and fed.

Sunday Brunch

See: Cafes; Food.

As an integral part of Sydney's "gone troppo" attitude, Sunday brunch affords a quiet opportunity for respite from the exhaustion of good living which the city offers in such generous amounts. Newspaper-toting groups head for cafes and restaurants to pass the time until lunch; what better suggestion can be made?

The Sun-Herald City to Surf Fun Run

See: Sports: Jogging; Tours Around Sydney: Bondi & Bay Explorer.

The second Sunday in August is always set aside for the city's biggest street party, an event firmly entrenched in its sporting and cultural life. This loosely termed "fun run" was initiated as a newspaper promotion in 1971, when a tiny two thousand and twenty-five participants made the fourteen kilometre dash from William Street in the City to Campbell Parade at Bondi Beach. In 1995, a record forty-three thousand people took part. The emphasis on the "fun" (as opposed to the "run") increases the further from the front you get: up in Group A it's all positional jostling and running with the aim of winning; those in Group B haven't yet broken the one hundred minute barrier and therefore want to run a good time to be promoted to group A the following year; and Group C, the mortifyingly named "Back of the Pack", walks in a mass of good cheer, silly hats and costumes. Swarming up William Street after the 10am mass start, the race sweeps through Double Bay and on to the long and steep incline of Heartbreak Hill, where one champagne-toting spectator was recently heard to exclaim, "I just love the smell of fresh sweat!" Along the route, jazz bands play from atop pub awnings, crowds cheer and party, children spray jets of water from garden hoses onto the crowd, and in true Sydney style, Bondi Beach erupts into an enormous party at the end.

Surf Lifesavers

See: Open Air Sydney: Beaches; Sydney By Area: Eastern Beaches; Walks Around Sydney: Bronte-Bondi Cliff Walk.

On almost every beach in Sydney are to be seen the letters S.L.S.C., behind which hides the great Aussie tradition of the Surf Life Saving Club, one which was started in 1894 and which has perpetuated the image of the deeply tanned bloke battling the waves ever since. The idea of parading up and down the beach wearing little more than a sun tan and a red and yellow cap was evidently one which appealed to many such 'blokes': by 1940, over ten thousand of them had joined the Life Saving Association and were competing in flamboyant surf carnivals watched by thousands of spectators. Those long, wooden, oar-driven boats crashing through the waves are still part of our beach culture, although rescue work is now done with outboard motor boats. However, the great job they do remains the same. Caught in a rip current? Too tired to swim back to shore? Raise your hand and a team of lifesavers will be there instantly to pluck you from your peril.

The Sydney Cricket Ground (SCG)

See: Sports: Cricket; Sydney By Area: Paddington; Tours Around Sydney: Bondi & Bay Explorer, Sportspace; Walks Around Sydney: Paddington.

Lacking a lengthy western history of courageous battles and conquering leaders, Australians have always turned their attention to the country's sporting fields for their dose of heroics. Only rarely are such deeds of derring-do overshadowed by the venues at which they take place, unless that place is the hallowed turf of the S.C.G., one of the country's best known sporting treasures. The very first game of cricket played in Australia took place here in 1854 between the Garrison and Royal Victoria Clubs, although the oval was then spare land used as a soldiers' cricket facility and garden. As the decades passed, rugby matches, athletics and even Aussie Rules found a venue here; perhaps it was this incursion which prompted the branding of the ground in 1894 'The Sydney Cricket Ground', placing an indelible priority on the original, noble game. The charmingly intimate ground oozes history as the stands proudly bear the names of The Greats: Noble, Bradman and O'Reilly, while watching a summer's day of cricket has an electric atmosphere unmatched by any other of the city's sporting facilities.

The Sydney Ferries

See: Sydney By Area: The Harbour; Tours Around Sydney: Cruises; Transport.

For a city which surrounds a large harbour, an efficient fleet of ferries is indispensable; if it is made up of good-looking green and yellow boats, so much the better. In the early years of residential Sydney, those needing transport across the water depended on individual ferrymen or their own muscle power, leaving a gaping gap in the market which, by the mid-nineteenth century, had been filled by a number of entrepreneurs and their commercial ferry services. However, this enthusiasm often resulted in several companies competing for passengers on the same route and engaging in price wars, leaving an unreliable and sometimes bankrupted (ie non-existent) service. Gradually, the services were taken over and regulated by the New South Wales Government. With the acquisition of the famous Manly ferry service in 1974, all Sydney Harbour ferries became part of the public transport network.

A number of the Manly ferries, such as the elegant *South Steyne* (in service 1938-1974, and now moored at Cockle Bay as a Sydney 2000 Olympic Showcase and Information Centre), were built in England and made the long journey to Sydney across the high seas under their own steam. However, the classic design of the Sydney ferry is based on the North Shore Steam Ferry company's 1859 world first double-ended propeller driven variety. Painted green and cream, they glide proudly, suavely and full of character across the water in and out of Circular Quay, faithfully serving the commuters of harbourside suburbs. Up until 1996, the ferries were allowed one day of wild abandon each Australia Day, when the Great Ferry Race saw them decorated with streamers and balloons and burning along the Harbour, battling it out to cross the line first in what was invariably a hilarious spectacle. Unfortunately, some little ferries couldn't take the pace and sank, prompting the authorities to end this crazy tradition.

Sydney Festival

See: Dance; Music; The Sydney Year; Theatre.

Information: Sydney Festival Administration (Level 11/31 Market St, City; ✆ 9265 0444).

One way to recover from a festive season hangover is to pick up the partying with renewed vigour. True to its energetically hedonistic character, Sydney does just that in the form of January's Festival: a month-long plethora of plays, concerts, performances, exhibitions and events to suit all tastes and budgets. Nearly fifty venues in Sydney's centre, ranging from the Opera House to Bondi Pavilion, offer the city opera, outdoor films, art showings, street theatre, writers' festivals and jazz, while the sheer energy of the event attracts all kinds of buskers and ring-ins to the city streets. Some of the most popular events take full advantage of the balmy summer evenings, such as the Bacardi Club, an open air dance and daiquiri club in the courtyard of Hyde Park Barracks, and enormous open air concerts in the Domain, such as Opera in the Park and Symphony under the Stars. The festival program is usually issued the preceding December, and tickets can be booked through any of the venues, FirstCall or Ticketek.

Sydney Opera House

See: Music; Sights To See; Tours Around Sydney; Walks Around Sydney: St Mary's to the Opera House.

Information: General (✆ 9250 7111); Box Office (✆ 9250 7777); Restaurants (✆ 9250 7578).

In 1956, Danish architect Jørn Utzon won an international competition for the design of the city's new Centre For The Arts, with a scheme praised for its combination of function and external beauty. Despite the popular theory that the building's design was purely based on the vision of sails on the harbour, Utzon did not visit Sydney before devising his design. Diverse inspirations guided him in its evolution, among them the huge, curved hulls of the ships on which his father had worked; the grand staircases of ancient temples; the amphitheatres of the Greeks; and the forms of clouds floating over the landscape. Fundamental to Utzon's approach was his understanding of the site, which is visible from passing boats, from the distant headlands and from the Harbour Bridge above. To Utzon (but to few of the other two hundred and twenty competition entrants) it was clear that the roof of the building would be exceptionally important, leading him to design it as a sculptural 'fifth facade'.

However, these sculptural shells were difficult to construct, as Utzon refused to allow his engineers to support them with columns, which would have cluttered the interior spaces in a way completely at odds with his design concept. Eventually, he solved the problem himself: if the shells were formed as sections of a single, imaginary sphere, they could be pre-fabricated in concrete from a set of moulds and would be self-supporting. The shells are covered by more than a million tiles of seventeen different types - white and beige, matt and glazed - all of which catch the sun's rays and maximise the constantly changing play of light over their surfaces.

The tallest of the concrete vaults rises to around sixty-six metres and covers the Concert Hall. The Opera Theatre lies under the second largest series of shells, and the Bennelong restaurant under the third and smallest set. The vast, granite-clad podium over which the shells soar rests partly on sandstone bedrock and partly on some five hundred and fifty piers. Utzon intended the podium's system of grand staircases and intermediate landings to provide patrons with a calm, progressive ascension to the fantasy world of his 'cathedral of culture'. To Sydney's great loss, a change of Government in 1965 led to political controversy and funding cuts which caused Utzon to close his office and return to Denmark. His complicated designs for the building's interiors (including his intricate systems of acoustic ribs) were never realised, and the work was finished by the local firm of Hall, Todd and Littlemore in 1973.

The clean lines of this triumph of modern architecture incorporate a complex of more than nine hundred rooms, including the major theatres of the concert hall (seating 2679), the Opera Theatre (1547), the Drama Theatre (544), the Playhouse (398), four restaurants and a reception hall. It was voted first among the seven wonders of the twentieth century by readers of *The Times* in 1991, and a well deserved nomination for World Heritage listing is being prepared.

SIGHTS TO SEE

Sydney is a visitor-friendly city, generous in that orientation and getting to know the place are easy. As a result of two centuries of haphazard yet centralised development, the main sights are clustered together accessibly in and around the City, so walking from one to the next is a great and easy pleasure. Surrounding the City are a number of dynamic and vibrant inner suburbs, where galleries, museums, parks, heritage areas and shopping precincts mix with cafes, bars and restaurants to form and support a cosmopolitan lifestyle full of living sights to see (See: Sydney By Area).

However, merely looking at buildings and sights out of context is not going to reveal all that the city has to offer; nor will it make visitors feel like locals. Also remember that much of Sydney's beauty and charm lies in the so-called everyday lifestyle that the city supports. So, rather than using this chapter to do a surface-scratching tour of Sydney, it should be used as a check list of the essential attractions which should not be missed. Consulting Sydney By Area and following up the cross-references listed with each sight will reveal each one's full context: seeing the sights need not make you a tourist.

BEACHES, GARDENS AND PARKS

Bondi Beach

Where: 7km east of the City on the Tasman Sea.
Map Reference: H11.
Transport: Train to Bondi Junction & bus 380, 382, 389; Bus 380, 382, 389 from Circular Quay.
See: Sydney By Area & Directory: Bondi; Open Air Sydney: Beaches; Tours Around Sydney: Bondi & Bay Explorer; Walks Around Sydney: Bronte-Bondi Cliff Walk.

Even those who know almost nothing about Sydney know about Bondi Beach. Seeing it for the first time, visitors stand dazzled by the waves rolling in over the clear turquoise bay, carrying surfboards and their riders in to the fine, white sand dotted with colourful bodies. In-line skaters glide past on the esplanade glancing at skateboarders who perfect arc turns on the stunt bowl. Overhead, a kite chews and rides the breeze, while behind on Campbell Parade, scantily-clad people drift in and out of cafes and restaurants. This is one of the city's most spirited and idiosyncratically charactered suburbs; however, it is not the only magnificent beach in Sydney. Even a short walk southwards along the cliff walk will lead to equally beautiful Tamarama and Bronte beaches.

Botany Bay National Park

Where: Kurnell Peninsula, 15km south of the City (✆ 9668 911)
Map Reference: 13km south of H12.
Transport: Car only.
See: History; Trips out of Sydney: The South Coast, Southern Highlands.

In 1770, British explorer Captain James Cook anchored in this protected bay on his way to Tahiti to observe an eclipse. Joseph Banks, a botanist accompanying Cook, was so deeply impressed by the abundance of hitherto unknown life forms that the bay was named Botany Bay, and it was energetically recommended to the British as a possible settlement site. It was in turn rejected by the leader of the First Fleet, Captain Arthur Phillip, in favour of what we now know as Sydney Harbour, but Cook's landing at this shallow bay contributed to the continent's being settled by the British, rather than the French or some other colonial power. As such, the landing place is preserved as a historic site, where a statue of Cook gazes out onto the water where oil tankers dock and aeroplanes roar overhead. Despite this, there are beautiful areas of reserve nearby where many families picnic.

Centennial Park

Where: 4km east of the City along Oxford St (✆ 9331 5056).
Map Reference: H7.
Open: 7 days: May to August 6.30am-5pm; September to April 6am-6pm.
Transport: Bus 389 or 280 from Circular Quay; Bus 378 from Railway Square, Central station.
See: Children; Open Air Sydney: Parks & Gardens; Sports; Walks Around Sydney: Centennial Park.

Centennial Park has been one of Sydney's favourite places for enjoying the fresh air ever since it was opened in 1888 as a celebration of the first century of European settlement in this country. Cyclists, in-line skaters, joggers, walkers and horse riders proceed steadily in a grand promenade along the many tree-lined tracks which circle and cross the enormous park, while all over are people playing games, picnicking, dozing or exploring. Throughout the park are delightful surprises, such as duck ponds and lakes, rose gardens, children's playgrounds and the Centennial Park Cafe, a favoured place for recovering from the exertions of the above, or from which to watch others exerting themselves.

Fort Denison

Where: In the middle of Sydney Harbour close to Mrs Macquarie's Point.
Map Reference: D6.
Transport: Only as part of a National Parks tour.
See: Tours Around Sydney: Harbour Cruises; Harbour Islands.

Fort Denison is a tiny fortified island with a ghoulish history. Originally named Pinchgut, it was used in the early days of the colony to punish convicts and to display executed criminals as a deterrent to insurrection. The island was fortified under Governor Denison's direction between 1841 and 1857 with a battery, store and Martello tower to increase the colony's security. Visitors can see one of the original cannons being fired each day at 1pm, and the tidal gauge used to measure the ebb and flow of the Harbour waters since the early 1800s. This is a fantastic vantage point from which to view the Harbour.

Hyde Park

Where: Between Elizabeth St and College St, City.
Map Reference: F4.
Transport: Train to Museum, St James or Town Hall station.
See: Walks Around Sydney: St Mary's to the Opera House, Macquarie St, City Centre.

When fenced and named by Governor Macquarie in 1810, Hyde Park marked the outskirts of Sydney. Today, flanked by the uneven spires of St Mary's Cathedral on one side and Centrepoint Tower on the other, the park is at the centre of a hurried metropolis. It contains one of the City's few irresistible fountains, the Archibald Memorial Fountain (1932), in which Apollo, Diana and others are rimmed by spitting turtles. (The significance of the figures is explained on a brass plaque facing the cathedral.) Further south stand a statue of Captain James Cook and the imposing art deco War Memorial (1934), designed by Bruce Dellit as a memorial to those who served in the First World War, and rededicated in 1984 to all Australian service men and women. The facade features poignant carvings, while inside, the Hall of Memory is lined with more than one hundred thousand stars representing each Australian who fought in the 1914-1918 war, and the Hall of Silence is dominated by a huge bronze sculpture. Between these imposing fixtures meanders a formal pattern of walking paths framed by huge, majestic trees and secluded lawns, offering many a peaceful retreat from the restless city.

The National Parks of the Sydney Region

Where: To the north, south and west of Sydney; around the Harbour.
See: Bushwalks; Open Air Sydney: Beaches, Picnics; Tours Around Sydney: Harbour Islands.

Hyde Park

The Top Five Photogenic Views of Sydney

Here are the top five vantage points from which to take the photos to send "the folks back home" into a spin.

Centrepoint Tower

A 360° view of the entire Sydney Basin. Not recommended on cloudy or foggy days.

Sydney Harbour Bridge Pylon

Looking directly down onto the Harbour, the Bridge and the Opera House, this is a classic lookout.

The Gap, South Head

Looking back over Watsons Bay across the Harbour and Eastern Suburbs to the City skyline from the highest point of South Head. Not recommended on smoggy days. A similar and equally stunning view is to be had from Dudley Page Reserve, Military Road, Dover Heights.

Fort Denison

A close up, water level, 360° view of the Harbour, Opera House, Kirribilli and water traffic.

Mrs Macquarie's Point

A postcard-perfect view of the Opera House with the Harbour Bridge behind, all conveniently within a single 35mm frame!

To go really over the top, a joy flight in a seaplane over the harbour and city can't be beaten.

Full details of the above can be found in Sights To See and Open Air Sydney.

Sydney is surrounded by luscious tracts of dense, green bushland which are maintained and protected as National Parks. Together, the Ku-Ring-Gai and West Head parks in the north, the Royal National Park in the south and the Blue Mountains National park to the west form a green retreat for bushwalking, rock climbing and nature observation. For those who prefer waterside strolls, the foreshore of Sydney Harbour is protected as the Sydney Harbour National Park, and offers picnic spots, secluded swimming beaches, walking paths and magnificent views, islands (see below), forts and weapons installations, all without the major exertions of an energetic hike: most involve only a short stroll from a car park! The Harbour islands (Shark, Rodd and Clarke) are usually empty and isolated, making great places to play castaways in the middle of one of the most beautiful harbours in the world. Goat Island is full of history with many convict built buildings remaining.

Royal Botanic Gardens

Where: East of Macquarie St, City, and reaching around the Harbour at Farm Cove (✆ 9231 8111)
Map Reference: E5.
Open: 7 days 6.30am to sunset.
Transport: Bus, ferry or train to Circular Quay.
See: Open Air Sydney: Parks & Gardens; Tours Around Sydney: Sydney Explorer; Walks Around Sydney: St Mary's to the Opera House.

Nestled around Farm Cove is an oasis amid the highrises and busy streets of the City, an exquisite and intriguing area renowned for its tropical and exotic plants and trees, Palm Grove, the pyramidical Sydney Tropical Centre, formal Rose Garden and Herbarium, while benches under enormous trees offer enticing places from which to gaze at the Harbour, the Opera House or watch the joggers go by. The central kiosk and famed Botanic Gardens restaurant ensure you can stay for hours, while picnics here can often turn into languid snoozes in the dappled sunlight. Surprises abound up near the rose garden, as statues appear behind shrubs and trees, and music from phantom instruments wafts out of the nearby Conservatorium's windows.

Taronga Zoo

Where: Bradleys Head Rd, Mosman (✆ 9969 2777)
Map Reference: B7.
Open: 7 days 9am-5pm.
Transport: Bus 250 from Miller St, North Sydney; Ferry from Circular Quay (wharf 4).
See: Children.

Sydney's award winning zoo is spread out over a leafy hill on the northern harbour shoreline, giving it one of the most attractive zoo settings in the world. The giraffes and elephants in particular have five star accommodation with panoramic harbour and city skyline views. Highlights of the zoo include Serpentaria, home to native and exotic reptiles, invertebrates and amphibians, the Orang-utang rainforest, Chester the white tiger and many Australian native animals, such as echidnas, platypuses and wombats. Visitors can be photographed with koalas at 10.30am and 1.30pm.

BUILDINGS

Centrepoint Tower

Where: Cnr Market St and Pitt St, City (✆ 9229 7444)
Map Reference: E4.
Open: 7 days 9.30am-9.30pm. **Cost:** $6/$3/$15 family.
Transport: Train to Town Hall station.
See: Walks Around Sydney: City Centre; Tours Around **Sydney:** Sydney Explorer.

Centrepoint Tower is the most logical place to go first after arriving in Sydney: from over three hundred metres up, visitors can familiarise themselves with the city's close relationship with the water, the lay of the land, the amount of vegetation, the National Parks to the north and south, the Blue Mountains to the west and the ocean to the east. See how it all haphazardly fits together through the high powered binoculars. Two revolving restaurants and a coffee lounge are on the three floors below the observation level. An alternative way to enjoy the tower is October's Sydney Tower Run Up, in which competitors from all over the country race each other up the 1385 stairs to the Observation level! Of course, should anyone prefer, there are three double lifts in continuous service.

Quarantine Station

Where: North Head, south-east of Manly (✆ 9977 6522).

Map Reference: North of A11.
Open: 7 days 1.10pm. Visitors must join this National Parks Tour.
Transport: Manly Bus Co bus from Manly Ferry Jetty 7 days at 1pm; Car to Quarantine Station; Ferry from Circular Quay (wharf 4) Sat-Sun January to Easter only.
See: Tours Around Sydney: Quarantine Station; Walks Around Sydney: Manly.
Experience the eerie silence of this historic hospital used to house disease-infected immigrants, and the mortuary and burial grounds used for those whose new life in New South Wales didn't eventuate. For the really brave, Wednesday, Friday, Saturday and Sunday night Ghost Tours take visitors around the station's facilities by kerosene lamp, telling ghost stories over the three hours. For those feeling chilled at the end, tea and damper are served.

The Queen Victoria Building (QVB)

Where: Cnr Market St and George St, City.
Map Reference: E4.
Open: 24 hours 7 days; shops open Mon-Sat 9am-6pm; Thurs to 9pm; Sun 11am-5pm.
Transport: Bus or Train to Town Hall.
See: Walks Around Sydney: City Centre; Shopping.
The Queen Victoria Building represents a particularly sympathetic and successful adaptation of a defunct historic building to a modern purpose. This is a five level shopping complex which incorporates immaculately restored elements of the architectural grandeur which once characterised Sydney's centre: sandstone building, stained glass, colourful tiling and an incredible dome of coloured glass. As it is joined to Sydney's main metropolitan transport hub, Town Hall station, the ground floor cafe under the dome, Bar Cupola, represents a great place to fuel up before beginning a day's touring and activity.

St Andrew's Anglican Cathedral

Where: Directly left of Town Hall in George St, City (✆ 9265 1661)
Map Reference: E4.
Open: Mon-Fri 7.30am-5.30pm; Sat 10am-4pm; Sun 8am-8pm.
Transport: Bus or Train to Town Hall.
See: Walks Around Sydney: City Centre.
St Andrew's is the oldest cathedral in Australia. It was founded in 1819, but due to political problems and a lack of funding, only the footings were built before work paused. Twenty years later, construction recommenced with the resolution of the problems, and St Andrew's was finally consecrated in 1868. Inside, visitors will find fine stained glass windows, numerous memorials, intricate stone and woodwork, and the sixteenth century English Great Bible. Lunchtime organ recitals are held here every Thursday at 1.15pm.

St Mary's Cathedral

Where: Cnr College St and Prince Albert Rd, City (✆ 9220 0400).
Map Reference: E4.
Transport: Train to St James.
See: Tours Around Sydney: Sydney Explorer; Walks Around Sydney: City Centre.
The construction of St Mary's faced extreme difficulties, not least the jinx that appeared to haunt the site: the original chapel which stood on the site burnt down in 1865, as did the subsequent temporary structure (1869), lasting success only being achieved by the current building, designed by William Wardell in Gothic Revival style. The building proceeded in stages until work finished in 1928, some sixty years after it began. Yet, it remains incomplete: notice how the two towers facing Cathedral Street lack spires. The luscious interior features two rose stained glass windows and a baptistery of Sienna marble with a one thousand ounce (roughly thirty kilograms) silver canopy. The crypt below hides a magnificent mosaic. Guided tours of the Cathedral are given every Sunday at 12noon, leaving from inside the College Street doors.

KOALAS & KANGAROOS

Where can you pat and feed koalas and kangaroos? Here are some of Sydney's native wildlife parks.

Featherdale Wildlife Park
217 Kildare Rd, Doonside (✆ 9622 1644; 24 Hour Information: ✆ 9671 4984)
Open: 7 days 9am-5pm. Cost: $8/$4.
Transport: Train to Blacktown, then bus 725 to the park.
Tours available (✆ 015-417 823)
A large number of native animals can be seen, patted and photographed.

Koala Park Sanctuary
Castle Hill Rd, West Pennant Hills (✆ 9484 3141)
Open: 7 days 9am-5pm. Cost: $8.50/$4.50.
Transport: Tours available from The Rocks (✆ 9251 6101)
Visitors can walk amongst free ranging kangaroos and pat koalas.

Taronga Zoo
Bradleys Head Rd, Bradleys Head (✆ 9969 2777)
Open: 7 days 9am-5pm. Cost: $9/$4.
Transport: Ferry from Circular Quay (ZooPass $12.60/$5.80)
Visitors can be photographed with koalas every day.

Waratah Park
Waratah Park Namba Rd (off Mona Vale Rd), Duffy's Forest (✆ 9450 2377)
Open: 7 days 10am-5pm. Cost: $11.90/$5.90/$32 family.
Transport: Train to Chatswood, then bus to the park (✆ 9986 3508)
Tours available with hotel pick up (✆ 9986 3508)
This is the home of Skippy The Bush Kangaroo; koalas can be patted every hour,
and kangaroos fed and patted at all times.

State Library of New South Wales
Where: Macquarie St, City, next to Parliament House (✆ 9230 1414; TTY 230 1541)
Map Reference: E4.
Open: Mon-Fri 9am-9pm; Sat-Sun 11am-5pm.
Transport: Bus or Train to Wynyard; Ferry to Circular Quay.
See: Tours Around Sydney: Sydney Explorer; Walks Around Sydney: Macquarie St; Wet Days.
The State Library is much more than just a mine of information. The Mitchell wing is housed in a grand old reading room, complete with shelf-lined walls and vaulted ceiling. Here are kept the thousands of prints and references which form the Australiana Collection, and a number of video computers on which reams of fascinating old photographs of Sydney are stored. The foyer is inlaid with an historic map of Australia. The new Reference Library has great facilities, even a genealogy centre in which the public can trace their family histories. It is easy to spend hours in the building, looking at exhibitions, learning how to use a microcomputer, listening to music, browsing in the library shop or taking a break in the Glasshouse Cafe.

Sydney Harbour Bridge
Where: between Dawes Point and Milsons Point, across the Harbour, due north of the City.
Map Reference: C4.
Transport: Bus, Ferry or Train to Circular Quay or Milsons Point.
See: Museums & Galleries: Pylon Museum; Sydney Icons: Harbour Bridge; Walks Around Sydney: City to Kirribilli.
Built during the Great Depression and opened in March 1932, the bridge cost around $20million by the time it was completed, and was not paid off until the late 1980s. Even today, motorists must pay a toll of $2 southbound to drive across, funding the continuous maintenance of the structure which includes bolt tightening and painting: it takes ten years to paint the whole bridge just once. The pylon closest to the Opera House is accessible via Gloucester Street, The Rocks, and has an open viewing platform with a spectacular view and a museum detailing the history of the bridge.

Sydney Observatory
Where: Observatory Hill, Millers Point (✆ 9217 0485)
Map Reference: D3.
Transport: Bus, Ferry or Train to Circular Quay.
See: Open Air Sydney: Tours Around Sydney: Sydney Observatory; Walks Around Sydney: The Rocks.
This is everyone's chance to leave the planet - gaze at the stars through the telescope under the copper dome in this historic building. The Observatory was built in 1858, and today it also houses a museum of astronomy with many hands-on activities. Evening programs run every night of the week except Wednesdays and include a short talk and tour of the buildings, films or videos and a telescope viewing of the sky. During the day, Observatory Hill is a fantastic spot to sit under enormous Moreton Bay Figs or in the old bandstand while gazing across the Rocks rooftops to the Bridge and Docks.

Sydney Opera House
Where: Bennelong Point, directly east of Circular Quay (✆ 9250 7111)
Map Reference: D5.
Transport: Bus, Ferry or Train to Circular Quay.
See: Dance; Music; Sydney Icons; Theatre; Tours Around Sydney: Opera House Guided Tours; Walks Around Sydney: St Mary's to the Opera House.
Believe it or not, the site of Sydney's most famous landmark, one of the Seven Wonders of the Modern World, was once a transport depot. Yes, a transport depot. Built over fourteen years to the design of Danish architect Jørn Utzon at the expense of over $100,000,000 (largely funded by lotteries), it was opened by Queen Elizabeth II in 1973. Who can deny it is one of the most striking buildings in the world? Inside you will find the performance spaces of the Australian Opera, Australian Ballet, Sydney Theatre Company and Sydney Symphony Orchestra. Outside on Sundays, you can hear a free performance or visit the markets. A close inspection and patient observation will reveal its many moods- bright sails white against the Harbour; orange in the sunset; eerie in the moonlight.

PRECINCTS AND SUBURBS

Circular Quay
Where: At the southern edge of the City on Sydney Harbour.
Map Reference: D4.
Transport: Bus, Ferry or Train to Circular Quay.
See: Tours Around Sydney: Harbour Cruises, Sydney Explorer; Transport; Walks Around Sydney: City Centre, City to Kirribilli.
Located half-way between the Opera House and The Rocks, Circular Quay is the hub of the Harbour, at which point all Sydney Ferries and their passengers depart and return. It is also historically significant as the first tents of the First Fleet settlement were pitched here. Nearby stands a plaque and flag pole marking the place where the British flag was hoisted on 26 January 1788. From this point, you can catch a ferry to Manly, Taronga Zoo, Hunters Hill, Balmain, the North Shore and most other harbourside locations. This is also where to join a harbour cruise or tour, while the Quayside Booking Centre and the State Transit Information Kiosk are useful resource centres to visit when co-ordinating a visit to Sydney. Apart from these functional aspects, the Quay supports an unique sub-culture of buskers, fishermen, and twenty-four hour cafes. It has a distinctive, slightly grotty character of its own.

Darling Harbour
Where: Surrounding Cockle Bay on the western edge of the City.
Map Reference: E3.

Sydney Harbour

Transport: Foot from the City along Market St; Monorail from the City.
Information: Darling Harbour Visitor Centre (✆ 9286 0111)
See: Museums & Galleries: Australian National Maritime Museum, Powerhouse Museum; Open Air Sydney: Parks & Gardens; Tours Around Sydney: Sydney Explorer; Walks Around Sydney: Chinatown, Darling Harbour & The Powerhouse Museum.
Darling Harbour sprang to life as the result of an urban regeneration project initiated as part of the 1988 Bicentennial frenzy, and includes some great attractions: exhibition and conference facilities, Harbourside shopping complex, the Australian National Maritime Museum and the Sydney Aquarium. Also within the frame of Darling Harbour, but away from the hype, are the excellent Powerhouse Museum, the magically exquisite Chinese Garden and the Pumphouse Tavern, all on the City side of Cockle Bay. Here also is moored the old Manly ferry, *South Steyne*, which sailed to Sydney under its own steam from England, and now holds the 2000 Olympic Showcase and Information Centre. The old Pyrmont Bridge, which leads pedestrians across the water, was one of the first electrically operated swinging span bridges in the world.

Manly

Where: On the north shore behind North Head, north east of the City along the Harbour.
Map Reference: 3km north of A11.
Transport: Ferry: the 30 minute ferry trip from Circular Quay is one of Sydney's longest and most famous.
See: Bushwalks: The Spit to Manly; Sydney By Area: Manly; Tours Around Sydney: Northern Beaches & Pittwater; Sydney Icons: Manly Ferry; Walks Around Sydney: Manly.
Most visitors to Sydney end up in Manly as the result of taking the highly recommended Manly ferry ride from the Quay, and soon after wonder why they have been directed to this somewhat grotty-looking suburb. 1920s and 1930s Manly was a very popular seaside resort, but has now largely fallen on commercialised times. However, what it does have are two beaches, one on the Harbour and one, very long, pine-lined, broad strip of fine golden sand facing the Tasman Sea, reached by walking straight through The Corso from the jetty. Once here, fish and chips eaten while sitting on the beach (and fighting off the sea gulls) or a walk around the coast along the mainly flat path to beautiful Shelly Cove are two lovely ways to experience the very positive aspects of Manly and to escape the rampant tourist trap atmosphere of the main drag.

The Olympic Site: Homebush Bay.

Where: 14km west of the City.
Map Reference: 12km west of D1.
Transport: Train to Strathfield Station (then a shuttle bus to the site).
See: Sports: Swimming; Sydney Icons: Sydney 2000; Tours Around Sydney: Homebush Bay Olympic Site.
Sydney went wild with all night revelling on a citywide scale (the likes of which had not been seen since the 1940s) when it won the right to host the 2000 Olympics. Perhaps it is too late for the party, but for those interested in where the Olympics' main events will be held, Homebush Bay is the place to go. The enormously popular swimming centre is in public use already, so a swimming costume is a good thing to take. Otherwise, the Sydney 2000 Olympics information centre in the old *South Steyne* ferry moored on the City side of Darling Harbour (above) is a highly informative alternative.

Picturesque, Old Inner Suburbs

Where: Balmain, Glebe, Newtown, Paddington, Woollahra, Watsons Bay and Hunters Hill.
Map Reference: D2, F1, H1, G6, G7, B11 and A1 respectively.
See: Sydney By Area: For each suburb; Directories; Walks Around Sydney: For each suburb.
Several of Sydney's inner suburbs are particularly well endowed with character and appeal. Generally it is these older suburbs, built when a shop or a pub on most corners was the norm, which have retained an interesting and haphazard mix of retail, residential and light industrial activity. Paddington and its neighbour Woollahra are where to find streets full of beautifully restored terraces; Glebe and Newtown feature many Gothic-style houses, large terraces and some graceful old mansions interspersed with a lively artistic

community; Watsons Bay and the Balmain peninsula are full of tiny workers' cottages and sandstone houses; and Hunters Hill contains almost exclusively beautiful historic sandstone cottages and residences set amongst leafy gardens and streets. All of these areas are easily accessible as far as transport and exploration are concerned, especially if the Good Life Guide's various walking routes are followed.

Sydney Harbour

Where: Smack bang in the middle of everything. It's the big blue bit on the map.
Map Reference: D7.
Transport: Bus, Ferry or Train to Circular Quay or Milsons Point.
See: Bushwalks: Northern Shoreline, The Spit to Manly; History; Sydney By Area: Sydney Harbour; Sydney Icons; Open Air Sydney; Tours Around Sydney: Bondi & Bay Explorer, Harbour Cruises, Sydney Explorer ; Walks Around Sydney: City Centre; City to Kirribilli; St Mary's to the Opera House.

Although Sydney divides itself into north, south, east and west around the Harbour, this fifty-two square kilometre blue oasis is much more than a geographical focal point. Few would argue that it is Sydney's heart, giving the city its character and focussing its identity. The water itself is by no means mute, and may appear vibrant blue on a sunny day yet murky grey under the clouds. It is no coincidence that many of the city's major icons and most spectacular events are located on and beside it. On this giant, glassy stage, lipped with golden beaches and verdant hills, ferries, racing yachts, cargo ships and runabouts perform, while slowly but surely changes the backdrop scenery of the City and houses.

The Old Finger Wharves & Docklands

Where: Walsh Bay (west of The Rocks) and Woolloomooloo Bay (east of the Botanic Gardens).
Map Reference: D4 & E5.
Transport: Walsh Bay: Foot from The Rocks; Woolloomooloo: Best viewed from Mrs Macquarie's Point.
See: Sydney Icons: Harry's Cafe de Wheels; Theatre: Sydney Theatre Company; Walks Around Sydney: Kings Cross & Elizabeth Bay.

Most of the old, grey wharves which jut out into the Harbour around Woolloomooloo and Walsh Bay are disused reminders of the great commercial activity which once took place all around the Harbour. Today, most loading and unloading of the cargo ships visiting Sydney is done near Pyrmont and beyond, in the Harbour's western coves. The Woolloomooloo wharves were predominantly used for passenger ships, and were for many migrants of the 1950s and 1960s the first place they stepped ashore in Sydney to begin a new life. Over in Walsh Bay, the old goods wharves are a fascinating area to explore, although access is greatly restricted. For a close inspection, it is best to head for the Sydney Theatre Company in Hickson Road (Pier 4). This wharf has been immaculately refurbished while maintaining the integrity of the original structure, and along its length are displayed the posters of past STC productions. Right at the end is the excellent Wharf restaurant and cafe, where a great view of the Harbour and the Harbour Bridge is spread before patrons.

The Rocks

Where: West of Circular Quay at the Harbour end of George St, City.
Map Reference: D4.
Transport: Bus, Ferry or Train to Circular Quay; Bus from George St to Millers Point.
Information: Rocks Visitors Centre (106 George St, The Rocks; ✆ 9255 1788; Open: 7 days 9am-6pm).
See: Sydney By Area: The Rocks; Museums & Galleries: MCA; Shopping; Tours Around Sydney: Sydney Explorer, Walking Tours; Walks Around Sydney: City to Kirribilli, The Rocks.

When the First Fleet stepped ashore where Circular Quay today stands, they looked to the west and saw an elevated rocky outcrop, the perfect spot, they thought, to begin European settlement at Sydney Cove. Quickly dubbed The Rocks, cottages, shops, and pubs were gradually erected. Over the following decades, the area developed into a Badlands of vice and disease while merchants established warehouses and, later, their residences. An outbreak of Bubonic Plague in 1900 and plans for the Harbour Bridge resulted in large scale demolition, a necessary evil nearly unnecessarily repeated in the late 1960s, when property developers eyed the area greedily. Thankfully rescued, The Rocks have been gradually refurbished, renovated and maintained by the ever vigilant Sydney Cove Authority, ensuring that any restoration or construction preserves the original buildings in their authentic state and integrity as far as possible. As a result of this painstaking care, The Rocks is a beautiful area through which to stroll, exploring curious narrow alleys and discovering jolly courtyard cafes. Laneways cut between colonial houses and mercantile buildings, where intriguing shops inhabit the previous domain of textile and wool stores. A strong sense of the past pervades Sydney's old town.

Highlights not to be missed are Cadman's Cottage, Susannah Place, the Lord Nelson pub and Sydney Observatory, but the best way to ensure the most is extracted out of The Rocks is to visit the Rocks Visitors Centre (above) to gather information, pick up a copy of the Sydney Cove Authority's self-guided walking route, or even better, book to join a guided walking tour of the area.

MUSEUMS & GALLERIES

Where: For full details and descriptions, See: Museums & Galleries.
See: Walks Around Sydney: Paddington.

Sydney has many excellent public, private and commercial galleries and museums. The larger of the public galleries include the Art Gallery of New South Wales and the Museum of Contemporary Art, both of which contain permanent collections and host temporary exhibitions. Of the city's museums, the Australian Museum displays the country's Aboriginal and European social history as well as being credited as one of the top five natural history museums in the world; the poetic Museum of Sydney charts the impact of European settlement on Sydney from its beginnings; and the Powerhouse Museum contains an eclectic sampling of popular, technological and social history. Beyond these are areas of living history and various historic houses administered by the Historic Houses and National Trusts, all of which impart a strong sense of Sydney's past.

STREETS & SQUARES

Art Gallery Road & Mrs Macquarie's Road

Where: Running north-east from Hyde Park to Mrs Macquarie's Point, City.
Map Reference: E4 & E5 to D5.
Transport: Train to St James station.
See: Museums & Galleries: Art Gallery of NSW; Open Air Sydney: Swimming; Walks Around Sydney: St Mary's to the Opera House.

Art Gallery Road has one of the most picturesque settings in the City. Beginning by St Mary's Cathedral and the Land Titles Office, it meanders through the luscious Domain, passing under huge Moreton Bay Fig trees on its way to the Art Gallery of New South Wales. After crossing the Cahill Expressway, the road passes the ornamental gates of the Botanic Gardens on the left and proceeds to the Andrew (Boy) Charlton swimming pool. It offers clear views of the old Woolloomooloo Bay finger wharves and Garden Island naval installation before rounding the corner towards Mrs Macquarie's Point. Here, set back from the edge, is the sandstone chair hewn by convicts for Governor Lachlan Macquarie's wife, and spectacular views across Farm Cove to the Opera House.

Martin Place

Where: From George St to Macquarie St, City.
Map Reference: E4.
Transport: Bus or Train to Wynyard or Martin Place station.
See: Walks Around Sydney: City Centre, Macquarie St.

Cutting an east-west swathe from Macquarie Street to George Street, this large, open square forms the human centre of the City. Addressing the General Post Office in the middle of the George Street block stands the Cenotaph (1929) flanked by Flanders poplars, Sydney's favourite and most intimate memorial to Australian soldiers, centre of services and commemorations every Anzac Day (25 April). The General Post Office itself was designed by James Barnet and built between 1866 and 1887. At the time the most extravagant and tallest building in Sydney, it features a colonnade with many highly detailed faces and figures carved into the Pyrmont sandstone, and a clock tower. Today, Martin Place is full of suited city dwellers, skateboarders trying out manoeuvres, and flower sellers, and the square comes alive each weekday lunch time with concerts in the central amphitheatre. Along the length of the square a number of installations, including the 1979 Dobell Memorial Sculpture (the seemingly precariously stacked kebab of steel cubes). A good point from which to observe the action is from the espresso bar on the first floor of Emporio Armani, opposite the General Post Office.

Macquarie Street

Where: From Hyde Park to the Opera House, City.
Map Reference: E4 to D4.
Transport: Bus, Ferry or Train to Circular Quay; Train to St James.
See: Tours Around Sydney: Parliament House, Sydney Explorer; Walks Around Sydney: City Centre, Macquarie St.

With Hyde Park Barracks, St James Church, the Supreme Court of New South Wales, the Mint, Parliament House, the State and Mitchell Libraries, several colonial administrative buildings and the Conservatorium as residents, this is Sydney's premier street for public buildings. Many of them were built during the governorship of one of the most influential of the colony's directors, Lachlan Macquarie, and designed by the convict architect, Francis Greenway, in the elegant and restrained style of the early 1800s, although certain modern additions provide an interesting contrast. Leading down from Hyde Park to the Harbour, the street imparts a strong sense of the City's colonial days, while simultaneously allowing a deep probe into its social history and present commercial life. All of these buildings and the museums contained inside them, can be visited as part of the Macquarie Street walking route.

Oxford Street

Where: Running south-east from the southern end of Hyde Park, City, towards Paddington.
Map Reference: F4 to H7.
Transport: Bus 380/382 from Circular Quay along Oxford St; Train to Museum.
See: Sydney By Area: Paddington; Markets: Paddington Bazaar; Shopping; Walks Around Sydney: Oxford St, Paddington.

Oxford Street is one of the most vibrant arteries in the city's cardiovascular system. It pumps along from the City through Darlinghurst's cafes, nightclubs and gay precinct, to enter the more serene territory of Paddington. Bookshops, clothing boutiques, cafes, restaurants, terrace houses, Saturday's Paddington Bazaar, and more clothing boutiques line each side as the road continues on its colourful and sprightly way towards Bondi.

LIVING SIGHTS: SYDNEY BY AREA

The easiest way to think of Sydney is to divide it into a few distinct geographical areas with the Harbour at the centre. Even though the demographic centre of Sydney is fourteen kilometres to the west, so central is the Harbour to the Sydney psyche that the other areas seem to peel away from it in a logical way.

Right on the Harbour at the southern end of the Harbour Bridge is the **City.** Here stand the high-rises and towers of Sydney's primary business district, interspersed with the historic buildings of the city's colonial past. The **North Shore** begins over the Harbour at the northern end of the Bridge, and extends around eighteen kilometres to Wahroonga and St Ives, where the bush meets many houses at their back fences. To the south of the City begin the **Southern Suburbs,** which spread around Botany Bay to the lusciously wooded Georges River and Port Hacking. Where the bushland of the Royal National Park comes towards the last houses of Sydney, the City is around thirty kilometres away. The small area of peninsula extending around the Harbour to the east of the City and south east to the coast forms the **Eastern Suburbs.** To the west of the Harbour, beginning where the port narrows into the Parramatta River, is Sydney's biggest growth area, the **Western Suburbs.** Here, the houses creep towards the Blue Mountains, ending over fifty kilometres from the city centre.

Over a total metropolitan area of twelve thousand four hundred square kilometres live close to four million people: that's an average of only three hundred people per square kilometre, yet the city is six times larger than Rome, twice as large as Beijing, and roughly the same size as London. As this suggests, Sydney is not compact; its residential areas are spread amongst a lot of empty, green space. Particular residential lifestyles are supported by separate areas of a variety of ages, characters and settings. Some suburbs were developed in the nineteenth century and are full of picturesque terraces, while others of a similar age are full of tiny workers' cottages, some feature sandstone mansions from the 1800s surrounded by large grounds and leafy streets; others were developed in the twentieth century, and still more are springing up regularly as new housing developments battle to house the growing population. The population of Sydneysiders is made up of the members of over one hundred and forty distinct nationalities and cultural groups, and each has left its mark on the social and cultural landscape of the city to varying degrees.

Where are the most interesting areas of Sydney? What are they like and why? What is there to see and do there, and where are the best places to have something to eat or drink?

By providing an overview of Sydney's best areas and cross-referencing to relevant detailed descriptions and listings elsewhere in the guide, these are the questions that this chapter answers.

CENTRE

Sydney Harbour

Map Reference: D7.

See: Bushwalks: Spit to Manly, Bradleys Head to Chowder Bay; History; Museums & Galleries: Pylon Museum; Sydney Icons; Open Air Sydney: Beaches, Picnics, Boat Hire; Sightseeing; Sports: Jogging, Sailing, Swimming; Tours Around Sydney: Cruises, Harbour Islands; Walks Around Sydney: Cremorne Point, St Mary's to the Opera House.

When the First Fleet arrived from England in 1788, Captain Arthur Phillip found Botany Bay (the site chosen by the British to establish the colony) to be shallow and exposed. Exploring to the north, he found a deep and protected inlet, glimpsed (but not explored) by Captain Cook in 1770. He decided to set up camp on the land surrounding a freshwater stream flowing into one of Port Jackson's many coves, and named it after England's contemporary Colonial Secretary, Lord Sydney.

This natural harbour is one of the finest in the world, with two hundred and forty kilometres of shoreline and a deepest point of forty-seven metres, near the Harbour Bridge. Surrounding the glistening water are tracts of natural bushland, parks, islands, picnic sites, lookouts, residential properties and naval installations, much of which are preserved and protected as a **National Park.** The **harbour beaches** offer a calm alternative to the rough surf of the ocean beaches, and include Balmoral, Chinaman's, Clontarf, Camp Cove and Nielsen Park, many with shark nets firmly in place. Many of the more spectacular events in the city's life have happened on this magnetic focus, and it is no coincidence that it also forms the backdrop for the city's primary icons recognised the world over: the Harbour Bridge (completed 1932), the Opera House (opened 1973) and indeed the City skyline itself: today it is almost impossible to imagine the Harbour without them. Nevertheless, it is fascinating to consider the enormous visual transformation which has gone on around this unchanging stretch of water. It is the city's stage, around which the surrounding scenery and players change continuously.

The City

Map Reference: E4.
See: Directory; History; Shopping; Sights To See: Centrepoint Tower, Hyde Park, Macquarie Street; Open Air Sydney: Parks & Gardens; Tours Around Sydney: Sydney Explorer; Walks Around Sydney: City Centre,

Stretching directly south of the Harbour from Circular Quay is the City, the business, administrative and retail centre of Sydney. It is surrounded by a belt of green formed by the Royal Botanic Gardens to the east, the Harbour to the north, Darling Harbour to the west and inner residential areas to the south. As well as providing a picturesque setting, the surrounding parkland meant that upwards was the only way the area could expand as Sydney burgeoned into Australia's business centre. So while the General Post Office in Martin Place was the city's tallest building around 1900, and although the City skyline remained relatively low until the 1970s, a

ARCHITECTURE: COLONIAL LANDMARKS

The buildings of Sydney's Colonial period (1788 to c. 1840) mirror the architecture which had developed in England between about 1727 and 1830 during the reigns of the country's first three King Georges. The early settlers' familiarity with this Georgian style led to its widespread adoption in the young colony.

Georgian buildings were formal in nature, generally rectangular in plan and elevation, and characterised by exposed brick or stone walls. Their style was essentially one of order, harmony and pleasing proportion with symmetrically arranged facades topped by simple, medium pitched, timber shingled roofs. Rectangular windows were divided into small panes, often sheltered by louvred shutters. Sometimes, verandahs were added to the facades.

Cadman's Cottage (1816; George Street, The Rocks), the oldest freestanding cottage in the City, clearly demonstrates the nature of the colony's early, small scale, detached houses. With its timber shingled roof and rubble stone walls, it stood at the edge of the harbour foreshore until Circular Quay was partly reclaimed and extended in 1854.

With Governor Macquarie as patron, convict architect Francis Greenway gave the appearance of Georgian Sydney a boost with his designs for many buildings throughout the town.

Greenway's Hyde Park Barracks (1817; Queen's Square) is a masterpiece of Georgian simplicity and restraint, with pale red face brickwork, sandstone trim and pilasters providing subtle relief from an otherwise flat front elevation. Further along Macquarie Street, the New South Wales Parliament House and Mint (both built 1811-1816 as part of the Rum Hospital), with their Greek inspired columns, demonstrate verandahed Georgian at its best. (See: Walks Around Sydney: Macquarie Street). Much less grand, but clearly representative of the style is the Lord Nelson Hotel (1834; Cnr Kent Street and Argyle Place, Millers' Point). (See: Pubs.)

Regency architecture, which was the final expression of the Georgian style, takes its name from the period 1811-1820 when George IV ruled England as Prince Regent. In reality, the style came to prominence around the turn of the century and continued until his death in 1830. Although very similar to their Georgian predecessors, Regency buildings can usually be distinguished by their pale, painted stucco (rather than face brick or stone) walls, and by the parapets with which their roof edges were often concealed. Other typical features are wrought or cast iron balustrades, slate (rather than shingle) roofs and French windows. Gentle projections and recessions in their external walls generally divided Regency facades into panels which framed windows and doors. St James' Church (1820-1824), also designed by Francis Greenway, clearly demonstrates this panelling of the facade and the subtlety and elegance of the style, although both interior and exterior were dramatically altered around the turn of the century. Elizabeth Bay House is another superb illustration of Regency architecture (See: Box: Marine Villas).

However, there was an alternative to this formality and moderation in the picturesque Gothick style, which was intended to excite an emotional, rather than intellectual, response in the viewer. With romantic silhouettes inspired by Gothic ruins and by contemporary literature (prone to evoking vivid images of the Middle Ages), these buildings were decorated with battlemented parapets, pointed arches, turrets, pinnacles and chimneys reminiscent of Medieval times. Greenway's Government House Stables (1817; now the Conservatorium, Macquarie Street) gives a clear indication of the characteristics of the style, while Government House, Lindesay and Carthona are also excellent representations (See: Box: Marine Villas).

Towards the end of the Colonial period, the fashion for archaeologically accurate Greek Revival buildings began to influence local design. Sydney's best example of this trend is the columned central portion of the Darlinghurst Courthouse at Taylor Square, designed in 1835 by Colonial Architect Mortimer Lewis.

large number of enormous highrises have gone up since that time, each one generally taller than the last. Unfortunately, many of the City's twentieth century buildings were built on sites where elegant stone buildings and terraces had stood, only to be labelled defunct and inefficient and torn down in the name of progress. The shape of the skyline is now formed by the Capita Centre, Chifley Square, Governor Phillip Tower, the MLC Centre, Grosvenor Place, and Centrepoint Tower.

The **major city streets** are George, Pitt and Castlereagh, all running parallel north-south, while across these cuts the main plaza of the City, Martin Place. Down in these modern day caverns are Sydney's major shopping complexes: the Queen Victoria Building, Skygarden, MLC Centre and the Strand Arcade. The most visually impressive precinct is Macquarie Street, where the New South Wales Parliament House stands flanked by the State Library, Supreme Court, Sydney Hospital, Mint, Hyde Park Barracks and St James Church, with St Mary's Cathedral nearby and Hyde Park at its end. There are still relatively few residential buildings in the City, so it is often deserted after business hours as Sydneysiders seek their food and fun elsewhere.

The Rocks

Map Reference: D4.

Information: The Rocks Visitors Centre (106 George St, The Rocks; ✆ 9255 1788).

See: Directory; History; Markets: The Rocks Market; Sights To See: The Rocks; Walks Around Sydney: City to Kirribilli, The Rocks, Walking Tours.

The Rocks area is Sydney's old town, one of the city's most vibrant, active and picturesque precincts owing to an abundance of restored and revitalised historic buildings. Occupying the peninsula to the west of Circular Quay under and near the City end of the Harbour Bridge, the area centres around George Street and Argyle Street, while many laneways and alleys criss-cross the area in an irregular pattern.

Throughout the Rocks, surprising views and contrasts confront the explorer as they look up from their own favourite laneways and courtyards to see the modern city looming above. Narrow terraces of varying ages line many of the streets, while Georgian residences and free standing sandstone cottages, such as **Cadman's Cottage,** are to be found elsewhere. Interspersed are stores and warehouses, such as the Argyle Centre, which were the backbone of the Rocks' commercial activity and continue this function today as shopping complexes. Tiny cobbled **laneways** with evocative names such as Ferry Lane and Nurses Walk lead explorers between buildings towards sounds of laughter and chatter coming from leafy courtyards, only to happen upon the tables and chairs of cafes gathered under sunshades. **Dawes Point,** once a military installation, is now a park, and its location directly under the bridge provides a clear view of this massive structure and across the palm trees to the Opera House. Yet, far from being a dry history lesson of a suburb, it is one of the most photogenic and vibrant areas in the city, with many fascinating **shops, galleries, pubs, cafes and restaurants.** Every weekend the extremely popular **Rocks Markets** are held under enormous tarpaulins in George Street, while strains of Irish music waft out of pub doors to greet the thousands of market browsers.

The **Rocks Visitors Centre** should be everyone's first stop in the area. Here, bookings to join a guided walking tour can be made, or a copy of the Visitors Centre's highly informative Self-Guided walking route can be collected. Exploring The Rocks' activities will bring the history of Sydney alive in an eminently enjoyable manner.

Balmain

Map Reference: D2.

See: Directory; Markets: Balmain Markets; Shopping; Walks Around Sydney: Balmain.

The Balmain peninsula extends into the Harbour on the western edge of the city centre. It is crammed full of historical buildings such as the Watch House, weatherboard and sandstone cottages and houses clustered around the narrow and hilly streets, and old industrial premises such as the Colgate Factory. Just over the back are the **docks** where giant cargo ships unload their weight of cars, while on the other side of the peninsula is the site of one of Sydney's most important historical docks, Mort's Dry Dock.

It is easy to see the evidence of the suburb's working class past; however, over the past few decades, more affluent residents have discovered Balmain's advantages and moved in. Consequently, many of the cottages have been renovated and refurbished to suit their new owners' demands, while others have been demolished to make way for modern residences.

Here and there are charming little parks with harbour views. The suburb is extremely busy on Saturdays, as some of Sydney's most popular markets are held in the grounds of **St Andrews** church in **Darling Street**, while the many pubs, cafes and restaurants of the area represent further enticements. Darling Street itself offers a large array of shops to browse in, and so it is safe to say that on a par with Paddington, Balmain is one of most popular suburbs for weekend strolling.

More than any other area, though, Balmain offers a clearly discernible mixture of old and new where contrasts are incorporated into a vibrant and highly enjoyable scene.

Chinatown

Map Reference: F3.

See: Directory; Markets: Burlington Centre; Sights To See: Chinatown; Tours Around Sydney: Sydney Explorer; Walks Around Sydney: Chinatown, Darling Harbour & the Powerhouse Museum.

Despite the more than one hundred and forty nationalities living in Sydney, it is only to certain extent that the city is truly multicultural. Many national and

Sydney Harbour: from the Pylon Lookout

cultural groups, particularly those whose members have arrived more recently, live clustered in particular suburbs or areas such as Cabramatta, known as the centre of the Vietnamese community. One of the largest 'ethnic' groups is the Chinese community, whose members first came to Australia during the Gold Rushes of the 1850s. Despite its very high level of integration, the community retains as its cultural and gastronomic focus the southern edge of the City centred around Dixon Street and known as Chinatown. Here is an extroverted visual display of national culture supporting a delightful concentration of excellent restaurants and eateries, intriguing herbal dispensaries, markets and clothing shops, enjoyed not only by the Chinese, but also extremely popular with the wider Sydney community.

NORTH

Hunters Hill

Map Reference: A1.

See: Walks Around Sydney: Hunters Hill.

If you're looking for **sandstone mansions and cottages, water views, luscious gardens and tree-lined streets,** Hunter's Hill can't be beaten. This is one of the premier suburbs in the city for a Sunday afternoon of aimless yet inspired wandering.

The tiny municipality was supposedly named after Captain John Hunter who sailed the Sirius into Sydney as part of the First Fleet in 1788, and who became Governor of the colony in 1795. It occupies the peninsula where the Lane Cove and Parramatta Rivers meet, and was known by the local Aborigines as 'Mookaboola', poetically and logically meaning 'meeting of the waters'. Among the first European residents to come to the area in the early 1830s was Mary Reiby, the colony's first woman retailer (featured on the Australian $20 note). Her cottage was built on Lane Cove River water frontage, but was moved (rather than demolished) when the Gladesville Bridge was being constructed in the 1960s.

1840s Hunters Hill was full of action: convicts escaping from the nearby Cockatoo Island penal institution often made a swim for Hunters Hill at low tide, hiding in the thick bushland of the peninsula until dark, while bushrangers combed the area. Simultaneously, a number of families were buying land and carrying out residential developments. Among them was Didier Joubert, a French immigrant of the 1830s who brought with him seventy Italian stonemasons precisely for this purpose. Others, such the Cobeos and Bordiers, joined him in erecting the gracious mansions and cottages which are still standing today under the National Trust's protection. The area became popular as an exclusive residential precinct at a very early stage, attracting doctors and lawyers in particular; today, the same degree of exclusivity is largely maintained by the real estate prices.

Cruising the streets beneath the trees and past the

magnificent houses, one cannot help but soak in the strong sense of community heritage. This is one of the most spectacular residential areas of the city, and a walk through its streets is the best way to discover it.

Kirribilli & Milsons Point

Map Reference: C5 & C4.

See: Open Air Sydney: Picnics; Sports: Swimming; Sights To See: Harbour Bridge; Walks Around Sydney: City to Kirribilli.

Sitting directly across the water from the Opera House and under the northern end of the Harbour Bridge are these two good looking, neighbouring suburbs. Both were developed by several land grantees, such as James Milson who built a number of houses, and a certain JGN Gibbes who, among other improvements, built a residence which caught the eye of the New South Wales Government. Duly acquired by same in 1885 and renamed **Admiralty House,** it began a twenty-eight year period as the official residence for the Admiral commanding the British Squadron in Australia. Today, it is used as the Sydney residence of the Governor General of Australia, the Queen's representative. Next door stands **Kirribilli House,** built by enigmatically named businessman Adolphus Feez in 1885. It is now the Prime Minister's Sydney residence. Both are highly desirable pieces of real estate: elegant sandstone buildings surrounded by manicured grounds looking straight across to the Opera House and directly up the Harbour.

Nearby is the **Royal Sydney Yacht Squadron,** formed in 1862 to co-ordinate the established scene of harbour racing which many had been enjoying since the 1830s. James Milson, son of the area's original land grantee, was regularly to be seen cutting through the water on his Era in the 1860s. Meanwhile in Milsons Point, the same entrepreneurial James Milson was operating his Milson's Point Ferry Company, shuttling people between the northern shore and the main centre. After selling the company in 1878, it became the North Shore Steam Ferry Company. By 1893, a fleet of vehicular ferries were constantly shuffling between Bennelong and Milsons Points, coping with the increased traffic which resulted from the development of the North Shore and increasing numbers of passengers using the extended North Shore Railway Line.

As the years went by and development and traffic continued to increase, it became evident that a more practical solution, such as a Harbour Bridge reaching across the narrowest and most central part of the Harbour was needed. At about the same time, **Olympic Pool** was built and proclaimed the finest salt water pool in the southern hemisphere, while **Luna Park** provided a place for wild abandon and raucous excitement, 1930s style. Unfortunately, this icon and important facet of Sydney's identity was closed down in March 1996.

Today, these two areas offer some of the most arresting sights and views of the City, and Kirribilli in particular is a popular residential area. Tall modern apartment blocks tower over little terraces, while small parks and the gaps between the buildings offer glimpses of the Harbour. It is a popular area for fish and chips and picnics, as well as sporting several good cafes.

Manly

Map Reference: 3km north of A11.

See: Bushwalks: The Spit to Manly; Open Air Sydney: Beaches; Tours Around Sydney: Quarantine Station; Walks Around Sydney: Manly.

Like Queensland's Gold Coast, Manly is a mixture of old world seaside resort and brashly commercialised development. Centred around a delicate isthmus separating the Harbour and the Tasman Sea, visitors alight from the famous Manly Ferry to see a small strip of unremarkable beach on the left, and wonder what the fuss is about. How could this have supported the very popular tourist resort which was promoted throughout the 1920s and 1930s under the banner of "a thousand miles from care"? However, persevering through **The Corso,** the real focus of the suburb is discovered: behold kilometres of clean, golden beach lined with tall pines and an esplanade, along which countless people in-line skate and stroll. **Fish and chips** eaten on the beach wall is one of the essential Sydney experiences, while a gentle stroll around to the right to Shelly Beach will reveal a quieter side of this seaside suburb. Up on North Head sit the imposing sandstone St Patrick's Seminary and Archbishop's House, while nearby is Quarantine Station and a lookout offering magnificent views down the Harbour.

The North Shore

Map Reference: North of map.

The North Shore consistently gets a bad wrap. Often touted as the stomping grounds of the ultra-conservative, boring and (above all) affluent, it can often be a disappointment to discover it is a relatively normal, sprawling residential area, much like the rest of Sydney. Big deal! The area most targeted is that which surrounds the upper reaches of the North Shore Line of the rail system: in particular Roseville, Lindfield, Killara, Gordon, St Ives, Pymble and Wahroonga. True, many houses have larger than usual blocks, but it is the lack of noise, lack of pollution and the thousands of trees densely covering most available spaces which are the major attractions. It is no surprise that there is an unusually high concentration of nurseries in this area, while one of the major attractions of the upper north shore is the Wildflower Gardens at St Ives. It was this area which was so ravaged by the shocking bushfires of January 1994, forcing many residents to help firefighters defend their homes at their back fences with their garden hoses, images which sped around the world.

SOUTH

The Southern Suburbs

Map Reference: South of map.

See: Bushwalks: Royal National Park; History.

ARCHITECTURE: GARDENS & SUBURBS

By the turn of the twentieth century, an ever improving public transport network facilitated the development of residential suburbs well beyond the earlier, compact, terrace-filled areas closer to town. Influenced by the development of the Garden Suburb in England and the United States, these newly spacious, healthy commuter havens were composed of rows of detached houses surrounded by gardens in leafy streets. Some suburbs, such as Haberfield, were laid out in their entirety in accordance with this model. However, the majority of Sydney's early suburbs evolved in a much more haphazard manner to become less formal representations of the ideal.

The houses of Sydney's suburbs have appeared in many guises, their varied forms demonstrating influences from numerous sources. A few of the more easily identifiable early suburban Sydney house styles are the following.

Federation style houses, built between about 1890 and 1915, are prolific in widespread suburbs such as Strathfield, Randwick, Roseville and Mosman. Influenced by the Queen Anne buildings of England and the United States, their design included an eclectic mix of features from seventeenth and eighteenth century Britain and the Art Nouveau movement.

These houses are built almost exclusively of red-brown face brickwork, and are easily distinguished by characteristic, ornamental timber friezes, turned timber verandah posts, and multi-paned windows, often containing coloured glass and leadlight. Equally characteristic are their picturesque roof forms composed of complex silhouettes of gables, verandahs and towers, topped by terracotta Marseilles tiles and tall, decorative brick chimneys.

The American West Coast style California Bungalow, with its distinctive, low-pitched roofs, overhanging eaves, liver coloured brickwork, deep verandahs, exposed rafters and timber battened gables, was keenly embraced in Australia in the 1920s and 1930s. These houses were designed to promote a relaxed, outdoor lifestyle and are often found in beachside suburbs such as Manly, Bondi, Bronte and Coogee, all of which developed during this period. The bungalows' brick walls were often relieved by sandstone bases, cream painted stucco, leadlight windows, timber shingles and earthy details.

The similarity of Sydney's climate to that of the Mediterranean led several architects, steered by Professor Leslie Wilkinson, to develop a style which combined some of the characteristic loggias, round headed arches and stuccoed, pale painted walls of the architecture of the Mediterranean region with many of the Georgian motifs from Sydney's own Colonial past.

In contrast to the face brickwork of Federation and California Bungalow dwellings, the walls of Mediterranean houses (often two storeyed) were bagged or smoothly rendered and painted in pale shades of cream or pink. Typical louvred shutters and Georgian style multi-paned windows were painted in dark colours, as were the style's wrought iron balcony railings. Unlike the picturesque roof compositions described above, the Mediterranean houses' terracotta tiled roofs were generally low pitched and simple. The Spanish Mission style, (See: Flats, above) shared many of these characteristics, and was sometimes used for single houses (See: Box: Flats & Apartments).

The romantic Old English house, with steeply pitched roofs and imitation 'half timbered' gable decorations, is another of Sydney's suburban styles. Although less prevalent than the styles described above, a large number of these residences are seen in Sydney's older Eastern and Northern suburbs. They are characterised by the reddish face brickwork, tiled roofs, diamond pattern leadlight window, and tall, medieval-looking brick chimneys characteristic of English rural and village architecture.

When Captain Cook first sailed into **Botany Bay** in 1770 and landed at what is now known as Inscription Point on Kurnell Peninsula, he saw a harbour of calm, clear waters surrounded by peaceful sandy shores. Today, the runways of **Sydney Airport** at Mascot extend into this polluted waterway on the northern edge and most of the major petro-chemical companies have their refineries and loading facilities on the southern edge. The bay itself represents the start of the southern suburbs which include **Coogee** and **Maroubra** on the eastern side, and extend beyond the beautiful Georges River through **Rockdale** to **Sylvania, Taren Point, Caringbah** and **Cronulla** at the start of the Kurnell Peninsula. As with the North Shore and the Western Suburbs, the south is predominantly a large residential spread, filled with neatly organised individual houses on standard size blocks. Along the coast of **Bate Bay** is a long sandy line incorporating Cronulla, Elouera and Wanda Beaches, popular with surfers. To the extreme south on the far side of Port Hacking lies the vast green expanse of the Royal National Park, where hiking and bushwalking tracks through luscious landscapes beckon. The **Royal National Park** claims to be the world's first National Park, as it was gazetted as such in 1879. Although Yellowstone (in the United States of America) was established in 1872, it was not designated to be a National Park until 1883. Although the distinction makes no difference to either area's beauty, the argument remains unresolved.

Sylvania Waters

Map Reference: South of map.

See: Tours Around Sydney: Cruises.

Just like the North Shore, the southern suburb of Sylvania Waters unwaveringly gets a bad wrap. Ever

Observatory Hill

General Post Office, Martin Place

The Gap

Maritime Museum

MCA Reflected in Rockpool

Below: Opera House

Below: Sydney Harbour

Bondi Beach

Royal Botanic Gardens

Nielsen Park Below: Long Reef Point

Farm Cove Below: Watsons Bay

Bronte Surf Pool

since the ABC and BBC got together to make a 'fly on the wall' series observing suburban life in a 'typical' Australian family household, the suburb, and the lives of the members of one family in particular, have been exposed to ridicule. Similar in appearance to the suburbs of Queensland's Surfers Paradise, Sylvania Waters is actually a large system of canals, whose many waterfront residences can be seen on a cruise along the **Georges River.**

EAST

The suburbs which extend around the peninsula east of Edgecliff prompt mixed reactions from Sydneysiders, and it is difficult to describe them accurately without resorting to popular cliches. While some are convinced they are a hot bed of big women with big hair, big nails, big cars and big houses, others adamantly maintain that quite normal people live here quite normally here.

What is undeniable is that **Darling Point, Bellevue Hill, Point Piper** with its enormous residences, **Rose Bay** with its yachts, **Vaucluse** and **Watsons Bay** possess enviable positions clustered around the Harbour, with some truly beautiful houses and some grotesquely ostentatious shockers. There are many trees, several yacht clubs, wide streets and a sense of calm comfort. **Double Bay** is the commercial and social/leisure centre of the area, where many are convinced the major action is people "doing lunch" while watching who is watching them. However, turn the corner at Watsons Bay at South Head, and head back along the cliff-lined coast, and it's a different story. Surf culture takes hold in increasing intensity the further south you go, progressing through sedate Dover Heights to Diamond Bay and down into Bondi.

The Eastern Beaches: Bondi & Bronte

Map Reference: H11.

See: Children: Beaches; Directory; Open Air Sydney: Beaches; Sights To See: Bondi Beach; Sydney Icons: Bondi Beach & the Icebergs; Tours Around Sydney: Bondi & Bay Explorer; Walks Around Sydney: Bronte-Bondi Cliff Walk.

Bondi is arguably Sydney's most famous beach and suburb, inherently collating and embodying its character: a bit dirty, gritty and rough around the edges, yet simultaneously cheeky in knowing it nevertheless manages to be suave.

ARCHITECTURE: FLATS & APARTMENTS

Dotting the hillsides of Sydney's inner, ocean and harbourside suburbs, the city's apartment blocks have increased steadily in number throughout this century, but most dramatically in the years between 1911 and 1933. It is the buildings of this period which make an important contribution to the city's urban character. The architectural styles of Sydney's 'blocks of flats' are eclectic and diverse, but many examples of these early residential towers are representative of one of three common types.

Federation architecture, characteristic of many of Sydney's early twentieth century houses, also found its way into the decoration of apartment blocks, although elements of the contemporary Art Nouveau and English Arts and Crafts movements, and of the California Bungalow, were often incorporated (See: Box: Gardens & Suburbs). Dark brickwork with cream painted stucco panels (often roughly textured) were typical of these buildings, while multi-paned windows, often arranged asymmetrically, were also common. Panels of shingles were sometimes added to facades, and rafters were often left exposed under the buildings' eaves, which were usually prominent. These buildings are seen mostly in Sydney's beachside suburbs, such as Bronte, Coogee, Manly and Bondi, where several examples can be seen at the southern end of Campbell Parade and in the surrounding streets.

Hundreds of 1930s blocks incorporated Art Deco style, and were characterised by deep red textured exteriors (sometimes combined with bands contrasting bricks) with inset decorative panels of herringbone or 'tapestry' brickwork. Decorative motifs were often inspired by Medieval architecture, and elements such as heraldic shields set in stained glass windows, or pointed 'Tudor' arches over garage doors are common. A vertical emphasis is among the most prominent features of these blocks, and was often achieved by stepping the facade into narrow, shallow wings to draw the eye upward and give the appearance of greater height. No better example of this verticality can be found than Birtley Towers (1934; 8 Birtley Place, Elizabeth Bay), one of the tallest Art Deco apartment buildings in Sydney. The Hillside Flats (1936; Edgecliff Road, Woollahra) are also representative of the style, although many such buildings can be seen in the suburbs of Bellevue Hill, Rose Bay and Double Bay, particularly the intersection of Ocean and Greenoaks Avenues.

Another style applied to the basic shoe box apartment building was the Spanish Mission style, influenced by contemporary architectural trends in California, where it had been popular since the 1890s. The style was being employed in Australia by the 1920s and 1930s, and can be seen in Drumalbyn Road, Bellevue Hill; Sir Thomas Mitchell Road, Bondi; and New South Head Road, Vaucluse, as well as in parts of the North Shore. Unlike the facades of Art Deco blocks, Spanish Mission walls were not left as face brickwork but were covered in a pale painted stucco, sometimes trowelled to give a rough decorative finish. Trios of arched openings separated by 'barley twist' columns and decorative capitals are typical, as are window shutters painted in a contrasting colour. Ornamental wrought iron and terracotta tiles (sometimes multi-coloured) are also characteristic of the style.

The area referred to as Bondi ("sound of waves breaking on the beach or over rocks") by the local Aborigines faced a sheltered cove, renamed Nelson Bay by the Europeans to honour the British naval hero, and was bought from its earliest private land owners by the government in 1856 for £4,500. Bondi Junction, meanwhile, was labouring under the embarrassing name of Tea Gardens, after an establishment which served tea and refreshments in (yes) its gardens, but was relieved of this sissy image when changed to The Junction with the advent of trams in 1881.

However, the essence of the area is the beach, and it is not disappointing. It hosts an entire inner city culture which retains and incorporates elements of the decades over which it has developed: white and turquoise water, traditionally dressed life savers, surfers, swimmers, sunbakers, seagulls, fibreglass mermaids, and in the grotty building at the end of the beach, the Bondi **Icebergs,** the famous winter swimming club. The Pavilion was built in 1906 to house the life saving club and changing rooms, and here also is the Bondi Community Centre, a venue for temporary art exhibitions. It is also worthwhile to see the photographs of Bondi Bathing Beauties, which plaster the upper walls in the foyer, as part of the obligatory walk along the entire esplanade and beach. The centre of the action is **Campbell Parade,** lined with slightly run down Victorian era buildings housing cafes, milkbars, restaurants and shops on their ground floors.

Just north of the beach on a rock in the grounds of the golf club are Sydney's most accessible, but by no means best, **Aboriginal rock carvings** (See: Box: Aboriginal Sydney). While those who may not get the chance to see any other rock art should definitely seek out these examples, it really is worthwhile to see the excellent and extensive collection of images in the West Head National Park (See: Bushwalks: West Head).

Many will notice that Bondi attracts some odd types, and this appears always to have been so. Two nineteenth century sisters devised a daredevil act in 1890: they would ascend in a hot air balloon and then parachute to earth. The idea was considered scandalous, and accordingly attracted considerable crowds. On the appointed day, Miss van Tassell floated into the air on a trapeze beneath the balloon, doing a series of manoeuvres on the way, and promptly parachuted expertly into the middle of a cricket game in nearby Coogee.

Bronte was the forty-two acre estate of free settler, Robert Lowe (later Viscount Sherbrook), who arrived in the colony in 1842 and bought the land around the beach from Colonial Architect Mortimer Lewis. Lowe built a residence facing Nelson Bay and named it 'Bronte House' to honour Lord Nelson, hero of Trafalga and Duke of Bronte (bestowed upon him by the Sicilian royal family). Lowe later returned to England having fought as a parliamentarian against the reintroduction of convict transportation and for the imprisonment of bankrupts. The house still stands in Bronte Road, owned by the National Trust but leased to private individuals (no public access).

These days, the area around Bronte Beach consists of a large grassy area, the sand and the surf, all packed with bodies in summer. Further attractions include a mini train offering toddlers rather sedate rides, and some criminally ugly changing rooms. However, even better than all this is the **surf pool:** a truly fantastic place with the appearance of a polar bear enclosure, cut into the sandstone under the hanging cliffs, from which pretty boys practise arc dives and little boys practise bombing each other, where swarms of Sydney children get their deep summer tans and 'dirty old men' 'perve' from the spectating benches. It is one of the city's best people watching places on a busy (sunny) day.

Darlinghurst

Map Reference: F5.

See: Directory; Gay Sydney; Nightclubs; Shopping; Tours Around Sydney: Bondi & Bay Explorer; Walks Around Sydney: Oxford St.

When known as Eastern Hill around 1800, this area of Sydney sported several large windmills grinding grain for the colony amongst the acreage of an Aboriginal reserve. It was consequently suburbanised as Henrietta Town, named after the second name of Governor Macquarie's wife, but was renamed for the subsequent Governor Darling according to fickle political 'loyalties'. It was once a fashionable and desirable suburb favoured by prominent Sydneysiders such as David Scott Mitchell (1836-1907), a wealthy bachelor and non-practising law graduate who bestowed his massive book and document collection to the state to establish the Mitchell library, and who lived unostentatiously at 17 Darlinghurst Road.

However, the local tone took a dive when Colonial Architect Mortimer Lewis' **Darlinghurst Gaol** (cnr Burton St & Forbes St) was built in 1841 to replace the original George Street lock-up. When it was completed, the prisoners were marched in chains to their new place of residence, jeered and sneered at along the way. Further dignity was lost when the first public hanging at the new gaol took place in October 1841. When four thousand citizens watched John Videle being hanged for murdering a debt collector and stowing the body in a sea chest (discovered when it split open on Circular Quay on its way to be dumped), and even greater crowds came to watch another murderer swinging and exiting this world, the establishment began to move away to more genteel areas, and the suburb's working class became the dominant influence. The gaol was closed in 1914, but was used as a security house for german refugees and innocent interns of german extraction during the First World War. These days, the buildings house the **College of the Arts** and its only interns are willing students. Next door stands the imposing and oppressive Court House (Oxford St at Taylor Square), opened in 1842.

The most dramatic change to the suburb this century happened when the **gay community** started moving in during the 1970s and 1980s. It is now the cultural and geographical centre of an extremely vibrant and expressive gay scene: the best known gay pub in the city, The Albury, is here, as are many specifically gay shops; the annual Gay & Lesbian Mardi Gras leads through its streets, while throughout the year, mobile police stations parked along Oxford Street attempt to deter bigoted individuals from expressing their intolerance with violence. In what proves to be an energetic overlap, the Darlinghurst section of Oxford Street is one of the centres of Sydney **night-life** and clubbing scenes.

Lower Darlinghurst (around Stanley and Yurong Streets) is more understated, forming a focus of serious **coffee** consumption, with one of the highest ratios of cafe to street surface in the city. In short, Darlinghurst is a gritty and slightly grotty inner-city suburb with an extroverted style of its own, definitely more attractive to some than others!

Darling Point

Map Reference: E7.

See: Open Air Sydney: Parks & Gardens; Tours Around Sydney: Bondi & Bay Explorer.

Darling Point stretches down to the Harbour from Edgecliff, centred around Darling Point Road which leads away from the modern world into the serenity of a bygone era. As it progresses past the charming St Mark's church (where the wedding scene of *Muriel's Wedding* was filmed) into the realm of noble terraces and grand residences, one begins to see why the point has always been favoured by the wealthy and prominent. Many notable citizens have lived here, such as the Tooth family (brewers), Samuel Hordern (retail giant) and Philip Bushell (tea and coffee importer). 'Carthona' was built by Surveyor General Sir Thomas Mitchell (1792-1855), while the Gothic-style **'Lindesay',** now owned by the National Trust, was home to pastoralist William Bradley and was one of the most noted social venues in the colony. More recently, the beloved Australian poet Dorothea Mackellar of *A Sunburnt Country* fame lived at 155 Darling Point Road until her death in 1968, while the Anglican Archbishop of Sydney's residence, **Bishopscourt,** is also here. Right at the end is McKell Park, a beautiful spot to listen to the water lapping against sandstone walls while lying on the grass and looking across to Clarke Island, Garden Island, the City and the northern shoreline. The suburb possesses a delightful charm, discreetly combining past and present, and is well worth exploring.

Kings Cross & Potts Point

Map Reference: F5.

See: Tours Around Sydney: Bondi & Bay Explorer; Walks Around Sydney: Kings Cross & Elizabeth Bay.

Kings Cross is Sydney's **red light district and backpacker centre,** and while this may put many people off venturing into this den of vice and grot, Kings Cross and its neighbour Potts Point have a lot to recommend them. The precinct's halcyon era was the 1940s, when American sailors based downhill at Garden Island led the onslaught of American culture here. Gaining the reputation as Sydney's most cosmopolitan suburb, the first espresso bars soon after began to appear, a tradition carried on today by the large number of cafes found here. Today, backpackers head for Victoria Street as soon as they arrive in search of cheap accommodation, while food buffs head for Bayswater Road or Macleay Street, two of the city's best loved 'eat streets'. Down the hill in Elizabeth Bay, the magnificent colonial mansion Elizabeth Bay House awaits inspection. Kings Cross is full of contradictions and well worth an investigation, even during the day.

Paddington

Map Reference: G6.

See: Directory; Markets: Paddington Bazaar; Shopping; Walks Around Sydney: Oxford St, Paddington.

Of all the suburbs of Sydney, it is probably Paddington which has undergone the most major demographic changes. Originally regarded as a wild and inhospitable place, several wealthy early colonials bought large land holdings on which they erected magnificent residences, bringing to the area a definite air of exclusivity. After it was decided that the soldiers barracks would be moved out of the City to a site on the Paddington ridge, cottages began to appear in the area, initially built for the **Victoria Barracks'** construction workers. In the second half of the 1800s, the large land holders began

Paddington terraces

carving up their lands and selling the sub-divisions to small-scale developers. They in turn were anxious to maximise profit by squeezing as many dwellings as possible onto each small plot. This necessitated the use of the terrace design, and over these years, middle class and working class families moved in in large numbers.

However, the cramped, dark and gardenless terraces lost popularity around the turn of the century, and as people moved out, Paddington degenerated into a slum. It was only resuscitated by the immigrants of the 1950s and 1960s, who soon set about reviving and restoring the suburb. From the 1970s, the streets of Paddington have progressively been beautified, gentrified and re-populated. As the old corner shops moved out, restaurants and cafes moved in; crowds were attracted to the weekly Paddington Bazaar and boutiques crammed into Oxford Street to capitalise on the constant crowds.

Paddington is now one of the most picturesque suburbs in the city, with steep streets lined with beautifully embellished **terraces** and occasional views down over the roofs to the Harbour. **Cafes, boutiques and galleries** crowd into the old buildings, making this one of the most popular and active residential areas of the city. It is one of the best places to take a stroll and to visit an excellent cafe, such as Elizabeth Street's Chocolate Factory. Saturdays' **Paddington Bazaar** is a vibrant and festive market where browsers can buy anything from exquisite jewellery to a plant, while the shops and boutiques of Oxford Street provide ample scope for a shopping expedition of mammoth proportions.

Watsons Bay

Map Reference: B11.

See: History; Open Air Sydney: Beaches, Picnics; Sydney Icons: The Gap; Tours Around Sydney: Bondi & Bay Explorer.

Watsons Bay is a quaint suburb tightly packed with tiny weatherboard cottages and minute beaches infused with a distinct village atmosphere. Clustered on the Harbour side of **The Gap** (South Head), it was named after Robert Watson (1756-1819) who came to Sydney with the First Fleet on the support ship *Sirius,* later to be appointed harbour pilot and harbourmaster of the Sydney Port in 1811, and first superintendent of Macquarie Lighthouse in 1816. He had lived in the isolated area since receiving a land grant in 1801 with a number of fishermen and other harbour pilots as neighbours.

Owing to the **South Head Signal Station,** this was a vitally important area of the early settlement. Governor Phillip's orders had been to establish the settlement at Botany Bay; however, he found it unsuitable and chose Port Jackson instead. With the Harbour hidden behind the tall cliffs of the Heads, it was a real risk that supply ships would arrive in Botany Bay to find no sign of life, and return to England without realising the settlement was in fact further north at Sydney Cove. To prevent such disaster (Sydney was desperately short of supplies), an enormous white column visible for miles out to sea was built in 1790, joined in 1791 by a tripod and iron basket for lighting a night signal fire. 1818 saw the construction of Francis Greenway's **Macquarie Lighthouse,** replaced in 1883 with James Barnet's improved, electric version, built to exactly the same design.

The most dramatic event in the suburb's history occurred in 1857 when fog caused *The Dunbar* to be wrecked on the cliffs nearby leaving one sole survivor of the one hundred and twenty-two passengers and crew; their memorial is still visible in Camperdown Cemetery.

Today, the popular suburb offers the Sydney Harbour **National Park,** The Gap and stunning Camp Cove and Lady Bay **beaches.** It is also extremely well loved for its harbourside beer garden and jetty fish & chips shop. Watsons Bay is also the home of **Doyles** seafood restaurant.

WEST

Glebe

Map Reference: F1.

See: Directory; Students: University of Sydney; Walks Around Sydney: Glebe.

The Eastern side of Sydney University is a fascinating mix of decades in its architecture, inhabitants and shops. A single street may contain tightly packed workers' cottages, tiny terraces and a massive Victorian mansion. Glebe embodies many such contradictions, so a walk around the area is definitely worthwhile.

The suburb's name means "church land for the maintenance of the parish", and in fact developed in the eighteenth century as a church estate attached to St John's, on the corner of St John's Road and Glebe Point Road. It was intended to be the Bishop of Sydney's residence; however the Church chose to capitalise on the land's value and sold much of it in the 1820s. The ensuing sub-division created an area (designed by Edmund Blacket in 1857) which facilitated the building of **workers' cottages, terraces and residences**, such as 'Toxteth House', 'Forest Lodge' and 'Lyndhurst', now the Headquarters of the Historic Houses Trust.

Down at the end of **Glebe Point Road** is Blackwattle Bay. Once a heaving, steaming swamp avoided at all costs (explaining the placement of the larger residences away from this end), it is now a peaceful area of the Harbour where the Pyrmont Bridge (Sydney's newest), a park, artists studios and The Blackwattle Canteen therein are to be found. This mixture summarises the jumbled character of the suburb, where **galleries, restaurants, cafes, immaculately restored houses, studios and shops** squeeze in together to form a distinct, neighbourhood ambience.

Leichhardt, Marrickville & Cabramatta

Map Reference: 2.5km west of H1.

See: Directory; Markets: Norton St.

Looking at the faces in the streets and the shopfronts,

you could be forgiven for thinking that these three suburbs are in different countries. Norton Street, the main thoroughfare of Leichhardt, is lined with gelato shops, **Italian** butchers, Italian cafes and restaurants such as the excellent Bar Italia and Italian supermarkets such as the Norton Street Market. A little further south in Marrickville and Cabramatta, one is instantly and effortlessly transported to **South East Asia,** as Vietnamese signs announce the location and produce of Vietnamese shops and restaurants. All over the inner west are independent cultural fortresses waiting to be discovered.

Newtown

Map Reference: H1.

See: Directory; Gay Sydney; Students: University of Sydney; Walks Around Sydney: Newtown.

Newtown's proximity to the University of Sydney ensures that it remains a vaguely run-down area comprised of second hand clothing and book dealers, as well as a variety of cheap eateries. Just how long it will stay like this, though, is questionable: Newtown is slowly being gentrified, stylised and renovated, and is becoming more and more like Paddington each year as its proximity to the City is appreciated as an appealing residential option. Nevertheless, Newtown has a style of its own, characterised by closely packed terraces, pan-global incense and candle shops, cafes, bookshops and varied inhabitants. Next to a run down pizza parlour may be a swank new brasserie, next to a second hand clothing bazaar may be a smooth hairdressing place: variety is the essence of this suburb.

What is now a crowded inner-city area began as a land grant named Burren Farm in 1794. Settlement gradually developed, and when a store was opened in the 1840s to service the growing area's three hundred and twenty-three houses and one thousand two hundred mainly Protestant inhabitants (plus one pagan), it was called the New Town Store. The name stuck and Newtown grew into one of the busiest suburbs of Sydney.

The atmospheric old **Camperdown Cemetery** attached to **St Stephen's Church of England** (consecrated 1874) holds the bones of may early settlers, including the memorial of the crew and passengers of *The Dunbar,* wrecked on 15 August 1857 after her captain mistook the rocks of The Gap for the opening to the Harbour. Another resident of the graveyard is Miss Donnithorne, the daughter of a judge who is said to have inspired the character of Miss Havisham in Great Expectations: jilted on her wedding day in the 1850s, she became a total recluse. Her wedding breakfast was never disturbed and remained set out until her death.

The main artery of Newtown is **King Street.** Walking away from the university, Gould's Book Arcade and Newsagency on the left is a massive emporium of second hand books: two floors crammed with publications covering all sorts of topics. **Georgina Street** is where you will find a stunning collection of enormous Newtown terraces and the elegant remains of an early residential estate project. Newtown is a favoured haunt of writers, artists and students, and has become a secondary centre for the gay community. It is a richly endowed historical area, well worth discovering by foot.

Redfern

Map Reference: H4.

See: History.

One are of Sydney most guides will not tell you about is Redfern, tucked in between Surry Hills and the back of the University of Sydney south of Central Station. Why? With its western half centred around **Eveleigh Street** known locally as 'The Block', it is well known as the centre of one of the most intense and concentrated Aboriginal communities in the city, controlled in the past with controversial methods by the police; needless to say, such extremes were met with great controversy. It is an intriguing and, to many, threatening combination of tiny terraces and a large **Aboriginal community** which is clouded by an atmosphere of great tension. Due to a severe lack of funding, many of the houses have fallen into disrepair and seem to cultivate a particular atmosphere and attitude, evidenced by the rubbish strewn on the streets. Often touted as the closest there is in Sydney to a no go area, the contrast between this area and the rest of the city is arresting, to say the least. You can draw your own conclusions.

The Western Suburbs

Map Reference: West of map.

As with the North Shore, the South and The Eastern Suburbs, The Western Suburbs have a particular reputation and evoke certain connotations amongst Sydneysiders from all areas. Looking at a map, the **Parramatta River** can be seen extending westwards from the end of the Harbour, and it was this waterway which encouraged early settlers to establish farms out of the main Sydney settlement. Early sandstone bridges still cross the river and several of Sydney's most important historic buildings of the early 1800s remain in and around **Parramatta,** administered by the National Trust. Among the most attractive are Elizabeth Farm and the original Government House. Stretching out from the centre through Concord and Auburn and beyond the Parramatta River, the Western Suburbs reach as far out as Blacktown, Eastern Creek and Emu Plains. Together, they form an enormous residential spread, and being the only direction in which Sydney can grow, they are constantly creeping towards the Blue Mountains foothills in the west and Campbelltown in the south. The Western suburbs are so large that they have their own Central Business District in the form of Parramatta, meaning that many residents increasingly have little to do with the 'true' City. This is where you will find the demographic centre of Sydney (fourteen kilometres west of the City), and the site of the 2000 Olympics, **Homebush Bay**.

MUSEUMS & GALLERIES

Whether it is due to Sydney's love of colour and form, the desire to bridge the gaps of time and distance from the world's other cultural centres, or the universal practice of providing spaces out of the sun devoted to aesthetic objects, Sydney has a wealth of museums, large, small, public and private. In addition are the various 'living museums' within the city - areas and landmarks which inherently speak of the city's social past (See: Sydney By Area). Many of the museums featured in this chapter are more than appropriate for children, with numerous push-button displays and interactive features (See: Children).

This chapter contains descriptions of the city's major museums, art galleries and historic houses. So whether you want to see a racing car, a warship, dinosaur, Aboriginal heritage, lie in a convict hammock or view the night sky, this chapter has the details of where to find them.

Unfortunately, there is no major Museum Pass is in existence, so separate entry charges must be paid for separate museums. The only such possibility is the Privileges Card (See: A~Z Practical Basics), the Historic Houses Trust's 'Ticket Through Time' (below) and entry to the Mint Museum which also includes entry to the Powerhouse Museum.

MUSEUMS & PUBLIC GALLERIES

Art Gallery of New South Wales

Art Gallery Rd, City (✆ 9225 1700)
Map Reference: E5.
Open: 7 days 10am-5pm. **Cost:** Permanent collection free; entry charged for special exhibitions.
Events: Art Express (selected final school leavers art major works) from January to February; Australian Perspecta Biennale (contemporary art in sculpture and other media) every odd-numbered year in February; Archibald, Wynne & Sulman Prizes (portrait, landscape, and genre/mural respectively) from mid-March to early May.

Within the gallery's numerous rooms and floors are to be found the works of many Australian artists (See: Box: Sydney's Culture Stock), highly interesting rooms of Asian and tribal art in **Yiribana**, and prints and etchings (usually downstairs) from the gallery's extensive collection. Upstairs is a **photography gallery** with changing exhibitions, while the bottom level contains an eclectic group of bizarre installations. The gallery **shop** is excellently stocked with art and history books, as well as cards and posters. Apart from the expensive restaurant on level 4, there is a good **cafe** serving great food on level 2 with views to Woolloomooloo. Don't forget, a visit to the gallery can be combined with a stroll down to Mrs Macquarie's chair via Boy Charlton pool to spectacular views of the Harbour, Opera House and Harbour Bridge.

Australian Motor Museum

320 Harris St, Ultimo (✆ 9552 1210)
Map Reference: F3.
Open: 7 days 10am-5pm. **Cost:** $8/$4.

Sydney's Motor Museum houses a diverse collection of cars and automotive memorabilia. Also note that each January, the NRMA holds a **Motorfest** in the Rocks as part of the Sydney Festival when hundreds of vintage cars are on display out in the open.

Australian Museum

Cnr College St & William St, City (✆ 9339 8111)
Map Reference: F4.
Open: 7 days 9.30am-5pm. **Cost:** $5/$3/$2; free after 4pm.

Established in the early 1800s, the Australian Museum is ranked as one of the top five **natural history** museums in the world. Thematically arranged exhibits cover Aboriginal Australia (from the Dream Time to the present day), Rituals of the Human Life Cycle, fossils, mammals, some reconstructed dinosaurs and specimens of wildlife, as well as temporary exhibitions such as the formidable 'Rediscovering Pompeii'. The **rooftop** affords great views of Eastern Sydney and Hyde Park, while the **bookshop** has a good collection of literature on matters Aboriginal. For a food stop, follow College Street along past Sydney Grammar School to Stanley Street, turn left and walk two minutes downhill: this is one of the city's best cafe precincts.

Australian National Maritime Museum

Darling Harbour (✆ 9552 7777)
Map Reference: E3.

Open: 7 days 10am-5pm. **Cost:** $9/$6/$4.50.
See: Children; Tours Around Sydney: Sydney Explorer; Walks Around Sydney: Chinatown, Darling Harbour & the Powerhouse Museum.
In this very popular museum can see first hand evidence of Australia's long-standing relationship with the sea, from fully rigged Americas Cup victor *Australia II* to floating destroyers and nineteenth century cutters. Organised into sections including the discovery of Australia, the long sea voyage to this country, commercial maritime activity and the Navy, this is a highly interactive museum where visitors can get their hands on all sorts of things from historic vessels to tunic buttons, lie in ship's quarters, look through periscopes, examine life on a convict ship, use computer games and watch films. Specific exhibitions are also held regularly. Finally, there is also a cafe attached to the museum by the waterfront.

Brett Whiteley Studio Museum
2 Raper St, Surry Hills (Thurs, Sat & Sun: ✆ 9225 1881; Mon-Wed & Fri: ✆ 9225 1738)
Map Reference: G4.
Open: Sat-Sun 10am-4pm. **Cost:** $6/$4.
The studio of one of Australia's most aggressively creative artists has been preserved as a museum, scattered with the objects of that creativity and evidence of his vibrant character. A wide selection of Whiteley's works are on display, while more can be found at the Art Gallery of New South Wales, above.

Justice and Police Museum
8 Phillip St, City (✆ 9252 1144)
Map Reference: D4.
Open: Sunday 10am-5pm. **Cost:** $5/$3/$12 family.
Here visitors can discover Australia's legal and police history in a building which has served as the Water Police Court (1856), the Water Police Station (1858) and the Police Court (1885). Cabinet displays show various tools of the trade used to apprehend crims, such as truncheons and pistols, while the charming accessories of yesteryear's crims, such as spiked metal balls and chains, are also on display. If nothing else, this museum will reveal how much more imagination and style past crims had- not for them the mundane kitchen knife. Homemade medieval weapons, probably crafted in a back shed with loving care, were so much more personal. The museum also incorporates a crime museum room, charge room, cells, and Magistrate's Court. The museum is part of the Historic Houses Trust, and is excellently set up and maintained, if a little gruesome in parts.

Living Museums
There are several precincts of Sydney which have particular historical or popular significance for the life and identity of the city. They include Paddington, The Rocks, the Opera House, Woolloomooloo wharves, The Harbour including The Gap, Bondi, Bronte and Glebe. Each of these forms the centre of a walking route (See: Walks Around Sydney), and is described in the chapter, Sydney By Area.

Museum of Contemporary Art
George Street, The Rocks (✆ 9252 4033)
Map Reference: D4.
Open: 7 days 11am-6pm. **Cost:** $8/$5/$18.
See: Sydney By Area: The Rocks; Tours Around Sydney: Sydney Explorer; Walks Around Sydney: City-Kirribilli.
The MCA is housed in the ex-Maritime Services Board headquarters and is devoted to a wide variety of contemporary art, whether it be from television, film, video, laser, design, sculpture or other forms of visual expression. Temporary exhibitions are regularly showcased in the museum, such as particular artists, photography and cartoon/comic art. Guided tours are led Mon-Sat 12pm and 2pm; Sun 2 pm. The **MCA Cafe** (Open: 11am-4pm) downstairs overlooks the Quay from one of the building's halls of vast proportions, and is very good for snacks, more substantial food, and refreshments. The gallery's **shop** is full of unusual books and things 'for the folks back home' as well as a good range of art books, magazines and arts papers.

Museum of Sydney
Cnr Phillip St & Bridge St, City (✆ 9251 5988)
Map Reference: E4.
Open: 7 days 10am-5pm. **Cost:** $6/$4/$15family; as the museum is part of the Historic Houses Trust, their 'Ticket Through Time' (above) can be bought and used here.
See: Box: Aboriginal Sydney; History; Walks Around Sydney: City Centre.
Sydney's most stunning museum is planted on the site of the colony's first Government House, constructed for Governor Phillip in May 1788. The early, turbulent years of the colony are the focus of the museum's exhibits, which take the form of highly poetic videos, LCD displays accompanying artefacts, story telling and beautifully designed installations. Concepts explored by the displays include 'Environment', 'Eora', 'Colony', 'Trade' and 'Gather', an amazing collection of stainless steel collectors drawers containing personal effects and artefacts recovered from archaeological digs around Sydney. Voices and birdsong haunt the interior of the building, while the **cafe** and museum **shop** offer excellent coffee, food, souvenirs and historical resources. Do not miss the open air installation in First Government House Place where tall poles of different building materials stand clustered together as a forest, with hauntingly melodic Aboriginal voices floating around in an expression how it must have been for the Sydney region's original inhabitants to see the white settlers step ashore. This is Sydney's most beautifully designed museum, carefully representing the abrupt and difficult transition of the country from the sovereignty of the Aborigines to the Europeans.

Powerhouse Museum
500 Harris Street, Ultimo (✆ 9217 0111)
Map Reference: F3.

Open: 7 days 10am-5pm. **Cost:** $5; free first Saturday every month.
This is an engaging, interactive museum of decorative arts, science, technology and social history contained in what used to be a power station for the city's trams. There are hanging aeroplanes, trams, cars (including a very suave 1929 Bugatti), videos to talk to, films to watch in a 1930s cinema, experiments to take part in, jars of Vegemite, clothing, even a locomotive engine. In successfully attempting to display the modern Australian experience by pursuing a broad-minded acquisitions policy, the Powerhouse has earned the reputation as being one of Sydney's most popular museums with the young and old alike. The museum also houses a cafe painted by Ken Done on an upper floor, where good food (ranging from potato wedges to Kangaroo steaks) is available.

S.H. Ervin Art Gallery

Observatory Hill, City (✆ 9258 0123)
Map Reference: D3.
Open: Tues-Fri 11am-5pm; Sat-Sun 12noon-5pm; Closed Mon. **Cost:** $5/$3.
See: Open Air Sydney: Parks & Gardens.
The S.H. Ervin gallery is located in the National Trust centre on luscious Observatory Hill. Here are displayed changing exhibitions of Australian and international art ranging from painting to sculpture and other media. The emphasis is on heritage and historical works, and strong promotion is given to Australian art, but this is not exclusive and a fairly varied series of exhibitions are scheduled every year, often incorporating contemporary international works.

State Library of New South Wales

Macquarie Street, City (✆ 9230 1414)
Map Reference: E4.
Open: Mon-Fri 9am-9pm; Sat 9am-5pm; Sun & public holidays 11am-5pm. **Cost:** Free.
See: Walks Around Sydney: City Centre, Macquarie St; Wet Days.
Few would classify the State and Mitchell Libraries as a museum. However, there is no other place in Sydney with such vast historical resources, and a little free range research on the very easy to use technology will make this a museum utopia: one where visitors can find out about issues and subjects which interest only themselves! Colonial records, a family research centre, exhibitions, free movies, newspapers and magazines, the journals of Captain Cook and Joseph Banks, as well as Captain Bligh's log from the 'Bounty', the picture files and, finally, the excellent Videodiscs where visitors can browse through decades of photographs of Sydney and print out small copies for twenty cents, are all to be found within the two wings of this magnificent resource centre. The Glass House Cafe in the centre of the building sits under a skylight dome, offering sugar hits, coffee, and more substantial food.

Sydney Harbour Bridge Pylon Lookout and Exhibition

Inside the pylon closest to Opera House (✆ 9247 3408) (access via the Argyle St steps, The Rocks)
Map Reference: C4.
Open: 7 days 10am-5pm (Closed Christmas Day)
Cost: $2/$1.
See: History; Sydney By Area: Sydney Harbour; Sydney Icons: Harbour Bridge; Walks Around Sydney: City to Kirribilli.
What more could anyone want than a walk along the Harbour Bridge, a climb inside its anatomy, displays and films showing its construction and history, dummies dressed up as maintenance riggers, a shop some Australian flags? All this can be yours inside the Tardis-like pylon, not to mention a utterly breathtaking **view** from the lookout. Late, fine afternoons are best for photographing.

Sydney Jewish Museum

148 Darlinghurst Rd, Darlinghurst (cnr Burton St)(✆ 9360 7999)
Map Reference: F5.
Open: Mon-Thurs 10am-4pm; Sun 12noon-5pm; Closed Jewish holidays. **Cost:** $5/$2.
See: Tours Around Sydney: Sydney Explorer.
Originally the NSW Jewish War Memorial Maccabean Institute, it now houses Sydney's Jewish Museum. Exhibits are spread over eight winding levels covering Australian Jewish history, Hitler's rise to power, ghettos, transportation to the camps, camps, liberation and, finally, reflection and remembrance. Formats include video, newspapers, sculpture, photography and artefacts, and together they compile a sobering chronicle of the social history of one of Sydney's important cultural groups, and a potent reminder of the value of cultural and religious tolerance.

Sydney Mint Museum

Queen's Sq, Macquarie St, City (✆ 9217 0311)
Map reference: E4
Open: 7 days 10am-5pm. **Cost:** $5/$2.
See: Walks Around Sydney: Macquarie Street.
The Sydney Mint Museum is housed in the elegant Colonial building which previously served as the Royal Mint. Here, the gold flooding in from the Gold Rush (1850s) diggings was weighed and smelted into sovereigns. Fully restored and refurbished, the building now houses a fascinating museum featuring a strongroom full of early coinage from Australia and around the world, early Australian gold and silver jewellery, and a coining factory. Here you will find Australia's first gold sovereign and a fascinating interactive computer display, through which visitors can access historic photographs and images of Circular Quay and the City. The museum also has regular special exhibitions and events, such as gold panning.

Sydney Observatory

Observatory Hill, The Rocks (✆ 9241 2478)
Map Reference: D3.
Open: Night sessions Thurs-Tues 6.15pm & 8.15pm; Booking essential ✆ 9217 0485); Day: Mon-Fri 2pm-5pm; Sat-Sun 10am-5pm; **Cost:** Night: $5/$2/$12

family; day: free.
See: Open Air Sydney: Parks & Gardens; Sights To See: Sydney Observatory; Tours Around Sydney: Sydney Observatory.
From this building, Australia's early astronomers studied the relatively unknown southern sky. Night time visits to the Observatory are highly recommended, as once inside this historic building, visitors are treated to a glimpse of the sky through the telescope under the copper dome, as well as an educational talk and video about astronomy. Further displays chronicle the history of timekeeping.

University of Sydney: Macleay & Nicholson Museums

University of Sydney, Parramatta Rd (✆ 9692 2812 & 692 2274 respectively)
Map Reference: G2.
Open: Tues-Fri 10am-4.30pm. **Cost:** Both free.
See: Tours Around Sydney: University of Sydney
The Macleay Museum of **Natural Science** and the Nicholson Museum of **Antiquities** constitute a large part of the university's collection. Egyptian artefacts including mummies, amulets and other jewellery, ceramic vases and many other Classical Greek and ancient Mediterranean items fill the Nicholson in the beautiful Quadrangle, while the Macleay comprises an oddly eclectic collection of stuffed animals, insects and other bugs, even lice from Captain Cook's ship, *Endeavour.* Hungry museum goers should stroll across Parramatta Road to Glebe Point Road, as the food on campus will not leave you with happy memories.

HISTORIC HOUSES

One way to gain insight to Sydney's social history is to visit the lavishly restored historic houses around the city, managed by the Historic Houses Trust. These buildings are of specific relevance to Sydney, and have therefore been painstakingly restored to their original condition and are immaculately maintained. The Historic Houses Trust's **Ticket Through Time** ($12/$8/$20 family) gives holders unlimited entry to all of the following Trust properties for three months from the date of its first use. It is available from all of the following Trust properties. All of the historic houses are closed on Monday.

Elizabeth Bay House

7 Onslow Ave, Elizabeth Bay (✆ 9356 3022)
Map Reference: E6.
Open: Tues-Sun 10am-4.30pm; Closed Mon except public holidays. **Cost:** $5/$2/$12 family.
See: Tours Around Sydney: Sydney Explorer; Walks Around Sydney: Kings Cross & Elizabeth Bay.
Once hailed as "the finest house in the colony", Elizabeth Bay House is a highly elegant villa which was built between 1835 and 1839 for Alexander Macleay. With an elliptical, domed staircase and dome, heavy wooden doors and a cool stone cellars and kitchen, the villa is furnished in the style of 1839-45. Visitors can discern a very strong sense of Sydney's colonial heritage. There is also a small park opposite the house where the estate's gardens used to reach down to the Harbour. Well worth seeing.

Elizabeth Farm

70 Alice Street, Parramatta (✆ 9635 9488)
Map Reference: 20km west of C1.
Open: Tues-Sun 10am-4.30pm; Closed Mon. **Cost:** $5/$2/$12 family.
See: History; Sydney By Area: Parramatta; Tours Around Sydney: Cruises.
Tucked into a quiet corner of this thriving business district are some of Australia's most significant historic buildings. Elizabeth Farm (1793) is the oldest European building in Australia, and its low reaching roof lines and simple design became the prototype for the Australian farm homestead. It is furnished in the style of the Macarthurs, the wool pioneers who were responsible for developing fine merino flocks and the basis of Australia's wool industry. The small garden of Elizabeth Farm is carefully tended with flowering plants and other species favoured in the 1830s. There are also some tea rooms.

Hyde Park Barracks

Queens Square, Macquarie St, City (✆ 9223 8922)
Map Reference: E4.
Open: 7 days 10am-5pm. **Cost:** $5/$3/$12 family.
See: Sydney By Area & Directory: City; History; Open Air Sydney: Parks & Gardens; Sydney Icons: Sydney Festival; Walks Around Sydney: City Centre, Macquarie Street.
Externally elegant and internally eerie, these Georgian barracks were designed in 1819 by convict architect Francis Greenway to accommodate his fellow convicts, but were later used to house single female immigrants. Today, the barracks' fascinating displays explore the occupants' lives and include a dormitory slung with hammocks in which visitors can lie and listen to ghostly fragments of convict conversation. There is also an excellent cafe in the courtyard, also the site of the hugely popular Sydney Festival Bacardi Club each January.

Rose Seidler House

71 Clissold Rd, Wahroonga (✆ 9989 8020)
Map Reference: 20km north of A3.
Open: Sun 10am-4.30pm **Cost:** $$5/$3
Rose Seidler House is one of Sydneys' most significant modernist residences. Built between 1948 and 1950, this pristinely minimalist house was the first Australian commission for Harry Seidler, the Austrian-born architect of several of Sydney's most distinctive buildings.

Susannah Place

58-64 Gloucester St, The Rocks (✆ 9241 1893)
Map Reference: D4.
Open: Sat & Sun 10am-5pm; 7 days in January 10am-5pm. **Cost:** $3.
See: Directory: The Rocks; History; Markets: The Rocks Market; Sightseeing: The Rocks; Sydney By

Area : The Rocks; Walks Around Sydney: The Rocks; Susannah Place is a terrace of four small dwellings and a corner shop. The buildings have a continuous history of occupancy by working class families, and so have been set up 'as found' to show how they were used between 1844 and 1990, and reveal the changes in working class domestic lifestyle over this period. The corner shop, with its polished wooden counter, has been recreated to depict the decade of 1910-20, and sells (newly made) contemporary goods including sweets and biscuits.

Vaucluse House

Wentworth Road, Vaucluse (✆ 9388 7922)

Map Reference: C10.

Open: Tues-Sun 10am-4.30pm; Closed Mon except public holidays. **Cost:** $5/$2/$12 family.

See: Open Air Sydney: Beaches, Parks and Gardens; Tours Around Sydney: Bondi & Bay Explorer.

Sitting in the middle of lushly designed gardens near the Harbour, the Gothic mansion Vaucluse House (1803) is one of the most enviable residences in the city. Luckily the public has access to it! This was the home of William Wentworth, father of the Australian Constitution (1901), and his family from 1829-1853. Again, the house is accurately furnished and meticulously maintained, and is surrounded by luscious gardens, also accurately restored. A visit here can be finished with one to the attached Vaucluse Tearooms, or a stroll down to the Harbour's edge at Nielsen Park.

COMMERCIAL GALLERIES

Sydney has a healthily active private and commercial gallery scene. The best source of information regarding these is the publication, State of The Arts, which details the current exhibiting artists and venues. The best area of Sydney for strolling around between galleries is Paddington which has the highest concentration of galleries in the country, and the walking route 'The Terraces and Galleries of Paddington' is designed to facilitate exactly this (See: Walks Around Sydney). A useful publication is the free 'Paddington and Environs Galleries' pamphlet which can be obtained from local cafes and bookshops; telephoning (✆ 9332 1840); or writing to PO Box 351 Paddington NSW 2021. Some of the city's better known small galleries are those which follow.

Coo-ee Aboriginal Art

98 Oxford St, Paddington (✆ 9332 1544)

Map Reference: G5.

Open: Mon-Sat 10am-6pm; Sun 11am-5pm.

Coo-ee contains a very large range of Aboriginal sand and bark paintings and sculpture by traditional and modern Aboriginal artists from all over the country. Also available to buy are didgeridoos, prints, books and gifts. Most of the profits are returned to the communities which produced the works.

Hester Gallery Espresso

355 King St, Newtown (✆ 9519 1608)

Map Reference: H1.

Open: 7 days 10am-6pm.

An art gallery and coffee, bagel and cake shop opened in April 1995 to show all sorts of stuff from drawings and photography to paintings.

Holdsworth Galleries

86 Holdsworth Street, Woollahra (✆ 9363 1364)

Map Reference: G7.

Open: Mon-Sat 10am-5pm; Sun 12noon-5pm.

The Holdsworth Galleries hold regularly changing exhibitions of established Australian artists' works.

Ken Done Gallery

George St, The Rocks (✆ 9247 2740)

Map Reference: D4.

Open: 7 days 10am-6pm.

Almost everybody knows of Ken Done's exuberant paintings and designs, and this gallery is the place to see and buy them.

Rex Irwin Art Dealer

1st Floor, 38 Queen St, Woollahra (✆ 9363 3212)

Map Reference: H7.

Open: Tues-Sat 11am-5.30pm; Closed Sun-Mon.

Major and important Australian and European contemporary artists' works are exhibited and sold here. Ask to see the private area upstairs, where the works of artists other than those exhibited downstairs can be viewed.

Robin Gibson Galleries

278 Liverpool St, Darlinghurst (✆ 9331 6692)

Map Reference: F5.

Open: Tues-Sat 11am-6pm.

Robin Gibson is known for gathering staggering collections of works from around the world, and the ensuing sales always attract great attention.

Roslyn Oxley Gallery

Soudan Lane (off 27 Hamden St), Paddington (✆ 9331 1919)

Map Reference: G7.

Open: Tues-Sat 11am-6pm.

This is one of Sydney's best known venues for exhibitions of contemporary art from Australia and overseas.

Sherman Galleries

1 Hargrave St, Paddington (✆ 9360 5566) & 16-18 Goodhope St, Paddington (✆ 9331 1112)

Map Reference: G6.

Open: Tues-Sat 11am-6pm.

Contemporary Australian and international painting, graphics and other works on paper. The gallery also has a sculpture garden.

Wagner Art Gallery

39 Gurner St, Paddington (✆ 9360 6069)

Map Reference: G6.

Open: Tues-Sat 11am-5.30pm; Sun 1pm-5pm.

The Wagner Gallery specialises in fine art whether by Australian or international, contemporary or traditional artists.

WALKS AROUND SYDNEY: DISCOVERING THE CITY BY FOOT

The best way to discover the true character of a city's lifestyle is to walk at your own pace through the streets and gardens, observing the people, buildings, shops and atmosphere. This is something you can't get without a bit of effort, but that doesn't mean it has to be unpleasant. The walking routes included in this chapter lead gently through the most interesting and beautiful areas of Sydney, dallying in cafes, pubs and shops, or meandering through gentle parkland. The lengths of the routes have been calculated by walkers of average fitness, not Olympic competitors. Taking time to linger over views, in museums and in cafes along the way will lengthen the excursion, but give you a break. The starting point for most walks is either Town Hall or Circular Quay, while alternative ways to cover the route are also included. Be sure to take a camera and wear comfortable shoes, sun screen and a hat; and avoid the hours around midday in the summer months.

CENTRE

City Centre Circuit

Description: This walk leads through the business centre of Sydney, past the City's most notable historic and modern buildings, through the various precincts and parks, and finishes in the middle of the retail area.
Starting Point: Circular Quay.
Map Reference For Walk: D4 to E4.
Length: Allow a day to leave time for museums, food, cafes and shopping along the way.
Best Time: Monday to Friday; the business district is a weekend ghost town.
Take: Camera and stamina.
Note: If you don't have time to devote a separate expedition to Macquarie St, this walk can be altered as follows to include it: after the Museum of Sydney, walk up Bridge St to the Conservatorium; then proceed along Macquarie St in reverse order to Hyde Park, adding Martin Place to the end of the walk. Those intending to visit several of the Historic Houses Trust's properties around Sydney should buy the Ticket Through Time (See: A~Z Practical Basics: Tickets).
Transport Alternatives: The City Circle train line loops the city centre; the Sydney Explorer bus tour covers many of the stops on this walk.
See: Directory; Film; History; Museums & Galleries: Australian Museum; Shopping; Sydney By Area: The City; Walks Around Sydney: Macquarie St; Wet Days.

Stepping off the train or ferry at **Circular Quay** and gazing ahead at the spire-like highrises, it is hard to imagine this scene of action as a completely natural cove, unmarked by human settlement. When the First Fleet decided to set up camp on the cove, known by the local Aborigines as the "Warrang", they looked for a spot where fresh water was in supply and found, roughly where the western edge of the Quay now is, a stream which they named the Tank Stream. Yet the precious water supply also caused problems: at high tide the entire area was under water and passable only by a single bridge, while low tide offered the enticing options of trudging through the mud, or paying someone a penny to trudge through the mud instead. The problem grew in seriousness as the town's population grew, so construction began in 1841 on what was to be the last major public project built using convict labour. The land was reclaimed and massive walls of Cockatoo Island sandstone, still visible, were erected to hold back the water. Reaching as far as the eastern bank of the Tank Stream, it was called 'Semi Circular Quay', and it was not until extensions were carried out in 1854 that it merited promotion to 'Circular Quay'. It was the commercial hub of the colony, but as passenger traffic increased, trading vessels were moved to other moorings and the Quay became one of the city's major ferry, rail and bus interchanges.

Leaving the Quay, cross Alfred Street directly behind it into Loftus Street (opposite wharf 4), stopping at the **Customs House**. Considering the colony's geographical position, trading by sea was bound to be the mainstay of its coffers. Relatively early in its history, Sydney became an important Pacific port continuously processing goods leaving and entering the colony. This

ARCHITECTURE: SKYSCRAPERS

Australian architects were not really influenced by the orthodox modern architecture until after the Second World War, by which time the style was several decades old in Europe and America. By the 1950s, however, fashionable, curtain walled office buildings were beginning to appear, and several examples remain in the City streets. The best is Qantas House (1958) at Chifley Square, with its sinuous curtain of glass following the contours of its curved site.

The Height of Buildings Act had limited the city's 'skyscrapers' to forty five metres (around fifteen storeys) since 1921, and it was the lifting of the Act in 1957 which was to be the greatest influence on the development of Sydney's skyline. The first building to exceed the old limit was the curved glass and aluminium tower of the AMP Building (1961) at Circular Quay.

Another event which would prove to have a dramatic effect on the city was the arrival of Austrian architect Harry Seidler, who commenced practice in Sydney in 1948. Seidler's circular Australia Square tower (1967) in George Street (between Bond Street and Hunter Street) was the first in his series of distinctive office buildings. Unlike most early Sydney skyscrapers, the tower was set above what has become a Seidler trademark, a sunny public plaza. Australia Square's plaza is a popular spot for city lunches and Friday night drinks even thirty years after its construction. Seidler's crisp, pale, octagonal MLC Centre (1978) also combines corporate and public spaces in a plaza opening onto Martin Place. The sculptural, structural concrete roof vaults and large modern artworks of the foyer are also Seidler hallmarks.

Seidler's steel-framed, granite-clad Grosvenor Place tower (1987; 225 George Street) is based on the quadrant shape. The curved facades are covered with sunshades, specifically positioned to achieve maximum sunscreening. The huge zig-zagging structural steel spire of Seidler's Capita Centre (1989; 9 Castlereagh Street) both braces the building and provides an eye-catching landmark above the its huge, angled, sun-trapping light well.

The King George Tower (1976; Cnr King Street and George Street) was designed by John Andrews. Its rugged brutalist style is very different from Seidler's towers, but it too addresses the problem of Sydney's sun, using a lightweight frame of angled sunscreening panels which contrast with the robust structure behind.

The gleaming Gateway Tower (the National Mutual building, opened 1990; Circular Quay) was designed by the firm of Peddle, Thorp and Walker, and provides the skyline with one of its more distinctive mirror buildings.

The Governor Phillip Tower (1993), Museum of Sydney and Governor Macquarie Tower (both 1995; bounded by Bridge Street, Phillip Street and Farrer Place) were designed by the firm of Denton, Corker, Marshall. The group demonstrates some sophisticated detailing in glass, steel, stone and timber, topped by a distinctive, criss-crossed cube of gleaming, metal fins.

Chifley Square's Chifley Tower (1993), with its steepled turret, is reminiscent of the 1930s Art Deco skyscrapers of Manhattan. Each facade of this Kohn Pedersen Fox/Travis Partners collaboration differs in its composition, and the combination of materials and Art Deco references are continued in the tower's glamorous shopping arcades and foyer.

Customs House was Sydney's fifth and was built in 1844 to a design by Mortimer Lewis. The building was given an extra two storeys and an upper verandah by James Barnet in 1885 during his office as Colonial Architect (1862-1890). Along with Lewis, Francis Greenway, Edmund Blacket and Walter Liberty Vernon, Barnet was one of Sydney's most prolific and important nineteenth century architects, even though the discovery of serious construction faults in a later building precipitated his resignation. This six storey sandstone building displays several characteristic Classical Revival details, in particular its polished granite columns, carved stone balusters and central pediment (decorated with a sandstone coat of arms). The clock face features a dolphin and trident motif, added in 1897. Adjacent to the building in Loftus Street stands a **flagpole,** estimated to be the very spot where the British Flag was first raised on 26 January 1788.

Walk up Loftus Street into the tree-lined **Macquarie Place** on the right. Although this is now only an island of green amid the bitumen acreage, it was originally conceived as an important public square by Governor Macquarie (1810-1821). Apart from the excellent Cafe Paradiso, the square itself contains a stone **obelisk** erected in 1818 to mark the point from which all roads in the colony were measured. Nearby stand the **anchor** and cannon of the Sirius, one of the First Fleet's escort ships. Off to the right lies Bulletin Place, a narrow laneway named after *The Bulletin*, historically Sydney's most significant journal which operated from the warehouse at No. 16-18. Some of Australia's best known writers worked for the journal, including Banjo Patterson, Henry Lawson and Norman Lindsay. The square is a regular Friday evening meeting place for legal, stock broking and suited city types, who gather to drink the Customs House Pub's brews under the trees. Indeed, you are entering the banking and stockbroking precinct of the Central Business District.

The square opens onto Bridge Street, roughly where the original crossing over the mud flats was located. Slightly to the right on the opposite side is **Pitt Street,** named after William Pitt, Prime Minister of England at the time New South Wales was settled and a champion of the new colony. Following Pitt Street a short distance, **Tank Stream Lane** becomes visible on the right, commemorating the original course of the stream, now enclosed in tunnels and invisible beneath the bulk of the buildings. Detouring into Bond Street on the right, walkers will find the **Sydney Stock Exchange,** where they can watch the value of the shares rise and fall on the giant screen which faces the front windows. Opposite is the large open space which forms part of **Australia Square.** This award-winning complex was designed by Austrian-born Harry Seidler (1923-), one of Sydney's most famous and interesting (if controversial) architects, whose many city landmarks include the Grosvenor Place tower, the MLC Centre, Capita Centre, and the much discussed Blues Point Tower on the northern harbour foreshore.

Turning left into Spring Street and following it to Loftus Street, walk along the side of the large sandstone building on your left back to Bridge Street. This is the **Department of Lands** building, designed by James Barnet and built in stages from 1876 into the 1890s. The facade of the building features alcoves in which **statues** of distinguished promoters of settlement (mostly explorers) are carved. A number were left vacant for future worthies to fill, but their emptiness presumably indicates that none has measured up to the standards set by the settlement's first **Governor Arthur Philip** (1738-1814) or explorer **Matthew Flinders** (1774-1814), who circumnavigated the Australian Continent between 1801 and 1803. The interior features a magnificent staircase with cast iron balustrades, a water-powered lift, inter-office speaking tubes, newly patented concrete flooring and pneumatic bells. Indeed, it was Sydney's most modern and technologically advanced building when it opened, and was even topped with a copper dome (originally intended to hold a telescope) to which the clock was added in 1938. The building is widely regarded as a classic example of nineteenth century architecture, and inside is a wide variety of aerial photographs of Sydney for sale.

Across Loftus Street stands the equally imposing **Department of Education** building, built around 1913. Although sharing some of the decorative characteristics of the Department of Lands, this free-standing early twentieth century building is less ornate, with simple rectangular windows marching around the Farrer Place, Bridge, Young and Loftus Street facades. The building's sandstone grandeur belies the fact that its structure is of reinforced concrete and steel. A stuccoed attic storey, a later addition, sits above the structure's central light well.

The corner of **Phillip Street** is a historic site of great importance as far as the European history of Sydney is concerned. This is where Sydney's first Government House was erected in May 1788, only four months after the First Fleet's arrival. By the 1800s, the six room house was in poor condition and Sydney's Governors were complaining about the rotting building, infested with insects and pests. It was eventually replaced with the second, luxurious model adjacent to the Conservatorium (See: Macquarie Street, below). The site spent much of the last two decades empty after construction excavations unearthed the historic foundations, and historians and authorities argued about how best to proceed. Today, part of the site is occupied by the spectacular Museum of Sydney, while the open square contains several interesting features. Close to Bridge Street is a covered stone mound containing a covered **viewing hole** down to the foundations below. To the left stands one of the most poetic of sculptural installations in Sydney, *The Edge of The Trees*. An assembly of columns built of varying materials stand in representation of Sydney Cove's original forest, and wandering through the 'trees', melodious Aboriginal voices murmur phrases and words. This expression of how it must have been for them to peer out from the trees and see the white settlers stepping onto their shores is a representation of the layers of memory and experience, and was assembled by Janet Lawrence and Fiona Foley.

Proceeding into the **Museum of Sydney** (✆ 9251 4611; Open: 7 days 10am-5pm), walkers will see the same lyrical quality used to explain various important aspects of Sydney's early history. Beautifully designed installations chronicle the original lifestyle of the region's original Aboriginal population; the goods and wares traded through Sydney; colonial Sydney's social life (portrayed by some of the city's finest actors); and fascinating stainless steel collectors' drawers containing numerous items recovered in archaeological digs on this and other historic sites around Sydney: pull one out and be surprised! No visit to the museum would be complete without investigating the museum shop on ground floor, one of the better and more imaginative souvenir shops in Sydney. Beside the shop and extending out into the square is the excellent **Museum of Sydney Cafe** (✆ 9241 3636; Open: Mon-Fri 7am-10pm; Sat-Sun 9am-6pm), the perfect spot for a restorative coffee or lunch.

After finishing at the museum, walk along Phillip Street to the right through the City's administrative precinct to **Chifley Square.** (If you are to do the Macquarie Street walk now, continue along Bridge Street to begin at the Conservatorium.) Named after Joseph Benedict Chifley (1885-1951), an engine driver who entered Labor politics in 1928 to become Defence Minister the following year, and who was Prime Minister from 1945 to 1949, it is also the site of Chifley Tower, one of the City's most prestigious office blocks, which in turn houses many slick retail outlets such as Tiffany's (See: Shopping).

Turn right into Hunter Street and then first left into Castlereagh Street. On the right stands the **Capita Centre** (Harry Seidler, above), with rotund stainless steel bracing zig-zagging up the facade. The skewed atrium was designed to catch the sun and fill the office spaces with natural light.

Continue along Castlereagh Street as far as **Martin Place,** noticing the polished granite columns and elaborate external fittings of the very solid

Commonwealth Bank on the left. Designed by Ross and Rowe Architects in 1928, the building incorporates monumental Classical details both internally and externally. Its Martin Place facade is clad in glazed terracotta tiles and is dominated by four huge Ionic columns. The grandiose and meticulously renovated banking chamber is worth a look.

Martin Place itself was originally a small laneway named after Sir James Martin, Chief Justice of New South Wales in the 1880s. However, when the General Post Office (below) was built in the 1870s, it became apparent that the lane needed to be widened. Under the *General Post Offices (Approaches Improvement) Act of 1889,* Martin Lane became Martin Place, paved with tessellated blocks of wood. Today it is the human centre of the City where flower sellers and city slaves relax under the trees as musicians of varying styles and ability perform during lunch time in the amphitheatre.

Walk down Martin Place to the block between Pitt and George Streets, passing the rather large **MLC Centre** on the left, another Harry Seidler number which contains the Dendy Cinema (See: Film), an excellent food court and great shops, many of them selling high quality clothing and goods.

The **General Post Office** is another of the Victorian architect James Barnet's works. Built between 1866 and 1887 directly over the path of the Tank Stream, it incorporates many Classical motifs, such as the semi-circularly arched colonnade and pediments. At the time, it was the most extravagant building in Sydney, and looking at the considerable decoration, it is easy to imagine that this was so. In particular, note the clock tower and the many highly detailed faces and figures carved into the Pyrmont sandstone. The building gives observers a sharp image of how the City has grown since the beginning of the century, as the clock tower was at that time the highest structure in Sydney. Today it is simply dwarfed by all the high-rises surrounding it. Opposite stands the Cenotaph, one of Sydney's favourite and most intimate memorials to Australian soldiers, and the centre of services and commemorations every Anzac Day (25 April). On the other side of the Cenotaph stands Challis House, home of Emporio Armani and its excellent first floor coffee bar and restaurant , a great place from which to observe the comings and goings of Martin Place. Many of the major Australian banks have their head branches in this vicinity.

From here, turn left into George Street and left again into King Street. This is a largely unremarkable stretch, but it leads directly past the Chanel boutique to the hallowed legal precinct of Phillip Street, home to hundreds of barristers and legal eagles. Some of the most desirable addresses, such as Wentworth Chambers and the law school of the University of Sydney, cluster around the high rise Supreme Court, which may be visited by the public (See: Wet Days). On the right hand corner of Elizabeth Street is Francis Greenway's **Old Supreme Court** Building, Australia's second oldest court building. Although it was begun as a school in 1819, the design was altered to create the courthouse and was eventually completed after Greenway's dismissal. A magnificent, domed, geometric staircase is contained within the building, the externally elegant proportions of which are one of Greenway's most popularly admired hallmarks. The colonnade was subsequently added by James Barnet.

Next door on the right is **St James Church** with its elegant copper spire. This was intended for use as a court, but was transformed into an Anglican Church when Governor Macquarie's excessive public works program was greatly curbed by Commissioner Bigge (for full details of the church, See: Macquarie Street walk, below). Walking to the front of St James in Queen's Square and crossing into Hyde Park, the top of the distant Art Deco Anzac Memorial is visible through the leafy trees. However, directly ahead stands the amazing **Archibald Fountain** which features a relaxed Apollo languidly pointing at St Mary's Cathedral (the temptation often becomes too great and Apollo has often been seen with a yoyo dangling from his hand over the years). The spitting turtles are simply noble, and their significance, as well as that of the other figures, is explained in a plaque on the cathedral side. JF Archibald, a founder of the Bulletin magazine, donated the fountain to commemorate the association of France and Australia in the first world war. It was designed by François Sicard and installed in 1932.

Hyde Park itself (See: Sights To See) was named after London's Hyde Park, and when fenced by Governor Macquarie in 1810, it marked the outskirts of Sydney. At one stage used as a racecourse, it was intended to function as Sydney's common. Today it remains as a calm, green oasis right in the middle of the noisy metropolis.

Cross College Street and walk to the right, turning left into Cathedral Street to walk up the imposing thirty-seven step entrance to **St Mary's Cathedral,** designed in Gothic Revival style by William Wardell. The construction of St Mary's faced extreme difficulties, not least the jinx that appeared to hover over the site. The site's original chapel burnt down in 1865, as did the consequent temporary structure (1869). This building proceeded in stages until work finished in 1928, some sixty years after it began. Yet, it is incomplete: the two towers facing Cathedral Street lack spires. The interior features two rose windows of stained glass and a baptistery of Sienna marble with a one thousand ounce (roughly thirty kilogram) silver canopy. The crypt below hides a magnificent Melocco Brothers mosaic. **Guided tours** of the Cathedral are given every Sunday at 12noon, leaving from inside the College Street doors (See: Tours Around Sydney).

Leaving the cathedral by the College Street doors, cross back into Hyde Park and walk down the central, tree-covered pathway all the way to the **Anzac**

ARCHITECTURE: EARLY CITY TOWERS & OFFICES

For most of the nineteenth century, architecture in Sydney was largely influenced by fashions current in England and Europe, but by the early twentieth century, the city's architects were drawing inspiration from contemporary architectural developments in the United States. Skyscrapers had evolved in America during the 1890s and were emerging as symbols of corporate prestige and success, their dramatic silhouettes against the sky providing instantly recognisable landmarks on city skylines.

While Sydney's early office towers were not really towers at all (building heights were restricted to forty five metres until 1957), the influence of their American predecessors can clearly be seen. The 1923 Chicago Tribune Tower had included a 'Gothic' lantern surrounded by 'Gothic' buttresses, and this initiated the fashion for medieval detailing demonstrated on the facade of the former British Medical Association House (1928-1930; 135 Macquarie Street). The building is clad in glazed, coloured terracotta, which was also used to form the complex Gothic inspired decorative motifs concentrated at eye level and on the skyline. The Grace Building (1930; Cnr King Street and York Street, with its crowning turret and Gothic inspired 'flying' buttresses, is another terracotta clad confection, while the former Sun Building (1929; 60-70 Elizabeth Street) and State Theatre (1929; Market Street) also illustrate the pinnacles, pointed arches and theatricality characteristic of the style.

Similar in their soaring verticality, but lacking the specifically medieval details of the Skyscraper Gothic buildings above, were the European-influenced Art Deco constructions of the 1930s.

The dramatic former City Mutual Building (1934-1936; Cnr Hunter Street and Bligh Street, was designed by Emil Sodersten, and incorporates the emphatic vertical piers and the crisp, shiny, modern materials which characterise the style. The building's continuous bands of zig-zag, metal-framed bay windows rise dramatically to an imposing corner tower, which incorporates decorative sets of parallel lines in a manner typical of the style. Below the tower, the building's monumental entrance is clad in black marble topped by a robust relief sculpture. Sodersten's Birtley Towers (1934; 8 Birtley Place, Elizabeth Bay) is a towering residential interpretation of the style, with decorative Art Deco forms modelled from dark red textured brickwork. (See: Box: Flats & Apartments.)

Ross and Rowe's design for the monumental, terracotta clad Commonwealth Bank Building (1928; Cnr Castlereagh Street and Martin Place) was influenced by the influential Parisian Beaux Arts school. Classical motifs, such as the huge Ionic columns and cornice of the facade, are typical of this style which, in contrast to Art Deco, looked to the past rather than to the future for its inspiration. The building's ground floor banking chamber was restored to its former splendour in the 1980s, and is well worth a visit. (See: Walks Around Sydney: City Centre).

The former Trust Building (1912, remodelled 1934) is representative of another American influenced style widely adopted by banks and other financial institutions. The architecture of this Commercial Palazzo followed Classical precedent, with a heavy, rusticated stone base, cornices and arches providing a dependable and timeless image. The former Bank of New South Wales (1932; Opposite Martin Place in George Street) is another example of the type.

Memorial. This is the City's largest and most significant war memorial, officially opened in 1934 after eighteen years of planning and fund raising. The Art Deco design was C.B. Dellit's competition entry and features various carvings representing the members of the forces- Army, Navy, Medical Corps and Air Force. Although built as a memorial to the First World War, it was rededicated in 1984 as a memorial to all Australians who have fought in wars. Inside are two halls: the Hall of Memory, featuring more than one hundred thousand stars representing each Australian who fought in the war, and the Hall of Silence dominated by a huge bronze sculpture.

From here, return to Park Street, turn left and walk to Elizabeth Street. Cross diagonally to the right and walk as far as No. 187, **The Great Synagogue** (Open: Tuesday and Thursday at 12noon). This immensely opulent building, a Byzantine/Gothic design of Thomas Rowe, was completed in 1878 and incorporates a melange of Medieval-inspired details. As the wrought iron gates are usually kept locked, visitors must walk around to the Castlereagh Street entrance, directly behind. The interior is not disappointing, made up of cast iron columns with capitals, plaster decorations to the arches, a panelled ceiling and stained glass windows.

From here, return to Park Street, this time turning right to walk towards the **Town Hall** in George Street, passing through magazine publishing land and a secondary legal precinct. The frou-frou Town Hall is the middle building of a group of three imposing Victorian sandstone edifices. Although Sydney City Council was formed when Sydney was declared a city in 1842, it was some time until it set about acquiring accommodation, particularly as the entire council was dismissed in 1858 over corruption allegations. The site chosen was also controversial: it was on top of Sydney's first cemetery, and the bodies and tombstones had to be moved to the Devonshire Street cemetery (and once again in 1900 when Central Railway Station was built). The foundation stone was unveiled in 1868 by the colony's first royal visitor, Prince Alfred the Duke of Edinburgh, and the building was completed by 1889. The exterior sandstone is actually only cladding over brickwork, and it shows many ornamental Classical Revival details similar to the ones you have already seen on other Victorian sandstone buildings on the walk. The accurately restored foyer is topped by an amazingly bright blue plastered dome with the kind of chandelier under which one would not want to be standing, should it fall! Beyond this is Centennial Hall, added in 1888-89, and the main auditorium, where concerts, recitals and tortuous school speech days are held. The Baroque-esque grand pipe organ contains more than eight and a half thousand pipes, and is one of the most powerful in the world. (The largest church organ in the world is in Passau, Germany).

Next door is **St Andrew's Cathedral** (See: Sights To See). Although Macquarie laid a foundation stone in 1819 and intended that Greenway should design and build the city an Anglican Cathedral, the project was shelved as a result of the Bigge report. This original foundation stone became the kernel of St Andrew's when work finally commenced in 1837 to a Gothic Revival design by Edmund Blacket. After progressing in stages, it was consecrated in 1868, but was not completed until almost ninety years later, after the towers, Chapter House and George Street entrance had been added by later architects. Despite the central city location, St Andrew's is one of the few city churches which has managed to retain the large open space all around it. Note the delicate pointed arches of the windows, decorative pinnacles, sturdy buttresses and well-proportioned towers.

Across Park Street stands the beautiful **Queen Victoria Building,** one of the city's most remarkable landmarks. This American-inspired late Victorian Romanesque building (constructed between 1893-98) was designed by City Architect George McRae on a grand scale. Covering an entire city block, it housed produce markets, a number of showrooms and corridors of offices, and was built to generate employment in the 1890s depression. However, the building was boarded up and fell into disuse over the years, standing semi-derelict until its refurbishment, restoration and re-opening in 1986. Light pours into the spacious voids from the barrel vaulted roof, intensifying the colours of the beautiful tile work, and it is one of the City's premier shopping venues, with Country Road, Polo Ralph Lauren, Red Earth, the Body Shop and the ABC shop among its favoured tenants (See: Shopping). Make sure you explore the building by riding the escalators to the top, and do not miss the incredible stained glass dome, best viewed from the ground floor. Indeed, right next to the dome is one of the City's great cafes, **Bar Cupola,** the perfect spot for another well-earned break where you can watch Sydney walk past.

From here, walk to the far end and turn right into Market Street. On the opposite corner stands **Gowings,** the boys and menswear store which has become a Sydney institution by occupying the corner under the motto "Walk through, no-one asked to buy" since the 1870s (See: Shopping, Sydney Icons). Next door in Market Street stands the amazing **State Theatre,** hailed as "the Empire's greatest theatre" when it was built in 1929 at a cost of £1 million. This 'Cinema Baroque' masterpiece was designed by Henry White as a wild fantasy specifically intended to lure people to it with its frothy, overloaded magnificence. Much of its splendour, such as the mosaic floor, marble columns, brass grille doors and statues, is visible in the entry lobby. Beyond the doors, the foyer and auditorium also exude incredible opulence. Today, it is used for concerts and many other events, especially the Sydney Film Festival each winter (See: Film).

The gleaming golden **Sydney Tower** (✆ 9229 7430; **Open:** 7 days 9.30am-9.30pm; **Cost:** $6/$3/$15 family; See: Sights To See) is the tallest building in the Southern Hemisphere. From this "three hundred and four point eight metre high" (as the employees will tell you) purpose-built crow's nest, visitors are treated to a three hundred and sixty degree, far-reaching (eighty-two kilometres) view of the Sydney basin, the Blue Mountains and the Tasman Sea.

At the base of the tower is the centre of the City's retail precinct. Both David Jones stores are further along the street , while the Pitt Street mall lies on the left, the axis of a number of **shopping arcades. Skygarden** is on the right, the Mid City Centre is on the left, and just beyond that is the magnificent Edwardian **Strand Arcade.** Sydney used to have a number of such elegant nineteenth century arcades, but unfortunately, ideas of 'progress' led to their demolition. Luckily, the Strand (c. 1891) survived with its cast iron roof trusses, elegant galleries, barrel vaulted glass roof, stained glass and colourful tiling, all of which were accurately restored after a fire nearly gutted the building in the 1970s. Again, this is one of the top shopping venues in Sydney for jewellery and clothing: Rox, Bracewell, Love & Hatred and Morrisey Edmiston are all here (See: Shopping).

Thus the walk ends in the middle of the City's shopping area, although the more exhausted walkers among the Good Life Guide's users may like to save the shopping for another expedition. Those searching for a pub should head for the exuberant Victorian **Marble Bar** (1893), originally part of the Adams' Hotel (demolished 1969) and now incorporated under the Hilton Hotel. Here, slabs of marble, stained pictorial glass, a vaulted ceiling, murals by well known Sydney artist Julian Ashton and copious amounts of cedar and walnut decoration, as well as a beer, await.

The Colonial Grandeur of Macquarie Street

Description: Flat and easy with a lot of inside stops, this walk glides through the city's most conspicuous and beautiful historic public buildings. A classic visitors' route.

Starting Point: St James Station (St James Road exit).

Map Reference For Walk: E4.
Length: Approximately 3 hours.
Best Time: While the buildings included in the walk have different opening times, they are open Mon-Fri 10am-5pm.
Note: Those intending to see a number of the Historic Houses Trust's buildings should buy the **Ticket Through Time** ($15/$10/$32 family) which gives entry to all the Trust's properties for three months (See: A~Z Practical Basics: Tickets).
See: Music: Classical & Opera; Open Air Sydney: Parks & Gardens, Picnics; Sights To See: Royal Botanic Gardens; Tours Around Sydney: Sydney Explorer; Walks Around Sydney: City Centre, St Mary's to the Opera House.

Lachlan Macquarie arrived in Sydney in 1810 to take over as fifth Governor of the colony. He looked around and saw a forsaken place, only barely self-sufficient- a perilous way to be when the nearest supplies are weeks away by sea- with poor roads, poor buildings, and helpless convicts being exploited by those in power and forced to work like slaves. He had big plans. During his eleven year governorship, the population tripled from eleven thousand five hundred to thrity-eight thousand eight hundred; land under cultivation grew fourfold from seven thousand six hundred acres to thirty-two thousand acres; numbers of sheep and cattle rocketed; the Bank of New South Wales (now Westpac) and a police force were formed; horse racing and cart registration were introduced; convicts were forced to attend church and an enormous public works program was planned.

However, in this area at least, he could not put his ideas into action single-handedly. One can imagine his glee when a practising architect was transported to Sydney for forging a signature following the collapse of a business. **Francis Greenway** probably did not imagine that this great misfortune would guarantee his

ARCHITECTURE: SYDNEY'S SANDSTONE

In 1770, Captain Cook (See: History) reported that the stone of the region where Sydney was later to be founded was well suited to building, and despite the First Fleet voyagers' lack of adequate tools and knowledge for exploiting the resource which surrounded them, sandstone has been used since the colony's earliest days. The number of skilled stonemasons grew as the colony expanded, and it was they who identified the high quality Yellow Block stone in Pyrmont in the 1850s, from which many of Sydney's grandest buildings were to be constructed. Yellow Block hardens and darkens after exposure to the buff, often becoming the almost orange colour which is characteristic of the city's sandstone buildings.

The second half of the nineteenth century was a time of progress in New South Wales, fed by the Gold Rush. Reflecting the confidence and relative opulence of the age, the 1870s and 1880s saw the construction of many exuberant Gothic and Classical Revival landmarks. Colonial Architects James Barnet and Walter Liberty Vernon were particularly influential in shaping the design of Victorian Sydney, and many of the city's public buildings were designed by either of these two luminaries.

Buildings in the Victorian Free Classical style display an eclectic mixture of the arches, columns, pediments, pilasters, sculptures and balustraded parapets found in the architecture of antiquity and the Renaissance, combined with little regard for historical precedent or accuracy. Barnet's Lands Department (1880; 97 Bridge Street), Colonial Secretary's Building (1878; Cnr Bridge Street and Macquarie Street) and General Post Office (1866-1890; Martin Place) are representative of this ebullient architecture.

Similarly energetic, but with an even greater profusion of decorative detail, in the form of French-inspired mansard roofs and coupled columns, is the Sydney Town Hall (1866-1889; 483 George Street), designed by J.H. Wilson and Albert Bond.

Much more restrained and serious are William Wardell's Gothic Revival St Mary's Cathedral (1868-1882; Cnr College Street and Cathedral Street), and Edmund Blacket's St Andrew's Cathedral (main structure 1837-1886; next to Town Hall). Both buildings show the pointed arches, stone window tracery, stained glass, pinnacles, wall buttresses and towers characteristic not just of Victorian design, but also of the centuries old great European cathedrals.

Following the turn of the twentieth century, Classical-inspired architecture was once more the fashion, although this time the individual components were generally carefully assembled to emulate their historical precedents. Walter Liberty Vernon's Art Gallery of New South Wales (completed 1909) has a columned and pedimented entrance clearly inspired by Greek temples, while his Premier's Office (completed c. 1896; now part of the Inter-Continental Hotel at the corner of Macquarie and Bridge Streets) is reminiscent of Renaissance palaces. Contemporary with this Classical Revival is the Queen Victoria Building (1893-1898; Cnr George Street and Market Street). George McRae's building, which borrows heavily from Medieval Romanesque architecture, was extensively restored in the 1980s to form one of Sydney's most popular shopping arcades.

During the twentieth century, the increasing expense of stone and the technological changes which have so altered the nature of building have meant that sandstone is now used primarily as a cladding material, as it is on the Art Deco inspired MSB Building (now the Museum of Contemporary Art, George Street, The Rocks). The building was designed in the 1930s and completed in 1952.

place in history; yet, collaborating with Macquarie, he was responsible for leaving Sydney the Hyde Park Barracks, St James Church and the first Vaucluse lighthouse, for which he received a conditional pardon, to name a few of his buildings. From 1816, he was in charge of overseeing construction, a task he carried out with such zeal that he was very unpopular with the workmen.

Macquarie's program extended to sixty-seven public buildings, spread over Sydney, Parramatta, Van Diemen's Land (Tasmania), and Bathurst; he constructed roads and bridges and generally managed to transform Sydney from a makeshift, forsaken prison camp to a permanent town with a future. However, not everybody thought this a good thing. Macquarie's so-called reckless extravagance prompted the commissioning of the Bigge Report by the British into the state of the colony. Especially contentious were Macquarie's liberalist attitudes which encouraged convicts to mend their ways by offering pardons; even more contentious was that many of them proceeded to make a fortune. This simply was not right: scum was scum and should have remained that way, preferably poor too! The report instigated Macquarie's resignation and Greenway was hit hard: Mortimer Lewis replaced him as Colonial Architect. Both died in poverty, having left a great legacy in New South Wales which unjustly went unappreciated for many years.

Along Macquarie Street are some of the city's most impressive public buildings, built with sandstone extracted from the Pyrmont quarries and drawn by a team of Clydesdale draughthorses to the site. Standing here at the edge of the park, they lie stretched out before you, reaching down to the Harbour. On the left is **St James Church** (original structure 1819-24), considered by many to be one of the most elegant buildings in Sydney. However, it has not always been a church: it was originally built as a Courthouse. The colony's early population was almost exclusively Anglo-Saxon, and as it grew, the need for an Anglican Cathedral was recognised. Macquarie and Greenway planned to build one in George Street, but as a cost-cutting measure, Commissioner Bigge arranged for the St James Courthouse to be transformed into a church. These days it cowers in the shadows of the **Supreme Court of New South Wales,** next door across Queen's Square. You can visit the courts if you wish (simply ask one of the people at the information desk what's on), but be warned: a lot of unintelligible appeal cases are heard here (See: Wet Days).

Over the road stand the **Hyde Park Barracks** (✆ 9223 8922; **Open:** 7 days 10am-5pm; **Cost:** $5/$3). Completed in 1819 and originally housing six hundred male convicts, the Barracks building has over the years housed free assisted settlers, served as an asylum for the 'insane', as a migrant clearing house and as a courthouse. Recent conservation and archaeological work has uncovered many belongings of previous occupants under the floorboards, either hidden there due to a lack of privacy or dragged to the sub-floor space by rats. Now the building incorporates a fascinating museum concentrating on the life of the convict workers- how they slept, ate, worked and relaxed- as well as changing exhibitions staged by the Historic Houses Trust. Here, visitors can lie in a hammock and close their eyes to listen to a soundscape of convict conversation. The courtyard cafe might be a good place to relax while reading of the history of the following buildings.

When Macquarie arrived, Sydney was in desperate need of a new hospital, so he awarded a contract in 1810 to Garnham Blaxcell, Alexander Riley & Dr D'Arcy Wentworth, who was to be surgeon in charge. Owing to the emptiness of the colony's coffers but the urgency of its inhabitants' desire for rum, Macquarie gave the developers the exclusive right to import forty-five thousand gallons of rum, which they then resold at a huge profit. From this they were required to construct the hospital, while the three shillings per gallon duty was refunded by the government as payment. **The Rum Hospital,** as its nickname became, originally consisted of three buildings in which conditions were Spartan: there were no bathrooms and the food was prepared in the wards with the patients. Unfortunately only two parts of the hospital remain as the Mint and the front section of the Parliament, while the central building was demolished in 1879 to make way for the new Sydney hospital, still in use.

Walk next door to the **Mint Building** (✆ 9217 0311; **Open:** Mon-Fri 10am-5pm; **Cost:** $5/$2/$12 family; also entitles visitors to entry to the Powerhouse Museum on the same day) on this side of the street, Australia's oldest public building. Gradually, the buildings of the Rum Hospital were seconded for other uses. First the elegant staff quarters became the Royal Mint in 1851, weighing the gold flooding in from the diggings as the Gold Rush gathered momentum, and smelting it into sovereigns. It was used for this purpose until 1927, while it has now been fully restored and refurbished, and opened as **The Sydney Mint Museum** in 1995. Early coinage from around the world is exhibited in a strongroom which originally housed the goldfields' spoils, early Australian gold and silver jewellery is displayed upstairs, and a coining factory is housed in a pavilion in the courtyard, all well worth a look. You will see Australia's first gold sovereign and find a marvellous interactive computer display with a map of the City and Circular Quay on its screen which visitors can touch to see various photographs and images of how those areas looked in the past. The museum also has regular special exhibitions and events, such as gold panning and actors.

Next are the buildings of the **Sydney Hospital** and **Eye Hospital,** built on the site of the central wing of the Rum Hospital. As magnificent as a brass pork chop can be, **Il Porcellino** was donated in 1968 by Marchesa Fiaschi Torrigiani, whose father and brother both served as honorary surgeons at the hospital. Sydney's favourite pig stands dribbling proudly on Macquarie Street, enjoying visitors rubbing its nose for good luck. Behind in the central courtyard stands an Art Deco fountain, donated by friends of British actor Robert Brough in 1907 and restored in 1988. The courtyard is a quiet, cool place to pause and listen to the sounds of the city.

The Principal Surgeon's quarters now form the centre front of **Parliament House** (✆ 9230 2111; **Open:** Mon-Fri 9.30am-4.30pm) of which several areas are open to the public (See: Tours Around Sydney). The New South Wales Legislative Council was formed by decree of British Government in 1823, made up of the Governor's appointees; representative government was not introduced until 1843. Under the *Australian Colonies Government Act* of 1850, the Legislative council was authorised to begin preparing a democratic constitution for New South Wales, accepted by the British Parliament in 1855. New South Wales has a Legislative Assembly (elections every four years; origin of most bills and legislation) and a Legislative Council (members elected for the duration of three parliaments). Cabinet consists of members chosen from the party currently in power; they are answerable to the parliament and therefore to the electorate. The building itself was first used by the executive in 1829 and was extended twice thereafter to accommodate the growing government. However, even more space was needed, so a 'temporary', pre-fabricated corrugated iron building was shipped from Melbourne and erected at the southern end of the existing building, much of it still in existence within the Legislative Council Chamber. Even the packing was not wasted, but was used to line the Council Chamber and adjacent offices. In the central courtyard stands an elegant fountain enclosed in glass, while the surrounding halls are full of portraits and reminders of the State's parliamentary history. Although not everybody's idea of a scintillating spectator sport, the luckiest of walkers may be able to watch a session of parliament. Those in attendance of the Information Desk near the front doors will direct interested parties to the chambers and explain the parliamentary process. Parliament usually sits in three week blocks from mid April to mid December.

Next door, the **State Library** (✆ 9230 1414; **Open:** Mon-Fri 9am-9pm; Sat-Sun 11am-5pm) is a mine of information stored on over one hundred and forty kilometres of shelving and copious amounts of computer data. The Australian Subscription library was started in 1826 to provide the isolated colonists with access to books and became a public library after acquisition by the government. Meanwhile, David Scott Mitchell was devoting his life to collecting books and documentation relating to Australia. His massive collection of over sixty thousand items was bequeathed with £70,000 to the State, on condition that a new library be built. Begun in 1906 and finished with the addition of the portico in 1941, the Mitchell Library's stately and suave book-lined **reading room** contains enormous Australiana collections. Videodiscs allow the public to view photographs of Sydney's past (ask the librarians for help), while Captain Bligh's log from *The Bounty* and Captain Cook's journals are kept elsewhere. The floor of its foyer contains an inlaid map of Abel Tasman's voyages and looks out beyond the building's sandstone columns to the Botanic Gardens. There is also a gallery on the first floor, which is renowned for its excellent exhibitions, while free films are shown every Friday. **The General Reference Library** was added in 1988 and contains enormous resources, such as a family history centre and a vast book stack. Tours can be arranged (✆ 9230 1603), and anyone finding themselves touristed-out one day should head for this haven of books, newspapers, magazines and quiet (See: Wet Days). The central, glass-roofed cafe is even further incentive to linger.

Across the road are the **Royal Botanic Gardens,** another of Sydney's treasures, where you can snooze or sit and admire the view. Continue down Macquarie Street to the first gates on the right, which are unusually grand; indeed, they almost look palatial. These are the **Palace Gates** which led to the Garden Palace, a massive timber and iron structure covering thirty-one thousand square metres built in 1879 to house international exhibitions. These were intended to show the world how far Australia, and New South Wales in particular, had come since the First Fleet sailed in and pitched their tents. More than a million people attended the exhibition, attracted by the domed and arched halls, observation towers, the enormous statue of Queen Victoria under the domed atrium and luxurious murals. It was all spectacularly grandiose, and it only took four hours for the entire thing to burn to the ground in 1882. The gardens are a sanctuary within the City, the perfect place to sit under a tree with a good book, and deserve a thorough exploration. If you do go in and have a look at this end, it is quite likely that you will hear the sounds of instruments carried on the breeze.

In the block opposite the Palace Gates are two large terraced buildings, originally houses, which remain from Macquarie Street's time as a desirable, elegant residential street. The **Royal Australian College of Physicians** building (No 145) was originally a two storey sandstone townhouse, built by 1848, which had two extra storeys added in 1910 to match the original details. **History House** (No 133), now the headquarters of the Royal Australian Historical Society, has an exterior characteristic of the 1880s, with elegant cast iron verandahs and carved cedar joinery inside, giving an idea of the elegance this street once had. Next door on the left stands the former **British Medical**

Association House (No 135). Designed in 1929, its terracotta facade incorporates detailing influenced by both the contemporary Art Deco movement and by medieval architecture.

The next stop on the walk is the **Conservatorium of Music,** the castle-like building next on the right. It can also be reached by walking through the Botanic Gardens' Rose Garden. Also part of Macquarie's works program, it was excessively (even provocatively) grand considering it was built as the Governor's Stables to house only thirty horses between 1817 and 1819. Commissioner Bigge was outraged, yet they remained in use until 1917, housing the Light Horse Infantry until the central courtyard was covered and it became the Conservatorium of Music. For years, 'The Con' has been the centre of musical education in New South Wales, and consequently, cheap concerts and master classes given by the stars of tomorrow (✆ 9230 1222) can be heard regularly. However, plans are afoot to move it to a new site.

Next to the Conservatorium stand the gates leading through more of the Botanic Gardens to **Government House.** It was built from a design by Queen Victoria's royal architect, Edward Blore, after a succession of Governors had complained about their accommodation: the existing Government House in Bridge Street (now the site of The Museum of Sydney) was rotten and infested with white ants. Governor Gipps was in the right place at the right time and opened the new quarters in 1845, although he retired twelve months later. Its picturesque and luxuriant detailing inspired by medieval architecture elevated it high above any existing buildings, containing under its towers and turrets thirteen bedrooms, cellars, kitchens, staff quarters and twelve public rooms, not to mention the ballroom, of course complete with orchestra gallery. Government House is still occupied by the Governors of New South Wales and its magnificently tended grounds have sweeping views over the Harbour and Opera House. Plans are afoot to oust the Governor from this dazzling residence and turn it over to public use.

The Hotel Inter-Continental, opposite in Macquarie Street, is an architectural curiosity. The sandstone base was used as the Treasury and Audit building in the past, but has now sprouted a modern, high-rise core as the hotel was planted solidly over the middle of the original building leaving the facade and atrium. The interior courtyard is a luscious spot for afternoon tea, preferably Devonshire Tea served with champagne!

As you cross the street in search of such delights, notice the **Colonial Secretary's Building** (not open to the public) designed by Colonial Architect James Barnet and built in 1875. This was where New South Wales' Executive Council met, and was at one time the office of Sir Henry Parkes (1815-1896) who entered the Colonial Parliament in 1854 and served as Premier five times between 1872 and 1891. He was central to the development of the Federation Movement (the joining of the States into one nation) and is therefore referred to as the 'Father of Federation'. His office has been restored to appear as it was when he was in office, and his portrait hangs over the fireplace. More recently, the chair has been kept warm by Sir Laurence Street, ex-Chief Justice of New South Wales.

This is the conclusion of the walk, and those not opting for the Hotel Inter-Continental's afternoon tea could continue down to the Opera House or keep walking to join this with the City Centre Circuit (above, recommended for extremely energetic walkers only). Those feeling like a cafe or pub stop should also cross Macquarie Street to Bridge Street, walking downhill to the tree-studded Macquarie Place on the right, where Bar Paradiso and The Customs House pub await.

The Rocks

Description: The Rocks is Sydney's old town, a fascinating mix of heritage buildings, shops, cafes and pubs.
Starting Point: The Rocks Visitors Centre (106 George St, The Rocks; ✆ 9255 1788; **Open:** 7 days 9am-5pm.
Map Reference For Walk: D4.
Length: Allow half a day.
See: Directory; History; Shopping; Sights To See: The Rocks; Sydney By Area: The Rocks; Tours Around Sydney: Sydney Explorer, Walking Tours.

The land surrounding this rocky outcrop was the first to be developed by the Europeans, and during the early years of the colony, a gaol, hospital and bakehouse appeared. By the time Governor Macquarie was in control of the colony (1810), the area was a crowded, disease-ridden and noisy slum, the domain of sailors, hustlers, petty thieves and transients from all over the globe. Sanitation was not a principal feature of the area, with many of the narrow lanes little better than open sewers. Suez Canal, for example, was named as a pun and was typical of the conditions which fostered the spread of the Bubonic Plague at the turn of the twentieth century.

Large scale demolition took place soon after to sanitise the area, and again in the 1920s to facilitate the building the Harbour Bridge, but the sweep of greater destruction was narrowly averted in the 1960s when the building of office towers in the area was mooted. One can only shudder to think what would have been lost had such plans gone ahead: not only irreplaceable architectural heritage, but also the local community. The controversy inspired the making of long term plans for the Rocks and the setting up of the Sydney Cove (Redevelopment) Authority in 1968. Contrary to initial fears by residents alarmed that restoration would see them evicted from their homes, most of the community remained in the area, either in their own houses or government housing, an example of which is tall apartment block above Playfair Terrace. Today, most of The Rocks' buildings have been reclaimed, restored and refurbished by the authority after detailed research into

ARCHITECTURE: WAREHOUSES & WOOL STORES

No buildings in Sydney give a clearer indication of the city's previous life as a bustling, booming seaport than the robust warehouses and woolstores which dot The Rocks, Pyrmont, Ultimo and the western fringe of the City to this day.

The earliest stores, such as Campbell's Store (original section built 1842-1861; Hickson Road, The Rocks) were built with sandstone, their thick timber floorboards supported by chunky posts and beams of native hardwood (often the aptly named Ironbark). Enormous triangulated timber trusses gave the roofs their characteristic zig-zagged profile. The former FL Barker's Store (Loftus Street) and the Hinchcliff Building (Loftus Lane; both just behind Circular Quay) are two further examples of this type.

The Argyle Bond Store (Argyle Street, The Rocks) is a collection of magnificent warehouses grouped around a central, cobbled courtyard. The complex began life in the 1820s when a house for Captain John Piper was commenced on the site. Never completed, the house was incorporated into the complex as it gradually enclosed the courtyard during the nineteenth century. On the northern side of the group, the Cleland Store was built in 1913 and is now integrated with the Argyle Bond. Recently conserved by the Sydney Cove Authority, the warehouses are a good demonstration of the sensitive adaptation of old buildings to new uses.

As the nineteenth century progressed, the increasing quality of locally made bricks was accompanied by the increasing expense of sandstone, inevitably leading to the displacement of stonework by brickwork by the final decades of the Victorian era. In 1876, the Australasian Steam Navigation Company commissioned prominent architect William Wardell to design its warehouse and offices at 3-5 Hickson Road, The Rocks. Completed in 1884, the building's distinctive Dutch-inspired gables, clock tower and richly coloured brickwork are still landmarks of the western side of Circular Quay. The company itself is long gone, but a visit to the Ken Done gallery now located in its warehouse will give a clear picture of the robust nature of a typical warehouse.

The prosperous 1880s were followed by a period of depression and drought, but the economic resurgence of the final years of the nineteenth century prompted a boom in warehouse building which continued until after 1910.

The warehouses of this period demonstrate the contemporary preference for simplicity of architectural detail. Their external walls were almost always of face brick, and the use of sandstone was restricted to the buildings' strongly emphasised bases and decorative details. Typically, facades were divided into vertical bays separated by massive piers and topped by recessed semi-circular arches. Although cast iron posts and wrought iron girders were beginning to replace the hardwood structures of the previous decades, the interiors of these warehouses, with grids of columns punctuating spacious storage areas, remained largely unchanged. The Farmers' and Graziers' Woolstore (commenced 1895; Wattle Street, Ultimo) is one of a number of mammoth turn-of-the-century warehouses in this area. Closer to the City and smaller in size are the many warehouses in Kent Street, particularly between numbers 346 and 372.

In recent years, many of Sydney's warehouses have been adapted to contemporary uses, aided by the simplicity of their original construction and the high quality of the materials. The location of the Kent Street buildings has enabled their easy and practical transformation into offices, while the mammoth Goldsborough store (1912) overlooking Darling Harbour is now being converted into apartments.

the buildings' original features. More than anywhere in the city, the visitor discerns a strong, community-wide sense of social and architectural heritage.

The Rocks is a complex web of architectural heritage, reconstructed social history, tiny back streets, archaeological digs and terraces. It would be impossible here to describe in enough detail all that should be seen of where Sydney's European settlement began in the 1700s. Instead, the best thing to do is to head straight for the **Rocks Visitors Centre** (above). The historians and architects of the Authority have put together a detailed **Self Guided Walking Tour,** which leads in an organised manner through the area's highlights. This, and many other information pamphlets, are available at the centre, where **Guided Walking Tours** can also be booked and joined. In either case, visitors should allow at least half a day to explore the alleys, shops, cafes, pubs, courtyards and buildings of The Rocks.

St Mary's Cathedral to The Art Gallery of NSW, The Royal Botanic Gardens & The Opera House

Description: This classic route is really only a gentle, flat stroll to the Art Gallery, Mrs Macquarie's Point, the Botanic Gardens and the Opera House. It is a very rewarding walk with stunning views, cafes and trees under which to relax or recover.

Starting Point: Hyde Park, by St Mary's Cathedral.

Map Reference For Walk: E4 to D5.

Length: 2-3 hours, depending on time spent in the Art Gallery and the gardens.

Best Time: Sundays, beginning at 12noon at St Mary's. This way, you will be able to join a tour of the Cathedral and a backstage tour of the Opera House, both only conducted on Sunday. Bookings are required for the Opera House backstage tour (✆ 9250 7250).

Transport Alternative: all points on the walk are on the Sydney Explorer route.

See: Music: Classical & Opera; Open Air: Parks &

Gardens; Sights To See; Museums & Galleries; Sports: Swimming; Sydney Icons; Tours Around Sydney: St Mary's, the Art Gallery, Sydney Explorer.

The imposing lines of the sandstone **St Mary's Cathedral** seem to reach over into Hyde Park, and as you cross the street and enter the cool, vaulted space of the Cathedral, a sense of establishment, rare for Sydney, is enveloping. The Cathedral's beginnings were dogged with trouble. Begun in 1821, both the original chapel and its replacement structure burnt down, and it was not until after sixty years of construction work from 1868 that it was finally opened. However, it is still incomplete: observant souls will notice that the two front spires are missing as they were never built. The stained glass windows, detailed altars and intricate stonework make this one of the most imposing buildings of the city. Unfortunately, the bells are only rung on Sundays and special occasions. Those interested can join a guided tour near the College Street doors on Sundays at 12noon (See: Tours Around Sydney).

Leaving the Cathedral, walk across onto the tree-lined Art Gallery Road, which leads past the **Domain** and, logically enough, to the **Art Gallery of New South Wales** (**Open:** Mon-Sat 10am-5pm; Sun 12noon-5pm; **Cost:** free with free guided tours; **See:** Museums & Galleries). The gallery's permanent collection covers European works, modern Australian works, prints, sculptures and installations; yet of particular interest is the new 'Yiribana' gallery of Aboriginal and Torres Strait Islander art and culture. There is also a good cafe on level two, offering views of Woolloomooloo Bay and Garden Island through its full length windows.

From here, continue along the water's edge path overlooking the grey **Woolloomooloo Wharves,** where many of this country's post-war immigrants arrived, **Garden Island Naval Base,** and **Andrew 'Boy' Charlton Pool** (**Open:** Mon-Fri 6am-8pm; Sat-Sun 6.30am-7pm; Closed winter; **Cost:** \$2/\$1). Garden Island is a bit of an enigma: it hasn't been a garden for one hundred and eighty years, and it hasn't been an island for half a century. All the relevance its name retains is as a reminder of the times before the island lost its simple beauty. Only sixteen days passed after the First Fleet's arrival at Sydney Cove before the crew of the *Sirius* used the island to plant the first crops in New South Wales (hence the name), and three sets of initials, FM, IR and WB were carved on a rock at the time, still visible today. But the British involvement in the Crimean War, Opium War in China and the Indian Mutiny prompted the desire for a permanent strategic base for the Empire, so Garden Island was handed over to the Royal Navy for the purpose in 1857 in exchange for Bennelong Point. However, the navy had difficulty in stopping picnickers from getting on to the island; today, guarded with boom gates, high fences, security cameras and water patrols, the problem does not arise. Instead, the view must be enjoyed from this road!

This peninsula is **Mrs Macquarie's Point,** where early colonial Governor Macquarie's wife liked to sit and take the air. Her chair is still here, carved in a large outcrop of sandstone set back from the end of the point and marked with a large inscription. This is a delightful area from which to gaze across the gleaming water of the Harbour, and a not insubstantial bonus is the usual pink presence of Sydney's best soft serve ice cream van. Yum.

From here, follow the stone steps down to the water's edge, and stroll along the footpath on the Harbour foreshore around **Farm Cove,** so called as this was where the first settlers started an experimental farm growing various crops and plants. This is part of the well signposted **Royal Botanic Gardens,** a city centre oasis of fresh air and calm established in 1816. There are plenty of trees and benches, and a central kiosk, so explore, take a rest or contemplate (**Open:** 7 days 8am-sunset; **See:** Parks & Gardens).

The sense of anticipation and wonder which arises while walking around from Farm Cove as the sails of the **Opera House** gradually emerge from behind the trees is awesome, and has been known to move people to tears. **Bennelong Point,** on which it stands, was named after one of two Aborigines patronised and voluntarily taken 'on tour' to England as social exhibits by Governor Phillip in 1792, and was, unbelievably, a bus depot before the construction of Jørn Utzon's masterpiece. Impeccably mirroring the sails on the Harbour beyond, the complex is the focus of musical activity in the city. (See: Sydney Icons.) Tours of the theatres and foyers leave regularly from the tour desk, lower walkway (7 days 9am-4pm; **Cost:** \$8.50/\$5.50). Special backstage tours are conducted on Sundays only (**Cost:** \$13; Bookings ✆ 9250 7250). While here, a visit to the box office would be a good idea. The chamber orchestras, symphony orchestra, opera, ballet and theatre companies performing here are of renowned quality. In addition, there are free concerts in the forecourt every Sunday at 12noon and 4pm.

All that stands between you and the **Sydney Cove Oyster Bar,** where slippery oysters and a slippery beer await, is the Opera House Forecourt Market (Sunday only). Once ensconced in the Oyster Bar, you can gaze across the ferries to Circular Quay, and contemplate the natural and man-made beauty you have seen on the walk!

Chinatown, Darling Harbour & The Powerhouse Museum

Description: This walk is made up of separable sections: Chinatown is an important part of the city, and the home of many fascinating elements of the Chinese culture which are easily explored. It then progresses towards Darling Harbour and on to the Powerhouse Museum.

Starting Point: Town Hall or the Queen Victoria Building.

Map Reference For Walk: F3 to E3.

Length: 3-4 hours for the whole walk, depending on stops.
Best Time: The best days for undertaking this walk are Saturday and Sunday, when the giant Paddy's markets are on and the people are out and about. Ideally, time the walk so that Chinatown and lunch time coincide.
Take: An appetite.
Note: Those intending to spend a considerable amount of time in Darling Harbour should consider buying the Darling Harbour Super Ticket ($29.50/$19.50) available from Darling Harbour Information Booths, the Sydney Aquarium and Matilda Cruises. It offers a two hour Matilda Harbour Cruise, a trip on the Monorail, entrance to the Sydney Aquarium and the Chinese Garden, a 10% discount shopping voucher for certain shops and food outlets.
Transport Alternative: Sydney Explorer.
See: Children; Directory: Chinatown; Markets: Food Markets, Paddy's Markets; Museums & Galleries: National Maritime Museum, Powerhouse Museum; Open Air Sydney: Parks & Gardens; Sydney By Area: Chinatown; Tours Around Sydney: Sydney Explorer.
Chinatown is reached by walking south along George Street towards Central from Town Hall, turning right into Goulburn Street and second left into the **Dixon Street** pedestrian zone. This is the decorative centre of Chinatown, with its traditionally exuberant gateway signalling your entrance into this city within the City. All around, and in the parallel Sussex Street, are roasted ducks, herbalists and acupuncture clinics, supermarkets loaded with exotic wares and foods and amazing restaurants: the Sussex Centre in particular is worth investigating in search of the establishments listed in the Chinatown Directory. At the end of Sussex Street is Hay Street, where the large building on the right houses **Paddy's Markets,** a huge network of undercover stalls selling everything from batteries to vegetables and leather goods.

A purposeless wander punctuated by ventures and stares into the windows of a couple of butchers to see what goes in and comes out is more than worthwhile. Both the **Burlington Supermarket** and **Yat San Vegetable and Grocery Shop** are in the Prince Centre (Thomas Street). Here you can view an amazing collection of Chinese vegetables and goods such as dried fish, green lip abalone and dried lotus root. Burlington also has a herbalist at the rear of the shop.

The best way to experience Chinatown is to taste it, and an integral part of any walk around Chinatown should be inseparable from **eating.** Wider Sydney has arguably the best selection of Asian eateries of any western metropolis. They serve top quality, authentic cuisines, not only from the provinces of China, but also Cambodia, Thailand, Malaysia and Singapore. Yum Cha has to be one of the best food concepts ever invented- abandoning oneself to the fate of the cooks, diners sit and select any number of dishes they feel able to cope with from the trays brought around to each table. Either an up front amount is paid or a dollar unit is stamped on each table's card for each dish selected. Either way it represents excellent value, entertainment and a challenge.

Of the many **restaurants** in the area, several are particularly popular with members of the community and those from further afield. **BBQ King** (18-20 Goulburn Street) is a sparingly decorated Mecca of fine yet inexpensive Chinese food, specialising in Chinese-style roast meats, but executing vegetable dishes such as stuffed tofu hot pot with flair. BBQ King is where those in the know go, and is accordingly extremely popular. **The Emperor's Garden BBQ and Noodle Shop** (187 Thomas Street) operates two take away windows as well as its restaurant, while **Golden Century Seafood** (393 Sussex Street) is mooted as one of the best overall Chinese restaurants in Chinatown: no mean feat. It offers reasonably priced seafood and a good selection of excellently cooked dishes from the simple to the staggeringly expensive and showy, such as shark fins. In the small **Happy Chef Phnom Penh Noodle** (1st Floor, Sussex Centre, 401-403 Sussex Street) eaters can find almost kind of noodle they desire, all delicious, authentic and cheap. **The Jing May Noodle Restaurant** (1st Floor, Prince Centre, Thomas Street) offers excellent simple noodle and won ton (dumpling) soups, made with flavoursome stock and fresh won tons daily. **Marigold** (299 Sussex St and 683 George Street) is so famous it is almost an institution, with what is reputed to be the best yum cha in Sydney. A staggering variety of snack sized dishes, famously fresh and quick dim sum, and good amounts of excellent food per dollar are to be found here. For early walkers, **Superbowl** (mid-Dixon Street) supplies simple traditional breakfasts of congee (rice and starch) and fried bread from 8am-2pm.

After eating through all this food, a **herbalist** may be the next best stop to make. Most have a qualified herbalist on duty who will instantly devise a remedy (usually an infusion) and prepare it in front of you, using mysterious ingredients taken from the hundreds of drawers, measured on old-fashioned scales, and calculated on an abacus. Two to investigate are the **Win Duc Chinese Herbal Co** (1st floor, Sussex Centre, Sussex Street), the genuine article, complete with abacus, and **Wing Chung Herbs and Food** (71 Dixon Street).

In summary, Chinatown looks interesting from the outside, but the real Chinatown lies within the buildings: in the food, the faces and the culture.

The **Chinese Garden** at Tumbalong Park is a fitting link between Chinatown and the modern development of Darling Harbour. Designed according to traditional principles, it was presented to Sydney as a bicentennial gift from Guangdong Province. To enter, visitors must pass through the screened temple; as bad spirits can only travel in straight lines, they will be left behind. Behind is a scene of serenity, with water trickling enticingly under curved bridges and willows, bamboo rustled by the breeze, and pagodas offering ideal book reading enclaves. A clear view of this bewitching garden can be found from the **Tea House,** purveyors of teas and Chinese cakes.

There is no denying that the **Darling Harbour** development, which transformed a disused wasteland to a pumping centre of activity, is a social success: one need only look around to see the popularity of the place. Here you will find the fountains, shops, pubs, restaurants, museums and above all, people. Hovering above is Sydney's controversial **Monorail,** unwanted by many locals and the butt of numerous jokes. Urban myths aside, it is still there and still discussed: 1994 saw the mooting of plans to relocate it underground.

The precinct itself consists of several separate entities. Before walking around to the main buildings, note that the **Sydney Aquarium** (✆ 9262 2300; **Open:** 7 days 9.30am-9pm; **Cost:** $12/$6/under 8 years free) is over on this side. It consists of two tanks moored in the Harbour which are viewed from the underwater walkway and a number of special aquatic exhibits (See: Sights To See). Also on this side of the bay is the ***South Steyne*** ferry. This historic Manly ferry was constructed in England and sailed to Sydney under its own steam. It is permanently moored here to serve as the 2000 Olympic Showcase and Information Centre. The Pyrmont Bridge linking the two sides of Cockle Bay is commonly referred to as being one of the earliest electrically operated swing span bridges ever built.

Around in the main centre, the Harbourside Festival Marketplace consists of a frenzy of over two hundred food and retail outlets. Its also a favourite haunt of jugglers, clowns and all kinds of bands, and the site of a permanent arts and crafts market (**Open:** Sat 10am-9pm, Sun-Wed 10am-7pm). **The National Maritime Museum,** adjacent to Pyrmont Bridge and with a large white sail-like roof, chronicles the country's past and present relationship with the sea. The museum incredibly houses several craft, either inside or moored outside, as well as the sternpost of Captain Cook's Endeavour. All boats can be boarded and inspected (**Open:** 7 days 10am-5pm; **Cost:** $9/$6/$4.50). **The Exhibition Centre** was designed in 1985 by the Sydney architecture firm of Philip Cox, Richardson, Taylor & Associates. A mast-like steel structure crowns a series of immense spaces and provides a venue for annual events such as the popular motor show.

The **Powerhouse Museum** is located a five minute stroll beyond the Darling Harbour convention centre (500 Harris St, Ultimo; & 9217 0111; **Open:** 7 days 10am-5pm; **Cost:** $5/$2 except first Sat every month free; See: Museums & Galleries). This is an enormous interactive museum of decorative arts, science, technology and social history, housed in what used to be the Power station for the now extinct Sydney trams. Here visitors young and old can engage in experiments, computer activities, demonstrations and films, while highlights include a flying boat frozen in mid-air, a racing Bugatti (not in mid-air), space travel exhibits, a cinema straight out of the 1930s, and very importantly, a display of brewing and pubs. You will need at least a couple of hours here, and for those rendered hungry and thirsty by the experience, there's a cafe on level three painted all over by Ken Done.

This is the end of the walking route, and from here, bus 443 will return you to the City.

NORTH

Circular Quay to Kirribilli over the Harbour Bridge

Description: A relatively level walk (apart from some steps), this classic route encompasses some of the finest and most spectacular views to be had in Sydney. A must.
Starting Point: Circular Quay.
Map Reference For Walk: D4 to C5.
Length: 2 hours.
Transport Alternatives: Train from Milsons Point back to city, or the Sydney Explorer.
Best Time: Any time; but if you want to be eating alfresco in Kirribilli when the light is richest, and the lights in the City start to come on, start around 3pm.
Take: Camera; swimmers in summer.
Transport Alternatives: Ferry to Milsons Point from Circular Quay; Sydney Explorer.
See: History; Museums: Pylon Museum; Sights To See: Circular Quay, The Harbour Bridge; Sydney By Area: Milsons Point & Kirribilli, The Rocks, Sydney Harbour; Sydney Icons: The Harbour Bridge.

Starting at Circular Quay, follow the Harbour foreshore around to the Museum of Contemporary Art, turning left up to George Street at the Passenger Terminal. Walk up Argyle Street in the Rocks as far as the big sandstone archway, the **Argyle Cut.** This passes directly under the traffic feeders of the bridge and was developed from a narrow, laneway cutting hacked through the cliff by convicts using only hammer and chisel from 1843. It was eventually finished using both free labour and explosives eighteen years after it was begun, and quickly became a favourite haunt of muggers. On the right hand side just before this is an arched stairway, where a blue sign points to the **Harbour Bridge Pylon Lookout.** At the very top, cross Cumberland Street and enter the grey concrete stairway. After a few flights of stairs, you should be on the footway (not the cycle path) of the Harbour Bridge. If not, it should be relatively easy to spot. The pylon you are heading for is the one closest to the Opera House.

As residential Sydney spread, increased numbers were commuting to the City for work; yet the North Shore railway line terminated at Milsons Point, leaving the passengers stranded on the wrong side of the Harbour. Privately run vehicular and passenger ferry companies shuffled continuously across the water, but as the years went by and traffic continued to increase, it was evident that a more practical solution, such as a bridge, was needed urgently. In 1912, a certain John Job Crew Bradfield was appointed Chief Engineer

ARCHITECTURE: 'FINGER' WHARVES

The aptly named 'finger wharves' which protrude into the harbour at Walsh Bay and Woolloomooloo are intrinsic to the character of Sydney, and although now largely obsolete, they are vivid reminders of the past importance of shipping to the commercial life of the city.

At the time of European settlement, the topography of Walsh Bay was marked by steep cliffs dropping straight to the water and preventing access by land, so the vessels which anchored there had to be serviced by boat. However, from the 1840s, land access to the shore improved with the construction of roads in the area, and the bay was progressively developed with wharves capable of servicing ocean-going vessels.

The origin of an outbreak of Bubonic Plague at the turn of this century was traced to the docks, so drastic measures (demolition) were immediately taken by the newly formed Sydney Harbour Trust in an attempt to halt the spread of the disease. The reconstruction of the area began in 1901, and culminated in the building of the distinctive grey, wooden wharves and storehouses themselves between 1910 and 1922. Their planning made a virtue of the dramatic level change behind the site by incorporating reinforced concrete bridges to span Hickson Road and connect the storehouses' upper storeys to Windmill Street. This arrangement, coupled with the buildings' up-to-date electrical cargo handling machines, effectively doubled the storehouses' capacity.

The economies dictated by the First World War affected both the construction program for the complex and the materials used to build it. Steel became unavailable, so native Ironbark had to be used in place of steel girders, and corrugated steel wall cladding was replaced on many of the facades by the timber weatherboards now characteristic of the wharves. The dark brick at the landward end of the wharves form a continuous, robust facade along Hickson Road, and contrasts with the lightness of the painted timber abutting the Harbour ends. The detailing of their imposing face brick walls, highlighted with bands of sandstone, is characteristic of the period, as are their multi-paned timber windows.

Further around the harbour at Woolloomooloo Bay is another finger wharf built by the Sydney Harbour Trust and completed in 1913 as a deep sea passenger terminal and storage area. Again, the wharf replaced an earlier facility made obsolete by the increased size and capacity of twentieth century cargo ships. Double storeyed sheds are made up of modular timber units similar in design to those at Walsh Bay, and the pier itself, over three hundred and fifty metres long, is supported over the harbour by piles of the native hardwood, Turpentine. Also obsolete, the Woolloomooloo wharf has been threatened with demolition, although the efforts of conservationists have so far scheduled the building for retention and redevelopment.

Redevelopment has also taken place at Walsh Bay, with Pier One being re-opened as a shopping centre in 1982, and Pier 4/5 opening as The Wharf theatre in 1984. The restaurant at the harbour end of the theatre complex is an excellent place to examine these buildings at close hand, while enjoying the dramatic views of the Harbour Bridge.

responsible for building an electric train system around Sydney and a bridge to cross the Harbour. His design was completed in 1916, but the project was shelved until 1923 when construction finally began. It was one of the biggest engineering feats of the period, continuing throughout the Great Depression of the late 1920s and early 1930s, generating badly needed jobs, and a badly needed cause for celebration, both culminating in the grand opening of March 1932.

The bridge rises across the Harbour with the appearance of a massive coat hanger, seemingly supported at each end by enormous granite pylons; yet they have no structural purpose. They were built purely to enhance the structure's aesthetic appearance. As PR Stephensen reminded readers of his book, *The History of Sydney Harbour,* "beauty is truth, and truth beauty", so you can ponder the validity of these phoney pylons as you stroll across the bridge. Regardless, the geometric patterns of steel and shadow, as well as the mind boggling number of bolts, are to be marvelled at. However, the best place to find out about the bridge's history and construction is the **Pylon Lookout and Museum** (**Open:** 7 days 10am-5pm; **Cost:** $2). The observation terrace at the top is a photographer's nirvana, not only because of the water **views** below, the ferries and sailboats crossing the Harbour, or the Opera House, but because of the close up look at the structure of the bridge itself which it allows.

Once you have emerged fully informed from the museum, continue along the footway to the northern shore, descending the stairs to **Kirribilli,** home of the official Sydney residences of the Prime Minister and Governor General. This is a lovely and popular residential suburb where a number of older apartment blocks mingle with the area's many terraces and cottages, while small parks and the gaps between the buildings provide views of the Harbour. The quiet streets emphasise the distinct village atmosphere, despite being the most densely developed area of the North Shore.

From the bottom of the Harbour Bridge steps, cross over Broughton Street to head to the left to **Fitzroy Street.** It is a happy coincidence that Fitzroy Street is representative of the suburb's character as well as being a food bonanza. On the corner you will find the excellent **Fitzroy Cafe,** while further along on the right is **Billi's Cafe,** and either will provide an excellent spot to have a break either now or when you complete the Kirribilli circuit as follows.

Turning right into Fitzroy Street, you will see the elegant large stone terraces on the left which are occupied by the **Community Centre**, juxtaposed with a number of small terraces both unrenovated and renovated, as well as a modern motel. This eclectic and seemingly haphazard collection of architectural styles is something you will see repeated all over the suburb. Fitzroy Street ends at **Carabella Street**, at which point you should turn left and walk as far as the large residence on the corner of Bligh Street. This is **'Balaclava'** , 'ancestral' home of one of the country's greatest legal dynasties, the Evatt family. Dr 'Doc' Herbert Vere Evatt lived here as a child before going on to become the first President of the United Nations and a Justice of the High Court of Australia; his son Clive was a Queen's Counsel and parliamentarian, while his grand-daughter Elizabeth was Chief Justice of the Family Court. Retracing your steps along Carabella Street, you will pass **Loreto Convent School** on the left, one of Sydney's better known Catholic girls' schools (est. c.1907), and on the corner of Parkes Street on the right, the National Trust listed mansion **'Burnleigh'** (c.1846). Beyond and below the school's buildings is the **Royal Sydney Yacht Squadron**, formed in 1862 to co-ordinate the established scene of harbour racing which many had been enjoying since the 1830s. By following the right hand footpath you will be treated to an elevated **view** over the roof tops, onto the apartment buildings and out to the Harbour.

Following Carabella Street, proceed to the intersection with Kirribilli Avenue and turn left. This ends in **Lady Gowrie Lookout**, a tiny but carefully tended garden park and the perfect spot from which to contemplate the Harbour and the view of Farm Cove and Mrs Macquarie's Point on the opposite shore. Unfortunately, the Opera House is a little too far around to the right to see from here; however, you may notice the high fence on the right topped with barbed wire and intimidating notices.

Behind here are the grounds of **Kirribilli House**, built in 1854-55 for businessman Adolphus Feez and narrowly rescued by the Commonwealth Government from demolition in the 1920s. Its location, steep gables and Victorian Gothic timber decorative details are partly why this is such a covetable residence. Yet we are out of luck: it has been used exclusively as an official residence (mainly for the country's Prime Minister) since 1956, and public access is restricted to almost zero. By continuing along Kirribilli Street, you will be able to gaze in through the elegant gates at this most desirable piece of real estate, with its sandstone buildings and manicured harbourside grounds. The spectacle is repeated next door by **Admiralty House**. Originally built as a single story house in 1842 by Lt. Col. John Gibbes, and added to between 1897 and 1900, it was acquired by the government of New South Wales from its private owner for use as an official residence for the Naval Commander-in-Chief for Her Majesty's Ships in the Southern Pacific (phew!), for which purpose it was used until 1913. Thereafter, it was lent to the Federal Government and is still used as the Sydney residence of the Queen's representative, the Governor General of Australia.

Kirribilli Avenue continues back towards the bridge with a fantastic photo opportunity at the **Beulah Street Wharf**, off to the left: it is directly opposite the Opera House and city, with the bridge looking enormous from this perspective off to the right. This part of the suburb is full of mid-sized apartment blocks, including the first block of flats to be built on the north shore (1 Waruda Street, c.1908). On the right is **St Aloysius College**, a boys' Catholic school established in 1903 by the Jesuit Fathers. The street ends back at Broughton Street, having passed the large vents which supply air to the harbour tunnel which runs across from that point and resurfaces just to the right of the Opera House. Few people know that the building of a tunnel under the Harbour was first suggested in the 1880s as a potential solution to the transport problem posed by the Harbour, but was rejected due to fears that such a structure would cave in or flood. You have now completed the Kirribilli circuit!

About one hundred metres away on the other side of the bridge (you can walk straight under it) is **North Sydney Olympic Pool** (See: Sports), which surely has one of the most amazing settings of any pool in the world. Backstroke is recommended to make the most of the view, but whatever the stroke, the salt water pool is a welcome sight at this point of the walk in summer. Next to it (hopefully still) stands the most famous face in Sydney, the entrance gates of **Luna Park.** Originally opened in the 1930s, the park had a chequered career spanning several lengthy closures and a tragic fire. It was reopened in early 1995 after a multi-million dollar facelift only to be closed again in March 1996 amid great controversy and disappointment.

Back on the shore, you can admire the view and consider what you have accomplished. Excellent fish and chips are to be found at **Kirribilli Seafoods Fish & Chips** (12 Fitzroy Street). All walkers will be forgiven for returning to the City by train (from Milsons Point station) or by ferry!

A stroll along the Harbour Foreshore at Cremorne Point

Description: An short, easy, almost flat stroll along the Cremorne Point Reserve to MacCallum Pool and the Cremorne Point lighthouse.

Starting Point: Bogota Ave, Neutral Bay at the beginning of the reserve; Milson Rd, Cremorne Point, at Sirius Street; or Cremorne wharf (from Circular Quay).

Map Reference For Walk: B6

Length: About 1.5km; allow an hour.

Best Time: The harbour changes character as frequently as the weather, although the expansive views across the water remain just as impressive.

Take: A picnic, a camera and a jumper.

See: Sports: Swimming; Sydney By Area: Sydney Harbour.

The walking track from Bogota Avenue to Cremorne Point leads along the narrow eastern edge of the narrow inlet, Shell Cove. Arched by leafy trees, it wends its relaxed way past several advantageously positioned park benches to MacCallum Pool. Surrounded by a green picket fence and wooden decking, this photogenic public pool offers uninterrupted views across the Harbour to the City. After passing Cremorne Wharf, the track abandons its genteel trees for the foreshore's original bushland, where wattle, bottlebrush and gum trees are being encouraged and preserved. A large children's playground offers younger walkers some diversion, while all should continue right to the end, where an elevated vantage point offers views beyond the photogenic lighthouse to the eastern suburbs. A very steep, slippery and treacherous ladder leads down to the water's edge, and to the lighthouse bridge. Taronga Zoo at Mosman is visible around to the left. From this usually windy point, there is little to do apart from admiring the view and returning along the same path.

Those seeking a more challenging, or more bushy, harbour foreshore walk should consult the chapter, Bushwalks. There they will find details of the tracks leading from the Spit to Manly and Bradleys Head to Chowder Bay.

Manly

Description: A flat stroll around this ocean resort suburb, from aquarium to galleries and restaurants and on to the magnificent pine-edged beach.

Starting Point: Take the famous Manly Ferry from Circular Quay to Manly Wharf. Ferries depart every 30 minutes and the trip takes half an hour. The faster Jet Cat is more expensive, and less fun.

Map Reference For Walk: 3km north of A11.

Length: 3.5km without North Head circuit or to North Head by car; walkers to North Head note the walk will be nearly 9km in total.

Best Time: Plan to arrive in Manly at around 12noon to allow time to investigate the Art Gallery or Ocean World before catching the bus to North Head.

Take: Swimmers in summer.

Note: North Head Quarantine Station can only be visited from Manly on the 1.00pm shuttle bus (as below) and must be booked in advance. Those planning to visit Ocean World should consider buying OceanPass (**Cost:** $17.80/$9/$47.60 family) a combined return ferry and Ocean World ticket with bonus food offer at the aquarium's cafe..

See: Bushwalks: The Spit to Manly; Markets: Manly Arts and Crafts market; Tours Around Sydney: Quarantine Station;

Named after the sighting by Captain Arthur Phillip and his men in 1788 of manly-looking Aborigines in the area, this erstwhile fishing village is an isthmus, with the Harbour on one side and a two kilometre beach fronting the Tasman Sea on the other. In between is a mixture of grit and grot which can largely be overlooked; however, there are several highlights of great charm which should be investigated.

Ocean World (✆ 9949 2644; **Open:** 7 days 10am-5pm; **Cost:** $12.50/$9/$6/$31 family) is located on the West Esplanade to left of the ferry wharf on arrival and offers a good chance to see a lot of the exotic sea life of the country in one place. Visitors are treated to a walk in a clear underwater tunnel to experience the joy of sharks and jelly blobbers (among other friendly items) swimming over and around their heads. Star attractions include the Giant Cuttlefish with three hearts, green blood and the ability to change colour, regular shark feeding and seal performances. Also here is **The Manly Art Gallery and Museum** (West Esplanade Reserve; ✆ 9949 1776; **Open:** Tues-Fri 10am-4pm; Sat-Sun 12-5pm; Closed Mon), one of Australia's oldest public galleries. It houses exhibitions relating the cultural landscape of Australia, while the museum is full of historical beach fashions, photographs and surf craft.

The large stone buildings visible up on the hill to the right are **St Patrick's Seminary** and **Archbishop's House**, formerly known as Cardinal's Palace. Both will be reached via Darley Road from the Corso later in the walk.

Leaving the ferry wharf, cross the road and walk straight ahead through the **Corso** pedestrian zone. At the end of The Corso, behold the **Ocean Beach**: two thousand metres of photogenic golden sand, seagulls and pine trees fronting the blue horizon. Sitting on the beach wall with fish and chips in hand (from the Corso) and watching the swimmers and surfers while fighting off the cheeky seagulls is such a classic Sydney experience that it almost encapsulates the essence of the city, and almost always inspires a rush of envy in visitors. It was not until 1903 that public bathing was allowed in daylight; before that time, bathing was only allowed before 6am and after 8pm, with men and women sternly kept at opposite ends of the very long beach. Reform came after a journalist decided to make a stand and bravely walked into the surf in broad daylight. When to his surprise he was not arrested, thousands adopted the previously risque practice with wild abandon. Surf culture now practically dominates the nation's leisure identity. Here also stands the **Manly Visitors Centre** (✆ 9977 1088; **Open:** 7 days 10am-4pm), the centre of the popular weekend **Arts and Crafts market** (Sat 12noon-7.30pm; Sun 8.30am-7.30pm; **See:** Markets). The visitors centre can help with information regarding sports equipment hire.

Manly became a popular seaside resort in the Edwardian era, attracting people from far and wide under the promotional slogan of "Manly - seven miles from Sydney, but a thousand miles from care". One short detour that will render the slogan reality is to head south along South Steyne Promenade to the short rock-edged shoreline path leading to the little beaches at **Fairy Bower** and **Shelly Beach**. Along the way, interesting history installations inform walkers of the tradition of the annual **Surf Carnival**. The latter is the home of beautiful and popular **Le Kiosk** (✆ 9976 3835) restaurant right on the beach, and **The Bower** (✆ 9977 5451), a very popular (and cheaper) place open for lunch (See: Directory). The path continues beyond the grassy cove and up to the top of rugged cliffs continually lashed by waves, and affords great views of the ocean.

Retracing your steps towards the Manly centre, there is access to a small street (Bower Lane) just beyond the swimming pool, and the more energetic should turn left here if planning to walk the two kilometres to North Head. This cuts out a large corner by turning left and across into College Street, right into Reddal Street, left into Addison Road and left again into Darley Road. (Those retrieving their cars first should join Darley Road via the Manly centre for access.) Darley Road passes through the middle of the two ecclesiastical buildings of the head. **St Patrick's Seminary** was built in 1885 and commands an enviable position at which point unbroken views to Terrigal in the north and Sydney in the south take the breath away. It was designed by Sheering & Hennessy in Gothic style and even from a distance, some of the arched narrow windows, colonnaded verandahs and bell tower are visible. The building's present use is a Hotel Management teaching college. **Archbishop's House** was also designed by Sheering & Hennessy, and was constructed as an integral part of the Seminary. This is a somewhat less intimidating building whose stone walls and decorations are more rounded to suit a domestic application of Gothic Revival style.

Also reached by Darley Road is **North Head**, part of the Sydney Harbour National Park. A scenic drive meanders right around the point almost as far as the head itself. From the car park, it is only a short stroll along the **Fairfax Walking Track** to reach the cliff edge lookout where spectacular views straight down the Harbour to the City are your reward. Nearby is the **Old Quarantine Station** (✆ 9977 6522; **Open:** By tour only 7 days at 1.10pm; **Cost:** $8/$6; **See:** Tours Around Sydney.) Visitors must join the single tour led by the National Parks and Wildlife Service to gain access to this facility which was used between 1828 and (would you believe it) 1984 to keep Australia isolated from the various contagious diseases carried by infected passengers arriving by sea. Here stand the eerily silent historic hospital, mortuary and burial grounds used for those whose new life in New South Wales didn't eventuate. The really brave among the Good Life Guide's walkers may like to come back on Wednesday, Friday, Saturday or Sunday night to join a Ghost Tour (not recommended for children; Booking essential; Cost: $17). These lead visitors around the station by flickering kerosene lamp, telling ghost stories over three hours.

Also on North Head are the **Tunnel Fortifications** (built in 1930 to protect the Harbour from attack) and **North Fort Museum** (✆ 9976 1138; **Open:** Sat-Sun 12noon-4pm by tour; Booking essential) which contains an extensive collection of artillery and memorabilia dating back to the mid nineteenth century. The Water Board's Water Pollution Control Plant, also up here, doesn't attract as many visitors although tours are available.

Events take place throughout the year in Manly. **The Manly Jazz Festival** (✆ 9977 1088; **See:** Music: Jazz) is held every year over the first weekend in October, the Labour Day long weekend. The festival features local and overseas acts in concert in various locations around the area: even the seal enclosure of Ocean World may be used! **The Manly Summer Festival** (✆ 9977 1088) takes place every year from mid December to late January, with events on the beach and jazz and brass bands around the area.

Ambling Around Old Hunters Hill

Description: This is a gentle stroll around one of the city's most historic and beautiful residential suburbs, full of sandstone mansions and cottages, water views and heavily wooded streets. It starts at the top of the peninsula, and leads down to the Valentia St wharf.
Starting Point: Hillman Orchard, next to Vienna Cottage, 85 Alexandra St, Hunters Hill.
Map Reference For Walk: A1.
Length: Allow around 2.5 to 3 hours, including stops; approximately 4 kilometres.
Best Time: Start mid-morning, have lunch at the mid-way break as suggested, and then a post lunch beer at the pub near the end.
Transport Alternatives: From Circular Quay, take the ferry (15 minutes) to the Valentia Street wharf. They run almost hourly Mon-Sat and every 2 hours on Sundays. Buses run up the hill of the peninsula from the jetty; catch one as far as the public school in Alexandra St. However, note that the buses do not run on Sundays. The walk can also be done as a car cruise.
See: Sydney By Area: Hunters Hill.
The old Hillman orchard is the perfect place to sit under the trees and read about the area's European history. The brothers Jules and Didier **Joubert** emigrated to Sydney in 1837 intending to develop land and build residences, and bringing with them the seventy stonemasons from Lombardy required to turn those plans into reality. Their efforts turned a wild peninsula of thick scrub and bush into what became known as the 'French Village'. Other developers, particularly the Cuneo family, joined in on the act, and continued to build fine houses and cottages from sandstone extracted from the nearby quarry. While many of the colony's professionals preferred to live in the city centre in the 1830s, semi-rural Hunters Hill offered the attractive prospects of gracious residences surrounded by peace and quiet, and thus it became a dormitory suburb for lawyers and doctors. Commuting was born; the peace was only broken by the occasional

escapee convict or prisoner from Cockatoo Island prison, just over the Parramatta River.

You are sitting in the centre of what is known as the **original village,** where most of the artisans working to build the grand residences of the area constructed their own, more humble dwellings. The walk will be coming back to this precinct, so for now, walk along Alexandra Street back towards the jetty until you come to the **Cuneo Building** and the **Garibaldi Inn**, Hunters Hill's first hotel. These buildings are on the right hand corner of Ferry Street. Built by the Cuneo family and so named to honour the Italian political leader, this was the Hunters Hill hot spot of the 1880s and 1890s. The tension between the different nationalities of the artisans, tradesmen and developers usually resolved itself here in the form of spectacular fights, demonstrating the problems of nineteenth century nationalism condensed into one pub. After examining the hotel from the front, you'll find at the rear of the building's courtyard a stairway surrounded by wooden railings. Looking down, you will discover the natural spring which gave the hotel its fresh water. It still runs to the extent that restoration work on the building in 1988 was endangered by the amount of water seeping out of it, so it has been piped under the street. As you walk out onto Ferry Street, notice the extremely fine stonework of the building; and the exquisite antiques shop on your right, **Clocks of Distinction** (32 Ferry St; & 9816 1401; Open: Mon-Fri 9am-5pm; Thurs to 7pm; Sat 9am-12noon; Closed Sun). Both are worthy of a thorough investigation.

Cross over into **All Saints Church**. Built in 1888, this sandstone Anglican church was designed by John Horbury Hunt, who was also largely responsible for St John's church in Glebe (See: Walks Around Sydney: Glebe). The interior has several points of interest. Firstly, notice the stone arches leading to the sanctuary and chapel. Horbury Hunt had a strained relationship with the building committee who had commissioned the Church, and although it had run out of money, Hunt insisted on and procured the unsanctioned inclusion of the arches; it cannot be denied that they add a lot to the interior. Money problems continued to plague the church: it was not until 1938 that the roof was finished, and the temporary structure extending from what is now the rear glass wall to the exterior wall could be removed. The stained glass windows are particularly beautiful; some were imported from England while others were designed locally. The exquisitely decorated organ was made by Bevington and shipped piece by piece. It is, in fact, the largest and most in tact Bevington organ remaining anywhere in the world. It is also badly in need of restoration!

Leave the church and turn left into Ambrose Street, passing the Rectory on your left. Further down on the right, on the corner of Passy Avenue is a **Gothic revival cottage** which was probably used as a coach house for an estate fronting the water. Unlike almost every other cottage in the area, this one was not named, suggesting that it was dependent on some larger residence. Continuing down Ambrose Street, you can see **St Peter Chanel** church (named after a South Seas martyr) through the trees to the right, and the Harbour Bridge straight ahead. Turning left at the bottom into Martha Street will lead you once more into Alexandra Street. Turn left, noticing the ferry wharf at the bottom of the hill. Access to the suburb used to be reliant on ferry services running to the City, and this remained largely the case until the Gladesville Bridge was built in the 1960s. At the peak of ferry use, there were seventeen wharves in Hunters Hill; now there are only two and the services are lamentably infrequent.

Lining Alexandra Street along the incline are some charmingly debonair cottages (Nos 68 and 66 being prime examples). This part of Hunters Hill mainly has small cottages lining its streets as this neck of the peninsula was the area's **utilitarian centre**. The tradesmen and artisans built their own housing around here before embarking on the large scale residences further down the point. Turning right into Lloyd Avenue, the cottages continue. No 1 (on the right) is apparently one of the most painted, drawn and photographed houses in the area, attracting sighs with its compact lines and efficient charm. On the corner of Campbell Street stands a prime example of the **French Provincial Cottages** built by Joubert and happily common in the area. Crossing to the other side of Lloyd Ave and turning left into the narrow Browns Lane, you will come to Ady Street.

Cross straight over into **Madeline Street**, noticing the mansion on the left hand corner. This was built by a certain Mr Tornaghi, a past Mayor of the municipality, and was allowed to degenerate into complete disrepair until a subsequent Mayor, much later, restored it to its current condition. It is a beautiful example of the two storey villas of the area. Walking along Madeline Street, notice **'Braemar'** (No. 29), a stunning, low-lying cottage with wooden shutters along the side windows, which remains unaltered from its original design, a largely untouched original. No. 25 features delicate tracery and iron verandah pillars; No. 23 was the original council meeting house before the area became a municipality and gained a town hall. Passing the bowling club on the right, and the Cuneo cottage at No.15 on the left, you will come to the intersection with D'Aram Street upon which stands a group of two storey dark brown flats. This complex was set up by local 'saint' Angus Bristow for the area's elderly, so that they wouldn't have to move away from Hunters Hill when no longer able to care for themselves. He also initiated several other programs, such as taking the residents on trips and excursions, before tragically being killed in an horrific bus crash near Kempsey in northern New South Wales. His great deeds are remembered fondly by all local residents.

Continuing along Madeline Street right to the end,

notice No. 3 on the left. This residence originally was two houses, but they have been meticulously restored and joined to form one extremely covetable residence. At the end of the street sits No. 1 in more ways than one: despite its relative lack of grandeur, **'Kyarra'** is one of the most arresting residences on the walk, and for many, its iron lace verandah decoration, louvred timber shutters, French doors, water views and trees epitomise the residential style of the area. It was constructed from sandstone quarried on site by Felix Cullen.

Retracing your steps back to Ferdinand Street, turn right and walk along to the High Gothic **Congregational church**, with its delicate detailing carved into the stone over the doorways and around the windows. Turn left at Alexandra Street, and walk along to the town hall on the left. As the parapet says, it was built in 1866 to C. Mayes' design , but unfortunately, the dry timber used in the construction facilitated the fire which destroyed all but the facade and shell of the building in 1978. There is a small but good museum of local history in the side wing. Further along Alexandra Street on the right at the corner of Ellesmere Avenue sits the original post office, opened in 1880.

On the left is the tiny, four roomed **Vienna Cottage** (No 38; ✆ 9817 2240; **Open:** Sat 2pm-4pm; Sun 11am-4pm) built in the late 1860s by John Hillman for his family of seven. Surprisingly few people owned Vienna Cottage over the years before it was saved from ruin by the National Trust and organised to show how its various owners lived over the decades. The back garden sports a homemade clothes line, based on the national emblem, the Hill's Hoist, while next door is the old Hillman Orchard where the walk began.

This completes the first section of the walk around what was the original village of Hunters Hill, so now is an appropriate time for a break! A little further along, back at the Cuneo building, is The **Stivell** restaurant and cafe (✆ 9879 4204; **Open:** 7 days all day).

Once refuelled, the second part of the walk takes you to the grand residences and mansions of the Hunters Hill peninsula, built largely by those who lived in the little cottages you have already seen. Again, private ownership means one's inspection must be restricted to subtle glances. This is one area of Sydney where the seasons are truly apparent, owing to the large number of deciduous trees planted over the past one and a half centuries, and whether spring or autumn, the streets have great atmosphere as you mender towards the water.

From Alexandra Street turn right into Ferry Street and follow this around to the left into Woolwich Road. The residences here are breathtaking, and especially enviable is **'Waiwera'** (No. 9). Built by Charles Jeanneret in the 1870s, Waiwera is part of a large semi-detached house , and to see its partner, **'St Claire'**, walkers must turn back left into Wybalena Road (No. 2).

With an iron lace crown on the roof, a tower with windows and a two storey cast iron verandah, this is widely regarded as a fine example nineteenth century domestic architecture typical of the Hunters Hill area. Continue around to the left into Glenview Crescent and left again into Jeanneret Avenue, where **'Wybalena'** (No. 3) is also worth a look. Built by Charles Jeanneret in 1874, it originally stood in twenty-five acres of grounds. As well as typical Victorian cast iron decoration, the smooth-faced sandstone building has curved, carved timber Gothic gable decoration.

Rejoining Woolwich Road, walkers will soon notice the elegant pair of houses on the right at numbers 27 and 29. The gardens contain two icons of old Australian gardens, the frangipani and the palm trees. Stylistically less ornate than many High Victorian houses, these houses nevertheless still show the eaves brackets and cast iron fringes typical of much Victorian architecture. Their comparative simplicity foreshadows the simplification of architectural design seen in the early years of the twentieth century. Around one hundred metres further along on the other side of Woolwich Road is a similar residence (No. 48).

From here, continue to the **Woolwich Pier Hotel** (✆ 9817 2204; **Open:** Mon-Sat 12noon-Midnight; Sun 12noon-10pm) for a rejuvenating beer and/or a barbecue in the beer garden. Some walkers may prefer a visit to **Bardeli's** opposite (✆ 9817 2198; **Open:** Mon-Fri 10am-10pm, Sat-Sun 8am-11pm) for some pasta or one of a menu of other Italian dishes.

Afterwards, walkers can stagger down to the Woolwich pier wharf and take the ferry back to the City. More energetic walkers may like to continue the final seven hundred metres to Valentia Street wharf before taking the ferry.

EAST

A Ramble Along Oxford Street & Queen Street

Description: Sydney's most dynamic street is true to the cliche 'something for everyone'. Its entire length is lined with clothing boutiques, bookshops, cafes, restaurants, pubs and cinemas, while Saturday's famous Paddington Bazaar draws in enormous crowds. Turning the corner at Centennial Park, the city's premier antiques street comes into view. When the light fades, the lights, music, cars, people, and noise of the hub of the city's club and pub district come to life.

Starting Point: Whitlam Square, corner of College St, Hyde Park and Oxford St.

Map Reference For Walk: F4 to G6.

Length: Greatly variable depending on the number of shops browsed in and cappuccinos consumed. Allow most of an afternoon, although a direct walk will only take an hour.

Best Time: Saturday is the best day to do this walk as the markets are on and the people are out and about.

Transport Alternatives: Bus 380 or 382 from Elizabeth St, City to Paddington, or taxi, but go only to the corner of Taylor Square and then walk: even a short distance by transport other than foot will mean you miss something.

See: Directories: Darlinghurst, Paddington; Markets: Paddington Bazaar; Shopping; Sydney By Area: Darlinghurst, Paddington; Walks Around Sydney: Paddington.

The corner of Hyde Park faces what is popularly known as the windiest intersection in Sydney: Whitlam Square was named after a Labor prime minister, Gough Whitlam, who served from 1972 until spectacularly dismissed from office in 1975 by the Governor-General after the Senate blocked his money bills. The Dismissal, as it is known, became the centre of major controversy which still rages, questioning the relationship between Government and the role of Governor-General. Oxford Street is the busy artery heading up the gentle slope ahead. The route is not difficult to follow: walk straight up Oxford Street on the left hand side (from the City), crossing over to the other side whenever something grabs your attention. However, several essential stops to make are as follows.

The first blocks of Oxford Street contain several clothing shops and boutiques worth investigating; however, off to the right is **Crown Street**, one of the city's most concentrated streets for young, trendy fashion labels and boutiques. A detour along here is likely to take some time, considering the length of the street and the number of windows to look in. Those interested would be well advised to make a separate journey after consulting the chapter, Shopping.

Continuing along Oxford Street and passing an odd collection of restaurants, health food shops and boutiques in the process, walkers will find themselves at **Taylor Square**, the nexus between Darlinghurst and Paddington. Around 1800, this slightly elevated area was an Aboriginal reserve named Eastern Hill, which sported several large windmills grinding grain for the hungry colony. Here today is the imposing facade of the **Darlinghurst Courthouse** and behind it along Forbes Street, the old **Darlinghurst Gaol**, both designed by Colonial Architect James Barnet. Both buildings were constructed in 1841 and played a large role in reducing the Darlinghurst area from one favoured by the wealthy establishment to poverty. The first public hanging saw John Videle exit for murdering a debt collector and stowing the body in a sea chest, discovered when it split open on Circular Quay en route to being dumped. Far from appalling the general public of the time, thousands of people began to watch the hangings, causing the Establishment to move away abruptly to more genteel areas. Today there are no such grotesque sights on offer and while the Courthouse remains in use as a criminal court, the gaol is used only as a **College of the Arts**.

Crossing Taylor Square diagonally, one begins to see the rainbow flags of gay pride flying on most shopfronts. Darlinghurst has been the centre of a very vibrant and expressive **gay community** since the mid 1970's and it remains a highly active residential precinct and social scene for clubs, bars and shops: the best known gay pub in the city, **The Albury**, is here; the annual Gay & Lesbian **Mardi Gras** leads through its streets, and throughout the year, mobile police stations are parked along Oxford Street to deter individuals from venting their bigotry with violence (See: Gay Sydney). An energetic and friendly overlap renders this section of Oxford Street one of the centres of the Sydney nightclubbing scene (See: Nightclubs).

A veritable United Nations of **restaurants** exists along this strip: Balkan, Vietnamese, Thai, Italian, Indian and American stand next to each other interspersed by two very good Art Supplies shops, where the smell of oil paint mingles with that of curry (See: Food).

The Paddington **Academy Twin** cinema beckons from across Bourke Street, joined in early 1996 by the **Verona**, a little further along. Both show Art House films, although the Verona is interesting not only as a venue of excellent films, but for its design. It was built from the remains of a 1940s paper mill using recycled hardwoods and natural materials to embrace the developer's creed of environmentalism and non-materialism. Within the modernist complex are four theatres, a yoga centre, a health shop, cafe and bar serving drinks and organic foods (wherever possible) in the form of zesty, quick dishes, and the extroverted Mambo Friendship store, on street level.

Book freaks will soon see that they are also well catered for here. **Ariel** (opposite the Verona) and **Berkelouw's** (opposite Ariel) are both favoured late opening browsing grounds who actively encourage customers to sit on the chairs and floor for a read. Berkelouw's concentrates on second hand books and even has its own cafe with floor to ceiling windows offering clear views of the scene below, while Ariel stocks a very large selection of fiction and non-fiction and has enviable sections devoted to visual arts and children (See: Shopping).

Continuing along Oxford Street opposite the Verona cinema, a collection of homewares and jewellery shops greets the walker. Here is also the renowned **Coo-ee Emporium** (No. 98), vendors of authentic Aboriginal artefacts, fabrics, bark and sand paintings. Opposite are the three metre high and thirty centimetre thick sandstone walls of **Victoria Barracks,** built with convict labour between 1841 and 1848 to Lt.-Col. Barney's Georgian design. This secure complex has been in continuous use since completion, with a number of elegant, verandahed buildings surrounding a huge parade ground. The Barracks are an appropriate way to approach Paddington, as the stonecutters and workmen who constructed them built and lived in the first cottages of the suburb, to be followed by shopkeepers and publicans (See: Paddington, below).

A short break in the action follows until the **Paddington Town Hall** appears on the right. As the suburb grew, a municipal Council was formed to administer it. Premises matching the large boom of the 1880s to house the council were built begun in 1890 to

JE Kemp's design. This is a fully restored example of a monumental Late Victorian Classical building, complete with classical balusters, colonnades, arched windows and pilasters. Before the main strip of shops commences, you will pass **Juniper Hall** (c. 1825) on the left. As the name suggests, the residence was built for the owner of Paddington's early gin distillery (down the hill in Cascade Street), Robert Cooper. (For full details of these three buildings, See: Paddington, below.)

The main **shopping** precinct of Paddington should be clear from the crowds and smart front windows. **Clothing** for all tastes is available in the many and varied boutiques, from the street cred Status Symbol to the hip and suave Bracewell. In between are outrageous fad-based Dotti and the elegantly conservative Australian staple, Country Road. A collection of shops such as Folkways music store, Loyal florist and the Reject China Shop pave the way to the **Paddington Bazaar**, held every Saturday from 10am in the grounds of St John's Church on the right. The stalls here can range from barbecues, wind chimes, toys, or old Chinese embroidered pyjamas to second hand books or pot plants; however, the emphasis is on crafts, jewellery and new clothing labels. Musicians perform under the adjacent trees as hundreds of people cram in between the vendors, seeking a piece of treasure.

Food in this stretch of road is more than adequate: the hamburgers at **Food Satisfaction** opposite the church are magnificent, and **the Golden Dog** (a few doors down) serves fresh and delicious Mediterranean food, drinks and milkshakes in real stainless steel cups. The only trouble may be getting a table.

Cafes in the area range from the post modern & image conscious, to the extremely well loved, suave, relaxed, jazz coffee, chocolate and cake altar, The **Paddington Chocolate Factory** (8 Elizabeth Street, Paddington; **Open:** Tues-Sat 8am-6pm; Sun 10am-6pm; Closed Mon).

Pressing on past more clothes shops such as Zimmerman, you will come to **Queen Street,** at which point turn left. This street is renowned for its galleries and **antique shops,** among which Appley Hoare, Copeland & de Soos and Anne Schofield are more than worth investigating (see Shopping: Antiques). Follow the street down to the Moncur Street crossroad, and on the left is the Woollahra Hotel and its Bistro Moncur, the perfect place to end your walk, have a drink and/or dine (See: Food).

From there, roll home by taxi, or walk back to Oxford Street, if you can, for a bus. Perhaps when you've recovered, another day could be spent navigating the Paddington and Woollahra walk, below.

The Terraces and Galleries of Paddington

Description: A stroll through picturesque and historic streets past notable residences, numerous art galleries and cafes, with glimpses of the Harbour and an insight into the area's history.
Starting Point: Chocolate Factory Cafe, 8 Elizabeth Street, Paddington.
Map Reference For Walk: G6
Length: About 4.5 km; allow half a day.
Best Time: Saturdays are best for the markets and the pubs, but be at Victoria Barracks at 10am on Tuesday if you want to see inside. The Chocolate Factory Cafe is closed on Mondays, as are most of the suburb's galleries.
Transport Alternative: Bus route 389 goes through Paddington via Five Ways; however, the walk leads through backstreets and a lot will be missed taking this option. The walk can't really be done as a car cruise due to the steps, lanes and one way streets.
Note: Parking restrictions in the suburb are many and zealously enforced at all times. Therefore, take care when parking a car, or it's likely you'll have a parking fine as a souvenir. This walk can be combined with the Oxford Street walk.
See: Directory: Paddington; Markets: Paddington Bazaar; Museums & Galleries; Shopping; Sydney By Area: Paddington; Walks Around Sydney: Oxford St, above.

The Chocolate Factory Cafe (8 Elizabeth Street; ✆ 9331 3785; **Open:** Tues-Sat 8am-6pm; Sun10am-6pm; Closed Mon) is the perfect place to muster enough energy to do the walk by stoking up on their excellent fares and coffee. While doing so, you can read up on the area's **history**. Paddington was originally regarded as a pitiful wasteland and was left uninhabited for many years after the European settlers arrived. The fact that it was ever developed and popularised can be traced to the Governorship of Lachlan Macquarie (1810-21), who declared it part of the Sydney Common in 1810, built South Head Road (now Oxford Street) through the area to Watsons Bay, and finally made a one hundred acre land grant to Messers Cooper, Forbes and Underwood, business partners who intended to build a gin distillery and mansion each. The gin distillery was duly established in 1818 at the foot of Cascade Street, where clear water flowed over the Glenmore Falls.

Yet it was not until 1838 that life really came to the area, when the colony's new barracks were planned here. These were to become the suburb's focal point and catalyst: as in Hunters Hill (above), the first houses built were those of the workmen. A smaller number of wealthy settlers chose the area to build their mansions and establish their grounds, eventually succumbing to the advantages of subdividing and selling off their holdings. Yet the land was steep and developers wanted to fit in as many houses as possible to maximise profit. The **terrace design** most suited these prerequisites, although various adaptations were needed to fit the Antipodean conditions, namely the addition of verandahs with French doors to block the sun and admit the breezes. Simultaneously, shops and services appeared and Paddington boomed: while the 1861 population was around two and a half thousand people living in five hundred and thirty houses, just thirty years

The Edge Of The Trees, Museum Of Sydney, On The Site Of First Government House

Georgian: Hyde Park Barracks, Macquarie Street

Sandstone: Department Of Lands Building, City

Woolstore Below:Deco: Former City Mutual Bldg

Gothic Skyscraper: BMA House Below: MLC Centre

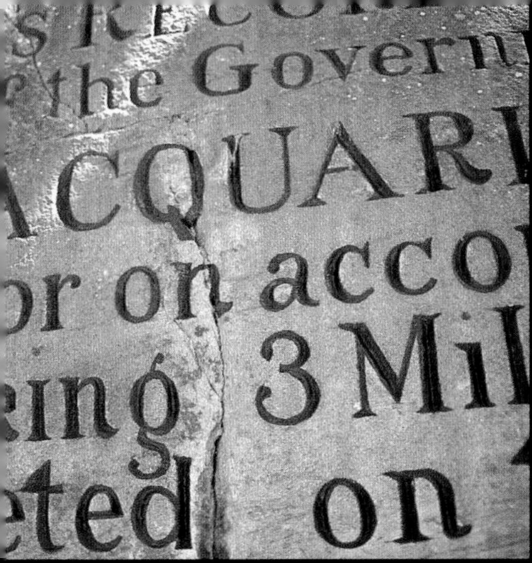

Mrs Macquarie's Chair

St Stephen's Church, Newtown

Finger Wharves, Walsh Bay Below: Opera House

Shelly Beach, Manly Below: Stock Exchange

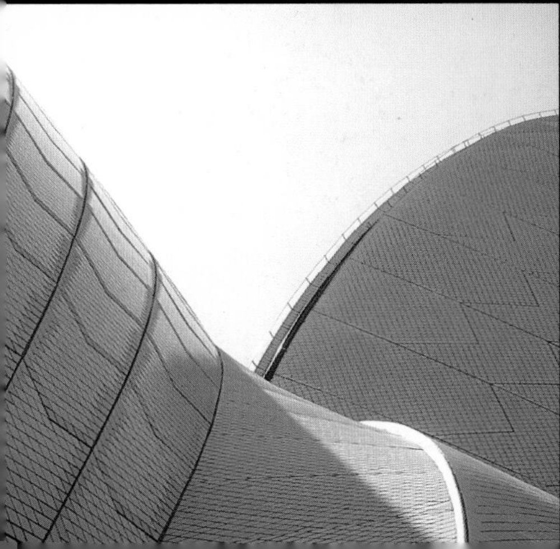

Balmain Bowlers

Clarke Island, Sydney Harbour

Watsons Bay Sunset

Below: City Skyline

Terraces,The Rocks Below: The Rocks

ARCHITECTURE: TERRACE HOUSES

Sydney's first European houses were makeshift huts of bark, reeds, thatch and sticks built by the early settlers, modelled loosely on the English cottages with which they were familiar. As the colony developed, materials and construction became less temporary in character and Sydney began to adopt some of the characteristics of the contemporary English Georgian town, including its rows of terraced houses. (See: Box: Colonial Landmarks.)

The colony's early terraces were built right up to the street boundary and had no verandahs, as they were designed for the gentle English climate in which there was no need to shelter the building from a burning sun. Although many have been demolished, there are several which survive to demonstrate the simplicity and elegant proportions of the style. The Jobbins Building (1854; 103-111 Gloucester Street, The Rocks) has typical multi-paned windows and louvred shutters, while 39-41 (1834) and 47-53 Lower Fort Street, Millers Point, are particularly refined examples.

It soon became clear that this style of terrace was not suited to the Sydney climate, and double storeyed verandahs developed during the Victorian period. Gradually, too, the individual houses in the terrace rows began to be set back from the street with small gardens in front.

The 1870s and 1880s were times of growing prosperity and confidence in Sydney, and speculative builders built many thousands of such terraces tightly packed into suburbs close to the centre of the town. This type of housing was well suited to speculation, as the shared roofs and walls allowed for lower construction costs, and for the compaction of as many houses as possible onto the rapidly subdividing estates and land grants of earlier settlers.

These later Victorian terraces were typically double storeyed and decorated with fringes, balustrades, columns and picket fences of cast iron, which transformed their verandahs into filigree screens. The walls were generally stuccoed and encrusted with moulded plaster details of Classical, Medieval or Italianate influence.

At the beginning of the Victorian period, cast iron detailing was simple and uncluttered in design, and much of it was imported from England. By the 1870s, however, Australian foundries were producing a comprehensive range of cast iron patterns of disparate influence. Some used the emblems of the British Isles - such as the rose, shamrock and thistle - revealing a lingering loyalty to those countries. However, the growing popularity of native Australian flora and fauna - flannel flowers, bush ferns, wattle birds, kookaburras and cockatoos - reflected a growing Australian nationalism. Many of these motifs can still be seen in the balustrades and fringes of terraces.

First floor balconies, with one or two pairs of French doors leading from the main bedroom, are typical of these houses. The impossibility of having windows on the sides of the house at ground floor level meant that the living area could only be two rooms deep, if it was to be naturally lit. Consequently, kitchens, laundries and washing facilities were originally located in narrow 'lean-tos' at the rear of the house.

The hillsides of Paddington were some of Sydney's first battlegrounds for the preservation of historic buildings and suburbs in the late 1960s and early 1970s. Fortunately, conservationist forces managed to ensure that the suburb's heritage was retained, and it is now one of Sydney's most popular living areas. The suburbs of Glebe and Newtown also contain many examples of terraced development. (See: Walks Around Sydney: Glebe, Newtown, Paddington.)

later there were nearly twenty thousand living in the area's four thousand houses.

However, there was no industry here. Paddington was not self-sufficient and residents had to go elsewhere for their employment. So it was that when terraces became unfashionable in the 1890s, there was nothing to keep the residents from moving away, and from 1915 to the early 1940s, Paddington was regarded as one of the country's worst slums. Yet it survived demolition, largely due to the immigrants of the 1950s who recognised the suburb's considerable advantages, unworried by its stigma. Paddington was gradually reclaimed over the following decades, the working class population eventually giving way to more affluent professionals. Meanwhile, the traditional shopping centre on Oxford Street gradually sprouted boutiques and cafes in place of serving local needs, much of the metamorphosis related to the changing demographics and the area's popularity with the wider city's residents.

The Chocolate Factory itself has an important part in the suburb's history. On the counter you will see a number of individual chocoiates wrapped in coloured cellophane. These were originally manufactured by Wladyslaw Pulkownik, a Russian immigrant, in his confectionery on this site. As his business thrived through 1930s Depression, Walter, as he was affectionately known, handed out free chocolaty treats over the counter to a whole generation of Paddington's children. Now manufactured in larger premises, the famous Paddington Chocolates are still made to Mr Pulkownik's original recipes and have rapture-inducingly smooth centres with evocative names such as Natasha Marzipan.

Leaving the Chocolate Factory, note the row of terraces opposite you, one of the most elegant stretches of residences in the suburb. These ones are comparatively wide and deep, set back from the road to squeeze in a patch of garden, and undoubtedly would have been built for wealthier residents, as you will appreciate when you see the size of the mini-terraces around the corner.

On the left is the first of the galleries you will encounter. **Stills** is devoted to changing exhibitions of photography (✆ 9331 7775; Open: Wed-Sat 11am-6pm). Pause at the corner of Underwood Street to admire the three storey **Grand National Hotel**, standing proudly under its elaborate parapet. This is one of the most unpretentious and honest Aussie pubs in Paddington, complete with traditional pub carpet, a regular local clientele and, usually, faithful old dogs waiting patiently by the door. Yet, typically of the area, out the back is an excellent and modernised bistro.

Turning left into **Underwood Street**, you will see a range of the famous terraces which give Paddington its character. This street was the centre of the hundred acre Underwood Estate, originally the land of Thomas Underwood, who had split from the Cooper-Forbes-Underwood distillery partnership after an argument. After he was declared bankrupt in the 1870s, it was subdivided with a regular street pattern, in contrast to other precincts, whose layouts had to skirt around estate boundaries and therefore are irregular. Notice the variety in terrace designs along here: some are right on the street while others are set back; some are elaborately decorated while others are quite modest. However, what is common to them all is the high density of living which people grew to detest around the turn of the century; it was the lack of garden and privacy which led to the suburb's decline!

At the corner of William Street stands the bright **London Hotel** (1875), one of the area's most popular watering holes and also a distinctive building: note the arch and pediment to the corner, the unusual windows and the floral moulding around the first floor windows. To the left is the charming William Street, lined at ground level with tiny and enchanting shops ranging from bed linens to hats and chocolates. Glancing above, you will notice the verandahs, iron railings, decorative parapets featuring urns and mouldings, and chimneys which give the buildings their character. It is worthwhile strolling up and down each side of the street before continuing. Proceeding along Underwood Street, the highlight is a row of original, single storey sandstone terraces with dormer windows, built in the 1840s to house the families of officers stationed at Victoria Barracks nearby.

From here, follow Underwood Street around to the left and turn right onto a most remarkable segment of **Oxford Street**. On the corner of Ormond Street stands the magnificent Georgian **Juniper Hall**, believed to be the oldest house in Sydney's east and one of the country's oldest surviving villas. It was built around 1824 for Robert 'The Large' Cooper who, transported in 1812 after smuggling French wines and silks into England, was pardoned, granted one hundred acres on which to build a gin distillery together with Underwood and Forbes, and went on to make a fortune and father twenty-eight children: altogether not a bad score. Cooper had promised his twenty year old (third) wife the finest house in Sydney and it was duly built, offering sweeping views of the Harbour to one side of the ridge and of Botany Bay to the other. In this shrine to the berry upon which he had based his fortune, the Coopers would entertain most of early Sydney's notables. It was later leased and renamed Ormond Hall to disassociate it from its ginny image (1831), used as an institution for children (1850s-1920s), converted into flats (1920s-1980s) and finally restored to its original state and protected by a permanent conservation order.

Directly opposite Juniper Hall is the original site of the **Paddington Reservoir,** built in 1864 to store and supply water piped from the Botany pump station to the growing suburbs. Apparently, the controller at Botany would observe a 'stand pipe' level with the reservoir through a telescope, and would stop pumping when he saw it overflow. This low-tech system was superseded by the bigger Centennial Park reservoir in 1899. Walking towards the town hall and looking down Oatley Street, you can see the impressive shrine to one of Sydney's favourite games: the **Sydney Football Stadium**. Designed by Philip Cox, Richardson, Taylor and Associates in 1986, its sweeping canopy and triangulated roof supports make this a landmark of the eastern region.

Across the intersection stands **Paddington Town Hall**. As Paddington hit its peak in the 1880s, it became Sydney's second wealthiest municipality (after Balmain), and its council decided it needed New South Wales' best Town Hall. An international design competition was held and won by local architect J.E. Kemp, whose plans gave rise to a grand Classical Revival building complete with a one hundred and seven foot clock tower (visible from Newtown), arched windows, Corinthian pilasters and columns, and a balustered parapet. Built at a cost of £15,000, its opening ironically coincided with the start of the depression of the 1890s and the decline in Paddington's popularity. In line with the rest of the suburb, it has now been restored. The late Victorian Post Office (c.1855) is also graced with Corinthian columns among its many decorative features.

Turning into **Ormond Street**, walkers are treated to a great view of a continuous line of terrace fronts and roof tops reaching down towards the Harbour, a typical streetscape in this part of the suburb. As you walk downhill, notice the intricate embellishment on the facades and in the cast iron railings, featuring a variety of motifs from Australiana (wattle, waratahs, and ferns) to the Classical (urns, scrolls etc) and the geometric. In particular, note **'Richmond'** and **'Turon'** (No. 32-34). This was the site of **'Engehurst'**, designed by early Sydney architect John Verge and built between 1832 and 1835 in the exclusive area known as Rushcutter Valley. The house was built in Georgian style for the grandly named Frederick Augustus Hely, Principal Superintendent of Convicts, and its stone flagged verandahs, roof garden, stables, and multiple rooms sat in seven acres of grounds. After Hely's death, it was acquired by John Begg for subdivision. All that remains today is a section of sandstone wall and a large stone cellar below an apartment block.

Proceeding downhill, turn right into Olive Street and walk towards the corner of Heeley Street. Here stands Begg's own mansion (now a kindergarten). **Olive Bank Villa** (c. 1869) was the last of the Paddington mansions to be built. Built of stone, it boasted its own reservoir and became the centre of the Olive Bank Estate, embracing the lands of Engehurst and Juniper Hall. Between 1875 and 1895, the land was subdivided and plots were bought by smaller scale developers and further divided. They gradually erected rows of terraces, living in one of them until they had enough capital to build further. Turning left into Heeley Street, you can see not only the results of the phenomenon, but the narrowness of the plots, maintained to ensure maximum profit to the developer.

Heeley Street leads into **Five Ways**, where a park bench beckons. From here you can admire the mighty **Royal Hotel** (c.1888) with its high degree of Victorian Classical Revival ornamentation, including the French doors leading onto the suave balcony with its delicate iron-lace railing. This verandah is a popular spot for a drink, and from here, you can gaze across the suburb's rooftops as you gather the energy to continue. A short detour down to 16-18 Goodhope Street, opposite, will take you to the **Sherman Galleries Goodhope** (✆ 9331 1112; **Open:** Tues-Sat 11am-6pm).

From whichever option you chose, proceed along Glenmore Road turning left out of Heeley Street. The walk will lead back through here shortly. On the opposite side between Nos 194 & 196 there is a narrow laneway leading to tiny Cooper Street, which walkers should follow. Another reminder of Robert Cooper, this street contains some lovely villas, mostly built in Victorian times. In particular, No. 4-8 deserve subtle attention for their bull-nosed verandahs, iron lace, entry tower and moulded embellishment. Adjacent stands well known Sydney architect Ken Woolley's radical yet somehow sympathetic modern structure, where design elements and scale are inspired by the lines and features of the originals, and therefore minimise impact on the streetscape. Unfortunately, such ideas were not in vogue at the time the adjacent flats were built! Walking along towards Brown Street, you can inspect the rears of the Glenmore Street terraces up on your left, and further along on the right, the Scottish Hospital. This was originally 'The Terraces', a stone mansion built in the 1840s for Justice Kinchella, whose drawing room was used until the early 1980s as the operating room! The typical wide verandahs and the slate roof are still visible through the fence. However, even grander were the extensive terraced rainforest gardens of rare trees and shrubs, a patch of which still stands at the corner of Cooper and Brown Streets. Some of these trees are over one hundred years old and include several Australian species such as Moreton Bay figs, Cabbage Tree Palms, Bangalow Palms and Norfolk Pines.

Turning left into Brown Street, pause opposite the end of Macdonald Street to admire the row of Edwardian Terraces. By the turn of the century, terrace living was no longer popular and Paddington was almost completely developed. Curiously, there was still a housing shortage and so these terraces came into being in 1910. They were among the last to be built in Paddington, and the lack of building activity at this time is evidenced by the comparative rarity of the Federation style in the suburb. The wooden slat and rising sun decoration on the gables is often seen on Federation facades. Turning right back into Glenmore Road, walk as far as **Gipps Street**, almost at Oxford Street.

This end of Glenmore is famous for its enticing antiques and clothing boutiques, but is best known as the site of the **original Paddington village**, where the cottages which housed the stonemasons and quarrymen constructing the Victoria Barracks were erected and clustered together in the 1840s. Reaching Gipps Street, turn left and pause on the corner of Prospect Street. Here (No. 1 and No. 3) are two of the oldest buildings still standing in Paddington. Completely simple and functional, these single storey sandstock terraces are largely in their original condition and stand on what was the first subdivision of the Paddington Estate (1842).

Continuing along Gipps Street to Shadforth Street, turn right and walk up to Oxford Street to cross carefully to the Barracks.

Victoria Barracks were designed by Lt. Col. George Barney after it was decided to move the troops out of the Sydney centre. Construction began in 1841 using two hundred tonnes of rough stone quarried from the site largely by convict labour, and they opened in 1848 after numerous difficulties and set-backs, not least the presence of a huge sand hill needing deep excavation before suitable foundations could be set. The soldiers were immune to the elegance of the barracks; in fact, they hated them: the distance from the city's delights and the eye infections caused by blowing sand rendered them less than receptive to issues of aesthetics! Perhaps the three feet thick sandstone walls, built to protect from surprise attack and therefore ten feet deep in some places, felt vaguely like a prison. Today, the barracks are the focal point for army activities in New South Wales, and the largest and best preserved complex of Georgian style buildings in Australia, in constant military use since 1848. A short detour along to 98 Oxford Street (towards the City) will lead you to the excellent **Coo-ee Aboriginal Art Gallery** and shop (✆ 9332 1544; Open: Mon-Sat 10am-6pm; Thurs to 8pm; Sun 11am-5pm; See: Shopping).

Cross back over Oxford Street into Shadforth Street and walk as far as Mary Place, at which point turn right. Here (No. 12) is the Mary Place Gallery (✆ 9332 1875; Open: Variable according to the exhibition, but most often Tues-Fri 11am-5pm; Closed Mon). The end of **Brown Street** is almost an enclave of magnificent Victorian Italianate terraces, overloaded with decorative details, yet retaining a great sense of grandeur and majesty.

After investigating this row of houses, turn right to follow **Glenmore Road** again for a while. Glenmore Road is one of the suburb's few streets which follow the topography, having been determined by teams of bullocks used by the Cooper distillery to haul loads of gin up from the bottom of the hill to Sydney. Along this street are some interesting variants in the kinds of dwellings built over the years: 1920s flat buildings which replaced large residences and took their names; an oriental-influenced pergola at Nugal Hall (No 190) whose Lord Howe Island Palms are remnants of the original garden; and substantial plain-fronted terraces crammed up against the street.

Walk through Five Ways and then bear right into Gurner Street, passing the excellent La Gerbe D'Or Patisserie, and leading to the **Wagner Art Gallery** at No 39 (✆ 9360 6069; **Open:** Tues-Sat 11am-5.30pm; Sun 1am-5pm). Those keen to photograph a typical Paddington street will find a short detour into **Cambridge Street** on the left very rewarding. Turn right into Norfolk Street and bear right again into **Suffolk Street** to admire the extremely suave streetscape offered by the terraces set back behind trees and gardens. From here, bear left and then right into Union Street, where a series of **Victorian Gothic Revival terraces** round the corner. Decorating these dwellings are elegant wooden carvings which draw the eye up to the steep and narrow gables. This street also contains an interesting collection of architectural styles: note the two storey terraces on the left and the starkly contrasted sandstone cottage at No 17.

At the end of Union Street turn left and walk one block along Underwood Street, turning left into William Street. From here, curve around to the right into Paddington Street. You are now in the home stretch!

Despite its name, **Paddington Street** is one of the few true avenues in the suburb: wide and lined with Plane trees, it has a feeling of space and regularity rare amongst the crowded streets you have walked through today. Cascade Street (on the left) was the original path of the stream which flowed down over the Glenmore Falls into the waiting mouth of the gin distillery. It is the steepest street in Paddington, and we avoided it for precisely that reason. However, a short detour down it to Hargrave Street will lead you to the **Sherman Galleries** (✆ 9360 5566; Open: Tues-Sat 11am-6pm). The view from the top across the suburb is magnificent. Directly opposite the end of Cascade Street are a number of beautiful terraces which have been modernised but not compromised in order to make them more comfortable. Terraces are extremely dark inside, having no windows apart from those at the front and back, so several of these have been opened out at the rear to allow the light to flood in.

As you walk along under the **Plane trees**, whatever the time of year, walkers will feel a real sense of season. In many areas of Sydney, evergreens and natives look the same all year; here, however, the vivid green of spring and summer is invigorating, while the rusty browns of autumn and winter are suitably thoughtful. Again, a great variety in styles and adaptation is evident in the terraces: many have been completely revamped and restored to combine the aesthetics of the last century with the advantages of the present. This is another photogenic street.

At the end of this street, turn right into Jersey Road, walking past one of Sydney's most successful florists on the left, Susan Avery. Approaching Oxford Street, you will find a row of **Victorian sandstone mansions** reminiscent of Hunters Hill. Incredibly, they were almost demolished to widen the road; however, they were thankfully saved by local pressure groups. As you look at these coveted residences smugly facing the still narrow street with their delicate iron lace, wooden detailing, generous verandahs and lush gardens, it is worrying to imagine the short sightedness which nearly destroyed them.

Opposite **'Westbourne'** stands the **Victorian Courthouse** and **Police Station complex**. Built to Colonial Architect James Barnet's Classical Revival design in 1888, the portico, columns and balustrades radiate authority and establishment.

From here, you can either turn right onto Oxford Street and then second right into Elizabeth Street to return for a refill at the Chocolate Factory, or continue on a short extension around neighbouring **Woollahra** as follows.

The noble character of the area continues into Woollahra, with many fine residences lining its main thoroughfare and original shopping centre, **Queen Street**. From the end of Jersey Road, turn left into Oxford Street and left again into the beginning of Queen Street, walking down the left hand side to admire the numerous **antiques dealers** such as Anne Schofield and Copeland & de Soos. Here is also **Rex Irwin Art Dealer** (1st floor No 38; ✆ 9363 3212; Open: Tues-Sat 11am-5.30pm). At the lights, cross Moncur Street diagonally, noting the **Woollahra Hotel** on the corner, home of the rightly famous Bistro Moncur, and then continue along the right hand side of Queen Street. Continuing a short distance further over Ocean Street at the next lights will lead you to a typical stretch of this suburb's residences, including terraces and semi-detached cottages. You may have noticed by now that most of the houses in this part of Queen Street bear brass plaques which state that they are listed on the Register of the National Estate as they are worthy of conservation and special care. Woollahra Council fights to ensure that modern developments are in sympathy with the suburb's heritage and village atmosphere, and that as few as possible of these buildings are altered or destroyed. **Waimea Street** off to the right is a particularly good example: with small cottages lining each side, it ends in the elegant sandstone villa **'Waimea'**, built around 1858. Each side of the short street has a row of terraced cottages which mirrors that on the opposite side. Their original brick walls have been painted in some cases, and some of the slate roofs have been replaced with tiles, but they still share bay windows, cast iron picket fences, and decoratively carved timber barge boards.

Returning up Queen Street, there are many delightful streets and shops to explore, such as Ocean Street and

Holdsworth Street where the **Holdsworth Gallery** is situated (86 Holdsworth Street; ✆ 9363 1364; **Open:** Mon-Sat 10am-5pm; Sun 12noon-5pm), although at this stage, the bus stop is probably what you want to see most!

Centennial Park

Description: Established as a celebration of Australia's centenary in 1888, Centennial Park is a bonanza of green where you can walk, in-line skate, ride a horse or bicycle, picnic, jog, eat at the kiosk or cafe, doze under a tree, talk to the ducks, smell the roses or play football. The park has perimeter walking, cycling and equestrian tracks, and most sporty equipment can be hired from establishments nearby.
Starting Point: Anywhere in Centennial Park.
Map Reference For Walk: H7.
Length: varies.
Best Time: Any time.
Transport Alternatives: The park is on Oxford St at Queen St on bus routes 380, 382, 394, 396, 398 from Elizabeth St, City; 311, 378 from Central.
See: Open Air Sydney: Parks & Gardens; Sights To See; Sports: Cycling, In-line skating, Jogging; Wet Days.
The site of Centennial Park led a chequered history before evolving into the genteel parkland you see today. The area, largely a natural swamp, was set aside in 1811 as a common in an attempt to deter individuals from grazing their animals in Sydney's formal parks and gardens. Between 1818 and 1825, several flour and paper mills were built in the area, after which the 'Lachlan Swamp' was used to supply water for the growing town. By the early 1850s, this water supply had become insufficient, and the reserve gradually became a dump for nightsoil and industrial effluent.

The *Centenary Celebration Act* of 1887 defined how Sydney would celebrate the first one hundred years of European settlement in New South Wales, and the decision to construct a large public park drew on English precedents.

The industrialisation of England had instigated a crisis in working class health, housing and amenity. Wealthy industrialists, who wished to support economic stability by keeping the working class contented, pronounced and realised programs of social reform and city beautification. The populist idea of 'Parks for the People' was mirrored in Sydney, in a convenient combination of the intellectual ideal of social reform and the aesthetic ideal of beautification. Together, they formed an irresistible electoral gimmick.

Charles Moore, director of the Sydney Botanic Gardens, was given the task of laying out Centennial Park. In keeping with English tradition, he incorporated a Grand Drive, tracts of dense woodland, specimen trees in isolation to allow the appreciation of their form, and a number of exotic flowering plants and trees. Large scale works realised by nearly six hundred labourers were required to put the plans into action. Up to eighteen kegs of powder were used in a single week to level the ground, remove rocks and mould the landscape to the smoothly undulating scene envisaged. Sandhills were removed and a third of an acre was blasted away purely for the official tree-planting ceremony at the park's opening.

The work was partly funded by the sub-division and sale of adjoining land for the construction of villas. Around one hundred acres were made available to the public, although rigid covenants setting minimum building standards dictated just which sectors of the public would be able to live there. Most of these villas were constructed between 1920 and 1925, and many are still visible in Lang Road.

There was also a firm idea fixed in the minds of the park's administration of exactly who should be using the park, and how. The genteel leisure classes were preferred over loiterers, wasters and loafers, while it was thought that cricket, golf, rugby union and polo were appropriate, gentlemanly pursuits. Rigid rules meant that these games could only be played by members of approved clubs, and gatherings of more than nineteen were forbidden, even for picnics. Also forbidden were tree climbing, the playing of unauthorised games, training for sports, performances and entertainment of any kind. Perambulators were not allowed, and wheelchairs were only admitted when the tracks were dry.

Nevertheless, Centennial Park became an important national focal point, attracting great crowds on the occasions of the proclamation of the Federal Constitution, the end of the First World War and the sesquicentenary of Sydney's establishment in 1938.

Over the subsequent decades, the park fell into steady decline, and only narrowly escaped 'improvement' by a number of building proposals. By the 1960s, the fences were damaged, the lakes were full of weeds and a basic staff was endeavouring to maintain the grounds in a reasonable state. A committee set up in 1964 set about replanting and revitalising the park, and it gradually regained its former splendour. Today, Centennial Park is enjoyed and loved by many who come to enjoy the riding, cycling and jogging tracks, picnic areas, open playing fields, beds of exotic flowers, the rosarium, palm trees, duck ponds, lakes and trees.

Maps are available near most park entrances, and the central kiosk dispenses excellent cafe fare and take away refreshments. The names and addresses of hirers of **sporting equipment** (cycles, in-line skates and horses) can be found in the chapter, Sports. This walk is not about the variety of the route: it is, after all, largely a circle. This one is what you make it: you're on your own!

The Bronte to Bondi Cliff Walk

Description: A different view of Sydney's most famous beach, offering spectacular ocean views. The walk hugs the rocky coastline around from Bronte, past Tamarama and on to Bondi, on concreted path with some steep steps.
Starting Point: Bronte Beach: the path starts with some steps at the Life Saving Club at the northern end of the beach (away from the pool); Bondi: the path starts at the

southern end, towards the pool.
Map Reference For Walk: H11.
Length: Around 40 minutes one way.
See: Directory: Bondi; Open Air Sydney: Beaches; Sights To See: Bondi Beach; Sydney By Area: Eastern Beaches; Sydney Icons: Surf Life Savers; Tours Around Sydney: Bondi & Bay Explorer.

Starting at either end of the walk will allow you to experience the strong winds that rush up the cliffs, admire the Prussian blue and turquoise green of the Tasman Sea, follow the surfers as they ride the waves into shore, watch the people on the sand and appreciate the beauty of the edge of this part of Australia. This is a popular path for walking, jogging and dog exercising, and many undertake it as a break from the hard job of lying on the beach. After all, at either end of the walk are a number of excellent cafes, bars and pubs to quench your thirst. In between is Tamarama Beach, alternatively known as Glamarama: the place where 'the beautiful people' choose to darken their skin tone and dip in the sea. This compact and good looking beach is also the home of an excellent cafe right on the sand, which always seems to play excellent jazz. The Cliff Walk may not be too long or challenging, but it is very popular precisely for this reason; you will often see people standing and simply staring out to sea.

Kings Cross & Elizabeth Bay

Description: A varied walk through Sydney's grittiest but undoubtedly most colourful suburb, to the regal colonial elegance of Elizabeth Bay and down to the 'loo.
Starting Point: The Coca Cola sign, Cnr Kings Cross Rd & Darlinghurst Rd.
Map Reference For Walk: F5 to E6.
Length: 3.7 km; allow 2 hours.
Note: Elizabeth Bay House is closed on Monday.
Transport Alternative: Bondi & Bay Explorer.
See: Markets: Kings Cross; Nightclubs; Sydney By Area: Kings Cross & Potts Point; Tours Around Sydney: Bondi & Bay Explorer.

Starting near the **Coca Cola sign**, and with thoughts of cultural imperialism in your mind, proceed down Darlinghurst Road towards the action and away from the chaotic seven-way intersection. Depending on the time of day, either calm or aggressive flesh pushing stares you in the face from most establishments, as well as what can only be described as a broad section of Sydney society. A prime backpacker lair and tourist spot, the backstreets of Kings Cross form a surprisingly quiet residential area characterised by leafy trees and grand old apartment buildings, as the middle of the walk will show.

At the spherical **El Alamein fountain**, the site of the Kings Cross Sunday markets, the road curves to the left and becomes **Macleay Street**. From here, continue along Macleay Street noticing the string of excellent restaurants on the left - Paramount, Pig and Olive, and the Macleay Street Bistro: these are some of the best in Sydney (See: Food). At Greenknowe Avenue, turn right and walk down the hill until you reach Ithaca Road on the left, and follow this street towards the water. At the end you will find the tiny waterfront **Beare Park**, which is perfect for reviving tired feet. This bit of waterfront may be temporarily yours, but not next door: this is the realm of two of Sydney's most fabled residences. Turning into Billyard Ave, the colourful wall on the right belongs to **'Boomerang',** a desirable and elusive waterfront property. It was designed in 1926 by Neville Hampson for Frank Albert, a music publisher known for his Boomerang Songbook and mouth organ, and incorporates many Hollywood elements such as pink stucco and elaborate columns. The garden is suitably exotic, dotted with palms and fountains.

Continue along Billyard Avenue and turn left up the hill into Onslow Avenue, home of the second residence in question, **Elizabeth Bay House**, now maintained by the Historic Houses Trust and open to the public (✆ 9356 3022; **Open:** Tues-Sun, 10am-4.30pm; **Cost:** $4/$2). The house was designed by John Verge for Colonial Secretary Alexander Macleay and built in 1835-38. An inspection of the furnished rooms and oval domed staircase reveals why it was known as 'the finest house in the colony', although it was actually never completed. The shuttered house has a serene symmetry to it, while the elliptical dome, paved with wedge-shaped stones, is described by The Heritage of Australia:: The Illustrated Register of The National Estate as one of the finest of its kind in early Australian architecture. The interior makes full use of cedar wood's lustre and is now furnished in the original manner. Astoundingly, the house was at one stage divided into sixteen flats before being rescued and expertly restored. Over the road is a lovely **park**, once part of the twenty-three hectares of land attached to the house.

Onslow Avenue continues uphill to meet Elizabeth Bay Road once more, and at this point, walkers should turn left and proceed around two hundred metres to **Macleay Reserve** to see the most fascinating microcosmic mixture of Sydney residential architecture in the city. Here stands a 1960s apartment block next to an Ocean Liner block of an earlier decade, next to an ultra modern house, next to wooden colonial huts, next to a grand sandstone residence. A stroll around will provide you with a short instruction on the city's major architectural styles.

From here, return up hill to Macleay Street, walk to the left and turn right into Hughes Street, walking under the trees past the terraces to the end where Victoria Street overlooks the City. **Victoria Street** is famous as the centre of the Kings Cross backpacking and cafe sub-cultures.

From this point you can end the walk in one of the area's restaurants, cafes or pubs, or walk down to Woolloomooloo as follows. At the right (lower) end of Victoria Street are McElthorne's Steps leading down to the loo's Cowper Street Wharf, which Australia's illustrious navy calls home. Down here also dwells **Harry's Cafe de Wheels**, a fixture on wheels serving world famous pies (the menu has been extended in recent years to pasties) since the 1940s. (See: Sydney Icons). Continuing around the waterfront are the Finger Wharves, and the Woolloomooloo Bay Hotel. From here, bus 311 will return you to the City.

WEST

Strolling Around Balmain

Description: Balmain is one of the city's most atmospheric suburbs, bursting with tiny workers cottages, sandstone houses and remnants of industrial activity.

Starting Point: Darling Street Wharf, Balmain. A 10 minute ferry trip from Circular Quay (hourly Mon-Sat & every 2 hours Sun); or bus No 442 from QVB, City; 401 from Market St; 433 from George St will deliver walkers to this spot.

Map Reference For Walk: D2.

Length: Approximately 4 kilometres or 2 hours including breaks and market browsing time.

Best Time: The best time is Saturday when the markets are on and the pubs are busy.

Take: Camera.

Information: Balmain Library, 270 Darling Street (✆ 9367 9211) & Balmain Watch House 179 Darling St (✆ 9818 4954; Open: Sat 12noon-3pm). This is the base of the Balmain Association, where guided tours can be arranged.

Transport Alternatives: Much of the interest is in back streets, so by foot is best. However, you can do the walk as a car cruise.

See: Directory: Balmain; Markets: Balmain Markets; Sydney By Area: Balmain; Tours Around Sydney: Harbour Islands.

Leaving the wharf, proceed to **Thornton Park** on the right for a brief history lesson. Accompanying the First Fleet on its treacherous voyage out from England was a bevy of medical staff, who, upon arrival, had the onerous task of maintaining life (and health, if possible) in the wilderness. One such officer was **William Balmain** (1762-1803), a surgeon's mate (full qualifications were not part of the job description), who, after finding favour by removing an Aboriginal spear from Governor Phillip's shoulder, served as Second Assistant Surgeon from 1788 to 1791 and was promoted to Principal Surgeon of New South Wales in 1796. He was later to serve as Principal Secretary to the Colony from 1797-1803. In April 1800, Balmain was granted five hundred and fifty acres of land by Governor Hunter. As the result of one of his numerous and complex business dealings, he sold the entire grant to a certain John Gilchrist of Calcutta for five shillings (approximately fifty cents, not considering inflation). These days, as many have pointed out in indignation, fifty cents does not even buy a beer!

Balmain saw little activity beyond cow grazing by settlers and fishing by Aborigines until the 1830s, when the land was first sub-divided and sold off. Yet, the lack of transport to the main settlement remained a deterrent to settlers: anybody who wanted to get there had to travel by rowing boat. However, when a ferry service was formed, Balmain became suddenly popular.

One attracted to the area was **Thomas Sutcliffe Mort** (1816-78), who established a dry dock at the end of Waterview Street in 1854 during the Gold Rush boom. Joined by other developing industries (a sawmill, coalmines, candleworks, a soap plant, chemical plant and other factories), there was soon little room for the cows. Hundreds of workers appeared on the scene, building and moving into cottages squeezed into narrow laneways near their workplaces.

While most of the industry which brought the suburb to life has disappeared, Balmain today retains the character of its haphazard development, with tiny cottages squeezed into unlikely blocks, flanked by larger stone residences, serviced by corner shops and numerous pubs, with the occasional 1960s red brick building thrown in. It is a resuscitated area, vitalised by the baby boomers who moved in in the 1970s, even though Balmain (Glebe & Paddington) had long been considered little better than slum. Now restored and supported by a rich collection of restaurants, cafes and shops, Balmain is one of Sydney's most coveted residential suburbs and its houses attract high prices.

This waterfront precinct is central to the area's early settled history. Leaving the park, cross Darling Street and go to the corner of Weston Street. **The Shipwright's Arms** (c. 1844) was the favourite haunt of the whalers, sailors and ferrymen of the area. It is easy to imagine that the relative peace of the pub's location was often shattered by the boisterous singing and shouting of its patrons when they weren't fighting, and boisterous shouting when they were. Opposite stands **Waterman's Cottage** (c. 1841), the residence of the waterman, or big-muscled rower, responsible for transporting people to Sydney Cove.

Start walking up the hill. **Darling Street**, named after Governor Darling, is Balmain's main axis, and it will form the centre of the walk, with various detours along the side streets.

The shops at this end of the street include one of the city's favoured wine merchants (**Sixty Darling Street**) on the left, and a great cafe (**Pelican's Fine Foods**; **Open:** Mon-Thurs 8am-4pm; Fri-Sat 8am-5pm; Sun 10am-3.30pm), on the right. Here you will find plunger coffee, burgers ($3.40/$3.90 with tofu), sandwiches with a choice of 24 fillings ($3.50), cakes and slices. Cooked breakfasts for $6.20 are extremely popular. Combined with the green grocer nearby, you have the makings of a fine picnic in Thornton Park at the conclusion of the walk, or **provisions** for along the way.

Proceeding along Darling Street, turn left into **Ewenton Avenue** at the bowling club. This green usually sees some hot action on Saturday afternoons and the bowlers are incredibly chatty. However, looking back to Darling Street across the green is one of the quintessential views in the suburb. Note the cobalt blue tinier than tiny worker's cottage cowering under the tall, pristine white modern residence. It is difficult to imagine achieving a greater contrast, yet this really characterises the area. Continuing to the end of Ewenton Avenue and turning left into Grafton Street, walkers will find **Hampton Villa** (No 12b). Built between 1847 and 1849, the sandstone villa with its green shuttered French doors, Doric columns and stone flagged verandah was the residence of **Sir Henry Parkes** between 1888 and 1892, while he served as Premier of New South Wales. Parkes (1815-1896) emigrated from Warwickshire in 1839 and became an eminent journalist and ivory trader before entering the Colonial Parliament in 1854. He held various offices and was, from 1872, repeatedly elected Premier of New South Wales. He was central to the development of the Federation movement (the joining of the States into one nation; See: History), and for this reason is popularly known as the Father of Federation. Returning to the end of Grafton Street, turn right into Adolphus Street to return to Darling Street.

At Darling Street, cross over to the **Watch House** (No 179). It was built in 1854 as a police station and lock-up to Colonial Architect Edmund Blacket's design, incorporating not so comfortable gaol cells into the guardroom structure. The 'dunny', 'privy', 'throne box', or 'outhouse' (all old Aussie colloquialisms for 'toilet') behind it must not be missed: constructed around 1878 using dressed sandstone blocks and topped with a chimney, it must have been one of the most structurally sound and luxurious in Sydney! The station was closed in 1887 and these days holds no prisoners. Used as a residence until 1950, it was acquired by the Balmain Association in the 1960, and is today the site of many exhibitions.

Turn into **Colgate Avenue** and proceed downhill as far as Caroline Street. Why is this street named after a toothpaste? Look closely down the hill and you will see the aged yet imposing advertisement blaring out the name on part of the factory structure! Again, this characterises the suburb, where residential and industrial elements are mixed and crammed onto the peninsula together. Many of the charming cottages in this little area were built with local stone, so stroll to the left into Caroline Street, and then turn right into **Waterview Street** to see a prime example. At No 46 stands **Balmoral House** which was built in about 1855.

At the bottom of this street is **Mort Bay**, the original location of Thomas Mort's massive drydock, established in 1854 and which grew into an engineering works and foundry, and which was even building locomotives and train carriages by the late 1800s. This was where the Australian Labor Party was formed in 1891. The area is now used to berth some of the tug boats which guide the thousands of huge cargo and passenger boats into and out of the Harbour every year. The next point jutting out into the Harbour on the left is Ballast Point, so named because of the particularly heavy rock quarried there and used as ballast on ships (to make them more stable) constructed in Sydney.

Straight ahead in the Harbour is Goat Island (See: Tours Around Sydney: Harbour Islands), site of notorious **'Anderson's Couch'**, the scene of one of the early colony's typically inhumane exercises in prisoner control. Anderson was a sailor in the British Navy who received head injuries in an accident and became violent. He was taken to Goat Island, placed in chains and tethered to a large rock. In this rock was carved a narrow ledge facing Balmain, partially sheltered by a rough wooden structure, to serve as his living quarters. Only free to wander at chain's length during the day, and with rations thrown at him from a distance, he was kept here for two years around 1838; yet his violence did not decrease (not surprisingly). He was eventually moved to Norfolk Island, where he was rehabilitated by Commandant Maconochie, and within a number of years, he was running the signal station single handedly.

From the water's edge, walk a short distance back up Waterview Street and turn right into Alexander Street. Turning left into Campbell Street and following it up hill, you will come to the **Presbyterian Church** (No. 5), built between 1867 and 1878 to the Gothic revival design of local mayor James McDonald. It is this church which possesses the octagonal stone spire visible from so may points in the suburb. At the top of the hill on the intersection with Curtis Road stands **St. Andrew's Church** (c. 1855). This Victorian Gothic landmark was designed to evoke the traditional English village church, and is the site of the Balmain markets, held every Saturday between 10am and 4.30pm. They are well worth a browse; walkers could even get a Chinese neck massage here ($10) before continuing! However, it is recommended that you first have a **break**, and this is a good spot to do it. In the church hall is a united nations of food stalls where hungry walkers can obtain Indian, Asian or European snacks and dishes. Across Darling Street to the left is the London Hotel, an inviting spot where patrons can perch on comfortably moulded tractor seat stools on the verandah and watch Balmain go past over the rim of a beer glass. This is one of the suburb's famously high quota of pubs: Balmain has more pubs than any other suburb in Sydney. Beyond the markets on Darling Street is Cafe Tatu, source of great big bowls of massive potato wedges with dips. Yum.

Once refuelled, the best thing to do is to stroll along **Darling Street**. In particular, you shouldn't miss: All our Yesterdays at No 209 (✆ 9555 9506), a sprawling second hand emporium and **Pentimento Bookshop** at No 275 (✆ 9810 070). There are also some excellent cake shops here such as the **Bay Street Patisserie** at No 323b (✆ 9555 9375).

Further up Darling Street on the left is the **civic precinct** of the suburb, where the post office (c.1885), police station, court house (built simultaneously and designed by the Colonial Architect's Offices under James Barnet) and town hall stand in a mighty assertion of authority beyond Montague Street. Leading from the tower of the post office, across the dome of the courthouse, and to the Town Hall (now the library), they are an imposing group of High Victorian monumental civic buildings (not often found in a suburban setting) with columns, stucco mouldings and other Italianate and Classical Revival details. Beyond this on the right hand side of Darling Street stands the late nineteenth century **fire station**.

Apart from this, there are still hundreds of little streets around the suburb to be explored. An unstructured wander is a great way to fill in the time before heading into one of the area's restaurants or pubs. Remember that several of Balmain's pubs, such as The Sackville, have excellent restaurants attached to them. Whatever you decide to do, the walk you have now completed has shown you the principal gems of the Balmain peninsula, one of Sydney's most atmospheric and picturesque suburbs.

An Architectural Ramble Around the Backblocks of Glebe

Description: A gentle but lengthy stroll around one of Sydney's most fascinating suburbs, passing many different styles of early Australian architecture and experiencing the strong sense of community through the pubs, cafes and galleries of the area.
Starting Point: Cnr Glebe Point Rd & Bridge Rd.
Map Reference For Walk: G2 to F1.
Length: A little less than 6km; allow a morning including stops and browsing.
Best Time: Saturday for Glebe markets and the Valhalla cinema 1pm matinees with jaffas and cordial included in the ticket price.
Transport Alternatives: Bus 432 from the City runs right down Glebe Point Rd, although the backstreets shouldn't be missed. The entire walk can be converted to a car cruise.
See: Directory; Film: Valhalla; Markets: Glebe Markets; Sydney By Area: Glebe.

Glebe lies tucked in under the shadow of the University of Sydney, a fascinating mixture of bohemian student life and gentrified, restored residences. The character of the suburb was always so, and its blend of architectural styles is evidence of its chequered history. The word 'Glebe' means 'church land', so it is not surprising to discover that the entire area belonged to the church until pressing economic needs prompted the land's sub-division in 1828. A number of wealthy merchants and professionals, eager to emulate the lifestyle of the English gentry, developed large estates. However, the depression of the 1840s forced many land holders to subdivide further and the large scale building activity which followed virtually destroyed the area's exclusive rural character, leaving Glebe as Sydney's largest suburb. A subsequent boom between 1871 and 1891 boosted the number of dwellings to three and a half thousand; this in turn encouraged the established families to move on to better, less populated pastures, and the social standing of the suburb declined accordingly. The slide continued into the Great Depression of the 1920s and 1930s, by which time the suburb represented the depths of social mediocrity, as described by the Glebe Society's 1988 pamphlet, Historical Glebe. Post-war town planners saw wholesale demolition as a good way to reutilise the land, and incredibly, it was not until the late 1960s that Glebe and its architectural treasures came to be appreciated. Luckily, the view quickly gained popularity, and today, it remains as one of the most beautiful areas in the city and a designated Conservation Area.

The suburb is divided into various precincts according to respective sub-divisions and developments. The walk leads through each of these areas, noting the differences.

Standing on the corner of Foley Park, it is hard to imagine this busy inner city suburb as a rural area dotted with large residences and their estates. Yet something had to give way for the transformation to take place and **'Hereford House'**, one of the area's earliest buildings (c.1830), was one such casualty. This park is the remains of the estate's grounds and the puny plaque on Glebe Point Rd is a sad testament to the phenomenon of 'progress'.

Next to the park is the Victorian Gothic Revival **Church of St. John the Evangelist**. Designed by Edmund Blacket, a Glebe resident who also designed the University of Sydney's Great Hall, it was built by John Horbury Hunt between 1868 and 1870 using stone quarried from nearby Pyrmont. The interior, furniture and pulpit were made to Blacket's original designs, while the upper half of the tower, choir, vestry and porch were added between 1909 and 1911.

Leaving the church onto St John's Road, you are facing the centre of the precinct known as Bishopthorpe, which has an unlikely historic connection with the poet William Wordsworth. Cross St John's Road to walk into **Derwent Street.** The father in law of one of Glebe's early Bishops was a close friend of the poet, who lived in the English Lakes District of Westmoreland, so Derwent and Westmoreland Streets were named in honour of the association, tenuous as it was! The buildings were built between 1856 and 1880 just after the Gold Rush, and are considered to be of particular interest because of the scarcity of information about that period of Sydney's architecture. Further, there is a mixture of styles, including post-Regency and Italianate terraces as well as tiny workers' cottages, evidence of the area's social diversity. Luckily, this was preserved by the Department of Housing's urban renewal program of the 1970s, which modernised and reconstructed many dwellings yet enabled long established families to remain in the area. **The Demeter Bakery** on the corner of Mitchell Street started operation in 1885, and is a good spot to obtain provisions for the walk!

Turning right into Mitchell Street and then right again into Westmoreland Street, walkers will pass a particularly attractive residence on the corner with patterned slate roof and verandah, which appears to have been built in the 1870s and added to at different stages. Continuing along this street, the evidence of sympathetic **renewal programs** is clear: elements of the old dwellings' design are incorporated into new housing projects. From here, proceed to St John's Road and cross over to the enigmatically named **Purves Street**, opposite. At this tiny street's entrance, look back across St John's Road to the town hall, with its elaborate facade laden with the mouldings and semi-circular arches of Classical Revival architecture. Lined with minute workers' dwellings, Purves Street leads straight through to Bridge Road via a narrow walkway.

Bridge Road was originally built as a private toll road by the Pyrmont Bridge Company to lead down to their new bridge, now used only for pedestrian access between Darling Harbour and the City. In line with nineteenth century practice, grand residences were common on main roads, so it contains some fine buildings. On the right of the walkway stands the **Presbyterian Church** (c. 1881; now The Abbey restaurant), which was moved here stone by stone from the noisy corner of Glebe Point and Parramatta Roads in 1927. Walking along Bridge Road away from Glebe Point Road, a string of Gothic houses will be seen: **'Reussdale'** and **'The Hermitage'** (No. 152-4, c.1868), both by Glebe architect and builder Ferdinand Reuss, followed by **'Hamilton'** (No. 156) and **'Mon Repos'** (No. 177). However, not everybody wanted or could afford a free standing house, so the variations of terrace design gained popularity. Italianate terraces, such as No. 179-181 and Party Wall terraces, such as Mitchell Terrace (No. 174-184) are frequently to be seen in the suburb. As most of Glebe was subdivided and developed at about this time, these are the bases of the major styles you'll see on the walk, yet the older, large residences are still relevant, as diverse uses for them have been found.

Continue up to Ross Street, turn right and walk along to meet Hereford Street, turning right again. You may remember that the walk began by bemoaning the 1960s demolition of **'Hereford House'**. This street also contains several elegant villas which survive to remind us of what was lost elsewhere. At No. 53 stands another 'Hereford House', this one built in 1874 by wheelwright William Bull who was the son of a First Fleet marine. 'Kerribree' (No. 55) was built in 1889 and shows many examples of ornate decoration such as cast iron tracery, corbelled eaves and verandahs.

Turn left into Walsh Avenue and walk through to **Wigram Road**, turning right and crossing over. Building activity in this precinct peaked in the 1880s, so most of the buildings originate from that period, characterised by late Victorian **Bay Type Terraces** (c.1890). The enigmatically named **'Alpha, Beta Gamma Delta and Epsilon'** (No. 63-71, c.1892) show early signs of Federation design in their gabled roofs. **'Federation'** refers to the style which flourished between 1895 and 1915, and is so named because of the contemporary Federation of Australian States in 1901. A further group (Nos 52-56) show the interesting way in which traditional terrace design was adapted to Australian conditions: large bay windows light the interior while verandahs give protection from direct sunlight. This is still a typical feature of Australian houses due to the macho nature of our sun. **'Minerva Terrace'** (No. 11a-17) features one of the most over the top facades in the suburb: those with a keen eye will note the balls, arches, balustrades and curved walls.

Turn left into Mansfield Street. Along the road you will come across **'Hauteville'** and **'Rageson'** (Nos 16 & 18), built in the Victorian Italianate style in 1884 by Glebe architect Lawrence Frost for a furniture dealer by the mysterious name of Mitchell Tartakover. Yet the prize for dwelling of the street goes to **'Tranby'** (No.13). This early Victorian cottage echoes the low lines and broad proportions of early colonial architecture, and was for many years the home of Wesleyan minister and philologist William Boyce. Indeed, Boyce Street, which cuts across Mansfield, is worth a short detour, not least to see the large Federation cottage **'Montana'** (No. 36). The suave wooden verandah posts and frieze work are typical of the period.

At the end of Mansfield Street is Toxteth Road, the boundary of the original Toxteth Estate, created by subdividing the grounds of Toxteth Park mansion (see below) between the 1880s and 1914 (try saying Toxteth three times quickly). In this precinct, one of the last to be developed, stand many Italianate villas and cottages designed by Joseph Walker and Thomas Sinclair. **'Toxteth Lodge'** (c. 1877) on the corner of Toxteth and Avenue Roads is a Gothic Revival cottage built from an 1860 'pattern book', the *Tarbuck Encyclopaedia of Practical Carpentry and Joinery*. The austere, steep roof and mysterious appearance of this, Toxteth Park's original gatehouse, may have lost some of their impact due to the shrinking of the surrounding land, but the enigmatic atmosphere remains as a ghost, standing at the top of the long dead driveway, Avenue Road. Walking left along Toxteth Road you will find lovely villas decorated with ceramic tiles and plastering done by skilled Italian tradesmen.

Turning right into Maxwell Road and then right again into Arcadia Road, the **Harold Park** trotting complex down in the valley to the left becomes visible. 'The Trots' have been part of Sydney life for many years and attract large audiences each night races are held (See: Sports). **Arcadia Road** itself contains an interesting mix of Federation and Italianate styles, and of particular interest are No. 1-9 (all c. 1895), which display great divergence in detailing: timber contrasting with iron fences at No1; gabled porches with filigree iron work at No. 3; timber balconies showing Federation influence at No. 5 and No. 9; and a circular tower on No. 7. Further up, No. 35 has intricate detailing in the form of native wattle and flannel flower motifs in the cast iron work and stained glass of the windows and doors.

On the corner of Arcadia and Avenue Roads stands **St Scholastica Convent**, as announced by the gateposts. Its main building, 'Toxteth Park', was constructed between 1829 and 1831 for George Allen, solicitor (founder of Allen, Allen & Hemsley, a large legal firm still practising in Sydney), Mayor of Sydney and moral campaigner for the reclamation of prostitutes, nourishment of seamen and total abstinence! Originally showing the characteristics of the Australian adaptation of the Georgian and Regency styles, the house was altered in the 1870s in Victorian Italianate style. It has long French windows opening onto Doric columned verandahs from where the owners could survey their magnificent grounds. These contained oak, fir and fruit trees as well as tracts of forest and a private cricket ground (no home should be without one). After a period of use as a residential college of the University of Sydney, it was sold to the Sisters of the Good Samaritan in 1901, after their convent was demolished to make way for Central Station, then under construction.

Following Avenue Road back to Toxteth Road, turn left and then left again into the charming **Allen Street**, whose elegant little houses sit in various stages of restoration and disrepair under leafy trees. At the end of Allen Street, do a left-right dog-leg into Edward Street. Here stands the **Sze Yup Temple**, a place of worship for Chinese Buddhists since 1904, whose exuberantly tiled, lion-flanked entry gates draw the curious gaze in towards the traditional Joss House main buildings.

This is the beginning of the Glebe Point precinct, and if you turn right into Pendrill Street, it will lead onto Glebe Point Road. Walking downhill to the left and into the corrugated iron **Artists' Studios** at the end on the right, you can be rewarded with a well-earned break at the **Black Wattle Canteen**(✆ 9552 1792; **Open:** Mon-Sat 8am-4pm; Sun 10am-4pm), one of the area's best cafes. Here await great pasta dishes, Italian snacks, a long list of beverages and a calm atmosphere imparted by gazing across the water of Blackwattle Bay to Sydney's newest bridge, opened in December 1995. Alternatively, **Rozelle Bay Bicentennial Park** on the water here is a good place for a snooze. (There's also a bus stop for those who can go no further.)

Once refuelled and/or rested, walk up Glebe Point Road as far as Leichhardt Street and turn left. A short distance along to the right is the post-Regency **'Margaretta Cottage'** (No 6, c.1848-50), the design of which shows colonial characteristics in its shuttered French windows and verandahs, flat cast iron stanchions on the verandah, and side gables. It was built for John Vannett using local sandstone and lime extracted from burning local sea shells; but he defaulted in his mortgage payments and the lot was sold in 1855 to an architect, Michael Golden, together with next door's **'Leichhardt Lodge'**.

Returning to Glebe Point Road and turning left, there follows a remarkable sequence of dwellings. No. 435-443 are ornate transitional Victorian/Federation terraces (c.1899-1900) with geometric wooden decorative work; **'The Doctors' Houses'** (Nos 216-224, c.1880), the neighbouring group (No.196-214) and the group at No. 385-389 highlight the great contrast between differing styles of **terraces** in the area. This is especially so with **Edith Villas** (Nos 226-8, c.1877), built in the parapet style with elaborate embellishment. The classically proportioned **'Bidura'** (No. 357; c.1860) was Edmund Blacket's home, and is now owned by the Department of Family and Community Services. **'Hartford'** (No. 244, c.1899) clearly shows the Federation style: note the cast iron work in particular. **'Lasswade'** (c.1893) next door is one of the earliest Federation buildings in the area.

From here, coast along Glebe Point Road and its shops as far as Ferry Road. Just a short distance more will lead you through the final precinct, the 'Lyndhurst Estate'. Turn left into Ferry Road and follow it downhill, veering right at the first bend into the tiny Quarry Lane. Emerging onto Quarry Street, turn right at the end into Taylor Street, and cross Bridge Road & Railway Street into Darling Street. Along here are Department of Housing projects built in a sympathetic style to replace randomly demolished 1880s cottages and terraces. Further along on the left is **Cardigan Street**, an extremely rare remainder of the original stone flagging with which the streets were paved. When you have turned left and ascended the incline, look back across the view of the suburb you have been exploring. On the right is the rear of the target: the second of the two surviving Regency villas in Glebe, **'Lyndhurst**' (c. 1835), designed and built in 1835 by John Verge, an architect famous for his elegant Sydney villas (Elizabeth Bay House is another example; See: Kings Cross & Elizabeth Bay, above). Walk around to the front, in Bellevue Street. The building's walls are brick, but are rendered and lined to simulate stone work, a typically Georgian device. As you circle the building, note the French windows on the terrace and the portico with Tuscan columns, both of which combine with classic Georgian lines and proportions to give the residence its poise.

This area was a large estate surrounding the residence of James Bowman, Principal Surgeon of the Sydney Hospital form 1819 and son-in-law of colonial grazier John Macarthur. When the Bowmans retired to the country after four years, the house became St James' College, the first theological college in Australia, later closed down due to the unpopularity of its leader's ideas and sympathies. It then became a distinguished Catholic school (1850s-70s) teaching a rigorous classical curriculum; was subdivided in 1878 and 1885; later became a hospital; and finally a church meeting hall. Tragedy nearly struck when Lyndhurst was acquired by the Department of Main Roads in 1971 for the construction of a North-West Freeway, but was saved by a State election promise. Eventually retrieved from its dilapidated state by a meticulous investigation and restoration process (headed by conservation architect Clive Lucas), the building is now the headquarters of the **Historic Houses Trust**. The modern flat steel columns on the verandah are indicative of the restoration approach. Rather than installing incorrect elements where the original details could not be accurately determined, modern substitutes were used to suggest the size and character of what may have been there.

Turning back onto Cardigan Street, you have a great **view** of the City's western skyline while a railway line cuts right under Glebe to emerge near Harold Park and the Sze Yup Temple.

Turn left into Darghan Street and then right into Lyndhurst Street. Antiques browsers may want to investigate **Fraser's Antiques** in the ex-flour mill (24 Lyndhurst St; ✆ 9660 3019; **Open:** Mon-Fri 10am-5pm; Sat-Sun 10am-4pm) before turning left into Darling Street, noticing the tiny yet intensely, even insanely coloured weatherboard cottage on the corner of the access lane between Darghan and Darling Streets.

St John's Road will lead you back to St John's church and Foley Park, where the walk began. As you reach the intersection, notice the police station, court house and post office, all of which were designed by Colonial Architect James Barnet in the 1880s, and share stuccoed facades with moulded Victorian Classical Revival details. From here, tired but satisfied walkers can head for The Nag's Head pub (162 St John's Road, four blocks away); another cafe such as Kafenio (72 Glebe Point Road, to the left); Gleebooks (49 Glebe Point Road, three blocks to the left) and maybe later a restaurant and a film at the Valhalla, happy in the knowledge that they have completed a long walk around one of the city's most important and socially interesting suburbs.

Meandering Around Old Newtown

Description: A stroll around another of Sydney's most interesting and historic inner suburbs, exploring the area's major draw cards and some quiet back streets which contain less obvious residential gems. On the route, you will discover some of the stories and urban myths of Newtown's past which form part of the area's rich social heritage. There are some surprising views and discoveries, and the route naturally leads past some good cafes.
Starting Point: Newtown Railway station, King St, Newtown.
Map Reference For Walk: H1.
Length: About 2 hours.
Transport Alternatives: The walk can be done as a car cruise.
Best Time: Saturdays are the most lively.
Take: Camera.
See: Gay Sydney; Shopping; Students; Sydney By Area: Newtown.
Like Glebe, Newtown began as a remote farming area after the colony's first Governor, Arthur Phillip, made an initial allotment in 1789 reserving specific areas for Crown, School, Church and farming use. As residential settlement began to spread away from Sydney Cove, the area known as Burren Farm spawned two settlements: O'Connell Town (at Missenden Road) and one near the current railway bridge. In the latter, John and Eliza Webster opened a store which they named the **New Town Store**. The name had stuck by 1832 even though unpopular, and the many subsequent attempts to change it are testament to the name's oddly enduring character. When the railway was built through the suburb in the 1850s, rapid and consistent development was further encouraged, attracting workers and the affluent alike. The area grew into a municipality by 1862, while by the 1920s, it was a thickly populated suburb with a number of factories and regularly serviced by trams. Today, Newtown is home to a population of heritage as mixed as the suburb's buildings. It is a fascinating inner-city precinct with strông ties to the students of the University of Sydney, a more honestly gritty version of Paddington.

From Newtown Station, turn right onto King Street and take the right hand fork in the road into Wilson Street. Proceed past the intersection with Erskineville Road. This is the beginning of the walking route.

Why are you walking along the busy and somewhat dilapidated-looking Wilson Street? Walking along you'll find a large white building, **'Alba'**, on the right. (No 69). While it has now been converted into apartments, it was a chequered path which led to its current state of domestic bliss. Built in 1888 and named **'Oddfellows Hall'**, its original use was exotic: Headquarters of the United Ancient Order of Druids! Between roughly 1910 and 1913, the small building on the right was a Church of Latter Day Saints; simultaneously, the larger building was used as a synagogue, although not exclusively. The arrangement often led to confusion and clashes caused by double-bookings. It is said that the Jewish community finally decided they needed a place of their own when a dog show was held on the Sabbath, thus preventing their service from taking place. The buildings do seem vaguely Sicilian in appearance, although they were designed in Victorian Tudor style. At one stage, the front surface featured a central eye-in-a-triangle motif in the round window, and a rising sun on the gable.

Wandering further down the street, walkers will come to the corner of Bucknell Street. The tall brick building on the right was built in 1898 as **Henry Henninge's Bakery**, Newtown's busiest and most successful. Known as 'the popular baker', it was regarded as one of the most efficient, safe and clean bakeries in operation, and produced up to five thousand loaves a day. The building has lost its iron filigree verandah, although it still displays several characteristics of the Victorian Filigree style in which it was built. Of particular note are the degree of embellishment and the lead light windows, while the parapet pediment on the corner still proudly displays the bakery's trademark sheaf of wheat. The building is now occupied by Original Finish, makers and restorers of some wonderful furniture and other wooden pieces, who will gladly show visitors the bakery's ovens.

Continue to Brocks Lane and turn left, following it through the right hand dog-leg until the T-junction with **Soudan Lane**, noting the backs of the tall terraces on the right- you'll see their fronts soon. The lane was a small pocket of industrial activity: Heiron & Smith's Billiard Table factory, Fred Gissing's joinery, and Olga's Lilywhite Laundry Company were all in operation here in 1915.

Turn right into **Soudan Lane**. This somewhat grotty little lane was named to commemorate the first overseas military expedition undertaken by New South Wales soldiers, when the Newtown Reserve Infantry was formed and sent to the Sudan in 1885. While the conflict was all over before they got there, the patriotic fervour displayed by the men was nevertheless regarded as significant, and so the lane was named in their honour.

The corner of Soudan Lane and **Georgina Street** was the site of **Cambridge Hall**, home of the woman at the centre of Newtown's greatest urban myth. Miss Eliza Donnithorne, the daughter of a judge, was jilted on her wedding day and became a total recluse: the wedding banquet remained undisturbed, spread out on the tables until her death in 1886. If this sounds familiar, it is not purely by coincidence: it is said that Great Expectations' Miss Havisham was based upon Eliza Donnithorne. How? Dickens is said to have known a settler who returned to England with the tale. While the link is tenuous and doubted by many, Eliza Donnithorne's unfortunate demise is recorded fact, and like all urban myths, it's a great story! The house was demolished in 1913 to make room for the Newtown Stadium; this in turn burnt down in 1915, and a warehouse was constructed. It has now been converted into residential apartments.

Turning right into Georgina Street will reveal one of the most interesting residential streets in the suburb. On the left stands the **Western Suburbs Synagogue** (No 18). After the dog show fiasco at **'Alba'** (above), the largely Eastern European Jewish community of the area set about acquiring a synagogue of their own. It was designed by Phillip Rosenblum to emulate the scale and simplicity of a village synagogue, and was completed in 1918.

Walking along under the Moreton Bay Figs, the grand **'Vis Unita Fortior'** terraces on the right are those whose rears could be seen from Brocks Lane. This is an unusually long row to find in tact, even if some are in better condition than others. Note the central terrace with the handshake and eye motifs on the pediment. The terraces were built in the 1880s as part of a planned development, L'Avenue Park Estate, which was to surround the park in imitation of the London Square pattern, transposed and adapted to the Antipodean conditions. **Warren Ball** Avenue was also to be part of the estate, while the large, Gothic house on the corner was the residence of George Brock, the estate's developer. The row of terraces along this street are notable primarily for their bizarre decorative embellishment: note the sea eagles, crabs and shells! **Hollis Park** itself was formed as part of the development and is an excellent spot for a break. It is a popular park with the community's children and their minders who are frequently to be seen picnicking or lying in the sun. There are surprisingly distant **views** to be had from here: to the right, the trees of the Royal National Park across the Georges River to Sydney's south; straight ahead the airport's runways; and diagonally left, glimpses of Paddington. The low-lying land between the three was the original position of Botany Road, established in the earliest months of the colony to facilitate the movement of supplies and materials from Botany Bay, where the Fleet first landed, to Port Jackson, where the colony was started.

Crossing the park diagonally to the bottom left-hand corner, turn left into Wilson Street and walk along until you reach Forbes Street on the left. The area you are now walking through was originally part of **Burrin Farm**, granted to Nicholas Devine, Superintendent of Convicts, by Governor Phillip. In his old age, he transferred the property to his servant, Bernard Rochford, in return for care and assistance until his death. Rochford duly inherited the property and began subdividing and selling, until an Irish nephew of Devine appeared and claimed the estate. Thus began a lengthy series of court battles which reached the English Privy Council before the parties settled the dispute. The case attracted such notoriety that it developed its own name, the 'Newtown Ejectment Case'.

Turning left into Forbes Street at the Royal Edward Hotel, you will see **Bladwell's Developments** built by Joseph Bladwell between 1884 and 1887, next to the pub on the right (No. 56-64). Having carried out a similar scheme in Glebe, he built and sold off each of these little houses forming **'Nottingham Terrace'** one at a time, except for **'Claverton'**, where he lived until 1892. The idea was not unique: thousands of small-scale speculative developers were in operation in the inner suburbs during the 1870s and 1880s, leading to a proliferation of this, the 'Victorian Filigree' style, also found in New Orleans, the West Indies and South Africa. (Those who have undertaken the Paddington walk will remember that similar schemes were responsible for most of that suburb's residential terraces.) A grander example of the style exists further up the hill on the right in the pale green **St Michael's Presbytery** (No 40). This private residence was occupied by the Sisters of Mercy from 1898 to 1901, when it became the Catholic Presbytery of nearby St Michael's. Several others owned it before being consecrated as a Melkite Catholic Church in 1981. The plain style complemented by fine decoration make this an attractive and elegant building.

Walk up to King Street, turn left and cross over at the lights into Little Queen Street, walking past the plain, unbalconied Colonial Regency terraces (c.1858-1864) on each side. Turn left into **Campbell Street** and gaze upwards to the left (No. 87 & 85). Side by side stand two buildings as disparate as they could be: one, a completely modernised and converted residence, and the other, the former **Trocadero Hall**. This amazing building was built in 1889 to house a skating rink, and one can only imagine just how extraordinary it must have been. Looking straight up the facade, a wheel is visible. This was attached to a pulley system, which in turn enabled the roof to be opened by sliding the iron sheeting down small tracks. Here at the rear was the glamorous 'Café Français' with a large fountain in its centre. After the rink closed, the building was occupied by a smash repairer and later a printer. Mutterings about knocking the Trocadero down and building a car park have started, as have much louder shouts in support of its preservation. Further along the street is the unmissably bright **Boquet Terrace** (Nos 25-43), built at the turn of the century.

Cross Missenden Road and turn into Longdown Street, noticing No. 5-7 on the corner of Stephen Street, a plain little Georgian terrace built in the 1860s featuring delicate wooden filigree decoration and sandstock bricks. Turning left into O'Connell Street, walk as far as the **Champion Textiles Building** on the right. Built in 1911 to house the New South Wales Railway & Tramway Recreation Club, this federation warehouse included a boxing ring, wrestling mats, bars, ladders, vapour baths, billiard tables and a reading room. But wait! There's more! There was even a twenty-five metre rifle range on the roof! Perhaps this was why alcohol and gambling were strictly forbidden: brawls could have ended in a shoot out!

Turn left into **Victoria Street**, and walk towards the spire of St Stephens, pausing at the corner of Hordern Street. The view towards the church from here is one of the finest in the suburb, while the two storey, wooden terrace on the right is extremely rare, and was built in the 1880s using weatherboard and corrugated iron on the roof, and features balconies with French doors and cast iron railings.

Continue straight ahead into the grounds of the **Anglican church of St Stephen**. Designed by Edmund Blacket (St John's, Glebe; The Great Hall of the University of Sydney), the Victorian Gothic Revival church of St Stephen is widely regarded as one of the best of his designs. The church has a cruciform plan and the elevation of the church renders its beautiful stone spire visible from afar. St Stephen's was built between 1871 and 1874 within the area of the existing cemetery, established in 1849, which holds the bones and memorials of many early residents of Sydney. Two of the more interesting graves include the mass grave of those drowned when **the *Dunbar*,** carrying 122 passengers from England, was wrecked off Sydney Heads at the Gap in 1857, leaving only one survivor (See: Sydney Icons: The Gap); and the unfortunate Eliza Donnithorne (above). This is a cemetery of great atmosphere.

Leaving the church gates, notice the massive Moreton Bay Fig Tree which shelters over the fascinating cemetery and the shingled lodge. Turn right into Church Street and right again into **Lennox Street**, which skirts along the edge of the Camperdown Memorial Rest Park. The park was originally part of the cemetery and under the very green, well fertilised grass, eighteen thousand people are reputedly buried. The majority of the cemetery was converted into a municipal park in 1948, when many of the headstones were moved to inside the safety of the sandstone walls. Lennox Street itself contains some interesting buildings. **Flower Terraces** (Nos 2-8), built in the economic boom around 1895, are so small that they are numbered by halves, while **May Terrace** was built at the turn of the century in early Federation style; note the painted wooden decorative frieze work. Slightly further along on the edge of the park stands a tree whose plaque states its dedication to a local Aborigine who was buried on the edge of the consecrated ground.

Turn left into Australia Street, noticing **Dibble's Commercial Building** on the corner, built in 1909. The building was used as a bakery by Dibble, a local Justice of the Peace and alderman, and set into the walls are art nouveau tiles. Further along is **Newtown Fire Station**, signalling the start of the civic precinct of the suburb. The area's first fire brigade was formed in 1875 and staffed by volunteers until professionals took over in 1892. The coloured glass, arched windows and two-tone brick work display federation warehouse characteristics. **Newtown Court House** (another of the ubiquitous works of James Barnet, built between 1883 and 1885) is very clearly Victorian Classical Revival style: who could miss that attractive bust of the former monarch drooping over the entrance. Clearly designed to ooze authority and intimidation, it contains two court rooms and their associated offices. In addition, the departments dealing with small debts, intestate estates, and births, deaths, and marriages were operating from here in 1915, at which time, nearly ten thousand dogs were being registered every year! At the end of the street sits the **Newtown Town Hall**, built as a School of Arts in 1865 and purchased by the council for £1,300 in 1868. The sale included the school's books and these formed the basis of the municipal library, the first established in New South Wales. While various changes have been made over the years, the building is now home to the Newtown Neighbourhood Centre: note the tiles made by local children and inlaid in the steps.

You are now at the end of the route, and should be on the opposite side of King Street from the railway station where you began. Those walkers with a little energy and curiosity left over may like to stroll along King Street's fascinating array of second hand and new clothing, antiques, and well-being shops.

Cruise the Harbour on the Scarborough

TOURS AROUND SYDNEY

Sydney's a top place and there's a lot of it. The difficulty for visitors is to plan a campaign which will allow them to see the maximum with a minimum of stress and effort. Joining a tour is a good idea, but doing so does not necessarily mean that you have to join a drive-by bus tour, as there are many ways to remain independent and flexible while still covering a lot of ground. This chapter includes information of several kinds. As well as specific tours to undertake, there are touring routes to explore and discover areas further afield in Sydney away from the centre and inner suburbs. A list of specific tours around certain attractions and sites is included as a check list, perhaps to give you some ideas of what to do; and finally, a number of tour operators are listed. Armed with this information, tourers can go for a coast ride on a Harley Davidson, discover tranquil Palm Beach (a.k.a. Summer Bay), eat their way through Chinatown, or spend a day on one of Sydney Harbour's islands.

INFORMATION & TOUR BOOKING CENTRES

National Parks & Wildlife Centre (Cadman's Cottage, 110 George St, The Rocks; ✆ 9247 8861)
New South Wales Travel Centre (19 Castlereagh St, City; ✆ 13 20 77)
Quayside Booking Centre (Circular Quay; ✆ 9247 5151)
The Rocks Visitors' Centre (106 George St, The Rocks; ✆ 9255 1788)
State Transit Information Centre (Opposite Wharf 4, Circular Quay; ✆ 13 15 00)
Sydney Visitors' Kiosk (Martin Place; ✆ 9235 2424)
For full details, See: A~Z Practical Basics.

CRUISES

With such a good looking harbour right in the middle of the City, it's no surprise to find that over eighty-five per cent of visitors to Sydney take a harbour cruise. However, if you think the Harbour looks good, wait until you see Pittwater, the Hawkesbury River and the Georges River.

Harbour Cruises

Each day, over thirty-eight different cruises share the Harbour, so whether you prefer a traditional Sydney ferry, a replica tall ship or an ultra modern floating restaurant, morning, afternoon or evening, something is bound to suit. However, one thing remains certain: the views are fantastic. The best place to examine the full range of cruises is the Quayside Booking Centre (Circular Quay, Manly Wharf and Darling Harbour; ✆ 9247 5151). Among the plethora of craft offering similar cruises, the following deserve special mention.

Sydney Ferries (✆ 9256 4670) run three different cruises, all of which represent good value and offer the most genuine harbour atmosphere. They cost $16/$14 for day cruises and $14/$10 for the evening cruise, food and drink are available on board, and a full commentary is provided throughout. **The Morning River Cruise**, (10am) tours around the Opera House, the Royal Botanic Gardens, Fort Denison and Shark Island, and then crosses under the Harbour Bridge to travel the Parramatta River as far as the Gladesville Bridge, and then ventures along the Lane Cove River before passing by Darling Harbour and returning to Circular Quay. **The Afternoon Harbour Cruise** (Mon-Fri 1.00pm; Sat-Sun & public holidays 1.30pm) tours past the Opera House and Fort Denison to the bays of the Eastern Suburbs as far as Sydney Heads, and then traverses to enter the maze of Middle Harbour. On the way, your trusty ferry will pass by luxury properties and luscious bushland hills. Both the morning and afternoon cruises last for around two and a half hours. **The Evening Harbour Lights cruise** (Mon-Sat 8.00pm) potters around the centre of the Harbour between Double Bay and Goat Island, with the lights of the City, the Harbour Bridge and the Opera House the main attractions. Especially in summer, when the long and late sunsets form a stunning backdrop, this is a spectacular cruise to take. Another option is to take the **Rivercat to Parramatta**. Although it is now a bustling commercial centre, several important historic sites are located here, including Elizabeth Farm, Hambledon Cottage, Experiment Farm, Old Government House and St Johns Cathedral. For

ARCHITECTURE: MARINE VILLAS

By the time the colony was around forty years old, there were enough residents with the income and leisure required to build and occupy grand houses. In Sydney, these took the form of Marine Villas, built on the town's outskirts with outlooks encompassing broad expanses of harbour. Generally constructed in the 1830s and 1840s on the hillsides of Darlinghurst, Paddington, Potts Point and Glebe, they were mostly designed in one of the two predominant architectural expressions of the period (See: Box: Colonial Landmarks).

The highly fashionable Gothick Picturesque villas were inspired by the contemporary popularity of the Middle Ages, both in literature, where melodramatic images were evoked by the poets and novelists of the time, and in architecture, where the picturesque qualities of ruins were admired. Romantic silhouettes with unpainted stone walls, turrets, battlements, medieval chimneys, pointed arches and stone window tracery were favoured. The elegant and more conservative Georgian Regency villa was characterised by pale stuccoed walls modelled gently into bays; subtle Greek-inspired columns, pilasters and pediments; a simple roofline; pleasing proportions; and overall restraint.

Several of these villas still survive on the harbour foreshores, and a harbour cruise on a Sydney Ferry is recommended as a good way of seeing them (See: Tours Around Sydney). Closest to Circular Quay is the two storey sandstone Gothick Government House, the historic residence of the Governors of New South Wales, looking eastwards over the harbour from the Botanic Gardens (See: Walks Around Sydney: Macquarie Street). It was built between 1837 and 1845 by architect Edward Blore and demonstrates the medieval motifs characterising the style.

Elizabeth Bay House (7 Onslow Avenue, Elizabeth Bay) was built between 1835 and 1839. The Regency style villa was originally set within huge gardens stretching to the water's edge. Its stuccoed facade is divided subtly into bays and painted in a pale stone colour. Contrasting deep green shutters complement the multi-paned windows and elegant French doors, while the entrance is defined by a columned portico capped by a triangular Greek-inspired pediment. The villa's elegant stair hall is elliptical in plan, with a stone floor and sweeping stair carrying the eye up to the lantern-topped dome.

Further around the harbour, peeping above the trees above the Darling Point ferry wharf, sits Carthona Avenue's Lindesay (1836), another mansion in the Gothick style. Lindesay, with a romantic silhouette created by decorative gables and Medieval chimney details, was the first house on the point. Also in Carthona Avenue is Carthona (1841), yet another Picturesque residence. The design of this sandstone house, located just above water level, was taken directly from a pattern book produced by fashionable English tastemaker John Claudius Loudon.

Vaucluse House (Wentworth Road, Vaucluse) is not visible from the ferry, but its battlemented facades, beautiful gardens and carefully restored interiors make it well worth a visit (See: Tours Around Sydney: Bondi & Bay Explorer). In its heyday, it was the centre of a five hundred acre estate, and its huge kitchen, cellars and stables provide a colourful glimpse into the lifestyle of an earlier era.

The colonnaded Admiralty House (Kirribilli Point) was built in 1842 and its top storey was added in the late 1890s. It is the Sydney residence of the Governor-General of Australia.

$8/$4, it is possible to catch Hopkinsons Coachlines' (✆ 9632 3344) **Parramatta Explorer**, which waits for the Rivercat at the Charles Street wharf from Monday to Friday hourly from (.30am to 2.30pm, and Saturday to Sunday at 9.30am, 10.30am, and hourly from 12noon to 3pm. The Ferries office at the Quay has information about this and the Rivercat timetable.

Captain Cook Cruises (✆ 9206 1111) offer a number of cruises on their boats, all departing from Circular Quay (wharf 6). Their **Highlights cruises** ($15) depart at 9.30am, 11am, 2.30pm and 4pm, and last just over an hour. The **Luncheon Cruise** at 12.30pm boasts a buffet lunch and offers around two hours of cruising for $38. **Coffee cruises** depart at 10am and 2.15pm.

Cruising The Hawkesbury River

The Hawkesbury River forms the northern frontier of Sydney, and opens out to the sea to the north of the Ku-Ring-Gai National Park by its estuary, Broken Bay. Much more than a single tract of water, it is an extensive network of beautiful waterways, beaches, secluded inlets and rugged sandstone outcrops. Shapely hills crowded with deep green eucalypts drop steeply into the water. A great sense of peace pervades this calm haven.

Brooklyn is easily reached by car from Sydney by heading north on the Newcastle Freeway, and following the Mooney Mooney turn-off signs beyond the Hawkesbury River Bridge (you must double back to Brooklyn). Train services run regularly to Brooklyn (Hawkesbury River station) although you may have to change trains at Hornsby (North Shore Line).

One of the best and most low key ways to cruise the river is with Australia's last **Riverboat Postman** (**Information & Bookings:** ✆ 9985 7566; **Cost:** $20/$15/$10 including morning tea), an affable, mid-sized chug chug boat operated by Hawkesbury River Ferries which plies the waters each weekday delivering mail and supplies to the remote houses of the area. The service has been running for over a century, although the boat has been updated. Departing at 9.30am, the postie boat travels some sixty kilometres over nearly four hours, passing Richmond and Windsor, and continuing up to Marlowe Creek near Spencer. On the way, passengers will be treated to pastoral scenery, sandy coves, luscious bushland and informed commentary.

Another way to cruise the river is to do it in the opposite direction with **Windsor River Cruises** (**Information & Bookings:** ✆ 9985 7566 or at the NSW Travel Centre, 19 Castlereagh St, City; ✆ 13 20 77; **Cost:** $45 including lunch & refreshments), departing from Windsor in Sydney's outer north-west and ending at Brooklyn after a full day's cruising. Their 'Bridge to Bridge' cruise spends all day passing Cattai National Park, Wiseman's Ferry, small fishing villages and historic buildings.

One last way to spend a day on the Hawkesbury with as little trouble as possible is the **Great Waterways Escape Tour** (**Information & Bookings:** ✆ 9247 5151 at the Quayside Booking Centre; or ✆ 9985 7566 at Hawkesbury Ferries; **Cost:** with return by train $35/$30/$100 family; both ways by ferry, bus and Jet Cat $50/$40/$100 family). Departing from Circular Quay, passengers will take a Jet Cat across the Harbour to Manly, where they will board the 'Boomerang Beach Bus' (below). The bus travels north along the Northern Beaches as far as Newport, at which point tour members will transfer to a ferry to cruise Pittwater, passing Scotland Island, Barrenjoey Lighthouse and Lion Island. Proceeding through Broken Bay, the boat will head into the Hawkesbury River. Finishing at Brooklyn, passengers can either return to Sydney by train, or by the same route of ferry, bus and Jet Cat. The tour departs from Circular Quay on Thursday, Saturday and Sunday at 10am, although passengers can also join it at the Newport Jetty at 11.45am.

Georges River Cruises

The Georges River runs into Botany Bay, and although it is more heavily populated than the Hawkesbury River, it nevertheless retains the same bushland character along much of its banks. However, delights of a different kind await up-river. Canal-carved Sylvania Waters (See: Sydney By Area) is perhaps Sydney's most unjustly ridiculed suburb. Ever since the ABC and BBC made a joint documentary of 'typical Australian suburban life' based on one hapless family resident here, the reputation of Sylvania Waters has never been the same. All this and more can be yours on a cruise of the Georges River. Departing from Sans Souci Wharf (7 days 10.30am & 1pm), cruises travel right up the Georges River to Como and Lugarno, detouring through Sylvania Waters as they go. (Information: Georges River & Botany Bay Cruise Information, Sans Souci Wharf; ✆ 9583 1284).

TOURING ITINERARIES WITHIN SYDNEY

While three of the following touring routes around Sydney are all organised for you, two require a little self-organisation in the form of transport.

The Sydney Explorer Bus

There are two Explorer Buses operated in Sydney by State Transit: the Sydney Explorer loops around Sydney's central attractions, and the Bondi and Bay Explorer loops around the bays and beaches of the Eastern Suburbs. With passengers able to get on and off as many times as they like to a total of one complete circuit, they offer an easy way to see a lot without being compelled to adhere to a tour leader's timetable. All passengers are supplied with notes and informed commentary; however, with a bit of true grit, pioneer spirit and energy, the potential of the tour can be expanded at each stop. The following notes offer only brief detail and suggestions of extensions, as full information is included else where in the guide (as indicated) and all passengers are provided with commentary and notes on the bus. Combining these two sources, tourism can be successfully combined with independent travelling.

Tickets for both Explorers cost $20/$15/$45family, and can be bought on the service, or at any State Transit office (Cnr Loftus St, Circular Quay; Carrington St, Wynyard Park; or York St, QVB). Vouchers can also be pre-purchased from selected travel agents. A twin ticket for both the Sydney Explorer and Bondi & Bay Explorers over two consecutive days is available for $35/$25/$70 family. Both Explorers are part of the Sydney Pass deal (See: A~Z Practical Basics; Transport).

Description: This good looking red bus (Route 111) travels around a thirty-five kilometre route of twenty-six central attractions and points of interest.

Note: Elizabeth Bay House is closed on Mondays.

Operation: 7 days from 9am to 7pm, every 20 minutes. The last circuit departs from Circular Quay at 5.20pm; however, it is best to start early to allow more time at each stop to explore.

Starting Point: Anywhere on the route.

Information: Sydney Buses (**Open:** 7 days 6am-10pm; ✆ 13 15 00).

Before starting at **Circular Quay (stop 1)**, stroll up Loftus Street to **Bar Paradiso** for a fuel stop of good coffee and a snack, as it may be a while before the demanding schedule you are embarking upon allows a break. While enjoying the small city centre oasis of Macquarie Place, read the City Centre walking route (See: Walks Around Sydney) for background information regarding Circular Quay. Alternatively, stroll along the active waterfront to begin the circuit at The **Opera House (2)**. This could be a good time to pick up a program or book some tickets at the box office. The Australian Opera, Australian Ballet and

Sydney Theatre Company all perform here, and are of the highest standards (See: Music, Dance & Theatre). Be sure to investigate the spectacular lines and angles of Sydney's most famous icon (See: Sydney Icons), paying particular attention to the intricate roof. There are many places at the top of the steps where admirers can come face to face with the tiles.

The bus will proceed up Macquarie Street which is lined with the city's most important public and official buildings, to stop outside **The Palace Gates of the Royal Botanic Gardens (3)** (See: Open Air Sydney: Parks & Gardens), where the rose garden, the statue of the colony's first Governor, Arthur Phillip, and sweeping views towards the water are the highlights. From here it is only a short stroll to the fascinating **State Library (4)** (See: Wet Days). You may like to follow the Macquarie Street walk (See: Walks Around Sydney: Macquarie Street), bearing in mind that this is the city's most important showcase of colonial heritage. Those interested in the law may like to investigate the Supreme Court building, where the public cafe on the fourteenth floor affords a great view over Macquarie Street to the Botanic Gardens and the Harbour beyond. The next leg of the journey directly passes **St Mary's Cathedral** and **Hyde Park** with its famous Archibald Fountain, so to investigate these two sights, do so before getting back on the bus.

The bus next passes beneath the leafy trees edging the Domain and the Botanic Gardens to proceed to **Mrs Macquarie's Point (5)**, right at the end of Art Gallery Road (See: Open Air Sydney: Picnics). Here, set back from the water on the side of the point away from the Opera House, is **Mrs Macquarie's Chair**, carved out of the sandstone by convicts for the wife of one of the colony's most influential Governors (See: History). Mrs Macquarie would often come to this spot to admire the view and tranquillity, both of which are marginally impinged upon by the constant stream of tourists being photographed in front of it. The view of the Opera House from this point across the placid and glistening water of Farm Cove is one of the most photogenic in the city. A stroll around the point to admire the might of the **Garden Island** naval installation (See: Tours Around Sydney: Harbour Islands, below) and the Woolloomooloo Bay wharves, and then down into the Botanic Gardens (See: Open Air: Parks & Gardens) is a lovely way to pass the time until another bus comes along. All along the water's edge are a number of sandstone outcrops to claim as your own private island for a few minutes at least.

The next stop is **The Art Gallery of New South Wales (6)**, where an impressive collection of Aboriginal works and artefacts, a large number of contemporary Australian works and excellent temporary exhibitions are waiting to be seen. The hungry and thirsty may like to proceed to the good cafe downstairs on Level Two. This is the last stop in the city centre, and from here, the bus proceeds into the wilds of inner Eastern Sydney, stopping at the perpetually and mysteriously popular **Hard Rock Cafe (7)**. A short detour by foot from this stop, around the next corner into **Stanley Street**, is suggested for a close encounter of the caffeine kind. This little stretch of road, lined on each side with cafes, is the territory of some of the city's most serious coffee fiends. Try The Arch, Alife, Three Frogs or Cafe Divino. One thing is for sure: after visiting a number of these cafes, you will really be rearing to go by the time the next Explorer bus pulls up. Another worthwhile detour to undertake from this stop is to walk up Liverpool Street to the **Sydney Jewish Museum** (See: Museums & Galleries). Interactivity takes on an intimate character here, as survivors of the Holocaust guide visitors through the exhibits and relate their experiences. On emerging, you may need to call in at one of the area's favourite cafes, **Dov** (cnr Liverpool St & Forbes St) to recover.

Back at the Hard Rock Cafe, board the bus once more and proceed to **Kings Cross (8)**, often touted as the city's most cosmopolitan area (See: Sydney By Area: Kings Cross & Potts Point). One option here is to follow the Kings Cross walking route (See: Walks Around Sydney: Kings Cross to Elizabeth Bay), or simply to walk down the main street directly to stop **The El Alamein Fountain (9)**, where the Kings Cross markets are held every weekend. The fountain is on the corner of Macleay Street, widely recognised as containing one of the city's best line ups of restaurants (See: Food).

Leaving the cosmopolitan grittiness of Kings Cross behind, the bus proceeds to **Elizabeth Bay House (10)** (✆ 9356 3022; **Open:** Tues-Sun 10am-4.30pm; **Cost:** $4/$2; **See:** Museums & Galleries: Historic Houses), a magnificent marine villa designed by John Verge and built between 1835 and 1838 for Alexander Macleay. Furnished in its original style, the villa is famous for its magnificent domed elliptical staircase. A lovely yet small park caps the hill in front of the property, a reminder of the property's original twenty-three hectares of grounds, and a suitably relaxing spot for a break. Elizabeth Bay has always been favoured by those building grand properties, and for a more modern example, tourers can stroll downhill into Billyard Avenue to reach the gates of **Boomerang:** privately owned, this 1926 Hollywood Villa (designed by Neville Hampson for Frank Albert) is one of the most fabled residences in Sydney.

Back up the hill at **Potts Point (11),** a glimpse of the suburb's residential past can be had by turning into Challis Street (off Macleay Street) and then turning left again into Victoria Street. Here are some lovely old terraces, many converted to backpacker hostels, and a large number of cafes. Worthy of particular note is The Piccolo, one of the first cafes in Sydney to serve espresso coffee back in the 1950s. The next stop at **Woolloomooloo Bay (12)** will reveal the beauty of the finger wharves, where many of the country's post-war immigrants stepped ashore for the first time. However, most recently, these grey wooden buildings have sparked a redevelopment controversy (**See:** Box: Finger Wharves).

At The **Australian Museum (13)** (**See:** Museums & Galleries), explorers can discover the natural history artefacts of Australia's unique environment. They can also cross the road into the southern block of Hyde Park and stroll through the gardens to the **ANZAC War Memorial** (**See:** Sights To See). Back on the bus and proceeding to **Central Railway (14)**, passengers will be treated to a close inspection of what was dubbed "the Paris end of Sydney" by a past Premier of New South Wales, Barry Unsworth. Strangely, property developers and restorers did not share his vision, and the area remains 'full of potential'. Most Sydneysiders pass through on their way to other areas of the city; however, this stop is the closest on the route to the Australian Opera Centre (**See:** Tours Around Sydney), where visitors can see scenery and costumes in production, and possibly gain access to rehearsals.

Back on the bus, **Chinatown (15)** (**See:** Sydney By Area; Walks Around Sydney: Chinatown, Darling Harbour and The Powerhouse Museum) offers the perfect opportunity to explore the focus of the city's large Chinese Community. The many noodle bars, supermarkets and traditional medical dispensaries make this a fascinating area to explore, and it may even be an idea to skip the next section of the bus route **(stops 16 to 18: the Powerhouse Museum, National Maritime Museum and Darling Harbour shopping centre)** and its attractions for another day (**See:** Walks Around Sydney: Chinatown, Darling Harbour and The Powerhouse Museum). Instead, walk to the City end of Dixon Street and turn left to reach the Entertainment Centre, opposite which is the exquisite **Chinese Garden (19)** (**See:** Open Air Sydney: Parks & Gardens), a fitting place to take a post-Chinatown break. You could even have tea and Chinese cakes in the tea house. From here, it is only a short stroll (or rejoining the bus, a short roll) to **The Sydney Aquarium (20)** (✆ 9262 2300; **Open:** 7 days 9.30am-9pm; **Cost:** $12/$6/under 8 years free), where visitors are able to glide amongst the sharks and fish from the safety of a perspex tunnel. Inside are also a number of 'feel tanks' and displays of Australian marine life.

The next leg of the route gives explorers a chance to mix it with the locals by navigating the eight lanes of Harbour Bridge traffic while speeding across to **Milsons Point (21)** (**See:** Sydney by Area), being sure to look directly up at the criss-crossing iron bars as you pass under the arch. This stop is right on the water and affords a stunning view across the Harbour to the City. It also is the perfect place to take a walking detour around nearby Kirribilli (**See:** Walks Around Sydney: City to Kirribilli), where charming terraces, cafes and fish and chips await. If it is summer, tourers requiring refreshment could even walk to **Olympic Pool** for a swim.

Back in the City, **Wynyard Park (22)** is not really worth stopping at, so continue to the **Queen Victoria Building (23)** (**See:** Shopping; Sights To See). This is a spectacular shopping complex in the heart of the City, housed in a renovated and refurbished Victorian Romanesque market building. With multiple levels of top quality retailers, it is a breathtaking picture of colour and movement. From here, the bus heads down George Street, stopping at **Wynyard Station (24)** (for Martin Place, the General Post Office building and the collection of historic bank headquarters), and continues to **The Rocks (25)**, the birthplace of Sydney's European settlement (**See:** Sydney By Area). However, it is strongly recommended that you stay on the bus until stop **The Rocks Visitors Centre (26)**, to pick up a copy of one of the Sydney Cove Authority's self-guided walking routes, or to sign up for a guided walking tour. The area is too fascinating and important to whizz through in a half-hearted manner, so it may even be a good idea to leave it for another day, and simply have a quick look around now. You could always stroll back to the Museum of Contemporary Art (**See:** Museums & Galleries), before collapsing into a big, deep armchair at the end of this most strenuous day's touring.

The Bondi & Eastern Bay Explorer

Description: This thirty-five kilometre route exploring the Eastern Suburbs and beaches (Route 222) is the one occasion where it is emphatically suggested that tourers abandon the idea of walking and submit to the flow of the tour bus. The best day to undertake the tour is Saturday, as there is more action on the beaches and in the beer gardens, and the Paddington Bazaar is in operation. As the ticket also entitles passengers to free State Transit bus travel back to, the City up to midnight, lingering in the Eastern Suburbs restaurant belt is a possibility (**See:** Food).

Note: Vaucluse House is closed on Monday. The route may differ slightly in summer (November-March) due to heavy traffic.

Operation: 7 days from 9am to 6pm, every 30 minutes. The last circuit departs from Circular Quay at 4.15pm. It is best to start early, to allow more time to explore each stop.

Starting Point: Anywhere on the route.

Information: Sydney Buses (✆ 13 15 00).

As the bus drives from **Circular Quay (stop 1)** (**See:** Sydney Explorer, above), through Woolloomooloo and on to **Kings Cross (2)** (Macleay Street), it might be a good idea to do some quick research into the area through which the tour will proceed (**See:** Sydney By Area: Eastern Suburbs). If you haven't done the Kings Cross walk, now might be a good time to do so. Otherwise, stroll around the Cross' main street, Victoria Road, to **Bayswater Road (3)**. Nearby stands one of the city's favourite restaurants, The Bayswater Brasserie (**See:** Food). These three stops coincide with the Sydney Explorer route (above).

After leaving Kings Cross, continue to the Cruising Yacht Club on **Rushcutters Bay (4)**. Originally a swamp, the bay gained its name as many rush cutters would gather reeds here to use in the construction of many of Paddington's early residences. Today, the park fronting the walled bay is a popular spot with joggers and informal footballers, and with the less active enjoying the small kiosk here. It is this marina which is the centre of preparations for the annual Sydney to Hobart Yacht Race (26 December).

As the route differs slightly from winter to summer, it is best to ask the driver if he or she will be stopping at **Darling Point** (**See:** Sydney By Area). If so, stay on the bus until then. However, if it will not be stopping there, the more energetic among The Good Life Guide's tourers are advised to walk towards the point from the Yacht Club and head up hill along Yarranabbe Road (still heading towards the point) and thereafter turn right into Thornton Street to reach Darling Point Road (one kilometre). From here, it is only a short distance to the left to **McKell Park** (**See:** Open Air Sydney: Parks & Gardens). The park occupies the Harbour frontage with wooden benches, luscious trees and verdant lawns. Despite being one of the most popular spots for observing the annual New Year's Eve fireworks, this is a charming and popular, yet quiet, park the rest of the year. Above its stands the National Trust's Gothic style **Lindesay**, historic home of pastoralist William Bradley.

Strolling back along the road away from the Harbour, tourers will be treated to a close inspection of one of Sydney's most remarkable streets. The point has always been favoured by wealthy and prominent citizens, whose houses contribute to the elegance of the area. More recently, the Australian poet Dorothea Mackellar, of "A Sunburnt Country" fame, lived at No. 155 until her death in 1968, while the Anglican Archbishop of Sydney's residence, **Bishopscourt**, is also here (on the right). On the corner of Greenaoks Avenue stands the lovely sandstone church **St Mark's**, which cinema buffs may recognise as the church in which the wedding scene of *Muriel's Wedding* was filmed.

From here, it is a short stroll downhill into **Double Bay (5)** (**See:** Sydney By Area) to rejoin the bus route, so walk down Greenoaks Avenue on the left hand footpath and take the steps to reach Ocean Avenue. Crossing Ocean Avenue into South Avenue will lead directly to the centre of this chic shopping precinct, Bay Street. Strolling through Bay Street, Knox Street, Cross Street and Transvaal Avenue, tourers will glimpse the gleaming scene which is constantly dogged by stereotypes: 'pretentious' and 'navel-gazing' are two which come to mind. However, it is the Sydney home of one of Sydney's most famous daughters, Elle MacPherson, and offers a number of boutiques to investigate. Cafes abound: try Twenty One or Dee Bees in Knox Street to experience the milieu. The Explorer bus stop is in New South Head Road, so rejoin it here.

Next, the bus drives around the Harbour to **Rose Bay Wharf (6)**, and unless you want to emulate the annual City to Surf (**See:** Sydney Icons) joggers, walkers and stragglers who struggle up 'Heartbreak Hill', it is worthwhile staying on until the next stop at the top of the hill, **Rose Bay Convent (7)**, where the view back to the City is breathtaking. Next stop is **Vaucluse Bay (8)** (Wentworth Road), which is definitely worth a lengthy visit at any time, but even more so on a warm and sunny day. Wentworth Road is the site of historic **Vaucluse House** (**Open:** Tues-Sun 10am-4.30pm; **Cost:** $4/$2; **See:** Museums & Galleries: Historic Houses). Built in 1803, and occupied by explorer William Wentworth from 1827-1853, it is an imposing example of the elegant style of nineteenth century Australian architecture. Over the road is **Nielsen Park** and its Shark Beach (**See:** Open Sir Sydney: Beaches, Picnics), home of the popular Italian Nielsen Park Kiosk (**See:** Food). Those feeling like a pleasant stroll should follow Wentworth Road in the same direction as that of the bus and turn right into Fitzwilliam Road. Off to the left, a narrow, walled footpath leads to **Parsley Bay**, a popular summer swimming spot where a very sturdy suspension bridge hangs over the deep-sided bay. To rejoin the bus, return to Vaucluse House by continuing in the same direction (it is a circuit) along Fitzwilliam Road, Boambillee Avenue and Olola Avenue.

Back on the bus, the next stop is **Watsons Bay (9)** (**See:** Sydney By Area). Home to several considerable attractions, this is also worth a lengthy stop. First up should be **The Gap** (**See:** Sydney Icons), which is really only a small indent on the cliff-lined coast. The route map will show Watsons Bay near the end of a peninsula tipped by South Head. Passage through The Heads is the only way into the Harbour from the Tasman Sea, and in the days before radar and computer navigation, these rocky cliffs represented a serious hazard. None more so than to *The Dunbar*, which, mistaking The Gap for the Heads, was wrecked here in 1857, leaving one single survivor out of more than one hundred. From the bus stop, take the footpath leading up to the top of the cliffs to explore the headland. The view across to North Head and Manly and back over the Eastern Suburbs to the City is magnificent. Watsons Bay is also the home of **Doyles** famous seafood restaurant (and their excellent fish & chips shop on the jetty), the best **beer garden** in the city (located between the two; **See:** Pubs) and a little beach lined with colourful rowing boats. For those with the time and the inclination, a short walk leads to **Camp Cove and Lady Bay Beach**, the latter brazenly nudist (**See:** Open Air Sydney: Beaches). To get there, turn right and immediately left into Cove Street at the end of Watsons Bay beach away from the jetty, then right into Victoria Street, then left into Cliff Street, and onto the beach. Lady Bay Beach is further along the cliff walkway to the north of the cove. The next stop on the tour is at the top of **The Gap Park (10)**, which offers confirmation of the spectacular view, and an inspection of the anchor of The Dunbar.

The bus now follows Old South Head Road through Dover Heights to **North Bondi Beach (11)**. Bondi is Sydney's most famous beach with a rich culture and many cafes, pubs, restaurants, bikini shops (**See:** Sydney by Area). Whatever you do, follow Campbell Parade up towards the main centre, not neglecting Hall Street on the right, and then up the hill. Most probably, you'll either want to spend a more than a few hours here, or come back another time and devote to it the attention it deserves. Now you can join the bus again and head for **Bronte Beach (12)**, home of one of Sydney's favourite surf pools and a few good cafes, such as The Bogey Hole and Bronte Cafe opposite the bus stop. Next is **Clovelly Beach (13)** (**See:** Sports: Diving) and thereafter **Coogee Beach (14)** (**See:** Open Air Sydney: Beaches), another two of Sydney's favourites. Coogee is a smaller and more intimate version of Bondi; however, around the southern tip of the beach lies **Wiley's Baths**, an exceptional example of the city's surf pools.

Heading back towards the City, the explorer ascends the coastal hills and enters Randwick, home of the **Royal Randwick Racecourse (15)** (**See:** Sports), where Saturdays in Autumn and Spring are a sight to see. On the other side of Alison Road is **Centennial Park** (**See:** Walks Around Sydney: Centennial Park), which is definitely worth investigating, although note that it is also accessible from Oxford Street (stop 17). Centennial Park is perhaps Sydney's grandest park, and a circuit around Grand Drive is a favourite with the locals fond of cycling, in-line skating, jogging and dog walking.

Next is the famous **Sydney Cricket Ground (16)** (**See:** Sydney Icons). Sports fiends may like to take a Sportspace Tour (**See:** below) and investigate the museum which concentrates on the Australian traditions of cricket, Aussie Rules, Rugby League and Rugby Union. Oxford Street in **Paddington (17)** is also worth a lengthy visit (**See:** Sydney By Area; Walks Around Sydney). If a tight schedule means it is unlikely that there will be time to come back another day, be sure to stroll by at least some of the shops here, which are occupied by the cutting-edge of Sydney's clothing designers, and venture down Elizabeth Street to the Chocolate Factory Cafe (**See:** Cafes) and beyond to Paddington Street, one of the suburb's most delightful residential streets lined with terraces. The next stop at Lower **Oxford Street (18)** offers the perfect opportunity to explore the area around and in Hyde Park (**See:** Sights To See). Amongst the green stand the ANZAC War Memorial and the statue of Captain Cook, while over College Street stands the Australian Museum (**See:** Museums & Galleries). A stroll down the length of the park to the Archibald Fountain and St Mary's Cathedral will bypass stop **Hyde Park North (19)**, while rejoining the Explorer to its final stop at Martin Place will leave you in the centre of the City. Phew!

Long Reef Head

Where: Approximately 15km north east of the City on the coast.
Getting There: By Car from the City, cross the Harbour Bridge and head for Manly. After crossing The Spit and reaching the large intersection of Sydney Rd, continue straight ahead (direction Brookvale). This becomes Pittwater Rd and continues to Long Reef. Turn right at Long Reef Golf Course into Anzac Ave. A small road leads up to the head. Bus 190 passes Long Reef on its way to Palm Beach from Wynyard.
See: Sports: Golf, Hang Gliding, Surfing.
Cliched as it may sound, there is something for (almost) everyone at Long Reef Point. Leaving the car park, a sheltered path enclosed by native plants leads to the exposed head. Off to the left, **model plane** fliers fine tune elaborate manoeuvres, and to the right, the frustrated **golfers** negotiate the golf links (a true links and a Grade 1 public course). Up ahead, on any windy day, **hang gliders** prepare to launch themselves into the air, and after leaping off the cliff, hover above and wave nonchalantly. **Surfers** walk past carrying their boards down to the sea, while children sit watching. Down below lies an enormous, flat and safe rock platform on which myriad life forms, numerous rock pools and their ecosystems exist. This is the **Long Reef Aquatic Reserve**, and it is a favourite with parents opening their children's eyes to natural science and beauty, and is easily accessible from Fisherman's Beach or the path at the end of the head. Further around the base of the point sits the slim, deep golden sand of a deserted (because windy) **beach**, marked with footprints, while on the other side, surfers jostle to catch a wave. Beyond this expansive blue view lies **North Head**, and hugging the coastline in between is a stretch of beaches: Dee Why and Curl Curl and Manly. From here you can follow the gentle Bicentennial **Cliff Walk** along the side of the golf course and down to Dee Why beach, discovering sheltered places to picnic or admire the view. All this within one square kilometre, and for free!

The Northern Beaches & Pittwater

Description: Those who do not know Palm Beach under this name may know it as Summer Bay, setting of the television series, Home And Away. However, Palm Beach and the surrounding area offer some of the most spectacular and pristine coastal and waterway scenery in Sydney, while nearby West Head National Park contains some of the region's best Aboriginal rock art.
Getting There: Palm Beach is around forty-five minutes north of the City. Allow a day to have time to

explore at a leisurely pace. By car from the City, head north via Military Rd (Mosman), to cross the Spit (Spit Rd), join up to Condamine St and Pittwater Rd (Route 14). This route runs up the eastern coast past Collaroy, Narrabeen and Mona Vale beaches. It is here at Mona Vale Beach that the following tour notes begin.

Transport Alternatives: The northern peninsula is easily accessible by bus. From Wynyard in the City, bus 190 will take you all the way to Palm Beach in about an hour. The bus route will give you access to many, but not all, of the area's best spots. Otherwise, you can join a tour with the Boomerang Beach Bus (**See:** below).

Note: Several walks in West head National Park are detailed in the chapter Bushwalks. If planning to do such a walk, it would be better to go to West Head first and then to Palm Beach.

The Northern Beaches peninsula is the north-east extreme of residential Sydney. Graced by the sparkling, protected waterways of Pittwater on the west and the Prussian blue splendour of the Tasman Sea on the east, it is easy to see the attraction which draws people up to the area. Clean, clear air, sea breezes, golden afternoon sunlight, and the voluptuous curves of densely wooded hills reaching into the water bring together an eclectic mixture of residents from extremely wealthy mansion owners to surfies (many of whom may also be extremely wealthy).

Driving up **Barrenjoey Road** from Mona Vale, glimpses of Pittwater on the left begin to appear. The sight of distant yachts and motor boats bobbing on the shimmering water is merely an indication of the splendour to come. After passing **Newport Beach** on the right, the road begins to wind up and around to Bilgola, giving distracting views back across to Bungan Head at the southern end of Newport. Immediately after rounding the sharp corner you will see a right hand turn-off down to **Bilgola Beach**, which you should take. This road (The Serpentine) cuts down through the bush to the thick palms of the bay and the charming, narrow beach itself. Leading up the other side of the inlet, The Serpentine leads to Bilgola Head where the **AJ Small Lookout** affords spectacular views of the very long stretch of beach-studded coastline. A brass plaque indicates what's what.

Meeting Barrenjoey Road again, turn right to drive past Avalon golf course on the left and Avalon beach on the right. Continuing further, you will next come to a section of road which literally skirts the side of **Careel Bay** on the left, where many of the area's little boats are stranded in muddy sand at low tide. The road then winds through several pockets of lush palms to pass many extremely covetable **houses** with magnificent views. This is the beginning of the suburb of **Palm Beach**, and it is a good idea to stop at the park on Sandy Beach on the left (preceded by a car park) opposite Barrenjoey House and the Palm Beach Fish Shop (**See:** below). Here is the jetty at which point **ferries** to The Basin and Mackerel Beach can be taken ($6/$3 tickets available on board; departures Mon-Fri every hour on the hour except 1pm; last trip at 4pm; Sat-Sun: hourly on the hour until 5pm Sat and 6pm Sun & Public Holidays/8pm in summer; Information ✆ 9918 2743 or 9974 5235). This lovely trip offers a close up view of **Pittwater** and **Ku-Ring-Gai National Park** on the opposite shore. The Basin is one of the city's best loved camping sites and stopping points for boat owners out for the day on the waterways: the smell of barbecuing steak, sausages and onions is quite dominant most weekends in summer! Alternatively, **Palm Beach Ferry Service** ferries depart from the jetty at 9am, 11am and 3.45pm on weekends for the thirty minute trip to Patonga (near Brooklyn on the Hawkesbury River). Day cruises to Bobbin Head (four and a half hours with a one hour stopover; **Cost:** $16/$12/$8; ✆ 9918 2747) also leave from here.

Back at Palm Beach, landlubbers may like to obtain some of the best fish and chips in the region from the aptly named **Palm Beach Fish Shop** opposite the park. The very fresh produce here constantly and consistently draws in the crowds, yet the food seems to taste even better when eaten gazing across the water from under the enormous pines which line the beach. Alternatively, **Cafe Ancora** (**Open:** Lunch: Tue-Sun from 11am; Dinner: Fri-Sat 7pm-11pm; Breakfast: Sat-Sun from 7am) offers dishes such as barbequed octopus with caramelised pumpkin or grilled polenta with mushrooms and basil ragout, as well as great desserts and coffee, served inside or in the leafy courtyard.

Rounding the end of the peninsula into Ocean Road, behold the glorious sight of the tour's destination: the long, narrow isthmus headed by the Barrenjoey Lighthouse, flanked on the right by clean **Palm Beach** with its gritty, orange sand (characteristic of the Northern Beaches), beachfront mansions, its surf pool and its huge rock platform. A walk along the impossibly long stretch of pristine coast is essential.

However, there is another side to Palm Beach with its own character, so after strolling around this side, return to where the road rounded the peninsula and turn right into Governor Phillip Park, passing the **Palm Beach Golf Course**, established by a group of campers nearly thirty years ago, to reach the sea plane depot. The more energetic among the Good Life Guide's users may like to stroll down the beach and cross the sand dunes to reach the same spot. **Barrenjoey Beach**, a favoured windsurfing area, lines Pittwater on the left, while at the jetty, you will find a charming **cafe** serving plunger pots of coffee on the water. You can also hire boats here from Barrenjoey **Boat Hire** (✆ 9974 4229). **Sea planes** depart for Rose Bay on the Harbour from this point, and also leave for scenic flights (South Pacific Sea Planes; ✆ 9544 0077).

This is also the starting point for an extremely rewarding twenty minute walk up to **Barrenjoey**

Lighthouse. Apart from some short, steep and uneven tracts of carefully arranged broken sandstone, it is generally an easy walk accessible to all ages and fitness levels, requiring about an hour for the return trip with time to sit and admire the views. The walking track begins at the rust coloured boat shed half way along Barrenjoey Beach and leads up through the National Park bushland, affording magnificent views back along the peninsula. Once at the top, unimpeded views across Broken Bay towards the beaches of the Central Coast (Killcare, Tallow Beach and Box Head), out to sea and across to Lion Island are the reward, while extremely accommodating flat rocks provide perfect vantage points for a picnic or bask. The buildings of the lighthouse complex themselves are interesting to explore, although access is restricted due to residents' privacy! Returning to sea level, it is an idea to explore the network of walking tracks cutting through the sand dunes (favoured Summer Bay filming spot) before leaving the area.

The next part of the journey requires a car, as bus 190 does not travel the small roads along the top of the peninsula. (If bus 193 to Avalon is running, you are in luck. Check the timetable at the bus terminus in Ocean Place.)Heading back towards the ocean side of Palm Beach once more, take the first right turn after rounding the corner (Palm Beach Road) to head up the hill. Continue around a very sharp and steep left corner and then fork first left into **Pacific Road**. This leads right along the top of the area and features some breathtakingly positioned houses. Continue until Pacific Road meets Norma Road, and turn left down to **Whale Beach Road**, at which point turn right. After passing the many cliff-top residences so favoured by celebrities, the road will rejoin Barrenjoey Road to return towards Sydney.

However, a worthwhile detour leads into the West Head National Park. At Mona Vale, turn right into **Park Street** at traffic lights (**direction Church Point**) and then turn right again at the roundabout into Pittwater Road. This leads directly around the bays and anchorages of Pittwater to **Church Point** where **The Waterfront Store and Top Room Cafe**, a charming little room looking out onto the water and to Scotland Island, awaits (1860 Pittwater Rd, Church Point; ✆ 9979 9670; **Open:** Mon-Fri 11am-4.30pm; Sat-Sun 8.30am-5.30pm).

Beyond Church Point, the road winds and curves through the eucalypts along **McCarrs Creek** to intersect with West Head Road. At this point, if you have time, turn right and drive to the entrance of **West Head National Park**, where the ranger on duty will be able to supply you with information regarding the park and its features. One particularly useful map details walking tracks and also marks the park's **Aboriginal rock carvings**. These are an absolute must to see in the park, and are quite extensive. Of particular note are the second group along West Head Road (Track 12 to The Basin; **See:** Bushwalks), which feature fish, turtles and human forms cut into large slabs of sandstone, not far from the road. West Head Road itself is the central axis from which almost all West Head walking routes begin (**See:** Bushwalks), and proceeds to **Commodore Heights** at the end, where there is a picnic area.

You will have to retrace the road to get out of the park turning right at the intersection with McCarrs Creek Road to lead onto Mona Vale Road. From here, the fastest way back to the City is to turn right onto Mona Vale Road and continue to the large intersection with **Forest Way**. Turn left and drive to the end, where it meets Warringah Road. Turn left and continue a short distance to the **Wakehurst Parkway**, at which point you should turn right. This major road cuts through bushland to emerge back near the Spit Bridge, from which point you should follow the signs to the City. Easy!

The Boomerang Beach Bus

Description: As a car-less alternative to the above touring route, the Boomerang Beach bus is unbeatable Operating on Thursday, Saturday & Sunday, the tour takes most of the day and costs $20/$15.

Starting Point: Four pick-ups are made in the City from 9.30am and take passengers to Manly, where they will have around forty-five minutes (**See:** Sydney By Area). The tour can also be joined at Manly Wharf at 11.15am. It returns to Manly at around 4.15pm.

Information & Bookings: (✆ 9913 8402).

With a spunky bus with roll up plastic sides for fine weather, commentary in four languages (German, Japanese, Cantonese and English) and extremely friendly and accommodating staff, this tour has a lot to offer. It progresses to North Head from Manly for spectacular views out over the Harbour, and then all the way up the coast to Palm Beach, allowing plenty of time to stop at lookouts and beaches. The good thing about this tour is that it goes to all the small places that Sydneysiders love, such as Bilgola and Church Point, and how much time is spent at several of the stops depends entirely on what the passengers want to do. At Palm Beach in particular, there will be a break of at least an hour and a half in which to hunt around for Home & Away cast and crew, or perhaps to walk up to Barrenjoey Lighthouse (**See:** Northern Beaches & Pittwater, above). For those who do not mind abandoning their independence for a day, the tour gives easy and inexpensive access to one of the most naturally beautiful areas of Sydney.

The Islands Of Sydney Harbour

Everyone can see them, but how do you get to them? Most are only accessible to the public as part of an organised National Parks and Wildlife Tour.

Fort Denison is the sandstone island fortification in the middle of the Harbour directly in front of the Opera House. Originally named Pinchgut, the tiny island inspired punishers with ideas of dastardly ways to punish convicts from the beginning of the settlement. In 1788, a convict was confined on the rocky outcrop for a week for stealing a biscuit. 1796 saw executed murderer, Francis Morgan, displayed on a gibbet flapping in the breeze on the island's highest point, creating what must have been a promising sight for new arrivals to the colony. Roll up, roll up! Welcome to Sydney Cove! Completed in 1857 and renamed after the Governor of the time, the fort was used to store gun powder and shot, and was intended to increase security following the Crimean war. One of the cannons installed at that time is fired daily at 1pm. Access to the island is only available with the tours run by the National Parks & Wildlife Service, which depart every day of the week from Pier 6 Circular Quay at 10am, 12noon & 2pm (**Information:** ✆ 9206 1166 Mon-Fri; ✆ 9206 1167 Sat-Sun; **Cost:** $8/$6).

Garden Island's name is a bit of an enigma: it has not been a garden for one hundred and eighty years, and it has not been an island for half a century. The island was given to the crew of the First Fleet ship Sirius, who crew planted the first crops in New South Wales just sixteen days after arriving, and harvested them in July 1788. When the Royal Navy became involved in the Crimean War, Opium War in China and the Indian Mutiny in the 1850s, it was decided that the colony would be a useful strategic base for the British Empire. Lacking a permanent naval installation, the colony's government handed over Garden Island to the Royal Navy for such a purpose in 1857, and a fleet of five warships was established to protect the region (1859). Despite the new official function of the island, the navy of the day had difficulty in stopping picnickers from descending; today, with boom gates, high fences, security cameras and water patrols, the problem does not arise.

Goat Island was called Mel-Mel by the Aborigines, but the pioneer British settlers, not surprisingly ignoring such heritage, called it Goat Island. Although the reason for bestowing the name is not decisively recorded, it seems likely that it referred to the fact that three goats, which had been brought with the First Fleet from Capetown in 1788, were put here to forage. In the early 1830s, the island was quarried by reconvicted convicts in leg irons, who at the time were living in squalor on *The Phoenix* while awaiting transportation to the ultra-penitentiary of Norfolk Island. They were later (1833-8) housed in huts on the island while building a naval installation, many of the buildings of which remain today in perfect condition. The island was used as a bacteriological safe haven and headquarters for the campaign against the Bubonic Plague (around 1900), and later was used by the Harbour authorities. **Access** to Goat Island is only available as part of a National Parks tour every Saturday and Sunday at 10.25am and 1.25pm, departing from the Harbour Master's Steps, Circular Quay, and at 10.45am and 1.45pm from the Harbourside Wharf, Darling Harbour. (**Information & Bookings:** Mon-Fri 8.30am-4pm ✆ 9555 9844.)

The following three islands are more independently accessible. Offshore to the north of Darling Point lies **Clarke Island** with its rock gardens, rock pools and native plants and trees. It was originally farmed by Lt. Ralph Clarke, who was constantly frustrated by thieves taking his produce. It is not hard to imagine why the local Aborigines could have believed the produce of the island, which they called Billongoola, was theirs. It is a top spot for a desert island picnic or for playing Treasure Island for a day. Facilities include natural bushland, a small grassy area, picnic tables, water and toilets. **Shark Island** lies between Rose Bay and Woollahra Point. Rocky soil supports a mixture of native trees and shrubs, and has in its time supported a number of hermits, including in the 1920s author, Con Drew. These days it sees action as a spectating spot for watching the racing yachts which use Shark Island as a rounding marker, and as a popular picnic ground. Facilities on the island include a picnic pavilion, tables, a grassy area, sandy beach, water and toilets. **Rodd Island** is right up near Birkenhead Point, and has picnic shelters, grassy areas, water and toilets.

Public Access to Shark, Clarke and Rodd Islands is available every day of the week, although it is not particularly easy or inexpensive. Bookings must be made with the National Parks and Wildlife Service (✆ 9555 9844) and a fee of $3 per person paid immediately by cheque, money order or credit card to: National Parks & Wildlife Service, Inside Box 500, Pyrmont, NSW 2009.

After paying, you must get yourself to these three islands, and it can be expensive. The best pick up point for Clarke Island is McKell Park, Darling Point; for Shark Island, Rose Bay; and for Rodd Island, Birkenhead Point. The prices below are per person from these points, and are for individuals and small groups; it is much cheaper for larger groups.

Banks Marine (✆ 9555 1222), who can also arrange hire equipment and hampers, will let you join non-exclusive groups who have chartered a service on weekends: to Clarke or Shark Island from $8 per person return;

Harbour Taxis (✆ 9555 1155) will charge to: Clarke Island around $5 per person; Shark Island $15 per person for the first person ✆ $5 per person thereafter; Rodd Island from Birkenhead Point $15 per person & $5 per person thereafter (one way);

Taxis Afloat (✆ 9955 3222) will charge around $30 per person;

Water Taxis (✆ 9810 5010) charge around $15 for the boat and then $5 per person (one way) to Clarke or Shark Islands.

Otherwise, you can hire a boat, but don't leave it in the water anywhere near the jetty (**See:** Open Air Sydney).

Further information can be obtained from the

National Parks & Wildlife Service, Sydney district office for Harbour Islands (✆ 9555 9901).

Sydney 2000 Olympic Site Tours

Where: Olympic Park, Homebush Bay (✆ 9752 3666)
When: Mon-Fri 10am, 12noon & 2pm; Sat-Sun by request and numbers permitting.
Cost: $6/$4/$16 family; booking required (✆ 9752 3666).
Transport: Train to Strathfield, Lidcombe or Homebush Station, then bus 401-403 & 404 to the Aquatic Centre. A new, direct train line is under construction.
Pool Open: Mon-Fri 5am-9.45pm; Sat-Sun & public holidays 7am-7pm.
Pool Cost: $3.50/$2.50/$9.50 family.
Sydney's newest, biggest, most expensive and most glamorous swimming pool was described by Juan Antonio Samaranch, President of the International Olympic Committee, as 'the best swimming pool in the world'. Highly informative tours are led around this magnificent and popular leisure facility, where the diving and racing pools which will be used for the 2000 Olympics can be viewed (and used). However, the centre contains much more: a training pool with a completely movable floor (so the depth can be altered from 2.5m to nothing at all); a leisure pool comprising a shallow paddling pool, mosaics, waterfalls, fountains and palm trees; a cafe; a fitness centre; child minding (and banana lounges for non-swimmers), so a great idea is to buy a combined tour and swim ticket (Cost: $7/$5/$29 family).

The **Olympic Showcase and Information Centre** (✆ 9267 0099) is a good place to find bulk information about Sydney 2000. Located in the *South Steyne* ferry (one of Sydney's historic Manly ferries) on the City side of Darling Harbour, visitors can see displays of Australians in past Olympics and the city's plans for 2000. Video presentations, touch screen computers and models mean that the showcase represents a comfortable 'information learned to effort spent' ratio. A large range of official souvenirs is also available from the centre.

Sydney 2000 Olympic Games Fact File

- Opening Ceremony: Friday 15 September.
- Closing Ceremony: Saturday 1 October.
- Athletes: 10,000 from about 200 nations.
- Team Officials: 5,000 from about 200 nations.
- Media: 15,000 visiting and local media.
- Tickets: 5.5 million tickets available for sale from 1999.

Events: Apart from the events which will take place in the stadium and facilities of the main Olympic site at Homebush Bay, the 42.2km marathon will be run across the Harbour Bridge, past the Opera House, around Centennial Park and Darling Harbour and then on to Homebush Bay; the Triathlon will start with a 1500m swim across the Harbour.

Sydney 2000 Paralympics

- Opening Ceremony: Saturday 21 October.
- Closing Ceremony: Wednesday 1 November.
- Athletes: 5,000.
- Team Officials: 1000.
- Media: up to 1000 visiting and local media.

The Olympic Site

- Where: Homebush Bay, 14km west of the City in the demographic heart of Sydney.
- How to Get There by Public Transport: Train to Strathfield station, then bus. A new train line leading directly to the site is under construction.
- What's There already: Athletic and aquatic facilities.
- Information Centre: In the old South Steyne ferry moored on the City side of Darling Harbour (Cockle Bay).
- Further Information: The Sydney Organising Committee for the Olympic Games (SOCOG) (✆ 9931 2000).

Gothic Sydney: The University of Sydney

Where: Parramatta Rd, Camperdown (Booking essential: ✆ 9351 4002)
When: Tours can be run for up to fifteen people as requested.
Cost: $10.
For a real, live Gothic experience, a tour of the University of Sydney's dark stone passages, grand staircases, enormous stained glass windows, secret passages, spiral staircases, four tonne bells and parts of sunken ships, is hard to beat. The guided tours generally lead through the older, sandstone buildings of the elegant Quadrangle, which were modelled on Oxford and Cambridge and begun in the 1850s, where the character of students and times past is easily discerned, particularly in the Great Hall and Maclaurin Hall, and as you pass the tennis ball which has been lodged between two sandstone details since the 1890s. From there, you will head up the spiral steps of the clock tower to the roof via the Clavier Room (from which point the mother of all glockenspiels, the War Memorial Carillon, is activated) for a fantastic view, not only of the university and wider Sydney, but of the fascinating decorative elements which adorn the structure. Here sits the world's only kangaroo gargoyle, as well as a crocodile and several equally attractive grotesques. Tour members can also visit the university's two main **museums:** the Nicholson Museum of Antiquities and the Macleay Museum of Natural Sciences, both beautifully housed and displayed (although they are closed during university holidays). At the latter, you can inspect lice from Captain Cook's ship and an enormous collection of insects bequeathed to the University by Alexander Macleay.

The tours can easily be adapted to accommodate participants' special interests by arranging access to various faculties and their museums around campus. The tour guides on duty are full of anecdotal information and have a wonderful sense of humour and campus history, making this a fantastic way to spend an afternoon: visitors will see many areas that the lowly students never get to see!

Scenic Flights

One way to take the photographs which will make 'the folks back home' wild with envy is to take a scenic flight over Sydney. **South Pacific Seaplanes (Information & Bookings:** ✆ 9544 0077; fax 9523 6919) take off with a roar from the calm water of Rose Bay for a range of scenic flights over the Harbour ($45 per person); the Harbour and Northern Beaches ($70 per person); the Harbour, Northern Beaches and Blue Mountains ($195p.p.); or scenic flights from Palm Beach around the Northern Beaches ($35 per person). Prices are all based on two adults taking the flight (children under 12 years fly for half price when accompanying two adults). They can also fly you to waterfront restaurants on the Hawkesbury and Pittwater, take you on aerial photography flights with the door off ($350 per hour; minimum $200), secluded beach flights, fishing excursions and romantic getaways. Note that Youth Hostels Association members travelling to the Pittwater Hostel can fly from the Harbour up to Pittwater for around $29.

TOUR OPERATORS

Those weary of organising themselves may like to put themselves in the hands of one of the following experienced tour operators. The range, quality and subject of tours on is so great that would be impossible to catalogue all of them here, so the best idea is to go to the Quayside Booking Centre or New South Wales Travel Centre (above) and find something amongst the myriad possibilities to suit.

Walking Tours

Heritage Week

When: Annually in April.

Information: National Trust of Australia (Observatory Hill, City; ✆ 9258 0123)

Heritage Week is a great opportunity for tourists and residents alike to get out and discover the treasures hidden in the back streets of Sydney's suburbs. As well as organising specific events in and around the city's historic buildings and sites, the National Trust co-ordinates popular walking tours led by individual heritage societies around Sydney. One to look out for is the South Sydney Heritage Society, which can be contacted at PO Box 2011, Strawberry Hills, NSW, 2012.

Maureen Fry's Walking Tours

15 Arcadia Rd, Glebe (✆ 9660 7157; fax 9660 0805)

Small, personally led walking tours on offer include Macquarie Street, the historic suburbs of Glebe and Balmain, Circular Quay and The Rocks, specific tours such as the cafes of Darlinghurst and Old Parramatta, and a number of excursions out of Sydney.

The Rocks Walking Tours

The Rocks Visitors' Centre, George St, The Rocks (✆ 9247 6678)

Group walking tours through the major sights of Sydney's old town, complemented by a full commentary of historical and architectural information, are organised through the Rocks Visitors' Centre. An excellent self-guided walking route is also available from the centre for free.

The Quayside Booking Centre and the New South Wales Travel Centre (19 Castlereagh St, City; ✆ 13 20 77) are the best places to go for further information.

Harley Davidson Tours

Those who want to get out on the road with the grunt of a Harley Davidson are in luck: several companies operate in Sydney purely for this purpose. The following will all pick passengers up from anywhere in metropolitan Sydney, will take tours at any time requested (within reason), all have insurance, all accept credit cards, and all supply helmets and jackets. However, the specifics of the tours vary, as follows.

All Bike Hire

Bookings & Information: (✆ 9796 2165)

All Bike Hire will take passengers wherever they like. The cost is $75 for the first hour, and $25 for each half hour thereafter. A little commentary is given wherever possible, but it is not a main feature of the tours.

Blue Thunder Bike Tours

Bookings & Information: (✆ 9977 7721)

Blue Thunder operates a wide range of tours at any time requested on their fifteen Harley Davidsons, whether a short drive around Sydney's eastern beaches, a City Explorer tour around Sydney's centre, a drive up to the Northern Beaches, or a full day's touring to the Hunter Valley, Blue Mountains or the South Coast. Full commentary, jackets and helmets are provided, a side car is available, and free city pick ups are made. The cost ranges from $65 for a one hour tour, to $290 for an eight hour (full day) tour, including lunch. Blue Thunder is Sydney's longest running Harley tour operator.

Dream Legends Motor Cycle Tours

Bookings & Information: (✆ 9584 2451)

Dream Legends will also take passengers wherever they want to go, whether to the South Coast or Palm Beach. The Cost for half a day is $200, and for a full day (including full lunch) $300. They do have a side car available, and a jacket is provided. A little commentary is provided where possible, although communication is a little difficult through helmets, and it is not promoted as a major part of the tour.

Eastcoast Motorcycle Tours

Bookings & Information: (✆ 9247 5151 or 9521 4519)

Eastcoast have a range of tours, varying from city

beaches to the Northern Beaches and further afield. The cost is $115 for two hours, $195 for a four hour tour to the South Coast and Royal National Park, and $325 for a full day's touring including the South Coast, Hunter Valley or Blue Mountains. Full commentary is provided as the helmets provided are equipped with speakers. Booking ahead is recommended.

CHECKLIST: GUIDED TOURS OF ATTRACTIONS AROUND SYDNEY

Here is an eclectic check list of popular tours organised by specific attractions and organisations around the city.

The Art Gallery of NSW
Art Gallery Rd, City (✆ 9299 1194)
See: Museums & Galleries; Tours Around Sydney: Sydney Explorer; Walks Around Sydney: St Mary's to the Opera House.
Free guided tours of the gallery's permanent collection (Mon 1pm & 2pm; Tues-Fri 11am, 12noon, 1pm & 2pm; Sat-Sun 1pm, 2pm, & 3pm).

Australian Museum
6 College St, City (✆ 9339 8111)
See: Children; Museums & Galleries.
Free guided tours of the museum's holdings (7 days 10am-5pm).

The Royal Botanic Gardens
Mrs Macquarie's Rd, City (✆ 9231 8125)
See: Open Air Sydney: Parks & Gardens, Picnics; Sights To See; Walks Around Sydney: St Mary's to the Opera House.
Free guided walks departing from visitors' centre (Wed & Fri 10am; Sun 1pm). Entry to the Tropical Centre costs $5/$2/$12 family.

The Great Synagogue
166 Castlereagh St, City (✆ 9267 2477)
See: Walks Around Sydney: City Centre.
Free guided tours of the Synagogue and museum (Tues & Thurs 12noon, except on religious and public holidays).

Historic Forts of Sydney
NPWS Cadman's Cottage, 110 George St, The Rocks (✆ 9977 6229)
The National Parks and Wildlife Service conducts tours exploring underground tunnels, gunpowder magazines and secret installations at various times (**Cost:** $6/$4).

The Opera Centre (not the Opera House)
480 Elizabeth St, Surry Hills (Booking essential: ✆ 9699 1099)
See: Music: Classical & Opera.
The home of the Australian Opera opens its doors in Surry Hills to reveal its wardrobe, millinery, wigs, sets and possibly a working rehearsal (Groups Wed; Individuals: Tues & Thurs; **Cost:** $8/$6).

The Powerhouse Museum
500 Harris St, Ultimo (✆ 9217 0111)
See: Museums & Galleries; Walks Around Sydney: Chinatown, Darling Harbour & the Powerhouse.
Free (with admission) tours of the museum's eclectic collection (7 days at 1.30 pm).

Sportspace Tours
Level 1, Members Stand, Sydney Football Stadium, Moore Park (Booking essential: ✆ 9380 0383)
See: Sports; Sydney Icons: The SCG.
One and a half hour tours of the Sydney Cricket Ground & Sydney Football Stadium, including areas to which the public does not usually have access such as players dressing rooms and security areas (Mon-Sat 10am, 1pm & 3pm; **Cost:** $18/$12). Professional actors lead the tours and play the roles of various characters along the way.

St Mary's Cathedral
Cathedral St & College St, City (✆ 9220 0400)
See: Walks Around Sydney: St Mary's to the Opera House.
Free guided tours depart from inside the College Street entrance (Sunday 12noon).

Sydney Observatory
Observatory Hill, City (Booking essential: ✆ 9217 0485)
Evening programs (every night except Wed 6.15pm & 8.15pm; **Cost:** $5/$2/$12family) include a short talk and tour of the buildings, films or videos and a telescope viewing of the sky .
Opened in 1858, this was the settlement's third observatory, and was originally responsible for recording weather and tidal information as well as observing the little-known southern sky. Daytime entry (Mon-Fri 2pm-5pm; Sat-Sun 10am-5pm) is free.

Sydney Opera House
Bennelong Point, City (✆ 9250 7250)
See: Dance; Music: Classical & Opera; Sights To See; Sydney Icons; Theatre; Walks Around Sydney: St Mary's to the Opera House.
Tours of the theatres and foyers (7 days 9am-4pm; **Cost:** $8.50/$5.50), departing from the lower concourse. Special backstage tours (a must) are conducted on Sundays only (9am-4pm; **Cost:** $13).

Sydney Theatre Company Complex
Pier Four, Hickson Rd, Walsh Bay (Booking essential: ✆ 9250 1700)
See: Cafes & Food: The Wharf; Dance; Theatre.
One hour tours (Mon-Fri; **Cost:** $5). If you're not a complete theatre freak, taking a stroll in the complex past the numerous production posters, enjoying the view of the bridge, and having something to eat or a coffee at the Wharf Restaurant and cafe at the end overlooking the Harbour will probably be sufficient.

Victoria Barracks
Oxford St, Paddington (✆ 9339 3176)
See: Walks Around Sydney: Paddington.
Open day at the barracks and access to the Army Museum (Thurs 10am-12.30pm & first Sun each month 1pm-4pm).

CAFES

Life is too short to drink bad coffee, and in Sydney, there is really no reason to do so. The change in Australia's affections from tea to coffee since the 1950s is a clear indicator of the change over from an essentially British food culture to that which was introduced by the post war immigrants, particularly the Italians. Cafes instigated and represented a gradual acceptance of the informal, Mediterranean (albeit relocated) lifestyle, and came to form an important part of the city's social fabric. Statistics of Apparent Consumption of Foodstuffs and Nutrients for Australia (1992-93) reveal that consumption of coffee increased from a third of a kilogram per person per year in 1938-39 to two kilograms in 1992-93, while the consumption of tea over the same period dropped from three kilograms to one kilogram. Thankfully, the ideology is today firmly entrenched in Sydney's lifestyle.

Sydney's east is where most of the cafe action is found. Here are the three legendary cafe streets: Oxford Street, Paddington; Victoria Street, Darlinghurst; and Stanley Street, East Sydney. However, excellent cafes abound throughout the city, and together, they support a vigorous cafe society which permeates the city with ambience and personality. So serious is the competition to distinguish one cafe from the next, that great pains are taken to infuse each with as much character as possible. To some, this means commissioning high profile architects and interior designers to create a striking modern space people will talk about. Others emphasise their retro character and music, still others make themselves as homey as possible, even offering shelves laden with witty collections of books and magazines. A lucky number of establishments are blessed with an incomparable location, and must constantly strive to live up to the exacting public's expectations and demands. All this means that almost anyone can find their cafe niche.

The cafes listed here have been singled out for their character, friendliness, atmosphere, comfort, and most importantly, the quality of the coffee, while in some cases, the presence of excellent food is a happy bonus. In fact, Sydney cafes offer a great and popular way to economise on eating expenses while not compromising on taste: many offer a perfectly viable alternative to restaurants. Two final notes: the average price of a coffee in Sydney is $2, and most cafes do not accept credit cards.

SYDNEY'S COFFEES

As it was the Italians who rescued Australia from coffee hell, the serving styles of coffee available in Sydney are almost exclusively of Italian origin.

Babycino Milk froth without coffee but with chocolate for the little ones to play with.
Caffé Corretto Usually espresso with a dash of liqueur in it.
Caffé Latte A flat white served in a glass and thus instantly more cosmopolitan. Equal espresso base & milk.
Cappuccino The ubiquitous frothy wonder.
Espresso A really good short black will have a layer of mocha cream (from the coffee) on top.
Flat White Most of Sydney's flat whites have a dense yet thin covering of creamed milk froth.
Macchiato Espresso served & marked with a dash of foamed or cold milk.
Ristretto A concentrated espresso, without unnecessary water.

CENTRE

Armani Express

1st Floor, Emporio Armani, Martin Place (✆ 9231 3655)

Open: Mon-Fri 10am-6pm; Thurs to 8pm; Sat 10am-5.30pm; Closed Sun. **Access:** Several entry steps, stairs to cafe.

A great way to combine window shopping and coffee consumption is to head for Emporio Armani. Proceeding through the racks of elegant subtlety and up the stairs, customers and non-customers alike will reach Armani Express, a small bar serving strong coffee and offering a good view down onto the city's main square and across to the fascinating lines and sculptures of the General Post

The Pick Of Sydney's Cafes

Bar Italia 169-171 Norton St, Leichardt (✆ 9560 9981)
Open: Mon-Thurs 9am-Midnight; Fri-Sat 9am-1am; Sun 10am-Midnight.

Bathers' Pavilion Refreshment Room The Esplanade, Balmoral (✆ 9968 1133)
Open: 7 days, 7am-11pm.

Bill's 433 Liverpool St, Darlinghurst (✆ 9360 9631)
Open: Mon-Sat 7.30am-4pm; Closed Sun.

Cafe Niki
544 Bourke St, Surry Hills (✆ 9319 7517)
Open: 7 days 7am-10pm.

Caffe Italia International Terminal, Sydney Airport (✆ 9669 6434)
Open: Mon, Wed & Fri 7.30am-6pm; Tues, Thurs & Sat 7.30am-9pm.

Centennial Park Cafe Grand Drive, Centennial Park (✆ 9360 3355)
Open: 7 days 8.30am-4pm.

The Chocolate Factory 8 Elizabeth St, Paddington (✆ 9331 3785)
Open: Tues-Sat 8am-6pm; Sun10am-6pm; Closed Mon.

Coluzzi Bar 322 Victoria St, Darlinghurst (✆ 9380 5420)
Open: 7 days 5.30am-7.30pm.

Dov Cnr Forbes St & Burton St, Darlinghurst (✆ 9360 9594)
Open: Mon-Sat 7am-10pm.

Hernandez 60 Kings Cross Rd, Potts Point (✆ 331 2343)
Open: 7 days 24 hours.

The Wharf Pier 4, Hickson Rd, Walsh Bay (✆ 9250 1761)
Open: Mon-Sat 9am-late.

BREAKFAST & BRUNCH HOTSPOTS

Part of the 'gone troppo' lifestyle of Sydney is the long brunch. Here are the names of a few particularly good establishments at which to pass a lazy morning of merrymaking, although there are many more where these came from.

Bayswater Brasserie 32 Bayswater Rd, Kings Cross (✆ 9357 2177)
Open: Mon-Sat 12noon-11.15pm; Sun 10am-10.15pm

Bar Italia 169-171Norton St, Leichhardt (✆ 9560 9981)
Open: Mon-Thurs 9am-Midnight; Fri-Sat 9am-1am; Sun 10am-Midnight.

Bathers' Pavilion Refreshment Room The Esplanade, Balmoral (✆ 9968 1133)
Open: 7 days, 7am-11pm.

Bill's 433 Liverpool St, Darlinghurst (✆ 9360 9631)
Open: Mon-Sat 7.30am-4pm; Closed Sun.

Cafe Niki 544 Bourke St, Surry Hills (✆ 9319 7517)
Open: 7 days 7am-10pm.

Le Petit Creme 118 Darlinghurst Rd, Darlinghurst (✆ 9361 4738)
Open: Mon-Fri 7am-4pm; Sat 7am-5.30pm;
Sun 8am-5.30pm.

For full details, See: Cafes and Food.

Office. The tables beyond the window bench are full of animated chatter at lunch times during the week, when the popular Italian restaurant here swings into action.

Bar Cupola

Grand Walk, Queen Victoria Building, George St, City (✆ 9283 3878)
Open: 7 days 7am-6pm. **Access:** Level entry to building & cafe, lift from car park.
As name suggests, the tables of Bar Cupola sit under the stained glass dome of the Queen Victoria Building, bathed in filtered light and surrounded by colour. The bar's design has a suave Italian flavour about it, making this one of the best spots in the City to refuel on an excellent coffee or one of many other beverages, delicious Italian cakes and pastries, antipasto rolls or other savouries, and watch the world go by.

Illy Caffe

Level 3 Skygarden, Pitt St Mall, City (✆ 9223 3448)
Open: Mon-Sat 7.45am-5.30pm; Closed Sun. **Access:** Lift to level entry.
Perched on a polished wooden walkway overlooking the light-filled atrium of this glossy shopping complex is Illy Caffe, purveyor of good, strong full flavoured coffee, well known as some of the most expensive beans around. Also on offer are excellent cakes, biscuits, and pastries, as well as small lunches such as soups, pates and the very popular cheese on toast.

Museum of Sydney Cafe

Cnr Phillip St & Bridge St, City (✆ 9241 3636)
Open: Mon-Fri 7am-10pm; Sat-Sun 9am-6pm. **Access:** Level entry & toilets.
Located underneath the museum and in the adjacent First Government House Square is one of the city's most congenial cafes, popular for refreshments and snacks throughout the day as well as for lunch and dinner. Jazz trios often serenade the patrons basking in the sunlight beneath the imposing building constructed on the site of the colony's First Government House, as they ponder the historical significance of the spot upon which they sit.

The Old Sydney Coffee Shop

Ground Floor Strand Arcade, City (✆ 9231 3002)
Open: Mon-Fri 7.15am-5.15pm; Sat 8.30am-4.30pm; Sun 11am-3.30pm. **Access:** Level entry.
This is a charmingly quaint cafe offering views out on to the colourful Victorian Strand Arcade. Not only does it serve specialty teas and coffees, delicious iced chocolates and a selection of small sugary snacks, it is the oldest coffee shop in Australia, and was opened in this same building in

1891. The great tasting, but no nonsense, house special blend drips constantly through the filter, and the aroma fills the arcade.

Paradiso Cafe

7 Macquarie Place, City (✆ 9241 2141)

Open: Mon-Fri 7am-6pm; Sat 10am-4pm. **Access:** all tables pavement seating.

Also at: Level 7 MLC Centre, cnr King St & Castlereagh St, City (✆ 9221 0527)

Open: Mon-Fri 8am-8pm (summer); Mon-Fri 8am-5.30 (winter). **Access:** Lift to level entry.

Also at: Darling Park, cnr Sussex St & Market St, City (✆ 9264 1729)

Open: Mon-Fri 8am-6pm. **Access:** Level entry to ground floor cafe; lift to level entry upstairs.

The original Paradiso at Macquarie place started it all - a relaxing place to sit outside in the City, have a coffee or drink and gaze into the trees. Now, the concept has been extended to the Darling Park complex, where tasty lunches can be eaten under the frescoed dome (Lunch Bar), coffee and cake ensconced in a deep leather sofa (Lobby E Bar) or while enjoying the view and bistro atmosphere of the Terrace. In short, three good places to eat or have coffee at each end of the City. The MLC Paradiso offers a seat on the bustling city piazza.

The Wharf

Pier 4, Hickson Rd, Walsh Bay (✆ 9250 1761)

Open: Mon-Sat 9am-late. **Access:** Advise beforehand for assistance, accessible toilets.

Right at the end of the converted pier housing the Sydney Theatre Company sits the Wharf restaurant, literally hanging out over the water. Light floods in through the enormous windows, bringing with it a view of the Harbour, the Harbour Bridge and the neighbouring pier. The restaurant's bar area dispenses coffee and cafe fare all day to those lingering in this magnificent setting.

NORTH

Bathers' Pavilion Refreshment Room

The Esplanade, Balmoral (✆ 9968 1133)

Open: 7 days 7am-11pm. **Access:** 2 entry steps to small interior, pavement seating.

What better way to start the day: sitting in the refreshment room, patrons can watch the sun glisten on the water between Sydney Heads, stay there as the beach fills and the boats and windsurfers speed past on the water, remain as the sun dips behind Mosman casting a golden haze over the bay and the moon rises between the heads. The Refreshment Room is one of the best cafes in Sydney, as it has very friendly staff, great coffee, biscuits and cakes; and lunches, such as the popular Beachman's Lunch of fresh baguette and a bowl of goodies (tomato, ham, rocket, cheese) or daily specials, in abundance. A loyal following enjoys the old beach shed atmosphere created by the building itself, the paintings, distressed furniture and beach frontage, simply because the cafe can't be beaten on a hot and sunny or wild, stormy day.

Brazil

46 North Steyne, Manly (✆ 9977 3825)

Open: 7 days 8am-Midnight. **Access:** Level entry to ground floor, stairs to first floor.

Brazil provides an eclectic menu of inexpensive (usually under $10) dishes during the day, and more formally devised interpretations of the modern Australian credo at night. Offering panoramic views of the famous pines, ocean beach and sparkling Tasman Sea through wide, louvred windows, Brazil is a top spot to visit for a drink or snack before getting back to the hard work of relaxing on the beach.

Candy's Coffee House

29 Belgrave St, Manly (✆ 9977 0816)

Open: 7 days 9am-Midnight. **Access:** 1 entry step.

Candy's takes its coffee seriously: the standard grind is a special Vittoria blend, while regional, organic and flavoured blends, gourmet espresso and a hazelnut blend are also available (for fifty cents extra). The warmly decorated room is lined with bookshelves containing volumes ranging from dream interpretation to Chomsky's Manufacturing Consent to In the spirit of Crazy Horse, all for the use of the cafe's guests while slouched comfortably in their cushion-laden chairs. International and local newspapers and magazines provide further reading material, while poetry or dream interpretation nights regularly take place to nourish the soul. The food on offer could include shepherds pie, lentil burgers or soups, while big cooked breakfasts and challenging slices of cake nourish the body, all for under $10. With a friendly staff on hand, Candy's has everything except a view.

Fitzroy Cafe

1 Broughton St (cnr Fitzroy St), Kirribilli (✆ 9955 3349)

Open: 7 days 7am-9.30pm. **Access:** 5 entry steps, small interior.

This elevated, cosy, light and airy space has a highly welcoming feeling to it, enhanced by friendly staff and excellent food. Weekend breakfasts are a treat here, with superb scrambled eggs topped with smoked salmon on thick toast and Megaccinos among the fare. Lunch and dinner are also extremely popular. Sach's herbal infusions provide a welcome alternative to coffee, and as you read the paper or gaze out onto the robust criss-crossing of the Harbour Bridge, you can prepare for a stroll around this lovely suburb.

Headmaster's Cottage

175 Rosedale Rd (cnr Porter's Lane), St Ives (✆ 944 6561)

Open: Mon-Sat 10am-5pm; Closed Sun.

The Headmaster's Cottage is a gallery and cafe

housed in a historic building which originally served as the headmaster's cottage of St Ives school, when the area was a rural orchard precinct. As well as very solid and very tasty home made cakes, Illy coffee and a selection of tea blends are on hand. Lunches here are popular with locals looking for gourmet pastas, frittatas, soups and salads.

SOUTH

Caffe Italia

International Terminal, Sydney Airport (✆ 9669 6434)

Open: Mon, Wed & Fri 7.30am-6pm; Tues, Thurs & Sat 7.30am-9pm. **Access:** Level entry to lift in terminal to level cafe entry.

For airport freaks (hello!), it can't get better than this shrine, located beyond the 'C' area of departures. With discreet whiffs of jet fuel on the approach, travellers and baggage, an atmosphere of blatant envy, excitement and internationalism, this is an excellent cafe. Caffe Italia, designed in the same mould as Bar Cupola (above), is a top spot to enjoy Grinders coffee, biscuits, cakes and pastries, savoury panini, pasta and foccaccia. Italian songs and opera often drift out the doors to the tables, where the clientele gazes wistfully through the full length windows to the aeroplane at Gate 52 and the runway beyond.

Honeymoon Patisserie

96 New Canterbury Rd, Petersham (✆ 9564 2389)

Open: Mon-Fri 8am-7pm; Sat-Sun 8am-5.30pm. **Access:** Level entry through back door.

The name is almost enough to merit a visit to this Portuguese sugar haven; however, on entering, patrons will be treated to the joyful buzz of happy consumers, the thick scent of fresh coffee, and row upon row of Portuguese pasteis (pastries) lined up eagerly in gleaming cabinets. Jackpot! With all the best loved pastries of the Portuguese repertoire on offer, it is hard to limit yourself to a short visit. Why not follow up an almond sponge with a chocolate roll or a few biscuits, and then move on to the famous almond and sweet bean tarts? All the pastries are made on the premises by local hero Luis Santos.

EAST

Bill's

433 Liverpool St, Darlinghurst (✆ 9360 9631)

Open: Mon-Sat 7.30am-4pm; Closed Sun. **Access:** 1 entry step.

Bill's is a beguiling place. A bright, white, sunny and an airy interior is startlingly tempered by the colours and shapes of flowers and customers, and by a buzz of contentment. As well as the conventional tables set up around the cafe's perimeter, a large common table, strewn with magazines, plates of food and coffee cups, occupies centre stage. Weekend breakfasts here have become such an institution that long queues of late sleepers always form outside the doors, so arrive early. Freshly home made food fills the menu.

Box

28a Bayswater Rd, Kings Cross (✆ 9358 6418)

Open: Mon-Fri 7.30am-4.30pm; Sat-Sun 8am-4.30pm. **Access:** 1 entry step, narrow inside.

Box is so minimalist that not only is its only sign simply scratched into the street-front wall, all clutter has been dispensed with. This is one of the longest, narrowest cafes in the city, flanked on one side by a continuous, cushioned bench and squeezed in between two of Sydney's most illustrious eateries: the Bayswater Brasserie and Darley Street Thai. Box may not fit the bill for those who prefer not to drink their coffee in an environment of treated concrete, light fibreglass fixtures and long benches, but for those who enjoy a modern atmosphere, Box is a find.

Cafe Crown

355 Crown St, Surry Hills (✆ 9331 2154)

Open: 7 days 7am-11pm. **Access:** 1 small entry step.

Set in stainless steel with a window-clad outlook and staffed with friendly people, Cafe Crown offers a winning formula: slick yet relaxed surroundings, good coffee, cheap yet good food, and a central location. Breakfasts of home made muesli, wood fired toast, jams, eggs and fruit are bound to give visitors a roaring kick start, while lunches and dinners are made up of a wide-ranging and regularly rotating menu. Cafe Crown is an excellent people watching spot too.

Where The Streets Are Paved With Beans

There are certain streets in Sydney which have a stronger connection with coffee than seems reasonable.

East Sydney, that tiny suburb between the City and lower Darlinghurst, has **Stanley Street;** Kings Cross has **Victoria Street;** Darlinghurst has **Victoria Street** and **Darlinghurst Road;** Paddington has **Oxford Street;** Bondi has **Campbell Parade;** Leichhardt has **Norton Street** and Glebe has **Glebe Point Road.**

Closely packed with cafes, they represent the main centres of the city's cafe society. Yet, faced with so many alternatives for their customers to patronise, each establishment must serve excellent coffee and snacks, distinguish themselves with decor, character and service, so cafe fiends are the winners.

Golden Dog, Paddington

Chocolate Factory Cafe, Paddington

Flat White

Bar Paradiso, City

Below: Courtyard, The Rocks

Below: Bathers Pavilion

Watsons Bay

Bistro Moncur

Sydney Fish Markets Below: Harbour View Hotel

The Australian Hotel Below: Centennial Park Cafe

Cafe Divino

70 Stanley St, East Sydney (✆ 9360 9911)

Open: 7 days 7am-Midnight. **Access:** 1 entry step.

Cafe Divino is one of the solidly popular establishments of the Stanley Street golden coffee triangle. Sip on a good coffee on the pavement terrace or under the back courtyard awnings and take part in consuming the brown bean in this, one of the city's highest coffee consumption zones. Busy from open to close, Divino also offers salads, focaccias and other light Italian meals.

Cafe Niki at Surry Hills

544 Bourke St, Surry Hills (✆ 9319 7517)

Open: 7 days 7am-10pm. **Access:** Small entry step.

Cafe Niki was created in Glebe by two heroes, Stefan and Peter, who kept much of Sydney University very well fed between 1989 and 1994. Two Niki ventures now exist: Kafenio (below) and Niki. Grinders coffee (beans also for sale), magnificent fruit whips and smoothies (ask for a pink one) as well as Italian soft drinks and fruit nectars are just some of the many popular drinks on offer. Focaccias are simply massive, and the soups and bagels are distractingly good. Numerous pastries, baked daily on the premises, and desserts such as very solid Greek cheesecake, are enough to keep patrons lingering. Add to this the friendly, comfortable atmosphere of the old corner terrace building, big windows and central exposed kitchen, and it's a winner! (See: Food).

Centennial Park Cafe

Cnr Grand Drive & Parks Drive, Centennial Park (Oxford St side) (✆ 9360 3355)

Open: 7 days 8.30am-4pm. **Access:** Level entry & accessible toilets.

Surrounded by green vistas interjected with a parade of cyclists, riders, in-line skaters, joggers and walkers flowing past the large open terrace, the Centennial Park cafe is a choice spot for flopping after exercising, or for watching others do so. The large, airy pavilion-like building draws Sydneysiders to its breakfasts, substantial meals or coffees and drinks year round.

The Chocolate Factory

8 Elizabeth St, Paddington (✆ 9331 3785)

Open: Tues-Sat 8am-6pm; Sun10am-6pm; Closed Mon. **Access:** Small ledge/level entry.

How to describe adequately the Chocolate Factory? Too many superlatives will inspire doubt as to the level of devotion inspired by this establishment; yet, simply put, this is one of the best cafes in Sydney. Where else is it possible to sit for hours reading the ample selection of magazines and papers, listening to impeccably cool music, sipping on Hernandez-roasted Spanish Espresso coffee, made by the most impossibly suave chrome Bo Ema machine, or perhaps sipping on a home made lemonade, or on a nectar or bitters or maybe an iced chocolate? Where else is it possible to eat home made brownies and blondies (just slightly gooey in the centre), towering chocolate cake, delicate biscuits, or lunch rolls perhaps filled with roasted eggplant, pastrami and salad? Where else offers all this and live classical guitar on Sunday, in a comfortably homely dark green and wooden interior, the main feature of which is a display case packed with chocolates, sweets and coffee beans. Nowhere, except the Chocolate Factory. (See: Sydney Icons: Paddington Chocolates.)

Coluzzi Bar

322 Victoria St, Darlinghurst (✆ 9380 5420)

Open: 7 days 5.30am-7.30pm. **Access:** 1 entry step, pavement seating.

Also at: Elizabeth St, City (✆ 9233 1651)

That well-worn looking place with the groovy lettering and the moulded plastic stools outside is one of the most famous coffee haunts in Sydney. Not necessarily for its coffee, though, but for being Coluzzi. Opened in 1957, this was one of the first places to serve real, live espresso when the city's new Italian community first began to save the rest of the population from a life of bad pseudo-coffee and tea. For that, we are truly grateful. Coluzzi is also a fabled people-watching spot.

Dov

Cnr Forbes St & Burton St, Darlinghurst (✆ 9360 9594)

Open: Mon-Sat 7am-10pm. **Access:** 1 high step and narrow door.

Dov is the bubbly home of a middle European/Mediterranean menu composed of such favourites as chunky onion tart and mountainous mixed plates. Breakfasts are suitably low key, while the coffee is good and strong. Dov's position over the road from the College of the Arts ensures an interesting crowd fills the cafe, while the sandstone walls create a cool, established feeling, juxtaposed by the stainless steel fittings.

Fez

247 Victoria St, Darlinghurst (✆ 9360 9581)

Open: 7 days 7am-10.30pm. **Access:** 1 small step.

Another resident in the Victoria Street coffee frenzy, Fez is a colourful and welcoming place which draws the active streetscape in through its large windows. Here guests can sit at any time of the day and enjoy a simple coffee or a meal of the cafe's fabled Afro-Mediterranean fare, while reading the paper and soaking in the atmosphere and buzz of the clientele. This is a sunny place, filled with the colours and textures of Morocco, the customers and the passing scene combined.

Golden Dog

388 Oxford St, Paddington (opposite St John's Church) (✆ 9360 7700)

Open: Mon-Fri 8am-11pm; Sat 7.30am-11pm; Sun 9am-11pm. **Access:** 1 entry step.

Dark wooden fixtures and tables, treated concrete floors inlaid with little brass golden dogs and vintage foreign beverage posters along the walls surround visitors to the Golden Dog. With large glass doors opening out onto Oxford Street and beyond to St John's Church, site of Saturday's Paddington Bazaar, the cafe can get noisy and amazingly busy. Here are to be found burgers, focaccias and other snacks, as well as more substantial pastas and Modern Australian mains. The coffee is good and strong, the hot chocolate great and the delicious milkshakes are served in suave chrome containers!

Gusto Delicatessen

Hall St, Bondi Beach (✆ 9304 565)

Open: Mon-Fri 7am-8pm; Sat 7am-6pm; Sun 7am-5pm. **Access:** High, fixed stools, very small interior.

Also at: Five Ways, Paddington (✆ 9361 5640)

As well as cabinets packed with zesty gourmet ingredients and a counter full of delicious take-away fare, Gusto has a snazzy street-side bar at which passers by can perch themselves and enjoy coffee, cakes, biscuits or even focaccias. This is an extremely popular place serving great food and goodies, so its few seats are often occupied.

Hernandez

60 Kings Cross Rd, Potts Point (✆ 9331 2343)

Open: 7 days 24 hours. **Access:** 1 entry step, narrow door & interior, inclined pavement seating.

Hernandez stays open all day every day, roasting and serving some of the best coffee to be found in Sydney. While this makes it extremely popular with discerning coffee fiends, the richly atmospheric decor, comprised of a eccentrically eclectic group of paintings, makes this cafe a joy, as well as something more than worth patronising and valuing. Even at four in the morning, Hernandez is busily serving up Spanish Espresso and drinks.

Jackie's

132 Warners Ave, North Bondi Beach (✆ 9300 9812)

Open: 7 days, 7.30am-Midnight. **Access:** Several entry steps.

Also at: 86-88 Bayswater Rd (cnr Waratah St), Rushcutters Bay (✆ 9332 2018)

Open: 7 days, 7am-Midnight. **Access:** Level entry.

Also at: Cnr Kent St & Liverpool St, City (✆ 9261 1439)

Open: Mon-Fri 7am-Midnight; Sat 8.30am-12.30pm; Sun 10.30am-12.30pm. **Access:** 2 entry steps.

The Jackie's empire extends to three separate cafes in Sydney, but Bondi is the original and best. Barefooted customers lazing away the hours reading, talking, sipping and eating dictate a very relaxed attitude, while the fruit smoothies would blow the socks off the patrons, if they were wearing any. Fabled spaghetti Bolognese is to be found at the Rushcutters Bay cafe, which maintains the relaxed style of Bondi, minus the sand on the floor. The City cafe offers an good and colourful spot to go before or after a movie.

24 HOUR SYDNEY

The following establishments are all open twenty-four hours, seven days a week.

The Bourbon & Beefsteak 24 Darlinghurst Rd, King's Cross (✆ 9358 1144)
Deriving its charm from its slightly grotesque nature, this eatery is the place for an enormous twenty-four hour menu.

Cafe Hernandez 60 King's Cross Rd, Potts Point (✆ 9331 2343)
With excellent, home roasted Spanish coffee in intimate and suavely eccentric surroundings, Cafe Hernandez is a great cafe at any time of the day or night.

City Extra Shop E4, East Podium, Circular Quay (✆ 9241 1422)
301 Church St, Parramatta (& 9633 1188)
These cafes continuously serve a wide range of food and drink continuously.
The Circular Quay outlet is a fascinating place to watch dawn yawning over the Harbour's transport hub.

Courthouse Hotel & Currency Exchange 189 Oxford St, Darlinghurst (✆ 9360 4831)
This pub serves beer and drinks all day and all night. Another useful service is the twenty-four hour currency exchange located in the hotel.

Sydney Harbour Casino Wharf 12 & 13, Pyrmont (✆ 9777 9000)
The flashing lights, glitz and beat of Sydney's casino never stop.

Lamrock Cafe

Cnr Lamrock Ave ✆ Campbell Parade, Bondi Beach (✆ 930 6313)

Open: 7 days 7am-Midnight. **Access:** 1 entry step, small interior.

The Lamrock Cafe has long been 'a scene' in Bondi, and this, combined with a front-row position for the observation of a passing parade of humanity along this famous stretch of beach, perpetuates it.

La Passion du Fruit

633 Bourke St (cnr Devonshire St), Surry Hills (✆ 9690 1894)

Open: Tues-Sat 8am-10.30pm; Sun 11am-4pm. **Access:** 2 entry steps, small interior, pavement seating.

Passion du Fruit's warmly colourful interior, filled

with people, magazines and flowers, is not the only attractive aspect of this gem of a place. Fantastic fruit concoctions or full flavoured coffee to drink, inexpensive meals and great desserts, such as the ever popular pear and polenta cake, ensure a loyal and well nourished following. (See: Food.)

Le Petit Creme

118 Darlinghurst Rd, Darlinghurst (✆ 9361 4738)

Open: Mon-Fri 7am-4pm; Sat 7am-5.30pm; Sun 8am-5.30pm. **Access:** Small interior.

While the popularity of the cafe for extended breakfasts sometimes results in 'a bit of biffo' in the competition for tables, Le Petit Creme offers a warmly and friendly chaotic atmosphere in which to scoff omelettes, croque madames and monsieurs, or bacon and eggs. Good, strong coffee can be ordered in a cup, glass or bowl at this unfailingly good bit of France.

Little West

346 Liverpool St, Darlinghurst (✆ 9360 5360)

Open: 7 days 12noon-Midnight. **Access:** 1 entry step.

Tucked into the city's golden triangle of coffee consumption, this is a frequent stop for late night dessert and coffee. Little West offers crumbles, sticky fig pudding, nut tarts and yes, good coffee.

Maltese Cafe

310 Crown St, Surry Hills (✆ 9361 6942)

Open: Tues-Thurs 7am-6pm; Fri-Sun 7am-7.30pm; Closed Mon. **Access:** 1 entry step.

The spare interior of this cafe serves only to heighten awareness of the greatly superior quality of the Maltese pastries available in this popular little cafe. Both savoury and sweet pastizzi (try the apple variety) bring a constant stream of loyal regulars through the door.

Picnic Cafe

3 Military Rd, Watsons Bay (✆ 9337 5221)

Open: Wed-Sun 12noon-9.30pm. **Access:** 1 entry step.

The best alternative to beer, fish and chips in Watsons Bay (See: Sydney By Area) is the Picnic Cafe, tucked into a quiet corner under the cliffs of the Gap. Here, locals enjoy a meal or a coffee inside or on the terrace. Good food leads to good desserts, perhaps creme brulee or warm lemon tart, making this a haven for those with a sweet tooth.

Rustic Cafe

Cnr Crown St & Devonshire St, Surry Hills (✆ 9318 1034)

Open: Tues-Sat 8am-11pm; Sun 9am-9pm; Closed Mon. **Access:** Small step, wide doors.

In an unmissably bright yellow building, the Rustic Cafe is a vibrant and popular spot for great Mediterranean food, coffee and drinks, cakes and snacks. Always busy and bustling, peak times may require a wait for a table (See: Food).

Sean's Panaroma

270 Campbell Parade, Bondi Beach (✆ 9365 4924)

Open: 7 days 7am-10pm (shorter hours in winter). **Access:** 1 entry step.

As well as being recognised as one of the best and most relaxed Modern Australian restaurants in Sydney, Sean's Panaroma is a friendly and delicious cafe by day. Fruit frappes, coffee and sweet snacks (not to mention the food; See: Food) and a view onto Bondi Beach make this one of the most enjoyable establishments of the area.

Speedos

126 Ramsgate Ave, Bondi Beach (✆ 9365 3622)

Open: 7 days 7am-10pm. **Access:** 3 entry steps.

Big breakfasts and great coffee close to the sand of Australia's most famous beach are a winning formula which invariably keeps this small and friendly cafe full. With advertising memorabilia of our national icon 'spray on' swimming costumes adorning the warm walls, refreshing fruit whips and thickly fluffy pancakes on the table, and delicious burgers walking out the door in take away boxes, Speedos is a great find.

Sports Bar

32 Campbell Parade, Bondi Beach (✆ 930 4582)

Open: Tues-Fri 12noon-Midnight; Sat-Sun 10am-Midnight; Mon dinner only. **Access:** 2 entry steps, narrow interior.

This is where the babes and hunks and their respective hunks and babes hang out in Bondi, the observation of which is a sport in itself, while seriously strange sports memorabilia hangs from most available spaces on the walls. A great place to see and be seen over the rim of a drinking vessel.

WEST

Bar Italia

169-171 Norton St, Leichardt (✆ 9560 9981)

Open: Mon-Thurs 9am-Midnight; Fri-Sat 9am-1am; Sun 10am-Midnight. **Access:** 1 entry step, pavement seating.

The original and best cafe on what is now the centre of Sydney's Little Italy, Bar Italia is a no frills, no-try-hard-design Mecca for Italian coffee, home made gelato, exquisite Italian pastries, cakes and fresh pasta dishes (from $6.50) which are not to be passed up. Bar Italia is an extremely popular Sydney Icon deserving great respect.

Blackwattle Canteen

Blackwattle Artists Studios, Glebe Point Rd, Glebe (✆ 9552 1792)

Open: Mon-Sat 8am-4pm; Sun 10am-4pm. **Access:** 2 steps, narrow wooden planks to level entry.

Another place which draws the relaxation out of the surrounding water and transfers it to its clientele is the Blackwattle Canteen, situated right at the very end of Glebe Point Road in the large tin sheds housing the Blackwattle Artists' Studios. Walking along the length of the building past intriguing studio doors and entrances to the far right hand corner, cafe goers are delivered to this beautiful 'canteen', whose windows look straight out on to the water and across to Sydney's newest suspension bridge, the Pyrmont Bridge. Strong coffee and a range of other refreshments such as nectars and soft drinks, tasty and fresh pasta, bruschetta, soups, cakes, and snacks make this an excellent cafe full of atmosphere.

Cafe Cinquecento

88 King St, Newtown (✆ 9557 1418)

Open: Mon-Thurs 7am-10pm; Fri-Sat 7am-Midnight; Sun 9am-10pm. **Access:** Level entry, high benches.

This is a neat little establishment designed in muted tones with tiny ceramic Fiat 500s adorning the walls. Apart from the full-flavoured coffee on offer, focaccias, pizzas, lasagne, pastries, fruit drinks and gelato make up the fare, and render this cafe one of the best options in this part of town.

Chester's Cafe in the Tin Shed

144 Beattie St, Balmain (✆ 9555 2185)

Open: 7 days 8am-4pm. **Access:** Level but uneven to outdoors eating, no access inside.

Winner of the prize for the most literal name, Chester's cafe is, not surprisingly, situated in a tin shed surrounded by several larger tin sheds full of second hand furniture, junk and antiques. The ground between them is covered with all sorts of trash and treasure, whether doors, park benches or suitcases. Breakfast here is a Balmain institution, offering eggs, bacon, sausages and tomato relish; or more healthy ways to rev up before sorting through the junk for that elusive piece of treasure, such as muesli, juices and home-made jams. Excellent, strong coffee, satisfying cakes and a strong menu full of zesty dishes keep the warmly decorated cafe full and lively most of the day, with any excess customers converting the surplus wheelbarrows and tricycles outside into temporary seats.

Glebe Coffee Roaster

In the Forest Lodge Hotel, 117 Arundel St, Forest Lodge (✆ 9552 6279)

Open: Mon-Fri 7.30am-6.30pm; Sat-Sun 8am-7pm. **Access:** Level to courtyard, 1 step inside.

A coffee fiend's magnet is this little place which has been, for years, a popular and conveniently located haunt of the students of the University of Sydney. Now operating from inside the Forest Lodge Hotel, the Glebe Coffee Roaster roasts its own delicious beans on the premises, and serves their noble brown brews from individual plungers. Guests can sit either in the bistro or in the courtyard.

Kafenío

72 Glebe Point Rd, Glebe (✆ 9552 3610)

Open: Mon-Sat 8.30am-6pm; Sun 11am-4pm. **Access:** 1 small step, low tables at rear.

This little gem constitutes half of the living remains of the original Cafe Niki (see below under East), where hungry patrons will find excellent pastries & cakes such as the legendary 'Louisiana Fat Boy Double Choc Fudge Brownie', excellently strong Glebe Coffee Roaster coffee, bizarre tea blends with intriguing names such as 'Arctic Fire' and delicious fruit whips and smoothies. Hunger can be pleasantly and definitely quashed with rosetta rolls, pizzettas, quiches and gigantic focaccias, towering with full-flavoured ingredients.

The Old Fish Shop

Cnr King St ✆ Church St, Newtown (✆ 9519 4295)

Open: 7 days 6.30am-Midnight. **Access:** Very small interior.

For those who enjoy really being part of the street scene, the Old Fish Shop could just be the niche you have been seeking. Full height, open windows bring busy King Street into the cafe's intimate space, whose local clientele help to pack the scene with warm colour.

Pelican's Fine Foods

81 Darling St, Balmain (✆ 9810 1966)

Open: Mon-Thurs 8am-4pm; Fri-Sat 8am-5pm; Sun 10am-3.30pm. **Access:** 1 entry step, pavement seating.

In this little cafe, occupying what appears to be an old butcher's shop, plunger coffee is accompanied by any of a range of delicious, home made cakes, biscuits and slices. Extremely popular gourmet burgers, sandwiches and cooked breakfasts form the cafe's more substantial fare, while a cabinet of picnic supplies make Pelican's a great stop to investigate while conquering the Balmain walking route (See: Walks Around Sydney).

Well-Connected Cafe

35 Glebe Point Rd, Glebe (✆ 9566 2655)

Open: 7 days 10am-10pm. **Access:** Level entry, stairs to second floor.

The Well-Connected cafe provides a happy mix of technology and coffee, by offering access to the Internet on one of its twelve computers at the rate of $12 an hour. Each computer's fair sized desk holds a mouse pad, keyboard and joystick, yet there is still room for a coffee and some cake. While the cafe's two storeys see a mix of earnest game-players and first time internet users, the place is extremely popular with tourists missing their Internet access. The atmosphere here is bohemian-intellectual, in a high-tech way.

FOOD

Sydney is home to a multitude of cultural groups and their taste buds. The happy result is that the city swarms with exotic foods which have over the years become 'normal'. But it was not always so. Before the waves of post-war immigration began, Australia was a comparative culinary wasteland, dominated by ubiquitous "Anglo-Saxon muck" with about as much imagination as a boiled potato. Thankfully, Sydney is now the place to be for those looking to enjoy a wide variety of excellent and inventive food whose quality is not dependent on ridiculous prices.

Looking through the following descriptions of the pick of Sydney's restaurants, readers may notice the large number of purveyors of **'Modern Australian'** food. So what is it? Perhaps it is best to define it by excluding what it isn't. Early Australian food would have been dominated by the above-mentioned Anglo-Saxon muck, sticking to regimented tradition without any cross-over between cuisines. Middle Ages Australian would have been the situation where foreign cuisines were widely spread throughout the city, but kept separate by their gastronomic traditions and usually run by members of those cultural groups. Modern Australian describes the happy, multi-cultural melange of Sydney's contemporary food in which ingredients, flavours and techniques from Italy, Thailand, France, Japan, California or the Outback are applied to any the fresh produce for which this country is famous. The result is that diners could be cutting into some lamb and associating the tastes with Morocco, while those at the next table could be enjoying barbecued octopus and tasting the flavours of Thailand. Above all, modern Australian food is confident, intensely flavoured, fresh and imaginative.

Most of the restaurants listed here are not expensive: it is possible to eat at most of them for around $20, especially as most restaurants serve many wines by the glass. However, there are certain restaurants in this gastronomic centre which merit a budget blow out, and for those seeking the finest and most elegant examples of the skill of the city's restaurateurs, there are many establishments among the following entries which will lead diners directly to exactly such an experience. However, each entry has details of the average prices of an entree, main course and dessert, so this shouldn't happen unexpectedly.

A final note: **"BYO"** denotes bring your own wine, as either the premises are not licensed, or permit this cheaper option. **"Lc'd"** means the restaurant is licensed to sell alcohol. If the listing doesn't say "book", there's usually no need to reserve a table. **"Access"** denotes that the restaurant is accessible to those using wheelchairs. Each listing also contains full details of credit accepted, opening hours and average prices. However, please remember that times change, and so do the details, so if you need to be absolutely sure about something, telephone the restaurant first.

CITY

Asturiana

77 Liverpool St, City (✆ 9264 1010) Spanish. Book.

Lc'd. Credit: AE BC D MC V. **Access:** Small ridge & narrow passage.

Open: Lunch: Tues-Fri & Sun 12noon-3pm; Dinner: Tues-Sun 5.30pm-10.30pm.

Average Prices: Entree from $5; Main $16; Dessert $7.

Situated in the heart of the Spanish area of the city, the traditionally rustic decoration of Asturiana makes this a favourite place to eat great tapas (from $4) and larger Spanish meals without having to fork out $$$. To become engulfed in the atmosphere, try the sangria and follow it with seafood, cider-poached sausage, tortilla, beef or risotto. House specials average around $15. ¡Olé!

The Bennelong

Sydney Opera House, Bennelong Point, City (✆ 9250 7578) Modern Australian. Book.

Lc'd. Credit: All. **Access:** Lift from stage door to level entry.

Open: Dinner only: Mon-Sat 6pm-11pm.

Average Prices: Entree $20; Main $30; Dessert $18.

BYO: The Great Aussie Tradition

Where a restaurant is denoted as "BYO", it means that you must "bring your own" wine or beer, as the establishment is not licensed to sell alcohol. Where it is listed as "Lc'd & BYO", the restaurant does have a wine list,but will also allow patrons to take the more economical option of bringing their own, although anything up to $2 will usually be charged for corkage. Many foreign visitors to these climes are often shocked by the apparent rudery of the BYO concept, especially in the realm of private parties. However, it can be explained as yet another example of the great Aussie pragmatism: why pay for other people's drinking habits when they could pay for it themselves? It could also be explained as self-preservation: Australians generally drink quite a lot.

With its very own shell of the Opera House under which to sit, the Bennelong is one of Sydney's most famous and spectacularly located restaurants. Entrees on offer could include a blue swimmer crab cake with coriander sauce; mains could be anything from roast pigeon, to salmon with green sauce, or a delicate breast of chicken with red wine vinegar and tomato sauce. Desserts might be grilled figs served with vanilla parfait; raspberries with sugar puff pastry; or a fabulous, flourless chocolate roulade. The Bennelong is the most expensive of the restaurants within the Opera House, but dining here represents a grand occasion.

Bilson's

Overseas Passenger Terminal, Circular Quay (✆ 9251 5600) Modern Australian. Book.

Lc'd. Credit: AE BC D MC V. **Access:** Ramps to level entry, toilet access.

Open: Lunch: Sun-Fri 12noon-3pm; Dinner: Mon-Sat 6.30pm-10pm.

Average Prices: Entree $15; Main $25; Dessert $13.

One of Sydney's most prominent restaurateurs in one of Sydney's most prominent buildings and positions makes for a famous restaurant. Bilson's offers panoramic views of the Quay, the Harbour and the Opera House from its perch in the Overseas Passenger Terminal, and a very highly regarded menu with an emphasis on seafood: rock oysters, lobster and mud crab, Yamba reef prawns with vermicelli, cashew and cucumber salad, or maybe some venison, guinea fowl or even lamb are all prepared with delicate flavours of great style. Bilson's offers guests a memorable dining experience.

Botanic Gardens Restaurant

In the middle of the Royal Botanic Gardens, City (✆ 9241 2419) Modern Australian.

Lc'd. Credit: AE BC MC V. **Access:** Ramp access.

Open: Lunch: 7 days 12noon-2.15pm; Closed evenings.

Average Prices: Entree $10; Main $17.50; Dessert $9.50.

For those who enjoy a lusciously leafy outlook and like listening to ducks, this is the place for lunch. Seated out on the spacious verandah under the vines, guests can eat to the quacks from a seasonal menu ranging from antipasto and salads to chicken confit with roasted buckwheat tabouli, or fish and chips with lime and lemongrass dipping sauce, the style varying according to the available ingredients.

Bouillon

City Hotel, cnr King & Castlereagh Streets, City (✆ 9299 4981) Book.

Lc'd. Credit: AE BC D MC V. **Access:** None.

Open: Lunch: Mon-Fri 12noon-3pm; Dinner: Friday only 6.30pm-9pm.

Average Prices: Entree $12; Main $17; Dessert $7.

This very popular, excellent value city eatery features long, skinny tables where perfect strangers mingle communally over their bowls of Tuscan sausage with spiced borlotti beans and mash, or snapper fillet topped with grilled fennel and accompanied by a mound of risotto, chosen from the short list of mains. Desserts are headed by a famed bread and butter pudding, an all time favourite. Separate banquettes and individual tables are also available for the less adventurous.

Brasserie Cassis

1st Floor, Chifley Plaza, Chifley Square, City (✆ 9221 3500) Modern Australian. Book.

Lc'd. Credit: AE BC D MC V. **Access:** Level entry from Bent St.

Open: Mon-Fri 11am-10pm; Closed Sat-Sun.

Average Prices: Entree $11; Main $17; Dessert $9.

Cassis' core is an ambitious menu stretching perhaps to include duck confit salad; sauteed prawns, champagne and saffron risotto, grilled tuna with tapenade sauce, roast lamb, or even salmon fish cakes. This is the lunch time Mecca of city go-getters, attracted to the smooth class of the big polished spaces of the split-level room. Excellent food and a relatively inexpensive wine list make this a great place to have lunch.

Criterion

Lobby level, MLC Centre, cnr King St & Castlereagh St, City (✆ 9233 1234)

Lc'd. Credit: AE BC D MC V. **Access:** Lift to level entry.

Open: Lunch: Mon-Fri 12noon-3pm; Dinner: Mon-Sat from 6pm.

Average Prices: Entree $13.50; Main $18; Dessert $8.

This is a predominantly, but not exclusively, Lebanese restaurant set in a warm, terracotta- floored conservatory-like room with a roll back screen for balmy days. It is a friendly, family-run place where patrons are equally welcome for a thick, sweet Lebanese coffee in the morning or an afternoon snack.

WATERSIDE EATING

Dining or sipping a drink by the water is a special pleasure readily available in Sydney. If you don't want to picnic, the following are some of the best waterside restaurants and cafes around the city. Full details can be found in the main text.

The Bathers Pavilion
4 The Esplanade, Balmoral (✆ 9968 1133)
Brazil
46 North Steyne, Manly (✆ 9977 3825)
Catalina
Lyne Park, Rose Bay (✆ 9371 0555)
Doyles
Watsons Bay and Watsons Bay Jetty (✆ 9337 2007)
Le Kiosk
Shelley Beach, Manly (✆ 9977 4122)
Nielsen Park Kiosk
Greycliffe Avenue, Vaucluse (✆ 9337 1574)
Onzain
2nd floor, Bondi Digger's Club, 232 Campbell Parade, Bondi Beach (✆ 9365 0763)
The Pier
594 New South Head Rd, Rose Bay (✆ 9327 6561)
Rimini Fish Cafe
35 South Steyne, Manly (✆ 9977 3880)
Sean's Panaroma
270 Campbell Parade, North Bondi Beach (✆ 9365 4924)

The mixed plate is delicious and extremely generous, easily feeding two. Specials may include seafood such as Atlantic Salmon or perhaps chorizo sliced on a bed of creamy mash and served with tomato, onion and zucchini relish.

Dendy Bar and Bistro
MLC Centre, 14-24 Martin Place, City (✆ 9221 1243)
Lc'd. Credit: BC D MC V. **Access:** Telephone staff before to arrange.
Open: 7 days 11am-"till late".
Average Prices: Entree $8; Main $12; Dessert $6.
A supplementary attraction of the excellent Dendy cinema is the possibility of a good nosh and a drink before the film. Here, the kitchen provides sustenance such as lentil, beef or chicken burgers, lamb, steaks and pastas from $8.50. Guests don't have to eat to have a drink either, as the bistro is also a licensed bar.

Edna's Table
Level 8, MLC Centre, Martin Place (✆ 9231 1400)
Lc'd. Credit: AE BC D MC V. **Access:** Level to lift, 1 step to restaurant.
Open: Lunch: Mon-Fri 12noon-3pm; Dinner: Mon-Sat 6pm-10pm; Supper: Mon-Sat 9.30pm-11pm.
Average Prices: Entree $6.50-$17.50; Main $20; Dessert $9.
Serving exclusively Australian produce and wines in a stunning interior decor (boomerang backed chairs and a rainbow serpent installation against a backdrop of glowing walls), Edna's Table has been known to present amazing concoctions such as gum-leaf smoked buffalo carpaccio, emu ravioli or barramundi coated with Macadamia nuts. Desserts such as lemon aspen ice cream with bunya nut praline are both a revelation and revolution in bush tucker!

Kingsley's
29a King St, City (✆ 9262 4155) Australian.
Lc'd. Credit: AE BC D MC V. **Access:** Ramp entry.
Open: Lunch: Mon-Fri 12noon-3pm; Dinner: 7 days from 6pm.
Average Prices: Entree $6; Main $12.50; Dessert $6.
Despite the not too subtle items of Australiana strategically poised around the restaurant, this is an energetic, classic Australian eatery which is dedicated to serving honest, meaty Aussie tucker - kangaroo, buffalo, beef, lamb, seafood and chicken dominate the menu, yet even vegetables make it onto the list. The food is of excellent quality, and will reveal why this is such a popular place with tourists and locals alike. Try the fish and chips, Big Red (kangaroo) burger or desserts, all Aussie favourites such as pavlova and lamingtons. The house wines are excellent.

Level 41
Level 41 Chifley Tower, Chifley Square, City (✆ 9221 2500) Modern Australian. Book.
Lc'd. Credit: AE BC D MC V. **Access:** Lift to restaurant's level entry.
Open: Lunch: Mon-Fri 12noon-2.30pm; Dinner: Mon-Sat 6pm-10.30pm.
Average Prices: Entree $15; Main $26; Dessert $9.50.
Level 41 is one of the city's most talked about restaurants, perched high up in an office tower with amazing views over the city, harbour and skies whether it be in sunshine or moonlight. But we're here for the food, and wow! Simple oysters and scallops with delicate Vietnamese dressings; perfectly roasted game; couscous encrusted Tasmanian Salmon; yellow fin tuna seared and served with buckwheat noodles and snow pea sprouts co-habit the menu in true modern Australian style. The influences are manifold and the result spectacular. Combined with the luxurious yet inconspicuous environment, diners slide into their extravagantly comfortable chairs with a grin of satisfaction. For a special eating event in Sydney, Level 41 is hard to beat.

MCA Cafe
Museum of Contemporary Art, 140 George St, Circular Quay (✆ 9241 4253) Modern Australian/Mediterranean.
Lc'd. Credit: AE BC MC V. **Access:** Ramp to lift to level entry from George St entrance.
Open: Mon-Fri 11am-5.30pm; Sun 9am-5.30pm.
Average Prices: Entree $12.50; Main $16.50; Dessert $7.50.

The exhibits forming the MCA's collection and the views from the outside terrace over the water of Circular Quay to the Opera House may be a distraction, but the MCA cafe's food deserves attention. Snacks and salads share the menu with antipasto plates, smoked salmon and eggplant lasagne, or maybe roast fish with olives and anchovies or pizze: olive oil abounds, except for on the desserts, and Penelope Sach herbal teas are a favoured extra on the usual menu of coffees.

Merrony's

Quay Apartments, 2 Albert St, Circular Quay (✆ 9247 9323) Modern Australian/French. Book.

Lc'd. Credit: AE BC D MC V. **Access:** Ramp to level entrance from Albert St, level interior.

Open: Lunch: Mon-Fri 12noon-2.30pm; Dinner: Mon-Sat 5.45pm-11.45pm.

Average Prices: Entree $15; Main $19; Dessert $9.

Merrony's has perfected the art of combining the modern Australian and French cuisines, offering in its airy and spacious restaurant dishes such as duck confit, the memorable crisp roast salmon with garlic puree and parsley sauce, and desserts such as perfect creme caramels, all of which can be eaten while enjoying the harbour views and watching the trains roll by silently at table level on the other side of a double glazed window. A great spot before or after an evening at the Opera House.

Museum of Sydney Cafe

Cnr Phillip St & Bridge St, City (✆ 9241 3636)

Open: Mon-Fri 7am-10pm; Sat-Sun 9am-6pm. **Access:** Level entry & toilets.

Average Prices: Dishes range from $6.50 to $18.50.

Located underneath and along the museum is one of the city's most congenial cafes, popular for refreshments and snacks throughout the day as well as for lunch and dinner. Jazz trios often serenade the patrons basking in the sunlight beneath the imposing building constructed on the site of the colony's First Government House, as they ponder the historical significance of the spot upon which they sit. Some of the zesty items on the menu could include anything from soups to chargrilled king prawns with steamed bok choy and chilli ginger dressing, various pastas and risottos or veal medallions with spring onions and mixed mushroom ragout and crisp potato cake.

The Palisade

35 Bettington St, Millers Point (✆ 9251 7225) Modern Australian. Book.

Lc'd. Credit: AE BC MC V. **Access:** None.

Open: Lunch: Mon-Fri 12noon-2.30pm; Dinner: Mon-Sat 6pm-10pm.

Average Prices: Entree $9.50; Main $18; Dessert $8.50.

Housed in an old, tall and skinny pub building on a cliff-edged peninsula, the Palisade is a sparingly decorated yet cosy, quiet, quaint little pub, with an undeniable 1930s atmosphere. The first floor bistro offers anything from hand-rolled pumpkin ravioli with butter and sage, Tasmanian Salmon pan fried with roasted tomato dressing, or perhaps Italian fennel sausages with cannellini beans and jus; to desserts along the lines of steamed lemon and semolina pudding, or sauterne creme with baked rhubarb. The wine list is well chosen and reasonably priced. All this in a bright, comfortable room with a great view onto the cargo docks and the historic buildings of The Rocks.

Rockpool

107 George St, The Rocks (✆ 9252 1888) Modern Australian. Book.

Lc'd. Credit: AE BC D MC V. **Access:** 1 steep entry step, ramp to restaurant.

Open: Lunch: Mon-Fri 12noon-2.30pm; Dinner: Mon-Fri 6.30pm-10pm, Sat 6.30pm-11pm.

Average Prices: Entree $25; Main $32; Dessert $15.

Rockpool is known for its inventive and celestial food. Entrees may range from a dozen freshly shucked oysters to spanner crab and preserved lemon ravioli with skordalia and rosemary jus, while main courses may include anything from roast Illabo lamb with braised vegetables, olives and aioli, to red emperor fillet cooked in a pot with coconut milk and garum marsala and served with snowpeas and semolina noodles. Dream-inducing desserts could include a honeyed grappa fruit compote with white pepper ice cream, or a coconut vacherin filled with mango and passionfruit sorbet, served with banana and lime sauce. This is one of Sydney's finest restaurants.

Sailors Thai

106 George St, The Rocks (✆ 9251 2466) Thai. Book downstairs.

Lc'd. Credit: All. **Access:** Level entry to both.

Open: Upstairs: 7 days 12noon-8pm. Downstairs: Mon-Sat 12noon-2.30pm & 6pm-10pm.

Average Prices: Upstairs: $10-$16; Downstairs: Entree $15; Main $20; Desserts $7.

Sailors Thai is the sister restaurant of Darley Street Thai, one of Sydney's most acclaimed restaurants, but it is popular in its own right. **Upstairs** is a suave noodle bar named the canteen, where speedy service and snappy presentation see guests enjoying delicious noodles at the long, central table or on the verandah. While the menu changes frequently, the canteen's pad thai, wines by the glass (from $4) and Thai beer are staple favourites. **Downstairs** is an equally slick but more formal restaurant, where the original sandstone of the historic Sailors Home building is juxtaposed with sumptuous wall panels. As with the canteen, there are some verandah tables here too, offering views across the International Passenger Terminal and Sydney Cove to the Opera House. On the menu could be entrees of grilled beef or green bean salads, or perhaps a Muslim curry, or even caramelised pork chops. The apparent simplicity of the dishes is deceptive, as the intense sensation greeting diners' tastebuds will prove.

Sydney Cove Oyster Bar

1 Circular Quay East, Circular Quay (towards Opera House) (✆ 9247 2937) Seafood.

Lc'd. Credit: AE BC D MC V. **Access:** Level. Waterside dining.

Open: 7 days 11am-11pm.

Average Prices: Half dozen $10.50; Dozen $19.

Let the oysters slide down the throat as the eyes glide over the smooth surface of the water across the ferries to the International Passenger Terminal, watching the sun slip down behind the City skyline; or chomp through prawns and crustacean critters, and arrive at the Opera feeling mightily content.

Thirty Something

31st Floor, Hotel Inter-Continental, 117 Macquarie St, City (✆ 9240 1275) Italian. Book.

Lc'd. Credit: AE BC D MC V. **Access:** None, split-level interior with stairs.

Open: Lunch: Mon-Fri 12noon-2.30pm; Dinner: Mon-Sat 6pm-10.30pm.

Average Prices: Pizza $15/$24; Pasta $10/$13; Dessert $8.50.

Those who ride the lifts up to the thirtieth floor of the hotel will find Sydney's most unlikely location for a pizzeria. Here, tasty gourmet pizzas and a range of pastas are served up with a side dish of panoramic views across the city, Opera House, Botanic Gardens and the Harbour.

T.T.T.E. Sarn

704a George St, City (✆ 9281 5683) Thai.

BYO. Credit: AE BC MC V. **Access:** 1 entry step.

Open: 7 days 11am-11pm.

Average Prices: Entrees $5; Mains $9; Steamboats $14.50.

This is a simple and calm Thai sanctuary squeezed in amid the noise of the City and Chinatown, where guests will find an almost confusingly extensive menu of standard and less common Thai dishes, all cooked with considerable skill and presented with flair and style. Lunch is always busy due to the Thai yum cha on offer (11am-3pm), in which a series of dishes (all $3-$4) from which to choose will stream past your table.

The Wharf Restaurant

Pier 4, Hickson Rd, Walsh Bay (STC) (✆ 9250 1761) Modern Australian/Mediterranean. Book.

Lc'd. Credit: AE BC MC V. **Access:** advise beforehand for assistance, accessible toilets.

Open: Mon-Sat: Lunch: 12noon-3pm; Dinner: 6pm-10.45pm; bar & cafe open all day.

Average Prices: Small dish $7; Large dish $14.50; Dessert $6.

Right at the end of the Sydney Theatre Company's converted pier sits The Wharf Restaurant, literally hanging out over the water of the Harbour. Enormous windows hover between wooden beams, letting the light and the harbour vista stream in unimpeded. The menu changes regularly, relaxedly covering dishes of varying size, heaviness and expense, while most wines listed are available by the glass. The menu could include pasta with roasted garlic and chilli, or ticino ham with fresh figs and rocket salad. Desserts range from fruit to luxurious mousses. Obviously a pre-theatre favourite, this is also a great place to linger during the day.

NORTH

Armstrong's

1 Napier St, Nth Sydney (✆ 9957 3011) Brasserie. Book.

Lc'd. Credit: AE BC D MC V. **Access:** entry ramp.

Open: Lunch: Mon-Fri 12noon-3pm; Dinner: Mon-Sat 6-10.30pm.

Guests can always expect a stunner of a meal in Armstrong's suave sandstone building: with uncomplicated yet intensely flavoured Modern Australian brasserie food, it is hard to go wrong. Renowned dishes include beautifully tender duck, luscious kangaroo loin, and the famous Armstrong Burger, while excellent fish and chips make choosing between seafood specials difficult. Desserts are great, as is the expansive wine list, many are available by the glass. Armstrong's at North Sydney is widely regarded as one of the best restaurants on the North Shore. Also at Manly, below.

Armstrong's at Manly

Manly Wharf, Manly (✆ 9976 3835) Modern Australian Brasserie.

Lc'd. Credit: AE BC D MC V. **Access:** Level entry and interior.

Open: 7 days 10.30am-10pm.

As well as the above food philosophy, Armstrong's at Manly offers beachside, waterside and ferryside outdoors dining under generous awnings. An excellent snack menu in the afternoons provides incentive to get to the end of the Spit to Manly walk (See: Bushwalks), as do the very good coffee and cakes.

The Bathers Pavilion

4 The Esplanade, Balmoral Beach (✆ 9968 1133) Modern Australian. Book.

Lc'd (extensive wine list). **Credit:** AE BC D MC V. **Access:** Level entry, 1 step to restaurant.

Open: Breakfast Sat-Sun 9am-10.30am; Lunch: Mon-Fri from 12noon, Sat-Sun from12.30pm; Dinner: 7 days from 6.30pm.

Average Prices: Entree $14; Main $23; Dessert $10.50.

It is almost impossible not to be infused with a sense of relaxed well-being while eating at the Bathers Pavilion. Housed in the white, glass-fronted beach-front building which gives the restaurant its name, the restaurant presents exquisitely chosen fresh produce and infuses it with Asian, North African and Italian overtones in a laid back and unpretentious style. This is a truly wonderful way to laze away an afternoon, gazing languidly out to sea or into a plate of: a seafood trio of oysters, scallops and fish with dipping sauces, or a slow roasted duck salad with coconut and ginger dressing. Main courses may be tuna cooked in a miso broth with pickled ginger and vinegared rice, some rare roasted venison in a salad with beetroot and cress, or perhaps roasted spatchcock with tamarind and sweet soy. Desserts are an essential experience, featuring stellar creations along the lines of honey and cardamom bavarois with poached apricots and honeycomb, or a sweet puff pastry tartlet filled with raspberries, peach and botrytis cream. Wow. The adjacent Refreshment Room is one of the best cafes in Sydney. Why move beyond Balmoral? This is Sydney's atmosphere encapsulated!

Brazil Cafe

46 North Steyne, Manly (✆ 9977 3825) Eclectic cafe.
Lc'd & BYO. Credit: AE BC MC V. **Access:** Level entry.
Open: 7 days 8am-Midnight.
Average Prices: Entree $7; Main $11; Dessert $4.50.
Despite the name, Brazil serves up delicious helpings of pan-Asian and Mediterranean food. The menu could include Balinese spiced fish, Singapore-style seafood laksa, or Mediterranean mezze plates. Favourites on the menu include an enormous vegetable and goats cheese lasagne, and crispy barbecued duck transformed into a curry and served with noodles, both bound to distract guests from the panoramic views of the Tasman Sea. A large variety of snacks are available for those looking only for a light meal.

Choyan

9 St Johns Ave, Gordon (✆ 9498 8698) Chinese. Book Fri-Sun.
Lc'd. Credit: AE BC D MC V. **Access:** Steep and long flight of stairs to restaurant.
Open: Lunch: Mon-Fri 12noon-3pm; Dinner: Mon-Fri 5pm-10pm, Sat-Sun 5pm-11pm; Yum Cha Sat-Sun 11am-3pm.
Average Prices: Vegetables $6.50; Meat $10; Dessert $5.
Although the Choyan faithfully delivers on Chinese dishes particularly popular with western diners, the key to this restaurant's enduring popularity is the Chinese menu. Here, hidden treasures await the intrepid guest, the secrets unlocked by the helpful and patient waiters who are adept at quick translations. It is on this menu that you will find excellent congee; amazing tofu, vegetable, shrimp, chicken and beef hotpots; slippery steamed oysters drizzled with a delicate shallot and ginger juice; or one of several traditional preparations of duck, chicken and beef. Lunch on Saturday and Sunday is simply not to be missed, as an excellent yum cha draws in the crowds from all over the North Shore. With a colour illustrated menu to decode the constant stream of delicious dishes being brought to the table, all guests are bound to walk away with a grin as broad as that of the jocular owner.

Cinema Cinema

1 Spit Road, Mosman (✆ 9968 1330)
BYO. Credit: AE BC MC V. **Access:** 1 small entry step.
Open: 7 days 6pm-10.30pm.
Average Prices: Entree $6.90; Main $10.90; Dessert $5.50.
For those who enjoy the often hilariously exuberant spectacle of Indian films and a bit of diversion while eating their dinner, Cinema Cinema is the place to go. The star eating option here is the spectacular banquet, with mixed entrees, curries, breads, rice and pappadams all served on a silver platter for around $14. The rest of the menu includes a number of less common dishes, such as the excellent dahi chaat (wheat crackers served with spiced yoghurt, potatoes, onions and chutney) and a variety of tava dishes (marinated meats cooked in the tandoor and then curried on the hotplate). However, what sets this establishment apart from the several others nearby is the rear wall of the restaurant: Indian films are screened continuously onto it. Add to that the proximity to the Mosman cinemas, and this is a great find for Indian food and film freaks.

Clareville Kiosk

27 Delecta Ave, Clareville Beach (on Pittwater) (✆ 9918 2727) Book.
BYO. Credit: AE BC MC V. **Access:** 4 entrance steps, split level interior.
Open: Lunch: Sun 12noon-3pm; Dinner: Wed-Sun 6.30pm-9.30pm.
Average Prices: Entree $11; Main $18; Dessert $8.
In this converted beach-side corner store lies a gem: warmed by a wood fire in winter and cooled by salty breezes flowing through louvred windows in summer, the Clareville Kiosk has been the setting for many very memorable lunches and dinners. Welcomed by the owners, guests are taken through a menu of bistro style dishes which are invariably delicious and create a satisfied and relaxed sense of benevolence. Beer battered prawns with tangy sun-dried tomato mayonnaise may begin the meal, to be followed by extra tender roast lamb on ratatouille and sage cream sauce, and then brandied fig ice-cream with drunken fig compote. It is out of town, but that's the charm, and the trip is more than worth the effort. A stroll onto the little Pittwater beach after a meal here is a perfect way to end the visit.

Eric's Fish Cafe

316 Pacific Highway, Crows Nest (✆ 9436 4907)
BYO. Credit: None. **Access:** Level entry.
Open: Mon-Sat 11.30am-9pm.
Average Prices: Entree $7; Main $12.
Eric's is a Sydney icon approaching Harry's Cafe de

Wheels status: no flash decor, no flash image, just good, fresh seafood cheap. The legendary (and legendarily inexpensive) seafood platter comes laden with calamari, prawns, steamed mussels, scallops and crab; sophisticated fish and chips arrive at the table grilled and delicately flavoured. Eric's is a good spot for those looking for honest seafood without any hype.

Fare Go Gourmet

69 Union St, North Sydney (✆ 9922 2965)

BYO. Credit: MC V. **Access:** 2 small steps.

Open: Tues-Sat 6.30pm-9.30pm.

Average Prices: Entree $15; Main $24; Dessert $10.

Looking at Fare Go, you may wonder why the food is more expensive than the decor would suggest. The answer is simple: the restaurant has refused to pander to the style pack's designer ideals, instead concentrating on its food, and we win because of it. Great produce receives magic wand treatment as it is transformed into the likes of grilled King prawns with Thai herbs, lime, palm sugar and eschalots; seared sea scallops on tangy roasted egg plant and tomato flesh; Venetian style calves liver; or exquisite glazed crispy duck with golden eschalot. The chef is also particularly fond of preparing unfashionable offal. Chunky glasses and basic cutlery remind diners that they are here for the food, not the decor.

Gourmet Pizza Kitchen

199 Military Rd, Neutral Bay (✆ 9953 9000)

Also at 60 Archer St, Chatswood ✆ 9411 8000)

Lc'd & BYO. Credit: AE BC MC V. **Access:** Level entry.

See under **East** for details.

La Goulue

17 Alexander St, Crows Nest (✆ 9439 1640) French. Book.

BYO. Credit: AE BC D MC V. **Access:** Level entry, toilets upstairs.

Open: Dinner: Tues-Sat from 6.30pm.

Average Prices: Entree $14; Main $21; Dessert $9.

La Goulue is an unassuming, low key restaurant where the most incredibly good French based food is anything but. A suave and smooth mixture of traditional French elements with Australian produce and inventiveness has created dishes such as 'salad' of pure white crab meat on a silky hazelnut dressing supporting a layer of intensely flavoured tomato flesh; roasted pheasant on a jus-laden forest floor of champignon and shitake mushrooms; and desserts such as gooey caramelised apple tart with calvados ice cream. La Goulue is a highly comfortable Sydney gastronomic institution of over twenty-three years standing, frequented by devoted regulars and well worth a visit.

Le Kiosk

Shelley Beach, Manly (✆ 9977 4122) Modern Australian. Book.

Lc'd. Credit: AE BC D MC V. **Access:** Ramp ✆ level entry to outside area, 1 interior step.

Open: Lunch: Mon-Fri 12noon-2.30pm, Sat to 3pm, Sun to 3.30pm; Dinner: Mon-Thurs 6.30pm-9pm, Fri to 9.30pm, Sat to 10pm, Sun 7pm-9pm.

Average Prices: Entree $14; Main $22.50; Dessert $9.50.

Enjoying the view from Le Kiosk of sunlight playing on the water of Shelley Cove, just around the corner from Manly's ocean beach, while holding a cool glass of white wine is one of the greatest summer pleasures to be found in or around Manly. Simple dishes, many of them seafood, create a short but broad menu. The food has a light touch, with tuna steaks accompanied by polenta, pesto and tomato relish, and pan-seared salmon served with coriander-dressed delicate lentils.

Pig and the Olive

318 Military Rd, Cremorne (✆ 9953 7512)

Lc'd & BYO. Credit: BC MC V. **Access:** Book front table.

Open: Lunch: Fri 12noon-2pm; Dinner: Mon-Sat 6pm-11pm.

See entry under **East.**

Radio Cairo

Cnr Military Rd & Spofforth St, Cremorne (✆ 9908 2649) African. Book.

BYO. Credit: AE, BC, D, MC, V. **Access:** 1 entry step.

Open: Lunch: Thurs-Fri from around 12noon; Dinner: Mon-Sat from 6pm.

Average Prices: Entree $7.50; Main $13; Dessert $10

Radio Cairo is one of the most colourful, vibrant, popular and unusual restaurants on the North Shore. Intoxicatingly beat-driven African music creates as strong an exotic feeling as the African, Sri Lankan and Caribbean food on the menu. This can range from South African marinated lamb fillets with spicy apricot dipping sauce, to Mozambique style marinated and grilled prawns, or an Africanesque creme caramel. There are no ordinary Italian coffee styles on offer here, but Abyssinian and Arabian spicy bean brews instead. Radio Cairo is frequently booked out weeks in advance for weekends, so a good idea is to head over the road to the restaurant's extension Cafe Cairo, where no bookings (or credit cards) are accepted, but the food is of equal style and quality. The problem is that the cafe is equally popular, so diners will have to arrive early to snare a table.

Rattlesnake Grill

130 Military Rd, Neutral Bay (✆ 9953 4789) SW American. Book.

Lc'd & BYO. Credit: AE BC D MC V. **Access:** 1 small entry step.

Open: Dinner: Sun-Wed 6pm-10pm, Thurs-Sat 6pm-11pm.

Average Prices: Entree $8.50; Main $15.50; Dessert $8.50

Way up north where the dried grass balls roll across the plains with the dust... Genteel Neutral Bay is home to another of the North Shore's most dynamic restaurants with an evocative name which is not disappointed by the menu or the food it contains. A Santa Fe coloured setting (washed terracotta oranges, pinks and yellows) echoes the hot and spicy, yet well balanced and controlled, flavours of the classic Mexican jalapeno chilli, nachos, quesadilla, tortillas, and traditional ingredients are revamped to form the ever-popular Rattlesnake Nachos (spicy, chilli-y chicken and capsicum smothered in cumin spiced guacamole and salsa), a dish best shared by at least two. Grills of beef, robust fish and buffalo steak may be served with spicy potato cakes, black beans and/or salsa, and desserts will usually include sugar and cinnamon sprinkled tostados, or something equally devastating smothered in a chocolate chilli sauce. The Rattlesnake also hosts a gospel music brunch on the first Sunday of every month. Spicy and colourful are the key words here.

Rimini Fish Cafe

35 South Steyne, Manly (✆ 9977 3880)

BYO Credit: AE BC D MC V. **Access:** 1 entry step.

Open: Mon-Fri 11.30am-11pm; Sat-Sun 8am-11pm.

Average Prices: Entree $9.50; Main $17.50; Dessert $6.50.

Flocks of hungry diners throng around Rimini, perhaps waiting for a taste of their flathead fillet tempura, maybe for some of the cafes many popular pastas or meats. The large menu ranges in variety and influences from Italy to China via Turkey.

Thip Thai

270 Pacific Highway, Crows Nest (✆ 9906 5735)

Lc'd & BYO. Credit: AE BC MC V. **Access:** Small entry step.

Open: Lunch: Mon-Fri 12noon-3pm; Dinner: 7 days 6pm-11pm.

Average Prices: Entree $6.50; Main $11.50; Dessert $4.

Thip Thai is a large and popular place. Intensely flavoured staples of the Thai repertoire will almost invariably include a range of delicious curried, whether red or green, meat or vegetable; fragrant stir-fries; delicate mixed entree plates of money bags, fish cakes and spring rolls; and barbecues. Specials extend the menu to embrace fresh seafood, whether traditionally served fish, or concoctions of fragrant basil, ginger, squid, prawns and vegetables.

SOUTH

Bay Tinh

318 Victoria Rd, Marrickville (✆ 9560 8673) Vietnamese. Book.

BYO. Credit: BC MC V. **Access:** Easy access to restaurant.

Open: Lunch: Mon-Fri 11am-2pm; Dinner: 7 days 6pm-10.30pm.

This unusually decorated Vietnamese restaurant is well known for its bonfires- pots of deeply marinated chicken or beef mixed with colourful vegetables and cooked in a blazing sizzle at your table. Unusual specialties are also on offer, such as snail shells stuffed with abalone, as are roll your own rice paper, anchovy and mint snacks. All this in a friendly neighbourhood restaurant where the owner is a previous chef of the South Vietnamese prime minister.

Perama

88 Audley Rd, Petersham (✆ 9569 7534) Greek. Book Fri-Sat.

Lc'd & BYO. Credit: AE BC MC V. **Access:** 1 step to restaurant & toilets.

Open:.Tues-Sat 6.30pm-10pm.

Average Prices: Entree $8.50; Main $14.50; Dessert $5.50.

Just teetering over into the south from the inner west is Petersham, where one of the surprisingly few very good Greek restaurants in the city is to be found: Perama. Perama is well known and loved for its simple and authentic food, and accordingly, its menu is full of delicious, lightened modern interpretations of traditional Greek dishes. Lamb features strongly, and may be succulently tender from a long marination in herbs, lemon and garlic and a slow grilling. The fabled desserts, ricotta cheesecake and halvas, are musts. Perama is a small, fresh, white icon of modern Greek cooking.

Tang Dynasty

127b Forest Rd, Hurstville (✆ 9580 0011) Chinese. Book.

Lc'd. Credit: AE BC MC V. **Access:** yes.

Open: Breakfast Sat-Sun 9.30am-3pm; Lunch: Mon-Fri 10.30am-3pm; Dinner: Sun-Thurs 5.30pm-10pm, Fri-Sat 5.30pm-11pm.

Average Prices: Around $19 per person.

With a chef specifically devoted to the production of delectable dim sums and an enormous kitchen churning out succulent Cantonese cuisine, this is a serious food find. Live seafood (lobsters and crabs) add to the list of traditional and authentic dishes of poultry, beef, vegetables, soups and rice. Duck specialties feature strongly, either stuffed Cantonese style, or crispy skinned Peking style, while a number of Westernised dishes feature on the menu for the less adventurous. Guests can also breakfast on congee. Tang Dynasty is a large island of Chinatown firmly anchored in of Hurstville, very popular with the Chinese and western locals.

391 Restaurant

391 Anzac Parade, Kingsford (✆ 9313 7663) Modern Australian bistro. Book.

BYO. Credit: AE BC D MC V. **Access:** 1 entry step.

Open: 7 days breakfast, lunch & dinner.

Set Price: 2 course dinner $25 .

391 is one of Sydney's best little casual neighbourhood BYO bistros. A large band of loyal devotees are kept happy by the very frequently

changing menu (usually once a week), making frequent return visits an appetising possibility. Large servings of imaginative food ranging from seafood to succulent sirloins include the ingredients of a variety of cuisines, blended together to form the phenomenon of Modern Australian food. In mid 1996, 391 is changing its opening hours to serve breakfast, lunch and dinner, staying open all day seven days a week.

EAST

The east of the city offers the most action as far as knives and forks are concerned.

Atlas Bistro & Bar

95 Riley St, East Sydney (✆ 9360 3811) Modern Bistro.

Lc'd. Credit: AE BC MC V. **Access:** Long flight of stairs to restaurant.

Open: Lunch: Fri only 12noon-2.30pm; Dinner: Tues-Sat 6.30pm-11pm.

Average Prices: Entree $7; Main $12.50; Dessert $6.50.

This boisterous bistro is one of Sydney's favourites for fantastic meats and seafoods from the grill, among the many other Mediterranean accented dishes on the menu. With a high-ceilinged, light and airy converted warehouse as its home, the bistro has a convivial feel about it, reinforced by the food. Try the filo pastries filled with olives, chicken and eggplant, the grilled lime spatchcock or one of the Atlas' amazing desserts, usually in the league of passionfruit bavarois with pear compote and lemon shortbread. Great value too.

Aviv

49 Hall St, Bondi (✆ 930 8302) Kosher. Book.

Lc'd & BYO. Credit: AE BC MC V. **Access:** Level & wide entry.

Open: Sun-Thurs 12noon-10pm; Sat sunset-11pm.

Average Prices: Entree $6; Main $15.

The emphasis of Aviv is on Middle Eastern dishes, and the Kosher menu accordingly features entrees such as a wonderful & huge dip plate of homous, tahini, baba ganouj, tabouli, eggplant and falafel, or interesting soups and goulashes. The whopping main courses from the grill may be fish, shasliks, veal or steak, and are accompanied by salad, chips and rice. Extremely generous servings and the imported Kosher wine (from $15) make this a great find.

Balkan Seafood

215 Oxford St, Darlinghurst (✆ 9331 7670)

BYO. Credit: AE BC D MC V. **Access:** Small entry step, two storeys.

Open: Tues-Thurs 6pm-11pm; Fri-Sun 6pm-Midnight

Average Prices: Depending on market prices: Entree $8.50; Main $17; Dessert $5.50.

The Balkan is a lively and colourful restaurant, where crowds gather to enjoy chargrills of octopus or fish steaks (perhaps tuna, Atlantic salmon or gemfish), or the contents of the specials board: maybe crisp, deep-fried whitebait, whole fresh-water trout, or John Dory. With a lively buzz filling the tightly packed room, the long-standing Balkan Seafood is one of the more popular of the Oxford Street restaurants, and worth investigating.

Bayswater Brasserie

32 Bayswater Rd, Kings Cross (✆ 9357 2177) Brasserie.

Lc'd. Credit: AE BC MC V. **Access:** 1 entry step, toilets up a flight of stairs.

Open: All day Mon-Sat 12noon-11.15pm; Sun 10am-10.15pm. Leafy courtyard & conservatory.

Average Prices: Entree $8.50; Main $17.50; Dessert $6.

As the brasserie which launched many imitators and one of Sydney's favourite eateries, the Bayswater has a special place in Sydney's culinary heart. It is consistently favoured for its prime people watching front conservatory, its roomy and suave atmosphere of palms and mirrors, friendly and professional service and exquisite food. The menu changes frequently, but will always contain the Bayswater classics of warm olive-filled bread and Thai style chicken curry; fresh seafood, whether it be shucked oysters or a perfectly grilled tuna steak; premium meats, whether Illabo lamb or sirloin; and traditional brasserie fare, whether sausages or pan-fried calves' livers, yet the waiters are unfazed if guests order only side of chips and/or a dessert. Magazines abound for day time coffee sippers, and a bar at the rear overlooking the courtyard offers smooth cocktails, wines and beers under subdued lighting. The Bayswater is a highly respected Sydney food icon.

Bill's

433 Liverpool St, Darlinghurst (✆ 9360 9631) Modern Australian cafe.

BYO. No Credit. **Access:** 1 step, small interior.

Open: Mon-Sat 7.30am-4pm; Closed evenings.

Average Prices: Breakfast $4.50; Entree $6.50; Main $9; Dessert $4.

Bill's is a beguiling place. The bright, white, sunny and an airy interior is as startlingly beautiful as it is comfortable, the flowers and customers adding their own colours and shapes to the neutrally elegant backdrop. The layout is unconventional, with traditional small tables surrounding one large common table in the centre, strewn with magazines and plates of food, where the snippets of conversation passively gleaned are fascinating. Guests could spend all day trying to choose from the wide ranging and long menu, part of the reason why Bill's is one of the city's favourite breakfast spots. Morning fare may include healthy coconut bread, cereals, yoghurts and fresh honeys, while the lunch menu is made up of a large number of sandwiches, frittatas and spicy noodles, perhaps with steamed bok choy and chicken.

Bistro Moncur

116 Queen St, Woollahra (Woollahra Hotel) (✆ 9363 2782) Modern bistro.

Credit: AE BC MC V. **Access:** Steps to restaurant.

EAT YOUR WAY ALONG THE STREET

There are certain streets in Sydney which are synonymous with eating. Go for it!

Bourke Street & Crown Street, Darlinghurst
Bourke Street and Crown Street are two of eastern Sydney's most popular streets for grazing. Here you will find Cafe Niki, Cosmos, Elephant's Foot, La Passion du Fruit, Mohr Fish, Rustic Cafe, Riberries and Yipiyiyo.

Glebe Point Road, Glebe
Glebe Point Road is very long and full of cafes and restaurants. Some of the better ones are Blackwattle Canteen, Cafe Troppo, Darling Mills, Kafenio, Le Chocoreve and Rose Blues.

Bayswater Road & Macleay Street
These two streets in Kings Cross and Potts Point are paved with some of Sydney's best and most popular restaurants. Among them are the Bayswater Brasserie, Darley Street Thai, Macleay Street Bistro, Mesclun Brasserie, Paramount, and the informal Pig and the Olive.

Dixon Street, City
Dixon Street is the focus of Sydney's Chinatown. Here are found numerous barbecue take aways, enormous restaurants serving yum cha, and supermarkets selling a fascinating array of exotic produce.

Norton Street, Leichhardt
Norton Street is the Italian centre of Sydney, the most concentrated expression of the community's food culture to be found in the city. Lining each side (and nearby Marion Street) is a string of popular cafes, such as the popular icon, Bar Italia; restaurants such as Castel Mola and Frattini; gelato shops and specialist food suppliers, such as the Norton Street Market, Amato's bottle shop, and the Buon Appetito pasta shop.

Oxford Street, Darlinghurst & Paddington
As well as a shopping Mecca, Oxford Street is packed with eateries. In the short stretch between Taylor Square and the Verona cinema alone, more than cafe 191, Perusco, The Balkan, several Thai and Indian restaurants and Verona's own cafe are awaiting exploration.

Victoria Street and Darlinghurst Road, Darlinghurst
Here is the city's most concentrated stretch of cafes and restaurants. Among them are Bar Coluzzi, Bill's, Fez, Fish Face, Fu-Manchu, La Bussola, Lauries and Tabac.

Willoughby Road, Willoughby
This is the North Shore's primary 'eat street', with many more restaurants and cafes than Thip Thai, Eric's Fish Cafe, Pasta Pronto, Fare Nosh, Sapporo, and Red Centre lining both sides and the surrounding streets.

Open: Breakfast: Sun 9am-12noon; Lunch: Tues-Sun 12noon-3pm; Dinner: Tues-Sun 6pm-10.30pm; Closed Mon.
Average Prices: Entree $10; Main $18; Dessert $8.
Entering by the Moncur Street stairs, guests immediately notice the airy space of the restaurant and its strikingly beautiful black and white mural spread down one side and mirrored in the opposite wall. A close second come the inane grins on the faces of the tables' occupants. This is a fantastic restaurant, with an impeccable menu whose exquisitely executed dishes skilfully blend French influences with Australian style and ingredients. While the bistro's classic dish is Victorian Sirloin with Cafe de Paris butter and fries, you will also find classic soups, Lyonnais sausages and charcuterie as good as they come. Desserts are hard to pass up. Bistro Moncur is a Sydney Institution not to be missed, and accordingly, diners should arrive early for a table or be prepared to wait in the suave pub next door.

Buon Ricordo

108 Boundary St, Paddington (✆ 9360 6729) Italian. Book.
Lc'd. Credit: AE BC MC V. **Access:** 1 small entry step, 3 steps to restaurant.
Open: Lunch: Fri & Sat 12noon-2.30pm; Dinner: Tues-Sat 6.30pm-11pm.
Average Prices: Entree $11.50; Main $22; Dessert $9.
This restaurant is frequently referred to as one of Sydney's best, and while the prices may reflect this, dining in these surroundings on this kind of food makes a little extra expense worthwhile. Here patrons will find top produce and refined cooking skills blended into a smooth mix of the classic and inventive, passionately presented in a proper dining room. Famed entrees include artichoke hearts dripping with wine-dark olive sauce or some hand made pasta, while exquisite mains such as lush Illabo lamb lead on to amazing desserts. See if Cioccolato Darenzo is on the menu: almost liquid chocolate in a delicate pastry shell dusted with ground coffee. This is one of the finest Italian gastronomic experiences on offer in Sydney, destined to leave guests with very happy memories.

Cafe Crown

355 Crown St, Surry Hills (✆ 9331 2154) Cafe.
BYO. No Credit. **Access:** 1 little step, spacious interior.
Open: 7 days 7am-11pm.
Average Prices: Cold dish $8.50; Hot dish $12.50; Dessert $4.50.
Set in smooth stainless steel with a window-clad outlook and staffed with friendly people, Cafe Crown offers a winning formula: suave surroundings, cheap yet luscious food, and a central location. Breakfast here is bound to give patrons a kick start, with a healthy menu built around home made muesli, wood fired toast and jams, eggs and fruit. Items on the long and frequently rotating menu may impose a number of culinary influences on anything from roast chicken

to whole baked trout, spicy sausages or seafood. Why move at all, when it is possible to sit in this bustling inner city cafe watching the fascinating world of Surry Hills pass by all day?

Catalina

1 Sunderland Ave, Rose Bay (✆ 9371 0555) Modern Australian.

Lc'd. Credit: AE BC D MC V. **Access:** With staff assistance.

Open: 7 days 12noon-11pm.

Average Prices: Small dish $15; Large dish $24; Dessert $10.

Catalina is an inspiring place to sit and contemplate the joys of Sydney eating: ensconced under a crescent moon-shaped awning reaching out into the Harbour's Rose Bay, the spectacular menu beckons. Creations such as smoked salmon with white bean puree, corn and polenta crackers and salmon roe, or a simple fish and chips may appeal to those looking for seafood, while delicate steaks served with pickled onion and potato salad, or roast herbed spatchcock with splitpea tabouli and roasted corn may satisfy meaty appetites. (A good number of items on the menu are available in small and large servings.) Desserts as smooth as the setting range from twenty-four carat gold jelly with mascarpone and muscatel biscotti to a chocolate candied orange mousse cake with mocha gelato. Catalina represents a perfect complement of food and setting, offering a dining experience which is the very essence of Sydney.

Cicada

29 Challis St, Potts Point (✆ 9358 1255) Modern Australian/Mediterranean & French . Book.

Lc'd. Credit: AE BC D MC V. **Access:** very difficult via the stairs or the kitchen.

Open: Lunch: Wed-Fri 12noon-2.30pm; Dinner: Mon-Sat from 6.30pm.

Average Prices: Entree $13; Main $20; Dessert $10.

Named for the exuberantly noisy winged insects whose droning ostinato fills the Sydney skies and trees each summer, Cicada's acclaimed seasonal menus waft between Eastern, Middle Eastern, Mediterranean and French influences in the form of elegant, simple food. Won tons filled with spinach and ricotta float in a clear consomme; Autumn may see exquisitely light flaky pastry rising above the satisfying, earthily garlicky mushrooms beneath; Summer could see tiger prawns, snow peas and preserved Moroccan lemon gracing a John Dory. Desserts such as pear ensconced in a rich, vanilla creme anglaise, or a souffle drizzled in citrus sorbet and cream, beckon persuasively. The open, vine-twisted front verandah of this high ceilinged, warmly sleek and gracious terrace is always in high demand.

Claude's

10 Oxford St, Paddington (✆ 9331 2325) French. Book.

BYO. Credit: AE BC MC V. **Access:** 1 entry step.

Open: Tues-Sat 7.30pm-Midnight. No smoking until 10.30pm.

Average Prices: Set price 4 courses $90.

The highly glossed black front door gives an inkling of what lies behind: solid, homely and highly polished, guests can expect a gastronomic trip of fantastic proportions and style at this, one of Sydney's most exquisite, serene, intimate and established restaurants. The chef at the heart of the experience is Tim Pak Poy, and it is his attention to detail and devotion to the art of food which make this dining room one of the most legendary in the city. Past creations have included delicate oyster broth topped with a fine layer of cream and wafer thin chives; velvety breast of pigeon accompanied by glazed mushrooms and currents; salt-baked farm chicken with potato gratin; and the celestial moulded almond milk jelly quivering in rose water.

Cosmos

185 Bourke St, East Sydney (just off William St) (✆ 9331 5306) Modern Greek. Book.

BYO. Credit: Amex, D. **Access:** 1 entrance step, small interior.

Open: Brunch: Sun 11am-3pm; Lunch: Fri 12noon-3pm; Dinner: Tues-Sat 6.30pm-11pm. No smoking before 10pm.

Average Prices: Dinner: 2 courses $23.50; Desserts $8.50.

Cosmos has been credited with introducing Sydney to real, live, modern Greek food, and this, coupled with the colourful Mediterranean atmosphere of the place, keep loyal dependants coming back. Brunches here are amazing- where else would sheep's milk yoghurt with honey and candied walnuts, or a cornmeal cake with orange and raisins be at the centre of the menu? For dinner, try roasted tomato and octopus on grilled olive bread, or maybe the rabbit and black olive pie, or lamb, or moussaka. You could then move on to frozen chocolate and orange tourta with orange blossom syrup.

Costi's Fish Cafe

355 Crown St, Surry Hills (✆ 9380 6044) Seafood.

BYO. Credit: AE BC MC V. **Access:** Level entry, spacious.

Open: 7 days 11am-10pm.

Average Prices: Entree $8; Main $12.50; Dessert $5.

A little more accessible and edible than the raw produce at Costi's fish markets outlet (See: Markets), the fish cafe offers all sorts of juicy fish and seafood in a friendly and bright environment. Tasmanian salmon, barramundi and tuna will usually be on the menu, along with a fish basket of calamari, prawns, flathead and chips. Yum. The superbly fresh fish is prepared according to the chef's daily whim, perhaps cased in a herby crust and served with a fresh tomato salsa and chargrilled vegetables.

Darley St Thai

30A Bayswater Rd, Kings Cross (✆ 9358 6530) Thai.

Book.

Lc'd. Credit: AE BC D MC V. **Access:** 3 entry steps, access to toilets.

Open: Lunch: Tues-Sun 12noon-2.30pm; Dinner: 7 days 6.30pm-11pm.

Average Prices: Entree $15; Main $25; Dessert $9.50.

Some of the most authentic and exquisite Thai food in Sydney is to be found here in this stunning, intensely coloured, box-like restaurant. The brilliant colours of the silks, flowers and strategic lighting echo the intense flavours of the renowned food: a taste of the prawns with chilli jam, lime juice, betel leaves and pork rind in omelette wrapping will explain the phenomenon. Incredible desserts, such as coconut and saffron dumplings, confirm it, and also explain the incredible popularity and fame of the establishment.

Dov

Cnr Forbes St & Burton St, East Sydney (✆ 9360 9594) Mediterranean & Mid European cafe.

BYO. No credit. **Access:** 1 tall step and a narrow door.

Open: Mon-Sat 7am-10pm; Closed Sun.

Average Prices: Entree $8; Main $11.

This extremely popular cafe is the home of a truly great onion tart and a magnificently mountainous mixed plate. Mains may cover crumbed chicken, goulash or fish of the day; breakfasts are suitably low key; and the coffee is good and strong. Its position over the road from the college of the arts ensures an interesting crowd, and the sandstone blocks of the walls create a cool established feeling, juxtaposing the modern stainless steel and complementing the pale wood of the interior.

Doyles on the Beach

11 Marine Parade, Watsons Bay (✆ 9337 2007) Seafood.

Lc'd. Credit: BC, D, MC, V. **Access:** Level entry and toilet access.

Open: Lunch: 7 days 12noon-3pm; Dinner: 7 days 6pm-9.30pm.

Average Prices: Entree $11; Main $22; Dessert $8.

It is definitely possible to obtain equally good seafood in this city without the hype of Doyles, but no other seafood restaurant has the position or the international fame. Doyles is where every family takes their visitors for an outdoors lunch or summer dinner of seafood platters "bigger than Ben Hur" (for two from $62), grilled fish or even fish and chips. Perched right on the edge of the Harbour behind a charming beach, Doyles is a fine place to enjoy an open air lunch. One way to guarantee waterfront Doyles dining is to opt for the inexpensive fish and chips and seafood from the Doyles wharf outlet (forty metres to the left) and eat it on the beach!

Edosei

22 Rockwell St, Potts Point (✆ 9357 3407) Japanese. Book.

Lc'd. Credit: AE BC MC V. **Access:** 1 entry step.

Open: Dinner: 7 days 6pm-10pm.

Average Prices: Entree $10; Main $22; Dessert $5.

Edosei is said to serve the freshest sushi in Sydney, famous not only for its beautiful presentation, but also for its freshness and intensity of flavour. The menu also includes appetisers such as smoked roe, as well as rice dishes, grills, and tempura, while fixed price menus offer good value.

Fez

247 Victoria St, Darlinghurst (✆ 9360 9581) N. African Mediterranean cafe.

Lc'd & BYO. No Credit. **Access:** 1 small step.

Open: 7 days 7am-10.30pm.

Average Prices: all dishes from $5.50 to $12.

A favourite resident in the Victoria Street golden triangle of food, Fez is a colourful and welcoming place which serves excellent food all day, dipped in the delicious dye of a strong north African Mediterranean influence. Breakfast may consist of a big bowl of couscous dripping with poached fruit, yoghurt and honey, or a few thick slices of gratifying toast. Feta and tomato omelettes are served with Turkish spicy sausage and capsicum; a mixed plate towers with homous, tabouli, falafel, olives, feta, lentil and eggplant; fragrant lamb is accompanied by vegetable couscous. This is a sunny place, filled with the colours and textures of the decor, the clientele and the passing scene combined.

Fishface

132 Darlinghurst Rd, Darlinghurst (✆ 9332 4803) Seafood.

BYO. No Credit. **Access:** 1 small step, high tables, narrow interior.

Open: Breakfast: Sat-Sun from 8.30am; Lunch: Tues-Sat 11.30am-3pm; Dinner: Mon-Sat 6.30pm-11pm.

Average Prices: Entree $8; Main $11.50; Dessert $6.

The day's fresh catches are cooked with flair in this tiny and much loved seafood restaurant. Here, guests can feast on mussels with white wine, shallots and garlic; deep fried calamari on a green leaf salad with roasted capsicum; or any of a wide range of imaginatively prepared fish. Weekend breakfasts will usually include such indulgences as fresh bagels loaded with smoked salmon, or pan-fired fish fillets. This is a suave place, small but light and airy, extremely popular, and worth queuing for or arriving early.

Flavour of India

120-128 New South Head Rd, Edgecliff (✆ 9326 2659) Indian. Book.

Lc'd & BYO. Credit: AE BC MC V. **Access:** Small entry ridge.

Open: 7 days 6pm-10.30pm.

Average Prices: Entree $7.50; Main $14; Dessert $6.

This fabled Indian restaurant offers reasonably priced and prize winningly good Indian food. Fine tandoors of marinated lamb or chicken with yoghurt and cashew puree feature strongly in the menu, as do more adventurous tandoors of fish marinated in lemon, ginger, garlic and spices. Spicy curries may be cooked with garam masala, fenugreek, tomatoes, red pepper and dhal. A banquet menu is also on offer.

Fu-Manchu

249 Victoria St, Darlinghurst (✆ 9360 9424) Pan-Asian noodlery.

BYO. No Credit. No smoking. **Access:** Small step, fixed stool seating.

Open: Mon-Sat 12noon-10pm; Sun from 5pm.

It's all red leather stools and stainless steel in this narrow eatery, matching the vaguely eccentric idea of the place. Purely devoted to noodles, Fu-Manchu has established itself as a great place to get great and inexpensive food fast. With over twenty noodle dishes on the menu, and for a bit of variety some steamed buns and fried tofu, Fu-Manchu is a fantastic spectacle for the eyes and taste buds.

Gastronomia Chianti

444 Elizabeth St, Surry Hills (✆ 9319 4748) Italian.

Lc'd. Credit: AE BC MC V. **Access:** 1 small step.

Open: Mon-Thurs 10.30am-5pm; Fri-Sat 10.30am-10.30pm.

Average Prices: Entree $9.50; Main $14; Dessert $7.

The beaming refrigerated counter lining the side of Gastronomia Chianti is a magnet for the eyes and imagination. Packed with deli goods, it holds the key ingredients of the food served here. Feast on antipasto plates or mushroom risotto, herb grilled chicken, or maybe a selection of pastas. Desserts are enough to make you weep, with delicate pancakes resting on layers of ground nuts, cream or rum a regular favourite. Wow. A stylish yet relaxed restaurant, with excellent Italian food and inspiring desserts.

Golden Dog

388 Oxford St, Paddington (✆ 9360 7700) Mediterranean influenced cafe.

Lc'd. No Credit. **Access:** 1 entrance step; narrow .

Open: Mon-Fri 8am-11pm; Sat 7.30am-11pm; Sun 9am-11pm.

Average Prices: Entree $9; Main $12; Dessert $6.50.

Golden Dog is a suave and extremely popular place, where the dark wood of the tables and chairs picks up the rich tones of the massive old advertising posters on the walls, and contrasts with the stainless steel bar. Golden Dog is bound to grab the attention with gourmet pizzas, pastas, steaks and risottos. It is also a popular venue for a simple coffee or a milkshake, although guests must be prepared to fight for a table on Saturdays, as the cafe is directly opposite the Paddington Bazaar, and a seat here is hot property in the people-watching stakes. The noise from Oxford Street can be a problem at the front.

Gourmet Pizza Kitchen

80 Campbell Parade, Bondi Beach (✆ 9365 7177)

Lc'd & BYO. Credit: AE BC MC V. **Access:** 4 entry steps.

Open: Sun-Thurs 12noon-11pm; Fri-Sat 12noon-Midnight.

Also at: 60 Archer St, Chatswood (✆ 9411 8000)

Open: Mon-Fri 11.30am-10.30pm; Sat-Sun 12noon-11pm.

Lc'd & BYO. Credit: AE BC MC V. **Access:** Ramp to level entry.

Also at: 199-201 Military Rd, Neutral Bay (✆ 9953 9000)

Lc'd & BYO. Credit: AE BC MC V. **Access:** Level entry.

Open: Sun-Thurs 12noon-11pm; Fri-Sat 12noon-Midnight.

Average Prices for all three: Main $11.90; Dessert $6.90.

The originators of the gourmet pizza topping serve delicious Jamaican (spicy chicken, snowpeas and roasted tomato), Nova Scotia (caviar, smoked salmon, creme fraiche, red onions, chilli, capers and spices) and even tandoori pizzas, as well as pizza crusts brushed with herbs, garlic or pesto, and, would you believe it, dessert pizzas such as cinnamon apple crumble with ice cream. Be prepared for a packed and noisy eating venue when coming to any of the GPK empire's pizzerias.

La Bussola

324 Victoria St, Darlinghurst (✆ 9331 4287)

BYO. Credit: none. **Access:** 1 entry step, small interior, pavement seating.

Open: Lunch: Mon-Fri; Dinner: 7 days from around 6pm.

Average Prices: Pizza $10; Pasta $7.50.

For those seeking authentically thin-crusted, yet inexpensive, Italian pizza, La Bussola is hard to beat. $10 is enough to see a generously proportioned medium, steaming, tasty pizza arrive at your table, perhaps with a hot 'diavolo' topping, or perhaps with the delicious vegetarian concoction of spinach, tomato, garlic, parmesan and herbs. Pastas are also on hand for only $7.50. La Bussola is an extremely popular place, and it is easy to see why.

La Passion du Fruit

633 Bourke St (cnr Devonshire St), Surry Hills (✆ 9690 1894) Cafe.

BYO. No Credit. **Access:** 2 steps to very small interior; pavement tables.

Open: Tues-Sat 8am-10.30pm; Sun 11am-4pm.

Average Prices: nothing over $11.

The colourful and warm interior filled with people, magazines and flowers is not the only attractive aspect of this gem of a place. Fruit concoctions to drink, fresh ingredients in the main dishes whether as onion tart or some baked vine leaves filled with mushrooms, roasted garlic and tomatoes served with freshly baked bread, while desserts such as pear and polenta cake ensure a loyal and well nourished following.

Lauries

Cnr Victoria St ✆ Burton St, Darlinghurst (✆ 9360

4915) Vegetarian.
BYO. Credit: AE BC MC V. **Access:** 1 entrance step.
Open: 7 days 12noon-11pm.
Average Prices: Entree $5.50; Main $8.50; Dessert $3.50.
Vegetarians and vegans will delight in Lauries' wide ranging and regularly changing menu. On offer in this relaxing and suave corner restaurant may be found any number of Indonesian, Jamaican, Japanese or Anglo-Saxon styled dishes. Stuffed mushrooms, sweet potato, mushroom and cashew bakes, spicy vegetable hotpots and stir-fries regularly feature on the frequently changing menu, while desserts may include crumbles, puddings and slices. The only problem with Lauries is the difficulty in choosing what to eat, as almost everything on the menu sounds delicious.

Macleay Street Bistro

73a Macleay St, Potts Point (✆ 9358 4891) Modern Australian.
BYO. Credit: AE BC MC V. **Access:** 1 entry step.
Open: Lunch: Tues-Sun 12noon-3pm; Dinner: Tues-Sun 6pm-11pm.
Average Prices: Entree $10; Main $18; Dessert $8.
Here live good, honest, inventive and delicious chargrills, roasts, pastas and salads. Mussels may be drizzled in white wine, lemon and herb sauce; pan-fried ocean trout may be tinged with a hint of chilli and resting on a bed of lightly steamed bok choy, while bread and butter pudding and bowls of deliciously chunky chips are two staples which consistently attract loyal followers to this small, lively and comfortable restaurant on one of the city's best food streets. While the restaurant's capacity is increased by pavement tables, intending diners should arrive early or be prepared to wait.

Mario's Restaurant

38 Yurong St, East Sydney (✆ 9331 4945) Italian. Book.
Lc'd. Credit: All cards. **Access:** 4 steps, staff will assist.
Open: Lunch: Mon-Fri 12noon-3pm; Dinner: Mon-Sat 6pm-11pm.
Average Prices: Entree $12; Main $18; Dessert $8.
As smooth, slick and cool as gelato, Mario's is full of slickly clad diners enjoying the converted warehouse space which has become one of the city's hippest restaurants. Exquisite, home-made sauces slide over the fresh pasta, excellent veal and poultry dishes dominate the menu on some nights while others are reserved for seafood. With desserts in the realm of tiramisu, zabaglione and chocolate mousse, Mario's offers a stylish dining experience.

Mesclun Brasserie

1st floor The Crescent, 33 Bayswater Rd, Kings Cross (✆ 9358 5582) Book.
Lc'd. Credit: AE BC D MC V. **Access:** Lift to first floor from car park below, level entrance.
Open: Mon-Thurs 6.30am-Midnight; Fri-Sat 6.30am-1am; Sun 6.30am-11pm.
Average Prices: Entree $8.50; Main $16.50; Dessert $7.50. 2 hours free parking underneath.
Mesclun feels more like a dining room than a restaurant: warm polished wooden floors and walls, pictures on the walls, and a glow of satisfied faces contribute to the feeling. Generous portions of classic brasserie dishes may include Lyonnaise sausage with beans, spinach and apple relish; veal tenderloin with crisp pancetta and sweet potato cake; juicy sirloin, and creme brulee with cumquats and lime. Mesclun is a popular yet relaxed up-market restaurant complemented by smooth service.

Metro

26 Burton St, Darlinghurst (✆ 9361 5356) Vegetarian restaurant & take-away.
BYO. No credit. **Access:** entry step and booth seating. No smoking.
Open: Wed-Fri 6pm-Midnight; Sun 6pm-11pm.
Average Prices: Entree $4; Main $6; Dessert $3.
Intending diners must arrive early or be prepared to queue at this extremely popular vegie haven. A weekly changing blackboard menu features enormous serves of laksa, Japanese tofu kebabs with vegetable and cucumber pickles, or maybe mains such as chilli cheese cornmeal turnovers with avocado and tomato salad. Desserts could be a crumble, a lime meringue tart, sago plum pudding, or maybe the excellent quince ricotta cake with toffee sauce. Very good vegetarian food at remarkably low cost!

Mohr Fish

202 Devonshire St, Surry Hills (✆ 9318 1326) Seafood bar & take-away.
BYO. No Credit. **Access:** Several entry steps, narrow interior & high tables.
Open: Mon-Fri 7am-10pm; Sat-Sun 9am-10pm.
Average Prices: Breakfast $6.50; Main $10.50; Dessert $4.50.
Breakfast on scrambled eggs mixed with smoked trout; move on to a lunch or dinner of mackerel with balsamic vinegary olives and chips, or maybe exquisite grilled salmon or poached reef cod, or perhaps octopus, mussels, squid or oysters, and then roll on to dessert of cherry or mud cake. Conveniently located near the Belvoir Street Theatre, Mohr Fish is even more packed than usual pre-performance time, and deservedly so. This is the spot to go to for extremely fresh and tasty seafood in a convivial environment where the laughter bounces off the old butcher's shop tiles.

Moran's

Cnr Macleay St & Challis Ave, Potts Point (✆ 9356 2223) Modern Australian. Book.
Credit: AE BC D MC V. **Access:** Level entry. Smoking at the bar only.
Open: Brunch: Sat-Sun 11.30am-3pm; Lunch: Wed-Fri 12noon-3pm; Dinner: Mon-Sat 6.30pm-11pm,

Sun 6.30pm-10pm. (Cafe next door open 7 days 8am-Midnight.)
Average Prices: Entree $11; Main $18.50; Dessert $9.
A discreet exterior broken by full height etched windows gives way to polished floors, central pillars and Prussian blue seats to create a light and airy yet cosy restaurant. There is a comfortable feel to Moran's, enhanced by the background buzz of animated voices. Mains could include beautifully tender suckling lamb on a bed of chopped vegetable ratatouille and fresh spinach, or corn fed chicken with pistachio stuffing. Seafood specials may be whole John Dory or other succulent fish, and the desserts are simply irresistible, always in the league of chocolate semi freddo with praline ice cream and toffee wedge. The wine list features some great local wines at reasonable restaurant prices, while wines by the glass can average $5 for white and up to $7.50 for a local red.

Nielsen Park Kiosk

Greycliffe Avenue, Vaucluse (✆ 9337 1574)
BYO. Credit: AE BC MC V. **Access:** Awkward, but possible with staff assistance.
Open: Brunch: Sat-Sun 8.30am-11am; Lunch: Tues-Sun 12noon-4pm; Closed evenings.
Average Prices: Entree $12; Main $19.50; Dessert $
A raised floor in this gorgeous beach kiosk (c. 1915) offer guests marvellous harbour views across Shark Beach, although the very fine Italian food on the plates inside is a fair distraction. Entrees could include Caponata Sicula (Sicilian salad of eggplants, onion, tomatoes, roasted pine nuts and slices of oiled bruschetta) or cured prawns in pomegranate vinegar, marinated on olive oil, scattered with slivers of radicchio and garlic flakes. Mains may be a feast of seafood (mussels, pipis, squid, yabbies, red rock cod, barbounia and ocean perch) served in a deep bowl, or a veal roulade thinly sliced, and enclosing a soft filling of ricotta, spinach and pancetta, garlanded with baked cannellini beans and scented with sage. Wow! Brunches (fixed price: adults $19.50, children $10.50) here are a languorous affair of pastries, fresh toasts, fruits, juices, sausages and omelettes from the buffet. The Nielsen Park Kiosk is a gem.

Niki

Bourke St, Surry Hills (✆ 9319 7517) Greek influenced cafe.
BYO. No credit. **Access:** 1 small step.
Open: 7 days 7am-10pm.
Average Prices: Entree: $4; Main $10; Dessert $3.50.
The food at Niki is proudly Mediterranean with a strong Greek slant, and the day time fare ranges from magnificent fruit whips to massive, towering focaccias and traditional soups. Additional night time specials may include field mushrooms seared and filled with garlic, smoked chicken and mustard seed tagliatelle in a white wine sauce or grilled snapper served with salad, potato and a roast tomato salsa. With home baked pastries and desserts, friendly staff, the comfortable (if slightly run down) atmosphere of the old corner terrace building, big windows and a central exposed kitchen, Niki is a gem. (See: Cafes.)

Noodle King

New South Head Rd, Double Bay (✆ 9328 1894)
BYO. No Credit. **Access:** 1 entry step.
Also at: 126 Campbell Parade, Bondi Beach (✆ 930 8822)
Credit: No Credit. **Access:** Level but narrow.
Both **Open:** 7 days 11.30am-10.30pm.
Average Prices: $6.50; nothing over $10.80.
This is the place for noodle-heads: generously large bowls of fresh pan-Asian soups, noodles and meat dishes fill the good value menu. Stretching between Chinese, Thai or Malaysian cuisines, the menu comprises dishes such as fishcake soup, Satay prawn soup, crispy fried noodles with shallots, ginger, seafood and chicken mixed in, and Thai fish curry all competing for attention. Peeking over the wall of the kitchen, diners will discover a rapid production line of wok filling, cooking and cleaning. With its polished wooden floors, light, fresh, modern interior, Noodle King is an extremely popular restaurant, and with the Double Bay cinema over the road, a pre- or post-movie favourite for dining in or take away.

Oh! Calcutta!

251 Victoria St, Darlinghurst (✆ 9360 3650) Indian. Book.
BYO. Credit: AE BC MC V. **Access:** Several entrance steps, narrow door.
Open: Lunch: Fri 12noon-4pm; Dinner: Sun-Thurs 6pm-10.30pm.
Average Prices: Entree $6.50; Main $13; Dessert $5.
Not content to restrict themselves to one particular type of food or menu, Oh! Calcutta! offers a long list of specials spanning the traditional foods of India, Afghanistan and Pakistan. As well as the usual popular dishes, this restaurant has a great Tandoor and is not afraid to experiment, a happy coincidence which produces such items as kangaroo stir fried with sesame seeds, chilli, garlic and lemon, or stir fried crab, or even southern Indian prawn curry with coconut and ginger. Yum.

Onzain

2nd floor, Bondi Diggers' Club, 232 Campbell Parade, Bondi Beach (✆ 9365 0763) Modern Australian.
Lc'd. Credit: AE BC MC V. **Access:** Lift from Campbell Parade entry.
Open: Lunch: Fri-Sat 12noon-3pm, Sun 12.30pm-6pm; Dinner: Mon-Sat 6pm-10.30pm, Sun 6pm-9.30pm.
Average Prices: Entree $8; Main $17.50; Dessert $7.50.
In this large, open dining room overlooking the waves and sand of the city's most famous beach through its

full height wall of windows, guests are treated to suave yet unpretentious and laid back food. Intensely flavoured roasted spatchcock with authentic potato galette, pale pink salmon boudin, grilled sirloin, duck and exquisite fish specials are likely to grace the menu.

Paramount

73 Macleay St, Potts Point (✆ 9358 1652) Modern Australian. Book.

Lc'd. Credit: AE BC MC V. **Access:** two entrance steps, then level.

Open: Lunch: 7 days 12noon-3pm; Dinner: 7 days 6.30pm-11pm.

Average Prices: Entrees $13; Main $19; Dessert $12.

One of the superstars of the Sydney restaurant scene, Chris Mansfield, is behind Paramount's superior food, managing to blend discretely the influences of various cuisines into a flawless melange. Try the oysters stir fried with bok choy, seaweed noodles and coriander pesto, the goats cheese tart, five spice duck and shitake mushroom pie with ginger glaze or a kangaroo steak and finish with an amazing dessert to see what the fuss is about. Add to this the striking style of a pale and sleek fibreglass interior, with a perfect, large, rectangular revolving door, and here is a momentous dining experience. It is widely accepted that the food here justifies the restaurant's name.

The Pier

594 New South Head Rd, Rose Bay (✆ 9327 6561) Modern Australian Seafood.

Lc'd. Credit: AE BC D MC V. **Access:** Level to restaurant, no access to toilets.

Open: Lunch: 7 days 12noon-3pm; Dinner: Mon-Sat 6pm-10pm, Sun 6pm-9pm.

Average Prices: Entree $16.50; Main $26.50; Dessert $11. (Surcharge: Sun $3.)

The Pier is one of the city's fabled restaurants, offering exquisite seafood in a stunning, airy waterside location on Rose Bay. Entrees could range from freshly shucked oysters, to a warm salad of South Australian squid, green beans, chilli and mizuna leaves, or, topping the list, the fabled freshly baked crab tart topped with caviar. Main courses continue the modern Australian eating experience with flair. Char grilled tuna steaks could be served with roasted egg tomatoes, green beans and chilli oil; grilled whole baby schnapper will arrive at the table glazed with soy and honey and accompanied by a watercress salad, while Yamba king prawns could be gently poached in a green curry and served with jasmine rice. More than suitable desserts are likely to include a delicate berry millefeuille drizzling with cointreau, or a simple creme brulee. Yum.

Pig and the Olive

71a Macleay St, Potts Point (✆ 9357 3745)

Lc'd & BYO. Credit: AE BC MC V. **Access:** 3 steps.

Open: Dinner: Mon-Sat 6pm-11pm; Sun 6pm-10pm.

Average Prices: Small $11.50; Medium $14.50; Large $17.50; Dessert $8.

Also at: Cremorne (see listing under North for details).

At last count the home of thirteen different eclectic gourmet pizzas, such as marinated lamb with fetta, harissa and fried onions or perhaps salami, goats cheese and artichokes, The Pig and the Olive generally sticks to the Mediterranean for inspiration. The menu also boasts excellent tapenade crostini and antipasto, mains such as great risotto and flavoursome meats, while desserts, such as steamed chocolate pudding with a white chocolate and praline sauce, or semolina and coconut cake with poached pears, are toothsome. This is a warm, colourful, noisy and extremely popular eatery, always packed with lively customers being served by efficient yet friendly staff swarming around the exposed kitchen.

Ravesi's

Cnr Campbell Parade & Hall St, Bondi Beach (✆ 9365 4422) Modern Australian.

Lc'd. Credit: AE BC D MC V. **Access:** Level entry, lift to first floor restaurant.

Open: 7 days 7.30am-11.30pm.

Average Prices: Entree $10; Main $18; Dessert $9.

With open balconies looking directly out over Bondi Beach and beyond to the placid, blue Tasman Sea, Ravesi's is a very popular place all day every day for a drink or meal with a view. Brunches are a suitably low key affair, with waiters donning sunglasses to cut the steady stream of sunlight pouring in from the sand beyond Campbell Parade. A traditional cooked breakfast or a more adventurous creamy polenta with spicy beans may provide the fuel to attempt a cross-bay swim before coming back for juicy fish and chips or char-grilled steak with aioli and English spinach. After a jog to Tamarama and Bronte beaches and back, dinner may seem an attractive prospect, and with the likes of seared John Dory with steamed Asian vegetables and lime butter on the menu, why not?

Riberries

411 Bourke St, Darlinghurst (✆ 9361 4929) Native produce, contemporary style. Book.

BYO. Credit: AE BC D MC V. **Access:** 2 entry steps.

Open: Lunch: Thurs-Fri 12noon-2pm; Dinner: Mon-Sat 6.30pm-10pm.

Fixed price menus: 2 courses $32; 3 courses $38 per person.

A chance to go on a wonderful armchair culinary tour of Australia via the tastebuds is Riberries, located in a suave sandstone terrace with the feel of a comfortable, private dining room far removed from the noise of Taylor Square outside. Riberries combines native produce and uniquely Australian ingredients to great effect, creating dishes such as kangaroo with Tasmanian alpine pepperberry sauce, the chocolate/coffee tasting wattleseed pavlova, or quandong and quince tart for dessert. Yum. The choice of ingredients is a serious devotion, far from a gimmick.

Rustic Cafe

Cnr Crown St & Devonshire St, Surry Hills (✆ 9318 1034) Mediterranean.

Lc'd & BYO. Credit: BC MC V. **Access:** 1 small entry step, wide doors.

Open: Tues-Sun 8am-11pm; Sun 9am-9pm; Closed Mon.

Average Prices: Entree $6.50; Main $11; Dessert $5.

In this unmissably bright yellow building are to be had generous servings of excellent Mediterranean food. The frequently changing menu ranges from entrees of stuffed mushrooms and grilled octopus, or a pasta; mains may include lamb souvlaki, chicken or seafood; desserts could be one of a large choice of cakes. Another bonus about the Rustic is its proximity (over the road in fact) to the 'Elephant's Foot', which is a top spot for a drink while waiting for a table.

Sean's Panaroma

270 Campbell Parade, Bondi Beach (✆ 9365 4924) Modern Australian. Book.

BYO. No Credit. **Access:** 1 entrance step.

Open: 7 days 7am-10pm (summer); Wed-Sun 7am-3pm & 7pm-10pm (winter).

Average Prices: breakfast to $10; Entree $9; Main $13.50; Dessert $6.50.

Sean's Panaroma burst onto the food scene with a bang, and quickly came to be recognised as one of the best Modern Australian restaurants in Sydney. The mood is comfortably lackadaisical, an impression emphasised by the pared down furnishings of aged wood and not quite matching metal chairs. However, there are no shortcuts when it comes to the food. The exposed kitchen turns out wonderful goodies to the cafe by day and restaurant by night, strictly adhering to a regimen of quality which keeps devotees returning regularly. Revel in breakfasts of toast and preserves, hash browns, spinach, mushroom and egg creations, fruit frappes or sheep's milk yoghurt with palm sugar, muesli and fruit, or even just a coffee. Lunch or dine on generous plates of antipasto or fried polenta with borlotti bean salad for entrees, and follow it with ocean trout, chicken, beef or even duck liver crostini with red onion confit and balsamic vinegar. Wow. Thursday, Friday and Saturday nights are revered events in the weekly mouth filling calendar- the set menu. Thursday is vegetarian, Friday is for Seafood and Saturday is reserved for Game and Livestock. The location does it no harm either, being at the northern end of Bondi Beach. All of this is bound to leave guests reeling from the experience, in the best possible way.

Tabac

379 Liverpool St (cnr Darlinghurst Rd), Darlinghurst (✆ 9380 5318) Modern Australian. Book.

Lc'd & BYO. Credit: AE BC D MC V. **Access:** Level entrance, narrow.

Open: Lunch: Fri 12noon-3pm; Dinner: 7 days 6.30pm-10.30pm. No smoking.

Average Prices: Entree $7; Main $15; Dessert $7.

This is a suave and small dining room, where the crisp tables, glistening tableware and the white panelled walls create a comfortable environment in which to be fed. The food looks expensive: luscious fresh ingredients in good looking arrangements, yet it is consistently inexpensive. Flavours are intense. Memorable noshes have included Jerusalem artichoke soup, Thai fishcakes, grilled octopus salad, chargrilled Atlantic salmon with fennel, rocket and orange salad, and finally, lime curd tart or baked anglaise with burnt sugar and cointreau.

Taylor Square Restaurant

Level 1, 191-195 Oxford St, Taylor Square (✆ 9360 5828) Modern Australian.

Lc'd & BYO. Credit: AE BC MC V. **Access:** Steep flight of stairs to restaurant.

Open: Dinner: Tues-Sun from 7pm; Closed Mon.

Average Prices: Entree $10; Main $16; Desert $7.

Here patrons can sit in the friendly atmosphere of a light, spacious interior filled with convivial patrons, while watching a sweeping view onto Taylor Square, and eating satisfyingly filling and hearty, yet inexpensive, food. As the lights of the cars swish past below, sup on succulent lamb or game, perhaps some seared Atlantic salmon with potato and chervil salad, char-grilled quail, rump steak or some great chips. Desserts may include a rhubarb brulee with orange and cinnamon salad or maybe a mocha parfait.

The Edge

60 Riley St, Darlinghurst (✆ 9360 1372) Casually chic Restaurant.

Lc'd. Credit: Amex, BC, MC, V. **Access:** 1 step.

Open: Lunch: 7 days 12noon-3pm; Dinner: Mon-Sat 6pm-11pm, Sun 6pm-10pm.

Average Prices: Entree $12; Main $17; Dessert $7.50.

Located in a quiet cul de sac just off William St, The Edge has a special atmosphere about it. Somehow, as the diners recline in their cane armchairs at glass tables surrounded by lime-washed yellow walls, they often seem to be paying more attention to who's watching them eat than watching what they're eating. The designer pizzas, with toppings such as roast pumpkin, prawns and basil; pasta of duck fettuccine with baby bok choy; prime sirloins, marinated grilled lamb and seafoods make choice a difficult word to put into practice. Desserts are simple yet accomplished, with apple tart served with luscious vanilla bean ice cream a regular favourite. The Edge is always good entertainment value for people watching.

Vamps

227 Glenmore Rd (Five Ways), Paddington (✆ 9331 1032) French Bistro. Book.

BYO. Credit: All. **Access:** 2 entry steps.

Open: Mon-Sat 6.30pm-10.30pm; Closed Sun.

FISH & CHIPS

Open air dining can provide some of the most memorable and inexpensive food experiences of the city. Apart from a picnic, the best way to do it is to find some fresh fish and chips and hit the sand, as follows.

Doyles Jetty
Watsons Bay Ferry Jetty (✆ 9337 1572)
Open: Mon-Fri 10.30am-5pm; Sat-Sun 10.30am-6.30pm.

Doyles At The Fish Markets
Sydney Fish Market, Blackwattle Bay, Pyrmont (✆ 9552 4339)
Open: Mon-Thurs 11am-3pm; Fri-Sat 11am-9pm; Sun 11am-5pm.

Kirribilli Seafoods Fish Shop
12 Fitzroy St, Kirribilli (✆ 9929 4680)
Open: Mon-Sat 10am-8pm; Sun 12noon-8pm.

Ocean Foods
Drummoyne 154 Lyons Rd, Drummoyne (✆ 9814 336)
Open: Tues-Wed & Sun 9.30am-8.30pm; Thurs-Sat 9.30am-9pm.

Ocean Foods
110 The Corso, Manly (✆ 9977 1059)
Open: Mon-Fri 9am-8pm; Sat 9am-10pm; Sun 9am-9pm.

Palm Beach Seafoods
1104 Barrenjoey Rd, Palm Beach (✆ 9974 4277)
Open: Mon11am-5pm; Tues-Fri 11am-8pm; Sat-Sun 10.30-8pm.

Average Prices: Entree $10; Main $18.50; Dessert $7.50.
Vamps is an ideal neighbourhood bistro: great food served by friendly staff in laid back yet suave surroundings. Looking directly onto the colourful scene of Paddington's Five Ways, Vamps is known for consistently delivering simple and honest bistro food with flair. Entrees may oscillate between anything from squid ink pasta to a fresh, Vietnamese-style spring roll filled with pork, crab and vegetables. Main courses may be roasted duck and potato red curry; pesto crusted rack of lamb with ratatouille; or marinated and baked baby snapper. Desserts will usually be along the lines of chocolate and orange tartlet, or creme brulee.

Wockpool
155 Victoria Rd, Potts Point (✆ 9368 1771) Modern Pan-Asian.
Lc'd. Credit: AE BC MC V. **Access:** noodle bar at street level, no access to restaurant or toilets.
Open: 7 nights 6.30pm-11.30pm.
Average Prices: Entree $14; Main $20; Dessert $8.50; Noodle Bar $9.
A suavely-clad crowd form the loyal clientele who regularly turn out to marvel over well presented Modern Asian food. This could include stir fried spanner crab omelette; red braised pork, or perhaps extremely tender Szechuan duck confit with mandarin pancakes, presented with slithers of cucumber and spring onion and a little bath of hoisin sauce. This is a slick restaurant made even better by the cheap as chips ground floor noodle bar, where excellent soups and noodle dishes are keenly consumed.

Yipiyiyo
290 Crown St, Surry Hills (✆ 9332 3114) Tex-Mex.
BYO. Credit: BC MC V. **Access:** 1 entrance step.
Open: Dinner: Mon-Sat from 6.30pm; Closed Sun.
Average Prices: Entree $8; Main $14; Dessert $7.
As the name might suggest, Yipiyiyo is a Tex-Mex stronghold. As this might in turn suggest, the standard fare here is made up of such exotics as quesadilla with roasted pumpkin, fetta, chilli and olives; buttermilk corncake; fish with fries and chilli sauce or 'fireworks chutney', or the Yipiyiyo combo with rellenos, taco, quesadilla, avocado and salsa. Desserts are hard to go past, including fig and coconut steamed pudding with bourbon sauce, passionfruit chilli sorbet or maybe key lime marscapone tart. With a vibrant and colourful interior and clientele, you'll leave shouting "yahoo"!

Yutaka
200 Crown St, Surry Hills (✆ 9361 3818) Japanese.
Lc'd & BYO. Credit: AE BC MC V. **Access:** Down six entrance stairs.
Open: Lunch: Mon-Fri 12noon-2pm; Dinner: 7 days 6pm-10.30pm.
Average Prices: Entree $5; Main $13.
Yutaka is widely regarded as one of the city's most authentic Japanese restaurants. Loved by foreigners (Australians) and natives (Japanese) alike, it is extremely popular and inexpensive. Here, you can eat sushi, sashimi, fermented soybeans, deep fried vegetables, skewered and grilled beef wrapped in bacon with garlic sauce, or even, if you feel like it, grilled eel. There are also two fixed price menus from $18.

WEST & INNER WEST

Bach Dang
46 Canley Vale Rd, Canley Vale (✆ 9724 6174) Vietnamese. Book Fri-Sat.
BYO. Credit: BC MC V. **Access:** 1 entry step.
Open: Lunch: Tues-Fri 10am-2.30pm; Dinner: Mon-Fri 5pm-10pm; All day: Sat-Sun 10am-10pm.
Average Prices: Entree $4; Main $6.50; Dessert $2.
Canley Vale is on the north eastern side of Cabramatta, the focus of Sydney's Vietnamese community. Bach Dang is very popular with the area's community in general, but even more so, the high number of Vietnamese eaters here indicates the calibre, quality and authenticity of the food. Vietnamese pancakes with vegetable, prawn or pork filling, a do-it-yourself cooked at the table beef wrapped in rice paper and served with vegetables, roast poultry and curries as well as many noodle

variations, are some of the dishes visitors will be likely to find on the menu. Desserts are limited to simply arranged fruits.

Camira

1/50 Park Rd, Cabramatta (✆ 9728 1052) Cambodian.
BYO. Credit: BC MC. **Access:** Level entry.
Open: 7 days 9am-9.30pm.
Average Prices: Entree $4; Main $9.50; Dessert $4.

Although the emphasis at this eatery is on Cambodian food, Thai and Chinese dishes are also prepared by the chefs, although the Thai food is not mentioned on the menu (ask the staff). Striking forward past the rows of barbecued ducks and chickens hanging in the window, behold the source of some great food. Barbecued poultry obviously features, but there are also a variety of soups, snacks, noodles and seafood dishes. Sweet and sour king prawns, beancurd hotpots, spicy squid and braised beef with almonds are all popular with the large band of regulars.

Castel Mola

286 Norton St, Leichhardt (✆ 9569 8814) Italian.
BYO. Credit: BC MC V. **Access:** 1 entrance step.
Open: Dinner: 7 days 6pm-10.15pm. Outside courtyard in summer.
Average Prices: Entree $10; Main $14; Dessert $5.

Leichhardt's Norton Street is one long stretch of Italian restaurants. One of these is Castel Mola, which offers traditionally good food without pretension. Pasta, seafood and meat (predominantly veal) dishes create a menu which ranges from the absolutely traditional to modern variations. Pastas of spinach fettuccine with basil, herbs, walnuts and garlic, and main dishes along the lines of tangy lemon pan fried veal baked in a tomato, mushroom and cheese sauce are complemented by a specials board full of choice items like the happily remembered rack of lamb in honey sauce. There is also a special menu from Monday to Wednesday of pasta and a veal dish for $15. If the restaurant's guests have room, the desserts include gelati, zabaglione and for a real pick me up, tiramisu.

Darling Mills

134 Glebe Point Rd, Glebe (✆ 9660 5666) Modern Australian. Book.
Lc'd & BYO. Credit: AE BC D MC V. **Access:** Ramp to level entry & accessible toilet.
Open: Lunch: Tues-Fri & Sun 12noon-3pm; Dinner: Sun-Thurs 6pm-10pm; Fri-Sat 6pm-11pm.
Average Prices: Entree $12; Main $21; Dessert $9.50.

With a comfortable and welcoming ambience, Darling Mills offers incredibly fresh produce sourced from the family farm and around Australia, given the magic wand treatment and turned into exceptional food. West Australian scampi, Tasmanian salmon, King Island beef and kangaroo represent arm chair travelling at its best, a culinary tour of the country taken from the exceptional comfort of a fireside table in winter or a garden terrace table in summer. Inventive combinations of unusual ingredients make up the menu: perhaps the asparagus, pea, nasturtium bud and corn salad in a walnut vinaigrette, the King Island beef, and the rarely found swordfish steaks. One of the most memorable desserts ever, a triple chocolate bavarois, happened here at one of Sydney's finest restaurants.

Fish Tank

119 King St, Newtown (✆ 9557 5627) Seafood. Book.
Lc'd. Credit: AE BC MC V. **Access:** 1 small entrance step.
Open: Mon-Sat 12noon-11pm; Sun 12noon-10pm.
Average Prices: Entree $7.50; Main $12.50; Dessert $5.50.

A very comfortable Fish Tank is exactly what this restaurant feels like- exposed and untreated concrete floors, tall glass and pale wooden doors and sharp white table linen protected with butcher's paper. The food of fellow finned friends here doesn't stick to the traditional ideas of how seafood should be cooked or served- entrees are imaginative and could include concoctions such as seared scallops on a bed of homous with tomato relish. Mains range from fish and chips (a class act, with chunky golden chips and a light batter), delicate whiting with ginger and broccoli fritters and spring onion dipping sauce, as well as simple grilled tuna steaks. Desserts are hard to ignore, particularly when faced with caramelised pear terrine with a dollop of double cream.

Frattini

122 Marion St, Leichhardt (✆ 9569 2997) Italian. Book.
BYO (bottle shop nearby). **Credit:** AE BC MC V.
Access: Level entry.
Open: Lunch: Sun-Fri 12noon-2.30pm; Dinner: 7 days 6pm-10pm.
Average Prices: Entree $9; Pasta $11; Main $17; Dessert $7.

Frattini is widely recognised as one of the most enjoyable Italian restaurants in Sydney. A warm interior and greeting from the staff make it exceptionally welcoming, and the vision of a restaurant packed with guests eating with broad grins on their faces is far from discouraging! Everything on the menu is worthy of attention, but perhaps the most popular dishes include salmon carpaccio, grilled field mushrooms stuffed with pure and noble garlic, agnolotti pasta with caviar and smoked salmon sauce, and veal filled with herbed cheese and barbecued with bay leaves and onions. The menu is complemented by a list of specials such as rabbit or grilled spatchcock. As for dessert - the blissfully fine crepes served with strawberries and drizzling with alcoholic sauce, or the profiteroles with poached pears and mascarpone, are a quasi-religious experience. Be sure to book as early as possible to avoid disappointment, as the restaurant is full every night.

Jiyu No Omise

342 Darling St, Balmain (✆ 9818 3886) Japanese.
Lc'd & BYO. Credit: AE BC D MC V. **Access:** 2 flights of stairs to restaurant.
Open: Dinner: 7 days 6.30pm-11pm.
Average Prices: Entree $6; Main $12.
Jiyu No Omise is a comfortable restaurant where the peaceful atmosphere of the interior and garden below is complemented by the care taken with the food. The menu has a large number of entrees and mains, all of which are impeccably presented. Particularly famed are the tuna and mushroom parcels wrapped in a delicate crisp pastry, while the sushi includes tuna, ocean trout, bream, squid, salmon and scallops and costs from $3 to $12 for a sushi-based main dish. Guests can also mix and make their own sushi. Jiyu No Omise has traded for over eight years, and has rightly earned a reputation as a popular, relaxing and intimate Japanese eating experience.

Peninsula Bistro

264 Darling Street, Balmain (✆ 9810 3955) French Bistro. Book.
BYO. Credit: AE BC D MC V. **Access:** 1 entry step.
Open: Lunch: Thurs-Fri 12noon-3pm; Dinner: Tues-Sun 6.30pm-11pm; Brunch: Sat-Sun 10am-3pm.
Average Prices: Entree $12; Main $17.50; Dessert $8.50.
One of the buzziest and brightest restaurants in Balmain is the colourful Peninsula Bistro. Here, fine renditions of bistro fare attract crowds who look almost as excited as the vibrant faces painted on exuberant wall mural. The menu may include intensely herby crumbed lamb's brains accompanied by cooled, grilled radicchio and a tangy lemon sauce, or perhaps a solid rump steak drizzling in a thick red wine sauce, the perfect accompaniment to a bowl of crispy, salty, steaming chips. French family classics, such as Skate wing with vinegared black butter sauce, and desserts, as well as cheese plates hovering near dessert status, make dining here a great experience.

Restaurant Manfredi

88 Hackett St, Ultimo (✆ 9211 5895) Northern Italian. Book.
Lc'd. Credit: AE BC D MC V. **Access:** Steep flight of entry steps.
Open: Lunch: Wed-Fri; 12noon-3pm; Dinner: Tues-Sat from 6.30pm.
Average Prices: Entree $15; Main $22.50; Dessert $9.50.
At the time of writing, Restaurant Manfredi was finalising plans to move to the top floor of The Argyle, Argyle Street, The Rocks. It is worth the effort to find: chef Stefano Manfredi and the Manfredi family support team have acquired an internationally fabled reputation for their restaurant, which provides a comfortable balance of modern formal and courtyard dining. Highly personalised interpretations of northern Italian food include reputedly unmatchable home made pasta, exquisite meats and game, and delectable desserts. Complemented by flawless service and a sommelier to guide patrons through the fine wine list, this is one of the city's most internationally applauded dining experiences.

Tetsuya's

729 Darling St, Rozelle (✆ 9555 1017) French/Japanese. Book.
BYO. Credit: BC MC V. **Access:** 1 step down. No smoking.
Open: Lunch: Wed-Sat 12noon-2.30pm; Dinner: Tues-Sat 7pm-Midnight.
Average Prices: Fixed-price lunch of 5 courses $60; fixed-price dinner of 6 courses (degustation menu) $75.
Everybody who has been to Tetsuya's categorically raves about the incredible, if not mythical, powers of Tetsuya 'the master' Wakuda, who performs the delicate art of coalescing the French and Japanese cuisines with great flair. The weeks-long waiting list for Saturday dinner is testimony to the legendary status his restaurant has acquired. Your main could be venison seared with chrysanthemum leaves, walnut oil, eschalot and port wine and sherry vinegar sauce. A creme brulee could be flavoured with just an elegant hint of ginger. Get the idea? This is an experience of the best kind.

Thai Pothong

294 King St, Newtown (✆ 9550 6277) Thai. Book or arrive early.
Lc'd & BYO. Credit: AE BC D MC V. **Access:** Stairs to restaurant.
Open: Lunch: Mon-Fri 12noon-3pm; Dinner: 7 days 6pm-11pm.
Average Prices: Entree $7; Main $12.50; Dessert $6.
Despite the concentration of restaurants and cafes lining each side of most of King Street, Newtown, Thai Pothong is definitely where the eating action is. With most of the neighbourhood in this colourful and vibrant eatery, it's not surprising how many people stop outside to have a look at what's going on in here. Not unexpectedly, the food is great and reasonably priced. Entrees could be fish cakes, marinated octopus, or stuffed chicken wings. Mains could well be amazing hot pot concoctions of chilli, lemongrass, and galangal with either meat or seafood as well as other Thai specialties. Vegetarians may be initially dismayed by the menu, yet the cook will prepare meat-free versions of any dish on request. This is a colourful and action packed place, and it can get crowded; yet the staff somehow manage to remain in control.

THE PICK OF THE PUBS

Recent statistics report that around ninety-five per cent of Australian residents live near water. If Sydney is anything to go by, it is easy to believe that a large proportion of this figure represents those living near 'watering holes' - pubs. The number, variety and quality of pubs (and beers available in them) reveal how important a national past-time pub-going is, and Sydney definitely has a more than an adequate number of great pubs to visit, and from which to select a 'local'. Below is a highly selective listing of the city's best pubs, categorised according to food, music, beer gardens, late opening hours and, first up, a list of the pubs which, for various reasons, really should not be missed.

THE BEST OF THE PUBS

The following pubs are the best in Sydney for various reasons, as detailed.

The Australian

100 Cumberland St, The Rocks (✆ 9247 2229)

Open: Mon-Sat 11.30am-11.30pm; Sun 11.30am-8pm. May stay open later Fri & Sat.

The Australian is a charming, traditional split-level pub where you can drink only Scharer's Little Brewery's boutique beers, brewed according to Bavarian tradition, taste and Beer Purity Law. These excellent brews, which are so delicious and intensely flavoured that they can almost be chewed, include: Scharer's Lager (caramelised malt flavour with hop bitterness); Burragorang Bock (very dark, very smooth, very treacly/malty, very drinkable); Berryblack (a concoction of strawberry liqueur and bock based in the tradition of Belgian fruit beers); and D'Lite (a dark beer with only 3% alcohol). Three packs are for sale. Also on offer are excellent gourmet pizzas sporting a wide variety of toppings from Thai style to Kangaroo. With the bonus of pavement seating looking directly across to the Harbour Bridge, this is altogether a truly top pub!

The Four in Hand

105 Sutherland St, Paddington (✆ 9326 2254)

Open: 7 days 11am-11pm.

Food: Bistro open 7 days 12noon-3pm and 6.30-11pm. Book.

Down the hill from the rest of the action in Paddington, the Four in Hand is a popular pub which is consistently full on Friday and Saturday nights. Decorated in a suave yet understated manner utilising pale, untreated wood and filled with the sound of conversations buzzing over up-beat music, the pub also has a popular restaurant attached serving widely varied bistro meals. The menu could include anything from roasted ocean trout to a steak or green curry, and mains average $16.50. Apart from the obvious, the bar serves wines by the glass, espresso and a large menu of cocktails ($10 av.), while the large doors swing open to reveal a streetscape at the heart of Paddington's leafy terrace house territory. The Four in Hand is a friendly and atmospheric pub in a typically good-looking inner suburban setting.

The Friend in Hand

58 Cowper St, Glebe (✆ 9660 2326)

Open: Mon-Sat 10am-Midnight; Sun 12noon-10pm.

Food: No Names restaurant; Cafe Bar upstairs; 'grill your own' BBQ downstairs.

This pub is one of the most wonderfully bizarre in Sydney, featuring weekly events such as Crab Racing on Wednesday nights (complete with a beer drinking competition), and the very popular Thong Clapping to Irish music on Sundays 3.30pm-6.30pm. The interior includes the Oar House (complete with surf boat, oars, old Bondi photos and courtyard), while on most available spaces stand and hang souvenirs and mementos sent back from all over the world. The No Names bistro reputedly goes through one and a half tonnes of pasta a week, consistently pleasing its large and loyal following of regulars with its broad range of Italian dishes. The grill your own Barbecue downstairs represents great fun and value, with enormous T-bone steaks and salad on the menu for $8. With so much going for it, it is no surprise that the Friend in Hand is so popular, and therefore not to be missed.

Hotel Bondi

178 Campbell Parade, Bondi Beach (✆ 930 3271)

Open: Mon-Sat 8am-4am; Sun 8am-Midnight

Food: Bistro (steak and salad currently about $4.00); 1st Floor Bistro.
Accommodation: Single $30; standard doubles $55; sea-facing double $65; sea-facing suite $75; sea-facing State Suite with cooking facilities $95.
The 1920s stained glass and high ceilings forming this fantastic, warren-like building on Sydney's most famous beach house so many different facilities that it is impossible to do anything but list them. Inside the Hotel Bondi are: a beer garden overlooking Campbell Parade and the sea, a Public bar, Casino Royal (card machines), Bistro (steak and salad currently about $4.00), Players Room for pool, City to Surf Bar, Champions bar with pool tables; Beach Club Disco which doubles as a movie theatre Monday 7-9pm; Sands Bar (1st Floor pool bar overlooking the sea with serious pool competition on Sundays and a Thai Bistro serving stir-fry for around $5. The accommodation represents good value. Hotel Bondi is almost Planet Pub with so many different rooms, real scene for energetic pub goers not necessarily looking for peace or quiet.

The Greenwood

Greenwood Plaza, Blue St, North Sydney (✆ 9964 9477)
Open: Mon-Sat 11am-Midnight; Closed Sun.
Favoured haunt of North Shore beautiful people and suited types trying to chat up the former, the Greenwood is a sight to see. With three bars housed in and around a sandstone school building and a deconsecrated church refitted with slick stainless steel bars and loud music, the Greenwood attracts so many patrons that hundreds spill out onto the comfortably large garden courtyard at the base of the enormous Optus Tower, fitted with tables and chairs sitting on warm sandstone amongst the garden beds. Blue light shines down from above, lending the entire scene a surreal atmosphere and adding to the already considerable spectacle. The Greenwood is especially popular on balmy summer Friday and Saturday nights, and earns its place as one of the pick of the pubs for the originality and character of its setting.

The London

234 Darling Street, Balmain (✆ 9555 1377)
Open: Mon-Sat 11am-Midnight; Sun 12noon-10pm.
Fronted by a wide-roofed verandah and situated opposite the Saturday market place on Darling St, the London is a spacious yet cosy, well stocked Victorian era pub. An enviable range of beers on tap include Dog Bolter, Cascade, Hahn, Redback and Coopers. Very comfortably formed tractor seats on the verandah provide the perfect viewing platform from which to watch the world go past, the perfect end to a stroll through the suburbs historic streets, shops and Saturday markets. The London is the perfect pub for those seeking peace and quiet with traditional atmosphere.

The London Tavern

85 Underwood Street, Paddington (✆ 9331 1637)
Open: Mon-Wed 11am-11pm; Thurs- Sat 11am-11.30pm; Sun 12pm-10pm.
Decorated with Ye Olde English beer posters, the London Tavern is Paddington's oldest pub, a very comfortable local, befitting the popularity and character of the pub on every second street corner tradition. The only intrusions of the modern age into this den of old world charm are a happy hour and pool competition. A large selection of beers on tap and a small day-time beer garden in the middle of this beautiful suburb, make the London Tavern a more than pleasant pub.

Lord Nelson Hotel

Cnr Kent St & Argyle St, The Rocks (✆ 9251 4044)
Open: 7 days 11am-11pm.
Food: Nelson's Brasserie; good counter meals also available from the bar.
Accommodation: See chapter, Accommodation.
The Lord Nelson is one of Sydney's best pubs for several reasons. The building itself is several storeys of historic sandstone, laden with of colonial atmosphere. Once through the heavy, glossy Prussian blue front door, patrons are greeted by naval flags hanging from the wooden beams, a portrait of Lord Nelson hanging over the fireplace where a log fire roars in winter, and many patrons enjoying their beer and conversations. The pub is also a brewery of renowned quality, offering tremendous concoctions such as Old Admiral (dark), Three Sheets (a full, wheat beer) and Quayle's Pale Ale. The Lord Nelson is the oldest licensed hotel in Sydney, and while busiest at weekends, it is consistently popular all week with those serious about their beer.

The Mercantile

25 George Street, The Rocks (✆ 9247 3570)
Open: Sun-Thurs 10am-Midnight; Fri -Sat 10am-1am.
Food: Bistro serving counter lunches 7 days; weekends sandwiches and salads.
Accommodation: Single $65; Double $85 (including breakfast).
One of the city's Guinness capitals and liveliest pubs, the Mercantile offers Irish atmosphere and music (rock, folk and Irish) on week nights and weekends. Sandwiches and salads served at the outside tables and chairs on weekends beside the Rocks Markets, and the pinnacle quality of the Guinness on tap contribute to the popularity of this great Irish pub. It is also the centre of St Patrick's Day celebrations in The Rocks (17 March).

The Oaks Hotel

118 Military Rd, Neutral Bay (✆ 9953 5515)
Open: Mon-Sat 10am-Midnight, Sun 12noon-10pm.
Food: Mon-Fri 12noon-3pm; 6.30pm-10pm; Sat 12noon-10pm; Sun 12noon-9pm. Grill your own steaks, chicken or fish in the bistro; select meats from the carvery; or enjoy gourmet pizzas under the oak tree ($9.50-$12).
The Oaks has one of the best atmospheres of all Sydney pubs: an enormous Oak tree dapples the sunlight over a tranquil and secluded beer garden, and the large, airy main bar carpeted with tartan and furnished with deep armchairs and old photographs. Upstairs is a series of

individual sitting rooms and pool rooms, each characteristically named and serviced by a gleaming chrome bar. The Kitchen, for example, features tiled walls and a highly glossed floor encasing an immaculate pool table. The pub itself has been a landmark on the North Shore since the 1880s, and remains one of the most popular in the city.

The Orient

Cnr George & Argyle Streets, The Rocks (✆ 9251 1255)

Open: Mon-Sat 10am-3pm; Sun 10am-Midnight

Cocktails: Rocktails, mezzanine level, from $5.

The Orient is a pumping pub, filled with flesh, music and action. Four bars serve a wide range of beers to a thirsty crowd. The Orient is a cleverly refurbished building which features central stairways, alcoves and grottos, through which live music wafts every night of the week. For those seeking faster action, the pub's disco, The Rhino Club, is a glassed-in fishbowl of pump and grind. Located in the centre of The Rocks pub strip, and apart from the quiet, open colonial beer garden, the Orient is more action packed than a Terminator movie.

The Nags Head

St John's Rd, Glebe (✆ 9660 1591)

Open: Mon-Sat 11am-Midnight, Sun 12noon-10pm.

This very comfortable, dark wooded, English style pub offers expertly poured Guinness in English style pint glasses, and has the bonus of two great garden areas, one inside and one on the roof, where ivy and ferns hang from all available surfaces. In addition, the pub has a good bistro famed for its steaks, 'the Nag's Chaff' and a small 'Loft' beer garden, filled with ferns, garden furniture and umbrellas. The variety of music featured from Wednesday to Sunday adds to the strong local atmosphere, and makes this pub worth a visit.

The Pumphouse

17 Little Pier St, Darling Harbour (✆ 9281 3967)

Open: Mon-Thurs 11am-Midnight; Fri -Sat 11am-3am; Sun 11am-Midnight.

Food: Bistro serving cheap but creative Australian food.

Another pub which brews its own concoctions is the Pumphouse, whose patrons can try before they buy. The building features enormous hydraulic accumulators in the bar area, relics from the era before electricity was on tap, when the building was a Pumping Station used to provide hydraulic power to the city. On tap are brews such as Golden Wheat Beer, Bulls Head Best Bitter, Pumphouse Extra and the aptly named Thunderbolt Ale (8% alcohol, and well worth the $6.50 a pint). The Pumphouse has live entertainment on Fridays and Saturdays from 10.30pm, and there is also a patio overlooking the palmed courtyard/beer garden. Brewery Tours are conducted by appointment.

The Royal

237 Glenmore Rd (Five Ways), Paddington (✆ 9331 2604)

Open: Mon to Sat 10am-Midnight; Sun 12noon-10pm.

Food: 1st floor restaurant with balcony.

Cocktails: Elephant Bar 2nd floor.

The Royal is a tall, open and opulently laced National Trust pub situated on the piazza-like Five Ways, right in the middle of residential Paddington. The pub's bars serve an enormous range of beers, making this a great pub to head for, especially when exploring the suburb by foot, and seats on the first floor verandah are hotly contested. The Royal Grill offers modern and traditional Australian lunches and dinners (Mon-Sat 12noon-11pm) such as rump steaks, chunky chips and innovative grills, in bustling surroundings.

Sackville Hotel

599 Darling St, Rozelle (✆ 9555 7555); Restaurant: 4 Wise St, Rozelle (✆ 9555 7788)

Open: Mon-Wed 10am-Midnight; Thurs-Sat 10am-2am; Sun 12noon-10pm.

Food: Damien Pignolet's bistro.

Cocktails: Cocktail bar with extensive menu from $4-$8.

Accommodation: $50 per night; $150 per week, with share facilities and continental breakfast.

This very comfortable pub has a lively yet calm atmosphere, centred around the buzz of conversation the gleaming public bar and its variety of beers attracts. However, the Sackville is also renowned for its food, and from the second half of 1996, the suave back area will become home to the second instalment of Bistro Moncur (see Woollahra Hotel, below). Damien Pignolet's trademark is delicately hearty modern Australian food with strong French tendencies, always greeted and devoured with relish by loyal diners.

Watsons Bay Hotel

1 Military Rd, Watsons Bay (✆ 9337 4299)

Open: Mon & Tues 10am-10pm; Wed-Sat 10am-Midnight; Sun 10am-8.30pm.

Food: Seafood and grills in the beer garden; take away fish & chips from Doyles on the Jetty.

Accommodation: Single $35; Double $55 per night.

On approaching the Watsons Bay Hotel, one could wonder why it comes so highly recommended. Forget the interior. Keep walking to the back garden and behold the beer garden with the most incredible and enviable view of any pub in Sydney. From the tables and chairs sitting directly on Watsons Bay beach on the Harbour, patrons can gaze across their beers to the water, the densely wooded northern shoreline, down the Harbour to the City skyline, watching ferries, cruisers and dinghies coming and going throughout the day, until the sun sinks red behind the City. Wow. The beer garden is especially popular on sunny weekends, and is best after a day on nearby Camp Cove beach or a walk to the Gap.

Paddington Inn

338 Oxford St, Paddington (✆ 9380 5913)

Open: Mon-Tues 11.30-Midnight; Wed-Fri 11.30am-1am; Sat 10am-1am; Sun 12noon-Midnight.

The Paddington Inn is a animated sardine can of a pub

on Saturdays when hundreds of people drawn to the Paddington Bazaar flow in for a beer. Mainly frequented by smart young patrons, it is pretty much the social centre of the Paddington section of Oxford Street. The strange mixture of columns, modern interpretations of traditional furniture, marbled turquoise paint and mirrors create a surprisingly comfortable atmosphere, and thus a great drinking spot.

BEER GARDENS

Although Sydney's climate makes it an ideal city in which to sit outside and consume, relatively few pubs, have embraced the 'garden' aspect as enthusiastically as might be expected. Many of the city's beer gardens are in fact roof gardens or terraces rather than Utopian, leafy fields sheltered by oak trees. Apart from the **Watsons Bay, Hotel Bondi and Pumphouse** above, the following pubs have the most popular and comfortable beer gardens in Sydney.

Birkenhead Point Tavern

11 Roseby St, Drummoyne (© 981 4238)

Open: Mon-Sat 11am-Midnight; Sun 12noon-Midnight.

Being next to the Birkenhead Shopping complex does nothing to hinder the success of the Birkenhead Point Tavern on weekends, and combined with a restaurant, two bars downstairs, a huge band venue, and access to one thousand car parking spaces, the tavern does a thundering trade. However, sunny weekends are particularly crazy as the multi-level beer garden overlooking the water becomes packed with patrons chasing beer, good food from the bistro and a good time. Further attractions and diversions include the Public Bar, packed with various forms of amusement such as pool, darts, pinball machines and video games; the saloon bar, overlooking the beer garden, with live entertainment on weekend evenings; and the Top Sail Bar upstairs, usually reserved for, but not restricted to, Blues music.

The Dolphin

414 Crown St, Surry Hills (© 9380 5614)

Open: Mon-Sat 10am-Midnight; Sun 12noon-10pm.

Pass the Dolphin's public bar and keep going to the back of the hotel. Here is the Dolphin Bar, famous for great meals from the Garden Bistro, and its open fireplaces. However, the main attraction at the Dolphin is the beer garden: unlike so many of Sydney's so called beer gardens without vegetation, this one is green. Plants, vines, pergolas, wooden tables and two levels of intimate little alcoves for alfresco dining and drinking fill the small area with good cheer. Unbeatable in the area on a sunny afternoon for a meal and a drink.

The Glenmore Hotel

96 Cumberland St, The Rocks (© 9247 4794)

Open: Mon-Wed 11am-10pm; Thurs-Sat 11am-Midnight; Sun 12noon-8.30pm.

Accommodation: Family room $80; double or single $60 per night; some have views.

The Glenmore is a traditional Rocks pub, with the traditional horseshoe shaped public bar, traditional beers on tap, and a traditional, local patronage. However, one of the further things that earns this pub its place in the top pubs of Sydney is the rooftop beer garden, offering spectacular views of the Harbour, Opera House, Circular Quay, the City and the Rocks. The best way to enjoy this pub on a warm evening is to get a beer, get some food from the bistro, and head up the steps to the rooftop. It's nothing slick or special to look at, but the pub has a definite charm, and the view certainly makes climbing the stairs worthwhile.

Kings Cross Hotel

248 William St, Kings Cross (© 9358 3377)

Open: 7 days 10am-5 or 7am, depending on the crowd.

The Kings Cross Hotel is definitely better at night than during the day. Even though quite large, the pub manages to feel comfortable due to its separation into a number of different areas. As patrons ascend the stairs they discover a new character and feel on each floor: the average ground floor bar, the first floor cocktail bar and on past a second set of doormen (paying a cover charge of up to $10), defying the dizzying, freaky, mirrored 'spin out' stairwell, emerging in the nightclub. Feeling like part of some giant board game, one reaches the goal: the Roof Top bar (open Thurs-Fri 9pm-4am) where an intimate and suave little bar plays suave, cool music, and serves suave, cool cocktails. Outside is the covered garden, offering great views of the Cross and the City. The pub is generally busiest at the end of the week, although Tuesday nights seem to be truly beautiful events especially popular with backpackers. Venturing into the Kings Cross Hotel is an experience.

Ravesi's Hotel

118 Campbell Parade (Corner of Hall St), Bondi Beach (© 9365 4422)

Open: 7.30am-10pm.

Accommodation: see chapter, Accommodation.

More a beer terrace than a garden, Ravesi's offers a spacious, sunny, first floor balcony sheltered from the wind overlooking Campbell Parade, all the action of Bondi Beach, and the deep blue Tasman Sea. This is a highly civilised place to have a meal or to sip on a long, cool drink or a coffee, favoured by those who don't feel like braving a pub. A great spot. (See: Food.)

Woolwich Pier Hotel

2 Gale St, Woolwich (© 9817 2204)

Open: Mon-Sat 12noon-Midnight; Sun 12noon-10pm.

A fifteen minute ferry ride away from Circular Quay is Woolwich jetty, and a few minutes walk from the jetty is the above hotel. What a voyage of discovery for a sunny day, terminus beer garden! Partially covered and paved in sandstone (with a playground), the garden is a great spot to spend an afternoon drinking and eating the generous portions of food served by the bistro (Open: Mon-Sat 12noon-3pm and 6pm-9pm; Sun 12noon-9pm). A strong family atmosphere pervades the establishment creating a cheerful place where the only thing missing is a big water view. However, the eyes' loss is compensated for by the ears' gain: jazz is played on Sunday afternoons and Thursday nights features rock and cover bands. The pub is a good end (or start) to a walk around the Hunters Hill area before catching the ferry back to the Quay.

HONEST AUSSIE PUBS

Sometimes a quiet drink in an ordinary pub, away from any glitz or glamour, is the best drink around. The following pubs are great, simply because they have adhered to the traditional Australian pub philosophy without being seduced by the slick lines or modernity.

The Grand National

161 Underwood St, Paddington (✆ 9363 3096; bistro: ✆ 9363 4557)

Open: Mon-Fri 10am-11pm; Sat 10am-Midnight; Sun 12noon-10pm

Food: Lunch: Wed-Fri from 12noon; Dinner: Mon-Fri from 6pm; All Day: Sat & Sun 11am-10.30pm.

This is a rare find in Paddington - a pub left to its own devices, basically untouched, yet no less inviting for it. The public bar of the Grand National is largely in its original state and has a not inconsiderable charm, increased by the faithful old doggies often to be seen waiting patiently by the door. However, modernity has come to 'the Nash' in the form of the bistro, which is extremely popular with the locals. The good value menu may range from Chinese spiced cured duck sausage, to home made tagliatelle with broad beans and pine nuts, to lamb cutlets with rosemary, roasted tomatoes and eggplant slices.

The Observer

69 George St, The Rocks (✆ 9252 4169)

Open: Sun-Thurs 11am-11.30pm; Fri & Sat 11am-2.30am.

The Observer is one of Sydney's historic pubs, located in the middle of The Rocks and containing the colonial sandstone Cellar Stairs in the tiny beer garden. The Observer is an honest pub with traditional, frosted glass doors announcing the 'BAR', a decorative iron ceiling and expertly poured Guinness on tap.

The Palisade

35 Bettington St, Millers Point (the end of Argyle St away from George St) (✆ 9247 2272)

Open: Mon-Fri 9am-11pm; Sat 9am-11.30; Sun 11am-9pm.

Housed in an old, tall and skinny building on a peninsula at the far end of Argyle Street, the Palisade is a sparingly decorated yet cosy, quiet, quaint little pub, with an undeniable 1930s atmosphere. The draw card here is the large picture window which frames the view down across the wharves to the Harbour Bridge, and two fires to keep patrons warm in winter while watching the sports television, constantly emitting a low hum in the background. The first floor bistro offers inexpensive, zesty food in a bright, comfortable room with a great view and a reasonably priced wine list. A very short stroll away are views down onto the cargo docks, a children's playground and the historic buildings of The Rocks. (See: Food.)

PUBS WITH THE BEST FOOD

Pub food can range from very simple greasy affairs to the sublime, yet it can be said that in Sydney, the pub bistro scene is pretty sophisticated. However, this does not necessarily mean expensive. Below is a selection of the pubs with the best food: some happen to be among Sydney's top restaurants, others are just as good, but a lot cheaper. Apart from **The Friend in Hand, The Grand National , The Palisade, The Royal and the Watsons Bay Hotel** (all above) are the following.

The Bellevue

159 Hargrave St, Paddington (✆ 9363 2293)

Open: Mon-Tues 11am-10 or 11pm; Wed-Sat 11am-Midnight; Sun 12noon-10pm.

Bistro Open: Mon-Sat: Lunch 12.30pm-3pm and dinner from 6.30pm; Sun 1pm-3.30pm. Book.

Approached from the outside, the Bellevue looks an innocent and quiet place. But open the doors and enter a den of drinking housed in an atmospheric interior of dark wood and marble. Touted as one of the city's most up-market betting arenas (after the Members Pavilion at Randwick racecourse), it is a comfortable pub frequented by patrons dressed in suits, shorts and joggers, jeans or fancy dress party costumes. Out the back is a very popular 'creatively Australian' bistro. A long term specialty of the house is a plate of extremely tasty (and enormous) sausages, mashed potato and peas, drizzling with onion gravy ($10), although a more delicate palate is also catered for by oysters, or perhaps fresh West Australian sardines and Roma tomatoes (average prices: entrees $8.50, mains $14) .The Bellevue Bistro is one of Sydney's best pub food experiences.

The Forbes Hotel

30 York St, Sydney (cnr King St) (✆ 9299 3703)

Open: Mon-Sat 10am-3am; Sun 12noon-10pm.

Grill Open: Lunch 7 days 12noon-3.30pm; Dinner: Thurs-Fri 6pm- 10pm.

Pasta Place Open: Lunch: Mon-Fri 12noon-3.30pm; Dinner Mon-Sat 6pm-9.30pm.

The Forbes is a multi-level pub, comprising a public bar at ground level, cocktail bar on the first floor, and our present focus... the second floor Grill and the third floor Pasta Place. Both are very busy at lunch time, as the pale decors fill with sunlight and conversation. The joviality would extend late into the afternoon if not for the call of the nearby offices, exerting their magnetic appeal on the pub's suited patrons.

Woollahra Hotel - Bistro Moncur

Cnr Moncur St and Queen St, Woollahra (✆ 9363 2782)

Open: 7 days 12noon-Midnight.

Bistro Open: Tues-Sat lunch & dinner; Sun breakfast, lunch and dinner; Closed Mon.

The Woollahra Hotel is a truly happy marriage of pub and food. Entering the main bar one is greeted by a light and airy space of pale wood and a gleaming stainless steel bar. Pushing through the heavy glass swing door into the adjacent Bistro Moncur, one finds something way beyond the average pub bistro: here is one of Sydney's favourite chefs and his restaurant, constantly filled with loyal diners fuelling up on Modern Australian food laced with a heavy French accent. This means that anything from oysters to magnificent Cafe de Paris sirloin ($17.50) or roasted Atlantic salmon could be on the menu. The long, slim room complements the dining experience with a striking black and white mural hugging one side wall, and pale wooden floor and furniture giving a suave yet relaxed feel. Service is some of the best in Sydney. Patrons intending to dine must arrive early to avoid disappointment or a long wait, as no bookings are taken.

BARS AND COCKTAIL BARS

In addition to the **Kings Cross Hotel's Rooftop Bar, the Sackville, the Royal and the Paddington Inn** (above) and the **Annandale** (below), are the following, recommended specifically for their cocktails.

Burdekin (Dug Out Bar)

2 Oxford St, Darlinghurst (✆ 9331 3066)

Open: Mon-Sat 11am-2am; Sun 12noon-Midnight.

The Burdekin is a starkly modern, beautifully designed, attitude-laden and very busy hotel with a young, artistic clientele. Downstairs is the Dug Out Bar, where a 1930's menu of cocktails is lapped up by the same largely up-market crowd. Cocktails from $8.

The Elephant's Foot

505 Crown St, Surry Hills (✆ 9319 6802)

Open: Mon-Sat 11am-Midnight; Sun Midday-10pm

A slick deco bar, the Elephant's Foot stands opposite the Rustic Cafe in a very happy twist of fate. The smooth interior of chrome, spaciousness and huge flower arrangements create a wonderful atmosphere through which wash waves of jazz and soul. Although the pub has its own good food, it is hard to resist the call of the bright yellow Rustic Cafe over the road (See: Cafes), and what better beginning to a meal there than a cocktail here? The Elephant's Foot's extensive list makes this a popular pub with its smart, young crowd. Cocktails from $7.

The Exchange (Safari Bar)

Cnr Beattie St & Mullens St, Balmain (✆ 9810 1171)

Open: Mon-Sat 12noon-Midnight; Sun 12noon-10pm.

Richly decorated with photographs of colonial India and Africa, furs, skins, weapons, trophies and the occasional (poor) stuffed animal, the Safari Bar and its verandah are a relaxing place to sip on cocktails and other long, cool drinks. Downstairs is the Beattie Street Bar- an honest, sporty pub, complete with photographs, memorabilia and beer. But why the safari bar? Because the old Balmain rugby league team was called the Balmain Tigers, so it's right in the heart of tiger country! Cocktails from $7.

Marble Bar

Under the Hilton Hotel, between George St & Pitt St, City (✆ 9266 0610)

Open: Mon-Wed 12noon-10.30am; Fri 12noon-2am; Sat 2pm-2am; Closed Sun.

Under the Hilton sits one of the city's most impressively grandiose 1890s bars, decorated with copious amounts of marble, mirror, stained glass and sculpture. The martini glasses are stacked in a tower, and the bar staff swear they can make any cocktail their patrons request. The bar has jazz on Thursday to Saturday evenings, and most importantly, ladies have been permitted since 1974. Cocktails from $7.

The Oxford (Gilligans)

134 Oxford St, Darlinghurst (cnr Bourke St) (✆ 9331 3467)

Open: Mon-Sat 3pm-2am; Sun 3pm-Midnight.

Found on the first floor of this rather anonymous-looking green building on Taylor Square is Gilligans - a plush pleasure dome where some of Sydney's best cocktails are served. Despite the men preferred policy of the public bar on the ground floor, Gilligans is not strictly gay. All sorts of people come here, from transvestites to the conventional. Cocktails from $8.50.

BEST MUSIC VENUES

Some claim that Melbourne has a more active pub music scene than Sydney. However, after a definite lull, the scene has rekindled energetically in this city. As well as the **Birkenhead Point Tavern** and **The Orient** (above), the following pubs are best known for regular live music. Current listings such as On the Street and Metro will have details of current performers (See: Media).

The Annandale

17 Parramatta Rd, Annandale (✆ 9550 1078)

Open: Mon-Sat 10am-Midnight; Sun 12noon-10pm

Music: generally Wed-Sat from8.30pm; Sun from 6pm.

At the centre of the Sydney University area music scene, the Annandale hosts a variety of bands every week, taking care to promote independent acts and alternative styles of music. Also attached is a 1950s cocktail bar serving over two hundred creations, priced from $4. Intending patrons are warned that the pub sometimes locks away all the alcohol to allow the underaged to patronise the pub music scene legally.

The Bridge

135 Victoria Rd, Rozelle (✆ 9810 1260)

Open: Mon-Wed 11am-Midnight; Thurs-Sat 11am-4am; Sun 12noon-Midnight.

Long established as one of Sydney's best live music venues, the Bridge sees a variety of music played from Thursday to Sunday evenings, with a cover anywhere between $3 and $20 being charged, depending on the act. Each of the two bars have live music, the Front Bar sparse and roomy with a large stage and two pool tables, and the relaxed Lounge Bar where Latin, rock and soul are to be heard. Occasional jam sessions and rap nights take place at other times.

The Coogee Bay Hotel
Cnr Coogee Bay Rd & Arden St, Coogee (✆ 9665 0000)
Open: Mon-Sat 9am-3am; Sun 10am-10pm.
Another restored historic pub pleasure palace is the Coogee Bay Hotel, home of Selina's, one of the city's premier live music spots. Elsewhere in this complex are the Sports Bar, the Beach Bar with views of Coogee beach, a huge beer garden, and a brasserie. Selina's is proud of its record as a music hot spot, and has been known to attract crowds of around three thousand to hear the big names in Australian music. The best known acts generally perform on Friday and Saturday nights, and between 8pm and 10pm when the bands are playing, the pub offers cheap drinks.

The Craig
Darling Harbour (✆ 9281 3922)
Open: Mon-Wed 10am-Midnight; Thurs-Sat 10am-2am; Sun 11am-Midnight.
The Craig's patrons can look out onto the boats of Darling Harbour through large plate glass windows while sipping their drinks to the beat. As an established music venue, Fridays and Saturdays see both bands and dance music alternating (there is usually a cover charge at these times).

The Harbourside Brasserie
Pier One, Hickson Rd, Walsh Bay (behind the Rocks) (✆ 9252 3000)
Open: Mon-Sun 6pm-3am.
The Harbourside Brasserie is known for supporting up and coming musicians, and for providing a great spot to dine or drink while listening to live music, which generally starts at around 9pm, except for Sunday afternoons when a cappella takes centre stage. The Harbourside Brasserie has the reputation of being one of Sydney's premier music venues.

Rose, Shamrock & Thistle (Three Weeds)
193 Evans Rd, Rozelle (✆ 9555 7755)
Open: Mon-Sat 11am-Midnight; Sun Midnight-10pm.
Live music is usually heard at the Three Weeds from Wednesday to Sunday, and while a wide variety of music is played at the pub, the Three Weeds is famous for its blues and folk rock bands. The public bar itself is a traditional, large room filled with pool tables and atmosphere.

The Strawberry Hills
453 Elizabeth St, Surry Hills (✆ 9698 2997)
Open: Mon-Thurs 11am-Midnight; Fri-Sat 11am-3am; Sun 12noon-10pm.
The Strawberry Hills is known for its dedication to jazz (See: Music: Jazz). While some nights of the week see modern and improvised jazz, others are reserved purely for traditional styles. A relaxed atmosphere makes this a popular and friendly jazz venue.

LATE OPENERS

As well as the Kings Cross Hotel (above), the following pubs stay open into the small hours of the morning.

Court House Hotel
189 Oxford St, Taylor Square (✆ 360 4831)
Open: 7 days 24 hours.
If insomnia or a lost house key makes a twenty-four hour opener an attractive prospect, the Courthouse may be just the thing. From the ground floor bar, patrons can contemplate the ebb and flow of night traffic passing through Taylor Square and the sandstone edifice of the courthouse over the road. A dark interior may just lull you to sleep.

The Forresters
336 Riley St, Surry Hills (✆ 9211 2095)
Open: Mon-Thurs 11am-1am; Fri-Sat 11am-4am; Sun 11am-10pm.
Polished wood, dim lighting, vintage beer advertisements, a pool table, and crowds until 4am on Saturday mornings is the Forresters: a great pub where a wide cross section of Sydney coincides for drinking purposes. There is also a smaller, quieter bar attached with low tables and chairs.

A DRINK WITH A VIEW

Here are the top five spots in Sydney for a drink, all with a truly inspiring view at which to gaze over the rim of a glass.

Watsons Bay Beer Garden
The beer garden's view yawns over the dinghy-lined beach onto the calm glistening water and straight down the Harbour to the City skyline.

The Horizons Bar
This bar at the top of the ANA Hotel has a view directly down onto the Harbour Bridge and across harbour from the thirty-sixth floor.

Bathers Pavilion Refreshment Room
This narrow room in the pavilion is the perfect spot for a glass of wine looking onto Balmoral beach, with the Harbour and Heads beyond, and the occasional Manly Ferry cutting across in the distance.

Centennial Park Cafe
For a day time glass of wine in the middle of this beautiful and enormous park, a seat on the terrace of the cafe pavilion while watching hundreds of people exert themselves by jogging, in-line skating, riding, cycling or walking around the track nearby, is perfect.

BYO
For a BYO drink with a view experience, obtain a bottle of wine, some glasses and a corkscrew and head for one of the beaches or waterside picnic spots around the city (See: Open Air).

All details of the above can be found in the chapters Pubs and Cafes.

SHOPPING

Sydney's brashness and vivacity continue into the realm of the commercial, with seven day trading and a large number of slickly designed and tenanted retail complexes scattered throughout the city. The quality of service is generally high and the range of merchandise available enormous; things worth investing in will confront shoppers at almost every turn, especially when visiting the cit' markets. Consequently, parting with your money can be both dangerously easy and enjoyable, with shopping qualifying as one of the major recreational pursuits of the city. For this reason, we have compiled the best in Sydney shopping, whether designer clothing, jewellery, music, books, antiques, homewares, children's goods, adventure equipment or souvenirs.

Opening Hours throughout Sydney are: Monday to Friday 9am to 5.30pm, Thursday trading extends to 9pm; Saturday 9am to 5pm; Sunday 11am to 4pm. However, the hours vary according to area and complex, and while most centrally located shops open on Sundays, not all do. **Sales** occur twice annually: immediately after Christmas and mid year, approximately at the end of June. As with anywhere, they can be manic, and usually last for about two weeks.

SYDNEY'S MAJOR SHOPPING VENUES

The following are the best general areas to head for when planning an aimless shopping expedition.

THE CITY

Map Reference: E4.

There are many enormous shopping complexes scattered throughout the city centre, and most major retailers have shops here. Whether flitting from the MLC Centre to the Queen Victoria Building, or from Skygarden to the Strand Arcade, glitz and pizzazz stare out from every perfectly polished shop window.

Chifley Plaza

2 Chifley Square, City.

The base of this suave office tower is filled with suave retail outlets, among which are Maker's Mark, Tiffany & Co, Max Mara, Nina Ricci and Astton.

MLC Centre

Cnr King St & Castlereagh St, City.

Between King Street and Martin Place lie concealed in the MLC Centre numerous wonderful shops, including purveyors of jewellery, shoes, accessories and clothing, many of them international labels such as Gucci and Moschino. With an open food court and a several cafes on Martin Place, the Dendy cinema and film shop in the basement and the Theatre Royal on the King Street side, the MLC is one of the city's premier shopping complexes. The intersection of King and Castlereagh Streets is also known as 'Luxury Intersection' where the big names in conspicuous consumption rub shoulders: Louis Vuitton, Loewe, Chanel, Celine, Hermès, Hardy Brothers and Gucci. Only a stone's throw away in Martin Place is Emporio Armani.

Queen Victoria Building

Cnr George St & Market St, City.

Originally built to house produce markets, this magnificent building lay idle for decades, but luckily escaped the bulldozers of progress. It is now the City's premier shopping arcade, with patterned floor tiling, wide walkways and terraces, and a magnificent stained glass central dome. The shops are predominantly clothing lines, such as Polo Ralph Lauren, Country Road, Jigsaw and Esprit, all on the ground floor, while Crabtree & Evelyn and the Body Shop are also tenants. The best cafe of the building is Bar Cupola on the ground floor under the dome, while the specially commissioned clock with marching figures inside it never fails to attract a large number of camera wielding tourists, and is best viewed from the second floor.

The Rocks

Far from being merely a collection of historic buildings, The Rocks is a vibrant shopping precinct. Spurred on by the weekly Rocks Market (Saturday and Sunday), several heritage warehouses have been converted for use as shopping centres. The Metcalf Bond Store (George

Queen Victoria Building, City

Berkelouw Booksellers, Paddington

The Rocks Markets   Below: Skygarden, City

Norton Street Market   Below: Balmain Markets

Start Of The City to Surf

Sydney Cricket Ground

Windsurfing on Pittwater Below: Bondi Skate Ramp

Long Reef Golf Links Below: Homebush Pool

Street), The Argyle (Argyle Street), and George Street itself are occupied by innovative and varied tenants, well worthwhile investigating for their arts, crafts, souvenirs and Australian fashions.

Skygarden

From Castlereagh St to Pitt St Mall, City.

Skygarden is full of polished parquet floors, an atrium 'bigger than Ben Hur', good clothing and homewares shops, Illy Caffe and the top floor's Skydining, where almost twenty purveyors of good food supply the lunchtime crowds with pasta, pizza, rolls and roasts under a massive glass roof. Among the centre's prestigious shops are Hermès, Hardy Brothers jewellers, Saba, Country Road and Blockbuster Music.

The Strand Arcade

412 George St (from George St to Pitt St), City.

The Strand Arcade is one of the few remaining Victorian arcades left in tact by the bulldozing carried out in the name of progress. After a near disastrous fire in the 1970s, careful restoration returned the patterned tiling, iron lace terraces, stained glass and wooden staircases to their original elegance, making this a beautiful place through which to stroll. Today, it is renowned for great jewellery and style conscious young clothing. While all floors are worth exploring, a trip to the top to get the full impression of the arcade is strongly recommended, as is a coffee stop in the charmingly quaint Old Sydney Coffee Shop, the oldest cafe in Sydney.

NORTH

Chatswood

Map Reference: 6km north-west of C4.

A suburb which seems to exist primarily for shopping, Chatswood can be a nightmare. However, David Jones, Grace Brothers, World 4 Kids, Khoumery jewellery, some great clothing shops in Westfield and the best Italian bakery on the North Shore, Il Gianfornaio, are all here. There is also a growing contingent of Chinese herbalists, restaurants and shops.

Military Road, Mosman

Map Reference: 1km north of A7.

A short distance up the hill from Balmoral Beach and Taronga Zoo lies a stretch of clothing, shoes and homewares boutiques. Country Road, Raymond Castles, Oxford Shop and Von Troska are some of its tenants.

North Sydney

Map Reference: B4.

The shopping scene of North Sydney is dominated by the glossy and highly polished Greenwood Plaza. Here, a large number of clothing retailers, ranging from Polo Ralph Lauren to Jigsaw, Oxford Shop and Esprit, dominate the centre's focus, while an excellent and varied food court, complete with cafe and bar, completes the scene.

EAST

The Eastern Suburbs are the clothing, galleries and antiques focus of Sydney. Young labels line Oxford Street and Crown Street, while the area around Queen Street is well known for its galleries and antiques shops.

Crown Street, Surry Hills

Map Reference: G4.

Crown Street (south of Oxford Street) is the place to go for the clothing of Sydney's young and most fashionable designers, such as Black Vanity, Dangerfield and Pepa Mejia.

Oxford Street, Paddington

Map Reference: G5 to G6.

A dense collection of clothing boutiques covering a wide scope of style and price, together with the fantastic Folkways music shop, the Paddington Bazaar on Saturday, and wonderful cafes, especially Elizabeth Street's Chocolate Factory, make up the Oxford Street shopping precinct. Also very important are its bookshops, Ariel, New Edition and Berkelouw's.

Queen Street, Woollahra

Map Reference: H7.

This is the prime spot in Sydney for purveyors of antiques.

INNER WEST

Glebe Point Road, Glebe

Map Reference: G2 to F1.

Another long street with wide variety and high interest is Glebe Point Road, home of Gleebooks, Architectural Heritage, the Valhalla cinema, and right at the end, the Black Wattle canteen, in the artists' studios.

King Street, Newtown

Map Reference: H1.

King Street is not as sanitised as Oxford Street and has much more variety, both in shoppers and shops. With its pan-global incense shops, second hand clothing shops, old wares dealers, new boutiques and cafes, interspersed with newsagents and hardware shops, King Street just holds on to its identity as the epitome of the Sydney suburban main street, a fast disappearing phenomenon.

DEPARTMENT STORES

David Jones

Flagship: Intersection Market St & Castlereagh St, City (✆ 9266 5544)

Open: Mon-Fri 9am-6pm; Thurs to 9pm; Sat 9am-5pm; Sun 11am-5pm.

Suburban Stores: Bankstown, Bondi Junction, Brookvale, Castle Hill, Chatswood & Parramatta.

The flagship stores are in the City, directly over the road from each other. The Elizabeth Street store is the women's store, and includes haberdashery, a ground floor cosmetics utopia, young fashions, designer clothing from Max Mara, Mani, Calvin Klein and Vittadini among others, women's and children's shoes, children's clothing and toys and up on the top floor, the quasi-untouchables of women's designer clothing. The Market Street store is supposedly the men's domain, including shirts and ties, shoes and casual wear, a fantastic suit department, electrical and household goods, kitchenware and computer and electrical equipment. All of this rests on the basement of the Elysian food hall. Together, these two are the city's premier department stores.

Grace Bros

Flagship: Cnr George & Market St, City (✆ 9238 9111)
Open: Mon-Sat 9am-6pm; Thurs to 9pm; Sun 11am-5pm.
Suburban Stores: Bondi Junction, Chatswood, Miranda, Parramatta & Roselands.
Grace Brothers is more functional department store, where less time is spent on the gloss and presentation than up the road at David Jones. The prices are the same, though. Highlights include the Miss Shop, full of quasi-disposable trendy clothes, a floor full of Australian and overseas designers, and Robert Clergerie shoes. Men's, women's and homeware items are combined in the one, sprawling store.

CLOTHING

Whether a suave suit or a tacky t-shirt, it can be found in Sydney. Following is a selection of the best clothing boutiques and labels for men (M) and women (W) available in this city. While the listings concentrate on local labels, a few overseas arrivals are also included.

Belinda (W)

8 Transvaal Ave, Double Bay (✆ 9328 6288)
Open: Mon-Fri 10am-6pm; Sat 10am-5pm.
Often described as a style haven, Belinda is a subtle suite of rooms filled with the best clothes of the season from overseas and local designers. The boutique concentrates on the more expensive and 'refined' lines.

Black Vanity (W)

Strand Arcade, City (✆ 9233 6241)
Open: Mon-Fri 9.30am-5.30pm; Thurs to 8.30pm; Sat 10am-4pm; Sun 12noon-5pm.
400 Oxford St, Paddington (✆ 9360 5130)
Open: Mon-Sat 10am-6pm; Thurs to 8.30pm; Sun 12noon-5pm.
182 Campbell St, Surry Hills (✆ 9380 6725)
Open: Mon-Sat 10am-6pm; Closed Sun.
Black Vanity can be relied upon for highly original clothing from various Australian and overseas designers as well as their own label. Evening dresses, dresses, trousers and jackets executed in exquisite fabrics makes this a magnet for any style conscious shoppers looking for clothing away from the main stream. The Surry Hills shop is the flagship store, complete with cafe.

Bracewell (M&W)

264 Oxford St, Paddington (✆ 9360 6192) (W)
274 Oxford St, Paddington (✆ 9331 2830) (M)
Open: Mon-Sat 10am-6pm; Thurs to 8.30pm; Sun 11.30am- 5.30pm.
Strand Arcade, City (✆ 9221 8882) (W)
Open: Mon-Fri 9.30am-5.30pm; Thurs to 8pm; Sat 9.30am-4pm.30pm.
Both stores are stocked with racks of suaveness. The women's lines include a wonderful home label and several local designers as well as Plein Sud, Demeulemeester and Dries van Noten, while the men's store stocks their own label, Indigo, Bettina Liano and some Bisonte. All Bracewell shops are a great place to find slick separates and ensembles, for casual, business and evening wear.

Country Road (M&W)

Queen Victoria Building, City (✆ 9261 2099) (M&W))
Open: Mon-Fri 9am-6pm; Sat 9am-5pm; Sun 11am-5pm.
Skygarden (Levels 1, 2 & 3), City (✆ 9223 7955) (M&W)
Open: Mon-Fri 9am-5.30pm; Sat 10am-5pm; Closed Sun.
Also at: Paddington (✆ 9332 3699), Mosman (✆ 9960 4633) & other locations.
Country Road is one of the best known labels in the country, and has dressed Australian men, women and their houses for nearly two decades. Classic designs and good quality fabrics are used to create timeless garments ranging from the now traditional and quasi-ubiquitous casual wear to business wear. Country Road 'Homewears' relaxedly capture the mood of Australian houses.

David Jones (M&W)

Elizabeth St and Market St, City (✆ 9266 5544)
Open: Mon-Fri 9am-6pm; Thurs to 9pm; Sat 9am-5pm; Sun 11am-5pm.
Spread over the floors of these two flagship stores you will find great selections of the entire spectrum of men's and women's clothing and accessories. The first floor of Market Street is where the men's designer clothes are (including Calvin Klein, Polo Ralph Lauren, Country Road and Paul Smith) while the second floor of Elizabeth Street is the equivalent for women (Max Mara, Calvin Klein, Vittadini, Mani).

Emporio Armani & Giorgio Armani (M&W)

EA: Challis House, Martin Place, City (✆ 9231 3655); **GA:** Cnr Market St & Elizabeth St, City (✆ 9283 5562).
Open: EA: Mon-Fri 10am-6pm; Thurs to 8pm; Sat

Clothing Sizes

Women's Clothing

Australian	**8**	**10**	**12**	**14**	**16**	**18**
American	6	8	10	12	14	16
British	8	10	12	14	16	18
German	34	36	38	40	42	44
Italian	40	42	44	46	48	50
Japanese	5	7	9	11	13	15

Women's Shoes

Australian	**36**	**37**	**38**	**39**	**40**	**41**
American	5	6	7	8	9	10
British	3	4	5	6	7	8
European	36	37	38	39	40	41

Men's Shirts

Australian	**36**	**38**	**39**	**41**	**42**	**43**	**44**	**45**
American	14	15	15½	16	16½	17	17½	18
British	14	15	15½	16	16½	17	17½	18
European	36	38	39	41	42	43	44	45

Men's Suits

Australian	**87**	**92**	**96**	**100**	**102**	**104**	**106**	**108**
American	34	36	38	39	40	41	42	43
British	34	36	38	39	40	41	42	43
European	44	46	48	50	51	52	53	54

Men's Shoes

Australian	**39**	**40**	**41**	**42**	**43**	**44**	**45**	**46**
American	7	7½	8	8½	9½	10½	11	11½
British	6	7	7½	8	9	10	11	12
European	39	40	41	42	43	44	45	46
Japanese	24½	25	25½	26	26½	27	27½	

10am-5.30pm; Sun 11am-5pm; GA: Mon-Fri 9am-6pm; Thurs to 8pm; Sat 10am-5pm; Sun 11am-5pm.

Apart from making available in Sydney the subtle lines and fabrics for which Armani is revered, there is even a fabulous Emporio Express coffee bar on the first floor of the Emporio, a popular restaurant where shoppers and browsers can lunch or snack on antipasto, pasta and desserts. The Giorgio Armani boutique up in Elizabeth Street offers more expensive expressions of the same design principles. Now Sydney too has access to the muted tones and subtle lines of the master.

Five Way Fusion (M&W)

205 Glenmore Rd, Paddington (near Five Ways) (✆ 9331 2828)

Open: Mon-Fri 10am-6.30pm; Thurs to 8pm; Sat 10am-5.30pm; Sun 12noon-5pm.

This is commonly referred to as the place in Sydney for the big names in men's and women's fashion: Dolce & Gabbana, Versace and Miyake hang amongst the best of them.

Gowings (M)

Cnr Market St & George St, City (✆ 9264 6321)

Open: Mon-Fri 8.30am-6pm; Thurs to 8.30pm; Sat 9am-5pm; Sun 11am-5pm.

The boys go to Gowings for socks, shirts, shoes, hats, jumpers, funny t-shirts and ties. This is a three level emporium of men's and boys' stuff. An independent department store of over one hundred and twenty-five years standing bearing the motto "Walk through, no one asked to buy", Gowings is a great place to shop, and an icon of the City (See: Sydney Icons).

Marcs (M&W)

280 Oxford St, Paddington (✆ 9332 4255)

Open: Mon-Fri 10am-6pm; Thurs to 8pm; Sat 9.30am-5.30pm; Sun 11am-4pm.

Also at: Pitt St Mall, City (✆ 9221 5575), Military Rd, Mosman (✆ 9968 1298) & Redfern St, Redfern (✆ 9319 7516).

As well as stocking several international labels, Marcs is famous for its own label's excellent quality shirts and t-shirts. With men's fashions dominant, but an excellent women's collection also in stock, Marcs is a popular haven.

Polo Ralph Lauren (M&W)
Ground Floor, Queen Victoria Building, City (✆ 9267 1630) (M)
1st floor David Jones Market St, City (✆ 9266 5681) (M)
Greenwood Plaza, North Sydney (✆ 9956 6828) (M&W)
From these three boutiques are available the unmistakable shirts, ties, trousers, shirts, polos, jumpers, jackets, skirts, dresses, blazers, accessories, caps and shoes of the Polo stables.

Riada (W)
118 Queen St, Woollahra (✆ 9363 0654)
Open: Mon-Fri 10am-6pm; Sat 10am-4pm; Closed Sun.
681 Military Rd, Mosman (✆ 9969 4269)
Open: Mon-Fri 9.30am-5.30pm; Sat 9.30am-4.30pm; Closed Sun.
Another restrained style haven, Riada offers the best in subtly elegant clothing sourced from labels here and overseas. Preferred lines are suave and understated, and include Alberta Ferretti, Mani and Rifat Ozbek as well as a number of local labels and a Riada label.

Saba (M&W)
Shops P2-3 Ground floor Skygarden, Pitt St Mall, City (✆ 9231 2436) (M); (✆ 9231 2183) (W).
Open: Mon-Fri 9.30am-6pm; Thurs to 9pm; Sat 9.30am-5pm; Sun 12noon-4pm.
Also at: 39 Bay St, Double Bay (✆ 9362 0281)
Open: Mon-Fri 9.30am-6pm; Sat 9.30am-5pm; Sun 12noon-4pm.
Although a Melbourne label, Sydney has three stores of its own, full of simple yet suave casual and elegant wear in fabulous fabrics. Highest quality materials and fibres make up pants, dresses, suits, jumpers, shirts and skirts, which are modern and impeccably suave.

INTERNATIONAL HOUSES IN SYDNEY

A number of international designers maintain boutiques in Sydney. Among them you will find Chanel (Castlereagh St, City); Gianni Versace (Elizabeth St, City;); Giorgio Armani (Cnr Elizabeth St & Market St, City); Gucci (Castlereagh St); and Max Mara (Chifley Plaza, City). Accessories made by the international houses can also be found here: Bulgari (Market St, City); Hermes (Castlereagh St, City); Loewe (Castlereagh St, City); Louis Vuitton (Castlereagh St, City); and Tiffany & Co (Chifley Plaza, City).

FASHION FOR SMART YOUNG THINGS

The best precincts for such slick numbers are Oxford Street, Paddington; The Strand Arcade, City; and Crown Street, Surry Hills.

Brave (W)
302 Oxford St, Paddington (✆ 9332 2940)
Open: Mon-Sat 10am-6pm; Thurs to 8pm; Sun 11.30am-5.30pm.
Shop 69 Strand Arcade, City (✆ 9221 5292)
Open: Mon-Fri 9.30am-5.30pm; Thurs to 8.30pm; Sat 9.30am-4.30pm.
Brave is largely what you've got to be to wear these directional pieces: tiny angora sweaters or spray on micro mini dresses may appear on the window mannequins, while crocheted bikinis and other eye catching objects lie at their feet. The label's men's line, introduced in winter 1996, follows similar principles of contemporary slick. This is a very distinctive and modern Sydney label.

Dangerfield (M&W)
330 Crown St, Surry Hills (✆ 9380 6924)
Open: Mon-Sat 10am-6pm; Thurs to 8pm; Closed Sun.
This label started in Melbourne to make and sell the op-shop treasures potential shoppers wanted but could not readily find. The stores consider themselves more a concept than shops, combining art gallery, music and alternative clothing in one place. The clothes are best described as hip, contemporary, unique exotic/bizarre/clubbing clothes.

Morrisey Edmiston (M&W)
Woman & Man 1st floor, Strand Arcade, City (✆ 9232 7606)
Open: Mon-Fri 9.30am-5.30pm; Thurs to 8.30pm; Sat 10am-4.30pm; Closed Sun.
These clothes are world famous: modern and slick, simple and funky dresses, t-shirts, shirts, skirts, trousers and jackets. The Morrisey Edmiston legend has reached New York and taken it by storm, but it started here!

Museum (W)
296 Oxford St, Paddington (✆ 9332 2030)
Open: Mon-Sat 10am-6pm; Thurs to pm; Sun 12noon-5pm.
Museum stocks the best in smart young things' wear, whether they be for day or evening. The boutique gathers its stock from around the world, and a browse is almost always vaguely intimidating but more than worthwhile, similar to their clothing.

Dotti (W)
227 Pitt St Mall, City (✆ 9223 4028)
Open: Mon-Fri 9.30am-6pm; Thurs to 9pm; Sat 9.30am-5.30pm; Sun 11.30am-4pm.
356 Oxford St, Paddington (✆ 9332 1659)
Open: Mon-Fri 10am-6pm; Thurs to 9pm; Sat 9.30am-6pm; Sun 11.30-5.30pm.
Dotti has to be seen to be believed. Purveyors of the pieces of every trend that comes into existence in Sydney, it is an invaluable source of cheap (almost disposable) clubbing and casual wear for women, priced from $10. They have even been known to stock Bavarian "mini-dirndls",

enthusiastically described as "really cool and cute".

Pepa Mejia (M&W)
318 Crown St, Surry Hills (✆ 9360 2463)
Open: Mon-Fri 10am-6.30pm; Thurs to 9pm; Sat 9.30am-6.30pm; Closed Sun.
Pepa Mejia is a great shop, not least because it stocks the clothing of around twenty small and independent Australian designers.

Sportsgirl (W)
Ground floor, Skygarden, Pitt St Mall, City (✆ 9223 8255)
Open: Mon-Fri 9am-6pm; Thurs to 9pm; Sat 9am-4pm; Sun 11am-4pm.
Also at: other locations (✆ 1800 801 334).
The Sportsgirl chain supplies relatively cheap interpretations of the trends in young clothing, accessories and shoes each season. The style is relaxed and casual, with some slightly more glamorous things as well. Upstairs are more sophisticated lines for grown up Sportsgirls, offering better fabrics and designs for business and leisure wear.

Tour (W)
Shop 217 Westfield Shopping Centre, Victoria St, Chatswood (✆ 9415 3440)
Open: Mon-Fri 9am-5.30pm; Thurs to 9pm; Sat 9am-4pm; Closed Sun.
Shop 73 Strand Arcade, City (✆ 9233 3180)
Open: Mon-Fri 10am-5.30pm; Thurs to 8.30pm; Sat 10am-4pm; Closed Sun.
Tour is an award-winning Sydney label spanning anything from funky separates to glamorous evening dresses.

Third Millennium (W)
Shop 65 Strand Arcade, City (✆ 9221 4089)
Open: Mon-Fri 9.30am-5.30; Thurs to 8.30pm; Sat 9.30m-4.30pm; Closed Sun.
328 Crown St, Surry Hills (✆ 9331 2490)
Open: Mon-Sat 10am-6pm; Thurs to 7pm; Closed Sun.
Third Millennium's label ranges from office wear, day wear, formal wear and "funky going out wear", but all items have a common, overriding classical tone.

Esprit (W)
Shop 28 Queen Victoria Building, City (✆ 9267 5444)
Open: Mon-Sat 9am-6pm; Thurs to 9pm; Sun 10.45am-5.45pm.
Also at: Pitt St, City (✆ 9221 8182) & Chatswood Chase, Chatswood (✆ 9411 1388).
It's the same the world over, and you can buy it here. Good items, comfortable yet snappy designs and great colours at low cost.

Paddington Bazaar (M&W)
St John's Church, Oxford St, Paddington.
Open: Saturdays only 10am-4pm.
This is the swamp out of which much of Sydney fashion crawls: scores of fashion design graduates start their own labels and sell them here. Some are better than you'll find in the shops! The entire left hand half of the markets is devoted to new clothing.

TRADITIONAL AUSTRALIAN CLOTHING

They may not be the height of fashion, but many Australians couldn't live without their 'RMs'. These elastic sided leather booties are worn all over the world, and the place to get them is here. 'Drizabone' coats are also a popular item out bush, as are Akubra hats and trousers. The following are not tourist traps, but where real, live Australians get their gear 'n' stuff.

Goodwood Saddlery
237 Broadway, Central (✆ 9660 6788)
Open: Mon-Sat 9am-5pm; Thurs to 8pm; Sun 10am-4pm.
The Goodwood Saddlery stocks the entire range, with a slightly more equestrian edge to it. Keep and eye out for frequent markdowns and specials.

RM Williams Bushman's Outfitters
389 George St, City (✆ 9262 2228)
Open: Mon-Wed 9am-5pm; Thurs 9am-9pm; Fri 9am-5.30pm; Sat 9am-4pm; Sun 11am-4pm.
Also at: Sydney International Airport (✆ 9313 4022) & Chatswood (✆ 9411 4388).
RM Williams is an Australian institution. The entire range of those funny, elastic-sided boots, those checked shirts, bushman's hats, off-white trousers, plaited belts and waterproof coats is available in these stores, in short, everything required to look like an original Aussie bushman.

Strand Hatters
Strand Arcade, Ground Floor, City (✆ 9231 6884)
Open: Mon-Fri 8am-5.30pm; Thurs to 8.30pm; Sat 9.30am-4.30pm; Sun 10.30am-3.30pm.
Here, you can not only buy the hats, but you can watch the movie too. Yes! The Strand Hatters constantly plays a video of how the world famous hats are made. Obtain a cake from the Boronia Patisserie, opposite, and watch the movie.

VINTAGE AND SECOND HAND CLOTHING

Reincarnation
169 Glebe Point Rd (✆ 9660 2092)
Open: Mon-Sun 10am-6pm; Thurs to 8pm.
Creations of many decades, from the bizarre to the very wearable, are to be found at Reincarnation among many silk shirts, jackets and outlandish dresses.

Recycle-Path
3/210 Darlinghurst Rd, Darlinghurst (✆ 9360 1484)
Open: 7 days 12noon-8pm
Also at: 131 King St, Newtown (✆ 9517 1789).

Recycle-Path is a great place to rummage around for Levis, Hawaiian shirts, t-shirts, dresses, leather and denim jackets, accessories and (new) caps.

Route 66

257 Crown St, Darlinghurst (✆ 9331 6686)

Open: Mon-Fri 10am.30-6pm; Thurs to 8pm; Sat 10am-5pm; Closed Sun.

Route 66 is a popular source of pre-loved vintage American clothing.

The Vintage Clothing Shop

149 Castlereagh St, Sydney (✆ 9267 7135)

Open: Mon-Fri 10.30am-6pm; Thurs to 9pm; Sat 10.30am-4pm; Closed Sun.

The Vintage Clothing Shop consistently stocks great suits, coats, dresses, trousers, accessories, jewellery and cases from the 1940s, 50s and 60s, tightly packed into a small area. A well selected collection of very high quality.

Zoo Emporium

332 Crown St, Darlinghurst (✆ 9380 5990)

Open: Mon-Sat 11am-6pm; Thurs to 8pm; Closed Sun.

Zoo is devoted to original 1970s psychedelia. Nowhere else will shoppers find boob tubes, sequined flares and stilettos glorified to such extremes and with such dedication.

More?

Don't forget the Paddington Bazaar (See: Markets) or King Street, Newtown.

JEWELLERY

The best spots for jewellery shopping are the City (particularly the Strand Arcade) and the Paddington Bazaar, which regularly has a number of excellent jewellers among its stalls. For antique jewellery, See: Antiques, below.

Community Aid Abroad Trading

Centrepoint L2, shop CM.05, City (✆ 9231 4016)

Open: Mon-Fri 9am-6pm; Thurs to 8pm; Sat 9am-5pm; Closed Sun.

CAA stocks a great selection of jewellery from all over the world, but particularly Africa, in the form of beads, silver and brass for the arms, neck and ears. The shop is a little difficult to find, tucked behind the escalators one level directly below the walkway into David Jones, but eminently worthwhile investigating.

Dinosaur Designs

Shop 73 Strand Arcade, City (✆ 9223 2953)

Open: Mon-Fri 9.30am-5.30pm; Thurs to 8.30pm; Sat 10am-4pm; Closed Sun.

Also at: 339 Oxford St, Paddington (✆ 9361 3776).

Dinosaur Designs is famous for fabulous resin jewellery in amazingly vibrant colours and cartoon-like shapes, as well as plain black and ivory-coloured designs. Rings, chokers, necklaces, bracelets and pendants form the staple core of the range, while utility pieces, such as serving spoons, also make an appearance. The designers started out at the Paddington Bazaar, and have been incredibly popular ever since. Their jewellery is not expensive.

The Family Jewels

46 Oxford St, Paddington (✆ 9331 6647)

Open: Mon-Sat 10am-6pm; Thurs to 7.30pm; Sun 11am-6pm.

If you're looking for it, it should be here. Almost gaudy plastic to beads to lapis and silver and some beautiful jewellery in the form of rings, necklaces and earrings form the Family Jewels' normal collection of stock.

Glebe Markets

Glebe Public School, Glebe Point Rd, Glebe (✆ 9660 6667)

Open: Sat 9am-4pm.

These markets have a smaller selection of jewellery than the Paddington Bazaar, concentrating on flea market, 'ethnic' or radical pieces.

Hardy Brothers Jewellers

77 Castlereagh St, City (✆ 9232 2422)

Open: Mon-Fri 9.30am-5pm; Sat 9.30am-3.30pm; Closed Sun.

Also at: 2 Guilefoyle Ave, Double Bay (✆ 9327 1366)

Hardy Brothers is one of Australia's best known jewellers, established in this country in the 1820s.

Jan Logan

36 Cross St, Double Bay (✆ 9363 2529)

Open: Mon-Fri 9.30am-5.20pm; Sat 9.30am-4.30pm; Closed Sun.

Jan Logan stocks a carefully selected, high quality collection of antique and new jewellery.

Love & Hatred

Strand Arcade, City (✆ 9233 3441)

Open: Mon-Fri 10am-5,30pm; Thurs to 8pm; Sat 10am-4pm; Closed Sun.

The very desirable (and very affordable in many cases) pieces in gold and silver are known for their elegant and witty designs. Here you may find devil's tails hoop earrings or medieval replica designs. Love & Hatred's collections also feature semi-precious stones and rose gold.

Maker's Mark

Chifley Plaza, 2 Chifley Square, City (✆ 9231 6800)

Open: Mon-Fri 10am-5.45pm; Sat 10am-3.45pm; Closed Sun.

Maker's Mark features the work of over one hundred Australian designers, from inexpensive trinkets to Broome pearls and precious work. Also worth investigating is a tasteful 'Australiana' section.

Margo Richards

1st Gallery level Strand Arcade, City (✆ 9232

3870)
Open: Mon-Fri 10am-5.30pm; Thurs to 7.30pm; Sat 10am-3.30pm; Closed Sun.
This shop is a delight for many reasons, not least its collection of antique and replica jewellery, including rings, watches and jet beads.

Paddington Bazaar
St Johns Church, 395 Oxford St, Paddington (✆ 9331 2646)
Open: Sat 10am-4pm.
A number of excellent jewellers are regulars at Sydney's best markets. In particular, seek out rose gold close to Oxford Street, a wide variety of pieces from Asia Minor, and striking silver and stone rings made by local designers.

Rox Gems & Jewellery
Shop31 Strand Arcade, City (✆ 9232 7828)
Open: Mon-Fri 9.30am-5.30pm; Thurs to 9pm; Sat 10am-4pm; Closed Sun.
Another famous Sydney jeweller, Rox creates striking modern designs, primarily concentrating on rings with large and colourful semi- and precious stones. This is a great window into which to gaze.

Tiffany & Co
Chifley Plaza, 2 Chifley Square, City (✆ 9235 1777)
Open: Mon-Fri 9.30am-6pm; Sat 10am-4pm; Closed Sun.
Sydney has its very own Tiffany's store full of mid-blue boxes and gleaming jewellery.

The Treasury Room
Mid City Centre, Pitt St Level, City (✆ 9223 6883)
Open: Mon-Sat 9am-6pm; Thurs to 9pm; Sun 11am-5pm.
A small shop tucked behind the escalators, the Treasury Room is crammed full of amethyst, amber, lapis, silver and other jewellery, primarily of broadly defined 'ethnic' origin.

COSMETICS & WELL BEING

Aveda Esthetique
Shop 16 Queen Victoria Building, City (✆ 9264 8925)
Open: Mon-Sat 9am-6pm; Thurs to 9pm; Sun 11am-5pm.
Aveda stocks a good range of its own top quality natural products, ranging from hair dehumectants and humectants to aromatherapy oils and cosmetics made from pure flower and plant essences.

The Body Shop
Shop 48-50 Queen Victoria Building, City (✆ 9264 1796)
Open: Mon-Sat 8.30am-6pm; Thurs to 9pm; Sun 10am-5pm.
Also at: Chatswood (✆ 9413 1793) Parramatta (✆ 9687 2377), Roselands (✆ 9740 4633) & other locations.
A bouquet of dewberry and rose scents greets visitors entering these heavily scented treasure chests full of natural creams, cosmetics, body goods, grooming goods, hair products and perfumes.

David Jones
Cnr Elizabeth St, Market St ✆ Castlereagh St, City (✆ 9266 5544)
Open: Mon-Fri 9am-6pm; Thurs to 9pm; Sat 9am-5pm; Sun 11am-5pm.
David Jones is a cosmetics, perfume and aftershave heaven: pale grey marble and mirrors reflect the gentle light, flowers burst out from above, the piano tinkles... and all those bottles and jars from scores of cosmetic and perfumery companies stand at enticing counters.

Red Earth
M12 Queen Victoria Building, City (✆ 9264 2420)
Open: Mon-Sat 9am-6pm; Thurs to 9pm; Sun 10am-5pm.
Also at: North Sydney (✆ 9955 6177), Hornsby (✆ 9482 3516), Bankstown (✆ 9796 1206).
The rich scent of Red Earth emanates from deep piles of unusual pot pourri mixes, featuring Australian leaves and blooms as well as the more traditional combinations. Red Earth also stocks body lotions, skin care, aromatherapy essences and all sorts of relaxation-inspiring items, such as brushes and massage rolls.

Sanctum
448 Oxford St, Paddington (✆ 9360 3895)
Open: Mon-Fri 10am-6pm; Thurs to 8pm; Sat 9am-6pm; Sun 11am-5pm.
As the name suggests, this is a retreat from the business of Oxford Street outside its doors and the City beyond, offering potions, infusions, lotions and aromas to assist one's quest for inner well being and relaxation.

FOOD & DRINK

BAKERIES, PATISSERIES & CAKE SHOPS

Bagel House
7 Flinders St, Darlinghurst (✆ 9360 7892)
Open: Tues-Sun 7.30am-4pm; Closed Mon.
This is the popular home of real bagels and an inviting bakery cafe.

Cafe Niki
Bourke St, Surry Hills (✆ 9319 7517)
Open: 7 days 7am-10pm.
Work starts at five in the morning at this wonderful cafe, as they bake their fantastic pastries and biscuits for other lucky cafes around Sydney. As an early opener, Niki is a top spot to pick up provisions before heading on a trip out of Sydney. (See: Cafes.)

Délifrance
Queen Victoria Building, City (✆ 9261 5582)
Open: Mon-Fri 7.30am-7.30pm; Sat 8am-7.30pm; Sun 8am-6.30pm.

Also at: Chatswood (✆ 9411 8414), Liverpool (✆ 9601 5321), Miranda (✆ 9524 1526), North Sydney (✆ 9955 0586) & other locations.
For those who can ignore the hungry looks of the thousands of commuters waking past to and from Town Hall station, this is a good place to indulge in French snacks, pastries and breads. Good coffee and refreshments are also on offer.

Il Gianfornaio
414 Victoria St, Chatswood (✆ 9413 4833)
Open: Mon-Fri 8am-7pm; Thurs to 9pm; Sat 8am-4.30pm; Closed Sun.
Also at: Skygarden, City (✆ 9231 2468).
Cuorgh! Shelves of Italian pastries and biscuits, loaves and loaves of Italian bread, fresher than fresh thin-crusted pizza constantly streaming out of the oven and hordes of hungry people elbowing each other to get to the counter make this the hottest bakery on the North Shore and in the City. Tables here are in high demand, especially as they serve Illy coffee.

La Renaissance Patisserie Cafe
47 Argyle St, The Rocks (✆ 9241 4878)
Open: 7 days 8.30am-6pm.
La Renaissance is famous for wonderful pastries and cakes, and equally great pies: the veal chasseur pie is legendary, as are the herbed, garlicky sausage rolls and the delicate quiches. Scrumptious pastries including amazing chocolate boxes filled with chocolate mousse, eclairs, religieuses, rum babas and tartlets, and there is a cool and calm back courtyard in which to eat the yummies, accompanied by a coffee or drink.

The Golden Pie
144b Glebe Point Rd, Glebe (✆ 9660 1794)
Open: 7 days 7am-6.30pm.
The Golden Pie is almost as legendary as the Golden Fleece, its fame based justifiably on its fruit and meat pies.

BOTTLE SHOPS & WINE MERCHANTS

Amato's Liquor Mart
40 Henry St, Leichhardt (✆ 9560 7628)
Open: Mon-Sat 9am-8pm; Sun 10am-6pm.
Amato's stocks a large range of premium Australian and imported wines and spirits, specialising in the Italian side of things. Less well known wines, perhaps from Chile and Greece, are also stocked.

Camperdown Cellars
21-25 Kingston Rd, Camperdown (✆ 9516 4466)
Open: Mon-Wed 9am-8.30pm; Thurs-Sat 9am-9pm; Sun 10am-8pm.
The mighty Camperdown cellars bill themselves as the house of fine wine, and judging by some of the labels available here, you may agree. However, apart from the usual tastings, they also offer 'master class' tastings with representatives of various houses.

Crown of the Hill
306-314 Willoughby Rd, Naremburn (✆ 9439 3902)
Open: Mon-Fri ✆ Sun 9am-8pm; Thurs 9am-9pm; Sat 8am-9pm.
Also at: Forestville (✆ 9451 6413), West Lindfield (✆ 9416 8711) & Harbord (✆ 9938 5122).
Crown of the Hill is worth journeying to as their shops stock large selections of Australian and imported wines, beers and spirits. Less common wines will often turn up on the shelves, while tasting bonanzas concentrating on a particular region, and specially labelled releases from vineyards, are further attractions to investigate.

Figtree Cellars
231 Burns Bay Rd, Lane Cove (✆ 9428 1899)
Open: Mon-Sat 8am-8pm; Sun 10am-6pm.
Another well respected wine merchant worth journeying to, Figtree stocks a very wide range of Australian and imported wines, as well as running a wine and food club which holds regular tastings and special events.

Kemeny's
137 Bondi Rd, Bondi (✆ 9389 6422)
Open: Mon-Sat 8am-9pm; Sun 9am-8pm.
A well stocked, well respected, well frequented and well informed wine merchant, definitely worth a visit, is Kemeny's. Occasional wine shows focusing on particular region, and a certain ability to find less common wines, make this a popular merchant.

Sixty Darling St Fine Wine Merchants
60 Darling St, Balmain (✆ 9818 3727)
Open: Mon-Fri 9am-9pm; Sat-Sun 10am-8.30pm.
This is a wonderful shop full of amazing wines and run by an enthusiastic expert. The front shelves and back section's bins burst with great wines from Australia and overseas (New Zealand, California, South Africa, France and Italy among others), ranging from the inexpensive to awe inspiringly unobtainable. Tastings are frequently held.

Theo's Liquor Markets
Shop 16 Neutral Bay Shopping Village, Military Rd, Neutral Bay (✆ 9908 1933)
Open: Mon-Sat 9am-8pm; Thurs-Sat 9am-9pm; Sun 10am-7pm.
Also at: Nth Bondi (✆ 9365 0666), Haberfield (✆ 9799 5533) & other locations.
Specialising in "a lot of wine", Theo's markets regularly have very good prices on great wines. A top spot with a wide selection.

Toohey Bros
223 Victoria Rd, Drummoyne (✆ 981 3789)
Open: Mon-Wed 9am-8.30pm; Thurs-Sat 9am-9pm; Sun 10am-7pm.
Also at: Annandale (✆ 9519 7227), Erskineville (✆ 9516 2563), Paddington (✆ 9332 1811) ✆

Willoughby (✆ 9958 1545).
Toohey Brothers is another group of good wine merchants in operation in Sydney. In addition to a wide selection of Australian and overseas wines, they often have self-labelled releases from various vineyards worth more than just trying.

Vintage Cellars
125 Bayswater Rd, Rushcutters Bay (✆ 9331 3223)
Open: Mon-Sat 9am-10pm; Sun 10am-7pm.
Also at: 548 Sydney Rd, Seaforth (✆ 9949 2072)
Vintage Cellars are particularly good for medium priced and expensive wines from Australia and overseas, as well as a wide selection of international and local beers and spirits.

Don't forget that most pubs around Sydney have bottle shops attached to them.

SPECIALIST COFFEE VENDORS & ROASTERS

The Chocolate Factory
8 Elizabeth St, Paddington (✆ 9331 3785)
Open: Tues-Sat 8am-6pm; Sun10am-6pm; Closed Mon.
As well as dispensing much needed excellent coffee from the cafe's gleaming Bo Ema machine, the Chocolate Factory sells several different freshly ground coffees from Hernandez (from $6.50 per 250g).

Forsyth Teas & Coffees
284 Willoughby Rd, Naremburn (✆ 9906 7388)
Open: Mon-Wed 9.30am-6pm; Thurs-Fri 9.30am-7pm; Sat-Sun 9am-6pm.
Naremburn's Forsyth Teas and Coffees is the source of eight pure coffees and fifty different blends. As well as stocking around ten different tea blends, Forsyth has a charming pavement cafe where patrons can try the brews.

Hernandez
60 Kings Cross Rd, Potts Point (✆ 9331 2343)
Open: 7 days 24 hours.
Apart from being a happy refuge for coffee fiends at all hours of the day and night, Hernandez is also the roaster of some very fine coffees. The Spanish Espresso, as served at the Chocolate Factory (above), is just one of twenty different blends roasted and/or sold on the premises (from $6 per 250g).

Bersten's Belaroma Coffees
457 Penshurst St, East Roseville (✆ 9417 5193)
Open: Mon-Fri 9am-5pm; Sat 8.30am-12.30pm; Closed Sun.
With sparkling coffee-making equipment lining the shelves and filling the window, cool and hot drinks served inside, surrounded by the bel aroma of rich, roasting coffee beans, Bersten's has been supplying fresh blends for over twenty-seven years. Coffees in the range include Australian, Indonesian, Nicaraguan, Columbian and Kenyan (from $6 per 250g).

Bravo Coffee
177 Enmore Rd, Enmore (✆ 9519 1204)
Open: Mon-Fri 7.45am-6pm; Sat 7.30am-1pm.
Bravo coffee sells its own roasts of A-grade coffee ranging from Brazilian to Ethiopian, or Kenyan to Espresso. A small cafe within Bravo offers cups of their brews and biscuits.

Brazilian Coffee & Nut Factory
34 Victoria Rd, Marrickville (✆ 9519 4984)
Open: Mon-Fri 8am-6pm; Thurs to 9pm; Sat 8am-3pm; Sun 10am-4pm.
With Columbian, Costa Rican, Arabica, Mocha, Nicaraguan, Australian and Indonesian just some of the many imported and freshly roasted blends in which the Brazilian Coffee Factory specialises, and with prices from around $4.50 per 250g, this is a great find. There is also a cafe attached.

Wyse & Alexander
Shop 110 St Ives Shopping Village (✆ 9988 4846)
Open: Mon-Fri 9am-5.30pm; Thurs to 9pm; Sat 8am-4pm; Sun 10am-4pm.
In this unlikely location is a great coffee roaster, coffee and tea purveyor and cafe. In the range are Brazilian, Dominican, Indonesian, Kenyan, and a number of blends, including an excellent, rich and rounded house blend. All eighteen types are roasted on the premises. A wide variety of teas, ranging from the everyday to the utterly exotic, such as Paradise and Rose Petal, is also on sale. The cafe attached is one of the very few very good ones in the area. Prices for coffee start at around $5.50 per 250g.

HEALTH & ORGANIC FOOD SHOPS

Eco-Farms Pty Ltd
Cnr Park Rd & Bedford Rd, Homebush (✆ 9764 2833)
Organic fruit, vegetables and dairy products are available here.

Go-Vita
Bondi Junction (✆ 9387 6395) & Chatswood (✆ 9415 2866)
Go-Vita is one of a number of health food store chains operating in Sydney, and stocks Natural Nutrition, Natures Own and Bio-Organics foods, tinctures, vitamins and products.

Healthy Life
S66 Queen Victoria Building, City (✆ 9264 3825)
Also at: Bondi Junction (✆ 9389 4449) & 12 other locations around Sydney.
Another chain, Healthy Life stocks vitamins, minerals, cereal mixes, nuts and fruit, as well as other snacks and drinks.

Macro Wholefoods
328 Oxford St, Bondi Junction (✆ 9389 7611)
Also at: Newtown (✆ 9550 5422).
Macro shops stock fruit, vegetables, dried fruits

and pastas, all organically produced.

Russell's Natural Food Markets

55 Glebe Point Rd, Glebe (✆ 9660 8144)

Also at: City (✆ 9267 3598), Dee Why (✆ 9982 4442), Neutral Bay (✆ 9953 5639) & North Sydney (✆ 9964 9420).

This is a seriously large emporium of health foods, snacks, drinks, natural dyes etc. There is also a large selection of organically grown vegetables, fruit grains and grocery items. Aromatherapy and other aids to promote inner well being are also sold, along with information.

There is also an organic food market held every week in Sydney (See: Markets).

MUSIC

CHAINS

Blockbuster Music

Pitt St Mall, City (✆ 9223 8488) including Classical Department (✆ 9223 8563)

Open: Mon-Fri 8.30am-6.30pm; Thurs to 9pm; Sat 9am-6pm; Sun 10am-5pm.

Also at: Darling Harbour (✆ 9281 3800).

Rock and pop compact discs, cassettes and merchandise; a separate jazz and soundtrack department; and a very good, large classical department, staffed by knowledgeable people, make up Blockbuster Music. All stock is marked down each March and September.

Brashs

Pitt St, City (✆ 9261 2555)

Open: Mon-Fri 9am-5.30pm; Thurs to 9pm; Sat 9am-5pm; Sun 11am-4pm.

Also at: Bondi (✆ 9369 1255), Chatswood (✆ 9411 7982) & other locations.

Downstairs are all the usual rock and pop compact discs, while upstairs is an emporium of pianos, organs, string, wind and brass instruments, sheet music and print music! Wow!

HMV Megastore

Lower level Mid City Centre, Pitt St Mall, City (✆ 9221 2311)

Open: Mon-Fri 9am-6pm; Thurs to 9pm; Sat 9am-5.30pm; Sun 11am-5pm.

Also at: Chatswood (✆ 9415 1288) & Parramatta (✆ 9891 4699).

Apart from all the usual stock, HMV has extensive jazz, world music and soundtrack sections as well as a wide-ranging classical department. HMV stores are always well stocked and have periodic markdowns, generally in early March and September.

SPECIALTY

ABC shop

Shop 48 Queen Victoria Building, City (✆ 9333 1635)

Also at: Chatswood (✆ 9950 3148), Parramatta (✆ 9635 9922) & other locations.

The retail outlets of the Australian Broadcasting Corporation ('Aunty') sell books, toys, games, t-shirts, compact discs and cassettes related to series and programs screened on the national broadcaster's television and radio channels. One of the most popular items on sale here are the 'Bananas in Pyjamas'

Ava & Susan's Records

Shop 20 Town Hall Arcade, City (✆ 9264 3179)

Open: Mon-Fri 9am-5.30pm; Thurs to 7pm; Sat 9am-2pm; Closed Sun.

This is one of the best shops in Sydney for soundtracks, film-related recordings and jazz. Ava & Susan's also stock some vinyl, among which the find of the year is sometimes to be made. The staff are also helpful in offering advice about rare recordings and finding something if it's not in stock.

Folkways

282 Oxford St, Paddington (✆ 9361 3980)

Open: Mon 9am-6pm; Tues-Wed ✆ Fri 9am-7pm; Thurs 9am-9pm; Sat 9.30am-6.30pm; Sun 11am-6pm.

Folkways is a top spot for contemporary, alternative, mainstream and jazz compact discs. A small but well chosen classical section lines one side of the store.

Jazz Plus

132 Victoria Rd, Rozelle (✆ 9818 4501)

Open: Mon-Fri 10am-5pm; Sat 10am-3pm; Closed Sun.

Jazz Plus, as the name suggests, are specialists in jazz, whether it be on record, compact disc or cassette. A very wide coverage of all types of jazz, but with less attention paid to funk, means this is a great place to browse.

Glenn A Baker's Time Warp

289 Clarence St, City (✆ 9283 1555)

Open: Mon-Fri 9am-6pm; Thurs to 9pm; Sat 9am-4pm; Closed Sun.

Time warp is a specialist store devoted to the music of the 1950s, 60s, 70s and 80s. The range also encompasses singles, t-shirts, videos, and memorabilia. You'll know when you're getting old when your favourite stuff turns up here! Auctions are also held here occasionally.

Michael's Music Room

Shop 18, Town Hall Arcade, City (✆ 9267 1351)

Open: Mon-Fri 9am-6pm; Thurs to 7pm; Sat 9am-2pm; Closed Sun.

Michael's is another great place to find classical, baroque, and opera discs. The large and comprehensive collection is highly distracting.

Recycled Records

37 Glebe Point Rd, Glebe (✆ 9660 1416)

Open: Mon-Fri 10.30am-6.30pm; Thurs to

LATE NIGHT BOOK CRUISING

If the noise and smoke of the city's more conventional 'nite spots' don't appeal, chances are you'll love the following bookshops for their late opening hours. In these revered sanctums, you can pick up a book or a stranger, eavesdrop on some conversations taking place over the shelves, practise self-control in spending, listen to some jazz and enjoy a cheap night out!

Ariel Booksellers
42 Oxford St, Paddington (✆ 9332 4581)
Open: 7 days 10am-Midnight.
This is a great midnight book stop, full of wonderful titles to spawn fascinating midnight conversations with perfect strangers in the night.

Berkelouw Bookdealers
19 Oxford St, Paddington (✆ 9360 3200)
Open: 7 days 10am-Midnight.
If second hand books are your thing, try over the road from Ariel amongst Berkelouw's shelves of second hand volumes spread over three floors.
You could always have a coffee in the first floor cafe to keep you going.

Gleebooks Second Hand Books
191 Glebe Point Rd, Glebe (✆ 9660 2333)

Gleebooks
49 Glebe Point Rd, Glebe (✆ 9660 2333)
Both Open: 7 days 8am-9pm.•
Crowds pack in on summer nights to listen to the jazz and read someone else's old, comfortable smelling books in the second hand shop; or the thousands of new editions in Gleebooks.

Gould's Book Arcade
32 King St, Newtown (✆ 9519 8947)
Also 493 Parramatta Rd (opposite Norton St), Petersham (✆ 9560 0363)
Open: 7 days 7am-Midnight.
Ensconced in the closely packed, chaotic aisles and piles of old books in the arcade, it could be 10am or 10pm and you wouldn't know. Gould's claims to have three hundred thousand books on over one hundred and forty different subject areas spread over nine thousand feet of arcade.

Lesley McKay's Bookshop
346 New South Head Rd, Double Bay (✆ 9327 1354)
Open: 7 days 10am (Sun from 9am) -10pm.
This is a prime pre- or post movies bookshop, opposite the Double Bay Village cinema.

For more bookshops around Sydney, See: Shopping.

9.30pm; Sat 10.30am-6.30pm; Sun 12noon-6pm.
Despite the name, this is not a second hand record dealer, but a specialist in new recordings of jazz, acid jazz, world music, independent, and dance music.

Red Eye Records
Shops 2 ✆ 5a Tank Stream Arcade Cnr King St & Pitt St, City (✆ 9233 8177 ✆ 233 8125)
Open: Mon-Fri 9am-6pm; Thurs to 9pm; Sat 9am-5pm; Sun 11am-5pm.
Red Eye specialises in imported and local compact discs, singles and records of independent and alternative music, as well as a number of t-shirts and posters associated with it.

SECOND HAND

Paddington Bazaar
St John's Church, Oxford St, Paddington
Open: Sat 10am-4pm.
There is almost always at least one dealer in second hand compact discs to be found at the bazaar.

Ray's Records
151a Bridge Rd, Glebe (✆ 9660 2384)
Open: Mon-Fri 10am-6pm; Sat 10am-4.30pm.
Ray's stocks an eclectic·collection of pop, rock, jazz, soundtrack and classical records and compact discs, all second hand.

BOOKS

Abbey's Bookshop
131 York St, City (opposite Queen Victoria Building) (✆ 9264 3111)
Open: Mon-Fri 8.30am-6pm; Thurs to 9pm; Sat 9am-5pm; Sun 10am-5pm.
One of the city's best bookshops, specialising in a large number of topics, including fiction, crime, classics, travel, music, history philosophy, psychology, poetry, biography and reference, is Abbey's. This book Utopia is rendered closer to bliss by the upper foreign language floor, stocking learning materials, literature and reference books in around fifteen languages. Abbey's also runs a mail order service.

Ariel Bookseller
42 Oxford St., Paddington (✆ 9332 4581)
Open: 7 days 10am-Midnight.
As a bookseller who truly realises and appreciates, the compulsion that is book browsing, Ariel not only keeps long opening hours, but they also provide comfortable chairs to make blatant browsers' reading comfortable. The staff are unperturbed by customers hitting the floor with a book and staying there all morning. For many, a visit to the Paddington Academy Twin or Verona (See: Film) would not be complete without a post film browse through the store's stocks of fiction, poetry, photography, art, design, travel, history,

media and children's books.

Dymocks
424 George St, City (✆ 9235 0155)
Open: Mon-Fri 8.30am-6pm; Thurs to 9pm; Sat 9am-5pm; Sun 10am-5pm.
It's big and it's full of books. Stock ranges from alternative health to law texts, and covers everything in between as well. Shelves of fiction, classics, poetry, photography, history, biography, travel, languages, philosophy and reference offer untold spending possibilities, and should it all get too exhausting, there is a cafe within the store on the first floor. Next door is the enormous Dymocks Stationery Superstore.

Gleebooks Bookshop
49 Glebe Point Rd (✆ 9660 2333)
Open: 7 days 8am-9pm.
Gleebooks is another large yet personal and comfortable book browsing magnet/trap, stocking hundreds of literature and non-fiction titles on a wide range of topics. Imports and journals are also kept, while children's and second hand books are kept up the road at 191 Glebe Point Road.

New Edition Bookshop
328a Oxford St, Paddington (✆ 9360 6913)
Open: Mon-Fri 9.30am-6pm; Thurs to 9pm; Sun 9am-6pm.
An intimate and well stocked bookshop is the New Edition. Also firm believers in the 'read before you buy' style of book selling, New Edition offers fiction, poetry, travel, photography, glossy coffee table books and a good selection of children's books.

Pentimento Bookshop
275 Darling St, Balmain (✆ 9810 0707)
Open: Mon-Wed 9am-8pm; Thurs-Sat 9am-10pm; Sun 10am-10pm.
A wonderful way to spend any Saturday is to cruise Darling Street, dividing the hours between the cafes, markets and second hand dealers in the street, and Pentimento. Pentimento also has an eminently comfortable sofa to facilitate a more detailed browse through their wide collections of fiction, non-fiction, design, art, cookery and children's books.

SPECIALIST BOOKSHOPS

Aquarian Bookshop
Basement 129 York St, City (✆ 9267 5969)
Open: Mon-Fri 9am-6pm; Thurs to 8pm; Sat 9am-5pm; Sun 11am-4pm.
Aquarian is the city's specialist in new age books, music and tarot cards.

Architext
3 Manning St, Potts Point (✆ 9356 2022)
Open: Mon-Fri 9am-5.30pm; Sat 11am-4pm.
This is the bookshop of the Royal Australian Institute of Architects. Suitably, it stocks architecture books and magazines.

Art Gallery of New South Wales Shop
Art Gallery Rd, Domain, City (✆ 9225 1744)
Open: 7 days 10am-5pm.
The shop in the gallery is fully and comprehensively stocked with covetable books covering almost every aspect and type of art.

Automoto Motoring Bookshop
154 Clarence St, Sydney (✆ 9299 2248)
Open: Mon-Fri 9am-5pm; Sat 9am-4pm.
Automoto is the source of a large collection of new and second hand motoring and aviation books, covering cars, motor cycles, restoration, models, racing and rallying, technical manuals, videos and other automobilia.

Comic Kingdom
71 Liverpool St, City (✆ 9267 3629)
Open: Mon-Fri 9.30am-5.45pm; Sat 9am-4pm; Sun 10am-3pm.
Also at: 135 Bathurst St, City (✆ 9267 3046)
The name says it all.

The Cookery Book
31 Albany St, Crows Nest (✆ 9439 3144)
Open: Mon-Fri 9am-5.15pm; Thurs 9am-6pm; Sat 9am-4pm.
A well displayed and wide selection of excellent cookery books, supplemented by an enormous catalogue and mail order list. The cuisines of most parts of the world are featured here.

Dendy Cinema Shop
19 Martin Place, City (✆ 9221 1242)
Open: Mon-Fri 11.30am-9.30pm; Sat 12noon-9.30pm; Sun 12noon 7.30pm.
The shop attached to the great Dendy cinema specialises in reference books, fiction, music and screen plays associated with films and the film industry.

Galaxy Bookshop
222 Clarence St, City (✆ 9267 7222)
Open: Mon-Wed ✆ Fri 8.30am-6pm; Thurs to 9pm; Sat 8.30am-5pm; Sun 11am-5pm.
Galaxy is Abbey's sibling, and specialises with thoroughness and flair in mythology, fantasy, horror, science fiction, film and television merchandise, reference and games.

National Trust Shop
National Trust Centre, Observatory Hill (✆ 9258 0154)
Open: Mon-Fri 9am-5pm; Sat-Sun 12noon-5pm.
The National Trust is responsible for the preservation and administration of the country's heritage, and accordingly, their shop specialises in Australian heritage, architecture, art, and gifts.

Travel Bookshop
20 Bridge St, City (✆ 9241 3554)
Open: Mon-Fri 9am-6pm; Sat 9am-5pm; Sun 11am-4pm.
The Travel Bookshop is Sydney's most respected

seller of maps, guides, histories and travellers' tales, and a favourite haunt of armchair travellers.

SECOND HAND BOOK DEALERS

Da Capo Music
112a Glebe Point Rd, Glebe (✆ 9660 1825)
Open: 7 days 10am-6pm.
Second hand music and music books are for sale at Da Capo.

Gould's Book Arcade
32 King St, Newtown (✆ 9519 8947)
Open: 7 days 7am-midnight.
Also at: 498 Parramatta Rd, Petersham (✆ 9560 0363).
Gould's Book Arcade has to be seen to be believed. Two densely packed storeys of second hand books are crammed into vaguely divided subject areas, piled in boxes and stacked on the floor.

Humanities Bookshop
240 Oxford St, Paddington (✆ 9331 5514)
Open: Mon-Fri 11am-7pm; Sat 10am-6pm; Sun 11am-6pm.
This bookshop specialises in second hand books ranging in subject over all aspects of the humanities.

Messrs Berkelouw
19 Oxford St, Paddington (✆ 9360 3200)
Open: 7 days 10am-midnight.
One of the best things about going down to Berrima south of Sydney has always been the possibility of going to Berkelouw's Book Barn- a massive structure surrounded by mysterious tall cypress pines and completely stuffed full with second hand and antiquarian books. Now they also have a city store, stocking collections or single items of importance, especially out of print scholarly books, art, film, travel literature, history. A large number of orange Penguin paperbacks are also kept, as well as a separate rare book collection. There's even a cafe on the first floor. For those who happen to be heading towards the Southern Highlands (See: Trips Out of Sydney), the address is 'Bendooley', Hume Hwy, Berrima (✆ 048-77 1370; fax 048-77 1102).

ANTIQUARIAN BOOK DEALERS

Louella Kerr and Lorraine Reed
26 Glenmore Rd, Paddington (✆ 9361 4664)
Open: Mon-Sat. 11am-6pm.
Right in the heart of the Paddington gallery belt, Louella Kerr and Lorraine Reed deal in fine and rare old books.

Tim McCormick
53 Queen St, Woollahra (✆ 9363 5383)
Open: Mon-Fri at various times; ring first or knock on the door.
Buys and sells Australiana, rare books and prints, paintings, photographs and manuscripts. The other bonus is the location in one of Sydney's best antiques grazing streets.

ANTIQUES

MARKETS & JUMBLE SHOPS

Unfortunately, there is no great antiques flea market in Sydney, so the best thing to do is to head for the city's markets to sort through the bric-a-brac (See: Markets). Balmain is the best central suburb for browsing through second hand wares shops because a number of them are close together. Walk the length of Darling Street and Beattie Street to discover a few.

Balmain Markets
St Andrews Church, Darling St, Balmain (✆ 9810 3712)
Open: Saturday 7.30am-4pm.
This market is probably the best for traditional flea market wares such as silver cutlery, clothes, comics and old wares, furniture and frames.

The Tin Sheds
144 Beattie St, Balmain (✆ 9555 2185)
Open: 7 days 8am-4pm.
Tucked away in a back street away from the main action of the suburb is this group of tin sheds full of second hand furniture, furniture made of recycled wood, junk and antiques. The ground between them is covered with all sorts of trash and treasure, while the extremely popular Chester's Cafe in the Tin Shed offers excellent, strong coffee, cakes and a great menu full of zesty dishes, with excess customers occupying spare wheelbarrows and tricycles outside if necessary (See: Cafes).

AUCTION HOUSES

Both **Sotheby's** (✆ 9332 3500) & **Christie's** (✆ 9326 1422) have offices in Sydney, and hold periodic jewellery, furniture and art auctions. Lawson's (✆ 9241 3411) hold auctions in their rooms at 212 Cumberland Street, The Rocks (See: Wet Days).

These are advertised in the Sydney Morning Herald classifieds, as well as the papers 'Antiques' and 'State of the Art', available from most dealers.

SHOPS

Woollahra's Queen Street is one of the city's premier antiques precincts, with a number of well established dealers lining both sides.

Anne Schofield
36 Queen St, Woollahra (✆ 9363 1326)
Open: Tues-Fri 10am-5pm; Sat 10am-2pm; Closed Sun-Mon.
Anne Schofield is one of Sydney's foremost specialised purveyors of antique jewellery, where prices may range from around a hundred to a few thousand dollars.

Architectural Heritage
62 Glebe Point Rd, Glebe (✆ 9660 0100)
Open: 7 days 10am-6pm.
One of the most fascinating fixtures on Glebe Point Road is this sprawling emporium of old bits and pieces from houses past. Doors are catalogued by measurements and wood type, and then stacked upstairs; church pews sit in corners; antique bath tubs wait for an owner in another corner, fireplaces are lined up in rows; marble lions sit purring; light fittings hang from the ceiling; and spare staircases are tied together for display and access to the upper floor.

Chippendale Restorations
505 Balmain Rd, Lilyfield (✆ 9810 6066)
Open: Mon-Fri 7.30am-5pm; Sat 9am-5pm; Sun 12noon-5pm.
This is another emporium of old and new bits of residences: doors, windows, light fittings, fireplaces and brassware provide excellent material through which to wade. Reproduction pieces are also available.

Clocks of Distinction
32 Ferry St, Hunters Hill (✆ 9816 1401)
Open: Mon-Fri 9am-5pm; Thurs to 7pm; Sat 9am-12noon; Closed Sun.
Clocks of Distinction is one of Sydney's most respected and amazing dealers in antique clocks, barometers, and music boxes of all ages.

Copeland & de Soos
66 Queen St, Woollahra (✆ 9363 5288)
Open: Mon-Fri 11am-6pm; Sat 11am-4pm; Closed Sun.
Specialising in fine and unusual Art Deco, Biedermeier, Art Nouveau and post war design including lighting, ceramics and sculpture, this is a wonderful shop if the twentieth century is your scene.

Country Trader
122 Oxford St, Paddington (✆ 9331 7809)
Open: Mon-Sat 10am-6pm; Sun 11am-5pm.
Several drool-inducing rooms are filled with exquisite pieces of furniture and household fittings sent back from France by the wandering owner.

Margo Richards
Shop 76 Gallery Level 1 Strand Arcade, City (✆ 9232 3870)
Open: Mon-Fri 10am-5.30pm; Thurs to 7.30pm; Sat 10am-3.30; Closed Sun.
Antique gold, silver and costume jewellery, dolls, china, buttons, clothing, and other items fill this treasure chest of a shop.

Paul Kenny Antiques
108 Hargreave St, Paddington (✆ 9363 9392)
Open: Mon-Fri 10am-5.30pm; Sat 10am-3pm; Closed Sun.
Paul Kenny's shop is renowned for exquisite antique furniture, predominantly of English origin.

The Art of Wine & Food
92 Queen St, Woollahra (✆ 9363 2817)
Open: Mon-Sat 9am-5 or 6pm; Sun 11am-4.30pm.
This shop is full of paintings associated with food, antique corkscrews, old French glass, decanters, labels and rare bottles.

ANTIQUES CENTRES

There are a number of antiques centres in Sydney which bring together a wide variety of separate dealers under their big roofs.

Sydney Antique Centre
531 South Dowling St, Surry Hills (✆ 9361 3244)
Open: 7 days 10am-6pm.
This centre is a bright yellow and red building housing over sixty dealers in furniture, books, sporting goods and literature, silverware, lamps, jewellery, toys, and Sydney's foremost dealer in corkscrews. The centre also has a cafe, making it more than easy to spend an entire morning or afternoon browsing.

Woollahra Antiques Centre
160 Oxford St, Woollahra (✆ 9327 8840)
Open: 7 days 10am-6pm.
Over fifty dealers in this centre sell furniture, jewellery, books, cutlery and silverware.

DESIGN & HOMEWARE GOODS

Bibelot
445 Oxford St, Paddington (✆ 9360 6902)
Open: Mon-Fri 10am-6pm; Thurs to 8pm; Sat 9.30am-6pm; Sun 11am-5pm.
Bibelot is the place to go for essential inessentials, such as Philippe Starck loo brushes, gleaming Alessi desirables, great tableware and other accessories for the house.

Country Road Homewears
332 Oxford St, Paddington (✆ 9360 2010)
Open: Mon-Fri 9.30am-6pm; Thurs to 7pm; Sat 9.30am-5.30pm; Sun 12am-5pm.
Also at: Skygarden, City (✆ 9223 7985) ✆ Mosman (✆ 9960 4633).
With a common feeling of relaxed style, Country Road Homewears capture the spirit of polite Australian houses in tableware, bed linen, furniture, fans, candlesticks, cutlery, crockery, glassware, fabrics and accessories.

David Jones
Cnr Market St ✆ Castlereagh St, City (✆ 9266 5544)
Open: Mon-Fri 9am-6pm; Thurs to 9pm; Sat 9am-5pm; Sun 11am-5pm.
Shoppers can find almost anything for the house in the Market Street store's multiple floors of homewares, whether it be a drink bottle or a crystal decanter, carpet or curtains.

Gamla Lan Interiors
114 Oxford St, Paddington (✆ 9360 2217)

Open: Mon-Fri 10am-6pm; Thurs to 7pm; Sat 10am-5pm; Closed Sun.
In between the Biedermeier, the modernist lines of the 1920s and 1930s, and Swedish country furniture are to be found glassware, tableware, and mirrors.

Homeworks

Shop 8, Queens Court, 118 Queen St, Woollahra (© 9362 0534)
Open: Mon-Sat 10am-6pm; Closed Sun.
This is a highly tempting and inviting little shop, crammed full of surprisingly affordable damask, sheets and pillowcases of cotton so fine they are cool to the touch, and all sorts of accessories to go with them.

Linen & Lace

213 Darling St, Balmain (© 9810 0719)
Open: Tues-Fri 10am-5pm; Sat 10am-4pm; Closed Sun-Mon.
This is a sweetly scented shop full of intriguing fittings and homewares, ranging from lamps to sheets and towels to soaps and linen clothing. Odds and ends, such as frames, antique china wares and even silk flowers scattered around, make for compulsive browsing, and a quiet respite from the nearby Saturday markets.

Paraphernalia

22 Strand Arcade, City (© 9231 2474)
Open: Mon-Fri 9am-5.30pm; Thurs to 8.30pm; Sat 9am-4.30pm; Closed Sun.
Paraphernalia is a dedicated stockist of Alessi goods and a wide range of classic designs in all sorts of shapes and functions, whether they be typewriters, toasters, pens, leather goods, soaps, jewellery or boules.

CHILDREN

TOYS

David Jones

Cnr Market St © Elizabeth St, City (© 9266 5544)
Open: Mon-Fri 9am-6pm; Thurs to 9pm; Sat 9am-5pm; Sun 11am-5pm.
An entire floor of the store is dedicated to children's toys and clothing.

Paddington Bazaar

Grounds of St John's Church, Oxford St, Paddington (© 9331 2646)
Open: Sat 10am-4pm.
The stalls of the Paddington Bazaar usually include a number of excellent toy makers. Toys range from brightly coloured snails on wheels to intricate puzzles and educational items.

Teach 'em Toys

55 Flinders St, Darlinghurst (© 9332 3134)
Open: Mon-Sat 8am-6pm.
Stockists of Ravensburger, Battat, Ambi, Brio; puppets, rocking horses, blackboards, play centres and mobiles, this shop aims to develop an intellect quickly and early.

World 4 Kids

Chatswood Chase Centre, Victoria Ave, Chatswood (© 9411 7411)
Open: Mon-Fri 9am-5.30pm; Thurs to 9pm; Sat 9am-5pm; Sun 10am-4pm.
Also at: Bankstown (© 9790 2733), Blacktown (© 9622 2000), Hornsby (© 9482 7566), Miranda (© 9526 0111) © Penrith (© 047-21 3399).
This is the mother of all toy shops, making up in variety for what it lacks in intimacy. Here are found aisles and aisles of bikes, computer games, dolls, board games, clothing and prams: in short, everything to keep a child stimulated and/or occupied and/or quiet.
For further information of children's activities in Sydney, See: Children.

OUTDOORS EQUIPMENT

Sydney's Golden Mile as far as outdoors equipment is concerned is to be found in the City along Kent Street between Bathurst and Druitt Streets (behind the Town Hall). Here are found the following retailers, many of whom stock their own brands as well as generic equipment, and undertaking the easy stroll from one to the next is the best way of comparing stock and prices. There are also many disposal stores around Sydney.

Kathmandu

Cnr Kent St © Bathurst St, City (© 9261 8901)
Open: Mon-Fri 9am-5.30pm; Thurs to 8.30pm; Sat 9am-5pm; Sun 10am-4pm.

Mountain Designs

499 Kent St, City (© 9267 3822)
Open: Mon-Sat 9am-5.30pm; Thurs to 8.30pm; Sun 10am-5pm.

Mountain Equipment

491 Kent St, City (© 9264 5888)
Open: Mon-Fri 9am-5.30pm; Thurs to 9pm; Sat 9am-5pm; Sun 11am-4pm.
Also at: Chatswood (© 9419 6955).

Paddy Pallin

507 Kent St, City (© 9264 2685)
Open: Mon-Wed 9am-5.30pm; Thurs 9am-9pm; Fri 9am-6pm; Sat 9am-5pm; Sun 10am-4pm.
Also at: Miranda (© 9525 6829).

Southern Cross Equipment

447 Kent St, City (© 9261 3435)
Open: Mon-Fri 9am-5.30pm; Thurs to 9pm; Sat 9am-5pm; Sun 11am-4pm.
Also at: Hornsby (© 9477 5467).

The Adventure Shop

69 Liverpool St, City (© 9261 1959)
Open: Mon-Fri 9am-5.30pm; Thurs to 8.30pm; Sat 9am-4pm; Closed Sun.

Wildsports

327 Sussex St, City (© 9264 2095)
Open: Mon-Fri 9am-5.30pm; Thurs to 9pm; Sat 9am-5pm; Sun 11am-4pm.

SOUVENIRS

If they have to be bought, they may as well be some typical and genuine articles rather than trinkets without integrity. Following are some suggestions of good places to look for presents and souvenirs, and some specific ideas of particularly Sydney products for the "folks back home".

Many shops around Sydney have large and varied collections of **social Australiana**, ranging from books, to audio items, clothing and other merchandise. Investigate the ABC Shop; the Australian Museum Shop; the State Library Shop; the Museum of Sydney shop; and the Powerhouse Museum Shop. Two shops worth investigating for souvenirs depicting Sydney's natural environment are the Australian Conservation Foundation Environment Shop (33 George St, City; ✆ 9247 4754; Open: 7 days 10am-5.30pm), which sells posters, diaries, post cards and books, natural cosmetic products, t-shirts and natural souvenirs; and the Australian Geographic Shop (34 Centrepoint, Pitt St Mall, City; ✆ 9231 5055; Open: Mon-Fri 9am-6pm; Thurs to 9pm; Sat 9am-5pm; Sun 12noon-3pm), a wonderful alternative shop for children and adults, with all merchandise bearing a strong relationship to the environment and/or animals and/or nature, whether they be gardening gloves, puzzles, inflatable globes, magic gardens or spinning tops.

Beautifully crafted **jewellery** and **hand crafts** can be found all over the city, but especially at Saturday's Paddington Bazaar, The Rocks Market (See: Markets), and specific handcrafts shops such as Craftspace (88 George St, The Rocks; ✆ 9241 3800). Makers Mark (above) stocks a large selection of Australian designed jewellery, and has a large Australiana section. The jewellery shops listed above in the general shopping information are also mainly Sydneysiders.

There are also a number of **Sydney products** which make particularly good souvenirs and presents. Firstly, **a copy of this book**. There is no better, easily transportable way to take home or give someone the whole of this fantastic city. How about ten copies? **Paddington Chocolates** (See: Sydney Icons) are delicious, big chocolates which have been made in Sydney since the 1930s. Favourites among the rich, creamy centres include Natasha Marzipan & Cointreau. The chocolates are available at the Chocolate Factory Cafe (8 Elizabeth St, Paddington) or from the factory in Camperdown, by the bag or individually. **Paper goods** such as photograph books, papers, blank books, covered pencils and other products are made by a variety of companies in Sydney, but particularly nice ones are made by Corban & Blair, and are available from The Ink Group and David Jones (Elizabeth Street). **RM Williams**, makers of those elastic-sided leather boots that such a high proportion of Australians wear and just about as many foreigners find amusing, are hard to beat for that classically 'elegant' Aussie bush wear look. Well made clothing and riding accessories are also available here. **T-shirts** are always a popular way to remember a city, so seek out something a little witty and desirable, perhaps from the Gowings, Ken Done, Paddington Bazaar or the ABC Shop. A bottle of exotic **wine**, whether souvenired from your trip to the Hunter Valley or bought from one of the wine merchants listed above, is always a good present.

ABORIGINAL ART, ARTEFACTS & GOODS

The maxim "buyer beware" is especially true in this area, not to mention the offence caused by buying fakes and supporting their manufacturers. Reputable dealers include the following.

Coo-ee Aboriginal & Oceanic Art Gallery & Shop

98 Oxford St, Paddington (✆ 9332 1544)

Open: Mon-Sat 10am-6pm; Thurs to 8pm; Sun 11am-5pm.

This wonderful shop incorporates an upstairs gallery featuring bark and sand paintings, as well as Aboriginal and New Guinea artefacts. Downstairs is a large selection of didgeridoos from $90 to $240 (instructions included!), clapping sticks, hand-painted fabrics, jewellery and ceramics. The work of several communities is sold here, the provenance of each major item is detailed, and the money returns to the community. It is likely your didgeridoo will be wrapped up in the colours of the Aboriginal flag!

Community Aid Abroad Trading

Shop CM-05 Centrepoint, cnr Pitt St & Market St, City (✆ 9231 4016)

Open: Mon-Fri 9am-6pm; Thurs to 8pm; Sat 9am-5pm; Closed Sun.

Also at: 36 The Corso Manly (✆ 9977 5391)

As well as selling jewellery and wares from all over the world, CAA Trading also sells a number of Aboriginal artefacts and musical instruments. As with Coo-ee, the origin of each piece is detailed.

OTHER SYDNEY SOUVENIRS

Compact Discs

Try some Sydney orchestras, such as the Sydney Symphony Orchestra, the Brandenburg Orchestra, the Australian Chamber Orchestra or the Australian Opera, or perhaps a recording or two by some Sydney bands. (See: Music.)

Books

Books in the State Library shop have a particularly Australian relevance, in many cases they're about Sydney specifically.

Homewares

Take home the feeling of Sydney houses with some Australian homewares, such as Country Road.

MARKETS

Whether your thing is bric-a-brac, incense, a massage, fluffy woollen car seat covers, the newest clothing labels, craft, jewellery, or toys, the markets of Sydney have it. In addition, the city suburbs are blessed with a large number of fresh food markets and international supermarkets, dealing in anything from Dutch clogs to a kilogram of fresh prawns or bargain pasta. The only thing missing is a really good antiques flea market, replaced by several large antiques centres (See: Shopping). We have found the best and most interesting markets in Sydney, listing them here in two groups: Traditional Markets and International Food Markets. Many of them are located in areas featured in Walks Around Sydney (as indicated), making a stroll around an easy complement to a market browse.

Saturday and Sunday are generally the city's best market days, but two world-wide market norms apply: quality depends largely on which dealers turn up and wet days can be messy.

TRADITIONAL MARKETS

Balmain Markets

St Andrew's Church, Darling St, Balmain (✆ 9818 2674)
Map Reference: D2.
Open: Sat 7.30am-4pm.
See: Directory: Balmain; Sydney By Area: Balmain; Walks Around Sydney: Balmain.
This market is probably the most diverse and the best for traditional flea market goods such as silver cutlery, clothes, comics and old wares; furniture; wooden mirrors and frames; incense; pottery; Chinese neck massages and other bizarre bazaar wares. Inside the church hall is an ethnic food extravaganza, full of ready to eat Indian, Middle Eastern, Asian and European food and snacks. Balmain markets are well worth visiting, and can easily be combined with a trip to the area's many second hand wares dealers (**See:** Shopping) or pubs, such as The London Hotel, all centred around the roundabout on the markets' corner. When a stroll around the suburb and a cruise down Darling Street are added to the itinerary, what better way to spend a Saturday is there?

Bondi Beach Markets

Bondi Beach Public School, Campbell Parade, Bondi (✆ 9398 5486)
Map Reference: H11.
Open: Sun 10am-4pm; Night markets: Thurs & Sun 5pm-10pm; Fri ✆ Sat 5pm-11pm.
See: Directory: Bondi; Sydney By Area: Bondi; Tours Around Sydney: Bondi & Bay Explorer; Walks Around Sydney: Bronte-Bondi Cliff Walk.
The Bondi Beach markets offer jewellery, clothing, crafts, arts, bric-a-brac, plants, and entertainment, and are worth a look if in the area. For those unable to resist any opportunity to rummage through other people's trash and treasure, the smaller Bondi Beach Night Markets may be hard to ignore.

Flemington Markets

Cnr Parramatta Rd ✆ Marlborough Rd, Flemington (✆ 9325 6200)
Map Reference: 11km west of F1.
Open: Flower Market: Mon-Sat 6am-10am; Produce Market: Mon 5am-10.30am; Tues-Thurs 6am-10.30am; Fri 6am-9.30am.
Flemington Markets are so huge that they have their own suburb (next to Homebush). Commercial sellers, the flower market and growers produce market are spread over several enormous buildings (**See:** Paddy's Markets, below), and are all open to the public.

Glebe Markets

Glebe Public School, Glebe Point Rd, Glebe (✆ 9660 6667)
Map Reference: F1.
Open: Sat 9am-4pm.
See: Directory: Glebe; Film: Valhalla; Sydney By Area: Glebe; Walks Around Sydney: Glebe.
This is how suburban markets should be: colourful and vibrant with a lively trade in second hand goods, records, furniture, arts, crafts, clothing, jewellery and bric-a-brac. In addition, large calico tents stand in place of stalls, their fabric flapping in the breeze to reveal patrons lying on mattresses having their joints and muscles kneaded and relaxed by trained masseurs! Glebe Markets are also at the centre of another great Saturday agenda: combine them with a stroll along Glebe Point Road through the cafes and bookshops to the Valhalla cinema's 1pm matinee ($7 ticket includes jaffas and cordial), and then on to the Harbour and the Blackwattle Canteen (**See:** Cafes).

Kings Cross Markets

El Alamein Fountain, cnr Macleay St & Darlinghurst Rd, Kings Cross (✆ 9368 1961)
Map Reference: F5.
Open: Sun 9am-7pm.
See: Sydney By Area: Kings Cross; Tours Around Sydney: Explorer Buses; Walks Around Sydney: Kings Cross & Elizabeth Bay.
Certainly one of the more interesting and less conventional markets is this one, where ethnic art and clothing,

handcrafts, jewellery and antiques combine with fortune tellers to attract a consistent crowd.

Manly Arts and Crafts Market

South Steyne (near the Tourist Information Centre), Manly (✆ 9977 1088)

Map Reference: 3km north of A11.

Open: Sat 12noon-7.30pm; Sun & public holidays 8.30am-7.30pm.

See: Sydney By Area: Manly; Walks Around Sydney: Manly.

Strictly handmade items are for sale at Manly's arts and crafts market, including ceramics, leather, woodwork and pottery. Sunday's market is generally the busier of the two, with more stalls and a bigger crowd.

Opera House Forecourt Market

In front of the Opera House, Bennelong Point, City (✆ 018-286 320)

Map Reference: D5.

Open: Sun 11am- 6pm.

The Opera House markets offer arts and crafts, jewellery, hats and souvenirs. The best idea is to stroll along these stalls, admiring the stunning view, and then walk around Circular Quay to the Rocks Markets (below).

Paddington Bazaar

St John's Church, 395 Oxford St, Paddington (✆ 9331 2646)

Map Reference: G6.

Open: Sat 10am-4.30pm

See: Directory: Paddington; Shopping; Sydney By Area: Paddington; Tours Around Sydney: Bondi ✆ Bay Explorer; Walks Around Sydney: Oxford St, Paddington.

For those with only enough time to go to one market in Sydney, make it this one. Amongst the organised chaos are to be found antiques, second hand clothing, new jewellery, old jewellery, ethnic jewellery, slick and modern jewellery, crafts, food, handmade wooden objects and toys, books, children's toys, music, hats and accessories. As a traditional rite of passage for clothing designers between college and label, the Bazaar is also one of the best places to pick up directional new clothing designed by the city's designers of tomorrow. Under the plane trees, a wide range of entertainers perform anything from fire breathing to comic music. At twenty years old, Paddington Bazaar is one of the most diverse and vibrant in Sydney, the centre of the chaotically busy theatre that is Oxford Street on Saturday.

Paddy's Markets

Parramatta Rd, Flemington Markets ✆ Hay St, Haymarket (✆ Information Hotline: 11589)

Map Reference: 11km west of G1.

Open: Flemington: Fri 10.30am-4.30pm; Sun 9am-4.30pm. Haymarket: Sat & Sun 9am-4.30pm.

This is one of the biggest and most famous markets in Sydney, dealing in clothing and accessories as well as an enormous amount of car seat covers, batteries, trademark infringing t-shirts, meats, vegetables and flowers. Almost anything can be bought here!

Parklea Markets

601 Sunnyholt Rd, Parklea (✆ 9629 3311)

Map Reference: 30km north-west of C4.

Open: Sat ✆ Sun 8.30am-4.30pm

Parklea markets are the biggest in the west and some of the largest in Sydney, offering hundreds of stalls selling a huge range of goods from fresh fruit and vegetables to fashion, homewares and pets, all under cover.

The Rocks Market

George Street, The Rocks (under the Harbour Bridge) (✆ 9255 1717)

Map Reference: D4.

Open: Sat & Sun 10am-6pm.

See: Directory: The Rocks; History; Sydney By Area: The Rocks; Tours Around Sydney: Sydney Explorer; Walking Tours; Walks Around Sydney: The Rocks.

Here, under the intricate steel work of the Harbour Bridge, are the great, varied and vibrant Rocks Markets. Complemented by the neighbouring pubs, in particular the Mercantile where Irish music wafts out the doors and joins the buzz, the Rocks Markets are some of the city's best for homewares, crafty souvenirs, antiques and collectables. There are lots of things to interest children too, such as magic tricks and toys. A stroll through the markets can easily be combined with a gentle ramble through the area's historic streets, alleys and courtyards.

Rozelle Markets

In the grounds of Rozelle Primary School, Darling St, Rozelle (✆ 9818 5373)

Map Reference: 1km west of D1.

Open: Sat & Sun 9am-4pm.

Rozelle Markets have only been running for two years, but they are known as an enthusiastic, old-fashioned place to rummage through second-hand and garage sale bits and pieces.

Trash & Treasure Markets

1895 Camden Valley Way, Preston (✆ 9607 5255)

Map Reference: 32km south-west of C4.

Open: Sun 8am-2pm.

Here, market grazers can search for treasure in the trash amongst the stalls, usually numbering between two hundred and four hundred, elbowing the estimated three thousand shoppers to get at the piles of second hand and new goods.

INTERNATIONAL & FOOD MARKETS

One of the cheapest ways to travel overseas without actually leaving Sydney is to head for one of the city's many international food markets, and come away with a large number of bargain purchases (souvenirs perhaps). Here is on offer deep insight to various cultures and communities which make up our population. How about flying down to a South American supermarket (complete with car sitting in the middle of it); or a Japanese supermarket for ready made sushi plus all the utensils you could possibly need to eat it; perhaps a quick trip to Holland for a spot of lunch eaten amongst cuckoo clocks and clogs? You don't need a passport, but only an open mind and a sense of curiosity.

Burlington Supermarket : Chinese
Thomas St, Ultimo (Chinatown) (✆ 9281 2777)
Map Reference: F3.
Open: 7 days 9am-7pm.
Also at: 285 Penshurst St, Willoughby (✆ 9417 2588)
Open: Mon-Sat 9.30am-7pm; Sun 10am-7pm.
Even without the mysterious herbal dispensary operating at of the rears of the Burlington markets, they are fascinating places to browse for dried seafood of indescribable variety, confectionery, cooking utensils, alcohol and above all, noodles. The Chinese vegetables are extremely fresh, and in the Willoughby outlet you will find an incredibly good barbecue shop where you can obtain a large container of delicious barbecued duck, chicken or pork with rice and bok choy for around $5. The butcher here stocks a wide range of extremely high quality meats. The Willoughby store even contains a cooking school. Wow!

Martinez Brothers : South American
33 Spencer St, Fairfield (✆ 9724 5509)
Map Reference: 20km west of H1.
Open: Mon-Fri 8.30am-5.30pm; Sat 8am-1.30pm; Closed Sun.
This market is known as a den of soccer watchers feasting on chorizo barbecues and cheering on the teams on the giant screen. This is, of course, especially so during World Cups, but the Fiat which sits in the middle of the large store is a permanent fixture. It isn't even the delivery van. Here, you will find South American tea as well as the proper items with which to drink it (metal straws and wooden bowls on stands). Sausages, empanadas filled with beef, onion and herbs, fruit jellies and an enormous range of items (both edible and utensils) fill the rest of the market, as well as a focaccia bar. Pick up a South American snack to chomp on while deciding what to buy.

Norton Street Market : Italian
55 Norton St, Leichhardt (✆ 9568 2158)
Map Reference: 2.5km west of H1.
Open: Mon-Sat 8am-7pm; Sun 8am-6pm.
Where else could you turn the corner of a supermarket aisle and be greeted by the comforting sight of a towering wall of giant, colourful olive oil tins (around $20), a wall of vibrantly labelled tomato tins (cheap!), a wall of pasta (79c/500g), a wall of very fresh vegetables, a wall of coffee beans or a wall of (mainly Italian) wine? Add to this enormous bins full of arborio rice and all kinds of beans, friendly staff, more Italian being spoken than English, and a great sense of community, and this is food shopping heaven! Parking is available inside the market.

Sydney Fish Market
Cnr Pyrmont Bridge Rd ✆ Bank St, Pyrmont (✆ 9660 1611) **Map Reference:** F2.
Open: Retail: 7 days 8.30am-5pm. Auction Hall: Sun-Thurs 6pm-7am.
The fish markets are a sight to **See:** hundreds of different types of seafood, from octopus to calamari to tuna to whiting to prawns to sushi, are available in the twenty or so dealers operating within the market complex. Prices for this excellent food are extremely cheap in Sydney, explaining the incredible popularity of the markets with the residents. Particularly busy vendors are Claudio's, De Costi and Peters, while shoppers can be sure of the freshness of the fare overall. You can also eat at the Doyles outlet, or enjoy the excellent fare cooked on the grill in Peter's. The markets also contain the extremely popular Sydney Seafood School (✆ 9660 1611) on site where you can learn the tricks of seafood cooking from some of the city's best chefs. Each class includes a cooking demonstration, recipe kits, free parking, and at the end of the class, your efforts are served with a glass of wine.

The Dutch Shop
85 Market St, Smithfield (✆ 9604 0233)
Map Reference: 25km west of H1.
Open: Mon-Fri 9am-4.30; Sat-Sun 9am-4pm.
Here it's all lacy curtains, tinkling shop door bells, trees of clogs, confectionery, cheeses, sausages, spices, Dutch newspapers and crosswords, furniture and the all essential matjes herrings for the herring salad. Yum! If all this proves too mouth watering to wait until you can cook it or use it, there is also a restaurant on the premises where you can obtain real, live Dutch food. This is a trip to Amsterdam without the expense and graffiti.

Organic Food Market
Parkway Hotel, Frenchs Forest Rd East, Frenchs Forest (✆ 9999 2226)
Map Reference: 8km north of C4.
Open: Sun 9am-2pm.
If pesticides, chemicals and artificial ripening are not the way you like to think of your food being produced, this market is for you. Purely organic fruit, vegetables, eggs, cheese, bread and cakes from producers all over New South Wales. A New Age and Alternate Therapies section, arts, crafts, antiques, plants and flowers are also found here.

Orion Lebanese Groceries : Lebanese
327 Penshurst St, Willoughby (✆ 9417 5493)
Map Reference: 5km north of C4.
Open: Mon-Sat 9am-9pm; Sun 9am-7pm.
Part of a cluster of middle eastern supermarkets and shops, Orion offers freshly prepared and absolutely delicious pastries such as baklava and ladies' fingers, Turkish delight, cheeses, syrups direct from Lebanon, freshly roasted nuts, beans, oils and local jams. Each turn at the end of an aisle reveals something new.

Tokyo Mart : Japanese
Shop 27, Northbridge Plaza, Sailor's Bay Rd, Northbridge (✆ 9958 6860)
Map Reference: 5km north of C4.
Open: Mon-Fri 9am-5.30pm; Sat 9am-5pm; Sun 10am-4pm.
Here is another market characterised by the 'walls of stuff to buy' approach of Norton Street: crockery, utensils, lacquer ware, instant noodles, fresh noodles and rice appear to be holding up the roof of the place. The kitchen up at the back of the market is the spot for hot snacks, while fresher than fresh sushi and meats are also for sale.

OPEN AIR SYDNEY

Blessed with a climate that many would describe as unnaturally good, the great outdoors forms one of the most important facets of the city's lifestyle. With golden beaches, glistening waterways and verdant parks and gardens, there are many facilities, both natural and man made, for making the most of it. However, take care to protect yourself against the summer sun: avoid it between 11am and 3pm, and wear SPF 15+ sun screen and a hat. Finally, bushwalks are contained in their own, separate chapter, as are all things sporty.

BEACHES

See: Sports: Surfing, Swimming; Sydney Icons: The Beach.

Closely associated with the sport of people watching, the beaches of Sydney bring the city's humanity out on display. Around thirty kilometres of golden sand form the city's Harbour Beaches, Northern Beaches, Eastern Beaches and Southern Beaches. Many of the ocean beaches are particularly popular with surfers (**See:** Sports), and also feature surf pool built on rock platforms and continually flushed with foaming sea water. Regarding flushing, the Tasman Sea around Sydney (many people are shocked to discover Sydney is not on the Pacific Ocean) is usually very clean, although the water of the inner harbour (west of Double Bay) is usually polluted. While choosing a favourite beach is a highly personal quest, here are some of the best.

HARBOUR BEACHES

See: Sydney By Area: Sydney Harbour.

Balmoral

The Esplanade, Balmoral (North Shore).

Balmoral Beach is a lovely, quiet, sheltered beach, complete with a little island to explore and a 1930s promenade. With no surf, Balmoral is highly popular with families, and is further improved by the proximity of one of the city's best cafes, the Bathers Pavilion Refreshment Room (**See:** Cafes). Popular throughout winter for its many sun traps, it's a relaxing place year-round from which to gaze at the Harbour and watch the distant Manly Ferries pass in front of Sydney Heads.

Camp Cove

Cliff St, Watsons Bay (Eastern Suburbs).

See: Sydney By Area: Watsons Bay; Tours Around Sydney: Bondi & Bay Explorer.

Camp Cove is a small, west-facing beach, which has retained a strong sense of privacy despite its popularity. Looking at the scenery here, we have a pretty good idea of the pleasure Captain Arthur Phillip, leader of the First Fleet, must have felt when he camped here after discovering the Harbour in January 1788. Sparkling water, views of the heavily wooded northern shoreline interrupted only by passing watercraft, yachts moored in the cove and a rocky foreshore to explore contribute to the atmosphere, while the beach-front kiosk and the cove's proximity to the Watsons Bay pub make this a lovely spot at which to while away a day.

Collins and Store Beaches

Collins Beach Rd, Manly (between Manly Cove & North Head, North Shore).

See: Sydney By Area: Manly; Tours Around Sydney: Quarantine Station; Walks Around Sydney: Manly.

Store Beach is legendary, with its sparkling, pristine emerald water, its thick bushland lining the beach, and its fine, golden sand and regularly arriving ice cream boat. Far from causing a problem, the difficult access (by foot around the rocky coastline) enhances the feeling that this is your private beach far from any city. Its neighbour, Collins Beach, is more accessible and a gem itself, boasting a trickling waterfall, a large yet slim slit of fine sand and shady grass. Collins Beach can be reached by clambering over the rocks from the end of Collins Beach Road, North Head. It is worth the effort.

Shark Beach, Nielsen Park

Greycliffe Ave, Vaucluse (Eastern Suburbs).

See: Tours Around Sydney: Bondi & Bay Explorer,

One of the greatest gems of the Sydney Harbour National Park foreshore is Shark Beach, which is backed by Nielsen Park. With sweeping views to the left to the City and to the right to Manly, this is an extremely popular place with parents looking for something to entertain their children, and peace, quiet and a beautiful setting for themselves. A favourite picnic spot (formal dining tables complete with candles surrounded by champagne-toting revellers have been seen here), Shark Beach has charm in abundant quantities.

THE EASTERN BEACHES

See: Tours Around Sydney: Bondi & Bay Explorer.

Bronte

Bronte Rd, Bronte (Eastern Suburbs).

See: Sydney By Area: Bondi & Bronte; Walks Around Sydney: Bronte-Bondi Cliff Walk.

Bronte has everything: surf, sheltered swimming, rock pools to explore, clean sand, clean surf-pool cut into the rocky cliffs into which waves crash discretely, cafes, bus access, and a child-sized model train on tracks complete with whistle.

Bondi

Campbell Parade, Bondi (Eastern Suburbs).

See: Sights To See: Bondi Beach; Sydney By Area: Bondi & Bronte; Walks Around Sydney: Bronte-Bondi Cliff Walk.

The beach with the most action and the biggest reputation is Bondi. Here, a graceful sweep of (generally) clean sand hugs the bay, dotted with people and colour, the water sparkles and the famous Bondi Icebergs winter swimming club sits defiantly at the southern end. Behind the beach on Campbell Parade is all the glitz and action of one of Sydney's most vibrant areas, including a large array of cafes and bars from which to choose.

Clovelly

Clovelly Rd, Clovelly (Eastern Suburbs).

See: Sports: Diving; Sydney For Disabled Visitors: Leisure.

Here is a beach with a difference: a large, deep and narrow rock pool naturally carved into the rock platform with a wall of rocks separating the swimming area from the Tasman Sea, yet allowing the waves to flow in; wide expanses of rock and concrete to lie on; a separate swimming pool infested with children; and a tiny little bit of sand on very flat water at the narrow end of the channel where families paddle. However, the huge attraction of Clovelly is the total wheelchair access to the water provided by a system of ramps and launches.

Tamarama

Between Bondi and Bronte Beaches, Waverley (Eastern Suburbs).

See: Walks Around Sydney: Bronte-Bondi Cliff Walk.

Also known as Glamarama, this is a tiny, narrow, intimate little beach where the beautiful people like to go. Equally famous for its dangerous rips (and for lifesavers who may be so intent on watching the above that they may not see swimmers waving for help out in the ocean), Tamarama is a gem. The beach-front cafe has excellent food, drinks and music, and can be visited as part of the gentle Bronte-Bondi Cliff Walk.

THE NORTHERN BEACHES

See: Bushwalks: Barrenjoey Lighthouse, West Head; Tours Around Sydney: Boomerang Beach Bus, Northern Beaches & Pittwater.

This name refers to a remarkable series of beaches which fill the many coves lipping the coastline north of Manly with clean, wide and long stretches of sand. Freshwater at Queenscliff, Curl Curl, Dee Why, Collaroy, Narrabeen, Mona Vale, Newport, Bilgola, Avalon, Whale and, finally, Palm Beach form this enviable string of beaches, around which a strong surf culture exists. While all of them are worthy in their own right, a few deserve special mention and attention.

Manly

North Steyne & South Steyne, Manly (not the small beach left of the ferry wharf).

See: Sydney By Area: Manly; Walks Around Sydney: Manly.

Manly was named by the members of the First Fleet who observed Aborigines of 'manly appearance' in the vicinity in 1788. The suburb's relative isolation from Sydney's centre made its a popular seaside resort throughout this century, and even though Manly's main drag has become highly commercialised and crowded in recent decades, the one and a half kilometre long beach has retained its integrity and may still be said to impart the feeling of being "a thousand miles from care".

Palm Beach

Barrenjoey Rd, Palm Beach.

Often referred to as the best beach in Sydney, Palm Beach is clean, very long (around two kilometres) and very wide, with a family oriented swimming pool at the southern end, and sand dunes and a nudist area at the other. On the ocean side of the peninsula, the surf is usually quite rough, while the rocks afford excellent fishing and rock pools to explore. On the Pittwater side, windsurfers speed across the choppy bay. A further attraction is the Barrenjoey Lighthouse , the exploration of which makes a great walk from the Pittwater side up to Barrenjoey Head, with highly rewarding views across Pittwater to the central coast. Palm Beach is also jokingly known as Summer Bay, as it is around this area that the television series *Home And Away* is filmed.

Shelly Beach

Bower St, Manly (North Shore).

Away from the noise and fast food of the main drag of Manly's seafront, Shelly Beach is a quiet, clean and popular beach with good swimming and shade areas. Short strolls up to the cliff tops allow a spectacular view of the Tasman Sea, while 'The Kiosk' provides the necessary refreshments to make the day half bearable. Yes, life's tough here, as the swimmers who lie gazing across to the pine trees of Manly, their view interrupted only by swimmers and moored boats, will attest.

THE SOUTHERN BEACHES

See: History; Sydney By Area: The Southern Suburbs. The Southern Beaches extend towards Botany Bay and beyond to Bate Bay. **Coogee Beach** is a delightful, more intimate version of Bondi Beach, with a smaller bay and a more relaxed scene of cafes and pubs behind it. **Wiley's Baths,** perhaps the most impressive and ultimate example of that Sydney Icon, the surf pool, cling to the cliff coast of Grant Reserve around the southern tip of the beach. Beyond Coogee lies the longer, more open stretch of **Maroubra** Beach, and on the southern side of Kurnell Peninsula, the northern head of Botany Bay and the site of Captain James Cook's 1770 landing, is the impossibly long stretch of **Cronulla Beach.** Divided into the four separate beaches of South Cronulla, North Cronulla, Elouera and Wanda, this roughly six kilometre stretch of sand is understandably the main focus of the group. Finally, the western edge of Botany Bay is lined by Robinson's Beach, more popular with aeroplane freaks than swimmers owing to the water quality and the proximity of the airport runways.

NUDIST BEACHES

Lady Bay

A short walk north from Camp Cove (above).
See: Sydney By Area: Watsons Bay; Tours Around Sydney: Bondi & Bay Explorer.
Lady Bay beach, one of the city's most famous male-oriented nudist beaches, is further around the coast line towards the Heads from Camp Cove. Be prepared for irregularly tacking boats steering through the bay with binocular-clad passengers perving across the water.

Cobbler's Beach

East of Balmoral Beach (above).
Cobbler's Beach has more of a family atmosphere about it, and the beach itself is beautiful, offering both a grassy strip and fine white sand. Boats hover near to shore again, but these passengers are usually also unclothed. The HMAS Penguin installation makes access a problem, unless visitors have a boat.

PICNICS

What better way can there be than to stride out into the fresh air armed with wine and food, and recline somewhere spectacular to laze away the hours? Whether it be for breakfast, lunch, dinner or a midnight feast, this is a great way to experience what natural Sydney has to offer. A number of the picnic spots suggested here even have food on site.

Desert Island Picnic: Shark & Clarke Islands, Sydney Harbour.

In the middle of Sydney Harbour.
See: Open Air Sydney: Boat Hire (below); Sydney By Area: Sydney Harbour; Tours Around Sydney: Harbour Islands (for details of access).
How does it sound to spend a day on a mid-harbour island in full view of the City, harbourside houses and passing water traffic, stocked with wine and food? These islands are where turn-of-the-century Sydneysiders played cricket, strolled along bush tracks, ate from hampers and paddled in rock pools, and while the surrounding scenery may have changed since then, the beauty of the setting has not been diminished.

Cremorne Point & Bradleys Head

Northern harbour foreshore, opposite Garden Island.
See: Sports: Swimming; Walks Around Sydney: Cremorne Point.
Easily reached by ferry from Circular Quay, Cremorne Point offers a leafy spot to recline and observe the Harbour traffic, while more energetic picnickers may prefer to clamber onto the Cremorne Point lighthouse for a unique picnic experience. For those who like the idea of combining a picnic with one of Sydney's most beautiful walks, take the ferry to Taronga Zoo, and walk around the shoreline to Bradleys Head. Here, the reward will be expansive views to the left and right, covering almost the entire harbour vista, as well as passing Manly ferries.

Balmoral Beach

The Esplanade, Balmoral (North Shore).
See: Open Air Sydney: Beaches & Picnics (above); Sydney By Area: North Shore.
At Balmoral, picnickers can relax on a small island and look directly out to the Heads, or recline on the sand and eat fish and chips from over the road. An excellent opportunity to avoid organising picnic food is to forget about sitting on the ground altogether and to go to the Bather's Pavilion Refreshment Room instead (**See:** Cafes).

Mrs Macquarie's Point & the Royal Botanic Gardens

Between Macquarie St, Cahill Expressway & Mrs Macquarie's Rd, City (✆ 9231 8111)
See: Museums & Galleries: Art Gallery of NSW; Open Air Sydney: Parks & Gardens (below); Walks Around Sydney: St Mary's to the Opera House.
A readily accessible spot for a picnic is Mrs Macquarie's Point, the leafy, breezy point on the eastern side of Farm Cove. Here, picnickers can enjoy uninterrupted views of the Opera House, the Botanic Gardens, Kirribilli House, Garden Island Naval base, the Woolloomooloo Finger Wharves, or even examine the insides of their eyelids. Diversions come in the form of cooling off at Boy Charlton pool, or visiting the Art Gallery of New South Wales.

Centennial Park

Between Oxford St, Lang Rd, Darley Rd & York Rd, Centennial Park (✆ 9331 5056)
See: Children; Open Air Sydney: Parks & Gardens (below); Sports: Cycling, In-line Skating; Walks Around Sydney: Centennial Park.
This big green area in central Sydney offers many varied opportunities to have fun on wheels and to picnic. **See:** Parks and gardens below for full details.

Nielsen Park, Vaucluse

Greycliffe Ave, Vaucluse (Eastern Suburbs)
See: Tours Around Sydney: Bondi & Bay Explorer.
Another beachside place with spectacular views for picnicking is Nielsen Park. A spot up on the grassy hills amongst the gum trees is hot property on a sunny day, not least because picnickers can look down on all the other picnics taking place on and around the sand. This is also a wonderful beach for drinks on warm summer evenings. (**See:** Beaches, above, for details.)

Watsons Bay

Western side of South Head (Eastern Suburbs)
See: Pubs; Sydney By Area: Watsons Bay; Sydney Icons: The Gap; Tours Around Sydney: Bondi & Bay Explorer.
Watsons Bay was Sydney's first fishing village, so it is appropriate that seafood feature on this 'picnic'. The harbour front is a picnicker's paradise, whether opting for BYO food and wine or not: boats anchored in the bay bob up and down, children play on the sand, the trees wave in the breeze, the grassy park is littered with picnic rugs and... Watson's Bay is the home of Doyles seafood restaurant. Picnickers can obtain fresh fish and chips from Doyles on the wharf, and eat it wherever they please: on the jetty, on the sand, in the grassy park or in the pub's beer garden. A stroll through the backstreets past the tiny 1800s weatherboard fishermen's cottages to Camp Cove beach, or up to the Gap cliffs for a spectacular view of the ocean, harbour and City, is the perfect end to the excursion.

West Head National Park

Directly west of Palm Beach across Pittwater (north eastern outskirts of Sydney).
See: Bushwalks: West Head; Tours Around Sydney: Boomerang Beach Bus; Northern Beaches & Pittwater.
For a grand scale excursion combined with a bushwalk, it is hard to beat West Head National Park. West Head Road cuts through the middle of dense bushland, forming the starting point of many spectacular walking tracks. One of the best to undertake with a picnic is to head down through the ferns and bush to Whitehorse Beach on Pittwater, where a fascinating rock platform and beach area sit almost undisturbed. However, there are more easily accessible picnic spots, and one of the easiest is right at the tip of West Head, at which point a panoramic vista across Pittwater to the Palm Beach peninsula awaits. Further information about the walks and the amazing Aboriginal rock carvings in the area can be obtained from the rangers at the park entrance.

Barrenjoey Lighthouse

At the northern tip of Palm Beach peninsula (north eastern outskirts of Sydney).
See: Tours Around Sydney: Boomerang Beach Bus, Northern Beaches & Pittwater.
Another option for enthusiastic walkers, Barrenjoey Lighthouse offers pretty much the same striking views as West Head, but without the cars, with fewer people, and with the lighthouse. The walk up the access track from the northern end of Barrenjoey Beach (the Pittwater side of Palm Beach) takes about forty minutes, and leads to very accommodating (large and flat) rocks to claim as your own on which to picnic. (Lightweight food is recommended due to the steady incline!) An alternative is to head for The Basin & Mackerel Beach, accessible only by ferry or boat. A short ferry trip leaving from the Sandy Beach wharf (on Barrenjoey Rd at Palm Beach) will take you across to two lovely spots to picnic at and explore (**See:** Tours Around Sydney).

Clareville Beach

Delecta Ave, Clareville (north eastern outskirts of Sydney).
See: Tours Around Sydney: Palm Beach,
Another aspect of inner Pittwater is to be found at Clareville: admire the quiet village atmosphere and the beauty of the lush, green, rounded hills as they sweep into the water, crowded with little boats and dinghies launched from the boat ramp and jetties. Public barbecues (bring wood fuel and aluminium foil to cover the hotplate) and a grassy area in front of the water make this a most acceptable spot to watch the sunset over a wineglass. For those who prefer not to organise food, the beach is also the home of the popular restaurant, the Clareville Kiosk (**See:** Food).

Royal National Park

Beyond the far southern edge of Sydney.
See: Bushwalks: Royal National Park; Trips Out of Sydney: The South Coast.
The many walking tracks, waterways and clearings of the luscious Royal National Park offer numerous possibilities for picnickers. As with West Head National Park (above), the best way to enjoy the park is to combine a walk with a lightweight picnic, and a number of walks detailed in Bushwalks are more than suitable for just such a purpose.

PARKS AND GARDENS

In addition to the thousands of trees which colour and revive the streets of suburban Sydney, there are a large number of public parks and gardens. Many of them are in otherwise highly developed precincts, and their fresh air and natural beauty is nowhere more apparent than in the city centre. The following public parks and gardens are particularly noteworthy for their views and historic significance. Entry to all of them is free except where indicated.

CENTRE

The Chinese Garden

Tumbalong Park, Cnr Pier St & Harbour St, Darling Harbour.
Open: 7 days 9.30am-Sunset. Cost: $2.
See: Sights to See; Sydney By Area: Darling Harbour; Walks Around Sydney: Chinatown, Darling Harbour

& the Powerhouse.
A serene oasis is a pretty good birthday present to give anybody, and Sydney was lucky enough to receive this unique garden as a bicentennial gift (1988) from the Chinese province of Guangdong. Orchestrated in a strictly traditional manner, it is entered through a screened pavilion: as bad spirits can only travel in straight lines, they are therefore kept out of the garden. Highly valued rocks have pride of place in this calm place, as water trickles enticingly through the little lakes, under bridges and over waterfalls. Pagodas extend over the water, offering ideal book-reading enclaves, while the view from the Tea House is not to be neglected, as are the tea and Chinese cakes. Surrounded by small scenes framed by branches of trees and windows, this is a truly wonderful retreat in which any visitor's pace is bound to be checked.

Dawes Point Park

Hickson Rd, The Rocks.
Open: 7 days 24 hours.
See: Sydney By Area: Sydney Harbour, The Rocks; Sights To See: The Harbour Bridge, The Rocks, Sydney Harbour; Walks Around Sydney: City to Kirribilli.
Right under the City end of the Harbour Bridge is Dawes Point Park, the perfect vantage point to gaze up into the structure's intricate yet brawny steelwork, or across to the Opera House. Palm trees grace the shoreline and frame the view, while further up the hill are five cannon, placed here during the Victorian era to upgrade the defences on Australia's oldest fortified position, established by the colony's first Governor, Arthur Phillip.

The Domain

Between St Mary's Cathedral, Sir John Young Cres, the Cahill Expressway & Macquarie St, City.
Open: 7 days 24 hours.
See: Music: Classical & Opera; The Sydney Year; Walks Around Sydney: St Mary's to the Opera House.
The first colonial Governor, Governor Phillip, set aside for public recreation the area now bordered by the Cahill Expressway, Sir John Young Crescent and the rears of Macquarie Street's official buildings. This prudence ensured a large, open, empty, green space for Sunday afternoon Soapbox speakers (along Art Gallery Road), annual January open air concerts such as Opera in the Park (**See:** Music), lunchtime soccer matches and joggers.

Hyde Park

Between St James Rd, College St, Liverpool St & Elizabeth St, City.
Open: 7 days 24 hours. Cost: free.
See: Sights To See; Walks Around Sydney: City Centre, Macquarie St;
The third of the City parks trio is Hyde Park, two blocks of formally and geometrically laid out gardens and trees. The park sits under the gaze of St Mary's Cathedral and the important-looking Land Titles Office at one end, the Great Synagogue in the middle, and the Anzac Memorial (to Australian and New Zealand troops) at the other end. The Archibald Fountain is also to be found here, complete with Diana, Apollo and spitting turtles.

Observatory Hill

Upper Fort Street, The Rocks.
Open: 7 days 24 hours. Cost: free.
See: Museums & Galleries: SH Ervin Gallery; Sydney By Area: The Rocks; Tours Around Sydney: Sydney Observatory; Walks Around Sydney: The Rocks.
Observatory Hill is one of those rare places which, despite its proximity to the city, remains calm and imbued with a strong sense of the past. Sitting under one of the hill's Moreton Bay Fig trees, visitors to the park can admire the **views** of The Rocks, the Observatory, the Docks, the City, the Harbour Bridge and the western Harbour. More observant visitors may notice the Lord Nelson Pub, below, the sequel to a snooze here.

Royal Botanic Gardens

Between Macquarie St, Cahill Expressway & Mrs Macquarie's Rd, City (✆ 9231 8111)
Open: 7 days 8am-sunset.
See: History; Walks Around Sydney: City Centre, Macquarie Street;
Stretching around the harbour's edge at Farm Cove, the Royal Botanic Gardens are the most spectacular of all. Originally the area was used to grow supplies to feed the stranded colony, (hence the name, **Farm Cove),** and over in the corner closest to the Art Gallery of New South Wales are to be found a recreation of the farm and a stone wall marking the location of Australia's first 'vegie patch'. They were formally laid out in 1816, with **South Pacific plants** in one area, **Moreton Bay Fig trees,** a formal **rose garden,** numerous **flower beds** and interesting specimens, **palm groves,** pyramidical **Tropical Centre** (**Open:** 10am-6pm summer, 10am-4pm winter; Cost: $5/$2/ $12family) and the central duck pond, and have the feeling of a series of intimate gardens rather than a huge, single mass. This is the perfect place to spend a sunny afternoon exploring, watching the clouds, lazing on a park bench or the lawns, book and wine in hand, with the splendour of the Harbour laid out before you. This is the City's premier picnic spot. Food can be obtained at the central **kiosk** and restaurant. An annual summer event is the production of *A Midsummer Night's Dream* in the gardens at night (**See:** Theatre: Open Air Theatre). There are also several **statues** of historic figures around the grounds, while the walk around Farm Cove to the Opera House is simply spectacular. The Botanic Gardens are an oasis in the midst of the City.

EAST

Centennial Park

Between Oxford St, Lang Rd, Darley Rd & York Rd, Centennial Park (✆ 9331 5056)
Open: 7 days, May-August 6.30am-5pm; September-

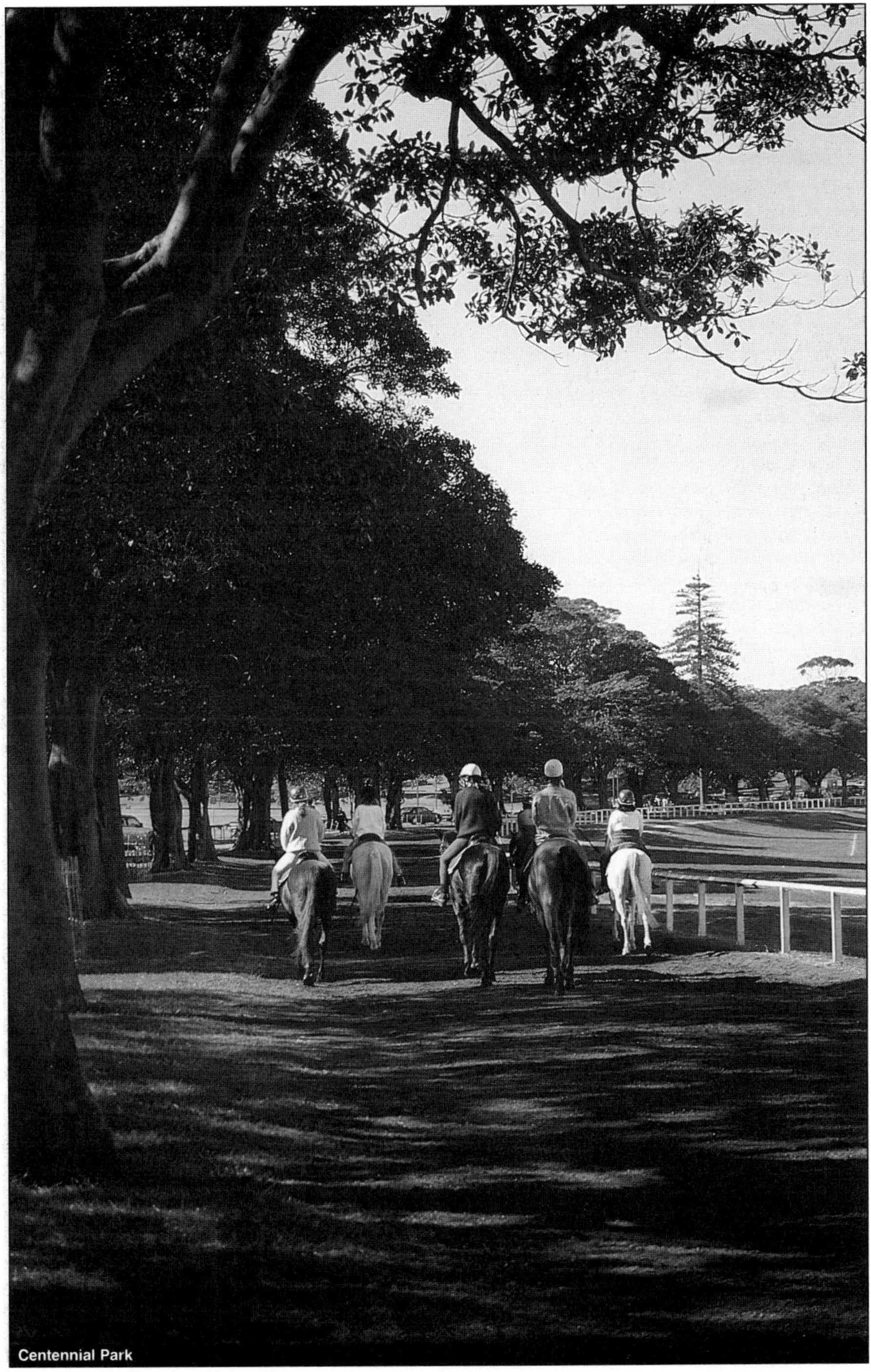

Centennial Park

April 6am-6pm. Cost: free.
See: Children; Sports: Cycling, Horse Riding, In-line Skating, Jogging; Tours Around Sydney: Bondi **&** Bay Explorer; Walks Around Sydney: Centennial Park.
Centennial Park covers an large area just to the east of the City in Woollahra, and incorporates several lakes, bicycle tracks, running/walking paths, a horse riding track, playing fields, picnic areas with barbecues, a cafe, and of course, hundreds of leafy trees. The grounds were opened in 1888 for the centenary of European-settled Australia, and are still extremely popular with Sydneysiders. While many take advantage of the sporting equipment available for hire nearby, whether a horse or a pair of skates (**See:** Sports), the park is also a favourite spot with many for simply relaxing.

McKell Park

Harbour end of Darling Point Rd, Darling Point.
Open: 7 days to 5.30pm.
See: Sydney By Area: Darling Point; Tours Around Sydney: Bondi & Bay Explorer.
This tiny, beautiful park is the perfect place to sit on a harbour **jetty** with the feet in the water, or to loll under the trees right at the harbour's edge enjoying the views of the City, the northern foreshore and Garden Island. The park is also a great place from which to watch weekend yacht races.

Nielsen Park

Greycliffe Ave, Vaucluse.
See: Open Air Sydney: Beaches & Picnics (above); Tours Around Sydney: Bondi & Bay Explorer.
Nielsen Park is blessed with an enviable beachside position, stretching along the Harbour in front of historic Vaucluse House. A spot up on the grassy hills amongst the gum trees is hot property on a sunny day, as picnickers jostle for position, while at any time, the park offers calm respite from the rigours of touring around the Eastern suburbs. It is also on the Bondi and Bay Explorer route, and the Nielsen Park offers a wonderful venue for breakfast or lunch (**See:** Food).

The National Parks

See: Bushwalks; Open Air Sydney: Picnics (above); Tours Around Sydney: The Hawkesbury River, Northern Beaches & Pittwater; Trips Out Of Sydney: Blue Mountains, South Coast.
The biggest parks of all in Sydney are on the outskirts, and together, they form a giant green ring in which no man-made development can take place. The Ku-Ring-Gai National Park marks the north eastern edge of Sydney; The Royal National Park marks the southern extremity, and the gorges and plateaux of the Blue Mountains National Park checks over-development at its foothills. They are the perfect places for bushwalking, observing Australia's native wildlife, examining Aboriginal rock carvings, and contemplating the impact of European settlement on the native environment of the Sydney Basin.

Private Gardens: The Open Garden Scheme

Information: Dorothy Friends Place, Bundanoon (✆ 048-83 6944)
Every year, a large number of private gardens throughout Australia are opened to the public on certain weekends as part of the Open Garden Scheme. A guide is published annually by the ABC (available at ABC Shops; **See:** Shopping), detailing all of the properties taking part, while weekly information is included in the *Sydney Morning Herald.*

SYDNEY HARBOUR BOAT HIRE

For those who like the idea of captaining their own boat around the secluded coves and bays of the harbour, there are several boat hire companies who can supply a variety of watercraft, even to those without licences. All of the following companies will impose certain limits on where hirers can go, and will advise about the harbour's shipping channels. Booking in advance is recommended for weekends, and fuel costs usually average around $10 for half a day.

Abbotsford Point Boatshed

End of Great North Rd, Abbotsford (✆ 9713 8621)
Open: 7 days 9am-5pm.
No licence is required for: 14 foot open boats ($35 half day/$50 full day); 14 foot canopy boats ($45/$70); 18 foot half-cabin boat ($60/$85). A $50 deposit is taken, and the cost of fuel used is deducted from it on the boat's return.

Balmoral Marine

2 The Esplanade, Balmoral Beach (✆ 9969 6006)
Open: 7 days 8am-5.30pm.
Balmoral Marine hires out anything from a tin dinghy or canoe to a yacht or cruiser, and charges from $22 per hour including fuel.

Elizabeth Bay Marina

1 Ithaca Rd, Elizabeth Bay (✆ 9358 2057 or ✆ 9358 2977)
Open: 7 days 8am-5pm.
No licence is required to hire: traditional launches with a sun awning ($55/$100), or half cabin cruisers ($240 full day). A $50 deposit is taken, and hirers must show some identification.

Rose Bay Aquatic Hire

On the beach, Vickery Ave, Rose Bay (✆ 9371 7036; or ✆ 018-259 733)
Open: 7 days from sunrise to sunset.
Rose Bay Aquatic Hire has catamarans ($25 per hour; no experience necessary); 14 foot aluminium motor boats ($40 for 2 hours, $10 per hour thereafter with a $40 refundable deposit; petrol extra) and windsurfers ($15 an hour) for hire, none of which require experience or a licence.

More?

For information regarding yachting in Sydney, **See:** Sports. For longer excursions of a more relaxed pace, several companies hire houseboats on the Hawkesbury River north of Sydney. The NSW Travel Centre (19 Castlereagh St, City; ✆ 13 20 77) can provide information.

BUSHWALKS

Surrounded by National Park on three sides, Sydney is bushwalker bliss. With walking tracks of varying length, difficulty and reward carved and carefully beaten into the bush in all directions, hikers can choose between rainforest pockets, canyons, cliffs, harbour foreshores, deserted beaches and Aboriginal rock art sites according to whim. The major walking areas are the Ku-Ring-Gai National Park, which includes Pittwater, to the north; the Royal National Park, the vast green space which separates Sydney from Wollongong, to the south; the northern foreshore of the Harbour; and, finally, the Blue Mountains to the west. This chapter includes details of thirteen of the best bushwalks the Sydney region has to offer, although hundreds more exist which are equally worthwhile.

Note Well

Australian bushwalks are generally rough. Whenever heading off into the wild, walkers must make sure they: take some nuts or chocolate and water; wear strong, sensible shoes; take note of bush fire danger classifications in summer; wear a hat and take a jumper and some swimmers as appropriate; and leave details of the walking route with someone.

Maps for the bushwalks can be obtained from the National Parks & Wildlife Service's centre at Cadman's Cottage (110 George St, The Rocks; ✆ 9247 8861; Open: Mon 10am-3pm; Tues-Fri 9am-4.30pm; Sat-Sun 11am-4pm), and at the entrance gates to the parks. Each walk has been tested and reviewed on site; however, a map is a very good idea.

Entry to National Parks is currently $7.50 per vehicle.

SOUTH

Bundeena to Little Marley Beach

Description: Little Marley Beach is legendary amongst Sydneysiders lucky enough to be in the know. Close to the suburbs, yet at the same time far removed from the City, it offers the perfect, short-term escape plan. A peaceful ferry trip from Cronulla to Bundeena, and a five kilometre walk through the Royal National Park passing Bundeena and Marley beaches (both famous for dangerous surf), lead to the safe waters of this scrap of paradise.

Starting Point: Cronulla Station ferry wharf, Tonkin St, Cronulla. Take one of the hourly ferries across Port Hacking to Bundeena (Cost: $4.20/$2.40 return; Timetable Information: ✆ 9523 2990).

Length: 10km return along mostly flat terrain; allow a day.

Transport Alternative: The ferry wharf is directly behind Cronulla train station.

Note: For a serious expedition, there is a campsite at Little Marley Beach, although drinking water is not available.

Of Sydney's three main waterways leading in from the Tasman Sea, **Port Hacking** is the farthest south. Chugging across Gunnamatta Bay into Port Hacking, the ferry crosses to Bundeena, where a suburban settlement clings to the coast: this is the extreme southern edge of residential Sydney. From the jetty, walk straight ahead along Brighton Street, turning at the second right into Scarborough Street. Walking onto the flat section of the street, look out for a small walking track on the left which leads along the fence line between scrubland and a private property. At the end is a rough four wheel drive track which leads uphill into the bush; follow this track to cross the sometimes swampy hollow bearing right from the fence. While walking up the hill, look out on the left for a well established foot track forking off to the left. This is the track which leads to Little Marley Beach.

Around one and a half kilometres from the jetty, another four wheel drive track turns sharp left and rounds the eighty-seven metre high **Jibbon Hill.** Soon enough, walkers will begin to see glimpses of the **South Coast,** including Little Marley Beach. The soundscape of the wind and birds, and the variety of vegetation in this part of the park, competes with expansive views for the attention.

Next, the track turns right and **follows the cliffs** to the north-east of Marley Beach at Marley Head, and emerges onto Marley Beach. Walking to the far (southern) end of Marley Beach, join the narrow track through the scrubland which leads off just behind the rocky shoreline to emerge at the destination: Little Marley Beach. Here is the perfect spot to swim, snooze, eat. explore and gaze at the view, gradually summoning the energy to return along the same route to Bundeena and Cronulla.

Heathcote to Karloo Pool & Audley

Description: This walk leads through the Kangaroo Creek bed past several swimming holes, large rock pools and sandy beaches, and finishes by crossing the Hacking River by bridge.
Starting Point: Heathcote train station. The walk is only in one direction, so check the train timetable between Royal National Park & Heathcote stations before setting out.
Length: 4.5km return to Karloo Pool only, or 11.5km one way (return by train) to Audley; allow a day.
Transport Alternative: Heathcote train station is very close to the Royal National Park and the beginning of this walking route.
Note: This bushwalk is best done between August and November when the wildflowers are blooming, or in summer so that the swimming holes are not too cold.

After obtaining a map from the Heathcote entrance to the **Royal National Park,** walkers should find and join the **Karloo Track** across Heathcote Brook, up over the Goondera Ridge and down into **Karloo Pool**, a deep, large rock pool carved by the water into the sandstone bed of the Kangaroo Creek where it meets the Heathcote Brook. This is a top spot, deep in the sandstone bushland to swim, picnic, rest and read. From here, there are two options: firstly, to return along the same track , or secondly, to continue to Audley (eight kilometres further) as follows.

From Karloo Pool, follow the **Kangaroo Creek bed** on the sandstone flats downstream towards Audley, detouring to the small tracks on the riverbank wherever the water is too deep or wide. Take note of how many large rock pools you pass. Soon after the **fourth big pool** after Karloo Pool, be sure to cross to the **right (eastern) bank** , as a long stretch of deep water follows where the Engadine Creek joins Kangaroo Creek. Two tracks to Audley exist; take the **high track to the right** up over the Gurrumboola Heights to the top of the ridge, where a track leading in from Uloola Falls will be seen. Continue downhill to the bridge which crosses the Hacking River. On the other side is a busy tourist area where picnic facilities, paddle boat hire, and a kiosk attract people like flies! To return to the beginning of the walk, follow the bitumen road out to the Royal National Park railway station. From here, catch a train back to Heathcote or back to Sydney.

NORTH

The Spit To Manly Walk

Description: The walking track opened in 1988 as part of the celebrations marking two hundred years of European settlement in Australia, and has come to be recognised as one of the finest and most beautiful in the area. The track leads through luscious native bushland, past secluded white sand beaches, rainforest pockets and broken cliffs: in short, some of the most spectacular scenery in Sydney.

Starting Point: At The Spit, park in or near Avona Crescent on the northern shoreline. The path begins here and follows the water's edge very closely, so head off confidently in the direction of the sea. A large metal plaque details the route at the beginning, blue posts mark the way throughout, and small signs provide notes on the vegetation at various points.

Length: 10km/3 to 4 hours one way only (recommended), allow half a day. It is best to do the walk from the Spit to Manly, not the other way around, and if you start at about 11am, you'll be in the right place at the right time for low tide, which shortens the walk near the end when you'll need it! Walkers will also emerge at Manly in time for afternoon tea: perfect!

Transport Alternatives: Bus 150 from Milsons Point or No 165-190 from Wynyard travel to The Spit. At the walk's conclusion, take the ferry back to Circular Quay; Bus 150 from Manly wharf back to Milsons Point; or one of buses 144, 150, 169 and 171 from Manly wharf back to the Spit.

The Spit marks the entrance to **Middle Harbour**, the opening bridge facilitating the passage of hundreds of sailing boats into the considerable marina here. It is a very busy waterway especially at weekends, and as you leave the Spit and commence the walk, you will have a good view of the action. **Fisher Bay**, next to The Spit, is contained by a thick pocket of sub-tropical rainforest- amazing considering the road traffic which goes through the area up the hill. Along the way are a number of **Aboriginal sites**, such as middens which consist of the remains of discarded shells (See: Box: Aboriginal Sydney). Follow the blue poles to **Clontarf Beach**, the quietly innocuous character of which belies its brief moment of scandal: Queen Victoria's son, the Duke of Edinburgh, was shot (but only injured) here in 1868. The site is now a popular picnic spot whose barbecues you must traverse to continue along the walk. If the barbecues excite pangs of hunger, there is also a small kiosk where provisions can be obtained.

The walk now enters a long stretch of beautiful, lush, thick bushland studded with natural lookouts offering across Middle Harbour to Balmoral Beach and its white pavilion. Eventually, the track emerges at **Grotto Point**, where a side track leads off to the right to the lighthouse, well worth the detour. Off to the left are some large, flat rocks which provide an

Aboriginal Sydney

The European settlers were not the first to find that the basin centred around this most magnificent harbour supported a very favourable lifestyle. Aboriginal settlement in the region now known as Sydney has been dated at around 20,000 years.

Sydney is like a enormous gallery: figures carved into rock appear on private properties, on golf courses, and in National Parks; trees scarred where bark was stripped off to make canoes or shields line the Hawkesbury River; and shell middens appear in seaside locations. Estimates place the number of rock art sites in and around Sydney at around five and a half thousand, the number of middens at two thousand, and sites showing previous occupation at several thousand. These relics give another dimension to the city, as we can see how the land was used before we came to it.

Aboriginal Hearths have been discovered at Shaws Creek on the Nepean River (15,000 years old); Randwick (8,000 years old) and Kurnell in the Southern Suburbs (12,000 years old; See: Sydney By Area).

Rock Art is found all over Sydney. The most accessible examples are to be seen on Bondi Golf Course (See: Sydney By Area), yet some of the best are in West Head National Park, where a huge number of figures, fish, whales and other animals are to be seen (See: Bushwalks). At the Gumbooya site in Allambie Heights are more than fifty carved figures; in the Royal National Park are numerous ochre and charcoal paintings as well as engravings (See: Bushwalks); and up in the Blue Mountains is the famous Red Hands Cave (See: Trips Out Of Sydney).

Occupation Sites are similarly numerous, and are to be found in the Blue Mountains at Leura's Lyrebird Dell (over 10,000 years old) and the Kings Tableland (grinding grooves over 22,000 years old; See: Trips Out Of Sydney); on Lane Cove River (4,000 years old); and in the Darling Mills National Park at West Pennant Hills (10,000 years old).

Shell Middens can be seen in many waterside locations, such as along the northern harbour shoreline (between The Spit and Manly; See: Bushwalks); Balmoral Beach (4,000 years old; See: Open Air Sydney); and in the Royal National Park (7,000 years old; See: Bushwalks).

However, for those who cannot get to see them first hand, a good place to gain a poetic insight into the lifestyle enjoyed by the Aborigines before the appearance of Europeans on these shores is the **Museum Of Sydney** (See: Museums & Galleries), whose installation 'Eora' is a delight to experience.

excellent resting spot, with breathtaking views across to the Tasman Sea, South Head and the Eastern Suburbs. Continue along the main track to **Dobroyd Point**, the site of kite and model plane flying most weekends, and a crazy palate of colour when the wildflowers bloom in Spring. **Forty Baskets Beach**, a tiny yet beautiful stretch of sand and sandstone formations, earned its name after a catch of forty baskets of fish made nearby in 1885 and presented to Sudanese troops in quarantine across the water at North Head. In this area are some stunning properties and houses. At about this point, it will seem that Manly is getting further and further away rather than closer, a fact made unpleasantly so by the lamentable absence of a ferry service directly across the water! However, after rounding the corner after Forty Baskets Beach into **North Harbour**, if the tide is low, walkers can cut across the sand flat to rejoin the path on the right. Otherwise, follow the path up the hill and around over a bridge.

However, you're nearly there! With a couple of detours through the streets to avoid private properties, the path leads straight along the shore into **Manly**, passing several monstrous apartment buildings (note the sky blue number by the **Fairlight Beach** pool) and the aquarium to finish at Manly Jetty. This is the site of **Armstrong's**, which is accustomed to welcoming walkers in off the track with their afternoon snack menu, coffee and cakes.

Bradleys Head to Chowder Bay

Description: More an easy stroll than a bushwalk, this harbourside walk leads around the northern shoreline from Taronga Zoo to historic Bradleys Head and beyond to Clifton Gardens, and then back along the same route.

Starting Point: Taronga Zoo ferry wharf off Bradleys Head Rd, Mosman.

Length: around 6km total.

Transport Alternatives: Take the ferry from Circular Quay, or bus 150 from North Sydney to the wharf.

Starting from the zoo wharf, turn right up the hill and veer off the road to follow the foreshore and walk. The path follows this instruction to the end without deviation! Having entered the Sydney Harbour National Park, the track follows the edge of Athol Bay around onto **Bradleys Head**, one of the more historically interesting headlands in the Sydney Harbour National Park. Having long served as a strategic observation post, the point near the **lighthouse** features the **mast** of the old HMAS Sydney, a light cruiser famous for its engagement with the German Emden in 1914. Below the mast stands a stone **column**, originally from Sydney's first Post Office and used to signify the distance of one nautical mile from the tower on Fort Denison.

Also here are the remains of a nineteenth century **fortification**. Comprising of a jetty, cannons and three gunpits with connecting galleries for riflemen, they were constructed using convict labour and completed in 1840. Having simply appeared 'out of the blue' and claimed this territory as British property, the early military colonists were apprehensive that another colonising nation, such as Spain, Russia or France, might decide to do the same. Thus, an extensive protection network along New South Wales' Tasman coast was established, of which these fortifications were part. The threat never became reality. From here, walkers can enjoy the views of the Heads, the City, the Manly ferries and many other craft plying their way through the water.

The path continues through a thick area of vegetation including many native and exotic plants to reach **Taylor Bay**. Here, you will undoubtedly notice a number of substantial residences which back onto the Harbour. A particularly grand example is the National Trust classified 'The Manor'. Beyond is **Chowder Head**. From here, the track leads through native bushland, in places meandering away from the water's edge, where large numbers of native birds are often to be seen and heard. At the end of the path is the small bay of **Clifton Gardens** with its fine beach and parkland at the base of a heavily wooded bushland hill.

At this point, walkers should return along the same route, and may like to walk beyond the wharf back at the start to investigate the adjacent Little Sirius Cove and its tiny sand beach, or explore the world famous **Taronga Zoo**.

Barrenjoey Lighthouse

Description: An easy walk to admire the expansive views of Palm Beach, the Tasman Sea, The Hawkesbury River and Pittwater.
Starting Point: northern end of Barrenjoey Beach (the Pittwater side of Palm Beach), around one hundred metres along from the seaplane depot. A sign painted onto a rust coloured shed marks the way to the lighthouse.
Length: 2.5km along a four wheel drive track; the grade is easy, but involves a steady incline; allow about an hour return.

At the northern end of Barrenjoey Beach begins the track up to the historic Barrenjoey lighthouse, another great picnic spot offering superb views across Pittwater to the northern coastline and its beaches. Similarly, looking back down along Palm Beach is a beautiful sight. Follow the track and enjoy the views at the top. (See: Open Air Sydney; Tours Around Sydney.)

KU-RING-GAI CHASE NATIONAL PARK

As with the Royal National Park, there are literally hundreds of walking tracks throughout the park, and even years of dedicated bushwalking wouldn't use them all. However, one of the most beautiful parts of the park is the area around West Head, which is also famous for its Aboriginal rock carvings (below). At the park gates on West Head Road, ask the ranger for a map showing where they are ($1). Further maps and books detailing the area's various walks are also available. Some of the best are the Elvina Bay track and the Whitehorse Beach via Flint & Steel Bay track. At the end of the road is West Head, from which point walkers can stare across to Palm Beach, Pittwater, and the Northern Beaches coastline.

For those who prefer to go on organised walks along the park's tracks, the National Parks and Wildlife Service co-ordinates guided walks, as well as various nature activities, throughout the year. Information can be obtained from local libraries. Also, a program of such activities in Ku-Ring-Gai Chase National Park can be obtained from the Chase Alive Volunteer Program, at the Kalkari Visitor Centre (✆ 9457 9853; PO Box 834, Hornsby, NSW, 2077). Most walks cost a $2 donation.

The following three walks are all within the park.

Bobbin Head Mangrove Boardwalk

Description: A short, level stroll or roll elevated above a mangrove swamp.
Starting Point: Near the Kalkari Visitor Centre, Bobbin Head.
Length: Less than 1 km.
As well as being a busy launch for all sorts of boats exploring the waterways of Pittwater, Bobbin Head has a fascinating Mangrove Boardwalk which leads through the mangrove forest (above the mud), its bird life, and the swampy, gooey, muddy roots of the trees. It is perfect for little children and for those restricted to flat, even surfaces.

Resolute & Mackerel Beaches

Description: A peaceful walk down through the bushland to the shore of Pittwater, visiting two of its most beautiful and secluded beaches.
Starting Point: Garigal picnic area, West Head Rd at West Head, Ku-Ring-Gai Chase National Park.
Length: 5km or 3 hours walking; easy grade.
Note: Those intending to camp must take all necessary equipment and drinking water.

This walk leads to two of Sydney's most secluded beaches, perched on the western edge of Pittwater with the National Park's hills rising steeply behind them. At the Garigal picnic area, look for and join the **Resolute Track**, which leads off to the south from a nature display building, and joins the Redhand Nature Trail. Soon after the track offers a spectacular view of Pittwater, it forks; bear to the right, looking out for the Aboriginal rock carvings at the point where the track turns to the right (west). At the foot of the **engraved rock**, a minor foot track cuts into the scrub heading south; take this path which short cuts a looping four wheel drive track. Soon after, it should reach the Headland Service Trail. At this point, turn left onto the trail and follow it to within a few metres of its end. Here is a small saddle with a narrow foot track leading directly to **Resolute Beach**. Take the track, which will lead onto a more major track leading around the Resolute Cove, but still high up above the beach (*). Turn right onto this track and after a few metres, double back and down to the beautifully secluded cove. This is the perfect spot for a restorative and contemplative break.

When ready to proceed, head back up the track to the track above at the point marked by (*). Follow this path around the shore and onto **Mackerel Beach** nearby. It is famous for its isolated residences and lusciously vegetated hillsides. After exploring the area, find and retrace the path back towards Resolute Beach, continuing past it to the next cove to the north, where a tiny trail, well worth investigating, detours down to the water. At this junction, the Resolute Track branches off steeply up a spur. By following it, walkers will rejoin the outward route just near the Garigal picnic area, where the walk began.

The Basin & West Head's Aboriginal Rock Art

Description: The Basin is one of Sydney's fabled camping and recreation spots, accessible only by water or walking. It boasts a beautiful, secluded beach at the end the cove. The walk begins by visiting some of the best Aboriginal rock art of the West Head National Park.

Starting Point: Post 12 along West Head Rd, Ku-Ring-Gai Chase National Park.

Length: 5.5km total, or around 3.5 hours walking, with a relatively easy grade.

Setting off from West Head Road along **Track 12**, follow the four wheel drive service trail until a smaller walking track appears on the right (a maximum of five minute from the beginning). This leads directly to some of finest and most extensive **Aboriginal rock art** in the area, featuring human and animal forms which are a treat to see. Returning to the **service trail,** turn right and head down to the Basin, around two and a half kilometres distant. The path leads directly through the typical sandstone country scrub of the area. Looking at the dry and dense vegetation which crowds the ground, it is painfully easy to appreciate how atrocious and destructive bushfires here can be. Those of early 1994 were particularly brutal, and the bush took a long time to regenerate after them. Descending to the water's edge, bushwalkers are privy to some lovely views over **Pittwater,** while at the bottom, the **Basin** and its beach await. After resting, picnicking and exploring, return to West Head Road by retracing the service trail.

WEST: THE BLUE MOUNTAINS

See: Trips Out Of Sydney: The Blue Mountains.

The major walking precinct to the west of Sydney is the Blue Mountains National Park, with its myriad tracks and trails leading through gullies, gorges, rainforest pockets and scrubland. Isolated villages where time seems to have stood still for decades are waiting to be discovered, as are many wonderful tea houses, the perfect places to go to recover after a long walk.

The Blue Mountains appear a hazy shade of Prussian blue especially in summer, as the oil, in high concentration in the eucalypts' leaves, evaporates in the heat and scatters the light rays. This creates an enormous bush fire hazard in the hotter months, so be aware of fire hazard classifications displayed along the side of the Great Western Highway. Many of the walks in the region are quite isolated and rough, and sudden weather changes can strike, so be prepared! The walks included here have been chosen for their variety and value, and between them, they include some of the best scenery of the region. Full historical and ecological background notes can be found in Trips Out Of Sydney: The Blue Mountains.

From Neates Glen To The Grand Canyon And Evans Lookout

Description: A very scenic descent through dense scrub into ferns and light-shy plants, along the canyon floor, through rock formations, past tiny sandy beaches and falls to the sound of gurgling water, and out the other end passing one of the most extreme views in the mountains. A very rewarding walk.

Starting Point: Take the Evans Lookout Road north off the Great Western Highway 2km east of Blackheath train station. About 2.8km along this road is a car parking area at the head of Neates Glen and the Grand Canyon. The walk begins its descent by the foot track into Neates Glen.

Length: 6km; medium grade, with some steep sections; allow a day.

Note: After completing the walk, it is only a short drive to the Wind Carved Cave (See: Trips Out Of Sydney: The Blue Mountains).

This Grand Canyon may not be anywhere as large as the American version, and is much greener in vegetation, and there are fewer tourists, but the name has stuck. To be fair, this two kilometre long canyon is quite deep in relation to its width, and, like its more famous big brother, its real grandeur lies in its natural beauty.

Leaving the car park, descend by the foot track into **Neates Glen** through a ferny gully, overhung with eucalypts: particularly lucky walkers may see the trees shrouded in mist. Neates Glen leads into the deeper Canyon by way of a sometimes slippery and wet track graded by a series of steps. After around four hundred metres, a clearing will come into view, offering the first glimpse of the magic canyon. This is **Greaves Creek**, whose many little ferny rock pools are interspersed by dry areas where lizards like to bask. From here, bear right to follow the path of the creek in the direction of the water's flow. Soon, the path should pass through a ten metre long rock **'tunnel'** where the stream goes underground, to emerge into the canyon proper. Continue downstream on the south bank noticing the ferny glades and rocky outcrops hanging over the canyon floor.

As the stream gathers momentum and descends more and more quickly, the path hovers above it in the drier vegetation. However, it soon returns to the canyon floor by a side gully, and thereafter follows the path of the creek closely to a **junction**. At this point, bear right to follow the creek as it swings left and then back to the right into another junction, overshadowed by some oversized rocks. Take the left branch **(the Rodriguez Pass track)** for about two hundred metres, emerging at some stunning cliffs, and views of Mount Banks and Beauchamp Falls. Retrace the track two hundred metres back to the boulder junction and descend the short path to the base of the **falls**, passing through the rock overhang. It is a good idea to have a break here!

From this point, **return** up the canyon and turn right onto the **Evans Lookout track**, ascending through magnificent tree and ground ferns. After around one kilometre, a service trail joins in from the right. Continue for a short climb to the Evans Lookout shelters, water tanks and picnic area. From this point, there is a spectacular view of the **Grose and Govetts Creek valleys**. The sheer cliffs, which drop some six hundred metres to the valley floor, are typical of the mountains, yet here they are more grand and extreme than anywhere else easily accessible. They are formed when sheets of rock split off the main body and slide down below to the valley floor. From this point, it is only a matter of returning to the starting point just over one kilometre back along the tourist road. After that, a drive along the Great Western Highway to Mount Victoria's **Bay Tree Tea House** is highly recommended for a Devonshire Tea of massive proportions (**See:** Trips Out Of Sydney: The Blue Mountains.)

Mount Wilson To The Wollangambe River

Description: Starting in one of the mountains' most beautiful towns, worthy of thorough exploration itself, the walk descends to the swimming holes of the Wollangambe River, whose banks are lined with narrow beaches of white sand, and proceeds along the rugged gorge through which the river flows.
Starting Point: Mount Wilson can only be reached from Bell's Line Of Road. On the main street (The Avenue) is a junction where the village hall stands opposite the bush fire brigade depot. Turn left and park nearby, as the walk commences just here on the right. There is a tourist information map in The Avenue further into the town, near the Post House.
Length: 5.5km return; easy grade.
Note: The legendary residences of Mount Wilson are also famous for their magnificent gardens, which are periodically open to the public. For details, See: Trips Out Of Sydney: The Blue Mountains.

From the starting point, walk around five hundred metres to reach the National Park, bearing left at the right-angled fence line. Follow the road another one hundred metres over a gassy slope to a **four wheel drive track**, turn right onto it and walk around thirty metres; then take the foot track which leads off to the left and straight to the **river bank**. Along the way, the path leaves the basalt-covered peak of Mount Wilson and leads down through the underlying sandstone around the head of the gully. The difference in vegetation will become noticeable as you descend: tall trees standing over carpets of ground ferns characterise the upper area, whereas smaller plants which prefer cooler, more sheltered conditions inhabit the deeper areas. The track then proceeds through a couple of saddles before forking into two paths, both of which descend to the river bank near the Wallangambe's confluence with the Bell and du Faur Creeks, over three hundred metres below the start of the walk.

After floating on an air bed, swimming in the icy water, exploring the little beaches and/or picnicking, **return** to Mount Wilson by the same path.

Ruined Castle

Description: The walk follows the Ruined Castle Track below the cut of the cliffs to a craggy rock outcrop which juts out into the Jamison Valley.
Starting Point: The car park of the Scenic Railway, Violet Street, Katoomba.
Length: around 4.5 hours; medium grade.
Note: The Golden Stairs which descend the cliff very steeply include a couple of short, wide-stepped steel ladders with railings. If this does not appeal, the walk can be altered to begin by descending the Scenic Railway, following the Federal Pass Track to the right, and later returning by the Scenic Railway.

Starting from outside the Scenic Railway, follow Violet Street to its intersection with Short Street and turn left. This leads directly to Glenraphael Drive to proceed out along the Narrow Neck Plateau. This stretch of the walk is necessary to make the route a loop, so persevere and enjoy a great moment in sightseeing: to the left of the road is the Megalong Valley, and to the right, the Jamison Valley. Where the road begins an incline, look out for the **Golden Stairs** to the left. It is a long way down to the floors of these giant gorges, but that is exactly where the Golden Stairs lead. Walkers who do not pay attention to the steep steps and ladders will be there a lot faster than intended, so be careful.

Having safely reached the bottom, turn south (right) and begin to follow the **Ruined Castle Track**, looking out for a fork in the path around two and a half kilometres from the base of the stairs. Bear right,

Wind-carved Cave, Blackheath, Blue Mountains

Blue Mountains Fern Glen

Spit To Manly Bush Walk

Valley Of The Waters

Blue Mountains Lookout

Below: Rock Art

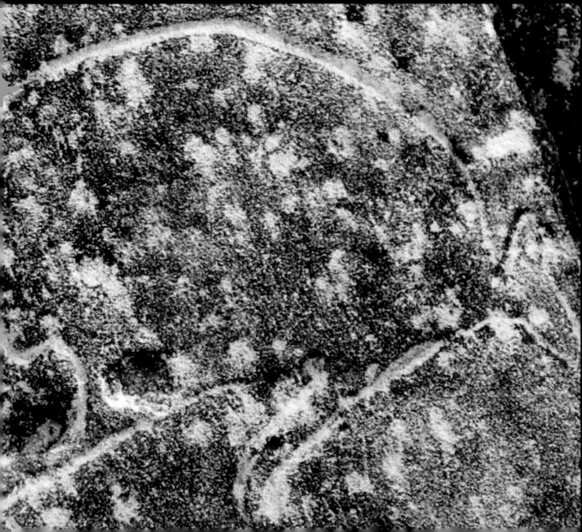

Below: Wentworth Falls

climbing steeply up the hill to a saddle. From here, it is around half a kilometre to the wide rock stacks of the romantically named Ruined Castle, where expansive views of the cliffs, valley and Three Sisters are the perfect accompaniment to a picnic.

From here, return the three kilometres to the base of the Golden Stairs. However, inviting as an upward climb may be, keep following the Federal Pass track around through the rainforest to the **rock slide** at Cyclorama Point. In this vicinity, the path passes a number of disused and sealed (but still visible) coal mines. Eventually it will reach the base of the **Scenic Railway**, from which point it is an easy ride to the top. The last ride up is at 4.55pm, although there is a track from the base station for those who miss it. (Those who have the energy may like to continue a short distance beyond the station to view some ancient trees and bubbling cascades.)

However the highlight of the walk is yet to come: leaving the railway, behold the amazing souvenir emporium! A browse through here is more than worthwhile and often highly entertaining. From here, it is a short drive into **Katoomba**, where an afternoon tea in the historic art deco Paragon Cafe and a stroll along the main street would be the perfect end to the day. (For full details, See: Trips Out Of Sydney: The Blue Mountains.)

Wentworth Falls

Description: A walk for thrill seekers, leading from the top of the tall Wentworth Falls down the cliffs and overhangs of the steep and deep escarpment to the valley bottom and up again. This is not a long walk, but in many places, a heart stopper.

Starting Point: Car park of Wentworth Falls, Falls Rd, Wentworth Falls.

Length: 3.5km; easy grade, but with a very steep descent and ascent. Allow half a day.

Note: This is not a good walk for the faint hearted, the unfit or those with sore knees.

From the car park at the falls, it is best first to walk to the road level look out where a map is displayed on a permanent board. A track leads off to the right to the **Princes Rock lookout,** from which point a clear view of the entire drop of the falls is to be had. A tentative and careful peek straight down over the edge is always inspiring. Looking towards the falls, the path leads along the left cliff top, across the top pool, and down the steps carved into the cliff all the way to the bottom.

At the point where the lookout outcrop joins the main cliff, a track leads off towards the falls. Follow this all the way around to some **lovely cascades** which flow along gurgling happily, unaware of the rather deep drop they are about to suffer. The track curves around to the right and leads onto the main water pool which feeds the falls Cross this to join the track on the far side, and begin the **descent** to the middle stage. This is a great place to explore, pleasantly pock marked as it is with deep rock pools. It is also a picnic spot with a difference. After resting and preparing mentally for the trip back up the stairs, go for it. A longer version of this walk is the Valley of the Waters track, following.

The Valley of the Waters Cliff Walk

Description: A descent into the Jamison Valley, leading past Valley of the Waters Creek and several sets of water falls along a stunning mid-cliff walking track cut into the sandstone, to Wentworth falls, up the steep stone steps, and back to the starting point.

Starting Point: Conservation Hut, end of Fletcher St, Wentworth Falls (off Falls Rd).

Length: 6km; easy to medium grade, with some steep sections; allow around 4 hours.

Note: As with the walk above, this is not for those with vertigo or faint hearts!

There is much interesting information available at the **Conservation Hut**, so take some time before striking off into the bush to read it. In particular, a leaflet is available by the door which details the native plants which line the track, so pick up a copy, or ask inside if stocks are depleted.

Clear signs point the way to the **National Pass track** leading into the valley. After passing through a gentle descent, the path suddenly emerges at a striking view: the track is now some way down from the cliff tops, and the rock faces and gorge ahead are literally stunning, particularly when shrouded in dense, foggy mist. A steep flight of metal stairs leads from Empress Lookout down into the **Empress Falls**, through luxurious fern gullies and (hopefully) pockets of vibrant wildflowers.

Further along, there is a fork in the walk (Vera Falls Walk), with the Sylvia, Lodore, Flat Rock, Vera and, eventually, Red Rock **waterfalls** lining the track, and making this one of the most spectacular stretches of walk in the Blue Mountains (around two kilometres). Unfortunately, it is a dead end, so it must be retraced to rejoin the National Pass, and to continue the walk.

It may be of interest to know that the track is perched on a **contour** of the sandstone on a rather small ledge, in places cutting through the cliff and tucking in behind waterfalls to edge along the Jamison Valley. It is impossible to ignore the uninterrupted **views,** yet be sure to watch your footing! Eventually, the track reaches the middle platform of **Wentworth Falls**, a great spot for a break. After exploring the rock pools and gazing up at the drop, tackle the many **carved sandstone steps** to the top of the falls. After crossing the pool, stick closely to the cliff edge, **bearing left** at any track junctions, to walk high above the outward bound track towards Queen Victoria Lookout. From here, head back to the Conservation Hut where the walk began.

SPORTS

Whether it be purely for the pursuit of a hole in one, or of the body beautiful, Australians are generally keen on sport. This is an understatement. Along with most other major cities, Sydney has a large number of excellent quality sports facilities providing equipment and venues for football, basketball, tennis, squash and swimming. However, unlike many other major cities, Sydney also has great facilities for golf, cricket, rock climbing and boating, to name just a few. In addition, Sydney's consistently mild climate means that open air sports are particularly popular. As Sydney gears up for the 2000 Olympics, the State Sports facility at Homebush bay is steadily being transformed to a world class venue. Already, the swimming centre is an extremely popular place with the city's residents. However, not everybody wants to get out there and sweat.

This chapter includes a variety of facilities where you can go and do all sorts of sports, as well as details of places where you can simply sit back and watch other people exerting themselves. They are organised alphabetically within the categories of water sports, ball sports, individual sports, leisure centres and gyms, and finally, four legged animal sports. A number of bushwalking routes are included in their own chapter (See: Bushwalks).

WATER SPORTS

BOATING AND SAILING

Sydney's harbour and meandering waterways facilitate a vast amount of boating activity, whether involving dinghies, cruisers or racing yachts. Of course, the cheapest way to have a day on the water is to take a long ferry ride or harbour cruise. However, for those who want to captain their own explorations around the Harbour, or just potter about and dangle a fishing line over the edge, there are a number of places to obtain a boat, whether to charter or drive yourself (See: Tours Around Sydney). If you can sail and want to crew, try the Cruising Yacht Club of Australia, New Beach Rd, Darling Point (✆ 9363 9731).

Spectating

The 18-Footers are a historic and colourful part of the Sydney Harbour yachting scene. Weekly competitions take place on the eastern side of the Harbour every weekend from late September to early March. The boats of the 18-Footers League of Double Bay (✆ 9363 2995) usually compete on Sundays, and a popular spectator ferry which follows all the action leaves from the Double Bay jetty at 2.30pm (Cost: $10/free). The boats of the Sydney Flying Squadron (✆ 9955 8350) usually race on Saturdays throughout the season, and a spectator ferry to watch this action leaves from the club (at 76 McDougall St, Milsons Point) at 2pm.

Learn To Sail

There are many organisations and marinas co-ordinating sailing schools. A few of the best known are the Anchorage Sailing School at Bayview (✆ 9979 5877), the Australian Sailing School at Mosman (✆ 9960 3077), and the Pacific Sailing School at Rushcutters Bay (✆ 9326 2399). See: Children.

Events

The Sydney to Hobart Yacht Race attracts boats and crews from all over and departs from the Harbour on Boxing Day (26 December). In a spectacular display of colour, thousands of craft pack the Harbour and much of Sydney turns out on the shores to cheer the competitors through the Heads. Every June long weekend, Sail Cancer holds its Three Island Race (Information & Entry: ✆ 9997 1022), in which boats of all types and sizes speed around Scotland, Lion and Dangar Islands on Pittwater, starting from the Royal Prince Alfred Yacht Club at Newport. For $25, you too can join the fifty to seventy-five boats raising money for cancer research.

DIVING

Equally fascinating underwater as above, the Harbour and coastline of Sydney have many great spots for diving and exploring marine life, reefs, sponge gardens and wrecks. Several shipwrecks lie off the Northern Beaches coast: the *Dee Why* ferry, sunk deliberately in 1976 off Narrabeen, which now forms a reef harbouring abundant fish life; the *Birchgrove Park,* a steamer which capsized in 1956 off Newport; and the *Catherine Adamson,* a clipper which sank in 1857 off North Head, in an area now renowned for its twenty-seven metre reef dive, with plenty of sponge life, fish life and wreckage.

Scuba diving schools and centres exist all over the city, and may be found in the Yellow Pages.

Dive Centre Manly (✆ 9977 4355; **Open:** 7 days 8.30am-7pm) organise dives for experienced divers as well as lessons. Pacific Coast Divers at Clovelly (✆ 9665 7427; **Open:** Mon-Fri 9am-6pm; Thurs to 8pm; Sat-Sun 7.30am-6pm) also arrange dives and lessons around this excellent diving and snorkelling area, as well as tours to other dive spots.

SAILBOARDING

Windsurfing is popular in Sydney, especially in the north. At Barrenjoey Beach (Pittwater side of Palm Beach), equipment and expertise in the form of lessons can easily be hired from Palm Beach Water Sports (✆ 018-86 2000), which operates from the car park directly on the water. They can also supply equipment and lessons associated with catamarans, surfing and sea kayaking.

The other most popular sailboarding venue in Sydney is Narrabeen Lake, which is free of the troubles caused by big waves and rips. Narrabeen Water Sports (11 Narrabeen St, Narrabeen; ✆ 9913 2636; **Open:** 7 days 9.30am-6.30pm) hires out "everything that floats" and is located only ten feet from the lake. Equipment available includes sailboards for $15 per hour or $50 a day.

SURFING

The waves of the Tasman Sea barrelling in towards the coast create many great surfing beaches, and consequently, surf culture is important to the life of the city. The clothing and accessories of Stüssy, Arnet, Quiksilver, Billabong, Ripcurl, Mambo and Hot Tuna grace the sand, sea and surrounds like nothing else. So whether it be body surfing, body boarding or board surfing you prefer, this is the place for you. Note that those using surf craft must stay out of the swimming area marked by the yellow and red flags. Bondi and Tamarama usually have some reasonable surf; the Northern Beaches of Narrabeen, Mona Vale and Bilgola are also popular, as are Collaroy and Cronulla, Palm Beach and Long Reef.

Instruction and equipment can be obtained form several operators, including Palawan Surf and Body boarding Coaching at Palm Beach (✆ 9918 3870).

SWIMMING

Andrew (Boy) Charlton Pool

Mrs Macquarie's Point (✆ 9358 6686)

Open: Mon-Fri 6am-8pm; Sat-Sun & public holidays 6.30am-7pm; Closed Winter. **Cost:** $2/$1.

The Boy Charlton public pool faces the Woolloomooloo Bay finger wharves and the Garden Island Naval Base With surrounding fig trees and a central location, Boy Charlton offers the charming possibility of visiting the Art Gallery, having a swim, strolling down to Mrs Macquarie's Chair, and relishing Sydney's best view.

MacCallum Pool

Cremorne Point Reserve, off Milson Rd, Cremorne Point (close to Cremorne Point jetty).

Open: 7 days 24 hours. **Cost:** Free.

MacCallum Pool must be one of the most spectacularly located public and free swimming pools around. Sitting right on the edge of the Harbour and surrounded by wooden slat decking, picket fencing, and luscious palms, the view shoots straight out and across the water to Fort Denison, Mrs Macquarie's Point, the City and the sails of the Opera House.

North Sydney Olympic Pool

Alfred South St, Milsons Point (✆ 9955 2309)

Open: Mon-Fri 6am-9pm; Sat-Sun & public holidays 7am-7pm. **Cost:** $2.70/$1.30.

A pool with a view which demands backstroke, Olympic Pool is right under the northern pylons of the Harbour Bridge, next to the Luna Park site and right on the Harbour. Easily accessible by train to Milsons Point, this fifty metre, very clean salt-water pool is a gem, equally so in winter when heated and covered with a large tent roof. The pool is part of Sydney's history, as its halls, lined with photographs of past swimming greats and not so greats, attest. There is also a paddling pool and a kiosk for the less sporty.

Sydney International Aquatic Centre

Olympic Park, Homebush Bay (✆ 9752 3666)

Open: Mon-Fri 5am-9.45pm; Sat-Sun & public holidays 7am-7pm. **Cost:** $3.50/$2.50/$9.50 family.

Tours: Mon-Fri 10am, 12noon & 2pm, Sat-Sun by request and numbers permitting; **Cost:** $6/$4/$16 family; booking required (✆ 9752 3666).

As yet very difficult to get to without a car (at least until closer to 2000), this is Sydney's newest, biggest, most expensive and most glamorous place to get wet. The diving pool and fifty metre competition pool built for the Sydney 2000 Olympics are already in place (and in use). However, the centre contains much more: a training pool with a completely movable floor (so the depth can be altered from 2.5m to nothing at all); a leisure pool comprising a shallow paddling pool, mosaics, waterfalls, fountains and palm trees; a cafe; a fitness centre; child minding; and banana lounges for non-swimmers. This is an immensely popular sporting and leisure venue, and considering Juan Antonio Samaranch, President of the International Olympic Committee, described this as "the best swimming pool in the world", it is not surprising. It looks absolutely fabulous too. A great idea is to buy a combined tour and swim ticket (**Cost:** $7/$5/$29 family; See: Tours Around Sydney). Access is by train to Strathfield, Lidcombe or Homebush Station and then bus 401-403 & 404 to the Aquatic Centre. A new, direct train line is under construction.

Wiley's Baths

Southern end of Coogee Beach, Coogee (✆ 9665 2838)

Open: 7 days 7am-7pm (summer); 7 days 7am-5pm (winter). **Cost:** $2/50c.

Wiley's Baths is Sydney's most spectacular surf pool, jutting out towards the sea on the rock platform, and cloaked by towering wooden decking. These beautiful baths have been fully and accurately restored and are protected by the National Trust. There is also a kiosk here.

Beaches
Don't forget the many other surf pools of Sydney's beaches, such as Bondi, Bronte and Mona Vale.

BALL SPORTS

BASKETBALL

Information: Sydney Entertainment Centre, Darling Harbour (✆ 9320 4200).
The National Basketball League competition attracts huge crowds during the March to October season. Sydney's team, the modestly named Sydney Kings, is no exception, and has its home stadium at the Entertainment Centre, where games are played on Friday and Saturday nights. Tickets are available from the venue before the game.

CRICKET

Information: New South Wales Cricket Association (✆ 9261 5155).
One of the strongest links to Australia's English heritage is the nation's obsession with cricket, and Sydney is home to the country's most historic cricket ground, the S.C.G. (See: Sydney Icons). Fuelled by the annual Test Series and 'World Series' one day matches, played against a range of opponents including Pakistan, Sri Lanka, England and the West Indies, much of the city's population is struck down by cricket fever between October and February. The New Year's Day one day match is a Sydney Institution, and is invariably sold out. To experience the electric buzz of the S.C.G., any of the England v. Australia clashes are hard to beat, although the 'Poms' don't tour here every year. The annual clash for the sacred Ashes, fought on the cricket pitches of each country alternating years, sees old rivalries workshopped on the pitch. Many of the most devoted cricket followers shun the hype of international matches, preferring the quiet Sheffield Shield contest, played between the teams of Australian states.

However, whatever the match, a day spent at the S.C.G. is a day well spent. Tickets are available from the ground on the day, or in advance (recommended for series finals and more popular matches) from Ticketek (✆ 9266 4800). Seats on the concourse mean you're close to the action and cost $25/$15/$36 family. In particular, a seat on Yabba's Hill guarantees a lively day of spectating, while seats in the stands afford a good overall view of the action.

FOOTBALL

Information: Sydney Football Stadium Moore Park Rd, Paddington (✆ 9360 6601); Match Information (✆ 0055 63133).
Footy Fever strikes every year from March to September, a disease whose symptoms include clothing oneself in colour-coded scarves and beanies, irrational feelings of patriotism and a lot of screaming. There are three codes of football: Aussie Rules, a highly athletic game vaguely related to Gaelic Football and more popular in the State of Victoria; Rugby Union (a vaguely more polite version of the following); and the big one, Rugby League: a big chunky game played by big chunky (yet very professional) blokes. The game's following is so huge and emotional that it almost sparked a civil war in 1995 as players and fans argued about the benefits or otherwise of the break away competition of Rupert Murdoch's Super League.

Rugby games are played every weekend of the season at various teams' home grounds around the city in an atmosphere which is always electric, noisy, fast and exciting, especially as the grand finals approach in September.

Tickets are available from the grounds, but it is advisable to pre-purchase them from Ticketek (✆ 9266 4800) in the gladiatorial frenzy of the finals.

GOLF

Information: New South Wales Golf Association (✆ 9264 8433).
More than ninety courses and mild weather make Sydney a haven for golf fanatics, and while it is a world-wide phenomenon that private clubs are adamantly protective of their mystic exclusivity, Sydney has a plethora of public courses, so golfers are in luck. Following is a selection of the best of the city's public and semi-public courses and driving ranges. The names of some private clubs, as well as the major golf events of the Sydney sporting calendar, are also listed.

Note that before attempting to play at any club or course, intending golfers must ring to verify visitors' days and to book a tee time. Many, but not all, of the following courses and clubs have open days, when anybody with a current, official handicap can play in the competition. All fees in the following listings are for a full round, and pars are for men/women respectively over a full round.

Ashlar
Springfield Ave, Blacktown (✆ 9622 4300)
18 holes. Par 71/72. Founded 1929.
Visitors: 7 days except Tues & Thurs morning. Green fees: Mon-Fri $20; Sat-Sun $25.
This course was named St Andrews until 1947, when a group of Freemasons bought the course and renamed it. Although relatively flat, Ashlar is known as a daunting course: every par three is over one hundred and seventy metres.

Asquith
Lord St, Mt Colah (✆ 9477 1266)
18 holes. Par 70/73. Founded 1938. Green fees: $25.
Visitors: Mon, Thurs, Fri; Tues & Wed afternoons with limits.
Asquith is a hilly course owing to the rugged terrain on which it was built, and a private club, although visitors are more than welcome at the above times. There are numerous trees, gullies, creeks, dams and sloping fairways, which makes for an interesting layout and a challenging game.

Bankstown
Ashford Ave, Milperra (✆ 9773 0628)

18 holes. Par 71/73. Founded 1928. Green fees: Mon-Fri $32, Sat-Sun $37.

Visitors: 7 days at limited times.

Bankstown is known as a pleasing yet vexing course with long and exacting holes, testing layouts and excellent greens. Situated a short distance from the Georges River in Sydney's south west, Bankstown carries a Group 1 rating.

Cammeray

Cammeray Park Ave, Cremorne (✆ 9953 2089)

9 holes. Par 33/34. Founded 1906. Green fees: $16.

Visitors: 7 days with restricted times on Tues, Wed, Fri, Sat & Sun.

Close to the City and known for its hilly holes and gullies, Cammeray is a short course, yet popular with locals and non-locals alike. Collared shirts must be worn when playing.

Gordon

2 Lynn Ridge, Gordon (✆ 9498 1913)

18 holes. Par 65/69. Founded 1936. Green fees: $14.

Visitors: 7 days except Thurs, Sat & Sun mornings.

Although it has a club attached to it, Gordon is maintained by Ku-Ring-Gai Council. Known as a leafy, charming and friendly course, it is situated right in the middle of the North Shore, so the outlook greeting golfers is a pleasant one as they tackle the dips, gullies and water hazards and bunkers.

Long Reef

Anzac Ave, Collaroy (✆ 9982 2943)

18 hole true links championship course. Par 71/72. Founded 1921. Green fees: $25.

Visitors: 7 days with limits.

Surrounded by the Tasman Sea on three sides on a point jutting out from the Northern Beaches, Long Reef is a famous championship links, and even if the strong winds, dog legs and gullies cause a certain amount of grief, players can still enjoy the views.

Moore Park

Cnr Cleveland & Anzac Parade, Waterloo (✆ 9663 1064)

18 hole championship course. Par 70/73. Founded 1920. Green fees: Mon-Fri $18; Sat-Sun $21.

Visitors: 7 days except Fri & Sun morning.

Prior to 1920, Moore Park was a grazing paddock for Sydney City Council horses. Located in the green triangle of the Sydney Cricket Ground, Moore Park and Centennial Park, but still very near the City, tree-lined fairways, large greens and hills comprise this popular and challenging public course.

Muirfield

Barclay Rd, North Rocks (✆ 9871 1388)

18 holes. Par 70/72. Founded 1954. Green fees: $30.

Visitors: 7 days at limited times.

Muirfield is not a public course, but does allow visitors at certain times. It is known for its compact layout, good-looking, narrow, tree-lined fairways, and pockets of natural bush, water hazards and deep rough. This is a Grade I course.

Palm Beach

2 Beach Rd, Palm Beach (✆ 9974 4079)

9 holes. Par 64/63. Founded 1926. Green fees: $12.

Visitors: Mon, Wed & Fri; other days at limited times.

With views to Barrenjoey lighthouse to north and a location right on Pittwater, Palm Beach golf course is a visual feast. It was established by a group of campers on some spare land, and has evolved into a popular course over the years. A compact layout demands precision.

Woollahra

O'Sullivan Rd, Bellevue Hill (✆ 9327 3683)

9 holes. Par 68/70. Green fees: $18.

Visitors: 7 days at limited times.

This is a very pretty course, with abundant trees and deep green fairways. The course is always in great condition, and has a common boundary with Royal Sydney (below). Relatively few bunkers, few creeks and some water carries make for a potentially relaxing game and a pleasant walk around one of Sydney's prettiest areas.

Very Private Clubs

These clubs, which represent the cream of the city's golf facilities, may generally only be played at with a personal invitation and introduction from a member. However, they sometimes host professional and amateur golf events.

The Lakes Golf Club (King St, Mascot; ✆ 9669 1311)

New South Wales (Henry Head Via La Perouse; ✆ 9661 4455)

Pymble Golf Club (Cowan Rd, St Ives; ✆ 944 2884)

Royal Sydney Golf Club (Kent Rd, Rose Bay; ✆ 9371 4333)

GOLF DRIVING RANGES

Although there are many driving ranges around Sydney, the following are very good and very popular.

City Golf

123 Pitt St, City (✆ 9223 2600)

Open: 7 days 7am-7pm. **Cost:** 50 balls Mon-Fri $8; Sat-Sun $5.

This is Sydney's most striking and centrally located driving range, whose opening shot was played by Brett Ogle! With forty-six undercover bays, a putting green with nine holes, and a safely netted building facade as the target, what more could you want? Perhaps a coffee from the cafe, whose windows offer a view of flying golf balls and the caged pick up van teetering all over the astro turf. Lessons, hire shoes and hire clubs are available.

Golf Paradise

1 Myoora Rd, Terry Hills (✆ 9450 2155)

Open: Mon 11am-10pm; Tues-Fri 8.30am-10pm; Sat-Sun 7.30am-9.30pm. **Cost:** 50 balls $5.

The confidently named Golf Paradise offers fifty-six undercover bays, a putting green and practice bunkers. For those completely discouraged by their progress (or otherwise), there is also mini-golf on site. Lessons and hire clubs are available.

Golf Events

The New South Wales Open (November), the New South Wales Medal and Amateur Championship (February), or even the Australian Open may be played in Sydney.

Golf Resorts Out Of Sydney

If the golf facilities of Sydney do not satisfy your golf appetite, there are a number of resorts in the country surrounding the city which cater for golf freaks. In the Southern Highlands, a number of public and semi-public courses await, while both Milton Park and Bowral Heritage Park have golf facilities attached to them (See: Trips Out Of Sydney: Southern Highlands). In the heart of Hunter Valley wine country is Cyprus Lakes golf and country club (See: Trips Out Of Sydney: Hunter Valley). A qualified travel agent should be able to suggest several more.

SOCCER

Match & General Information: Australian Soccer Federation (✆ 9597 6611).

Sadly, soccer has never attracted the numbers devoted to the visually more spectacular 'grunt and sweat' world of Rugby in Australia, so the National Soccer League games are held at a number of smaller grounds around the city. With teams named Sydney Olympic, Sydney Croatia and Marconi, it may be apparent that soccer in Sydney is an intensely nationalistic affair in which teams and supporters are generally of distinct national groups and loyalties, with the Italians and Croatians leading the stakes. This makes for energetic and vocal crowds!

The season runs from the last weekend in October to April, with the grand final held in May.

The Australian Soccer Federation (above) will let you know which matches will be played where and when are on any given weekend. The major venues are Marconi Stadium, Bossley Park (✆ 9823 2222), Sydney Croatia Sports Centre, Edenser Park (✆ 9823 6418), and Leichhardt Oval, Leichhardt (✆ 9810 1030).

Those wishing to join an amateur soccer team should contact the association and/or buy one of several soccer magazines and newspapers available in most major newsagents.

SQUASH

Information: New South Wales Squash (✆ 9660 0311).

High impact, efficient exercise of this type can be had at a large number of squash centres around Sydney. The following are centrally located.

Balmain Shipshape Gym, Squash & Fitness Centre

340 Darling St, Balmain (✆ 9810 3393)

Open: Mon-Thurs 6am-10pm; Fri 6am-9pm; Sat-Sun 7.30am-7pm. **Cost:** $16.50-$20 per hour.

Bondi-Waverley Squash Club

8 Denison St, Bondi Junction (✆ 9387 1452)

Open: Mon-Fri 10am-9.30pm; Sat-Sun 9am-9.30pm. **Cost:** $8-$16 per hour.

Mosman Squash Courts

7a Vista St, Mosman (✆ 9960 3918)

Open: Mon-Fri 10am-2pm & 4pm-10pm; Sat-Sun 9am-6pm. **Cost:** $14 -$18 per hour.

Squashlands Gym, Fitness & Squash Centre

4 Norfolk St, Liverpool (✆ 9601 4844)

Open: Mon-Fri 6am-10.30pm; Sat 8am-9pm; Sun 9am-12noon & 4pm-9pm. **Cost:** $11-$13 per hour.

Surry Hills Squash Centre

525 Crown St, Surry Hills (✆ 9699 3233)

Open: Mon-Fri 6am-10pm; Sat 8am-8pm; Sun 9am-8pm. **Cost:** $15-$19 per hour.

Most squash centres co-ordinate a number of graded teams to play in the Sydney regional competitions, and will be able to provide information to those interested in joining the competition.

Squash Events

Every December, the World Outdoor Open attracts the big names in international squash to the outdoor court erected in the City's Martin Place. New South Wales Squash will be able to give information or send a calender regarding dates and other events (✆ 9660 0311).

TENNIS

Another sport rendered extremely popular in Sydney by the comfortable climate is tennis. There are hundreds of courts around the city which can be hired, and a large number of tennis clubs. A selection of those offering casual bookings is listed.

Darling Harbour Tennis Centre

Cnr Day St & Bathurst St, Sydney (✆ 9212 1666)

Open: Mon-Fri 6.30am-10pm; Sat-Sun 9am-6pm. **Cost:** $20 per hour.

Miller's Point Tennis Court (Sydney City Council)

Kent St, The Rocks (✆ 9256 2222).

Open: 7 days 8am-9.30pm. **Cost:** $16 per hour.

Positioned below a vine-clad sandstone cliff in the Rocks district, surrounded by terraces and leafy trees, this is a great court.

Mosman Tennis Centre

4 Bickell Rd, Mosman (✆ 9968 1888)

Open: 7 days 7am-11pm. **Cost:** $12-$14 per hour.

North Sydney Tennis Centre

1a Little Alfred St, North Sydney (✆ 9371 9952)

Open: 7 days until 10pm. **Cost:** $17-$19 per hour.

Tennis Events

New South Wales Open

White City, 30 Alma Rd, Paddington (✆ 9331 4144)

From the second week of January each year, this international tournament takes place at White City and attracts many big names as a warm up for the Australian Open (held in Melbourne). Tickets are available from White City or Ticketek (✆ 9266 4800) and cost $27/$16/$42 for the finals.

INDIVIDUAL SPORTS

CYCLING

Many individual councils have mapped and signposted cycling routes around their areas of Sydney. Information can be found by ringing the relevant council. **Bicycle New South Wales Inc** (L2/209 Castlereagh St, City; ✆ 9283 5200) organises regular road tours and races in and around Sydney and New South Wales.

However, for those who prefer to avoid riding on the

street, the ideal cycling place in central Sydney is Centennial Park: it's big, flat and leafy (See: Open Air Sydney; Walks Around Sydney). There are also a number of bicycle hirers in the vicinity.

Centennial Park on Wheels
26 Clovelly Rd, Randwick (✆ 9314 6460)
Open: Mon-Fri 10am-6pm; Sat-Sun 9.30am-6pm. **Cost:** $8 for 1 hour, $12 for 2 hours.

Woolys Wheels
82 Oxford St, Paddington (✆ 9331 2671)
Open: Mon-Fri 9am-6pm; Sat 11am-4pm; Sun 9am-4pm. **Cost:** Varies.
Woolys hires out good cycles and mountain bikes, and is in the perfect position for exploring Paddington, Centennial Park and the surrounding area (depending on the rider's fitness level) on two wheels.

HANG GLIDING AND PARAGLIDING

If this is your idea of fun, you're in luck. Bald Hill at Stanwell Park, about an hour south of Sydney (See: Trips Outs Of Sydney: The South Coast), is one of the best places in the world to hang glide or paraglide. As well as experienced gliders with their own equipment, Stanwell Park has a number of instructors and organisations on site taking novices on tandem flights, so no prior experience or organisation is necessary. Although booking is recommended, it is usually possible to sign up for a tandem flight once you get to Bald Hill on weekends.

Active Air Sports
PO Box 183, Helensburgh NSW 2508 (✆ 042-9942 999 or 018-423 069)
Active Air Sports offer tandem flights, introductory courses and licence courses in both hang gliding and paragliding. The instructor and tandem flier is a freestyle hang gliding champion, a member of the Australian paragliding team, and a level two instructor.

Sydney Hang Gliding Centre
PO Box 180, Helensburgh NSW 2508 (✆ 042-9942 545)
The HGFA accredited centre claims to be the longest established school in the country, and organises tandem flights and courses using Moyes gliders and a level two instructor.

Up & Away
7 The Drive, Stanwell Park NSW 2508 (✆ 042-9943 240 or 042-9943 533)
Up & Away, whose instructors are fully accredited by the HGFA, offer long instruction courses as well as single tandem flights and introductory days. Motorised paragliding courses are available for pilots with an Intermediate Pilot certificate.

IN-LINE SKATING

The best places for in-line skating are Bondi Beach Esplanade, a long, flat and wide promenade above the sand complete with a stunt bowl for the more adventurous, and Centennial Park, graced with the circuit road around the entire park covered with trees and serviced by a central cafe. All equipment (skates, helmets and padding, but not skill) can be hired for these two locations at the following shops.

Bondi Boards and Blades
230 Oxford St, Bondi Junction (✆ 9369 2212)
Open: 7 days 10am-6pm. **Cost:** $10/1st hour then $5 per hour.
Also at: Shop 2/148 Curlewis St, Bondi Beach (✆ 9365 6555)
Open: 7 days 10am-6pm. **Cost:** $15 for 1st hour then $5 per hour.

Centennial Park on Wheels
26 Clovelly Rd, Randwick (✆ 9314 6460)
Open: Mon-Fri 10am-6pm; Sat-Sun 9.30am-6pm. **Cost:** $9 for 1 hour, $15 for 2 hours.

JOGGING

The best and most picturesque routes for jogging in central Sydney are the following.
1. Along Art Gallery Road, around Farm Cove to the Opera House and back to the City, as experienced by hundreds of office dwellers every lunch time. See: Walks Around Sydney: St Mary's to the Opera House.
2. Along the cliff walk between Bronte and Bondi beaches. See: Walks Around Sydney: Bronte-Bondi Cliff Walk.
3. Around the peripheral and central tracks of Centennial Park. See: Walks Around Sydney: Centennial Park.

Jogging Events

Sun-Herald City to Surf Fun Run
On the second Sunday in August, the annual City to Surf Fun Run takes place. It is the biggest community sporting event in Australia, in which approximately forty thousand participants run, walk or crawl the fourteen kilometres from Hyde Park through the Eastern Suburbs to Bondi Beach, forming an amazing spectacle and the city's biggest mobile street carnival. (See: Sydney Icons.)

ROCK & MOUNTAIN CLIMBING

City Crag Climbing Centre
499 Kent St, City (inside Mountain Designs) (✆ 9267 3822)
Open: Mon-Fri 9am-9pm; Sat 9am-6pm; Sun 9am-5pm. **Cost:** $12 casual; memberships and climbing courses available.
To gain expertise and experience before endangering life and limb on a hundred foot cliff, City Crag offers "T Wall" holds mounted all over the sides of a fifteen metre deep, glass-sided 'cavern', giving three hundred square metres of climbing surface, complete with boulder problems and difficult angles. The centre can also advise about expeditions and locations around Sydney and New South Wales for intending climbers.

SPORTS CENTRES & GYMS

City Gym
107 Crown St, East Sydney (✆ 9360 6247)
Open: 7 days 24 hours. **Cost:** $8 per casual visit.
Centrally located, the gym's large windows provide some

diversion for drivers frequently stuck in traffic on Crown Street. This is a tightly packed den of weights, treadmills, fitness classes, steam sauna, solarium and massage, widely known as the gym of 'the beautiful people'.

Contours Ladies' Health & Fitness Centres

100 Church St, Parramatta (✆ 9687 1233)

Branches at Brookvale, Miranda, Pymble, Wynyard and Willoughby.

This is a highly popular chain of women only gyms operating in Sydney with special exemption from the Human Rights and Equal Opportunity Commission. Members and visitors can take advantage of child minding and hairdressing services, as well as the usual equipment and facilities. No casual visits; memberships only.

Healthland RCM

Level 9, Bondi Junction Plaza, Bondi Junction (✆ 9387 4244)

Open: Mon-Fri 6.30am-9pm; Sat 7am-7.30pm; Sun 9am-12noon & 4pm-7pm. **Cost:** $8 per casual visit.

Healthland is a popular gym offering a fully equipped gym, World and Australian aerobics champions as instructors, and even a child minding centre.

Squashlands Gym, Fitness & Squash Centre

4 Norfolk St, Liverpool (✆ 9601 4844)

Open: Mon-Fri 6am-10.30pm; Sat 8am-9pm; Sun 9am-12noon & 4pm-9pm. **Cost:** $7 per casual visit.

This is a large fitness centre which includes squash courts, a large gym with all the latest equipment, a circuit room with thirty-two stations, an aerobics room capable of fitting one hundred people, spas, saunas, showers and child minding.

Sydney International Aquatic Centre

Olympic Park, Homebush Bay (✆ 9752 3666)

See: Swimming, above.

Willoughby Leisure Centre

Small St, Willoughby (✆ 9958 5799)

Open: Gym: Mon-Fri 6am-10pm, Sat-Sun 8am-7pm. **Cost:** Varies according to activity.

With a swimming pool, aquarobics classes, a gym, basketball court, aerobics instructors and a whole host of other activities under one roof, Willoughby is an extremely popular leisure and fitness centre.

FOUR-LEGGED ANIMAL SPORTS

GREYHOUND RACING

Wentworth Park

Wentworth Park Rd, Glebe (✆ 9552 1799)

Open: Mon & Sat; first races around 7pm.

Information: check the yellow form guide in Saturday's *Sydney Morning Herald.*

A sport with a cult following among certain sectors of the Sydney population, and increasingly with Japanese visitors, is Greyhound racing. Consistently solid crowds flock to the track on race nights to watch sleek doggies chase a fake rabbit on a stick, while Derby nights (usually Saturday) are positively packed with thousands of punters watching the greyhounds compete in each of twelve races. If this is your scene, you can also wander around the kennels and watch the dogs on parade.

HORSE RACING

Information: Sydney Turf Club (✆ 9799 8000).

Sydney's four race tracks are host to pumping thoroughbred muscle throughout the year and particularly during the Autumn Racing Carnival, whose highlights include the Golden Slipper at Rosehill, and the Sydney and Doncaster Cups at Randwick. The races at Randwick, Sydney's most central racecourse, can be a particularly glamorous affair on Saturdays in the members enclosure, but in any case, they're always a great experience. The Spring Carnival is a sight to see. The Sydney Turf Club will be able to provide information about the following tracks.

Canterbury Park Racecourse

King St, Canterbury (✆ 9799 8000)

Randwick Racecourse

Alison Rd, Randwick (✆ 9663 8400)

Rosehill Racecourse

Grand Ave, Rosehill (✆ 9799 8000)

Warwick Farm Racecourse

Hume Hwy, Warwick Farm (✆ 9602 6199)

Listings of upcoming race meetings can be obtained from one of the many T.A.B. (Government betting body) outlets, all of which are listed in the White Pages, or in the form guide in Saturday's edition of the Sydney Morning Herald.

HORSE RIDING

Centennial Park (See: Open Air Sydney) is the most central place to ride in Sydney, with a number of companies operating out of the stables at the showground corner of the park (over Lang Road) . The maximum speed allowed around the park is a trot, although there are jumping facilities in the centre. Lessons run for around an hour, and provide a different experience of this wonderful park.

Centennial Park Horse Hire and Riding School

'A' Pavilion RAS Showground (✆ 9361 4513)

Cost: $20 for park ride; Lessons $40 (private) or $30 (group of two or three); Jumping $45.

This company offers pretty docile horses for park rides, dressage and jumping. Helmets and children's leads are available. Booking essential.

Eastside Riding Academy

'D' Pavilion RAS Showground, Paddington (✆ 9360 7521)

Cost: $20 for park ride; Lessons $40 (private) or $30 (group of two or three).

Eastside is well organised and has contented-looking and well groomed horses available for park rides for those who can ride already and lessons for those who can't. They also provide helmets and leads if required. Booking essential.

MUSIC: CLASSICAL & OPERA

Although the ill-informed shibboleth, that Australia is a cultural wasteland, is often heard when discussion turns to music and "the yarts", it is frequently he case that those bemoaning this country's supposed lack of 'kultcha' don't know where to look. In Sydney, it can be found at every turn.

Apart from the many orchestras and artists who are permanently based here, a large number visit regularly on tour from all over the world. Under the auspices of Musica Viva, for example, we are treated to the likes of the Beaux Arts Trio, the Kalichstein-Laredo-Robinson Trio, the Moscow Soloists, Les Arts Florissants, Hesperion XX, or divine visitations by Teresa Berganza or Victoria de los Angeles. The venues most frequently used for classical music are generally the larger, formal halls around the city, especially the Opera House. However, a large number of smaller venues are also frequently used.

This section contains details of the major concert facilities to hear classical music, as well as particulars of orchestras and ensembles to look out for in Sydney.

LISTINGS

The Sydney Morning Herald has daily entertainment pages, but Friday's Metro section is the most comprehensive weekly listings in Sydney. An excellent, free quarterly, State of the Art in Music, has a national concert guide and articles regarding concerts series, musicians and events. If you can't find a copy, telephone the publishers (✆ 9221 4321).

TICKET AGENCIES

ABC Shop

Queen Victoria Building, cnr George St & Market St, City (✆ 9333 1635)

Open: Mon-Sat 9am-6pm; Thurs to 9pm; Sun 11am-5pm. Credit: All.

The ABC (Australian Broadcasting Commission) Shop box office handles reservations and tickets sales for all concerts associated with the ABC. This mainly involves the Sydney Symphony Orchestra, although tickets for the orchestra's concerts are also available from the Opera House box office.

First Call

State Theatre, Market St, City (24 hour phone bookings ✆ 9320 9000)

Open: Mon-Sat 9am-5.30pm. **Credit:** All.

First Call is a large agency handling a wide variety of music (and theatre) bookings. The State theatre outlet is only one of a network of offices around Sydney.

Half-Tix

Martin Place, City (✆ 0055-26655)

Open: Mon-Fri 12noon-5.30pm; Sat 10.30am-5pm.
Credit: All.

Each morning, various venues alert the Half-Tix booth of available seats for performances that evening. These are listed on a recorded message on the above number after 11am, and advertised on the booth's boards. When the booth opens, they're sold off at half price. Half-Tix give purchasers a coupon which is then swapped at the venue for a ticket. While the allocated seats can be less than brilliant, the saving makes it worthwhile. Half-tix also handles all advance bookings at normal prices.

The Opera House Box Office

Opera House, Bennelong Point (✆ 9250 7777)

Open: 7 days as late as performances run. **Credit:** All.

Tickets for all Opera House events are available from its box office. Student Rush tickets are generally available thirty minutes before the performance in question, unless sold-out. Rush tickets are usually around $20 for the opera, and are priced from $10 for orchestral concerts.

Ticketek

State Theatre, Market St, City (✆ 9266 4800)

Open: Mon-Sat 9am-5.30pm; Closed Sun. **Credit:** All.

The mother of all ticket agencies handles bookings for musical events (not only musical theatre), although be wary of fees for telephone credit card bookings.

THE MAJOR VENUES

The ABC: Eugene Goossens Hall

700 Harris St (✆ 9333 1500)

This is the venue for excellent talks on matters musical, where experts on various composers come to share their knowledge with interested members of the public. However, concerts are also held here regularly throughout the year. For example, this is the home base of Synergy, Sydney's highly energetic percussion ensemble.

The Churches of Sydney

Each year, and particularly in Spring, Sydney's

churches play host to a variety of musical diversions. Others have regular events throughout the year, and the listings publications above will provide details. Look out for series of concerts by the Australian Chamber Orchestra doing the nomadic 'Bach at Twilight' around Sydney in April, and series in St James mid-year. Organ recitals can be heard in St Andrew's Cathedral every Thursday at 1pm, and in St Stephen's every Tuesday at 1.10pm.

Australian Chamber Orchestra (See: below)

St James (173 King St, Sydney (✆ 9232 3022)

St Stephen's (179 Macquarie St, Sydney ; ✆ 9221 1688)

St Andrew's Cathedral (cnr George St & Bathurst St, Sydney; ✆ 9265 1661)

The Conservatorium of Music: Verbrugghen Hall

Macquarie St, Sydney (✆ 9230 1222)

'The Con', government stables in a previous, colonial life, is always interesting to explore, but especially good to visit when concerts are on. Both professionals and students regularly give recitals in this, the main auditorium of the complex.

The Domain

Art Gallery Rd, City

Particularly in January, when the Sydney Festival is in full swing, the breeze is awaft with music from open air concerts and performances. The Domain sprouts a massive stage where operas, symphonic concerts, choirs and jazz performances take place. The order of the day is to arrive as early as possible to secure a good spot, and then to impose territorial markings; food, wine and friends should arrive soon after.

Sydney Opera House

Bennelong Point, Sydney (✆ 9250 7777)

You can be sure that there is always something going in this, one of the world's most impressive buildings, whether it be ballet, chamber, orchestral, operatic or recital. The **Australian Opera** has two seasons per year- Summer: early January to mid March; Winter: early June to end October. In the interval between the two, the Opera moves to Melbourne, and the **Ballet** has its season- Winter: March to May; Summer: December.

Chamber Music is well catered for, with Musica Viva and the Australian Chamber Orchestra's concerts held here during much of the year. The **Sydney Symphony Orchestra** frequently performs in the Concert Hall. Further details in monthly programs available from the Opera House.

Seymour Theatre Centre

Cleveland St, Chippendale (✆ 9364 9400)

This rather functional building primarily hosts theatre events. However, a second series of Musica Viva chamber concerts take place here, next to the University of Sydney.

The Universities

Both Sydney and NSW universities hold concerts in their halls, museums and auditoriums. These may range from performances by student choirs and orchestras to professional orchestras and recitals. The **Chamber Choir of the University of Sydney** (Parramatta Road, Camperdown; ✆ 9692 2222) is very highly regarded, and performs a series of works each year in the historic Great Hall (information: Box 229 Wentworth Building, University Of Sydney NSW 2006). The University of New South Wales' John Clancy Auditorium (Anzac Parade, Kensington; ✆ 9385 4872) is the home of the Australia Ensemble (below).

SYDNEY'S ORCHESTRAS & CONCERT SERIES

Australia Ensemble

John Clancy Auditorium, Anzac Parade, Kensington (✆ 9385 4872)

Resident at the University of New South Wales, the Australia Ensemble is regarded as one of the country's foremost chamber group. With the leader of the pack Dene Olding, it comprises a string quartet, flute, clarinet and piano, and has performed all over the world. Their subscription concerts, held in the John Clancy auditorium, are paired with lunchtime workshops on the Tuesday and Thursday preceding each concert, led by musicologists and conductors, with the ensemble illustrating the discussion.

Australian Chamber Orchestra

50 Darlinghurst Rd, Darlinghurst (✆ 9368 1712; box office ✆ 9357 4111)

Based in Sydney, the ACO has acquired an international reputation for exquisite musicianship. They can be heard playing around Sydney in all sorts of locations, from nightclubs such as the Basement to the Concert Hall of the Opera House, but always to the same excellent musical standard.

Australian Opera

480 Elizabeth St, Surry Hills (✆ 9319 6333; bookings ✆ 9319 1088 or 9250 7777)

Based in Sydney and performing in the Opera Theatre of the Opera House, the AO is a very fine company with a remarkable stock of performers. Productions vary from the traditional to the outrageously provocative and confrontational, but are almost always extremely well received. Some of the better known stars, past and present, of the AO include Deborah Riedel, Miriam and Clare Gormley, Joan Carden, David Hobson and Geoffrey Black.

Musica Viva Australia

120 Chalmers St, Surry Hills (✆ 9698 1711)

This revered organisation co-ordinates over two thousand chamber concerts a year, bringing international and local artists to numerous Australian stages and schools. Sydney is therefore lucky enough each year to hear heroes such as the Quartetto Beethoven di Roma, the Guarneri ensembles, Emerson string quartet, Kalichstein-Laredo-Robinson trio and many others of equal calibre. At the Opera house concerts, pre-concert musicology talks are given in the back foyer on the carpeted steps.

Sydney Spring International Festival of New Music
Information: Eugene Goossens Hall or Sir John Clancy Auditorium (both above).
Every October, the Sydney Spring festival of new music features around fifteen concerts to showcase recent Australian and overseas works, many of them performed by the composers themselves. The concerts could involve anything from string ensembles to piano solos, jazz groups or masterclasses.

Sydney Symphony Orchestra
700 Harris St, Ultimo (✆ 9333 1600; box office ✆ 9264 9466)
This is our city's symphony orchestra, led for many years by the late much loved and revered Stuart Challender, and now under the baton of Edo de Waart. The orchestra runs several concert series simultaneously, and performs all year in the Concert Hall of the Opera House.

Synergy
700 Harris St Ultimo (✆ 9333 1600)
Synergy is Sydney's famous percussion ensemble, which, as well as playing with specific orchestras and in different venues, has its very own concert series. These concerts are held at the Eugene Goossens Hall of the ABC's Ultimo HQ, and are guaranteed to plant a beat firmly and permanently in every audience's collective chest.

FOR OPERA FREAKS

Tours of the Opera Centre
The huge headquarters of the Australian Opera regularly opens its doors in Surry Hills, revealing wardrobes, millinery, wigs, sets and even working rehearsals. Booking is required (✆ 9699 1099). For full details, See: Tours Around Sydney.

Opera In The Pub
Cat & Fiddle Hotel, Cnr Darling St & Elliott St, Balmain (✆ 9810 7931)
Occasional series throughout the year.
Opera In The Pub aims to make opera more accessible and relaxed. In this, they definitely succeed, with members of the Australian Opera performing extracts and arias from various operas with piano and beer accompaniment. Excellent, if rare.

JAZZ, ROCK, FOLK, WORLD MUSIC & CABARET

On any night of the year, there is live music of some sort to be heard: Sydney is the home of an extremely energetic live music scene, ranging from indie to rock to folk to blues to jazz. Whether it's any good or to your taste is another matter, so the following information is intended to help you to find your niche.

LISTINGS

For this hemisphere of the musical world, there are several listings guides around. Drum Media, On The Street and The Beat, are free publications covering most live music acts around the city, but concentrating on rock, jazz, world music and everything in between. The other listings guide, 3D World, concentrates on dance music and the rave scene. All of these are available for free from music stores such as HMV (Pitt Street, City); various pubs; and book stores such as Ariel (Oxford Street, Paddington). For full details, See: Media.

TICKET AGENCIES

As above, Ticketek and First Call are the major booking outlets for such tickets. Most music venues simply charge a cover at the door on the night, although if it's going to be hugely popular, they're available in advance. The listings (above) will have the details.

JAZZ

JAZZ VENUES

The Basement
29 Reiby Pl, Circular Quay (✆ 9251 2797)
Open: From 7.30pm: Mon-Thurs to 1am; Fri-Sat to 3am; Sun to 1am.
A Sydney Icon deserving and receiving the greatest respect, The Basement has seen and heard it all. It is dedicated to jazz, but occasionally makes exceptions for other greats, such as the Australian Chamber Orchestra. However, more often than not, you will find the greats of jazz performing for a vastly appreciative audience. Admission varies, but is usually around $10.

Cricketers' Arms Hotel
58 Botany Rd, Alexandria (✆ 9698 3168)
Open: Mon-Sat 11am-late; Sun 12noon-10pm (24 hour licence)

This is another famous jazz spot, which also welcomes folk music onto its stage. Friday and Saturday nights, and weekend afternoons, see a variety of acts playing to the mixed yet appreciative crowd.

The Harbourside Brasserie

Pier One, Hickson Rd, Walsh Bay (behind the Rocks) (✆ 9252 3000)

Open: Mon-Sun 6pm-3am.

The Harbourside Brasserie is known for supporting up and coming musicians, and for providing a great spot to dine or drink while listening to jazz. The music generally starts around 9pm, although Sunday afternoons are purely a cappella from around 4.30pm.

Real Ale Cafe and Tavern

66 King St, City (✆ 9262 3277)

Open: Mon-Thurs 9am-Midnight; Fri-Sat 9am-3am; Closed Sun.

Situated right in the middle of the city is one of Sydney's best jazz venues, with a reputation built on hosting regulars such as Tommy Emmanuel, James Morrison, Galapagos Duck and any international act passing through the neighbourhood. All ages come to this dimly lit long thin underground room framed with jazz murals and filled with the lingering ghosts of music past! Check current listings for its program. Cover charges vary between $5 and $20, as set by the performers.

Round Midnight

2 Roslyn St, Kings Cross (✆ 9356 4045)

Open: Mon-Fri 6.30pm-4.30am; Sat-Sun 6.30pm-5.30am.

Live music: every night interspersed with DJs on Fri & Sat.

Round Midnight is a cool club more often than not featuring top jazz and funk of varying descriptions. However, the live music heard every night of the week is interspersed with DJs on Friday and Saturday nights.

Soup Plus

383 George St, City (✆ 9299 7728)

Music: Mon-Thurs 7.30-11.30 pm; Fri & Sat 8pm-1am.

This dark little basement with attitude in the heart of the city is devoted to jazz, which wafts up out onto the street above. Mondays are reserved for jam sessions, and the management stresses families are welcome.

The Strawberry Hills

453 Elizabeth St, Surry Hills (✆ 9698 2997)

Open: Mon-Thurs 11am-Midnight; Fri-Sat 11am-3am; Sun Midday-10pm.

The Strawberry Hills is known for its dedication to jazz. Tuesday and Wednesday hear contemporary and improvised jazz, weekends (Fri-Sun) are reserved for traditional jazz. Although a cover charge is in place during the week (usually $5), weekends are free. A relaxed atmosphere makes this a casual and popular jazz venue.

The Unity Hall Hotel

292 Darling St, Balmain (✆ 9810 1331)

The Unity Hall Hotel became known as a jazz venue over twenty years ago, and remains resolutely so on Friday nights from 9.30pm and Sunday evenings, although R & B is admitted occasionally.

FOR JAZZ FREAKS

The Manly Jazz Festival (✆ 9977 1088)

The Manly festival, held over the October Long Weekend (first weekend in October) is the highlight of the Sydney Jazz year, with over eighty performances in three days and nights of music by the sea. Venues range from Ocean World's seal house to the Park Royal's Grand Ballroom, and performances feature the cream of the jazz world.

The Kiama Jazz Festival (✆ 042-32 3322)

This popular jazz festival takes place to the south of Sydney every February, always including the greats of Australian and overseas jazz.

Jazz In The Vines (✆ 049-38 1345)

Wine and jazz are a good mix, and this is an annual late September event in the Hunter Valley, featuring top Australian jazz acts. With guests planted on blankets, feasting from their hampers, it is a great event held between the vines of the Tyrrells's Long Flat paddock.

SYDNEY'S JAZZ ACTS & GROUPS

DIG

Directions in Groove has been smoothing the air waves for several years with their eclectic brand of modern jazz. A couple of CD releases have helped them on their way to deserved stardom, and if they're on, go and hear them. Regular venues include the Sydney Festival Bacardi Club, the Basement ✆ Kinselas.

James Morrison

James Morrison is Australia's foremost jazz trumpeter, so if he's performing, every effort should be made to hear him.

Vince Jones

Jones is one of Australia's most famous and established jazz singers, famous for a voice which frequently ranges from gutsy to chocolate mousse smooth, but always delivers punctiliously shaped phrasing, and is accompanied by his painfully cool band. He has been known to tell the audience that he'll go home if they don't stop talking.

Where To Buy?

Birdland (3 Barrack St, City; ✆ 9299 8527)

Good Groove (350 Crown St, Darlinghurst; ✆ 9331 2947)

ROCK

Sydney regularly attracts big, international names in rock. The advertising for such events is usually so noisy that information here would be superfluous. Instead, this section contains details of the city's smaller rock venues, most of which are pubs.

LIVE ROCK VENUES

The Annandale Hotel

17 Parramatta Rd, Annandale (✆ 9550 1078)

Open: Mon-Sat 10am-Midnight; Sun Midday-10pm

Part of the University of Sydney scene, the Annandale can be relied on to host a variety of original, independent and alternative bands every week. A bonus is the 1950s deco cocktail bar serving over two hundred creations. Be warned that the pub sometimes locks all alcohol away so that the underaged may legally patronise the Sydney music scene.

The Bridge

135 Victoria Rd, Rozelle (✆ 9810 1260)

Open: Mon-Wed 11am-Midnight; Thurs-Sat 11am-4am; Sun 12noon-Midnight.

Examine the walls to see evidence verifying the Bridge's reputation as one of Sydney's most active live music venues: their past line up has included the greats. The pub's two bars are doused in music, with the relaxed Lounge Bar perhaps featuring a Latin band, Rock or Soul. Whether this or one of the occasional jam sessions and rap nights, there is usually something going on here.

Harbourside Brasserie

Pier 1, The Rocks (✆ 9252 3000)

Open: 7 days varied hours between 6pm-3am.

As well as being the home of a cappella and jazz, the Harbourside has established itself as one of the top (if hard to find) venues for live music in Sydney. It is a hive of musical activity during January's Sydney Festival, while the rest of the year sees special and discerningly selected acts performing regularly on stage.

Metro

624 George St, City (box office ✆ 9264 2666)

Open: Varies.

This venue has emerged as the premier place for indie, rock, dance and folk music, and even better, it's centrally located. Past acts have included our national heroes/icons, Midnight Oil, as well as many other famous acts, such as Jamiroquai.

Orient Hotel

Cnr Argyle St & George St, The Rocks (✆ 9251 1255)

Open: Mon-Sat 10am-3pm; Sun 10am-Midnight.

This multi-level pleasure dome includes several bars, viewing platforms and a dance floor; but there is also live music playing every night in the public bar. Jazz gets a look-in here on weekend afternoons.

Rose, Shamrock & Thistle (Three Weeds)

193 Evans Rd, Rozelle (✆ 9555 7755)

Open: Mon-Sat 11am-Midnight; Sun 12noon-10pm.

While a wide variety of music is played at the pub, the Three Weeds is famous for its blues and folk rock bands. The public bar itself is a traditional large room filled with pool tables and a calm atmosphere belying the energetic hive of musical activity which lies nearby.

Selina's: The Coogee Bay Hotel

Cnr Coogee Bay Rd ✆ Arden St, Coogee (✆ 9665 0000)

Open: Mon-Sat 9am-3am; Sun 10am-10pm.

The Coogee Bay Hotel is a restored historic Sydney pub/pleasure palace, in which, amongst the numerous bars and lounges, is to be found Selina's: one of the city's fabled rock spots. The better known acts amongst the pub's line up generally perform on Friday and Saturday nights. although the constant line-up of acts makes this one of the city's most intense pub music venues.

Don't forget the various Universities and Leagues Clubs around the city.

WHICH ACTS TO HEAR LIVE?

Midnight Oil, the national icons, are always worth hearing, although appearances are becoming less frequent; Boom Crash Opera are a resuscitated 1980s pop band who are constantly reviving themselves and mutating their sound; world famous Nick Cave & the Bad Seeds regularly tour nationally; silverchair has a mass following; Ed Kuepper is recognised as an extraordinary songwriting talent; Hunters & Collectors are nationally recognised as one of the country's great acts, while Def FX are a blend of basic guitar and dance. Others worth looking out for include The Cruel Sea; Things of Stone & Wood; Weddings, Parties, Anything; Single Gun Theory; and Trout Fishing in Quebec.

FOR LIVE MUSIC FREAKS

Every January usually around the time of the Australia Day long weekend, the Big Day Out takes place. This nomadic concert travels between Australian cities and is always greatly anticipated. A colossal line up of enormously popular live acts rotate on several stages according to the style of the band's music. Information is broadcast in the time leading up to the event on all major radio stations, but especially on JJJ (105.7FM), while tickets are usually available from major agencies, such as Ticketek (✆ 9266 4800).

FOLK & ACOUSTIC

The folk and acoustic scene in Sydney is not as active as it could be, and tends towards the Irish. Venues are concentrated in pubs and leagues clubs around the city, and the best listing for it is the Sydney Morning Herald's Metro section.

VENUES

Friend in Hand Pub

58 Cowper St, Glebe (✆ 9660 2326)

The friend is a friend indeed for Irish music lovers: every Sunday from 4pm you'll find the familiar beat pumping out the doors. (See: Pubs.)

Observer Hotel

69 George St, The Rocks (✆ 9252 4169)

Open: Sun-Thurs 11am-11.30pm; Fri & Sat 11am-2.30am.
Being rather attached to Guinness and things Irish, the Observer often features Irish folk bands among its otherwise standard musical fare. Browsers in the Rocks Markets will often hear this pub's attractive music wafting out the door.

The Three Weeds, Rozelle
193 Evans Rd, Rozelle (✆ 9555 7755)
Open: Mon-Sat 11am-Midnight; Sun Midnight-10pm.
See above.

The Basement
29 Reiby Pl, Circular Quay (✆ 9251 2797)
See above. Sometimes, but not often, folk musicians are allowed to tread the hallowed stage!

More?

Bandemonium
Beginning every June long weekend and continuing until mid July, this festival of jazz, rock, folk, country and world music fills Darling Harbour with music and people taking advantage of the free, open air performances.

WORLD MUSIC

Having discovered that being home to over one hundred and forty nationalities can mean more than just good restaurants, Sydney is a veritable carnival when it comes to finding world music acts on stage. Below are listed some of the city's major venues, acts and retail outlets; however, as the world music scene grows in stature in Sydney, the turnover of artists is increasing, so keep an eye on the current listings (above; See: Media).

VENUES

Most of these overlap with the above information, so brief details only are provided.
Harbourside Brasserie (Pier 1, The Rocks; ✆ 9252 3000)
Rose, Shamrock & Thistle (Three Weeds) Hotel (193 Evans Rd, Rozelle; ✆ 9555 7755)
The Bridge Hotel (135 Victoria Rd, Rozelle; ✆ 9810 1260)
Cyprus Hellene Club (150 Elizabeth St, City; ✆ 9264 6802)
Metro (624 George St, City; box office ✆ 9264 2666)
Bondi Pavilion (The Esplanade, Bondi Beach; ✆ 9365 1253)
The Basement (29 Reiby Place, Circular Quay; ✆ 9251 2797)

WHICH ACTS TO HEAR LIVE?

The World Music scene in Sydney is a veritable United Nations, with representatives from all over the world performing regularly. Papalote (Latin American), Ashok Roy (Indian), Bu Baca (Senegalese), Yungchen Lhamo (Tibetan), Slivanje (Macedonian), Valanga Khoza (South African), Utungan Percussion (Australian/New Guinean), Mark Atkins (Australian, playing Didgeridoo) are just some of the more established performers. Others are bound to arrive!

WHERE TO BUY?

Several music retailers have particularly good reputations for stocking a large range of world music recordings. These include: Birdland, City; Fish Records, Darlinghurst, Paddington; Good Groove, Surry Hills; Folkways; HMV, City; Recycled Records, Glebe and Bondi; and The Record Plant, City. (See: Shopping.)

FOR WORLD MUSIC FREAKS

One World
Information: SCC City Promotions (✆ 9265 9110)
1995 saw the first One World concert take place in Sydney, and its subsequent popularity has launched it on its way to becoming an annual event. A large number of the finest world music performers from around the globe, and around the corner, come together in February in an intoxicating mix of frenzied energy and raw musical power.

CABARET

Outside the drag/camp scene, the city really doesn't have a strong tradition of cabaret. However, while the scene isn't exactly overactive, a number of cabaret venues exist. For current listings, see Metro.

Kinselas
Taylor Square, Darlinghurst (✆ 9331 6200)
Everything else goes on in here, so it is no surprise to find cabaret performances too. (See: Nightclubs.)

The Cat & Fiddle Hotel
456 Darling St, Balmain (✆ 9810 7931)
The Cat & Fiddle is fast acquiring a reputation as a very active pub, whether the attraction is opera, folk music, rock, or cabaret.

The Performance Space
199 Cleveland St, Redfern (✆ 9315 5091)
The Performance Space is primarily a theatre, but occasionally hosts cabaret acts, usually as part of the Gay & Lesbian Mardi Gras Festival (See: Gay Sydney).

The Tilbury Hotel
Cnr Forbes St & Nicholson St, Woolloomooloo (✆ 9358 1295)
This is probably the most active cabaret venue in Sydney. Geraldine Turner, one of the country's finest cabaret performers, is a regular act here.

The Sydney Festival and The Gay & Lesbian Mardi Gras
Both of these mammoth events in the Sydney calendar produce a rush of cabaret performances in the city. Their programs will have the details of acts and venues around Sydney (See: Sydney Icons).

DANCE

There is no denying that Sydney loves to boogie. With dance classes, dance venues, clubs and parties, it is easy to believe that the whole of the city is gyrating to a pre-programmed beat (See: Nightclubs). The energy continues into the realm of professional dance, and Sydney is home to several famous and less well-known companies, which together make up a feast of both classical, contemporary and experimental works.

CLASSES

There are too many academies offering dance classes throughout Sydney to list them here. However, one well-established, central and diversified centre teaching all sorts and levels of dance is the **Sydney Dance Company Dance Classes** (The Wharf, Pier 4, Hickson Rd, Walsh Bay ; ✆ 9867 9721) where students can learn to dance classical, jazz, afro, or simply stretch their muscles. Beginners are welcome.

EVENTS

Dance Week

Information: Ausdance, Pier 4, Hickson Rd, Walsh Bay (✆ 9241 4022)

At the end of April every year, Dance Week explodes over Sydney scattering a range of free lunchtime performances in Martin Place, performances by professional companies, seminars, classes, workshops and demonstrations throughout the city. The week long festival is an initiative of Ausdance (the Australian Dance Council), which sets up an information telephone number close to the time.

The Sydney Festival

Information: Level 11/31 Market St, City (✆ 9265 0444)

During January's arts celebration, many distinguished dance companies from around the country and around the world visit Sydney to perform various works. This is the busiest time in Sydney for dance activity, and the venues for these performances are spread right around the city. The annual festival program will have the details.

VENUES & COMPANIES

The Australian Ballet

Sydney Opera House, Bennelong Point, City (✆ 9250 7777)

Australia's revered national dance company has toured extensively throughout the world to rave reviews, and Sydney is lucky enough to have regular access to their brilliance. The Australian Ballet is famous for stunning productions of both classical and more modern works, and performs two annual seasons at the Opera House: Winter, from March to May, and Summer, from December. Some of the national stars are Justine Summers, Vicki Attard, Steven Heathcote and David McAllister.

The One Extra Dance Company - Dance of Ideas

St Georges Hall, 354 King St, Newtown (✆ 9212 6549) or Ticketek (✆ 9266 4800)

What started in 1976 as an opportunity for choreographers and dancers to try out new ideas has blossomed into one of the country's most respected dance groups. Their performances treat audiences to modern dance verging on the experimental, often exploring themes central to the Australian psyche, and featuring specially commissioned music. This fully refurbished Victorian hall (c. 1887) is central to the burgeoning of the Newtown arts precinct.

Sydney Dance Company (Graeme Murphy)

Pier 4, Hickson Rd, Walsh Bay (✆ 9250 1777)

Over the past two decades, the Sydney Dance Company has earned the reputation as one of the country's most enigmatic and commanding contemporary dance and music groups. Many of the company's productions have acquired legendary status, simultaneously for the specially commissioned music, costumes, outstanding choreography, innovative production designs and propitious collaborations. The company shares Pier 4 with the Sydney Theatre Company for rehearsal space, and performs in the Opera Theatres of the Opera House. Not to be missed.

The Capitol Theatre

13 Campbell St, Haymarket (✆ 9320 9000)

This big theatre is the venue for the big names in dance visiting Sydney, especially during January's Sydney Festival (See: above).

The Performance Space

Cleveland St, Redfern (✆ 9319 5091)

This theatre annually features the works of Sydney's independent dancers and choreographers in a co-operative performance, the Dance Collection.

The Seymour Centre

Cleveland St, Chippendale (✆ 9364 9400)

Occasional dance acts feature among the usual line up of theatre and chamber music.

SYDNEY'S CULTURE STOCK

Sydney is lucky to be home to a large number of writers, musicians and visual artists who have formed the rich and varied landscape of Sydney's cultural life. In the following selection, you will find writers, performers and visual artists, as well as books and poetry to prepare and recall your visit to Sydney. Look out for them in the theatre listings, concert programs and art galleries as you make your way around the city.

Writers

Kenneth Slessor (1901-1971) is one of the most enduringly popular of Sydney's poets. His love of Sydney harbour, the streets and people of the city provided the inspiration for much of his poetry, the best known selection of which was published in 1944 as *One Hundred Poems*. Five Bells, in which he pours out his love for the Harbour, is widely regarded as one of the finest Australian poems ever written. **Ruth Park** (b.1923), who was born in New Zealand and moved to Australia around the age of twenty, became particularly famous for her trilogy of novels *The Harp in the South* (1947) describing life in the slums of Surry Hills, *Poor Man's Oranges* (1949) and *Missus* (1986). Her *Companion Guide to Sydney* (1973) is a sensitive journey through the city's social history, while *Playing Beatie Bow* is an extremely atmospheric adolescents' novel drawing on the history of The Rocks district. **Thomas Keneally** (1935-) is a prolific and gifted author, most recently in the public eye after his book *Schindler's Ark* (1982) was made into the film *Schindler's List*. Among his many other novels, the themes of oppression and displacement are explored. **Robert Hughes** (1938-), an internationally renowned critic, was born and studied in Sydney, where he also began writing and drawing for a number of periodicals. Two of his most popular books are *The Art of Australia* (1966) and *The Fatal Shore* (1987), a best-selling history of the transportation of convicts to Australia. A collection of his essays on art and artists appeared in 1987 under the title *Nothing if Not Critical*. **David Williamson** (1942-) is widely regarded as the country's most famous playwright currently working. Born in Melbourne and originally trained as a mechanical engineer, his first plays to receive recognition were *The Removalists* and *Don's Party* (1971), while other works have also entered the national cultural estate, for example *Emerald City* and *Gallipoli*. A new Williamson production is always greeted with great anticipation and expectation in Sydney, which has claimed this popular playwright as its own.

Performance Artists

Dame Joan Sutherland (1926-) was born and trained in Sydney, and made her debut here in 1947 as Dido in Purcell's *Dido and Aeneas*. Transferring to London in 1951 to continue her training, she joined the Royal Opera in 1952 and made her debut in that city as First Lady in *The Magic Flute*. Her interpretations of Lucia di Lammermoor and performances in Handel's *Samson* gained her international reputation, and established her as the most famous opera singer Sydney has yet produced. The current crop of Sydney's musicians includes **Paul Dyer**, director of the Australian Brandenburg Orchestra, one of Australia's leading musical archaeologists and specialists in period styles. **Simone Young** is a young, dynamic and internationally acclaimed conductor; **Richard Tognetti**, director of the Australian Chamber Orchestra; and, finally, **Joan Carden** and **Yvonne Kenney**, both acclaimed opera singers.

Owing to the location of the National Institute of Dramatic Arts (NIDA) at the University of New South Wales, the city has enjoyed and continues to enjoy a large collection of excellent resident actors. Some of the more famous include **Ruth Cracknell, Judy Davis, Colin Friels, Hugo Weaving** and **Henry Szeps**, while the current crop of the city's stage actors includes **Jacqueline McKenzie, Richard Roxborough, John Howard, John Bell, Linda Cropper** and **Donald MacDonald.** In the world of dance, the city's most famous and innovative choreographer is **Graeme Murphy**, Artistic Director of the Sydney Dance Company. He has also taken part in several Australian Opera productions.

Visual Artists

Lloyd Rees (1895-1988) was born in Queensland, but worked extensively in Sydney at the studio of Ure Smith from 1917 before travelling in Europe. He has a close connection with Sydney in that his first exhibition was held here, and many of his works depict the early pearly light of Sydney harbour. **Brett Whiteley** (1939-1992) was born in the Sydney suburb of Paddington, and went on to travel and work abroad particularly in New York and France, before winning the prestigious Archibald prize in 1976 and again in 1978, the Sulman prize in 1976 and 1978 and the Wynne prize in 1977 and 1978. Famous for using and abusing substances to open the doors of perception, Whiteley's works have been the subject of large retrospectives and are keenly sought after by collectors. **David Moore** (1927-) is Sydney's foremost photographer, a recorder of Sydney's metamorphosis to metropolis. Works of these artists can be found in the Art Gallery of New South Wales, so keep an eye out for them.

Sydney is the centre of Australia's film industry, with most of the country's film production and financing centred here. Some of the world famous productions to have come directly and indirectly out of Sydney include (roughly in chronological order from the late 1970s to 1996): Patricia Lovell's **Picnic At Hanging Rock**; Gillian Armstrong's **My Brilliant Career**; George Miller's **Mad Max**; Peter Weir's **Gallipoli**; Paul Hogan's **Crocodile Dundee**; Baz Luhrmann's **Strictly Ballroom**; Jane Campion's **The Piano**; Stephan Elliott's **Priscilla, Queen of the Desert**; and George Miller's **Babe.**

THEATRE

Sydney is the lucky home of a year-round, hyperactive theatre scene. While the best known companies, such as the Sydney Theatre Company, the Belvoir Street Theatre and The Bell Shakespeare Company, embrace modern productions as well as the traditional, the city is also fortunate to have a large collection of innovative companies. This chapter lists the major theatres and theatre companies of Sydney; details of their current productions can be found in any of the city's listings papers (See: Media), or the venues themselves. However, a great night out at the theatre involves food, and for this reason, included alongside each theatre are the names of a few nearby places to eat. Full details can be found in the chapters Food and Cafes. Ticket prices are listed here for full price and concession, although they may vary according to the production.

COMPANIES & THEATRES

Bell Shakespeare Company

Information: (✆ 9241 2722)

Tickets: Prices vary according to venue.

Highly regarded productions of Shakespeare's masterpieces are the centre of this specialised company. Established by John Bell in the early 1990s, it has since rightly earned the reputation as one of the city's finest groups. The performance venues vary, yet they are often to be found at the Footbridge Theatre of the University of Sydney.

Belvoir St Theatre

Belvoir St, Surry Hills (✆ 9699 3444)

Tickets: $30/$15. **Food:** Cafe Niki; Gastronomia Chianti; Mohr Fish; Rustic Cafe.

This is a building and a company with a history. The theatre itself was originally a tomato sauce factory, became the home of the Nimrod Theatre Company, and was later earmarked for demolition. Luckily saved from that terrible fate, it is now one of the premier theatres in the city. Upstairs, the Belvoir Company's productions sap the talents of many of the city's best directors, actors and designers to create a program of plays at once popular and stimulating. More experimental and less formal works by small companies are staged downstairs, often focussing on Aboriginal, multi-cultural and women's issues.

Crossroads Theatre

159 Forbes St, Darlinghurst (✆ 9332 3649)

Tickets: Around $18. **Food:** Atlas Bar & Grill; Cosmos; The Edge.

The Crossroads Theatre is particularly known for drama classics, whether Sophocles' 'Antigone', staged in full mask and with musical accompaniment, or an adaptation of 'Wuthering Heights'. The theatre also runs an annual Irish comedy festival for St Patrick's Day.

Ensemble Theatre

78 McDougall St, Milsons Point (✆ 9929 0644)

Tickets: Around $33/$21. **Food:** Billi's Cafe, Fitzroy Cafe, Kirribilli Fish Shop.

As well as housing an acting school, the Ensemble is a very well established theatre which consistently produces top notch plays.

Genesian Theatre Company/ Kent Street Theatre

420 Kent St, City (✆ 9529 5333)

Tickets: $16/$12. **Food:** Chinatown has myriad possibilities.

Formed in 1944 and performing in this historic building since 1954 , the Genesian Theatre Company claims to specialise in everything: dramas, comedies, thrillers and "a general range of works".

Lookout Theatre

Woollahra Hotel, cnr Moncur St & Queen St, Woollahra (✆ 9362 4349)

Tickets: $20/$15. **Food:** Bistro Moncur, The Bellevue, Golden Dog.

Perhaps oddly placed above a pub, The Lookout (almost chamber) Theatre has acquired a reputation for compelling productions in a truly intimate setting. Past productions have included Mitterer's 'Siberia' and Burrell's 'Hess', while cabaret also makes an occasional appearance.

Marian St Theatre

Marian St, Killara (✆ 9498 3166)

Tickets: depending on the play, $30-$20. **Food:** There is a restaurant within the theatre.

Two of the country's great theatre personalities, Googie Withers and husband John McCallum, perform regularly with the company in what are usually extremely well-received productions. Other well-known actors also perform with the company, such as Judi Farr and Jane Harders.

New Theatre

542 King St, Newtown (✆ 9519 3403)

Tickets: $16/$11. **Food:** Fish Tank, Thai Pothong or other King St eateries.

This is Sydney's oldest, and therefore most inappropriately named, theatre company! Now in its sixty-third year, its history of producing anything from radical, social conscience challenging works to Shakespearean classics, has made it famous. Here you will find an emphasis on Australian works performed by its core of 'resting' professional actors.

NIDA Theatre
215 Anzac Parade Kensington (✆ 9697 7613)
Tickets: Vary. **Food:** 391 Restaurant.
Based at the University of New South Wales, this is the National Institute of Drama, where many of the country's current theatrical stars received their training. Student performances are usually exceptional; several of them have since gone on to become massive commercial successes, such as Baz Luhrman's film Strictly Ballroom.

Opera House Playhouse
Bennelong Point (✆ 9250 7777)
Tickets: Usually between $32 & $45. **Food:** Bennelong, Merrony's, Rockpool, Sydney Cove Oyster Bar.
The Playhouse sees a number of productions by different companies and formations, ranging from pure drama to musical works. The Opera House's monthly programs will have the details. See also the Sydney Theatre Company, below.

The Performance Space
199 Cleveland St, Redfern (✆ 9319 5091)
Tickets: Vary. **Food:** Cafe Niki; Rustic Cafe.
Various performance groups stage their productions here throughout the year, yet all share a common thread of contemporary issues and social examination. Some are purely experimental and outlandish. Also using the Performance Space is the Theatre For The Deaf, whose demonstratively visual style makes theatre accessible to all.

Stables Theatre
10 Nimrod St, Kings Cross (✆ 9361 3817)
Tickets: $20/$16. **Food:** Bayswater Brasserie, Fez, Fu Man Chu, La Bussola, Mesclun, Tabac.
This reputable little theatre does good quality productions of an eclectic range of plays, from classics to moderns and experimental works.

Sydney Theatre Company
The Wharf Theatre, Pier 4, Hickson Rd, Walsh Bay (✆ 9250 1777)
Tickets: Vary between $28/$24 and $46/$36. **Food:** The Wharf Restaurant
Some of the greatest names in Australian theatre are associated with the STC. To name a few, Ruth Cracknell, Jacki Weaver, Linda Cropper and Hugo Weaving can all be seen in what are usually excellent productions of a wide variety of plays. The theatre company particularly likes contemporary works, and the faithful audiences particularly like the company.

More?
The Western Suburbs is regarded by many as the big developing area of Sydney as far as theatre is concerned. Here, you will find **grass roots** companies such as the Death Defying Theatre, Open City Inc, the REM Theatre For Young People, Q Theatre and the Sidetrack Performance Group.

OPEN AIR SUMMER THEATRE

Midsummer Night's Dream
Royal Botanic Gardens, City.
Bookings: (✆ 9250 7666) or through Ticketek (✆ 9266 4800). **Tickets:** $22.90-$34.90.
Shakespeare in the Royal Botanic Gardens beneath the stars kissed by the summer breeze... aah! This has become an extremely popular annual event, to which the audience is required to bring a blanket, cushion and a hamper.

Shakespeare By the Sea
Balmoral Beach Rotunda and surrounds.
Information (✆ 9557 3065). **Tickets:** Vary.
The plays being performed each summer vary, although Shakespeare's classics remain the focus. Recline on a blanket while sipping wine and delicately chomping food as the performance unfolds under the white rotunda beside Balmoral Beach in the Esplanade Park.

MUSICAL THEATRE

The resurgence of the musical has definitely been seen in Sydney, where the following theatres are dedicated to the big, international productions. Tickets are generally available through the booking agencies FirstCall (✆ 9320 9000) and Ticketek (✆ 9266 4800), while the numbers below are those of the respective theatres.

Capitol Theatre
13-17 Campbell St, Haymarket (✆ 9320 9122)
Tickets: Vary depending on the production. **Food:** Asturiana, Chinatown, TTTE Sarn.
Recently reopened and refurbished, the Capitol is the grandest of all Sydney theatres, veritably dripping with the romanticised sculptures, gilding and chandeliers of its original design. Big international musicals, such as West Side Story and Miss Saigon, look set to dominate the stage indefinitely.

Her Majesty's Theatre
107 Quay St, Haymarket (✆ 9212 3411)
Tickets: Vary depending on the production. **Food:** Asturiana, Chinatown, TTTE Sarn.
What will happen to the name of this theatre when (or if) Australia becomes a republic is open to debate. However, for the time being, it is the home of more musical drama activity.

State Theatre
Market St, City (✆ 9373 6655)
Tickets: Vary depending on the production. **Food:** Cassis, Dendy Bar & Bistro, Edna's Table (special pre-theatre menu), Illy Cafe, Kingsley's, Level 41, Paradiso.
The glorious State Theatre is one of the most astounding buildings in Sydney, where a wide range of productions from performing soloists to musicals take place. The building itself is definitely worth seeing for its nicely grotesque picture palace opulence.

Theatre Royal
MLC Centre, King St, City (✆ 9202 2200)
Tickets: Vary depending on the production. **Food:** Cassis, Dendy Bar & Bistro, Edna's Table, Illy Cafe, Level 41, Paradiso.
The home of the 'Phantom of the Opera' is a red carpet, glittering walls, shiny brass and lacquered black fittings kind of theatre, well suited to the glitz of big productions.

FILM

Sydney is home to many mainstream, art house, independent and bizarre independent cinemas. The foreign film scene here extremely active considering our multicultural society, although it is really dominated by French film. It is very rare in Australia that foreign films undergo the degrading experience of dubbing, so while the visual sphere may be encroached upon by the sub-titles, at least the integrity of the actors is left unviolated. The cinemas in George Street generally screen mainstream movies, and exude an aroma of popcorn long past, well trodden into the plush red and black carpet. The exception to this rule is the Dendy cinema in George Street, which shows foreign and art house films. However, the majority of the more interesting cinemas can be found in the inner city suburbs: Paddington's Academy Twin and Verona, Glebe's Valhalla, North Sydney's Walker Street Cinema, and Kings Cross' Movie Room. The Sydney Film Festival happens once a year, featuring experimental, Australian, foreign release, documentary and rare films. All screenings are at the State Theatre in Market Street.

Programs and session details for the following cinemas are best found in the daily entertainment pages of the Sydney Morning Herald (see: Media). Tickets are usually $12/$9/$6.50, while Tuesdays are often cheaper.

MAINSTREAM

Village

545 George St, City (✆ 9264 6701)
Session Details & Information: For all cinemas (✆ 0055 51121)
Also at: Blacktown; Double Bay; Gosford; Parramatta.
Hearing help

Hoyts

505 George St, City (✆ 132 700)
Session Details and Information: For all cinemas (132 700)
Also at: Bankstown; Chatswood; Eastgardens; Roxy; and Warringah.
Hearing help is available at all cinemas.

Greater Union

525 George St, City (✆ 9267 8666)
Session Details & Information: For all cinemas (373 6666)
Also at: Pitt Street, City; Blacktown; Castle Hill; Mosman; and Parramatta.
Hearing help is available at all cinemas.
These cinemas are all pretty much adjacent and identical, even down to the popcorn perfume, a block down from Town Hall towards Central, in amongst noisy entertainment arcades.

ART HOUSE & INDEPENDENT

Academy Twin Cinema

3A Oxford St, Paddington (✆ 9361 4453)
Ticket Deals: The Acad Pass: 6 films for $48 (not valid day of purchase).
No Hearing help.
Widely recognised as the core of Sydney's foreign and discerning film scene, the Academy Twin has consistently screened the best films in Sydney on its two screens. A further advantage is its location on Oxford Street, where myriad restaurants, cafes and pubs beckon. A location over the road from Ariel and a few doors down from Berkelouw bookshops makes for an eminently enjoyable evening.

Chauvel/Australian Film Institute (AFI) Cinema.

Cnr Oxford St & Oatley Rd, Paddington (✆ 9332 2111)
True film enthusiasts find ,satisfaction here in the AFI's educated selections which encompass all nationalities and schools of film. The cinema regularly runs festivals following particular themes or honouring a particular film maker. A calendar is available from the cinema, while weekly schedules are published in Metro.

Cremorne Orpheum Picture Palace.

380 Military Rd, Cremorne (✆ 9908 4344)
Ticket Deals: Orpheum Ticket: 10 films for $80/$50 concession.
On the north shore, this cinema boasts something the others don't have: a genuine, massive Wurlitzer cinema organ, which rises thundering from the bowels of the theatre with flashing lights like some

kind of wild creation (complete with organist wearing underwear visible through white trousers). The films on show are good, whether American or European mainstream, art house or classics, but the double bills (perhaps *2001 Space Odyssey* with *Clockwork Orange)* are always memorable. Before or after film food stops can be made at Radio Cairo or Cafe Cairo, over the road (see: Food).

Dendy Cinemas

Ticket Deals: Club Dendy: $40 per year for $2.50 reduction on tickets, 10% off bistro meals and at the store, free newsletters and catalogues.

Revamped in its bunker under the MLC centre (Martin Place, City; ✆ 9233 8166), the Dendy complex comprises a bistro and bar (Open: 7 days 10am-late), and a store stocking screenplays, soundtracks, videos, books and t-shirts related to the film industry. Also a stayer in the independent cinema scene, the Dendy consistently screens great films almost always. The Dendy George Street (Upstairs 624 George St, City; ✆ 9264 1577) and Dendy Newtown (261 King St, Newtown; ✆ 9550 5699) complete the Dendy's line up.

No Hearing help.

The Movie Room

112 Darlinghurst Rd, Darlinghurst (✆ 9360 7853)

A unique phenomenon, the Movie Room is a great place where patrons have been known to be offered foot massages by fellow patrons as they recline in their armchairs in the tiny theatre. However, it is tiny, so early arrival is compulsory. No program is advertised; the best thing to do is pick up a copy of their calendar from the cinema itself, or just turn up and be surprised, but rarely disappointed.

Valhalla

166 Glebe Point Rd, Glebe (between Bridge Rd and Hereford St) (✆ 9660 8050)

Ticket Deals: Cheaptix: 5 tickets for $30, valid immediately (for 6 months) for use at any session Monday to Thursday. Also: 3 Cinema Pass: 10 films for $70, for use at the Rialto, Chauvel and Valhalla.

Hojotoho! No Wotan or Walküre, but just as exciting. The Valhalla is the home of the quirky movie: *Dial M for Murder* in 3D (glasses provided), *Thunderbirds, Chopper Chicks in Zombietown* and the classics, whether *Casablanca, ABBA The Movie* or *Clockwork Orange.* Tickets for Saturday afternoon sessions are usually $7, and include jaffas and cordial. Sunday evening doubles are usually very well paired.

The Verona

Cnr Verona St & Oxford St, Paddington (✆ 9360 6099)

Ticket Deals: 6 films for $48; can also be used at the Academy Twin and Walker.

The Verona is a New Age cinema aiming to clothe, feed and cure the soul. In what must be the ultimate recycling operation, it was built from the remains of a 1940s paper mill using recycled hardwoods and natural materials, to embrace the developer's creed of environmentalism and non-materialism. Within the modernist complex, there are four movie theatres, a yoga centre, a health shop, cafe/bar serving drinks and organic foods (wherever possible) in the form of zesty, quick dishes, and a Mambo store. The Verona offers not just entertainment in the form of art-house films, but a total environment in which to linger. **Hearing help available.**

The Walker

121 Walker St, North Sydney (✆ 9959 4222)

Ticket Deals: Walker Pass: 6 films for $48.

Associated with the Academy Twin and Verona, the Walker offers film of a similar nature to its Paddington siblings. Wednesdays $7.50. **No Hearing help**.

FILM FESTIVALS

The Sydney Film Festival

When & Where: Annually in June at the State Theatre, Market St, City.

Information & Tickets Festival Office: 405 Glebe Point Rd, Glebe (✆ 9660 3844; fax 9692 8793); or PO Box 950 Glebe NSW 2037.

Every winter, the Sydney Film festival beckons and draws its fans into a total frenzy of local and foreign feature films, new releases, documentaries, old television episodes, experimental work and theme programs. Bleary-eyed devotees are visible at all hours of the day and night in the vicinity of the ornate State Theatre, looking vaguely disoriented as they wait for the next feature to start. Ticket options include subscriptions of varying numbers of days and sessions, as well as separately ticketed special nights and events. Daytripper & nighttripper tickets for various days are also available. Tickets sell quickly in May, so get organised and get on the mailing list!

The Tropicana Film Festival

When & Where: Annually for one Sunday in mid February at and outside The Tropicana Coffee Lounge, 227bVictoria St, Darlinghurst (✆ 9360 9809).

Information: At the Tropicana, close to the time.

The Tropicana film festival is an annual celebration of very short film. Unknown and up-and-coming film makers expose their creativity to the judging panel and large crowds in what has become an internationally renowned event.

NIGHTCLUBS

Sydney is the home of an energetic club scene, and this chapter is intended to allow club-goers to make informed decisions about where to go before being trapped on the other side of a cover charge. While we have sought out the most consistent and established nightclubs, note the disclaimer: novelty is the primary requirement of fickle club crowds and consequently, what we recommend here might now be a dry cleaner's shop. The greatest concentration of good clubs is to be found in Darlinghurst, however the best thing to do when planning a foray into the throng is to consult the current listings papers. These will have reviews and details of current music and DJs.

The free weekly paper **3D World** is devoted to the weighty subject of what's on where in the worlds of techno, ragga, hip hop, house, jazz, funk, indie, style, clubs, raves, film, food and the arts, all of which is communicated in an opinionated, attitude-laden style. **On the Street** and **The Beat** are also good, although they concentrate more on live bands than the club scene itself. All are available widely in clubs and bars. Three places that always have them are Folkways music store (Oxford St, Paddington), Ariel Booksellers (Oxford Street, Paddington), and the HMV Megastore (Pitt Street Mall, City). (See: Media.)

CITY

The Basement: 29 Reiby Place, Circular Quay (✆ 9251 2797)

Open: from 7.30pm: Mon-Thurs to 1am; Fri-Sat to 3am; Sun to 1am. **Cover:** Usually $10.

Sydney's best known and longest running jazz venue (See: Music: Jazz), the Basement is a dark and comfortable space equipped with bistro and well stocked bar, fitted with tables and seating, and walls plastered with jazz memorabilia. The main attraction is the music, with different acts performing as advertised in Sydney Morning Herald's Friday supplement Metro (See: Media). A must for jazz followers.

Blackmarket: 111 Regent St, Central (✆ 9698 8863)

Open: Sat from 10pm; Sun Day Club from 6am. **Cover:** $10.

A dodgy-looking building in a dodgy-looking area of Sydney near Central station, home to the Hellfire Club on Thursday nights (from 10pm), is the Blackmarket: two levels, each with its own dance floor, said to be where the city's glamorous set goes. Looking at it from the outside, you'd be forgiven for thinking otherwise. The club claims to be "pro choice" in dress standards, although just whose choice it is is not specified. Some degree of suavity is required.

Jackson's On George: 176 George St, Circular Quay (✆ 9247 2727)

Open: 7 days & nights 10am- around 4am. **Cover:** To $5.

Jackson's is consistently popular, and at least if 1970s dance & music is your thing, then there is guaranteed to be at least one night a week when you can 'shake your groove thing'.

Juliana's: Hilton Hotel, 259 Pitt Street, Sydney (✆ 9266 0610)

Open: Tues-Sat 9pm-3am. **Cover:** To $15.

Situated off the lobby of the Hilton, Juliana's is a well established night club featuring modern dance music. Frequented by all ages, but most popular with the more mature international crowd of the hotel , the club is comfortable in atmosphere, serving relatively expensive drinks and a light supper menu.

Neo Pharaoh: 121 Sussex St, City (✆ 9299 3777)

Open: Mon, Tues & Thurs 6pm-2am; Wed, Fri & Sat 6pm-4am; Sun 6pm-Midnight. **Cover:** To $15.

Neo Pharaoh claims to have the latest in light & sound systems in Sydney, as well as some of the city's best DJs. Music and patronage can vary between the latest energetic dance music and a young crowd to cool jazz and groove enjoyed by a smoothly dressed clientele, but the common factor linking all guests is adherence to the 'smart casual' dress code.

Riva: Castlereagh St, City (between Market St & Park St (✆ 9286 6666)

Open: Wed-Sat from 10pm. **Cover:** Wed $7; Thurs-Sat $12.

Riva tries very hard to be suave, as most clubs do, and succeeds, as many don't. Two separate chambers feed onto a large, open area with plush seating around the large cocktail bar (with suitably flamboyant bar tenders), and supply high energy dance music and funk. There's even a sense of occasion as successful door applicants are ushered in by the headset-bemicrophoned doormen advising the desk below of their arrival.

NORTH SYDNEY

Blueberries: 107 Mount St, North Sydney (✆ 99544919)

Open: Mon-Wed 12noon-2am; Thurs 12noon-3am; Fri & Sat 12noon-4am. **Cover:** Usually none.

Blueberries is a relaxed club consisting of an inexpensive brasserie (also operating during the day), a large cocktail bar, dance floor and lights. The clientele seem to enjoy Blueberries' lack of attitude.

Metropolis: 99 Walker St, Nth Sydney (✆ 9954 3599)
Open: Tues 8.30pm-late; Fri 12noon-late; Sat 7.30pm-late. **Cover:** $10.
The club, apparently inspired by the 1920s futurist silent film of the same name, consists of three dance floors and a totally sound proofed room, The Works. The young, slick, trend-conscious crowd who come here appreciate the excellent light and sound systems which contribute to the energetic yet comfortable atmosphere of North Sydney's best club.

SURRY HILLS, DARLINGHURST & PADDINGTON

Bentley Bar: 320 Crown St, Surry Hills (✆ 9331 1186)
Open: 7 days 'till late'. **Cover:** None.
The Bentley Bar is famous for consistently packing the 'in' set in. Popular every night with intangibly dressed young patrons, weekends are even busier with excellent off-beat music, the cream of the DJ stockpile, pool, pinball and video games, and an unbeatable atmosphere.

Club 77: 77 William St, East Sydney (✆ 9361 4981)
Open: Fri & Sat 6pm-around 3am; music starts at 11pm. **Cover:** Between $7 & $15.
Club 77 is bizarre phenomenon on the Sydney club scene, known for its energetic pursuance of various themes. For example, past extravaganzas have included Ancient Roman parties and all night soul and funk extravaganzas. The club has a mixed clientele, veering towards the very young on some nights, and maintains a relaxed dress code. Club 77 is the spot for driven music and serious dancing without unnecessary attitude.

DCM: 33 Oxford St, Darlinghurst (✆ 9267 7036)
Open: Thurs-Sun 11pm-between 6am & 9am; Closed Mon-Wed. **Cover:** Between $5 & $20.
DCM is firmly established as one of Sydney's most engaging clubs, especially engaging for those displaying their expertise on the tall dance floor podiums. The atmosphere pumps and throbs, fuelled by the club's renowned sound and light systems, and while most clothing will get intending guests through the door, more up-market dress is preferred. Busiest from Thursday to Saturday, the club occasionally sets aside nights for cabaret.

Kinselas: 383 Bourke St, Darlinghurst (✆ 9331 3299)
Open: Mon-Sat 8pm-3am; Sun 7pm-Midnight. **Cover:** Top floor only, between $7 & $10.
If you go to only one club in Sydney, make it Kinselas. A multi-level pleasure palace devoted to the myriad principles of music-bound leisure, the club is a melange of night club (top floor), bar, cafe (downstairs), and theatre. But even more impressive is the epic splendour of the building (formerly a funeral 'palace'), echoing the emphasis on aesthetics shown by the young, hip crowd and their attire. Definitely worth a visit.

Mr Goodbar: 11 Oxford St, Paddington (next to STA) ✆ 9360 6759)
Open: From 6pm Wed-Mon; Closed Tues. **Cover:** Mon & Wed $3; Thurs $5; Fri-Sun $8.
Mr Goodbar sees itself as the most hip club in Sydney, and if the door staff oblige by stepping aside, it is worth a visit. A favourite haunt of the members of the Sydney modelling scene, often on Sunday nights, it sees itself as cool personified.

Zoom: 163-169 Oxford St, Taylor Square (✆ 9360 2528)
Open: 6pm-late. **Cover:** Between $5 & $15.
Speed on up the long, wide flight of stairs to Zoom, a popular spot where the large, spacious interior of pale wood and chrome fills with the thrills of its young, groovy clientele, the lasers, lights, podiums and pumping music.

KINGS CROSS & POTTS POINT

Cauldron: 207 Darlinghurst Road, Kings Cross (✆ 9331 1523)
Open: Tues-Sat 6pm-3am. **Cover:** Between $5 & $10.
Cauldron is convinced it is one of Sydney's best, longest running and most popular up-market clubs, and hosts a mixed and interesting bunch of smoothly dressed patrons. DJs and live bands feature all week, while the club's bistro serves Italian influenced food until the early hours. The atmosphere is (relatively) easy-going and (relatively) friendly, although the club is not as slick as it once was.

Round Midnight: 2 Roslyn Street, Kings Cross (✆ 9356 4045)
Open: Mon-Fri 6.30pm-4.30am; Sat-Sun 6.30pm-5.30am. **Cover:** To $10.
Certainly with some of the longest opening hours in Sydney, Round Midnight is dedicated to live jazz & funk club music (with bonus DJs on Fridays and Saturdays), and to generating successfully a smooth, late night atmosphere. The inner city, up-market crowd come to listen and move minimalistically (owing to the crowds) to the smooth music. A great spot.

Soho Bar & The Site: 171 Victoria Street, Potts Point (✆ 9358 6511)
Open: 7 nights 6pm-4am. **Cover:** Between $5 & $20 depending on the band.
The Site is the domain of imported dance tracks, while the attached Soho Bar concentrates on jazz, funk, and suave, unruffled drinking with a city skyline view. A creative and energetic clientele readily file in to hear the groove generated by the top DJs and live bands. An otherwise generous dress code requires some degree of smoothness.

Tunnel Night Club: 1 Earl Place, Potts Point (✆ 9357 3331)
Open: Wed-Sun 9pm-3am. **Cover:** To $10.
This small, sauna-like club features state-of-the-art light, sound and video systems, funk, soul, R&B and American dance music, and an up-market crowd controlled by a strict door policy: those not wishing to be left on the footpath must dress smartly casual or casually smart. A bonus is the (almost) soundproofed area.

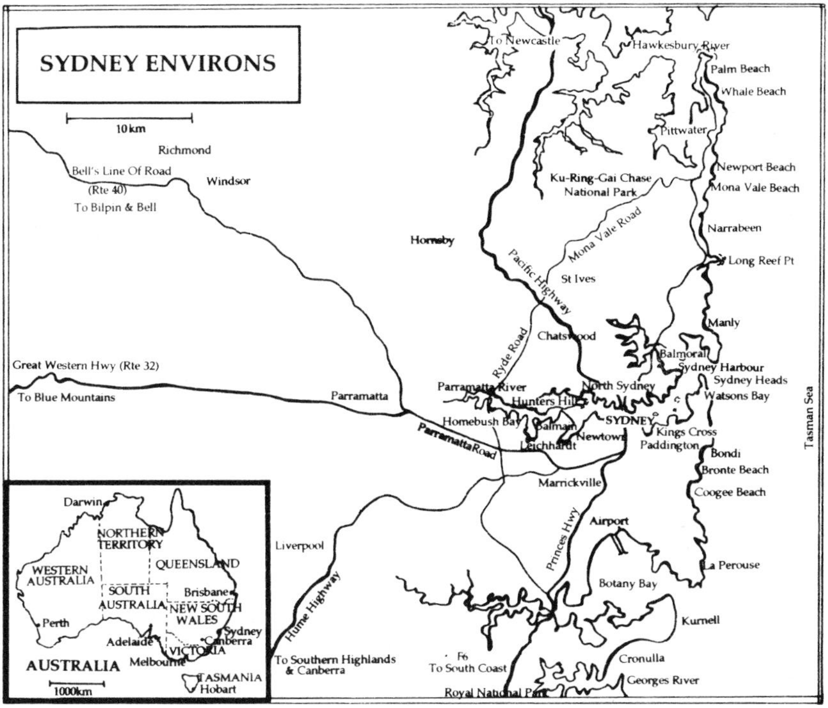

DAY TRIPS OUT OF SYDNEY

Surrounded by greatly contrasting regions to explore, it is little wonder that the big day out is an important part of Sydney's suburban lifestyle. To the north lies the Hunter Valley wine region, with dozens of wineries to visit and hundreds of wines to taste. On the opposite side of Sydney lie the Southern Highlands with their luscious grazing lands and heritage towns; the stunning South Coast with its turquoise water and dairy towns, and further beyond, the nation's capital, Canberra. To the west stand the imposing Blue Mountains, dotted with walking tracks, lookouts and tea houses. Yet all of these areas have two things in common: astounding beauty and easy access from Sydney.

This chapter details seven of the best day trips out of Sydney, generally within two hours drive from the City. Each itinerary has clear directions for car and alternative transport, background notes, a full description of the sites and attractions to look out for, and of course, a number of places to eat along the way. For those who have a little extra time, some suggestions of places to stay are also included. The two final trips may seem a little unusual: not many would think it possible to visit Antarctica or any of Australia's other major cities in one day. Read on, and find out how.

THE BLUE MOUNTAINS

Description

One and a half hours directly west of Sydney lie the quaint towns and arresting bushland gorges of the Blue Mountains, one of Sydney's favourite retreats.

Not so much a series of mountains as plateaux intersected by deep gorges, most of the area is part of the two hundred and fifty thousand hectare Blue Mountains National Park, which edges the Wollemi and Kanangra-Boyd National Parks to the north and south-west respectively. Together, these three parks make up New South Wales' largest wilderness area. However, it is the region directly west of Sydney adjacent to the Great Western Highway and the Bell's Line of Road which is commonly referred to as 'The Blue Mountains', and it is this area on which the following itinerary concentrates. The mountain towns are packed with charms: sights to see, gardens to inspect, a network of bushwalking tracks to conquer, picnic spots and numerous tea houses doing a roaring trade in scones, jam and cream.

Starting Off & Getting There

From the City, drive west along Parramatta Road past the University of Sydney, through the suburbs of Leichhardt, Ashfield and Strathfield among several others. Stay on Parramatta Road until the enormous sign pointing right onto the **M4** for **Katoomba** appears. Point the car and drive. This freeway turns into the Great Western Highway (Route 32) which leads all the way through the mountain towns. The mountains can be reached in about two hours by **train** from Central Station between 5am and 11pm (**Information:** ✆ 13 22 32). Trains going as far as Katoomba depart hourly (**Cost:** $7.60/$3.80 return), while trains for beyond Katoomba depart almost every two hours. Be warned that most walks and attractions are difficult to get to without wheels. A great idea for those without a car is to take a tour to places such as Anvil Rock, the Wind Eroded Cave and Pulpit Rock on a 1940s Jeep with Compass Four Wheel Drive Tours (✆ 047-824 649 or 047-825 610). For Harley Davidson Tours of the mountains, See: Tours Around Sydney.

Before You Go

The Blue Mountains are an adventure lover's paradise. While several of the region's popular hiking routes are included in the chapter **Bushwalks**, the help, expertise or equipment of adventure co-ordinators may well be required for abseiling, canyoning, rock climbing and mountain biking. The better known operators in the area include the following. The Blue Mountains Adventure Co (190 Katoomba St, Katoomba; ✆ 047-821 271) offers abseiling, rock climbing, mountain biking, canyoning, caving and bushwalking. The Australian School of Mountaineering (182 Katoomba St, Katoomba; ✆ 047-822 014) offer excursions and instruction in abseiling, rock climbing, canyoning and mountaineering. Finally, note that even when stiflingly hot in Sydney, the weather can be very cool in the mountains. The average maximum temperatures up here are as follows: November-March 21°; April 16°; May 13°; June-August 10°; September 14°; October 17°. Sudden changes of weather mean adequate supplies when walking are necessary.

Information Centres

The **Blue Mountains Visitor Information Centres** at Great Western Highway, Glenbrook (✆ 047-396 266; fax 047-396 787; Open: Mon-Sat 8.30-5pm, Sun 8.30-4.30pm) and also at Echo Point, Katoomba (✆ also 047-396 266; Open: 7 days 9am-5pm) dispense good maps, information, accommodation information and souvenirs. The Glenbrook centre should be your first mountain stop, as they can locate and reserve accommodation. In Sydney, the **New South Wales Travel Centre** (19 Castlereagh St, City; ✆ 13 20 77; fax 232 6080) can provide general information on the region as well as help with accommodation and camping. The **National Parks Information Centres** in the mountains (Govett's Leap Rd, Blackheath; ✆ 047-878 877; Open: 7 days 9am-4.30pm) and in Sydney (Cadman's Cottage, 110 George St, The Rocks; ✆ 9247 8861; Open: Mon 10am-3pm; Tues-Fri 9am-4.30pm; Sat-Sun 11am-4pm) can help with camping, walking routes and ecological information regarding the park and its Aboriginal sites.

Ecology, History & Background

The huge cliff faces of the Jamison and Grose Valleys reveal cross sections of sand, gravel and pebbles laid down on the delta of a massive river system around two hundred million years ago. These eventually hardened and compressed to form sandstone, the predominant rock of the region. When the Great Dividing Range was formed (around sixty million years ago), the delta was uplifted, while lava flow from volcanoes left basalt and rich soils on a number of peaks. The two types of mountain sandstone - Narrabeen (in the Grose Canyon & Echo Point to the west) and Hawkesbury (in the Glenbrook Gorge to the east) - broke down into distinct soils, in turn supporting different plants and, indirectly, animals.

Archaeological discoveries suggest that the Daruk and Gandangara peoples originally came to the mountains seasonally for hunting or religious purposes. While it is estimated that some six thousand of these tribespeople were living in the area when the Europeans first arrived, their numbers were quickly depleted following contact with settlers, their weapons and their diseases.

As the European population of Sydney grew, pressure on food supplies also increased, yet the settlers could neither rely on locally grown crops nor supply shipments from India. More agricultural land was needed; however, the settlement was hemmed in by impenetrable geographical barriers on all sides. While convicts wishfully believed China (and escape) lay over the western mountain range, officials suspected that arable land lay on the other side, so they set about finding a crossing through the gorges. A number of expeditions culminated in success when Gregory Blaxland, William Charles Wentworth and William Lawson sighted potential pastures on the far

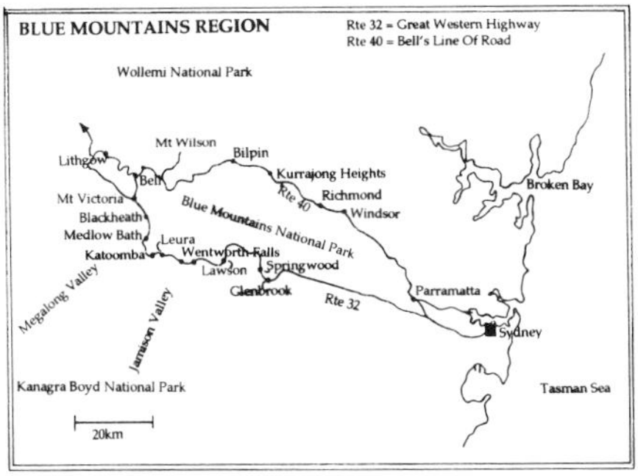

side in June 1813. Convict gangs completed a road by 1815, yet it was not until the 1870s that much progress took place: Sydney's wealthy discovered the fresh air and scenery, and the construction of a railway allowed the area to flourish. The mining of shale and coal around Katoomba generated further development, while the official designation of Wentworth Falls, Govett's Leap and the Three Sisters as tourist attractions in turn led to the area becoming a honeymoon and tourist Mecca by the 1930s.

Wildlife is conspicuous in the mountains. Crimson Rosellas, King Parrots, Cockatoos, Honeyeaters, Kookaburras and Lyrebirds can all be heard if not seen. Reptiles of the region include Geckoes, Skinks and Eastern Water Dragons. A large number of snakes are found here, many of which are venomous. (Bites generally occur when an attempt to kill a snake is made, so the best way to deal with one is to assume it is poisonous and wait quietly for it to disappear into the bush.) Grey Kangaroos, Swamp Wallabies, Sugar Gliders and Ring Tailed Possums are the most visible marsupials; Wombats, Echidnas and Platypuses live here too, although it is rare to see them. While Banksias, Waratahs, Sassafras, Coachwood and Tree Ferns are common, mostly in patches of temperate rainforest, the most visible plants are the eucalypts. The valleys support enormous communities of Blue Gums, Blue Mountain Ash, Stringybark and Angophora, and it is the refraction of the sun's rays (known as 'Rayleigh's Scattering') in the oil which continually evaporates from the Eucalypt leaves that gives the mountains their blue tinge and their name. Wildflowers bloom all year, although late spring to summer is the best time to see them.

The Big, Bad Banksiamen

When walking in the mountains, you will probably come across the grotesquely ugly seed pods of the Banksia. Named after Sir Joseph Banks, a botanist who accompanied Captain Cook on his voyage to the southern continent in 1770, their malevolent appearance inspired May Gibbs to cast them as the villains of her classic children's book, The Complete Adventures of Snugglepot and Cuddlepie, first published in 1942. They were responsible for all kinds of mischief, not least the kidnapping of the Gumnut Babies.

Aboriginal Sites

The following sites may be visited, although the greatest care and respect must be exercised.

Red Hands Cave, Glenbrook, is a heavily protected site featuring ochre hand stencils between five hundred and fifteen hundred years old alongside Campfire Creek. Access: from the Visitors Centre at the Bruce Avenue entrance to the National Park, proceed to the Red Hands Cave picnic area. The cave is a short walk from here. The Kings Tableland Grinding Grooves were used for sharpening stone tools, and are found near a twenty thousand year old rock shelter. Access: from the Great Western Highway east of Wentworth Falls, follow the brown King's Tableland sign. See: Box: Aboriginal Sydney.

The Tour

Ascending into the increasingly fresh mountain air as the highway climbs and winds through the gum trees, the first mountain town encountered is **Glenbrook**, where you'll find the **Visitors Information Centre** (above) on your left, and the Red Hand Cave site (above).The climb progresses gradually but surely through Blaxland and Warrimoo (273m.a.s.l.), generally following the crest of the plateau which has the Jamison Valley to its south and the Grose Valley to its north. Soon you will come to **Faulconbridge** (447m), famous for the **Norman Lindsay Gallery and Museum** (14 Norman Lindsay Crescent; ✆ 047-511 067; **Open:** Wed-Sun and public holidays 11am-5pm). **Turn right into Grose Road** (Blue Mountains Drive 2) beyond the shops and station. Lindsay (1879-1969) lived and worked for most of his creative life in this stone cottage which now houses a collection of oil paintings, watercolours, etchings, sketches and drawings, as well as a large number of personal effects. The Magic Pudding Room and the artist's studio are especially worth seeing. The town is also noted for the grave of Sir Henry Parkes (the Father of Federation) and the interesting **Corridor of Oaks**, where a tree has been planted by every Prime Minister of Australia (both on the other side of the railway line). Proceed through Faulconbridge, noticing the deep valleys and gorges which made finding a way through the mountains difficult. At this stage, glimpses between trees on either side into the valleys and back to distant Sydney begin to appear. As the road leaves the lower mountains and enters the mid mountains, the general character of the area begins to emerge: old houses, old pines clustered around them, old gardens, tea houses, antique dealers and old wares shops abound. Antiques fiends may like to stop at **Lawson** at investigate Badgery's Antiques (Badgery's Crescent, Lawson; ✆ 047-592 686; **Open:** Thurs-Mon 10am-5pm; Closed Tues-Wed) and their stocks of vases, stripey jugs, old ceramic bread bins, bizarre salt and pepper shakers, old food signs and Australian

The Cliff Drive

The beginning of this famous eight kilometre route is reached by following Leura Mall to its end and turning right along either Gordon Road or Olympian Parade. The drive continues to Echo Point and beyond Katoomba's Cyclorama Point, revealing a panorama of the Megalong and Jamison valleys, Narrow Neck's cliffs and the Ruined Castle, Saddleback and Mount Solitary. On particularly clear days, Mittagong in the Southern Highlands is visible in one direction and the sands of Sydney's Botany Bay in another, each at least ninety kilometres away. The Megalong Valley is visible through clumps of roadside gums on the way to the Narrow Neck Plateau, which reaches out into the Jamison Valley, with sheer cliffs of pink and rust coloured sandstone lipping the vast blue valley.

meat safes.

The town of **Wentworth Falls** marks the beginning of the upper mountains, the most visited part of the region where the biggest gorges, highest falls, and most expansive views are found. Just before entering Wentworth Falls, turn left into Tableland Road (marked by a brown touring sign pointing to King's Tableland) and then turn right into Yester Road to reach **Yester Grange** (Yester Road, Wentworth Falls; ✆ 047-57 1110; fax 047-57 3528; **Open:** Mon-Sat 10am-4pm; Sun & Public holidays 10am-5pm; **Cost:** $5/$4/$2.50/$1). Built in 1888 by Sir John See, Premier of New South Wales from 1901 to 1905, Yester Grange represents the mountains' past as a retreat for Sydney's Establishment. The residence looks out into the Jamison Valley, and, sitting directly above the three hundred metre falls, it is common to see sprays of water shooting up from the bottom of the garden. The house is fully furnished as a Victoriana museum, while a cellar art gallery displays works for sale. Upstairs in the Kauri-lined ballroom you will find Devonshire teas and lunches, either on the verandah or by the log fire, depending on the weather.

Rejoin the highway for a short stretch, and then turn left into **Falls Road** to reach a spectacular vantage point from which to view **Wentworth Falls**. The road-level lookout offers stunning views into the Jamison Valley; however, for a full length view of the falls, you must follow the easy fifteen minute (return) track to the Princes Rock Lookout. The Falls Reserve area is the starting point for a network of walking tracks, the most rewarding and spectacular of which is the Valley of the Waters walk (See: Bushwalks). Otherwise, a short walk to the top of the falls is recommended.

Back on the Great Western Highway, continue towards Leura, but before entering the town, turn left onto the **"Alternative Route to Leura & Katoomba"** immediately before the railway underpass for a much more picturesque route into town. Proceeding to the main street, Leura Mall, you will find several highly recommended eateries (See: Mountain Food, below). Despite its proximity to Katoomba, Leura has retained its own, quieter character, due to its large residences and their gardens, many of which are open to the public as part of the Leura Garden Festival (nine days from the weekend after the October long weekend). Of particular note are the National Trust's **Everglades Gardens** (37 Everglades Ave; ✆ 047-841 938; **Open:** 7 days 9am-sunset; **Cost:** $4/free). Created by Danish master gardener Paul Sorensen in the 1930s, this six acre garden's terraces, grotto and conifer-winged amphitheatre are bewitchingly calm and delightful, secret corners. They are especially favoured in Spring for the blossom and late Autumn for the rich leaf colours. Equally important is **Leuralla** (Olympian Parade; ✆ 047-841 169; **Open:** Wed-Sun & holidays 10am-5pm), the former residence of H.V. "Doc" Evatt, former head of the Labor Party and first president of the United Nations, which now houses memorabilia and a toy and railway museum. Follow the signs to Sublime Point for a breathtaking view, and then take the scenic route to Katoomba, the Cliff Drive.

The Cliff Drive reaches **Katoomba** at Echo Point (around two kilometres south of the town centre), site of the famed **Three Sisters rock formation**. The Three Sisters are the symbol of the mountains, and have been spot-lit since the 1930s when the area was developed as a tourist centre. The views from here are some of the best of the Jamison Valley, explaining why this is the most visited lookout anywhere in Australia. There is an easy footpath leading to the stairs which descend the cliff to a bridge across to the first sister (Honeymoon Point).

Leaving Echo Point, tourers can either drive around the cliffs to Cyclorama Point (and then on to the town centre via Echo Point Road and Lurline Street), or follow the Cliff Drive to the **Scenic Railway** (around one kilometre west of Echo Point): the steepest incline railway in the world at fifty two degrees. Originally built in the 1880s to take miners and coal up and down the four hundred and fifty metre cliff face, today it transports visitors to the base of the Jamison Valley and the starting points of a number of walks. A short stroll to the left of the valley floor railway platform will reveal the Katoomba Falls and a number of ancient trees, while a longer walk to the right will take you to the site of the famous landslide (and for those with a few hours to spare, the Ruined Castle Walk: See: Bushwalks). Two hundred metres above the gorge glides the Scenic Skyway, giving brave souls (cardiac) arresting views of the Jamison Valley, Orphan Rock and Katoomba Falls.

The town centre of **Katoomba** (1017m a.s.l.) features many 1920s-30s shopfronts and buildings designed in Art Deco style, most notably the **Carrington Guest House** (renovation under way) and

the Paragon (65 Katoomba St; ✆ 047- 822 928; **Open:** 7 days 9am-5pm). Established in 1916, the cafe's perfectly preserved 1930s decor comes complete with wooden booths, classical sculptures and reliefs, and an amazing cocktail bar at the rear. The homemade Paragon chocolates are beautifully packaged and rightly famous, making this an extremely popular stop on any tour through the region. A stroll along **Katoomba Street** makes for a fascinating walk past several second hand and old wares dealers, the best of which is Bygone Beauty's in street adjacent to the railway line (122-124 Main St; ✆ 047-821 018). For food, try Pins and Noodles (See: Mountain Food, below), the Savoy, Trocadero or Florida Cafes, or the Carrington Pub's upstairs bistro, all in Katoomba Street. Picnic supplies such as cheeses, pates, pickles, bread, coffee, prosciutto, tarts and puddings (or hampers complete with corkscrew) can be obtained from **Divino Deli** (177 Katoomba St; ✆ 047-82 6083).

Heading west on the highway once more, take a short detour to the left along **Narrowneck Road**, to head out into the valley along a ridge. Along here you will find the Golden Stairs, the starting point of several walking tracks (See: Bushwalks). Back on the highway, you will also pass the Explorers' Tree marked with Blaxland, Lawson and Wentworth's

The Legend of the Three Sisters

Long ago in the Blue Mountains lived three Aboriginal sisters, Meenhi, Wimlah and Gunedoo. Their father, Tyawan, was a Witch Doctor, and they lived happily together with the other people of the mountains. They feared only one creature: the bunyip. Tyawan had to pass the Bunyip's cavern on his way to collect food in the valley, so he would leave his daughters safe, high up on the cliff behind a rocky wall. But one day, while the sisters were waiting, a centipede crawled out of the bush and frightened Meenhi. She threw a stone at it which rolled away over the cliff, crashing into the valley and causing the rocky wall to crumble to a mere ledge. From deep below in the valley came a terrifying rumble: the furious Bunyip had been woken from his sleep and was searching for the culprit. High up on the ledge he spied the three terrified girls, and lurched forwards to devour them. Tyawan heard his daughters' cries, and in a frantic panic, pointed his magic bone to turn them to stone so that they would be safe until the Bunyip had gone. However, the Bunyip became so enraged that he chased Tyawan and trapped him against a large rock. Changing himself into a lyrebird, Tyawan scurried into a cave to hide. Everyone was safe, but Tyawan had lost his magic bone. As his search continues to this day, he is to be heard calling to his daughters, who watch silently from above.

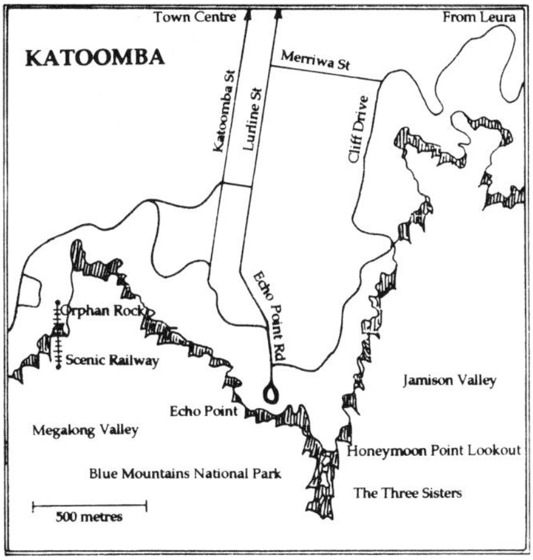

initials, but not really impressive enough to merit a stop.

The next town worthy of attention is **Medlow Bath**, home of the melodramatic **Hydro Majestic Hotel** (Great Western Highway; ✆ 047-881 002). Opened in 1904 as a health resort offering rejuvenating water treatments, the building also featured a ballroom and casino, still in existence. A viewing of the Megalong Valley from the hotel's terrace is one of the best ways to see it when the weather is bad.

Blackheath has escaped the bustle of Katoomba and retained its quiet village atmosphere, even though it is known to possess some of the most awesome sights and walks of the region. **The Grose Valley** (best seen from Evan's Lookout and Govett's Leap), Bridal Veil Falls (the highest in the mountains), **Pulpit Rock, Anvil Rock** (without chorus) and the astounding **Wind Carved Cave** are all reached via Hat Hill Road. The aptly named **Perry's Lookdown** is the starting point of the shortest route to the Blue Gum Forest in the valley bottom (around four hours return). There are also several charming bed and breakfasts (See: Accommodation, below). In the town, tourers will also find Keith Rowe (Unit 7,134 Station St, Blackheath; ✆ 047-877 220; **Open:** Sat & Sun 10am-4pm), a potter who takes his inspiration from the natural surroundings of the Blue mountains, whether flood or fire. West of Blackheath at Shipley is **Peter Rushforth** (Le Varu, Mt Blackheath Road, Shipley; ✆ 047-877 040), a potter who is dedicated to the use of a traditional wood fired kiln and of the materials provided by the Megalong Valley such as gum ash and limestone. Vases, bowls, teapots and plates of exquisite skill and design are available for viewing on request, and range in price from $50 to $1,500.

On the western side of the ridge lies the aptly named **Megalong Valley**, reached by turning left off the highway over the railway line and immediately turning left again into Station Street. Much of valley has been cleared for grazing, but a drive down through thick pockets of rainforest is a worthwhile detour. **Megalong Valley Farm** (Megalong Road; ✆ 047-879 165; **Open:** 7 days 10am-5pm; **Cost:** Sat-Sun & Public Holidays: $6/$3; other days half price) is a fifty hectare farm at which demonstrations of sheep shearing, milking of dairy cattle, handling of beef cattle and a special Clydesdale Draught Horse show take place. Horse and cart rides and tractor tours of the farm make this a favourite with children.

Mount Victoria (1111m.a.s.l.) is a charming historic town. Opposite the Victoria & Albert Guesthouse stands the ever popular **Bay Tree Tea House** (26 Station Street; ✆ 047-871 275; **Open:** Fri-Tues 10.30am-5pm; 7 days during school holidays), home of the most legendary, biggest, freshest and best tasting scones in the mountains: the kind that steam pure enjoyment when broken open. Station Street is also where you will find a number of excellent second hand book and wares dealers, while over the highway at the head of Station Street stands the wonderful Twentieth Century Antiques shop.

By continuing westwards along the Great Western Highway one further kilometre, you will reach the right hand turn-off to **Mount York**. This several kilometre long detour is more than worthwhile, as the lookout offers a spectacular, clear view of the grazing land discovered and made accessible by the European explorers. A further ten kilometres west along the Great Western Highway is **Hartley**, a charming yet somewhat spooky town whose fifteen historic buildings give a clear idea of what rural New South Wales rural life was like in the 1830s and 1840s. To return to Sydney, you must retrace the road back to Mount Victoria and turn left into Station Street.

Station Street continues directly onto **Bell's Line of Road,** which will lead back to Sydney. Along this route are spectacular views, but keep a lookout for the turn-off to **Mount Wilson**, to the left. A narrow, winding, bush-encased road leads along a ridge before sharply turning and ascending through a magical pocket of tree ferns into the town, where enormous eucalypts rise out of the rich soil. This luxurious growth, both natural and cultivated, is the result of the basalt capping of the mountain by volcanic activity. The town has been a haven for gardening enthusiasts since last century, and boasts a collection of stunning residences and grounds. In particular, **'Yengo'** in Queen's Avenue, demands a visit. These twenty acre gardens were designed and laid out in 1877 by the first director of Sydney's Botanic Gardens, Charles Moore, and include an exquisite walled garden and trees from all over the world. A stroll or drive along Church Lane will lead you to 'Nooroo' and 'Sefton Cottage' gardens, as well as a lovely lookout, while Queen's Avenue boasts some mysterious gates, beautiful cottages and gardens, and a forty five minute circular rainforest **Waterfall Track**. A thorough exploratory stroll around the town is a must, although note that Mount Wilson's gardens are generally only open at specific times from September to November. Check by calling: Cherry Cottage (✆ 047-562 067), Nooroo (✆ 047-562 018), Sefton Cottage (✆ 047-562 034), Yengo (✆ 047-562 002) and Lindfield Park (✆ 045-781 804).The Mount Irvine Road leads to the Cathedral of Ferns, where giant tree ferns stand clustered together, and further still to 'Lindfield Park' gardens.

To continue to Sydney, you must retrace your path to **Bell's Line of Road** and turn left onto it. It leads past the **Mount Tomah Botanic Garden** (Bells Line of Road, via Bilpin; ✆ 045-672 154; **Open:** 7 days Mar-Sep 10am-4pm; 7 days Oct-Feb 10am-5pm **Cost:** $5 per car). This cool climate exotic garden, associated with the Royal Botanic Gardens of Sydney, sits tucked into a basalt-capped peak which nurtures and protects its tree ferns, azaleas, alpine flowers, waterfalls and mouth watering native rainforest. There are also special conifer and rhododendron collections, a formal garden, visitors centre, cafe and picnic area. Further still towards Sydney is Bilpin, whose rich soil supports a vigorous orchard industry; you will often find fruit and honey stalls along the road here.

After Bilpin, the road progresses through Kurrajong Heights, and begins a dramatic descent onto the coastal plain through Bellbird Hill. Emerging at Richmond, itself an area rich in heritage, follow the signs for Sydney along the often drab road.

MOUNTAIN FOOD:
A BLUE MOUNTAINS DIRECTORY

The fresh and at times biting air of the mountains will invigorate, refresh and inspire visitors as they explore the region, and undoubtedly leave you with a mountainous appetite. Luckily there are a number of excellent cafes, delicatessens and restaurants which demand as important a place on the day's the itinerary as the sights and walks!

Cleopatra's

Cleopatra St, Blackheath (✆ 047-87 845) BYO. Book.
Open: Lunch: Sat from 1pm; Dinner: 7 days from 7.30pm.

Cleopatra's has operated as one of the most revered restaurants of the region for the past ten years, offering food with flair and passion along the lines of melting buckwheat tartlet with baby beetroot, apple and quail egg, or perhaps salmon enveloped by a smooth tapenade. Their Bilpin sugar plum tart is famous.

La Normandie

124 Wentworth Ave, Blackheath (✆ 047-87 6144) BYO. Book.
Open: Lunch: Fri & Sun 12noon-2.30pm; Dinner: from 6.30pm.

As the name suggests, butter and apples feature prominently on the Modern Australian/French menu here, while the house specialty of duck leg with caramelised apples and sauteed potato is renowned.

The Mount Inn

Bells Line of Road, Bilpin (✆ 045-67 1354) Lc'd. Book.

Open: Lunch: Wed-Mon (closed Tues); Dinner: Fri-Sat.

Many day trippers head back to Sydney by this route, speeding through this beautiful apple and fruit growing area in the dark, unaware of the gems which lie hidden from view. One particularly worthy of notice is the Mount Inn. Creamy blue swimmer crab with saffron and mussels, pan roasted ocean trout with field mushrooms and chervil; boned spatchcock with wild rice and mountain mushrooms or perhaps the lemon-poached rhubarb tower with mascarpone and brandy snap biscuit make it easy to understand why! For a more relaxed experience, coffee and focaccia are available all day, and children are always welcome.

Pins and Noodles

189 Katoomba St, Katoomba (✆ 047-82 3445) BYO.

Open: Lunch: Mon-Sat 11am-2.30pm; Dinner: Mon-Tues & Thurs-Sat 5.30pm-8.30pm; Closed Sun.

Pins and Noodles is a popular eatery where Japanese style noodles star on the menu alongside linguini boscaiola and fettuccine alfredo. Large or small servings of the noodles, made daily on the premises by the Scottish proprietor, are available.

Silks Brasserie

128 Leura Mall, Leura (✆ 047-84 2534) Lc'd. Book.

Open: 7 days 12noon-3pm & from 6pm.

This high-ceilinged yet demure room is the home of many a great meal: corned tenderloin of veal with horseradish sauce and mash; game crepes and alluring desserts, often involving hot butterscotch sauce, will provide enough fuel for a twenty kilometre walk, provided you can leave the open fires, 1930s music, fresh flowers and friendly staff.

Terrafirma

201 Leura Mall, Leura (✆ 047-84 1734) BYO.

Open: 7 days, 10am-9.30pm Sun-Thurs; Fri -Sat 10am-10pm.

Terrafirma is a popular and comfortable, made comfortable by the sunny courtyard and happy buzz. Pizzas, pastas, foccaccia, solid cakes and good coffee make this a good spot to seek out in Leura.

Whistle Stop Cafe

8 Station St, Wentworth Falls (✆ 047-573 161) BYO.

Open: Mon-Fri 8am-4pm; Sat-Sun 9am-4pm.

Fried green tomatoes feature prominently on this menu, albeit accompanied by a strapping pesto, while chunky chips, plum sauce spare ribs, hearty burgers and enormous "glory" muffins offer enough tempting choices to make missing your train a distinct probability.

ACCOMMODATION

Below is a small number of places to stay in the region. The visitors information centres (above) have details of many more, and can arrange reservations

A large number of guesthouses are in operation here. **Balmoral House** (196 Bathurst Rd, Katoomba; ✆ 047-822 264), reputedly the oldest guesthouse in the Blue Mountains, was built in 1876 and fully restored in 1983. **Balquhain** (161 Govetts Leap Road, Blackheath; ✆ 047-877 026) a is suavely converted 1883 country manor with enormous gardens, offering luxurious yet homely accommodation. Grand breakfasts include juice, fresh fruit, yogurt, cereal, croissants, brioche, toast, bacon, eggs and tea or coffee. **Cleopatra Country Guesthouse** (Cleopatra St, Blackheath; ✆ 047-87 8456) is a National Trust listed home set in secluded gardens featuring century old trees and a tennis court. **Lilianfels** (Lilianfels Ave, Katoomba; ✆ 047-801 200/008 024 452) is centred around a country house built by the Lieutenant Governor of New South Wales in the 1860s near the Echo Point escarpments. Eighty six new rooms and suites have been sympathetically added around the original residence, while fireside lounges, a reading room and full recreational facilities are at guests' disposal. **Withycombe** (Cnr The Avenue & Church Lane, Mount Wilson; ✆ 047-562 106) was the late author Patrick White's childhood home, and contains a library tightly packed with first editions of his works, while enveloping arm chairs face the open fire. Afternoon tea complete with 1860s silver tea pot is accompanied by the owner's cheddar biscuits; breakfast of bacon and eggs, home made jam and bread and great coffee is the perfect preparation for one of the local walks. Dinner is an eminently sociable affair with wine and conversation shared between guests lingering over the great food and atmosphere.

Of many bed and breakfasts, **Rose Lindsay Cottage** (113 Chapman Parade, Faulconbridge; ✆ 047-514 273) is near the Norman Lindsay gallery and house, and offers a bush theme and a breakfast to match: hot poached fruit, local jams and honeys and home baked muffins. Backpackers are also catered for here.

Walkabout Backpackers (190 Bathurst Rd, Katoomba; ✆ 047-824 226) offers budget accommodation in a nineteenth century home with an open fire and kitchen facilities, as well as trekking and travel information. Twin rooms are available. **The Blue Mountains YHA Youth Hostel** (66 Waratah St, Katoomba; ✆ 047-82 1416) is in a converted guesthouse, and offers twin, family or share rooms with private bathroom facilities, a dining room, lounges and television room, equipped kitchen, log fires, pool table and heating throughout.

THE HUNTER VALLEY

Description

This trip takes day trippers one and a half hours to the north west of Sydney to the Hunter Valley and leads through the best vineyards of the area. It is a good idea to pack a picnic and buy some wine to accompany your food when you get there, although details of a number of food stops are also included. The wineries included have been selected for the quality or significance of their wines: to attempt to taste at every winery in the valley would render you unable to return to Sydney. Should this nevertheless be the case, accommodation options are also listed. Drivers must bear in mind that the blood alcohol limit for drivers in NSW is 0.05%. As a guide, this means that men should drink no more than two standard drinks (100ml wine or 60ml fortified wine) in the first hour and no more than one standard drink per hour thereafter, while women should drink no more than one standard drink per hour.

Starting Off & Getting There

Join Pennant Hills Road from the west of Sydney or the Pacific Highway from the east and north, and head north towards Wahroonga. There is a large sign pointing onto the Sydney-Newcastle Freeway (Route 1). Turn right onto it, point the car, and drive.

Information Centres

Apart from the **New South Wales Travel Centre** (19 Castlereagh St, City ✆ 13 20 77; **Open:** Mon-Fri 9am-5pm; Sat phone only 9am-1pm), the Hunter Valley Tourist Information Centre Aberdare Rd, Cessnock (✆ 049-904 477; fax 049-906 954; **Open:** Mon-Fri 9.30am-5pm; Sat-Sun 9.30am-3.30pm) can organise accommodation as well as dispensing enormous amounts of information. The touring route passes this centre.

History & Background

The valley of the Hunter River embraces over twenty towns, many of which were established by pioneers in the early 1820s. Cessnock in particular quickly attracted many emancipated convicts and free settlers as the land was cleared, and they began to exploit the richness of the landscape above and below ground by grazing, timber cutting and grape growing. Yet it was the coal industry which was eventually to give the region economic, if not social, stability.

By the 1800s, Sydney had all but lost control to rum- most transactions were conducted with the spirit rather than real currency, and the great availability of the spirit had a degenerative influence on the productivity, propriety and sobriety of the colony's population.

When a certain James Busby published *A Treatise on the Culture of the Wine*, and the Art of Making Wine, the colonial administration granted him a two thousand acre plot in the Hunter Valley, hoping that this would encourage production of a more moderate and gentile beverage than rum. Busby travelled to Europe and obtained over seven hundred vine cuttings, and while he gave half to the Botanic Gardens in Sydney, he used the other half to found the wine industry which today includes over fifty wineries and utilises around seven thousand acres of land. The region is particularly known for its white wines and light reds.

The Tour

Leaving the north of Sydney, the freeway skirts past the Ku-Ring-gai National Park on the right, and leads up to the spectacularly beautiful Brooklyn area and Brisbane Water National Park on the **Hawkesbury River** (See: Tours Around Sydney: Cruises). Note the oyster beds. Yum. Continue straight on despite short gaps in the freeway (still destination Newcastle) until the turn-off to **Kurri Kurri/Cessnock (Route 82)** appears. Take Route 82 and follow the signs to Maitland/Cessnock and then Branxton/Cessnock. On entering Cessnock, the visitors centre will be visible on the left. After collecting some information and a map, follow the signs for **Branxton** through the town to the T-junction traffic lights. At this point, turn left and then second right into **Mount View Road**. This takes you to the first wineries of the tour.

Follow the right hand gravel road up the hill to one of the best small wineries of the region: **Petersons** (✆ 049-901 704; **Tastings & Sales:** Mon-Sat 9am-5pm; Sun 10am-5pm). Since they made their first wines in 1981, Petersons have won over one hundred and fifty medals and trophies in National and International shows. The wines are made from grapes grown on the forty acre vineyard, and are generally not available through retail outlets. Their Chardonnay, Semillon and Botrytis Semillon are particularly famous.

From here, go back to Mount View Road and turn left onto **Marrowbone Road**. This leads to **McWilliam's Mount Pleasant** (✆ 049-987 505; **Tastings & Sales:** Mon-Fri 9am-4.30pm; Sat-Sun 10am-4.30pm). Here you can taste both aged and young Hunter wines next to a roaring fire in the 'homestead', or join a guided tour of the winery operations (Mon-Fri at 11am & 2pm). As with Petersons, many of these wines cannot be found in retail outlets, so be sure to try the Semillon, for which McWilliam's Mount Pleasant are well known. Leaving Mount Pleasant, turn left back onto Marrowbone Road, proceed to Oakey Creek Road where you should turn left, and then right into **McDonalds Road**.

The next winery on the tour is **Lindemans**. One of the region's earliest vignerons, Dr Henry Lindeman, planted his first vines in 1843 on this site, then known as "Carrawa". These days, the Lindemans operate over one hundred and thirty hectares and are one of the most famous of the Hunter wineries. One reason for this is a peculiar piece of Australian viticultural history, **Ben Ean Moselle**, which achieved huge sales in Australia and throughout an ever thirsty export market. What makes this so amazing is the extremely sweet flavour and the curious after-effect of drinking the wine, often likened to a kind of high. When pressed for an explanation, the Lindemans wine tasting staff replied that the undisclosed ingredients are "a bit of this and a bit of that", and stated that it is no surprise that every vintage has tasted the same. When the export of Ben Ean ceased recently, an unceasing flow of hate mail started to flow in, particularly from Canada. It really is worthwhile to try a part of Australia's social history and one of this country's cultural icons here at the source, as well as their many excellent wines, such as the White Burgundy, Semillon, and Reserve Porphyry. The tasting area joins a large museum which is full of historic winemaking implements and tools gathered from the district.

From here, proceed to **Broke Road** and turn left, continuing as far as **Tyrrells Vineyards** (✆ 049-987 509; **Tasting & Sales:** Mon-Sat 8am-5pm; Closed Sundays). The winery has been run by the same family since 1858, and remains largely as it has been for the past century. Even the 1864 slab hut still stands in the grounds, although the family has moved to more comfortable lodgings and the estate has grown to incorporate over two hundred hectares of land. Try their Semillon Chardonnay and join a winery tour (Mon-Sat at 1.30pm). There are also picnic and barbecue facilities here.

Retracing Broke Road to the intersection, cross McDonalds Road and continue along Broke Road to the **Rothbury Estate** (✆ 049-987 555; **Tasting & Sales:** 7 days 9.30am-4.30pm) on the left. Apart from being able to taste a variety of wines here, the **Rothbury Cafe** upstairs is a lovely place for afternoon tea while looking out over the vines (✆ 049-987 363; **Open:** 7 days 12noon-3pm).

One last stop before you drop is reached by turning right off Broke Road shortly after Rothbury's to Historic Pepper Tree, which consists of **Murray Robson Wines**, the Convent Guesthouse (✆ 049-987 764; fax 049-987 323) and Robert's Restaurant. Robson's wines are available in limited releases only, and despite the late stage of the day, really shouldn't be missed. Robert's restaurant offers fresh local produce transformed into French-Italian cuisine, and the building itself, an 1876 slab cottage with polished floor and exposed beams, contributes to an excellent food experience (✆ 049-987 330).

This is the end of the tour, and if you're not staying overnight, from here it's back to Sydney: follow Allandale Road (Route 82) back to Cessnock and beyond to the freeway, following the Sydney signs.

Accommodation

Below is a small selection of places to stay in the region, although the visitor information centre (above) has the details of many more, and can organise reservations.

The Carriages Guesthouse (✆ 049-987591) is a popular yet small guesthouse with eight suites set in lovely gardens. In addition to the swimming and tennis available, horse drawn carriages can be chartered for gourmet picnics. **The Casuarina Country Inn & Cottages** (Hermitage Rd, Pokolbin; ✆ 049-987 888) comprises a number of tasteful and authentic fantasy suites such as the Asian Room, complete with nineteenth century opium bed. The buildings of **The Convent at Pepper Tree** (✆ 049-987 764) afford accommodation in a grand style: beautifully appointed rooms, full country breakfast, pre-dinner drinks and canapes, as well as tennis, spas, swimming and riding. **Peppers Guest House** (✆ 049-987 596; fax 049-987 739) is set amongst vines and fragrant gardens, with fifty one suave yet homely rooms appointed with antiques and flowers. Guests can eat on the vine-covered verandah, and take advantage of special arrangements between the guesthouse and Cypress Lakes golf resort next door. There are also many hotels in the area, with which the staff at the visitors information centre (above) can help.

Cycling The Hunter Valley

For those who extend the trip beyond a day, an excellent idea is to travel the reasonably flat ground between vineyards by bicycle. Grapemobile Bicycle Hire (✆ 049-987 639) hires out bikes and helmets for $25 per day or $15 per half day. It's a good idea to make a note of the wines you like, and after the cycling is over, do a scoop in the car to collect them.

THE SOUTH COAST

Description

This trip heads to the stunning coastline to the south of Sydney. Following the Coast Road from the world famous soaring site at Bald Hill, where the more adventurous among the guide's users can undertake a tandem flight, it proceeds through a string of pretty and historic towns towards Bulli. Rounding Wollongong, the tour proceeds to Gerroa and Seven Mile Beach National Park. From here, a number of options are available. Those with adequate time may proceed to the spectacular Jervis Bay and Hyam's Beach, while others may prefer a shorter drive through Nowra, Cambewarra Mountain and Jamberoo Valley back to Sydney.

Starting Off & Getting There

From the City, head towards Sydney Airport on Southern Cross Drive, continue around Botany Bay along General Holmes Drive through Brighton Le Sands, and turn right onto Ramsgate Road. This meets the **Princes Highway (Route 1)**. Turn left and stay on this road through a number of suburbs and eventually onto the F6 Freeway. After around ten minutes driving, take the exit leading off to the right, signified by a brown sign for **Helensburgh and Stanwell Park**. This is the old Princes Highway and the beginning of the sixty nine kilometre long **Tourist Drive 10** (Route 68), much of which you will be following today.

Trains (**Information:** ✆ 13 15 00) run regularly between Sydney and Wollongong, and with sweeping views of the coastline, it is one of the most popular train rides in New South Wales.

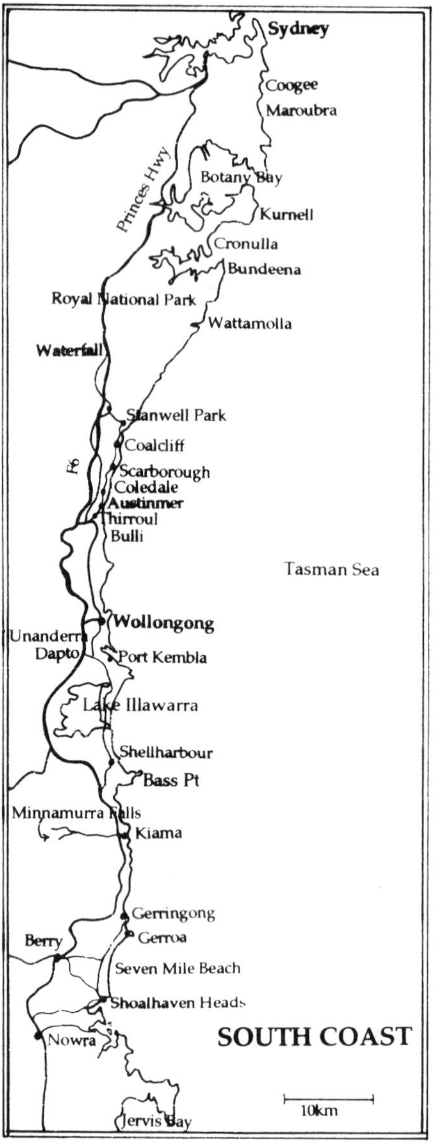

Information

The enormous area covered by the itinerary means that the best way to obtain information about accommodation is to contact any of the following local visitors centres: Kiama Visitors Centre (Blowhole Point, Kiama; ✆ 1800 803 897); Shellharbour Tourism (Lamerton House, Shellharbour Square, Blackbutt; ✆ 042-21 6169); or Tourism Wollongong (93 Crown St, Wollongong; ✆ 042-28 0300). In Sydney, the New South Wales Travel Centre (119 Castlereagh St, City; ✆ 13 20 77) can also help.

BEFORE YOU GO

Bundanon

Information & Bookings: Shoalhaven Tourist Centre (✆ 1800-024 261).

Open: First Sunday of every month (maximum 250 people). **Cost:** $12/$8.50.

One of Australia's best known artists, Arthur Boyd, generously made a gift of his extensive grounds, house, studio and artworks to the Australian nation. 'Bundanon' has become a living arts centre where musicians, dancers and artists can work, perform or exhibit. The estate is open once a month, when visitors are guided by the artist through the timber and stone house with its numerous artworks, and will maybe have the opportunity to watch Boyd working in his studio shed. The beautiful gardens are also an ideal picnic spot. Note that bookings are essential, and must be made through the Shoalhaven Tourist Centre well in advance, as places are often full six months in ahead.

The Kiama Jazz Festival

Information & Bookings (✆ 042-323 322)

This immensely popular jazz festival is held over two weeks each February with a large number of acts and fringe events featuring Australian and overseas jazz. The Gala Family Day is always a highlight, well worth investigating by those with children.

Minnamurra Rainforest

Budderoo National Park via Jamberoo (✆ 042-360 469)

Open: 7 days 9am-5pm (no access to Rainforest Walk after 4pm). **Cost:** $7.50 per car.

Minnamurra is a remnant of the ancient subtropical rainforest which once covered the entire eastern coast of Australia. Giant stinging trees, rare ferns, palms, flowering plants and strangler figs can be observed from the elevated, meandering Rainforest Walk and the Minnamurra Falls track. Those wishing to visit the rainforest should allow at least an hour. It would best be reached on this itinerary by detouring to Jamberoo (via Jamberoo Road) from Kiama.

History & Background

Due to the suddenness of the Stanwell Park turn-off from the freeway, tourers would be well advised to put off reading these background notes until comfortably ensconced on a viewing bench at Bald Hill (below).

The occupation of the South Coast region by Aborigines has been dated at around seventeen thousand years. Archaeological excavations around what is now known as Shellharbour have uncovered large numbers of tools and artefacts which are among some of the oldest found in Australia outside the tropics. At Bass Point, an axe more than three thousand five hundred years old was recently uncovered. The rich marine life which supported the local Aborigines also attracted Europeans. Whalers in particular came to the area, and it was George Bass

Northern Beaches Coastline

Hawkesbury River

Olympic Aquatic Centre Below: To The Lighthouse

Nielsen Park Below: University Of Sydney

Flightseeing

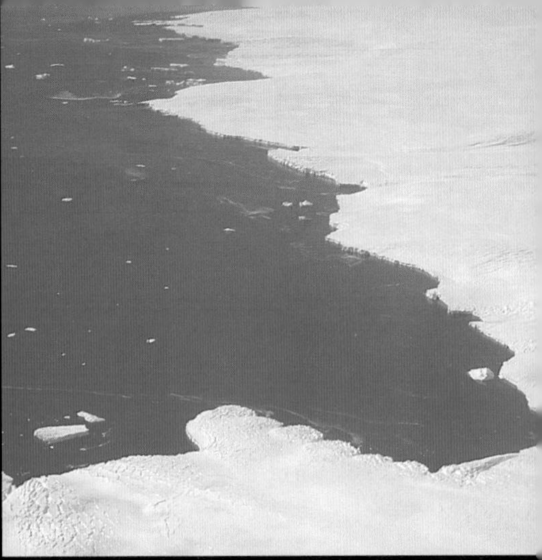

Antarctica

Hunter Valley

Berrima Gaol

Below: The Three Sisters

Below: Canberra

who recorded the first European reference to Kiama and its famous Blowhole (1797). After a basic settlement was set up here, timber getters arrived to clear the forests of their hard wood, particularly cedar, which was in high demand for furniture. Venturing inland with their saws, land was gradually cleared, allowing cattle grazing to develop; quarries began to extract bluestone from the area's hills; and in turn, support industries and businesses were established. Gold was discovered in the region around the Shoalhaven River in the 1850s, and the European population continued to grow.

Meanwhile, shipwrecked sailors stranded on a beach further north had spotted a black seam in the cliff face (1797). Investigations proved this to be part of an enormous coal seam which extended under much of the region. Today, Australia's largest company, BHP, operates gargantuan processing and steel plants, and coal loaders fill cargo ships in Port Kembla, giving many residents their livelihoods and the region its prosperity.

Despite the clear trend of extraction and exploitation of the area's natural resources by the Westerners, the South Coast remains largely a naturally beautiful stretch of countryside. Clean beaches lapped by turquoise water contrast with the solid might of the Illawarra Escarpment, under the shadows of which plump dairy cattle munch on lush pastures. Holiday houses line the coast, and day trippers flow in from Sydney. Elsewhere, pristine tracts of National Park give an idea of the area's original identity.

The Tour

After the road meanders through the Royal National Park and cuts back under the freeway, look out for **Lawrence Hargrave Road** to the left. Winding its way to the coast, and offering occasional glimpses of the sea, the road emerges from the bushland at Bald Hill. This is the first stop on the tour.

Bald Hill, located directly north and above Stanwell Park, is a world famous soaring site, where hang gliders and paragliders turn perfect arcs out over the intensely blue water of the Tasman Sea. Several reputable and established companies operate from here, taking novices on tandem flights. On fine weekends, it is usually possible simply to sign up on the spot without booking in advance, although tourers are advised to book during the week. (For details of operators, See: Sports.) The spectacle of daredevils preparing their colourful equipment and then simply launching themselves over the very tall cliffs makes for compulsive viewing. For this reason, custom-built, backwards-tilting wooden benches facilitate the most comfortable viewing position, nearby plaques explain glider aerodynamics, the theory of thermal and lift currents, and the history of paragliding and hang gliding, and refreshments are available. The nearby memorial to Lawrence Hargrave, inventor of the box kite and one of the 'founding fathers' of modern aviation, reveals the area's ties to the development of modern aviation.

This considerable airborne spectacle takes place in front of a wonderful backdrop. Stretching away to the south, you should have a very clear **view** of the coastline you will be exploring on this tour.

Leaving Bald Hill and retracing fifty metres to the intersection on the left, turn left to wind down to the town of Stanwell Park. Here begins the spectacular Coast Road, which continuously winds in and out of rugged inlets. The views back along the coast would be worthy of photographing, if only the numerous warning signs (complete with pictures of falling rocks) didn't state "Do Not Stop" so unequivocally . Despite the hype, this is a safe road offering a tame and beautiful seaside drive.

It leads to the charming, unpretentious seaside town of Coalcliff, where a short detour via Paterson Road will reveal a lovely beach. Coalcliff is famous as the site of the first coal discoveries in the region, made by chance in 1797 when some shipwrecked sailors noticed the signs of a rich seam as they stood on the beach. The discovery eventually led to the exploitation of the very rich seam of "black diamond" which underlies much of the Illawarra region, and still supports the giant steel and coal industries of Port Kembla and Wollongong. Clifton, Scarborough and Coledale are all overlooked by the looming Illawarra Escarpment, and are fronted by clear turquoise waters. Austinmer also has a lovely beach, although unlike many others nearby which are often empty, this one is regularly busy. Despite the wealth of the region's resources, this particular part of the South Coast was overlooked by developers even after direct rail access to Sydney was established in 1888, and has retained its simple charm. It is now the centre of the holiday home belt.

Further south in Thirroul stands the ocean-edge bungalow rented by DH Lawrence in 1922 while writing **Kangaroo**. It is to be found at 3 Craig Street, so turn left off the main road into the Esplanade, turn left into Cliff Parade, round the corner into Surfers Parade and turn left into Craig Street. Although the private house is not really visible from the street, tourers may like to stroll along the tiny park one house block along to look across at the garden and appreciate the ocean views which Lawrence so enjoyed. You can also follow the steps down onto the beach and rocks, one of the novelist's favourite walks. From here, turn left back into Surfers Parade and take the first right and first left (Station Street) to lead back to the town centre. Bearing right at the station and ascending the small ramp will lead you back onto the main road. Turn left.

Rejoining Tourist Drive 10, the road proceeds into **Bulli**, where a collection of historic buildings await. On entering the town, temporarily disregard the signs directing the Tourist Drive 10 to the left. It is worthwhile to admire the **Bulli Family Hotel** on the main road at the same intersection. This Victorian hotel (1889) was a popular resting place for travellers, sightseers and miners who had negotiated the steep and treacherous Bulli Pass (which still cuts through the escarpment, today reaching the freeway) on their way to Wollongong. Its filigree cast iron railings which line the verandah, local brickwork, and frosted and engraved bar windows contribute much to the building's landmark status, recognised by the National Trust when they classified it.

Although the Tourist Drive enters a short distance of monotony at this point, it is best to stay on it. Such persistence will be rewarded by seeing the massively mighty **BHP steel works and Slab and Plate Mill**, through which the drive proceeds. Although the plant is not open to the public, there is a visitors centre further along off Springhill Road (✆ 042-75 7023; **Open:** 7 days 8am-4pm). To find it, look out for the large entrance to the Slab and Steel/Flat Products Plant at some traffic lights, flanked by monstrously large BHP and Australian flags. Inside, you will see informative models and displays detailing the operations of this enormous plant, and some information about BHP, one of Australia's biggest primary resources companies. A two hour **guided tour** by bus and foot through the plant can be joined on Fridays at 9.30am, although booking in advance is essential and sturdy, safe clothing must be worn.

Back on Tourist Drive 10, the surrounding suburbs reveal an interesting mix of industrial and suburban land use, while the beaches lining the ocean near the Port Kembla coal loading facility seem oblivious to the heavy industrial scene behind them. Continuing southwards towards Shellharbour, a left turn off the main road will take tourers to Shellharbour and its Bass Point Reserve, the site of numerous Aboriginal middens and archaeological finds. Carbon dating of artefacts has dated Aboriginal occupation of the site at around seventeen thousand years ago, while excavations uncovered a edge-ground axe over three thousand five hundred years old, one of the oldest ever found outside Tropical Australia. An important part of the local indigenous people's diet was seafood, and once eaten, they would discard the shells onto a pile; over time, the piles became buried in the earth. These middens, really only refuse piles, are visible in many parts of Australia as crumbling white and grey matter in concentrated layers in the earth. They are important because they reveal much about the prehistoric environment and its occupation by indigenous people.

Returning to the Princes Highway via Five Islands Road, continue to the hilly and picturesque town of **Kiama**. It is worthwhile going first of all to the **Visitors Centre** at Blowhole Point (above) to pick up a copy of the comprehensive leaflet **Heritage Walks of Kiama and District**. To reach it, drive down the

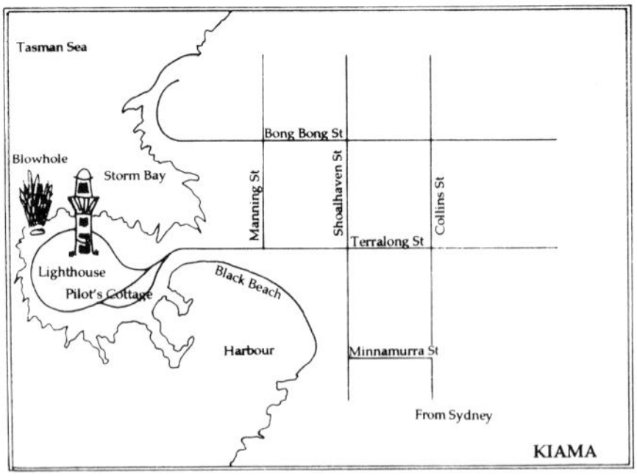

hill to the roundabout and turn left into Terralong Street. Follow the signs on this road to the Blowhole, where the **Visitors Centre** (✆ 042-32 3322; **Open:** 7 days 9am-5pm) will be visible on the left. There is also a good cafe here, whose outside tables offer the perfect opportunity to admire the jetty, town and harbour. Despite its natural appearance, the harbour was constructed over sixteen years by joining Blowhole Point to the mainland. Next to the cafe stands the Pilots Cottage Museum (**Open:** Wed-Mon 10am-4pm), where displays related to the area's maritime history and heritage are to be found. Down on the jetty is a renovated cargo shed, which today houses a popular fish shop.

The town's name is thought to have originated from the word used by the local Aborigines, Kiarama-a, meaning 'where the sea makes a noise'. The Blowhole nearby was also noticed by George Bass, when he anchored his whale boat here in 1797 and recorded the first European reference to the site. The abundance of Cedar trees nearby later attracted timber getters, who became the first Europeans to settle here permanently. By the 1870s, dairying and basalt quarrying had become important industries for the area, and continue to be so to this day.

A visit to Kiama would not be complete without a visit to the **Blowhole**, although it is highly likely that this famous landmark will be silent and inactive when you visit, as it seems only to perform properly when the wind blows precisely from the south-east. It is just as likely that scores of hopeful, camera-toting tourists will be standing there in vain! On Blowhole Point stands the **lighthouse**, established in 1887 to assist the safe passage of coastal shipping. However, the best way to see Kiama's other historic sites is by foot, so drive back to Terralong Street and park near the corner of Terralong and Manning Streets.

Here stands the richly coloured Post Office. Built around 1888 in Victorian Italianate style, it seems it tries to compete for grandeur with the **Court House** (1860) and **Police Station** (1884), adjacent in Terralong Street. Passing under the iron railway bridge (1892), you will reach **Scots Presbyterian Church** (dedicated in 1863 and completed with the addition of the spire in 1898). On the other side of Shoalhaven Street stands the local **Fire Station** (1925), built to replace the tin shed which had housed the town's hand-drawn fire cart for nearly twenty years. The building is now used as a Community Arts Centre, but the original shed is still visible at the rear. The corner diagonally opposite the station is occupied by the Kiama Inn, built in 1888 and originally known as Tory's Hotel. Turning right into Collins Street will lead you directly to **The Terraces** (✆ 042-32 1149). This row of cottages was built around 1886 to house the town's quarry workers, and is a very rare example of a weatherboard terrace. It now contains a popular group of craft shops and tea houses. Turning right into Minnamurra Street, you will find the **Kiama Infants School** (1871), whose buildings are constructed of bluestone. Turning right again into Shoalhaven Street to head back towards Terralong Street, you will pass some of the original **railway tracks** used by trams to carry basalt from the quarry to the harbour. This completes the Kiama circuit, although after retrieving your car, you may like to take a short drive up Manning Street to see the Council Chambers/Town Hall and the Grand Hotel on the corner of Bong Bong Street, which has operated here under the same name since 1891. The jolly seaside town of Kiama really does represent a breath of fresh air after the industrial might Wollongong, and looking at a map of the town, it is impossible to ignore the fact that it looks like something out of a children's story or game.

From Kiama, the tour follows the Princes Highway (Route 1) once more towards Nowra, passing rich, rolling hills dotted with dairy cows, and rounding the cliffs where the Illawarra Escarpment meets the coast. A brown sign points to the left and announces **Tourist Drive 6** to Gerringong, which you should follow directly to **Gerroa**. On reaching the **Kingsford Smith Lookout**, turn left to park in the car park. Here, tourers are treated to a spectacular view of the full, arching sweep of **Seven Mile Beach**, and the distinct band of bushland which separates it from civilisation. It was from this beach, now a National Park, that Kingsford Smith took off for New Plymouth on 11 January 1933, to make the first commercial flight between Australia and New Zealand. At the southern end the enormous bay, the Beecroft Peninsula marks the beginning of Jervis Bay. At the eastern end of the town is an enormous **rock platform** (reached by following this side road to the end), famous for the many fossils of plants and animals which can be seen on its surface (after a bit of searching and luck). Returning to the tourist drive at Kingsford Smith lookout, turn left and follow it down to the coastal flat. After crossing over the Crooked River, the road becomes lined with trees, and several turn-offs to the left allow access to the magnificent beach, the perfect place for a stroll.

Continuing along Tourist Drive 6, maintain a lookout for **Beach Road** on the right, which leads some seven kilometres to the town of Berry. **Berry** is a delightful town with a main street lined with historic buildings, and many avenues of oak, elm and beech trees, planted by the area's original settlers. The town was named in honour of Alexander Berry who had explored the south coast with Hamilton Hume and was granted a four thousand hectare property in the region, which he named Coolangatta. His great activity developed the estate into two hundred and sixty thousand hectares, and did much to allow the town to prosper. Berry was an important centre for hard-living, whip-cracking timber getters, whose bullock teams dragged countless loads of hardwood to the mill on Broughton Creek. From here, the planks (and anything else leaving the town) would journey down-stream at high tide to reach the ocean and a passage north to Sydney. Those ready for a restorative break may like to head for either the charming Postmasters' Coffee House, opposite the Bunyip Inn Guest House, or the Espresso cafe on Hotel Berry's covered verandah, opposite the **Berry Museum** (135 Queen St; ✆ 044-641 551; **Open:** Sat 11am-2pm; Sun 11am-3pm; Holidays 11am-2pm). This building was designed by architect William Wardell and built as a bank in 1886. Unusual Flemish brickwork and a stepped facade make this a distinctive building, inside which displays educate the visitor about Berry's past.

Other historical buildings, which point to the town's past as a bustling centre, include the **Post Office**, the **Court House** (1891), and most distinctively, the **CBC Bank** building (1889), now the Bunyip Inn Guest House. This is one of the town's greatest landmarks, a two-storey Classical Revival bank with an elegant pillared verandah. The charms of the village can be easily discovered by simply strolling up and down the main street, Queen Street. Two of the town's best **restaurants** include the Modern Australian Baker and Bunyip Restaurant (23 Prince St; ✆ 044-64 1454) and The Silos Restaurant (Princes Highway, Jaspers Brush, Berry; ✆ 044- 48 6160). Tourers may be lucky enough to be in town for one of Berry's regular **events**. Antiques and craft shopping is at its best on the first Sunday of each month, when the local showground is the site of a **Country Fair** with hundreds of stalls and activities. Once a year in February, the showground becomes the scene of the large annual **Agricultural Show**, reminding all who see it that the town's prosperity relies to a large extent on the black and white dairy cows prevalent under gum trees, munching on luscious green grass.

The best way to proceed from this point is to head for the lovely town of Kangaroo Valley, and the most scenic way to do so is to head south out of Berry and drive towards Nowra until meeting the large roundabout almost at the town's entrance. Turn right to join the southern end of **Tourist Drive 7**, which is Cambewarra Road (direction Moss Vale). This will lead through some lovely countryside to begin the long, gently winding, fern-lined ascent to **Cambewarra Mountain** (678m.a.s.l.), which offers views over Nowra, the Shoalhaven Valley and Jervis Bay. On a clear day, it is apparently possible to see up to one hundred and fifty kilometres.

From here, turn right back onto Cambewarra Road and wend your way into Kangaroo Valley, named because of the large number of Australia's national icons encountered by the early settlers. The region was first explored by Charles Throsby (see Trips Out of Sydney: Southern Highlands, below) in 1818, and was prepared for settlement and exploitation by the 1830s. Cedar cutters cleared the ground of its rich bushland, enabling cattle grazing to commence by the 1850s. The increasing activity in the area required a number of official buildings, such as a Post Office (1870) and school (1871). This in turn attracted others, and so the population and industry grew: a butter factory had been established by 1888, and the Hampden Bridge was built over the pretty Kangaroo River in 1898. Today, the town has a number of delightful cafes, tea rooms and craft shops to explore, and the banks of the Kangaroo River are as picturesque a spot as anywhere to have a break. Adventurous types may like to drive the winding fifteen kilometres to the dramatic Fitzroy Falls, from which point breathtaking views of the Moreton National Park are on offer. Those doing so should return to Sydney via the Hume Highway. Those preferring to travel back to Sydney through the more gentle countryside of the south coast region should follow either Kangaroo Valley Road or the longer Woodhill Mountain Road back to Berry, enjoying the lovely views towards the coast. From Berry, simply follow the Princes Highway beyond Kiama and on to Sydney via the F6 freeway.

The Far South Coast

Below Jervis Bay are idyllic coastline and country towns, impossible to reach on a day trip form Sydney. Those with more time might like to explorer the territory covered by heading south to Bawley Point, Bateman's Bay, Twofold Bay, Narooma, the gorgeous Tilba Tilba & Central Tilba. Then take the Bermagui turn-off to Tathra, rejoin the highway at Bega, continue south to Merimbula, Eden and Boydtown. Most importantly, this is a particularly scenic route to keep in mind if heading towards Melbourne.

THE SOUTHERN HIGHLANDS

Description

This trip heads south from Sydney past Wollongong, up through the Macquarie Pass to Robertson (around which much of the film Babe was made), through the lush countryside surrounding the historic towns of Moss Vale, Berrima, Bowral and Mittagong, and returns to Sydney by the freeway. The area has a subdued yet definite beauty: lush grazing paddocks meet historic estates and residences; heritage cottages and buildings line the streets of leafy towns, some occupied by bed and breakfasts, others offering epicurean delights. Waterfalls and gorges in one area carve a landscape which is, elsewhere, tamed by golf courses and country clubs. A popular way for Sydneysiders to enjoy the area is to rent a house from one of the many real estate agencies here, or simply to travel between bed and breakfasts at whim. It is more than easy to spend a number of days here in the invigorating air, absorbing the atmosphere of the towns, doing a bushwalk and indulging in a hearty meal.

Before You Go

One of the best places to eat is The Briars Inn (Moss Vale Rd, Bowral; © 048-681 734). In this extremely popular 1845 pub, guests can choose and grill their own lunch and make their choice from the salads and vegetables. Tandoori lamb, beef fillets and rump steaks, whole trout, gourmet sausages and chicken are usually on the menu (mains around $15), while chef cooked entrees such as pate, curry puffs, tempura fish average around $6.50. The children's menu ($4.50 - $6.50) may include spaghetti, sausages, roasts or fish & chips, while desserts, such as hazelnut meringue cake, are around $5. The pub contains a number of warmly wooded rooms with fireplaces and rich burgundy walls, and the eating areas (inside and out) are full of large wooden tables and extremely happy eaters and drinkers. The Briars Inn positively buzzes, and is so popular that two sittings on Sunday are required, so booking is recommended.

Starting Off & Getting There

This is a long day trip, so start off early. By car from the City, head south towards Sydney Airport on Southern Cross Drive, continue around Botany Bay along General Holmes Drive through Brighton Le Sands, and turn right onto Ramsgate Road (direction Wollongong). This meets the Princes Highway. Turn left and continue straight ahead onto the F6 freeway/Route 1 Princes Highway. It is about forty kilometres to Wollongong. By train, the area can be reached by a two hourly service from Central to Picton, Bowral, Mittagong & Moss Vale. Return trains depart every two hours (**Information:** CityRail © 13 15 00). Buses run regularly between the towns of the region, usually departing from the railway stations (**Information:** Berrima Coaches © 048-713 211). This is necessary to reach Berrima, as the town is not on the railway line. A third option is to take the train to Unanderra (two stops south of Wollongong) and then join the historic Cockatoo Run (**Information:** © 9699 2737) train up the Illawarra Escarpment to Robertson and on to Moss Vale.

Information Centres & Events

Apart from the New South Wales Travel Centre (19 Castlereagh St, City; © 13 20 77; **Open:** Mon-Fri 9am-5pm; Sat phone only 9am-1pm), there are several visitors centres in the Southern Highlands which can help with general information and accommodation.

These can be found at Fitzroy Falls (✆ 048-87 7270; **Open:** Mon-Fri 8.30-4.30; Sat-Sun 8.30am-5pm); Berrima Courthouse (Argyle St, Berrima; ✆ 048-77 1505; **Open:** 7 days from 10am-4pm); Mittagong (Winifred West Park, Old Hume Highway, Mittagong; ✆ 048-71 2888; **Open:** 7 days 8am-5.30pm); and Sutton Forest (Shell Service Centre, Hume Highway, Sutton Forest; ✆ 048-78 9369; **Open:** Fri-Sun 9.15am-4.15pm)

The Moss Vale Agricultural Show takes place in mid March each year, featuring the produce of the district. At about the same time takes place the Southern Highlands Antiques Fair, usually held in Bowral. Bowral is also Tulip Festival capital every year from late September to early October. Bendooley Street's Corbett Gardens are the centrepiece of the show, while many private gardens participate in the festivities.

History & Background

The Southern Highlands (650-860m.a.s.l.) are approximately one hundred kilometres south of Sydney, and topographically range from gently undulating grazing slopes to rugged cliffs and gorges of the Illawarra escarpment and the Morton National Park in the South-East.

After Aboriginal inhabitation began around forty thousand years ago, this became the tribal area of the Wadi Wadi, who roamed the area hunting and gathering possum, kangaroo, berries, roots and the Burrawang Palm nut, leaving behind established paths and tracks.

When European pioneers came to the area, all efforts were made to find a safe way to cross the ranges to link with the coastal settlements, and although it was known that the Aborigines had such a track, it could not be found. Eventually, a self-educated Aborigine, Dr Ellis Karadgi, revealed the route, which the Macquarie Pass Road follows to this day. Further co-operation between the settlers and the Aborigines took the form of accompanying explorers, and it was on such journeys that their names were left in places such as Wingecarribee (flight of birds) and Berrima (black swan to the south). Unfortunately, the settlers were not as helpful in return, and displaced the Aborigines firstly by bringing diseases with them which devastated the Wadi Wadi population, and secondly by establishing houses, towns, farms and fencing systems- they were unable to travel or hunt their land or to visit sacred sites for ceremonial purposes, and eventually a large part of their culture was lost.

The first European to visit the area is thought to have been John Wilson, a convict who lived and roamed the lands with the Aborigines. In 1798 he led an expedition to disprove the now laughable convict theory that China lay over the ranges! Extensive exploration took place between 1814-1820 (notably by Hume and Throsby), yet settlement was discouraged. In fact, it was an offence to pass beyond the Nepean River without a permit between 1803 and 1821. The grazing potential of the area was realised during these years, and a eventually, number of properties were established near Bowral, Oxley's Hill and Sutton Forest. When the Railway was built in the 1860s, settlement and farming activity on the rich volcanic soil increased rapidly, especially after the **Robertson Land Act** of 1861 encouraged settlers to buy and clear land for £1 an acre. Most of the architectural heritage of the region remains from this time.

The Tour

Driving through the beautiful, densely gummed National Park, the road descends by a long, steep hill, revealing the Port Kembla coal loading facility in the distance. Where the road forks just before Wollongong, bear right (direction Nowra, remaining on Route 1), or you will become entangled in Wollongong. Continue through Unanderra and Dapto, pass Lake Illawarra on the left, and then turn right onto the **Illawarra Highway** (**Route 48**; direction Robertson & Moss Vale). Stay on the Illawarra Highway, enjoying the luscious green pastoral scenery dotted with dairy cows as the road approaches the base of the Illawarra escarpment.

The road now begins a spectacular climb as it leaves the coastal plain and winds up and over the Macquarie Pass, winding through thick pockets of rainforest and passing trickling waterfalls where billowing mist clings to the steep escarpment (recommended music, Schubert: Death and the Maiden).

Occasionally, glimpses back to the coast catch your eye, until suddenly, you will emerge at the top, the landscape will open out again, and the road rolls on a short distance to **Robertson**. Here dwell two eminent residents, the Big Potato and the famous Robertson Pie Shop, where tourers can obtain an enormous range of excellent pies for around $1.90. Be warned: hungry customers may have to join the queue out the door. Robertson was known as "Yarrawa" until the success of the Robertson Land Act in settling the area prompted a name change, and its halcyon era was at the end of the 1890s, when the Robertson Butter Factory, a Bacon factory and a Sawmill were thriving, and supporting an infrastructure of builders, butchers, auctioneer, blacksmith, bootmaker, doctor, newspaper, plumber, saddler, tobacconist and a population of five hundred. Today, the big potato is representative of the town's fabled high quality vegetable produce, which can be bought at the Country Market on the second Sunday of each month. However, since early 1996 Robertson has become known as the home of Babe, the world famous piglet who found success under the motto, 'a little pig goes a long way'. Much of the film was made in the countryside around Robertson, and although at the time of writing no specific Babe sights or tours are yet in operation, the popularity of the film suggests it will not be too long before they spring up nearby. It is therefore worthwhile checking with the visitor information centres, above.

Staying on the Illawarra highway, proceed through Robertson and five kilometres out of town; then turn off left to **Burrawang** (three kilometres away), another melodious Aboriginal word meaning "place of love". Aah! 1880s Burrawang consisted of a school, three churches, bank, two bakers, two hotels, a tailor, blacksmith and butcher. The **General Store** with its unique structure of a huge Baltic pine lining, Mansard roof, Kauri pine counter and Australian cedar fixtures and drawers, was established in about 1860. One of the oldest buildings of its kind in Australia, the store has a large collection of antique groceries (past their use by date) and signs. The post office section has not been changed since last century. The old school house (on the main road) contains a delight: Dining Room Antiques (✆ 048-86 4500; **Open:** Sat-Sun 10am-4pm) is a delicious collection of tableware, whether china, picnic hampers, cutlery, linen or furniture. The charming proprietor has established a gorgeous cafe amongst the antiques, focussed on an impossibly suave espresso machine, but also serving light lunches and cakes. Sunny days may see chairs and tables spread under the trees in the garden. From here, follow the signs to Wildes Meadow and continue to the eighty two metre high **Fitzroy Falls**, some of the best looking waterfalls in the state. There are two walking tracks of approximately one to two hours duration, but the falls are visible only one hundred metres from the car park. The excellent Visitors Information Centre here dispenses copious amounts of information on the region and its wildlife.

From the falls, follow **Route 79**, passing Yarrunga, to rejoin the Illawarra Highway. Turn left and head for Moss Vale. As you come into **Moss Vale**, on the right is one of the oldest houses of the area, Throsby Park (c.1834), site of Dr Throsby's one thousand acre land grant given in recognition of his services as a pioneer. This magnificent, privately owned house was given the National Trust's top classification when listed, and is built of local sandstone and cedar. For a clear view of the house and grounds, continue to the roundabout and turn right. Just over the railway bridge (around fifty metres) is a little Apex Park. Looking along the valley from here, the pale purple house is clearly visible among trees on a rounded hill top. [Note: Those proceeding to The Briars Inn (above) for lunch should continue along this road for around three minutes until its sign becomes visible on the left. After lunch, retrace the road back into Moss Vale.]

Retracing the road back over the bridge and across the roundabout will lead to the centre of **Moss Vale**, one of the prime rural centres in New South Wales for sheep, cattle, goats and horses. The town's prosperity developed in the 1890s after the railway was built, and after the Earl of Belmore, then Governor of NSW, chose nearby residence 'Hillview' as his official country residence. Several wealthy individuals from Sydney took note of this stamp of status and built their own estates around the town. Along Moss Vale's main street, you will see the Post Office, the fully restored Railway Station (1867), and a number of charming commercial buildings, now housing antique, art and craft shops, cafes and tea rooms.

Continue along the Illawarra Highway towards Sutton Forest, an area renowned for its grand residences and estates, such as 'Hillview', barely visible through the trees off and up to the left of the road. This town is the centre of an area founded by Governor Macquarie in 1820 to supply Sydney with agricultural produce while emulating an English pleasure ground. Despite his frequently ridiculed penchant for naming buildings, streets and towns after himself, Macquarie named the town after the Speaker of the House of Commons in England, the Right Honourable Charles Sutton. Although a government village was planned, Sutton Forest grew along the highway, so this is where most of the town's historic buildings are visible today. As well as old shop fronts and commercial buildings, **All Saints Church** (1861) is worth investigating for its historic cemetery, as is the nearby Public School (1879).

Next, retrace one kilometre and turn left to reach the Hume Highway. Cross the southbound traffic carefully and turn right onto the highway, immediately taking the turn-off to Berrima.

Berrima was settled in 1829 on the Wingecarribee River, and was intended to become the administrative and industrial centre of the region. The official surveyor, Robert Hoddle, designed Berrima in the style of a typical English village, the central elements of which are the common and the market place, both still visible today. The town's position on the southern road supplied it with a constant stream of hungry, thirsty and tired Cobb & Co coach travellers, explaining the number of inns and pubs established here. **The Surveyor General Inn**, in particular, was established in 1834 and claims to be the oldest continuously licensed hotel in the country. This is an

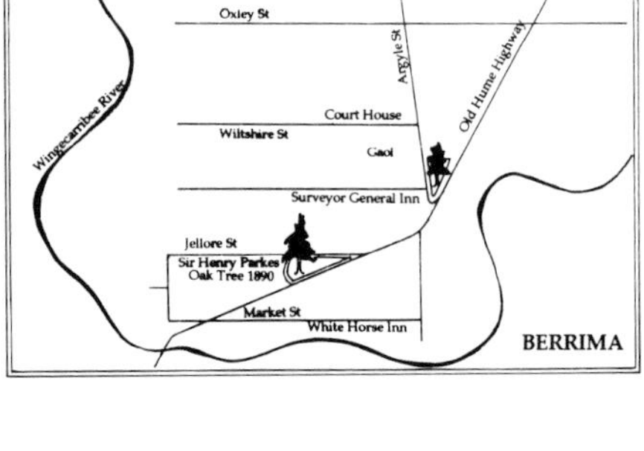

exemplary early colonial town, maintained in its original state and protected under a National Trust preservation order.

Entering the town and passing the Catholic Francis Xavier Church on the right, pull over by the grassy area on the left, just after the bridge. This is the original village green, and is the perfect spot to park while strolling around the town as follows.

Start by walking around the green to the left, where the small **Berrima Historical Society District Museum** beckons (**Open:** Sat-Sun and public holidays 10am-4pm). Here is to be found information about the town's past, including the internment of German Australians during the First World War in the nearby gaol.

Lining the green are a number of elegant cottages and buildings. Turning left off Bryan Street, you will discover the sandstone Berrima House (c. 1835, private), the school house (1840s) and even a nursery tucked into the trees. Rounding the corner into Jellore Street, a succession of charming inns and cottages leads back to the main road. On the corner of the Old Hume Highway stands an oak tree planted in 1890 by Sir Henry Parkes, the 'Father of Federation' (See: History). To the left is the Post Office (originally a toll house) and beyond, the main row of shops, including 'Berrima Cottage', a quaint shop tightly packed with antiques, vintage and new clothing and accessories, fabrics and furnishings.

At the end of this row of shops beyond the Surveyor General Inn, are the **gaol** and **Court House**, both magnificent sandstone buildings designed by Colonial Architect Mortimer Lewis and completed in 1838-39. The Berrima Gaol is still in use, while the courthouse includes a museum, open colonial cells and a visitors information centre (above). While looking at the front of the Court House in Wilshire Street, note the famous bull's head fountain on the opposite wall. Across on the other side of the Old Hume Highway is a long row of colonial buildings housing craft shops, galleries and tea houses, such as the Old Bakery, beyond Wingecarribee Street. From here, you can stroll back towards your car, detouring along Argyle and Market Streets to have a look at the **White Horse Inn** (1840s) and **Magistrate's House** (1870s).

As the Old Hume highway leaves Berrima to the north, it passes Harper's Mansion (1834) on the left. This National Trust classified building was constructed for the first licensee of the Surveyor General Inn. Out in the countryside once more, continue on past the Bowral turn-off and drive three hundred metres or so to **Berkelouw's Book Barn** on the left ('Bendooley', Hume Highway, Berrima; ✆ 048-77 1370; fax 048-77 1102; Open 7 days from 9.30am), surrounded by tall pines and devoted entirely to the storage and sale of second hand books from the cheap to the rare and expensive. There are few bookshops with as much atmosphere as this one.

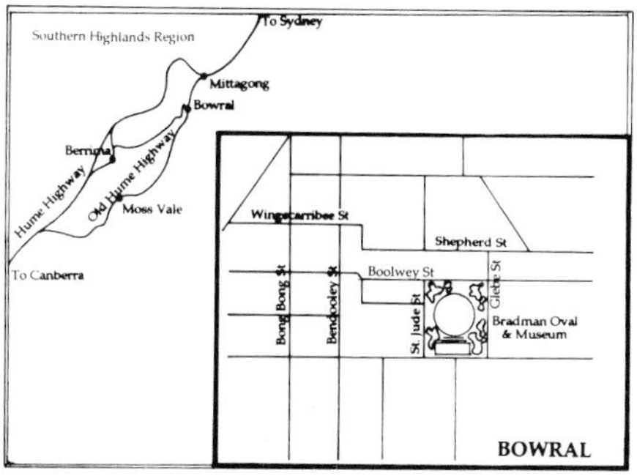

Return to and take the **Bowral** turn-off (**Oxley's Hill Road**; Route 31), which cuts through some lovely countryside to reach the escarpment and proceed down into the town itself. Named from the Aboriginal name for nearby Mount Gibraltar, Bowral began as a trading centre, and attained a certain gentility when John Oxley, Surveyor General, acquired his lands here. His heir recognised the town's potential when the railway was planned to pass through it, and sub-divided the estate in 1863 . The town boomed, encouraging and requiring the building of many of the buildings which today give the town its historic character.

Coming down from Oxley's Hill, turn right to cross the railway line, and then left to reach **Bong Bong Street**, the town's enigmatically named main street. And yes, it's time for a well-earned food or coffee break. **Epicure** at 337 Bong Bong Street (to the right)(✆ 048- 61 4705; **Open:** Mon-Sat 8.30am-5pm; Sun to 4pm) is an excellent, relaxing cafe where restorative and excellent afternoon teas or more substantial meals are to be found. Also in this street nearby at 327 Bong Bong Street is Gallery J (✆ 048-622 310; Open Mon-Sat 10am-5pm; Sun 10am-4pm), a wonderful shop specialising in Australian handcrafts in the form of hand blown glass, ceramics, woodwork, hand painted silk and jewellery.

Turn left off Bong Bong Street into Bowral Street to reach **Bendooley Street**. Turning left at the historic cemetery, you will see that this is a beautiful, tree-lined street graced with big old houses and **historic buildings**. The Courthouse, built in 1896 from trachyte quarried on Mount Gibraltar above, the library of 1890, St Jude's Church of England and cemetery of 1887, and the public school, opened in 1863, all stand more or less in a single row. However, cricket fans will know that Bowral is a most important focus for Australian cricket history. **Sir Donald Bradman**, 'The Don', spent his childhood and first played cricket in this very town. From Bendooley Street, you need only turn right into Boolwey Street, which will lead you straight to the **Bradman Oval**, where you may also be lucky to see a cricket game in progress: such is the importance of the oval that as well as local matches, international teams also play here on occasions. Here, you can visit the **Bradman Museum** (✆ 048-62 1247; **Open:** 7 days, 10am-4pm) in the pavilion of the oval, which also contains a large amount of cricket memorabilia of wider application, from Alan Border's helmet to a 1750s oak bat. Specifically Bradman objects include the bat he used at Headingley in 1934 to score his second highest test innings of 304. You can also undertake a short **Bradman Walk** (or drive) to see where he lived. 52 Shepherd Street and 28 Glebe Street are both nearby.

Returning to Bong Bong Street, turn right and head along the Highland Highway (Route 79) towards **Mittagong**, the last town on this itinerary. The town began between 1835 and 1860 as a group of inns servicing nervous travellers emerging from the bushranger-infested bushland. Mittagong is a pretty town with a number of gracious buildings, as a brief drive through around will reveal. From here, it is an easy drive straight onto the expressway and back to Sydney.

Accommodation

Below is a small selection of places to stay in the region, although the visitor information centres above have access to the details of many more. They can also organise reservations.

Bed & Breakfasts in Berrima include **Jellore Cottage** (Jellore St, Berrima; ✆ fax 048-83 4 001), a beautiful colonial cottage in a fragrant garden, the **Coach and Horses Inn** (Jellore St, Berrima; ✆ 048-77 1242), a sandstone cottage overlooking the river, and **Parsley Cottage** (Oxley St, Berrima; ✆ 048-77 1427) is near the old courthouse. Bowral also has a number of bed and breakfasts, such as **Bowral Cottage Inn** (22 Bundaroo St; ✆ 048-61 4157), a Victorian house offering an open fire and full, hot breakfasts with champagne, served in the conservatory. There are several luxurious Country Resorts and Guest Houses in the region, such as **Milton Park Country House** (Horderns Rd, Bowral ✆ 048-61 1522; fax 048-61 4716), a beautiful residence with forty deluxe rooms and suites surrounded by three acres of immaculate gardens, tennis courts, a croquet lawn, a heated pool, riding and golf. **Bowral Heritage Park** (9 Kangaloon Rd, Bowral; ✆ 048-61 4833; fax 048-61 4966) is another luxurious resort set in acres of gardens, offering suite accommodation with individual spas and fireplaces. The original mansion houses the lounging and dining areas, while recreational facilities include a gym, tennis, squash, swimming, bicycles and golf.

Golf

Golf is a popular pursuit in the Southern Highlands, so as well as the resorts listed above, there are a number of publicly•accessible courses. As with any course, intending golfers should ring ahead to book a tee time. The three clubs below all have clubs and buggies for hire. **Bowral Country Club & RSL** (Boronia St, Bowral; ✆ 048-61 1946; 18 holes, par 70) is a well-designed course, varying from hilly to gentle slopes. **The Highlands Golf Club** (Old Hume Highway, Mittagong; ✆ 048-71 1995; 18 holes; par 69) is said to have the best greens of the district, as well as six dams and creeks to add a bit of spice. **Moss Vale Golf Club** (Arthur St, Moss Vale; ✆ 048-68 1811; 18 holes; par 71) is a well kept, challenging and picturesque course.

CANBERRA

Description

Originally a cold, windy isolated paddock, Canberra was chosen as the site of the nation's capital in the early 1900s and was transformed by American architect Walter Burley Griffin into a meticulously planned city. Canberra is at once loved or loathed by the country's citizens; nevertheless, with the Australian National Gallery, the Science and Technology Museum, Parliament House, the embassy precinct of Yarralumla and the beautiful Lake Burley Griffin, it is a great place to spend a couple of days. Although further afield than the other day trips in this chapter (bar Antarctica), Canberra is of such significance that undertaking the two and a half hour journey down the freeway is more than worthwhile.

Starting Off & Getting There

From the City, drive west along Parramatta Road past the University of Sydney through the suburbs of Stanmore and Petersham, looking out for the large green signs pointing left for **Liverpool Road (Route 31). Turn left.** This is the beginning of the Hume Highway which will lead through many suburbs as it winds its way through Sydney's south west. Eventually, the road turns into the **South Western Freeway** (Toll $2) and continues almost all the way to Canberra. Drivers need only follow the signs. Turn-offs to the Mittagong, Berrima and Bowral area are signposted along the freeway, and this is a beautiful area to explore (See: above). Further south (another turn-off via the Old Hume Hwy) is the large town of Goulburn, traditional mid-way stopping point for Sydney-Canberra travellers. Driving into town, you will see the large jail on the right, and as the old Hume Hwy leaves the town to rejoin the freeway, you will have a beautiful view of one of the country's most aesthetically pleasing items: the pure new concrete **Big Merino**, a testament to this country's obsession with Big Things. Where the highway forks much further south, follow the **Federal Highway (Route 23; direction Canberra)** and soon after enjoy the spectacle of **Lake George** rimmed by steep mountains. On reaching Canberra, keep driving straight ahead along the same road **(Commonwealth Avenue)** and it will lead right through the city and on to its centre point: Parliament House.

Canberra can be reached by **coach** within four and a half hours, and services run regularly. Fares with Greyhound Pioneer (✆ 13 20 30; eight departures every day) for adults are $30 one-way and $54 return, and for concessions, $21 one-way and $42 return. Canberra can also be reached by **train** (Information & Bookings: Countrylink ✆ 13 22 32) from Central Station for $51.80 for adults or $25.90 for concession in first class, and for $37.80/$18.90 in second class. There are three departures a day and the journey takes five hours, travelling through the southern highlands. The station is in Kingston, a south-eastern suburb of Canberra, and passengers must then take a bus to the centre.

Information Centres

The **Canberra Tourism Commission** Visitor Information Centre (✆ 1800-026 166; fax 06-205 0776) can help with general information and accommodation by mailing a number of publications. There is a visitors centre at Northbourne Avenue, Dickson (**Open:** 7 days 8.30am-5pm).

History & Background

The limestone plains of the Canberra region were explored in the 1820s by Charles Throsby Smith, who set out to confirm Aboriginal descriptions of lands made rich by the Murrumbidgee and Molonglo Rivers in the vicinity of Lake George. These were first settled by a certain Joshua Moore, who named his property 'Canberry' after hearing the word "Kamberra" in local Aborigines' conversation meaning "meeting place" and referring to the gathering of tribes to feast on Bogong Moths. Another major settler was Robert Campbell, who had been granted land here as compensation for the wrecking of his ship, the Sydney, while under government charter. Naming his property 'Duntroon', he built a wide-verandahed, single storey cottage, surrounded by gardens which included a maze, orchard, conservatory and vineyard. Today, it is the centre of the Royal Military College of the same name. (Guided tours available April-Oct Mon-Fri at 2.30pm.) By the 1830s, large scale pastoral development had created a number of self-sufficient, but remote, settlements. One such property was Lanyon Homestead, built by John Lanyon and now fully restored (below). Life was hard on the isolated plains, and while all supplies had to come overland from Sydney, the bullock wagon 'road' linking providing access was so bad that it frequently disappeared. Prosperity and greater activity finally came in the 1860s, following the area's link to Goulburn by railway.

When Federation took place on New Year's Day 1901, Australia's separate colonies became States within one nation: a national capital was needed. It is often said that neither Melbourne nor Sydney was chosen to avoid fuelling the strong rivalry between the country's leading cities. Yet the rivalry continues to this day, probably precisely because it was not resolved at the turn of the century. However, perhaps as a partial victory to Sydney, the selection criteria stated that the seat of government should be "within the state of New South Wales and... distant not less than one hundred miles from Sydney". Over forty districts were mooted, but the choice eventually rested on the empty plain of Canberra. An international competition for a city plan was won by Chicago-based architect Walter Burley Griffin, whose plan aimed to achieve unity between landscape and civic necessities. The concept saw the site as an enormous amphitheatre formed by mountains reaching down to a stage of water. The monumental buildings required by a capital would build up to Capital Hill, and the backdrop to the whole would be the distant mountains ranges. With a large artificial lake in the centre, the city was to be geometrically radial and completely ordered. Construction progressed from 1913 through to the 1960s, during which time all of the decorative and functional buildings and monuments essential to a capital city were erected from scratch, including a temporary parliament house (1927). The current Parliament House, occupying Capital Hill, was only opened by Queen Elizabeth II in 1988.

The city is dotted with official buildings and important national institutions, such as the High Court, the diplomatic missions of Yarralumla, the National Library, National Art Gallery, many museums, and national monument, such as the National War Memorial and James Cook Memorial. Looking at Canberra today, it is amusing to consider that just over eighty years ago, none of it existed at all. The Australian National Capital is notoriously full of 'attractions' and 'things to see', so the best way to experience the city is to make your own way around the following list of 'things to do' as you please. A sightseeing itinerary around some of Canberra's most picturesque suburbs also follows.

THINGS TO SEE & DO

Australian Institute of Sport

Leverrier Cres, Belconnen (✆ 06-252 1444)

Open: 7 days at 11am & 2pm. **Cost:** $2.50/$1.50.

Here you can see where our Olympic hopefuls and elite athletes train. Hour long tours of the Institute, led by the athletes, are available daily at 11am & 2pm, leaving from the AIS shop.

Australian National Botanic Gardens

Clunies Ross St, Black Mountain (✆ 06-250 9540)

Open: 7 days 9am-5pm. **Cost:** free.

More than six thousand species fill the gardens, creating a Rainforest Gully, Rockery, Eucalypt Lawn, Mallee Shrubland, Tasmanian Garden and an Aboriginal Trail. In expressing the major types of Australian vegetation, the gardens are both worthy of a visit and an unusual delight. Strolling guides available from Visitor Information Centre.

Australian War Memorial

Anzac Parade (✆ 06-257 1068 or 243 4268)

Open: 7 days 9am-5pm/6pm in summer. **Cost:** free.

The nation's memorial to its war dead incorporates a Hall of Memory, Tomb of the Unknown Soldier and a museum documenting the participation of Australians in war by way of relics, models, paintings, photographs and film.

Calthorpe's House

24 Mugga Way, Red Hill (✆ 06-295 1945)

Open: By tour Tues-Thurs at 9.30, 11am, 1.30 & 3pm; Sat & Sun: Open house 1.30-4.30pm.

As an example of domestic history, Calthorpe's House (c. 1927) is excellent: furnishings, fixtures, appliances and personal affects have been maintained to display typical Canberra life in the early days of the city. The gardens and air raid shelter are particularly worthy of attention.

Floriade

Information: (✆ 1800-020 141) or PO Box 1119 Tuggeranong ACT 2901.

When: September to October annually. **Cost:** free.

Over half a million flowering plants are on open display each year around the city, centring on Commonwealth Park on the foreshore of Lake Burley Griffin, creating a mass of colour.

High Court of Australia

King Edward Terrace, Parkes (✆ 06-270 6811)

Open: 7 days 10am-4pm. **Cost:** free.

The High Court is the highest court in the country, and the decisions made here form precedents to be followed in the Australian law. Inside are three courtrooms and a number of offices, all centred around a huge atrium. Guides are on hand to explain the building and its function in the Australian legal system.

Mount Ainslie Lookout (842m)

Mount Ainslie Drive (NE of Lake Burley Griffin).

Open: 7 days 24 hours. **Cost:** free.

An initial orientation stop at a lookout is a good way to begin, and this one provides panoramic views of Walter Burley Griffin's 'amphitheatre'. Mount Ainslie looks straight down Anzac Parade beyond the War Memorial, across the lake to the High Court and National Gallery, and on to Parliament House: a top spot for a photo.

National Aquarium and Australian Wildlife Sanctuary

Lady Denman Dr, Scrivener Dam (6km SW of City Hill) (✆ 06-287 1211)

Open: 7 days 9am-5.30pm. **Cost:** $10/$6/$32 family.

Here you will find a comprehensive display of Australian freshwater and salt water fish as well as a large range of native wildlife species to get close to in six and a half hectares of grounds. Kangaroos are on hand to be fed and patted.

National Film and Sound Archive

McCoy Circuit, Acton (✆ 06-267 1711)

Open: 7 days 9am-5pm. **Cost:** free.

This museum houses the nation's archival collection of historical film and sound media, revealed through interactive displays, sound recordings, historic footage and historic radios.

National Gallery of Australia

King Edward Terrace (next to the High Court) (✆ 06-271 2502)

Open: 7 days 10am-5pm. **Cost:** $3. Free guided tours available from the lobby.

As well as hosting major visiting exhibitions, the gallery houses the National Art Collection which ranges from Aboriginal art, Australian colonial art, 1940s-60s Australian art, contemporary Australian art, early European art, international art, contemporary international art, Asian art, works on paper and open air sculpture gardens.

Old Parliament House

King George's Terrace, Parkes (✆ 06-270 8222)

Open: 7 days 9am-4pm. **Cost:** $2/$1/$5 family.

This building was Australia's seat of government from 1927 to 1988, and consequently is where most of the country's parliamentary history has taken place. Tours lead through the Parliamentary chambers, Kings Hall, Prime Minister's Suite, Cabinet Rooms and press gallery, while visitors can also investigate the rose gardens and regularly changing exhibitions. The building also houses the National Portrait Gallery.

Parliament House

Capital Hill (✆ 06-277 5399)

Open: 7 days 9am-5pm (later when parliament is sitting). **Cost:** free.

Canberra's focal point is a fascinating building to explore, even if it is at times completely overwhelming. However, the most interesting thing to watch is a session of Parliament in either the House of Representatives or the Senate. Tours are available.

Questacon (National Science and Technology Centre)

King Edward Terrace, Parkes (✆ 1800-020 603)

Open: 7 days 10am-5pm. **Cost:** $8/$4/$20 family.

Hundreds of highly interactive displays and exhibits spread over six, interconnected galleries make the centre a museum experience to rival all others. Each different aspect of science is explored and explained by way of a variety of items. An earthquake simulator, lightning bolt, tornado, mirror maze and countless other experiments and games captivate young and old visitors for hours, so if possible, allow half a day.

Royal Australian Mint

Denison St, Deakin (✆ 06-202 6999)

Open: Mon-Fri 9am-4pm; Sat-Sun 10am-3pm. **Cost:** free.

In the mint, visitors can track the history of Australia's coinage as well as seeing how it is made today, and can also make their very own $1 coin on the public presses.

Tidbinbilla Space Tracking Station

Paddy's River Rd, Tidbinbilla (40 minutes from the city on Tourist Drive 5) (✆ 06-201 7800)

Open: 7 days 9am-5pm (to 8pm in daylight saving). **Cost:** free.

Run by NASA, this is one of only three such tracking stations around the world, and features memorabilia of early space missions, videos and programs, models and the latest space news.

MORE THINGS TO DO: A CANBERRA DRIVE

For those who do not like the idea of running, cycling or in-line skating along the track which lines Lake Burley Griffin, a drive around the city's main attractions may appeal. One of the most pleasant ways to spend an afternoon in Canberra is to cruise the suburbs in a vaguely structured way, coming across architectural delights and tragedies. The following is a suggested itinerary.

Starting at **Parliament House**, do a circuit of Parliament Drive (inside Capital Circle) around the building. When you have gone full circle, and perhaps ventured inside to explore the building, drive back down onto Commonwealth Avenue and get onto the larger, fully encircling State Circle. Take the Perth Avenue turn-off for **Yarralumla**, turn first left into Moonah Place and soon after fork left into Turrana Street. This is the precinct where most nations have their embassies, and it is interesting to drive around the area looking at these architectural expressions of national style. In this street alone you will find the embassies of the Philippines, Sweden, the United States of America, Israel and Germany.

Next, turn left into Empire Circuit and then first right into Schlich Street, following it all the way to the end through the middle of one of the city's most desirable suburbs. Turn left into Banks Street to pass the **Forestry School**, noticing the trees and plantations of suburban woodland. If doing the drive on a weekend, fork right into Maxwell Street and then right again into Denman Street to the excellent **Canberra Antiques Centre** (Old Canberra Brickworks, end of Denman St, Yarralumla; ✆ 06-285 1432; **Open:** Sat-Sun & most long weekends 11am-5pm). The centre houses six dealers within giant, old kilns, selling a wide variety of domestic artefacts, furniture, old wares, ceramics and jewellery. The brickworks themselves were constructed between 1913 and 1916 to produce building materials for the new national capital. They ceased production in 1976, whereupon they began use as the antiques auction venue. Each easter there is an Antiques, Arts and Crafts fair, where additional exhibitors and dealers add to the permanent wares on offer.

From here, follow Denman Street to its other end, turning left into Kintore Crescent and then right onto Novar Street to cross over Adelaide Avenue. Turn left into Strickland Crescent and left again into Stonehaven Crescent, which soon afterwards turns into **Mugga Way**. Here there are several old houses with large grounds such as the National Trust's **Calthorpe's House** (above). From here, turn left into Flinders Way and left again just before the large, circular Manuka Park into **Franklin Street** for a coffee & food stop. This is the Double Bay of Canberra which feels in several ways quite cosmopolitan, except for the Canberra touch of being able to see the very ordered streets of suburbia lurking fifty metres away in either direction. Try **My Cafe** opposite the **Capitol cinema** for great soups, bagels and focaccias, **La Grange bar & brasserie** opposite, or **Rolls Choice** nearly next door (all generally **Open:** Sun-Wed 8.30am-10.30pm; Thurs-Sat 8.30am-Midnight).

From here, the northern side of **Lake Burley Griffin** beckons, so get back onto the State Circle via Canberra Avenue, skirt around Parliament House and head off over the Commonwealth Avenue Bridge, turning off onto Barrine Drive to reach **Regatta Point**. From here you have an uninterrupted view of the **Captain Cook Memorial Water Jet**! Briefly back on Commonwealth Avenue, take the Parkes Way turn-off to lead along the shore of the lake towards Anzac Parade, at the head of which stands the imposing **National War Memorial**. After reaching the end of Anzac Parade, turn right onto Fairbairn Avenue to reach Mount Ainslie Drive, a direct route up to the lookout. From here, you can survey all that you have seen and explored!

PLACES TO EAT

Barocca Cafe

Cnr Marcus Clarke St & Barry Dr, Canberra City (✆ 06-248 0253)

Lc'd and BYO. Credit: AE BC D MC V. Access.

Open: Lunch: Mon-Fri 12noon-2pm; Dinner Mon-Sat 6-9.30pm.

Full-flavoured quail risotto or perhaps an aromatic lamb curry with Moroccan lemon consistently draw in the crowds to this large, airy, glass-fronted restaurant, ensuring an energetic buzz. Next door is the less expensive lunch-stop deli, the source of great coffee, pasta and foccaccia.

Cafe Chaos

Cnr Ainslie Ave & City Walk, Canberra City (✆ 06-248 5522)

Lc'd. Credit: AE BC D MC V. Access & pavement tables.

Open: Mon-Sat 10am-10pm; Brunch Sun 10.30-3pm.

Not only does this somewhat mad corner cafe have some of the best coffee in Canberra, but the modern Mediterranean food is also great. The menu offers pizzas, salads, fresh oysters and mezze plates, as well as more substantial dishes, such as rump beef kebabs with mushrooms, or perhaps herb-crusted sardines. The cakes are pretty good too.

The Chairman and Yip

108 Bunda St, Canberra City (✆ 06-248 7109)

Lc'd and BYO. Credit: AE BC D MC V. Access.

Open: Mon-Sat 12noon-11pm; Sun 5.30-11pm.

The Chairman and Yip offers amazing dishes such as baked pork chops with spicy strawberry and bean sprouts, Vietnamese style veal hotpot, or perhaps even steamed prawn dim sum modernised with salmon roe.

Hyatt Hotel Canberra

Commonwealth Ave (✆ 06-1234) Book.

The Buffet Breakfast at the Hyatt's Promenade Cafe (7 days 7am-10.30am) is legendary, offering endless coffee or tea, juices, fruits, cereals, pastries and cooked dishes. The cost for those not staying at the hotel is $21.50 for enough food to last you all day. Equally suave is 1920s High Tea served in the piano-graced Tea Lounge or on the adjacent verandahs.

Ottoman Cuisine, The Edge & Kismet

8 Franklin St, Manuka (✆ 06-239 6754) Book.
Lc'd & BYO. Credit: AE BC D MC V. No Access upstairs.
Open: Lunch: Mon-Fri 12noon-2.30; Dinner Mon-Sat 6pm-10pm.

The Ottoman Cuisine is an extremely popular restaurant serving popular, fresh and flavoursome Turkish food. The inviting scent of lemon mingled with garlic hovers over the comfortable room, complementing the flavours of the famed char-grilled seafood platters. The empire also includes The Edge (a brasserie) and Kismet (a delicatessen and take-away) downstairs, equally good and equally popular.

The Republic

20 Allara St, Canberra City (✆ 06-247 1717)
Lc'd. Credit: AE BC D MC V. Access.
Open: Lunch: Wed-Fri from 12noon; Dinner: Mon-Sat 6pm-10pm.

This bistro is one of the capital's favourites, with an energetic yet comfortably subdued ochre interior complemented by exquisite design. The menu combines modern Mediterranean and traditional French elements, with occasional Asian influences. In other words, Modern Australian cuisine.

Tu Tu Tango

124 Bunda St, Canberra City (✆ 06-257 7100)
Lc'd. Credit: AE BC MC V. Access.
Open: 7 days 10am-late.

This is the young, funky and bright Tex-Mex/Santa Fe hot spot of Canberra, where diners can find Tasmanian salmon burritos, mash and chorizo turnovers or perhaps a south western burger. Napa Valley wines complement the menu.

The best street for cafes is **Franklin Street**, Manuka (behind Parliament House) where several establishments offer excellent coffee, great food, and a cosmopolitan atmosphere, not often discovered in these parts. Worthy of attention is My Cafe, where the coffee's strong, the soups and focaccias are delicious, and even Sydney-style black bottomed cup cakes make an appearance.

Places To Stay

There are a large number of grand hotels in Canberra. However, one of the best is the **Hyatt Hotel Canberra** (Commonwealth Ave, Yarralumla ACT 2600; ✆ 06-270 1234; fax 06-281 5998), a terribly suave, five star deluxe hotel, where it is possible to sit in deep armchairs while taking high tea to the tinkling of a piano in the elegant Tea Lounge, exercise in the glass-encased pool spa, saunas or gym, hire bicycles, play tennis and partake in mammoth buffet breakfasts. All this in an intimate and friendly 1920s Art Deco building near Lake Burley Griffin. **University House** (Cnr Balmain Cr & Liversidge St, Acton ACT 2601; ✆ 06-249 5275; fax 06-249 5252) is a cheaper option ($75-$100 per room), located in the leafy grounds of the Australian National University, and offering spacious rooms and suites. This unique building was, until recently, the domain of a few privileged academics, politicians and professionals, but after renovation and refurbishment, it now represents a great accommodation alternative. Guests also have access to University sporting facilities. **The colleges of the ANU** (Bruce Hall & Burton Hall ✆ 06-267 4700, and Burgmann College ✆ 06-267 5202) also offer accommodation for under $50. One of the cheapest options is the **Canberra YHA Hostel** (Dryandra St, O'Connor; ✆ 06- 248 9155; fax 06-249 1731), a modern and clean hostel with twin and share rooms, a well equipped kitchen and a YHA Travel Desk. The hostel's bush setting belies its proximity to the city. This is only a small selection of places to stay in the city; further information is available from the Canberra Tourism Office (above).

MYSTERY FLIGHTS

Both Ansett and Qantas operate Mystery Flights out of Sydney airport as an ingenious and eminently enjoyable way of filling spare seats. Passengers must book and pay in advance as below, and simply let the airlines surprise them as to the destination. Mystery Fliers could end up in Adelaide, in Melbourne or on Hamilton Island!

Ansett

Information & Credit Card Bookings (✆ 13 13 00); other bookings through travel agents.

Day Flights must be booked fourteen days in advance, even earlier for weekends, and cost $129 per person. Passengers must telephone at 2pm the day before travelling to find out what time they must be at the airport. The destination will only become known on boarding. Overnight Mystery Packages run only on Friday, Saturday and Sunday, and are available in either standard (Three star accommodation) ($199 per person for one night, or $259 per person for two nights) or elite (4/5 star accommodation for $229 per person for one night or $329 per person for two nights). The flight, accommodation and continental breakfast are included in the ticket. With these, ring the day prior to travel at 2pm to find out the departure time and destination. For all mystery flights, payment must be made on the spot, and the ticket cannot be changed.

Qantas

Information(✆ 13 13 13); bookings through travel agents and Qantas agents.

Day Flights should be booked between fourteen and three days in advance, and cost $119 per person.

Passengers must telephone the day prior to travel to find out the departure time and destination. Overnight Mystery Packages with Qantas are available in standard ($199 per person for one night, or $259 per person for two nights) and First Class ($229 per person for one night or $329 per person for two nights). Flight, accommodation and continental breakfast are all included in the price. These must be booked between nine and three days before travel, and passengers must ring the day before travelling for departure time and destination information. As with Ansett, payment must be made on the spot, and the ticket cannot be changed.

ANTARCTICA

Description

Unlikely as it may seem, it is possible to see the icebergs, glaciers, mountain ranges and station huts of this mesmerising continent on a day trip from Sydney on a Qantas 747-400. This is an unabashed 'flightseeing' tour, which enables a new breed of Antarctic explorers to see a great variety of the continent's landscape without getting cold, and, most importantly, without interfering with the continent's environment. Flying time for the round trip is around twelve hours, educational videos about the exploration, exploitation, wildlife and scientific research of Antarctica are played during the flight, and Antarctic experts provide a full commentary during the three and a half hours spent flying over the continent. Full on-board service is provided by the Qantas crew.

Details

When: Approximately nine tours depart each summer from late November to late January.

Cost: Three economy fares are on offer (Centre $999; Standard $1,199; Premium $1,399), as well as Business Class ($2,199) and First Class ($2,799).

Viewing: A seat rotation policy means that those with an economy standard or economy premium seats will spend half the flight in a window seat; economy centre seats are not rotated. All first and business class seats are window or aisle with no rotation. However, passengers on the flights are encouraged to share the viewing and windows (and do so), and almost everybody is up and around the plane for the majority of the flight . The aircraft flies "figure eights" over particular points of interest to allow viewing from both sides.

Information: Travel Agents will have brochures detailing the current dates and fares.

Booking: Tickets must be booked through Croydon Travel (34 Main St, Croydon, Victoria 3136; ✆ 1800-633 449; Fax 03-9723 9560) as they are the only operators in the world of such flights. They charter Qantas aircraft and crew. Bookings in advance are recommended as seats on the flights are in great (and increasing) demand.

History & Background

When thinking of Antarctica, images come to mind of extreme cold, ice, blizzards, and hapless, frostbitten explorers battling the relentlessly unforgiving continent to claim glory for their countries. The image is not without basis.

Antarctica's remoteness has excited a fascination in generations of explorers. Captain James Cook sailed south towards Antarctica in 1773, and although he did not sight land, he concluded that it must lie under the ice cap. Antarctica's existence as a continent was not confirmed until 1821, and in the years that followed, a number of explorers such as Dumont d'Urville (1790-1842), Charles Wilkes (1798-1877), Henrik Bull (b.1844) and Carsten Borchgrevink (1864-1934) took part in expeditions, the latter two being the first ever to set foot on the continent in 1895. Robert Falcon Scott (1868-1912) set out for the South Pole with four companions in 1911, arriving on 18 January 1912 to find the Norwegian flag already flying: Raoul Amundsen (1872-1928) had put it there on 14 December 1911. Ernest Shackleton (1874-1922) made his first Antarctic expedition in 1901-04, and located the South Magnetic Pole in 1906. In 1914, he commenced an ambitious expedition to traverse the continent, but his ship was crushed in ice and he was forced to cross the wild Scotia Sea to get help at South Georgia, eight hundred miles away. Sir Douglas Mawson (1882-1958) set out in 1912 to explore King George V Land, but after both his companions lost their lives, he was forced to discard all non-essential equipment, cut his sledge in half, and make the hundred mile journey to Commonwealth Bay alone, arriving to see his ship steaming away. (Luckily, five men had remained behind and he was rescued.) Richard Byrd (1888-1957) spent four and a half months alone in a small hut south of the Ross Sea in 1934. Having left his hut in minimal clothing to check the instrument shelter during a winter blizzard, he returned to find he was locked out, and desperately clawed his way in from certain death through a reinforced skylight.

Antarctica is a land of extremes. The **coldest** temperature ever recorded on Earth, -89.6°C, was recorded here at Vostok in 1983. The almost exclusively white surface of the ice cap causes much of the sun's radiation to be reflected back into space, and combined with low humidity levels in the rarified, high altitude air, there is very little opportunity for that heat to be absorbed. Consequently, the continent has an annual mean temperature of -49°C, and significantly influences world weather patterns. Antarctica is also the world's **driest** continent, with an annual amount of moisture equivalent to that falling on the Earth's hot desserts falling here, even though the continent's icecap holds up to 75% of the world's fresh water. Winds race down the coastal slopes at speeds of up to 320 kilometres an hour, earning it the reputation as the **windiest** continent on the planet. It is also the **highest**, with an average elevation of 2,300 metres (Australia's average elevation is only 340 metres), and a highest peak of 4,897 metres. Much of this is made up by the ice, which has an average thickness of 2,160 metres (4,700 metres at the thickest point). Were the ice to melt, it is estimated that the continent would eventually rise by around one thousand metres, and the planet's seas would rise by around sixty five metres.

Antarctica was once part of the great Gondwanaland super-continent located in the northern hemisphere. Forced apart by the movement of the Earth's crust, one section drifted towards the South Pole, taking with it its indigenous and developing plants such as ferns, and animal life forms, such as fresh water fish, amphibians and reptiles. In its new geographical position, exposed to months of continuous winter darkness, freezing winds roaring off the surrounding oceans, and smothered by an ice cap, Antarctica's original and early life forms eventually became extinct and are now only present as fossils. However, even after Antarctica had arrived in its present location, around three to two and a half million years ago, vegetation similar to that of Tasmania's cold temperate rainforests grew near the South Pole.

Despite a similarity in appearance, the life forms of Antarctica and the Arctic are not the same, and people are often surprised to learn that there are no polar bears here. Antarctica's marine life is rich and diverse. Krill is present in abundant quantities spread over an area four and a half times as large as that of Australia. Some Antarctic fish have no red blood cells and others contain antifreeze, enabling them to survive the extreme temperatures. Despite the hunting of over one million whales in the region this century, blue, humpback, fin and sperm whales are all still present in Antarctic waters. On land, over five hundred species of algae, one hundred and twenty five species of lichen (most growing extremely slowly) and thirty mosses have been found in continental Antarctica. Several kinds of seal live on the continent, among them Crabeater Seals, Fur Seals and the largest of all, the Southern Elephant Seals, whose adult males can grow to four and a half metres and weigh as much as four tonnes. Over one hundred million birds breed around Antarctica's rocky coastline, including three species of penguin, petrel, skuas, gulls, terns and albatross.

The Tour

It is this unique environment and its wildlife which draw scientists from Argentina, Australia, Belgium, Chile, Germany, France, Japan, New Zealand, Norway, Poland, South Africa, UK, USA and Russia, to the continent under the Scientific Committee on Antarctic Research (SCAR). The other modern day Antarctic expeditioners are tourists, many of whom have the hard work taken care for them; none more so than those of us reclining in our comfortable seats, drink in one hand and camera in the other, ten thousand feet above in a Qantas 747-400! Many have voiced concerns that the encouragement of tourist operations on the continent (let alone flying overhead in a fuel-guzzling aeroplane) is not environmentally responsible. Greenpeace International is not in fact opposed to Antarctic tourism activities, although it urges all intending tourists carefully to assess their decision to go in the context of the region's value as a pristine area practically undefiled by human impact. Before these flightseeing tours commenced, a detailed Preliminary Assessment of Environmental Impact s of tourist overflights was submitted to the Australian Antarctic Division in accordance with the Antarctic Treaty (Environment Protection) Act 1980. The results stated that such activity was "likely to have no more than a negligible impact on the environment", and imposed carefully planned operational conditions. Compared with the impact on penguin colonies and the continent caused by ground-borne tourists, airborne sightseeing is regarded as the most environmentally acceptable way for tourists to experience Antarctica. As we sip our drinks and chat excitedly to each other up in 'our' aeroplane, our senses of comfort, adventure and responsibility are reconciled.

One condition of operation is that the plane must maintain a minimum altitude of ten thousand feet (roughly three thousand metres). What can passengers expect to see from this height? How much of an Antarctic Experience does the flight really represent?

Arriving at Qantas' domestic terminal in Sydney in the early morning, several signs indicate that this will be no ordinary flight. Most conspicuous is the unusual chattiness of the passengers in the departure lounge drinking their complimentary orange juice, tea and coffee, and quizzing each other as to why they joined the tour. Some, it transpires, are here for a once in lifetime experience, some are scientists who have previously been stationed on the continent and want to share and explain their experiences with friends and family, some are here for the thrill and status factor and some to photograph, but it seems that most have one goal in common: to see the most remote continent on Earth, one of the few remaining mysteries of exploration. Everywhere else has been colonised by the human race except Antarctica. Indeed, this is the only place on Earth where humans are not indigenous. What is actually there? What does it actually look like at the end of the Earth?

The safety demonstration of how to put on a polar survival suit shows us once again that this is no ordinary flight (and that we need not have brought our thermal underwear). Taking off and flying southwards along the eastern coast of Australia, we are shown two educational videos about the wildlife and environment of Antarctica, while we eat our brunch. It becomes apparent that these are no jaded travellers when the great land mass of Antarctica first appears on the bottom of the map in the cabin. People jump up excitedly to video and photograph the map as the little red line shows our trusty plane speeding steadily towards the great unknown. A little while later, the two Antarctic experts on board bring out their expedition equipment for us all to try on. With no show of embarrassment, adults queue up to don thick insulated jackets, chunky gloves and full head protection. Most have their photograph taken. How odd (we would normally think) trying on someone else's sub-glacial gear on an aeroplane in front of three hundred strangers. But nobody seems to care; this is an Antarctic expedition, and for an Antarctic expedition, you have simply got to have the right equipment.

As we boldly go where few have gone before, our aircraft carries us surely over the 'roaring forties', 'furious fifties' and 'screaming sixties' towards the South Magnetic Pole, nearly four hours after we left Sydney. Here, the plane's compass spins and searches continuously for north, and finds it in every direction. Here too begins in earnest our expert's constant, informative and entertaining commentary. Not only do we hear about explorers, expeditions, tragedy, success, geology, history and wildlife, all coloured and illustrated with his personal experiences, but the Captain makes contact with the Australian base at Casey, whose scientists tell us about their activities.

Suddenly, the impossibly intense deep Prussian blue sea is marked by an improbable dash of white, floating innocuously on its way. Gradually, the incidence increases until delicate ice berg tongues are roped in by a fine sheen of sea ice coating the surface and catching the glinting sun. As those of us without window seats pile up against each other and blatantly invade others' seat territory, we all share the access without question. This is totally unabashed sightseeing, but the excitement of seeing Antarctica overwhelms any scruples. After all, for most of us, this is the only time we're ever going to see it apart from on a television screen. Just as we become used to these scenes of proud, silent integrity, the stark shock of the edge of the ice cap draws gasps from us all: we've reached the edge of Antarctica!

Crossing over Dumont d'Urville, 'our' captain turns a figure eight to allow both sides of 'our' plane to see this amazing sight. The shocking slash of deepest blue against purest white looks so calm down below, a stark contrast to the adversity faced by the early explorers. Tracking across glimmering waters with the appearance of Italian marbled paper, we head across the mouths of giant glaciers where the rock base beneath gives way to sea and the unimaginable weight of the ice calves massive bergs, and launches them into the sea. We fly over the ruins of Mawson's hut at Commonwealth Bay, in his words "the windiest place in the world", from which point he led the Australasian Antarctic Expedition (1911-1914) to carry out mapping and research missions, establishing the first direct radio link between Antarctica and the outside world, and reaching the roving South Magnetic Pole in 1912. We cover the same distance in only an hour, and continue beyond Fisher Bay over the Ninnis Glacier, heading inland over King George V Land.

As we cut across towards Inexpressible Island, we have glimpses of the astounding Transantarctic Mountains, which effectively carve the continent in two. Haggard, rocky peaks poke through the ice, reminding us that there is land somewhere underneath all these forms and gradations of white. Looking at our maps, issued to each of us as part of our Antarctic Information Kit, we check our progress as we happily eat our ice creams, served over the ice of course. Two hours after we first crossed over the coastline, we reach Inexpressible Island and Terra Nova Bay on the opposite side of the northern peninsula and fly a figure eight over the Italian base down below. Summoning the scientists on the radio, the Captain converses with them about their programs and experiences, and we think we hear an espresso machine gurgling in the background!

Continuing northwards along the coast (north is in just about every direction from here), we view the Admiralty Range and its highest peak, Mount Minto (4,163 metres). Near Cape Washington, we pass Mount Melbourne, a quiescent volcano still issuing steam, and a number of glaciers, to reach the Borchgrevink Coast, home of the USA-NZ base, Hallett. Continuing to Cape Adare, we fly over the site of the first landing on the Antarctic continent (1895) and the headquarters built by the Southern Cross Expedition (1898-1900), the first party to winter on the continent. It is now three hours and twenty minutes after we first crossed the edge of the ice cap, and crossing it once more, we leave Antarctica behind. We seasoned expeditioners, glancing away from our conversations, dinners and drinks, have become almost blase to the lonely icebergs we can see once more which caused so much excitement on our way south.

It really is not possible to explain logically the emotion inspired by seeing Antarctica. Perhaps it is the improbability of our having been there which joins us together in our awe struck admiration of the essentially white scene below, or our common desire to see its pristine integrity preserved. Perhaps it is the recognition of what is unknown of the only continent on Earth almost free of the impact of unchecked human population and exploitation. Perhaps it is the pure thrill of going somewhere where very few humans have been. In fact, none of us has actually been to Antarctica today, but you can't tell us that: everyone is elated. Organised with such sensitivity and dedication, this tour represents armchair travelling at its best.

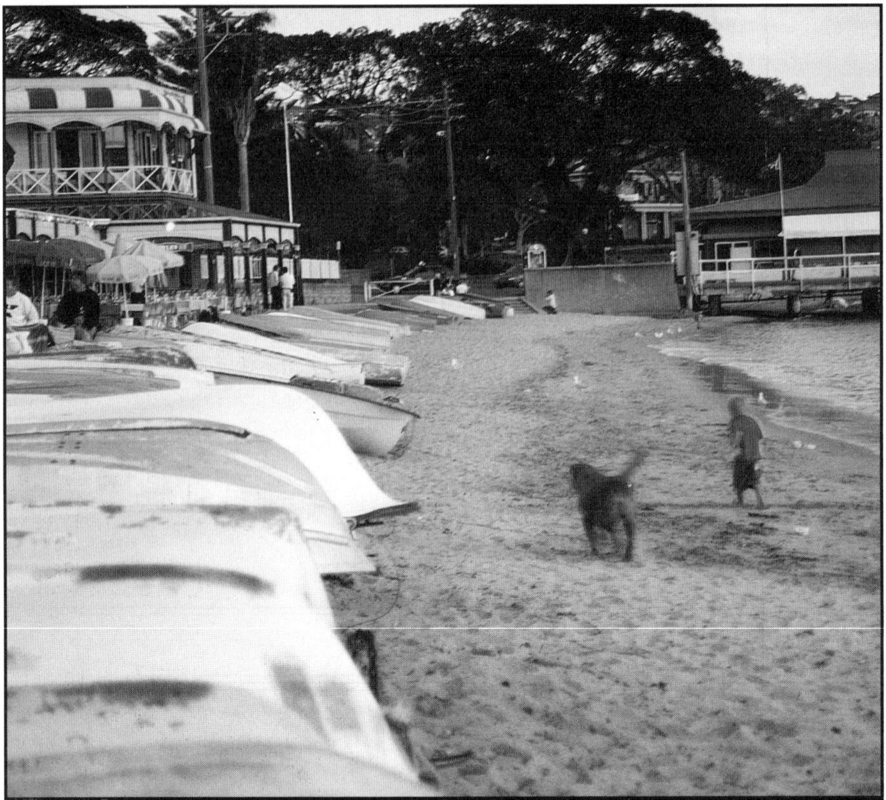

Watson's Bay

SYDNEY FOR CHILDREN

With a consistently mild climate, fresh air, large open spaces and safe streets, Sydney is a particularly child-friendly city. Many facilities are designed specifically with them in mind, and the possibilities for cheap, open air fun are endless. Many of the city's museums are highly interactive, allowing little hands to press buttons and be placed firmly on the exhibits. For this reason, the Powerhouse, Australian National Maritime and Australian museums are especially popular with children. Parks and gardens are numerous and usually have playgrounds within them, while many run specific children's holiday programs. There are also many arts institutions, puppet shows and theatres catering specifically for children around the city. Adults with accompanying children are unlikely to attract scowls in restaurants except for the very elegant establishments; nevertheless, several particularly child friendly food stops are listed here. Armed with the following information, the "I'm bored" problem should be a thing of the past.

TRANSPORT & CONCESSIONS

While most trains are two-storey, all have large areas at ground level inside the doors for passengers with baby baggage. However, the train stations mostly have steps to the platforms, so a mild struggle is almost inevitable. Buses are a little difficult, being narrow and crowded; some, but not all, have luggage areas inside.

On public transport, children under four travel for free, and those between the ages of five and sixteen travel for half price. Those over sixteen must pay full fare. School and university students qualify for public transport concessions, but only if they have a valid Concession Pass, granted on enrolment. No other card will obtain a concession fare, and while ticket inspections infrequently take place, the fines for fare avoidance are hefty ($100).

LISTINGS & NEWSPAPERS

A free newspaper, Sydney's Child (✆ 9484 5334), appears around town every month. In it, all sorts of articles and information are collated and supplemented with advertisements for various services, companies and activities. Subscriptions are available, but the paper can be picked up for free from locations such as municipal libraries and children's shops.

BASICS

Baby Equipment Hire

The Roads and Traffic Authority (RTA) requires babies to be carried in cars in capsules.

There are several companies offering nursery and baby equipment for hire (see Yellow Pages). A large, reputable and approved company is Hire For Babe: (✆ 043-55 1280), with offices in the North, Inner West, and City.

Baby Sitters And Child Minding

The Yellow Pages lists professional baby sitting organisations and companies. Hotel concierges should be able to recommend a baby sitter.

Chemist: Soul Pattinson

160 Pitt St Mall, City (✆ 9232 7166)

Open: Mon-Fri 8.15am-6pm; Thurs to 8.45pm; Sat 9.30am-5pm; Sun 11am-5pm.

Most chemists carry large ranges of baby basics such as nappies, formula and various potions. This is a particularly large and central pharmacy, although almost every suburb in Sydney has at least two chemists. Many belong to chains, such as Soul Pattinson, Amcal and Chem-Mart. The Yellow Pages has a chemist locality guide.

Children's Hospital

Hawkesbury Rd, Westmead (✆ 9845 0000; Emergency ✆ 000)

The hospital is approximately twenty-one kilometres west of the City, and just over one kilometre west of Parramatta. In an emergency, dial 000 for an ambulance.

David Jones (Elizabeth St store)

Cnr Elizabeth, Market & Castlereagh Streets, City (✆ 9266 5544)

Open: Mon-Fri 9am-6pm; Thurs to 9pm; Sat 9am-5pm; Sun 11am-5pm.

The Elizabeth Street store has baby changing facilities on the third floor, while the fourth floor is devoted to toys and children's clothing. Children's shoes are on the fifth floor.

THINGS TO DO

MUSEUMS

Several of Sydney's museums go to great lengths to engage young imaginations and curiosity. This means a hands-on, interactive approach and generally a lot of noise. Those listed below are particularly popular with little visitors, although don't forget Sydney's historic houses as well, such as Susannah Place. (For full details of the following, See: Museums.)

Australian Museum

Cnr College St & William St, City (✆ 9339 8111)

Open: 7 days 9.30am-5pm. **Cost:** $5/$3/$2; free after 4pm.

The grand Australian Museum is famous for the interesting and accessible way in which it educates visitors, especially young ones, about the natural history of Australia. Aboriginal Australia (from the Dream Time to the present day), Rituals of the Human Life Cycle, fossils, mammals, reconstructed dinosaurs and specimens make up the bulk of the museum's exhibits, while the museum shop is well stocked with topical and educational items, many of them suitable for children.

Australian National Maritime Museum

Darling Harbour (✆ 9552 7777)

Open: 7 days 10am-5pm. **Cost:** $9/$6/$4.50.

The Australian National Maritime Museum is a highly interactive museum (especially at child's-eye level) where visitors can get their hands on all sorts of things; lie in a ship's quarters; look through periscopes; experience life on a convict ship; use computer games; walk through a destroyer, complete with sirens and the sounds of loading guns; watch a simulated battle; or play a huge board game which takes players through gale force winds to test sailing skills.

Justice and Police Museum

1 Albert St, City (✆ 9252 1144)

Open: Sunday 10am-5pm. **Cost:** $5/$3/$12 family.

For slightly ghoulish children, the Justice and Police Museum displays past criminals' tools of the trade, such as truncheons, pistols, spiked metal balls and chains, and other charming homemade medieval-style weapons. The museum also incorporates a crime museum, charge room, cells, and Magistrate's Court.

Powerhouse Museum

500 Harris Street, Ultimo(✆ 9217 0111)

Open: 7 days 10am-5pm. **Cost:** $5; free first Saturday every month.

The Powerhouse is an interactive museum of decorative arts, science, technology and social history, where a broad minded acquisitions program has resulted in aeroplanes hanging from the vaulted ceiling, trams, cars (including a Bugatti), videos to talk to, films to watch and experiments to conduct. There are numerous items to play with, use and sit in, and the museum always seems to be full of little people running around and enjoying themselves.

Sydney Harbour Pylon Lookout and Exhibition

Inside Pylon of the Harbour Bridge closest to Opera House (✆ 9247 3408)

Open: 7 days 10am-5pm. **Cost:** $2/$1.

An easy walk along the Harbour Bridge and a climb up the stairs inside will lead visitors to displays of artefacts and films showing the construction and history of the bridge. The view from the top balcony looks straight onto the Harbour and passing cars below.

Sydney Observatory

Observatory Hill, The Rocks (✆ 9241 2478)

Open: Day: Mon-Fri 2pm-5pm; Sat-Sun 10am-5pm; Night: (booking essential ✆ 9217 0485) Thurs-Tues 6.15pm & 8.15pm. **Cost:** Day: free; Night: $5/$2/$12 family.

The Sydney Observatory offers a hands-on introduction to astronomy. Night time openings mean that visitors can view the skies through the telescope after an informative talk and video. Looking out to space as the friendly guides explain what it is exactly that they are looking at, children always seem to be fascinated here. Further displays chronicle the history of timekeeping.

ANIMALS

Sydney has two stunning aquaria, one at Darling Harbour, and the other at Manly. Both have clear, underwater tunnels which enables visitors to walk amongst the stingrays, sharks, little fish and seaweed. As any interaction with a shark may be rather one-sided, the interactive tradition is limited to 'feel tanks', which provide the opportunity for little (and big) hands to poke and prod patiently tolerant starfish and corals.

Sydney Aquarium

City side of Darling Harbour (✆ 9262 2300)

Open: 7 days 9.30am-9pm. **Cost:** $12/$6/under 8 yrs free.

The Sydney Aquarium offers an excellent opportunity to look at creatures of the deep close up from inside the safety of a clear tunnel walkway. Two tanks permanently moored in the Harbour are respectively inhabited by harbour marine life and exotic marine life, while feel tanks and displays inside exhibit Barrier Reef and seashore animals and their habitats.

Ocean World

West Esplanade, Manly (✆ 9949 2644)

Open: 7 days 10am-5.30pm. **Cost:** $12.50/$9/$6/$31 family.

Events: Shark feeding & performing seals (ring for details of schedule).

Manly's aquarium features sharks, jelly blobbers and other friendly items swimming over and around visitors' heads as they glide along in an underwater tunnel. However, the star of the show is the suave Giant Cuttlefish with three hearts, green blood and the ability to change colour.

Taronga Zoo

Bradleys Head Rd, Bradleys Head (✆ 9969 2777)

Open: 7 days 9am-5pm. **Cost:** $9/$4; ZooPass (return ferry, bus & zoo entry) $12.60/$5.80 available from Circular Quay.

Taronga Zoo is a large, award-winning park, stretched out over the harbourside hills where the elephants' and giraffes' accommodation comes with million dollar, panoramic views. Visitors with children are advised to take the cable car or bus on arrival by ferry from Circular Quay to the top gate, and make their way downhill through the zoo! Of particular interest to children is Friendship Farm, where they can pat lambs, fluffy ducklings and other baby animals. The zoo also houses in luxury all kinds of furry, scaly & feathery animals, and some cool seals in an enclosure which resembles Bronte Beach surf pool.

PARKS & PLAYGROUNDS

Sydney is covered with green spaces. The **Royal Botanic Gardens** are great for stretching (and exhausting) little legs, as there are ducks to feed in the central pond, the Tropical Centre pyramid to explore and a kiosk in the centre. **Hyde Park** has a fascinating fountain as well as lôts of Ibis and seagulls wandering around to chase, while **Centennial Park** offers space to ride bikes, in-line skate or to ride horses. The **Domain** has swings and a playground on Art Gallery Road in the corner closest to St Mary's Cathedral. For full details of Sydney's parks and gardens, **See:** Open Air Sydney.

The **National Parks** of the Sydney region have many educational and recreational facilities for children. Apart from the easy mangrove board walks and bushwalks around Bobbin Head and Apple Tree Bay on Pittwater to the north, the National Parks and Wildlife Service runs a co-ordinated program (especially around school holiday times) of discovery tours and activities in the National Parks in and around Sydney. For full details, See: Bushwalks.

Australia's Wonderland

Wallgrove Rd, Eastern Creek (✆ 9830 9100); 24 hour information line (✆ 9832 1777)

Open: Weekends, school holidays and public holidays 10am-5pm. **Cost:** $29.95/$21.95/children under 3 years free. Car parking $4.

The mother of all playgrounds may be a fair way out of Sydney, but many residents happily make the journey to 'play' on the tamely named roller coaster, The Demon, the Pirate Ship or perhaps the friendly-sounding Bush Beast, as well as to take advantage of the entertainment and wildlife enclosure, all of which are included in the admission price.

BEACHES

Surf beaches can be a bit scary for uninitiated children. However, **Bronte Beach** has a shallow area enclosed with large sea rocks to break the waves especially for children. **Clovelly Beach,** next along the coast to the south, is a paddler's delight: there are no waves at all in this enclosed rock cutting with a wide and very shallow sandy end. Both of these beaches also have swimming pools. **Watsons Bay,** on the Harbour, provides very calm paddling and is very popular with the kiddies (or maybe with their parents: note the beer garden next door). On the North side, **Balmoral Beach** is very calm and has a shark net, while nearby **Cobblers Beach** is a family oriented nudist beach. **Long Reef Point** offers a beach, a safe rock platform to explore, surfers, hang gliders and golfers to watch, and an easy coast stroll to do. If children swim with their parents and between the flags, they should be safe. For full details, See: Open Air Sydney.

FILM

Films suitable for children are **listed** with the rest in the Sydney Morning Herald's Metro (Friday) and in the newspaper's daily entertainment pages (for full details, See: Media).

Macquarie University (✆ 9971 6020) runs children's and family movies, including blockbusters such as 'Lassie'. Otherwise, **municipal libraries** often show children's films, as does the **State Library** in Macquarie Street, City, most often during school holidays. The most action in this respect is to be found during school holidays (January, April, July and September).

Censorship ratings are: G (general exhibition); PG (parental guidance recommended); M (for mature audiences 15yrs+); MA (under 15yrs not allowed in); R (restricted to adults 18+).

THEATRE & CIRCUS

Permanent children's theatres are hard to find, although a number do exist in Sydney.

Marian Streeters Children's Theatre

Marian St Theatre, Killara (✆ 9452 2139)

Seasons of theatre dedicated to children (generally between three and nine years old) feature performances such as 'Sleeping Beauty', 'Albert the Dragon' and 'Fairytale Fantasy'. They usually run during the school holidays.

JAM theatre

Information (✆ 9764 4805 or 9823 3222)

JAM stages performances throughout the year in different locations, usually parks or public spaces. Past productions have included 'The Toymaker' with original, live music, Australian animal characters, magic spells and trolls in Centennial Park, and 'Charlotte's Web'. It is best to ring to find out what's on when, as JAM is most active during school holidays.

The Rocks Puppet Cottage

Kendall Lane, The Rocks (✆ 9241 2902)

Open: Sat-Sun with performances at 11am, 12.30pm, 2pm & 3.30pm; more often during school holidays.

With their collection of handmade marionettes, shadow, arm and rod, and glove puppets, the cottage stages half hour shows which never fail to delight the young audiences.

Circus Oz

Undoubtedly the best circus in Australia is Circus Oz, which travels around the country and usually arrives in Sydney during January's Sydney Festival, and setting up near the SCG. The newspapers' entertainment pages will have details and advertising of performances.

ACTIVITIES

Sports

The Australian **Sailing** School (✆ 9960 3077) runs five day camps teaching children (and adults) how to sail, including all the relevant theory. The Anchorage Sailing School (✆ 9979 5877; fax: 9997 1324) has learn to sail courses and classes for mother/son and father/daughter pairs. Outward Bound (✆ 9261 2200 or 008-267 999) is a famous and established organisation spanning twenty-three countries. Outward Bound runs a variety of courses for adults and families, as well as excellent adventures for twelve to sixteen year olds, teaching bushcraft, meal planning, water activities such as rafting and canoeing, rock climbing and abseiling. They also run a Marine Course teaching sailing techniques on their hundred foot schooner (that's a big beer), Challenge of Outward Bound.

A number of companies offer **children's sports programs** and gym classes; one to investigate is Kidsports (✆ 9418 9222). There are many organisations and stables providing riding courses and camps. One such is Otford Farm Trail Rides (✆ 042-941 296), which has in the past offered week-long camps for children between the ages of eight and sixteen, in which they feed and groom the horses, milk the cows, do sporting activities and toast marshmallows over a campfire. For those who want to learn to **in-line skate** with a pack of like-minded and like-skilled people, Manly Blades (✆ 9976 3833) run holiday programs especially for this! **Tennis Camps** (and their advertising) can be found all over Sydney during the school holidays. **Cricket Coaching Camps** (✆ 9955 8306) are regularly held during school holidays at Riverview and Barker schools, where children can begin their ascent into cricket stardom. This group has in the past boasted among its coaches Tony Grieg, Ian Chappell, Doug Walters, Brian Taber, Greg Chappell, Barry Knight, Len Pascoe, David Colley and Jeff Thomson!

Visual and Performing Arts

Many centres around Sydney offer art classes for children. One particularly well known establishment is the Workshop Art Centre in Willoughby (✆ 9958 6540), which offers art and craft courses for four to eleven year olds.

Local councils will be able to provide information on performing arts classes and courses taking place throughout the year in their administrative area. TAFE-run classes in drama, dancing, singing and many other activities for children throughout the year. Two independent centres with established reputations include the St Laurence Arts Centre (505 Pitt St, Sydney; ✆ 9212 6000) and the Sydney Theatrical Centre (2 Ennis Rd, Milson Point; ✆ 9922 4455). The latter has been offering training in all performance arts for four to eighteen year olds since 1979.

Holiday Programs

Many public bodies and community centres organise holiday and term time programs for school children.

Royal Botanic Gardens (✆ 9231 8134)

The Royal Botanic Gardens' programs provide children with fascinating science workshops, art workshops, walks, scavenger hunts and topical storytelling.

Mosman Community Centre

Cnr Short St & Myahgah Rd, Mosman (✆ 9968 2869)

This group runs baby ballet, playgroups, pre-school music, kindy gym, languages and after school classes in a range of disciplines, such a Tai Kwon Do, chess and basketball.

Sydney Opera House Bennelong Program Plus

Sydney Opera House, Bennelong Point, City (✆ 9250 7777)

The Opera House program offers an introduction to orchestral music for six to twelve year olds, usually run during school holidays.

Taronga Zoo

Bradleys Head Rd, Bradleys Head (✆ 9969 2777)

The education office of the zoo co-ordinates engrossing holiday programs involving the children in the lives of the animals, craft projects, zoo administration and many other animal-related activities.

EATING

Being accompanied by children doesn't mean parents need to resort to fast food & grease mega-chains. Most restaurants listed in the chapters Cafes and Food will welcome restaurant-friendly children into their dining rooms, and will generally not stoop to service with a snarl unless the small diner begins flinging spaghetti Bolognese into orbit around the room. However, if a listing says book, this indicates a degree of formality in the establishment, and intending diners should ask about children when reserving a table.

Almost without exception, any **Chinese** restaurant, particularly in Chinatown and especially at Yum Cha time, will welcome children. The **Centennial Park Cafe** has a separate children's menu and welcomes little patrons. **Gourmet Pizza Kitchens** also welcome children, and have high chairs. **Doyles** at Watsons Bay do have a (pricey) children's menu, although their fish and chips outlet on the jetty next door has equally good and much less expensive food. **Mohr Fish** (Surry Hills) welcomes children constantly. Also remember that much of Sydney's best and inexpensive food is found in informal cafes, and here, children are almost always welcome. **Cafe Niki** (Surry Hills), **Cafe Crown** (Darlinghurst), and **Dov** (Darlinghurst) are a few to consider.

Particularly child-friendly **cafes** are **The Chocolate Factory** (Paddington) with its very friendly staff, great cakes and counter full of sweets; **The Black Wattle Canteen** (Glebe) with its calming views, kid sized dishes and commitment to serving babycino (milk froth minus the coffee); and the **Bathers' Pavilion Refreshment Room** (Balmoral Beach) for its paddling paradise beachside location and patiently calm staff. However, most cafe staff's patience depends on the behaviour of the children involved.

STUDENTS

The dirty jeans and smelly shoes brigade appear to be everywhere, and Sydney is certainly no exception. There are currently over one hundred and twenty-five thousand students at Sydney's major tertiary institutions alone. However, they may appear a little younger than in other countries. With an average school leaving age of seventeen, no military service, and most undergraduate courses taking only three years to complete, it is possible to be in and out of university by the age of twenty-one. The result is an unusually young and energetic band of students feeling either as though they are still at school and disinterested in campus politics, or unusually young, vaguely rebellious and energetic students determined to protest against everything, join every action group and discover themselves in the process. Although the Vietnam War gave urgency and necessity to student response in Sydney, prompting debates and demonstrations against the war and conscription (introduced in 1964), the halcyon era of student activism has passed. Causes taken up since then have largely concentrated on environmental concerns and government-student-university funding relations.

Student accommodation generally consists of privately rented flats and houses residential colleges within the universities. The latter can be expensive and can verge on the luxurious: some colleges even have maids to clean the students' rooms. However, a large number of students live at home. One of the reasons for this is the government study allowance, Austudy. It is not available to all, as qualification is partly based on means testing parents' assets until the age of 23, by which time many have finished university. Every student must pay HECS, the Higher Education Contribution Scheme, on a course by course basis. This frequently runs into the upper reaches of between $1000 and $2000 a year.

THE MAJOR UNIVERSITIES

Macquarie University

Balaclava Rd, North Ryde (✆ 9850 7111)

Set among the gum trees in the far north of the city, Macquarie University looks the picture of absolute calm; yet, the centre of the city's student activity lurks under the surface. While management, business and science courses form the core of the university, the students take advantage of the many leisure facilities on and around the campus, not least the subsidised bars.

University of New South Wales (UNSW)

Anzac Parade, Kensington (✆ 9385 1000)

Founded in the 1960s, the UNSW has acquired an excellent reputation not only for practical and modernised legal education, but also for NIDA, the national drama institute for which annual auditions are heavily oversubscribed.

University of Sydney

Parramatta Rd, Camperdown (✆ 9692 2222)

The University of Sydney is the city's, and indeed Australia's, oldest university. Largely characterised by golden sandstone Gothic buildings, its large grounds provide places to lie in the sun much more tempting than attending the often large and anonymous lectures. The central quadrangle, with its famous Jacaranda tree, houses the administration and some lecture halls, while the medical, education, sciences, languages and humanities faculties are spread over the sprawling campus. It even has its own postcode.

University of Technology (UTS)

1 Broadway, Ultimo (✆ 9330 1990)

UTS started life as the Institute of Technology and grew over the years to become one of the most highly regarded learning institutions in the city. Some would say that this is where the really useful courses are: the marketing, communications and visual arts diplomas and degrees are among the most highly esteemed and practice-oriented programs available.

INFORMATION

Universities Admissions Centre (UAC)

3 Rawson St, Auburn (✆ 9330 7200)

This central, administrative body governs the applications and placements of students in the various courses at all of the State's universities and colleges. All information regarding courses, qualifications, applications and enrolments can be obtained from the individual universities' Student Centres.

UNIVERSITY & STUDENT BOOKSHOPS

Co-op Bookshop

Head Shop: 80 Bay St, Broadway (✆ 9212 2211) General, text and medical.

University of New South Wales: Quadrangle Building (✆ 9663 4024)

University of Sydney: Transient Building (✆ 9692 8666)

UTS: 3 Broadway, Ultimo (✆ 9212 3078)

The Co-op bookshops give a healthy discount to anyone who takes out membership; the fee usually pays for itself within a couple of visits. As well as a wide selection of literature titles, the Co-op stocks prescribed texts for all faculties within each institution. They are simply great places to browse.

For second hand bookshops, See: Shopping. There are also numerous specialist bookshops around Sydney, all of which are listed in the Yellow Pages.

BARS & PUBS

Students and subsidised alcohol are at best an ugly mix. Each university has subsidised bars; you can visit them if you like, although happy hour may resemble a war zone. Pubs in surrounding areas are a slightly more restrained and possibly more suave way to do one's student drinking, and while the universities act as a magnet in attracting watering holes, some are better than others.

UNIVERSITY OF NEW SOUTH WALES

UNSW is at the centre of a disappointingly sparse scene.

Squarehouse Union Bar

The Squarehouse, UNSW (✆ 9663 9184)

Open: Mon-Fri 12noon-Midnight during semester.

The Squarehouse bar hosts the usual collection of students enjoying cheap beer, highlighted by bands, dance music and Oktoberfest celebrations.

Coogee Bay Hotel

Cnr Coogee Bay Rd & Arden St, Coogee (✆ 9665 0000)

Open: Mon-Sat 9am-3am; Sun 10am-10pm.

The Coogee Bay Hotel is also the home of the fabled Selina's Night club. For details of this sprawling complex, See: Pubs.

The Regent

418 Anzac Parade, Kensington (✆ 9663 2248)

Open: Mon-Sat 10am-3am; Sun 10am-10pm.

The most popular of the pubs surrounding UNSW, The Regent's public bar offers pool competitions, darts competitions and a wide range of beers on tap. The Circus Bar is the pub's hot spot, hosting alternately a nightclub, band venue and pool venue in a circus interior.

UNIVERSITY OF SYDNEY

Wentworth Bar

Wentworth Building, City Road (✆ 9660 1355)

Open: Mon-Fri 12noon-8pm during semester.

A large bunch of engineers make up the stable clientele at this subsidised union bar, where a sometimes ugly display of humanity is on view: happy hour can explode into a war of schooner sized plastic cups emptied of their cheap beer. Consistently popular.

Manning Bar

Manning House, Manning Rd (✆ 9563 6122)

Open: Mon-Fri 12noon-8pmduring semester; occasional weekends.

Manning House is full of surprising sub-cultures, not least those located around the bar. Local and overseas bands play regularly to large crowds, not only students, and bring the scene to life. Again, the effect of the cheap plastic schooners is a sight to see.

The Alfred Hotel

51 Missenden Rd, Camperdown (✆ 9557 2216)

Open: Mon-Sat 11am-3am; Sun 12noon-10pm.

Just over the road from the hospital which, apart from many other functions, has an intensive de-tox unit frequently used by students of the university's nearby colleges, The Alfred is very popular for its walled and roll-back-roofed beer garden at the rear.

The Annandale

17 Parramatta Rd, Annandale (✆ 9550 1078)

Open: Mon-Sat 10am-Midnight; Sun 12noon-10pm.

This is the major music venue near the University of Sydney. For full details, See: Pubs.

The Excelsior

101 Bridge Rd, Glebe (✆ 9660 7479)

Open: Mon-Sat 11am-Midnight; Sun 12noon-10pm.

In the centre of the residential area of Glebe is the Excelsior, a hot spot where free 'champagne' for the 'ladies', schooners for the price of middies, Trivia nights, half price cocktails and happy hours make an unbeatable line up.

The Nag's Head

St John's Rd, Glebe (✆ 9660 1591)

The Nag's Head is a great pub, and usually attracts more subdued students to its roof beer garden, excellent bistro, and Guinness on tap. For details, See: Pubs.

CHEAP TICKETS

How far a **student card** can go and how much it can get depends largely on the benevolence of the person behind the ticket window. While some insist on the official cinema card to obtain concession tickets, others are happy to accept international student identification cards or university student cards. Other cheap options exist for specific **cinemas:** The Valhalla has $6 tickets if you buy a book of five; the Academy Twin also has a similar deal. The **Opera House** box office is used to foreign students flashing obscure student cards at them to obtain the excellent value student rush tickets to the opera ($20) and orchestral concerts (from $10), available half an hour before performances. Queue up to the right of the box office windows. **Theatres, other Concerts and venues** are also broad-minded about student cards, and generous concessions are available for most performances. It is always worth asking! Travel on **public transport** at concessional rates is only available with the specific NSW Public Transport concession card issued on enrolment. While ticket inspections are infrequent, the fine for fare avoidance is around $100.

UNIVERSITY LIBRARIES

Fisher Library

University of Sydney (✆ 9692 2993)

Open: Mon-Fri 8.30am-8pm; Sat 9am-5pm; Sun 1pm-5pm.

Fisher library apparently contains the largest book stack in the Southern Hemisphere, and at fifteen storeys, it looks like it. Add to this large collections of music scores and research data bases, and it is a great institution. Specialised faculty libraries are located around campus.

UNSW Library

University of New South Wales (✆ 9385 2667)

Open: Mon-Fri 8am-10pm; Sat-Sun 12noon-5pm.

This is the main library of the university, operating in conjunction with the specific faculty libraries around campus.

SYDNEY FOR DISABLED VISITORS

This chapter contains practical information which may be required by disabled visitors to Sydney. It also indicates where to obtain further particulars and detailed access maps. The comprehensive book published by ACROD, Accessing Sydney, is the best source of information for this purpose.

USEFUL PUBLICATIONS & ORGANISATIONS

Access Committees

Most municipal councils around Sydney have Access Committees, which can assist with information regarding access and services in their particular areas. For central Sydney, contact Sydney City Council (✆ 9265 9338).

ACROD: Accessing Sydney

55 Charles St, Ryde NSW 2112 (✆ 9809 6517; TTY 9809 4488)

This is the State association co-ordinating providers of disabled services, and is literally a mine of information. Accessing Sydney is a comprehensive access guide published by ACROD and available from bookshops and libraries. It features complete access details and specifications of facilities and services all over Sydney, from the functional to the frivolous.

Directory of Disability Information Services in New South Wales

This is available from DINA (✆ 9230 1540; TTY 9230 1541; fax 9232 4816).

Easy Access Guide

Details of ramps, lifts and toilets of the train system available from all CityRail ticket offices.

Getting Around the City of Sydney

This mobility map, available from the Council of the City of Sydney (Town Hall House, Sydney Square NSW 2000; ✆ 9265 9027; fax 9265 929), details the best ways to get around the city centre.

Outdoor Access for Everybody

This publication details access to New South Wales' various National Parks, and is available from the National Parks and Wildlife Service (✆ 9585 6333 or 9585 6555).

PRACTICAL BASICS

Emergencies

Telephone: Police, Fire, Ambulance (✆ 000)

TTY: Police (✆ 9211 3776), Fire (✆ 9690 111), Ambulance (✆ 9211 3048)

24 Hour Pharmacy (✆ 9438 3333)

24 Hour TTY Relay Service

Deaf Society of New South Wales (✆ 9633 9718)

This enables communication with a non-TTY telephone user.

EQUIPMENT HIRE AND REPAIRS

Audio Loops

SHHH Hearing Resource Centre (TTY/✆ 9447 586)

Baby Capsules

BC Hire, Mona Vale (✆ 9997 4602)

Jumping Jacks Playtime, Mosman (✆ 9960 4602)

Electric Wheelchairs and Scooters

Bee Technical Services (25 Broderick St, Camperdown; ✆ 9953 0303; fax 9953 9191)

Bee can also carry out repairs, supply spare parts and supply power converters for international visitors' powered wheelchairs.

Manual wheelchairs are available for hire from:

Barrere Surgical Co (55 Wentworth St, City; ✆ 9281 0511; fax 9281 0711)

Exercise Equipment Australia (368 Eastern Valley Way, Chatswood; ✆ 9417 5100)

Gillespies Hire and Sales (13 Elizabeth St

Artarmon NSW 2064; © 9419 2081 or 9413 3616)
Wheelchair repairs can be done by bicycle shops such as:
Clarence St Cyclery (104 Clarence St, City; © 9299 4057).

TRANSPORT

Trains

It has taken many years to realise that train stations with flights of stairs are not accessible to everyone. Consequently, development of an 'Easy Access' network has been started, although at this stage it is limited: Circular Quay is actually the only central station in the scheme already fully operational, while Central and St Leonards have ramps suitable for wheelchair use. Until the Easy Access system is in operation, CityRail suggests that disabled travellers telephone the relevant station prior to their journey so that the staff can assist with access, and travel during off peak times (9am-4pm) to avoid the crowds.

Free suburban bus, ferry and rail travel, as well as concessional rates on country travel, are available to visually impaired passengers. In addition, seeing eye or hearing dogs travel free.

Buses

Only a limited number of kneeling buses are operational, for example on the Airport Express routes (See: Transport). Standard buses are not accessible to those using wheelchairs.

Ferries

Sydney ferries are accessed by unstable ramps from the jetty. The Manly ferries, being the largest in the fleet, have wide level entrances to the bottom level. Sydney Ferries suggest that those using wheelchairs should contact them before travelling (© 9956 4670 or 9256 4672), and ask wharf staff for assistance.

Taxi

Multi-purpose taxis (with raised ceilings and hoists) operate all round the city through a central booking number (© 1800 043 187 or 9339 0200). Subsidies for residents are available for taxi use on application (consult ACROD, above). Ordinary taxis can be ordered or hailed in the street (See: Transport).

CAR HIRE

Two major car hire companies have hand controlled vehicles available. For all other hire vehicles, See: Transport.

Avis Australia Car Rental

214 William St, Kings Cross 2011 (© 9353 9000; toll free 1800 225 533; fax 9353 9090)

Automatic cars ranging from hatches to large sedans can be fitted with hand controls at no extra cost. Bookings must be made seven days in advance through the Kings Cross office.

Hertz Rent a Car

Cnr William St & Riley St, Sydney 2000 (© 9360 6621; fax 9360 5145)

Also at: Sydney Airport (© 9669 2444 or 9693 5829).

Hertz can only fit automatic station wagons with hand controls. Bookings must be made in advance through either of the above offices.

City Parking

Concessional rates are available at the following parking stations in the City:
Domain Parking Station (© 9232 6944)
Kent St Parking Station (© 9265 9124)
Goulburn St Parking Station (© 9212 1533)

Street parking for drivers displaying the disabled sticker is available all over Sydney in reserved spaces, designated by a bright blue sign with a white wheelchair on it.

LEISURE

Details of access to restaurants, cafes, cinemas (including hearing help) and theatres are included with each entry in the relevant chapters. However, the city's swimming facilities merit special attention here.

Of the city's beaches, **Clovelly** is the most accessible. A gradual ramp leads to a wooden platform over the calm water in a long rock cutting, which is sheltered from the waves by a wall of rocks. **Bronte** beach has a beautiful surf pool with metal rails to facilitate access; there are reserved parking spaces nearby and ramp access from the road to the pool. Several **swimming pools** around Sydney are fully accessible. In the Western Suburbs, the **Sydney International Aquatic Centre** at Homebush Bay (© 9752 3666) has seven hoists around the main pool and further ramps and hoists for the other pools. On the North Shore, **Willoughby Leisure Centre** (© 9958 5799; fax 9958 0189) has hoists as well as ramps to the changing rooms. For full details of these centres, See: Sports: Swimming.

For details of other sporting facilities, **Disabled New South Wales Sports Council** (State Sports Centre, Homebush Bay; © 9763 0155; fax 9746 3224) is the best association to consult.

GAY SYDNEY

Every February, the Gay and Lesbian Mardi Gras Festival revs into life with several weeks of events culminating in the world famous, jaw-droppingly extroverted and, for some, eye-opening Mardi Gras parade. East Sydney stands still as thousands of people cram the streets to watch and cheer the bizarre floats and dance in the streets to join in the celebration of this important aspect of the city's community. This chapter contains an outline of Sydney's gay services and social scene. Current details can be found in the publications listed below.

BACKGROUND

Many international visitors are convinced that Sydney's gay scene is the most happily open and accepted anywhere in the world. However, it was not always so. As homosexuality was still classified as a criminal offence in New South Wales in the 1970s, it took the work of several politicised groups to pressure the government of Neville Wran to implement anti-discrimination legislation, and instigate a corruption clean-up of the few gay bars and clubs that were in operation in Kings Cross. 1978 saw the first small Mardi Gras parade to commemorate the Stonewall Inn uprising, widely considered to be the origin of the gay rights movement, but ended in riot when a bevy of police and paddy wagons turned up uninvited. Subsequent demonstrations only fostered widespread vilification.

The metamorphosis from covert to overt continued as the community gradually took over lower Oxford Street around Darlinghurst. Clubs, pubs, restaurants and shops opened, and in turn attracted more gay residents to the area. As community activity increased in the 1980s, the Mardi Gras gathered momentum with the appointment of a co-ordinating body and a decision to concentrate on celebratory rather than political concerns. Gay culture received a boost from the establishment of the Sydney Star Observer, the city's first gay newspaper, to which the task soon fell of providing up to date information on the AIDS dilemma. After the death of Gay Olympian Bobby Goldsmith was publicly acknowledged as AIDS-related (1984), a fund set up by relatives and friends to care for him in his last months was transformed into the Bobby Goldsmith Foundation, today the largest HIV/AIDS charity in Australia.

However, despite increasing acceptance of the community by society at large, some remained adamantly against it. Fred Nile and his Call to Australia party still continues to campaign against what they regard as the vice and lasciviousness of the community. The 1990s have so far been dominated by debate about labelling, representation, and participation in gay events by those who are not part of the gay community. While the original agenda has largely been met, legal recognition of gay partnerships in the realm of superannuation and succession law is still to be gained.

Politics aside, what most Sydney residents see is the overactive so-called 'Pink Precinct' stretching over the original community areas: Darlinghurst, Surry Hills, Paddington and Newtown. These days, the Mardi Gras serves as a celebration of gay pride and to raise the profile of the remaining reform goals. The community is both visible, vocal and largely supported; the scene is positively jumping.

PUBLICATIONS, INFORMATION & COMMUNITY

Accommodation

As is to be expected of the most active gay city in the Southern Hemisphere, accommodation operators are generally both aware of the value of the gay market, and polite and friendly to gay guests: the two usually go together. However, a couple of specifically gay hotels are in operation, concentrated in Darlinghurst, Paddington and Surry Hills. Demand is greatest in

February, during the Mardi Gras festival.

For long term accommodation, try **Share Space** (263 Oxford St, Paddington; ✆ 9360 7744; fax 9360 4818; **Open:** 7 days 10am-7pm; 24 hour current listings and prices ✆ 9361 0590), who use a database to assist personality compatibility. Short term needs may be met by **The James Hotel** (86 Flinders St, Darlinghurst; ✆ 9380 6633; fax 9380 5016), a specifically gay and lesbian luxury boutique hotel where facilities include a swimming pool, bars, lounges and regular social events. **Sydney Star Accommodation** (275 Darlinghurst Rd, Kings Cross; ✆ 015-22 8444) bills itself as a "gay friendly" and stylish pensione, and offers single, twin and double suites, each with kitchen and television, in a security building.

Help

The **Gay & Lesbian Counselling Service of NSW** (✆ 9360 2211 or 008 805 379; Open: 7 days 4pm-midnight) is a phone advice, information, counselling and referral service operated by trained counsellors. **Police** (Dial 000) at 222 Australia Street, Newtown and 151 Goulburn Street, Surry Hills are both staffed with Gay Liaison Officers attached to them.

Publications

Sydney's major publications concerned with serious, political and frivolous gay issues are *The Sydney Star Observer* and *Capital Q Weekly* (which also includes the Xtra arts guide). Both are free and available from Ariel Booksellers (Oxford St, Paddington); inside the George St doors of the Museum of Contemporary Art (City); and most gay social venues (See: below).

Travel Agents

A number of travel agencies are particularly geared to service the community. Silke's Travel
(636 Oxford St, Darlinghurst; ✆ 9380 6244; fax 9361 3729) is able to offer advice and help with accommodation, the community and activities. They also have a useful Sydney map full of addresses and services for gays.

What's On

There are two recorded what's on lines currently operating in Sydney. Gay & Lesbian Information Line (✆ 9361 0655) is theoretically accessible twenty-four hours a day. The Lesbian Line (✆ 9550 0910) is staffed on Fridays between 6pm and 10pm, while recorded information is available at all other times. It is best to pick up a copy of one of the newspapers above.

The **Gay Calender** usually begins with an enormous New Year's Eve dance party. February sees Shop Yourself Stupid and the beginning of the month-long Mardi Gras Festival of concerts, theatre, exhibitions, sporting events, and March, the Mardi Gras parade. Sleaze Ball is the next big event of the year, usually held in October.

LEISURE: CLUBS, PUBS & VENUES

The area around Taylor Square is where many gay clubs and venues are found, although most in Sydney would be very quiet if they didn't welcome gays.

The Albury Hotel

6 Oxford St, Darlinghurst (✆ 9361 6555)

Open: Mon-Thurs 2pm-1am; Fri-Sat 2pm-2am; Sun 2pm-12 midnight.

The Albury is perhaps the best known and most popular social scene in Sydney's gay community, where meeting, socialising, drinking and riotous entertainment (often drag shows) draw in enormous crowds. The Albury is an icon.

The Oxford Hotel & Gilligan's

Cnr Oxford St & Bourke St, Taylor Square (by the paper stand) (✆ 9331 3467)

Open: Mon-Fri 5pm-2am; Sat-Sun 5pm-3am.

Gilligan's is a class act with a cocktail menu boasting a long list of luscious drinks, engulfing sofas and an often fascinating spectacle: it consistently attracts exquisitely dressed drag queens among its clientele. Down on the ground floor, dance music pumps with the beer, as this hot spot revs into life.

There are many other gay social venues around Sydney. These include **Bank Hotel** (324 King St, Newtown; ✆ 9557 1280; **Open:** Mon-Thurs 10.30am-1.30am; Fri-Sat 10.30am-4am); **Beauchamp** (267 Oxford St, Darlinghurst; ✆ 9331 2575; **Open:** Mon-Tues 12noon-Midnight; Wed-Sun 12noon-1am); **The Beresford** (354 Bourke St, Surry Hills; ✆ 9331 1045; **Open:** Mon-Wed & Sun 12noon-Midnight; Thurs 12noon-1am; Fri-Sat 12noon-3am) **The Courthouse** (Cnr Oxford St & Bourke St, Taylor Square; ✆ 9360 4831; **Open:** 7 days, 24 hours); **Imperial Hotel** (35 Erskineville Rd, Erskineville (✆ 9519 9899; **Open:** Mon-Wed & Sun 9.45am-3am; Thurs 9.45am-5am; Fri-Sat 9.45am-8am); **Newtown Hotel** (174 King St, Newtown; ✆ 9557 1329; **Open:** Mon-Sat 11am-12 midnight; Sun 11am-10pm); and **Taylor Square Bar** (L2 Cnr Oxford St & Flinders St, Taylor Square; & 9360 5828; **Open:** 7 nights 6pm-3am). More are bound to appear, so check the social pages of the newspapers above.

FOOD

Exclusively gay restaurants are very scarce; however, there are regularly more gays than straights in the eateries of the original Golden Mile along **Oxford Street, Darlinghurst,** and **King Street, Newtown** (See: Food). One establishment right at the centre of the Darlinghurst scene is the very popular **Cafe 191** (191 Oxford St, Taylor Square; ✆ 9360 4295; **Open:** 7 days 8am-around 12.30am), where a predominantly gay clientele enjoy zesty food and copious amounts of coffee. For a broad spectrum listing of Sydney's restaurants and cafe food scene, **See: Food.**

A ~ Z PRACTICAL BASICS

AIRLINES & AIRPORT INFORMATION

All the international airlines servicing Australia have offices in the City. Their numbers can be obtained from the telephone directories or from directory inquiries (✆ 013).

The two major domestic airlines operating in Australia are the domestic arms of Ansett Australia (32 Martin Place, City; ✆ 352 6444) and QANTAS (Cnr Hunter St & Philip St, City; ✆ 13 13 13).

Recorded information regarding international and domestic flights is updated regularly (✆ 0055 51850).

BANKS, MONEY & CREDIT CARDS

There is no limit on the amount of currency visitors can bring into Australia, although all money above $5,000 must be declared. The **Australian Dollar** ($AUD; made up of 100 cents) is the Australian currency. Notes are issued in $5, $10, $20, $50 and $100 values; coins in 5c, 10c, 20c, 50c, $1 and $2.

Most **credit cards** are widely accepted in Sydney, although MasterCard and Visa are the most popular. Almost all shops accept American Express, Bank Card, Diners Club, JCB, MasterCard, and Visa. In addition, Eftpos (Electronic Funds Transfer at Point Of Sale) allows users whose credit cards are linked to bank accounts to debit them directly and by-pass their credit accounts.

The major **Australian banks** and their city locations are as follows. **Banking hours** are from 9.30am to 4pm Monday to Thursday, and 9am to 5pm on Friday.

ANZ: 275 George St, City (✆ 9290 0700)
Commonwealth Bank of Australia (CBA): Corner Pitt St and Martin Place, City (✆ 13 22 21)
National Australia Bank (NAB): 343 George St, City (✆ 13 22 65)
State Bank of New South Wales: 52 Martin Place (✆ 13 18 18)
Westpac Banking Corporation: 341 George St, City (✆ 9260 6666)

See: Currency Exchange, below.

BOOKING & INFORMATION OFFICES

Before You Go

The **Australian Tourist Commission** operates a number of **Helplines** around the world, which are intended to help organise a trip to Sydney and New South Wales. They can also direct you to your nearest "Australian Specialist" travel agent. They are:

Asia: Hong Kong (✆ 852 802 7817); Singapore (✆ 65 250 6277; trade: 852 802 7817)
Europe: Frankfurt (✆ 069 274 0060; trade 069-274 00621); Paris (✆ 1 45 79 80 44); Rome (✆ 06 329 3697); Zurich (✆ 01 920 3310)
Japan: Tokyo (✆ 03 3585 0707; trade: 03 3585 0659)
New Zealand: Auckland (✆ 09 302 7721)
United Kingdom: London (✆ 0181 780 2227)
United States of America and Canada: Chicago (✆ 708 296 4900); Los Angeles (800 433 2877)

In Sydney

Halftix Kiosk

Martin Place, City (✆ 0055 26655; **Open:** Mon-Fri 12noon-5.30pm; Sat 10.30am-5pm).
Half price tickets to various theatres and events available on the day.

National Parks & Wildlife Information Centre
Cadman's Cottage, 110 George St, The Rocks (✆ 9247 8861; **Open:** Mon 10am-3pm; Tues-Fri 9am-4.30pm; Sat-Sun 11am-4pm). Information about the parks and bushwalks, flora & fauna.
New South Wales Travel Centre
19 Castlereagh St, near Martin Place (✆ 13 20 77; **Open:** Mon-Fri 9am-5pm; Sat phone only 9am-1pm).
Accommodation and travel information from the government tourist body.
Rocks Visitors Centre
106 George St, The Rocks (✆ 9255 1788; **Open:** 7 days 9am-5pm).
Information about the buildings and area, booking centre for guided walking tours, leaflets and maps, books, souvenirs.
Sydney Visitors Information Kiosk
Martin Place, City (✆ 9235 2424; **Open:** Mon-Fri 9am-5pm).
The other half of the Halftix kiosk dispenses transport information, maps and leaflets.
Quayside Booking Centre
Wharf 2, Circular Quay (✆ 9247 5151; **Open:** 7 days 8am-6.30pm).
Bookings for a very wide range of tours and activities. No fees.
Travellers Information
Sydney International Airport (✆ 9669 5111; **Open:** 7 days 5am-11pm).
Information & bookings for jet lagged new arrivals on accommodation and travel.
YHA Membership & Travel Centre
422 Kent St, City (✆ 9261 1111; **Open:** Mon-Fri 9am-5pm; Thurs to 6pm; Sat 9am-12pm; Closed Sun).
Information regarding youth hostels and travel.

CONSULATE OFFICES

All addresses are in the city centre, unless otherwise stated.
Austria: 2a Kingslans Rd, Bexley (✆ 9567 1008)
Belgium: 2a Trelawney St, Woollahra (✆ 9327 8377)
Britain: 1 Macquarie Place (✆ 9247 7521)
Canada: 111 Harrington St (✆ 9364 3000)
China: 539 Elizabeth St (✆ 9698 7929)
Denmark: 1 Alfred St (✆ 9247 2224)
France: St Martins Tower, 31 Market St (✆ 9261 5779)
Germany: 13 Trelawney St, Woollahra (✆ 9328 7733)
Greece: 15 Castlereagh St (✆ 9221 2388)
Indonesia: 236 Maroubra Rd, Maroubra (✆ 9344 9933)
Italy: 1 Macquarie Place (✆ 9247 8442)
Japan: 52 Martin Place (✆ 9231 3455)
Malaysia: 67 Victoria Rd, Bellevue Hill (✆ 9327 7565)
New Zealand: 1 Alfred St (✆ 9247 1999)
Norway: 5 Gresham St (✆ 9251 6628)
Philippines: Ferrier Hodgson House, 55 York St (✆ 9299 6633)
Spain: L 24/31 Market St (✆ 9261 2433)
Sweden: 44 Market St (✆ 9299 1951)
Switzerland: Plaza II Tower, 500 Oxford St, Bondi Junction (✆ 9328 7511)
U.S.A.: 19-29 Martin Place (✆ 9373 9200)

ELECTRICITY

Domestic electricity in Australia is 240 volts, 50 Hz. Plugs have three flat pins; however, adaptors for foreign appliances are readily available.

EMERGENCY & CRISIS

Ambulance, Police, Fire (✆ 000) (free call)
Chemist Emergency Prescription (✆ 9438 3333)
Dental Emergencies (✆ 9692 0333)
Immigration and Ethnic Affairs (88 Cumberland St, The Rocks; ✆ 9258 4555)
Interpreter Service (✆ 9221 1111)
Legal Aid Commission (✆ 9219 5000)
Lifeline Counselling (✆ 9264 2222 or 9951 5555)
Poisons Information (✆ 9519 1466)
Rape Crisis Centre 24 hours (✆ 9819 6565)

HOSPITALS

Children's Hospital: Hawkesbury Rd, Westmead (✆ 9845 0000)
Dental Hospital: 2 Chalmers St, Central (✆ 9282 0200)
Eye Hospital: Sir John Young Crescent, City (✆ 9228 2111)
Royal North Shore Hospital: Pacific Hwy, St Leonards (✆ 9438 7111)
St Vincent's Hospital: Victoria St, Darlinghurst (✆ 9339 1111)
In an emergency, dial 000 (free call).

MEDICAL

Travellers from New Zealand, Sweden, Italy, the Netherlands, Malta and the United Kingdom are entitled to receive "immediate emergency treatment", whether by a general practitioner or hospital, through the government's Medicare system (✆1800 801 901). This does not cover dental work, although your travel insurance may.

Doctors and dentists are listed in the white and yellow pages. Otherwise, try the Hotel Doctor (✆ 9962 0333) or Travellers' Medical & Vaccination Services (advice) 7th Floor, Dymocks Building, 428 George St, City (✆ 9221 713 or 9221 7210).

PARKING

Parking in Sydney can be expensive and problematic. In the city centre, street parking is

CURRENCY EXCHANGE

Travellers cheques are a secure way to carry money while travelling. Most common travellers cheques are readily cashed by banks and bureaux de change, although Thomas Cook, American Express and Visa are the most widely accepted. Commissions and charges vary from one establishment to the next, as follows.

Banks

Of the major banks operating in Australia, several will charge a fee for cashing travellers cheques; however, some do not.

Bank	$AUD TC - $AUD cash	Foreign TC - $AUD cash	Foreign cash - $AUD cash
ANZ*	no charge	$6.50 total fee	no charge
CBA**	$5 total fee	$5 total fee	no charge
NAB***	$5 total fee	$5 total fee	$5 total fee
State Bank	Greater of 1% or $10	Greater of 1% or $10	no charge
Westpac	no charge	no charge	no charge

* ANZ cashes all Visa travellers cheques without charge.
**CBA cashes travellers cheques without charge if opening a Tourist Account and depositing money directly into it.
*** NAB deals only in Thomas Cook and American Express travellers cheques.

Currency Exchange Companies

Currency exchange kiosks in Sydney are generally operated by four companies. Following are their central locations.

American Express

92 Pitt St, City (✆ 9239 0666; **Open:** Mon-Fri 8.30am-5pm; Sat 9am-12noon; Closed Sun).
73-79 Mount St, North Sydney (✆ 9957 2277; **Open:** Mon-Fri 8.30am-5pm; Closed Sat-Sun).

Interforex

140 George St, The Rocks (✆ 9247 5555; **Open:** 7 days 8am-9pm).
Jetty 6, Circular Quay (✆ 9247 2082; **Open:** 7 days 8am-9pm).
Pitt St Mall between Market St & King St, City (✆ 9233 7159; **Open:** 7 days 9am-6pm).

Thomas Cook

Shop 22 Queen Victoria Building, George St, City (✆ 9264 1133; **Open:** Mon-Sat 9am-6pm; Thurs to 9pm; Sun 11am-5pm).
509 Kingsgate Shopping Centre, Kings Cross (✆ 9356 2211; **Open:** Mon-Fri 8.45am-5.15pm; Sat 9am-1pm; Closed Sun).
Sydney Airport International Terminal (✆ 9317 2100; **Open:** 7 days 5.30am-9.30pm).

Travelex Australia

32 Martin Place, City (✆ 9221 2942; **Open:** Mon-Fri 8.30am-5pm; Closed Sat-Sun).
182 George St, City (✆ 9241 2372; **Open:** Mon-Fri 8.30am-6pm; Sat-Sun 8.30am-5pm).
37-49 Pitt St, City (✆ 9241 5722; **Open:** 7 days 7am-7pm).
48 Darlinghurst Rd, Kings Cross (✆ 9357 3604; **Open:** 7 days 8.30am-5.30pm).

24hour Currency Exchange is found in the Courthouse Hotel, Taylor Square (✆ 9360 4831; no charge).

Company	$AUD TC - $AUD cash	Foreign TC - $AUD cash	Foreign cash - $AUD cash
Amex	no charge	No charge	no charge
T Cook*	$5 total fee	$5 total fee	Greater of 1% or $4
Travelex	Greater of 3% or $4	Greater of 3% or $4	Greater of 3% or $4
Interforex	5%	5%	5%

* Thomas Cook do not charge for cashing Thomas Cook travellers cheques.

heavily restricted and generally hard to find. In many areas, parking meters are in use; some take only $1 coins while others accept all coins. Be warned that hourly limits are zealously enforced by squadrons of parking officers who constantly roam the streets slapping hefty fines ($65-$130) on illegally parked cars. Parking in clearways will see your car disappearing in an undignified manner pulled by a tow truck. You will have to telephone the Roads and Traffic Authority to find out where they have taken it (usually close by) and pay the towing bill.

If you still want to park in the street, the best streets for city parking are Art Gallery Road and Haig Avenue near Hyde Park.

Parking Stations in central areas charge as much as $6 per hour. Early bird rates are sometimes available (enter before 9am), while most have flat rates on weekends. The cheaper city parking stations are in York Street, and the Opera House car park charges $4 per hour (max $10) during the day (exit before 6pm).

POST

The General Post Office (GPO) is located on the corner of Martin Place and Pitt Street (✆ 9230 7033; **Open:** Mon-Fri 8.15am-5.30pm; Sat 8.30am-12noon). The Poste Restante service is in the ground floor foyer; hopeful mail recipients should type their name into the computers to see if there is any mail, and if so, take the receipt to the counter. All general Post Services are on the first floor. Join a queue. Enjoy the muzak. Wait for the bell to toll.

Suburban post offices are open Monday to Friday from 9am to 5pm.

Postage rates for post cards/light letters respectively are currently:
U.S.A. (95c/$1.05)
UK/Europe ($1.00/$1.20)
NZ (70c/75c)
Japan (90c/95c)
Postage within Australia for cards and letters is 45c.

TELEPHONES

Calls from public telephones cost either 30c or 40c. Most public telephones take both **coins and Phone Cards,** which are available from newsagents everywhere. Public telephones which can be charged directly to a credit card can generally be found in hotels and post offices. There is a **twenty-four hour Telephone Centre** at 100 King Street, City.

Sydney's two major **telephone directories** are the White Pages, listing all private numbers alphabetically, and the Yellow Pages, listing businesses by subject.

Operator assistance can be found as follows: directory and operators: local (✆ 013), Interstate (✆ 0175), overseas operator (✆ 0103), and reverse charges (✆ 0107). Long distance callers should note that international charges are lowest overnight from 10pm, and interstate charges are lowest after 6pm and on weekends.

TICKETS

There are not many combined tickets available for travellers to Sydney. One which will give you significant discounts including 2 for 1 admission at a large range of museums, shops, transport, entertainment and food is the **Privileges Card** (Cost: 3 days $15, 7 days $20, 1 month $25, 12 months $60). It is available from NSW Travel Centres (in Sydney: 19 Castlereagh St, City; (✆ 13 20 77).

The **Historic Houses Trust Ticket Through Time** (Cost: $12/$8/$20 family; valid 3 months) offers considerably reduced entrance fees to all their properties around Sydney. These include Hyde Park Barracks, Vaucluse House, Elizabeth Bay House. Elizabeth Farm, the Police and Justice Museum, Rose Seidler House and the Museum of Sydney, in short, some of the most important historic sites and buildings in the city. It is available from any Historic Houses Trust property.

There are many **transport ticket deals** available. The most comprehensive is the Sydney Pass (Cost: 3 days $50/5 days $70/7 days $80), which includes return Airport Express, unlimited use of the Sydney Explorer, Rocks - Darling Harbour shuttle bus, Sydney Ferries (including the Zoo ferry, Manly ferry and ferry harbour cruises), JetCats and all regular state transit Sydney Bus and Sydney Ferries services. It is available on all State Transit services which are included in the ticket; State Transit ticket offices; the New South Wales travel centre (19 Castlereagh St, City ✆ 13 20 77); and travel agents. (For further details, See: Transport.)

TIME

Sydney is on Australian Eastern Standard Time, which is **GMT+10 hours.** Despite the conviction prevalent in other Australian States that it confuses the cows and fades the curtains, New South Wales switches to **Daylight Saving** from the last Sunday in October to late March. For this period, the clocks go forward by one hour.

TRANSPORT AROUND SYDNEY

Covering an area of over 12,380.64km², Sydney is bigger than Los Angeles and Rome. After the Harbour Bridge was built in the 1930s, residential development on the North Shore boomed. Sydney spread northwards towards St Ives to cover land previously used for orchards, and westwards across towards Hornsby. The West spread similarly, although its growth started in the early days of the colony, and this vast, sprawling area of suburban Sydney has now almost reached the foothills of the Blue Mountains. To the South, Sydney has reached the waterways of the Georges River and the National Park; to the East is the ocean. Indeed, the huge Sydney Basin is almost full; some would say it is overflowing.

Consequently, Sydney has an extensive public transport system of trains, buses and ferries, run by CityRail, Sydney Buses and Sydney Ferries under the umbrella of the State Transit Authority. The trains alone run two thousand five hundred services daily over one thousand seven hundred kilometres of track, and in 1994 carried two hundred and forty million passengers. Such is the need that many private transport companies fill in the gaps left by the public network: taxis, private ferries, water taxis, buses and hire cars are all available. This chapter details Sydney's major transport operations, concentrating on the State Transit system. **The How To Get To...** list is a quick and easy reference tool to use while on the move; but remember, passers by, shop keepers and bus drivers are easy targets to stop and ask for help, and most will respond usefully!

ARRIVING IN SYDNEY BY AEROPLANE

Sydney's airport is only fifteen minutes south of the city centre. The international terminal includes several bureaux de change and the Travellers' Information Service (✆ 9669 5111; Open: 7 days 5am-11pm) which can help with accommodation, sightseeing and oversized baggage. Inter-terminal shuttle buses run every ten minutes (Cost: $2.50/$1.50) to transfer passengers between the international and two domestic terminals (Ansett and Qantas). These are located on the other side of the tarmac and service all flights from and to Australian territories and states. Car hire agencies are located in each.

Several transport services depart from outside each terminal for the City, as follows.

Airport Express

Cost: Return (valid two months) $8/$4; One Way $5/$3.

Booking: No booking is necessary; passengers board at any point where the green and yellow Airport Express sign appears along the route.

These green and yellow public buses take approximately twenty minutes to reach the City and Kings Cross, departing approximately every thirty minutes as follows. Route 300: Airport to Circular Quay via City (first trip 5.53am, last trip 10.55pm) and Circular Quay to Airport (first trip 5.15am, last trip 9.57pm). Route 350: Airport to Kings Cross (first trip Mon-Fri 6.35am (Sat-Sun 6.30am), last trip 10.55pm) and Kings Cross to Airport (first trip 4.53am from Century Radisson, Victoria St, last trip 10pm). Both routes include a stop at Central Station.

Note: after 9pm, the Airport Express routes become one combined service, and the southbound George Street stops (direction Airport) are replaced by the northbound George Street stops (direction Circular Quay) on the opposite side of the road.

Clipper Airporter Shuttle Service (✆ 9667 3800)

Cost: Return $10/$6; One Way $6/$4.

Booking: No booking is required for airport to hotel service; however, passengers must book at least two hours before requiring the hotel to airport service.

The Clipper Airporter shuttles to and from the airport picking up and dropping off at a number of City, Darling Harbour, Glebe and Kings Cross hotels as required seven days a week (5am to 8.00pm).

Taxi

A taxi to the City will cost approximately $18, and should take about fifteen minutes.

Hire Car

If using a hire car, the route to the City via Southern Cross Drive is well signposted with large, green and white, easy to understand signs. If the trip takes more than around twenty minutes, seek help.

ARRIVING BY TRAIN

Sydney Rail Terminal (Central Railway Station) is on the southern edge of the city centre near Chinatown. It is the first station out of the city centre and contains a Travellers' Information Centre (cnr Eddy Avenue & Pitt Street; ✆

9281 9366). Transport from Central to the City is as follows.

Train

From Central Station's metropolitan platforms, passengers can take a City Rail train on any line in the system. These include the City Circle for Town Hall, Wynyard, Circular Quay, St James and Museum in the City; the Eastern Suburbs Line for Martin Place, Kings Cross, Edgecliff and Bondi Junction; or the Northern Suburbs Line for stations north of the Harbour Bridge on the North Shore.

Bus

Central Station is also serviced by many metropolitan bus routes. These depart from the corner of Eddy Avenue and Pitt Street. Here you can also pick up a copy of the State Transit Bus Guide, for routes, terminals and frequencies. Bus 430 goes to Circular Quay via George St (city centre).

ARRIVING BY COACH

Several coach terminals are located around Sydney.

The **Sydney Coach Terminal** is on the corner of Eddy Avenue and Pitt Street at Central Station(above). Several companies operate from here, such as Firefly & Kirklands, and access to the City is as above.

The **Greyhound Pioneer** terminal is on the corner of Riley Street and Oxford Street, Darlinghurst. This is near Hyde Park on the eastern edge of the City, which can be reached by taxi (three minutes) or walking (ten minutes). Alternatively, buses run along Oxford Street to the City and the Eastern Suburbs. See Public Transport System (below) for details.

The third is at Circular Quay West on the Harbour at the northern edge of the city centre, which may be reached by bus from Alfred Street (parallel to Circular Quay) or by foot along George Street (fifteen minutes).

THE PUBLIC TRANSPORT SYSTEM

Information

Timetable, fare, service and ticket information can be obtained from the following sources.

State Transit Information Kiosk, Circular Quay (✆ 13 1500)

Train, Bus and Ferry Infoline (Open: 7 days 6am-10pm; ✆ 13 1500). The Infoline is a useful number to remember when out and about and lost.

Concessions and Fare Avoidance

Concession fares are available for children under four years of age (free travel) and for five to sixteen year olds (half price). Those over sixteen must pay full fare unless they have a State Transit concession pass. No other card will earn a concession fare. Fare avoidance is vehemently punished in Sydney: inspections frequently take place on buses and ticket collectors guard most station exits, so there is little scope for escape. The fines imposed are hefty ($100).

Train

All train lines radiate from the City, except for the city circle which loops it, and rail services run regularly from around 4am to midnight (for night travel, see below). Tickets must be bought before travelling from the ticket windows or ticket machines at all stations. Fares start at $1.20, while off-peak fares (Mon-Fri 9am-3pm; Sat-Sun all day) offer worthwhile discounts. A particularly picturesque train journey within Sydney is along the North Shore Line from Wynyard station in the City, which leads over the Harbour Bridge offering a superb view of the western side of the Harbour and down onto Olympic Pool. You could even continue up through the North Shore as far as Gordon to see how a large part of leafy suburban Sydney lives. The train trip to Wollongong (See: Trips Out Of Sydney: The South Coast) offers some of the best scenery in the region.

Bus

Buses fill the gaps left by the train network, most notably the eastern suburbs and beaches, the inner west and the northern beaches. Public buses are blue and white and usually run regularly. Tickets for single journeys are bought on board from the driver, while combination tickets and multiple journey passes must be bought from newsagents or train stations (see below). Particularly good-looking bus routes include **bus 389** from Circular Quay to Bondi Beach via Paddington's back streets and Woollahra; **bus 380 or 382** from Circular Quay to Military Road, Dover Heights for a panoramic view of the City skyline. However, for sightseeing value and ease, the **Sydney Explorer** (bright red, route 111) and **Bondi & Bay Explorer** (silver and blue, route 222) are hard to beat. On each service, tourers can cruise Sydney, boarding and alighting at any stop on the circuit all day. (See: Tours Around Sydney.)

The **Night Ride** bus system takes over from the trains between midnight and dawn. The City Shuttle (N1) operates between Town Hall, St James, Circular Quay, Martin Place and Wynyard, while the North Route (N90) services Hornsby via North Sydney and the North Shore Line. Other services cover much of the train system: a map is available from information offices. Any valid CityRail return ticket can be used on the service, however Night Ride bus tickets can be bought from the driver.

Ferry

Sydney's suave ferries radiate to the many little coves and bays of the Harbour from the jetties of **Circular Quay,** providing an eminently relaxing way to travel. Tickets for travel from Circular Quay or Manly must be bought before travelling, and are available from either the ticket windows or ticket machines on the jetties. Tickets for travel from small jetties around the Harbour must be bought from the machines on the jetties of Circular Quay or Manly after travelling. **Particularly good ferry routes** to cruise include the famous Manly Ferry and the services to Hunters Hill and Balmain. A harbour cruise on a Sydney Ferry is a delightful way to spend an afternoon on the water (See: Tours Around Sydney: Cruises).

MULTIPLE TICKETS & PASSES FOR ALL STATE TRANSIT SERVICES

In addition to the outlets listed below, the following tickets are all available from State Transit ticket kiosks. In the City, these can be found at Circular Quay (cnr Loftus Street and Alfred Street); Wynyard Park (Carrington Street); or behind the Queen Victoria Building in York Street.

BusTripper

Cost: $7.80; Available: Newsagents is an all day bus pass allowing unlimited use on all government buses (except the Explorers and Airport Express).

SydneyPass

Cost: 3 days $50/5 days $70/7 days $80; Available: State Transit ticket offices; all services included in the ticket; New South Wales Travel Centre, 19 Castlereagh St, City; travel agents) is a single tourist ticket including return Airport Express, unlimited use of the Sydney Explorer, Rocks-Darling Harbour shuttle bus, Sydney Ferries (including the Zoo ferry, Manly ferry and ferry harbour cruises), JetCats and all regular state transit Sydney Bus and Sydney Ferries services. Phew! The ticket need not be used on consecutive days.

TravelPass

Cost: Varies; Available: Newsagents & train stations. This is a weekly ticket for seven days of unlimited travel on Sydney buses, ferries and trains. It cannot be used on either of the Explorer buses or the Airport Express.

TravelTen

Cost: Varies; Available: Newsagents & train stations on and around the City Circle line. These are tickets of ten bus trips of a particular length, valid for an unlimited time. They are available from newsagents and train ticket windows near public bus routes, and must be inserted in the validation machine on entering the bus.

More?

Special combined tickets to various attractions, such as AquariumPass, OceanPass and ZooPass are also available. They include the ferry fare and admission to the attraction, and constitute a good saving; all are available from Circular Quay and Manly.

CAR HIRE

Car hire in Sydney need not be exorbitantly expensive, although some dealers are cheaper than others. The best place to go to shop around in person is **William Street** between Hyde Park and Kings Cross, where several operators have offices. A number of specialist, prestige and sports car hire operators can be found in the Yellow Pages or through a travel agent. The major car hire operators in Sydney, most of which have multiple branches, include the following.

Avis (214 William St, Kings Cross; ✆ 9357 2000)

Bayswater Car Rental (120 Darlinghurst Rd, Kings Cross; ✆ 9360 3622)

Budget (93 William St, Kings Cross; ✆ 13 27 27)

Crown Rent-a-Car (83 William St, East Sydney; ✆ 9361 0555)

Delta (77 William St, East Sydney; ✆ 13 13 90)

Hertz L2, FAC House, Keith Smith Dr, Mascot (24 hour reservations ✆ 13 30 39)

Thrifty (75 William St, Kings Cross; ✆ 9380 5399; toll free 1800 652 008)

MONORAIL

Cost: $2.50 each circuit or part circuit; Day Pass $6 unlimited travel between 8am and closing.

Open: Winter (mid April to late September): Mon-Wed 7am-9pm; Thurs-Sat 7am-Midnight; Sun 8am-9pm; Summer (late September to mid April): Mon-Sat 7am-Midnight; Sun 8am-9pm.

Information: (✆ 9552 2288).

The monorail operates every five minutes to link the city centre with Darling Harbour. The one-way route covers a loop of seven stations including City Centre (Cnr Pitt St & Market St); Darling Park (near the Sydney Aquarium); Harbourside (at the Darling Harbour end of the old Pyrmont bridge); Haymarket (near Chinatown at the Entertainment Centre).

TAXI

Taxi drivers are usually good value for a 'talking to a local' experience, even if they seem to think that they own the road and lean the right elbow on the open window frame while steering with the left wrist draped languidly on the top of the wheel. Do not worry, your driver is not asleep. Sydney's major taxi operators are the following.

ABC (✆ 132 522); **Legion** (✆ 13 14 51); **Premier Taxis** (✆ 13 10 17); **RSL** (✆ 9581 1111); **St George Cabs** (✆ 13 2166); and the best to ring, **Taxis Combined Services** (includes ABC, St George and Southern Districts) (✆ 9332 8888).

Cost

For all taxis, the starting price on the meter is $2.00; for taxis ordered by telephone, there is an additional $1 charge. For all taxis, the charge thereafter is $1 per kilometre, while waiting time usually costs around $28 per hour.

How To Get One

Taxis can be either ordered by phone, caught from taxi ranks, or hailed in the street as they drive by. The larger taxi ranks in the city centre include Market Street at David Jones, and The Regent Hotel, George Street.

If a complaint arises regarding a taxi service, call the Taxi Complaint Hotline (✆ 9916 5244). Special taxis suited to transporting passengers with wheelchairs are available, and should be ordered in advance (✆ 9339 0200; See: Sydney for Disabled Visitors).

WATER TAXIS

Several water taxi companies operate on the Harbour . The major ones include the following.

Banks Marine (✆ 9555 1222); **Harbour Taxi Boats** (✆ 9555 1155); **Taxis Afloat** (✆ 9955 3222); and **Water Taxis Combined** (✆ 9810 5010). Fares are calculated as a basic charge plus a smaller amount per additional passenger, so they are usually better value for groups.

DISABLED TRAVELLERS

For full information of accessible transport around Sydney, See: Sydney For Disabled Visitors.

How To Get To...

The Sights & Suburbs By Public Transport

Where	How To Get There	What's There
Airport	**Airport Express** Bus 300 from Circular Quay (George St) or 350 from Kings Cross; or **Bus** 400 from Bondi Junction Interchange.	
Avalon, Palm Beach & Pittwater	**Bus** 190 from Wynyard (Carrington St), City.	Pristine beaches; boating; 'Summer Bay'.
Balmoral Beach	**Bus** 257 from Chatswood (limited service); **Ferry** to Musgrave Street wharf from Circular Quay (wharf 4) then bus 233; or **Ferry** to Balmoral Beach wharf from Circular Quay (summer only).	Bathers Pavilion cafe and restaurant; Esplanade; Island.
Balmain & Birchgrove	**Bus** 441 from Town Hall (Mon-Fri 9am-5pm); **Bus** 432 from George St (7 days after 5pm and all day Sat-Sun); **Bus** 442 to Balmain only; or **Ferry** to Darling St wharf from Circular Quay (wharf 5).	Historic Area; Saturday markets; Shopping; Pubs; Food.
Bondi Beach	**Bus** 380, 382, 389 direct from Circular Quay; or **Train** to Bondi Junction; then bus 380, 382, 389 from Bondi Junction Interchange.	Beach; Cafes; Coast Walk; Aboriginal Rock Art.
Bondi Junction	**Bus** 380, 382, 389 from Circular Quay; **Bus** 378 from Railway Square (Eddy Ave); or **Train** to Bondi Junction.	Shopping; Transport Hub.
Bronte Beach	**Bus** 378 from Railway Square (Eddy Ave) via Oxford St & Bronte Rd.	Beach; Cafes; Bronte-Bondi.
The City	All roads lead to Sydney's centre. The major city train stations are Wynyard, Town Hall and Martin Place. Bus terminuses are Circular Quay or Railway Square at Central Station, while the QVB is a good central spot to alight. All ferries go to Circular Quay; from here walk (15 minutes) or take a bus along George Street to the city centre.	Centre of Sydney: Major Sights To See; Cafes; Centrepoint Tower; Highrises; Museums; Opera House; Shopping; Theatres.
Coogee	**Bus** 373, 374 from Circular Quay; **Bus** 313 express from Bondi Junction Interchange; **Bus** 314 from Bondi Junction Interchange via Randwick.	Beach; Cafes; Historic Wylie's Baths.
Cremorne Point	**Ferry** to Cremorne Point wharf from Circular Quay (wharf 4).	Cremorne Lighthouse; MacCallum Pool; Nature Reserve.
Darling Harbour	**Ferry** to Darling Harbour from Circular Quay (wharf 5) **Foot** from city centre via Market St & directly onto the old Pyrmont Bridge; **Monorail** to Harbourside station; or **Rocket** from Circular Quay.	Aquarium; Chinese Garden; Convention Centre; Powerhouse Museum; Shopping; Street Theatre.
Dover Heights	**Bus** 380, 382 from Circular Quay via Bondi Beach.	Panoramic city views.
Elizabeth Bay	**Bus** 311 from Railway Square (Eddy Ave) via Oxford St & Darlinghurst Rd; **Bus** 311 also from Circular Quay via Castlereagh St, Haig Ave & Woolloomooloo; **Train** to Kings Cross then foot (5 minutes).	Elizabeth Bay House; Macleay Reserve.
Fort Denison	**See** Tours Around Sydney.	Historic fort; Harbour and City views.
Glebe and Glebe Point	**Bus** 431, 433, 434 from Millers Point in the Rocks via George St & Railway Sq.	Historic Suburb; Bookshops; Cafes; University of Sydney.
Harbour Islands:	**See** Tours Around Sydney.	

Where	How To Get There	What's There
Hunters Hill	**Bus** 506 from Circular Quay; or **Ferry** to Alexandra St or Valentia St Wharf from Circular Quay (wharf 5).	Historic Sandstone Mansions & Cottages.
Kings Cross	**Bus** 324, 325, 327 from Circular Quay via William St; **Bus** 311 from Railway Sq. via Taylor Sq.; or **Train** to Kings Cross station.	Backpackers' Focal Point; Cafes; Red light District; Restaurants.
Kirribilli	**Ferry** to High St or Kirribilli wharf from Circular Quay (wharf 4); **Foot** via the Rocks and Harbour Bridge (30 minutes); or **Train** to Milsons Point; then foot (4 minutes).	Historic Suburb; Cafes.
Leichhardt	**Bus** 436, 438, 440, 470 from Circular Quay via George St & Parramatta Rd.	Italian Community; Cafe & Food Focal Point; Food & Wine Markets.
Manly	**Ferry or JetCat** (faster but not traditional) from Circular Quay (wharf 2/3).	Beach; Coast walk; Manly Ferries; Ocean World; Spit-Manly Bushwalk.
Neutral Bay	**Bus** 247 from Wynyard (Carrington St); or **Ferry** to Hayes St or Kurraba Point wharf from Circular Quay (wharf 4); then bus along Ben Boyd Rd.	Restaurants; Shopping; Transport.
Newtown	**Bus** 422, 423, 426, 428 from Circular Quay via Castlereagh St & City Rd; or **Train** to Newtown station.	Cafes; Historic Suburb; King St Shopping; Markets.
North Sydney	**Ferry** to North Sydney wharf from Circular Quay (wharf 4); or **Train** to North Sydney station.	Shopping; Transport Hub.
Paddington	**Bus** 380, 382 from Circular Quay via Elizabeth St & Taylor Sq; **Bus** 378 from Railway Sq; **Bus** 380, 382 from Bondi Beach & Bondi Junction Interchange; or **Foot** from Hyde Park along Oxford St (40mins)	Art Galleries; Cafes; Oxford St Shopping; Historic Terrace Houses & cottages; Paddington Bazaar; Pubs; Restaurants; Sydney Cricket Ground & Football Stadium; Victoria Barracks.
The Rocks	**Bus** any City bound bus or any northbound bus along George St; **Ferry** to Circular Quay; or **Foot** from Circular Quay or the City.	Birthplace of European Sydney; Cafes; Harbour Bridge Pylon & Walkway; Historic Buildings; Museum of Contemporary Art; Markets; Pubs; Shopping.
Taronga Zoo	**Bus** 250 from North Sydney (Miller St) via Military Rd; or **Ferry** to Taronga Zoo wharf from Circular Quay (wharf 4).	Award-winning Zoo; Harbour Views.
Vaucluse	**Bus** 324, 325 (to Vaucluse House) from Circular Quay.	Nielsen Park beach & kiosk; Vaucluse House.
Watsons Bay	**Bus** 324, 325 from Circular Quay; or **Ferry** from Circular Quay (wharf 4 Mon-Fri; wharf 2 Sat-Sun).	Beaches (Camp Cove, Watsons Bay & Lady Bay); The Gap National Park; Historic Fishermen's Cottages; Beer Garden.
Woollahra	**Bus** 380, 382 from Circular Quay to Queen St, then 2 mins by foot; **Bus** 389 from Circular Quay to corner of Queen St & Moncur St; **Train** to Edgecliff station; then bus 327, 387 or foot up Ocean St (5 minutes).	Centennial Park; Historic cottages & terraces; Queen St antiques shopping; Restaurants.

Notes: Bondi Junction Bus Interchange is behind Bondi Junction station parallel to Oxford St; **Circular Quay buses** depart from Loftus St, Pitt St and Alfred St; **Millers Point terminus** in The Rocks is at the top of Argyle St, diagonally opposite the Lord Nelson pub; **Railway Square** is at Central Station; buses going to the Eastern Suburbs depart from Eddy Ave.

MEDIA

The Australian Press is largely controlled by two rival media barons, Rupert Murdoch and Kerry Packer, but with increasing interest and acquisitions by media concerns and owners outside Australia, the debate about foreign ownership levels in this country is never far from the surface. This chapter provides information of the various media servicing Sydney, with particular emphasis on newspapers and listings publications. It also details where to obtain foreign papers.

NEWSPAPERS & NEWS MAGAZINES

There are two major **national newspapers.** *The Australian* (Murdoch) is published in Melbourne Monday to Saturday. This most patriotically named daily offers good coverage of national issues and world news. Saturdays are a bonanza, with thick arts, topical, news and employment sections as well as a colour magazine. The *Financial Review* (Fairfax) is almost purely business news, but Friday's edition is always full of interesting articles covering a wide scope of topics, including a great world news section. A colour magazine is published and included with the paper every month.

Two major daily **Sydney papers** are published, covering the nation but emphasising this city. The large format *Sydney Morning Herald* (Fairfax) appears from Monday to Saturday covering Australian politics and events as well as world news and sport, and includes special sections each day. Particularly good are Tuesday's Good Living for new restaurants, food, wine and fashion, and Friday's Metro, for a comprehensive listing of all entertainment venues and sessions. Like The Age, Saturday's *Herald* includes great features, more comprehensive news coverage, and a colour magazine. Sunday's *Sun-Herald* is published as a thick, small format paper with articles covering world news, Sydney and national news, sport, food and fashion. The *Telegraph Mirror* (Murdoch) is a small format tabloid full of large headlines announcing brief articles covering national and local news, sport, and general topics, which appears from Monday to Saturday. On Sundays it is published as the *Sunday Telegraph* and includes a wide range of news, sport and general topics.

There are two major Australian news magazines, both of which are available in Sydney newsagents. The *Bulletin with Newsweek* and the Australian edition of *Time* both appear weekly full of topical, politics, legal and general comment.

A large number of small newspapers are published in Sydney by various national groups to cover local and national news in foreign languages. Die Woche in Australien, La Fiamma, Le Courrier Australien, Cosmos, the Greek Herald, and a number of Portuguese and Spanish papers are generally available from the large newsagents. Try the Wynyard Station (City) newsagent on the station concourse.

FOREIGN MEDIA

A large number of foreign newspapers and magazines are widely available in Sydney, either to buy or to read without buying. Here's where to find them.

Sydney Library

Level 3 Town Hall, 456 Kent St, City (✆ 265 9694)
Open: Mon-Fri 8am-7pm; Sat 9am-12pm.
The Sydney Library is located within Town Hall House and receives a fair range of major daily newspapers from overseas.

World News Centre

402 Harbourside Festival Marketplace, Darling Harbour (281 3707)
Open: Mon-Fri 8.30am-9pm; Sat 9am-9pm; Sun 9am-7pm.
For those who prefer to buy, this newsagency stocks a very large number of American, English, New Zealand, Asian, and European newspapers and magazines.

ENTERTAINMENT LISTINGS

To keep abreast of the myriad possibilities Sydney

offers your free time, there are a number of listings papers available, generally for free.

Metro

Metro is included in the Sydney Morning Herald every Friday. Listing film, dance, theatre, cabaret, opera, musicals, concerts, recitals, folk, country, jazz, rock, comedy, it is indispensable and wide ranging.

On The Street; The Drum; 3D World

All three are issued weekly and are available for free from many cafes, bars and independent cinemas in the east and inner suburbs. Between them, they comprehensively list the city's club, dance and live music scene, combining attitude-laden comment and critique. Ariel Booksellers at 42 Oxford St, Paddington (✆ 9332 4581) always has a number of each.

The Opera House Program

It is a good idea to get one of these as early as possible, see what's coming up and plan ahead for the ballet, theatre, concerts, opera and free forecourt events. The programs are available for free from the Opera House Box Office and ticket agencies around Sydney.

Various Theatre Programs

FirstCall ticket agency regularly puts out a theatre guide which details all theatre's current plays and shows. They are available from FirstCall ticket agencies around Sydney.

TELEVISION

Sydney has five channels and three pay television operators, Foxtel, Galaxy and Optus Vision.

Of the publicly accessible channels, **SBS** deserves special mention for its dedication to providing information and entertainment in a large number of languages with English subtitles. Its superb international news coverage includes not only daily bulletins in English but also foreign language news broadcasts every morning from 7am. Foreign films and programs are featured at all times. The Australian Broadcasting Corporation (ABC), affectionately known as 'Aunty', and three commercial stations (7, 9 and 10) fill the other airwaves.

RADIO

Sydney's two major classical radio stations are both excellent: ABC FM (92.9) and 2MBS FM (102.5), the latter a non-government venture staffed by knowledgable volunteers. Of the city's rock and pop music stations, 2 Day FM (104.1) and 2MMM (104.9) are the major ones. Triple JJJ (105.7) is run by the ABC and plays off beat music. The AM band is filled with talk back stations staffed with opinionated announcers, easy listening music stations and three excellent ABC news stations: 2BL (702), Radio National (576) and Parliament & News Network (630).

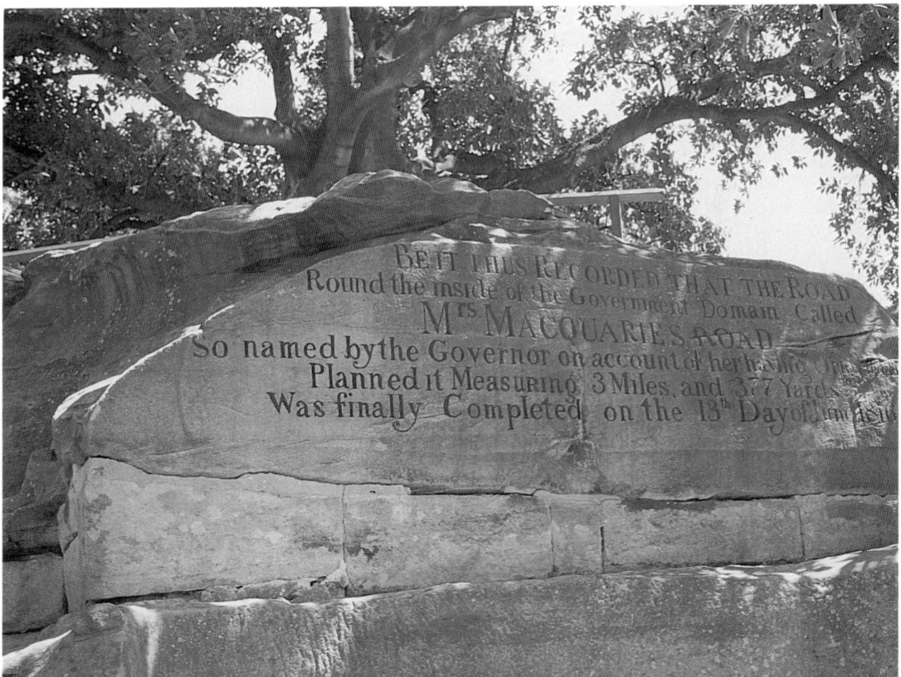

Sit and read the paper on Mrs Macquarie's Chair

ACCOMMODATION

There is a very wide range of accommodation available in Sydney, so whether you prefer a luxurious five star hotel or a small, family-run guesthouse, you should be comfortable. Although not particularly common in Sydney, there are a number of booking agencies co-ordinating bed and breakfasts in Sydney homes. Serviced apartments offer extremely good value in that most have facilities worthy of luxury hotels and equipped kitchens in each room. Booking as far in advance as possible is highly recommended, particularly in peak seasons.

The accommodation included in this chapter has been selected for value, location, facilities and character. They are organised according to type: boutique, budget, bed and breakfast, luxury and serviced apartments. Accommodation listed in these groupings are divided into the geographical divisions of north, south, east and west. Finally, the price bracket listed with each entry is for a double room per night including breakfast, although long stays and corporate clients may attract cheaper rates.

The New South Wales Travel Centre (below) has enormous resources and ability to pinpoint and secure appropriate accommodation in Sydney. Furthermore, they often have special deals with many hotels (including those listed below with NSWTC), resulting in lower room rates; it is worth while investigating the possibilities.

Explanation of Symbols & Ratings

Price Ratings (for a double room per night, including breakfast):

$	under $50
$$	$50-$80
$$$	$80-$150
$$$$	$150-$250
$$$$$	over $250

Other Symbols:

NSWTC The accommodation is affiliated with the New South Wales Travel Centre, and special rates may apply.

INFORMATION & BOOKING CENTRES

Apart from accredited travel agents, the following sources should be able to provide further information and options.

The Travel Centre of New South Wales

19 Castlereagh St, City (✆ 13 20 77)

This is the flag ship of the state run, official tourist body, Tourism New South Wales, where very helpful staff can recommend, find and book accommodation. They can also provide masses of information on all sorts of tourism related topics.

Youth Hostels Association Membership & Travel Centre

422 Kent St, City (✆ 9261 1111; fax 9261 1969)

Central bookings for Sydney and Australia (✆ 9267 3044).

BOUTIQUE HOTELS & GUESTHOUSES

Small hotels offer a kind of intimacy and connection to the city that enhance and become part of your stay, rather than simply performing a practical function. Sydney has many excellent small and charming establishments, a selection of which are listed below.

CENTRE

Harbour Rocks

34-52 Harrington St, The Rocks (✆ 9251 8944; fax 9251 8900). **Map Reference:** D4.

Rooms: 54. **Stars:** 3fi. **Rates:** **$$$$**. **Credit:** All. **Views:** Some rooms harbour views.

The Harbour Rocks is a small, friendly hotel which has been created within a heritage-listed one hundred year old building in the heart of The Rocks district. All rooms have their own bathrooms, tea and coffee making facilities, television and video. The hotel contains a bar and a restaurant.

The Lord Nelson Brewery Hotel

19 Kent St, The Rocks (✆ 9251 4044; fax 9251 1532). **Map Reference:** D3.

Rooms: 5. **Rates:** **$$$**. **Credit:** All. **Views:** The Rocks, Observatory Hill, Harbour Bridge.

At the quiet end of the historic Rocks area is one of Sydney's most loved and quiet brewery pubs, the oldest continually licensed hotel in Australia. Included in its beautiful, convict-built sandstone building are a bistro and five hotel rooms, decorated in colonial style. A stay here will impart the atmosphere of the city's early days with the comforts and convenience of the modern. The only draw back is that the bathrooms are across the passageway.

The Russell

143A George St, The Rocks (✆ 9241 3543; fax 9252 1652). **Map Reference:** D4.

Rooms: 29. **Rates:** **$$$**. **Credit:** All. **Views:** The Rocks, Opera House.

The Russell exudes charm, personality and friendliness right in the middle of the historic quarter. Although classified as a bed and breakfast, the suave Russell comprises twenty-nine prettily decorated rooms across three buildings and centred around the quaint, historic turreted and pointy roofed original building. The Russell's excellent restaurant, Boulders at The Rocks, roof garden and guests' sitting room with a bar, make this an extremely well appointed and popular place to stay.

NORTH

Cremorne Point Manor

6 Cremorne Rd, Cremorne (✆ 9953 7899; fax 9904 1265). **Map Reference:** B6.

Rooms: 30. **Rates:** **$$** (stays of 1 week pay 6 nights only). **Credit:** BC MC V. **Views:** The Harbour.

This recently refurbished federation mansion (c.1900) sits calmly above the Harbour's edge on Cremorne Point. From the nearby ferry jetty, it is a peaceful nine minute ride into the City. Close by are numerous harbourside walking tracks and the lush vegetation of the northern shore line. With cooking, laundry facilities and en suite bathrooms, this is affordable, convenient and atmospheric accommodation.

Kirribilli Court

45 Carabella St, Kirribilli (✆ 9955 4344). **Map Reference:** C5.

Rooms: 35. **Rates:** **$**; weekly rates available. **Credit:** AE MC V. **NSWTC**. **Views:** Some rooms harbour views.

Kirribilli is a friendly hotel located in a leafy residential street, close to the ferry jetty and from that point only a five minute journey to the City. An old, low house has been transformed and refurbished, with common facilities of coin laundry, kitchen, dining room, video and television room at the disposal of guests. Kirribilli Court is a good option for those looking for good value.

Neutral Bay Motor Lodge

45 Kurraba Rd, Neutral Bay (✆ 9953 4199). **Map Reference:** B5.

Rooms: 20. **Rates:** **$$** (weekly rates also). **Views:** Some rooms Harbour views.

Although it sounds like a highway horror, this is actually a rambling old house converted to hold twenty rooms, about half of which have their own bathrooms. A few rooms do have harbour views, and all are clean and equipped with television and refrigerator. With friendly staff too, the lodge is often full.

Periwinkle Manly Cove Guesthouse

18-19 East Esplanade, Manly 2095 (✆ 9977 4668; fax 9977 6308). **Map Reference:** 3km north of A11.

Rooms: 17. **Rates:** **$$$**. **Credit:** BC MC V. **Views:** Some rooms harbour views, some rooms courtyard outlook.

With high ceilings, brass beds, iron lace edged verandahs and glimpses of water views, this charming bed and breakfast welcomes guests to its federation style (c. 1895) and calm respite from the noisy city. Apart from a lounge room with an open fire and a leafy courtyard, the guesthouse offers 'help yourself' breakfasts of croissants, juices, coffee, tea and cereals from the well stocked pantry, eaten in the dining room overlooking Manly Cove, or in leafy courtyard. Over here at Manly, it's all beaches, water, Norfolk Pines and fresh air, although it is thirty minutes by ferry (or ten minutes by Jet Cat) to the City. Nevertheless, the quieter corners of Manly are lovely places to stay, and the Periwinkle is one of the best.

EAST

The Hughendon Boutique Hotel

14 Queen St, Woollahra (✆ 9363 4863; fax 9362 0398). **Map Reference:** H6.

Rooms: 37. **Stars:** 4. **Rates:** **$$$**. **Credit:** All.

Located in Sydney's premier antiques street, only fifty metres from Centennial Park and a two minute walk to Paddington, the city's cafe and gallery suburb, the Hughendon is a beautifully restored, charming mansion (c. 1876) run by a dedicated family team. The glass-enclosed terrace serves as a breakfast room and cafe serving excellent afternoon teas (Quaife's). The Hughendon is one of the most suave and atmospheric places to stay in Sydney.

L'Otel

114 Darlinghurst Rd, Darlinghurst (✆ 9360 6868; fax 9331 4536). **Map Reference:** F5.

Rooms: 16. **Rates:** **$$$**. **Credit:** All. **Views:** Darlinghurst streetscape.

L'Otel is a very "homey" hotel, offering reasonable rates despite the central location. All rooms have en suite bathrooms and full room facilities, French provincial furniture and friendly staff. Although the hotel does not have any fitness facilities, there are several gyms nearby. One factor to consider is that L'Otel is located on a busy street in the heart of the restaurant and cafe district, so those looking for quiet of a residential suburb should look elsewhere. Small standard rooms and larger suites are available.

Morgan's

304 Victoria St, Darlinghurst (✆ 9360 7955; fax 9360 9217). **Map Reference:** F5.

Rooms: 26. **Stars:** 4. **Rates: $$$. Credit:** All.

The accommodation at Morgan's includes studios and one bedroom apartments, all with kitchen and en suite, situated right on the "hip strip" of Victoria Street, Darlinghurst. While the outside noise level can be a problem, the street life, bars, cafes and restaurants are not. Morgan's restaurant is a popular spot with the city's residents. Striking, modern decor and a central location make this boutique hotel stand out.

Ravesi's on Bondi Beach

Cnr Campbell Parade and Hall St, Bondi Beach (✆ 9365 4422; fax 9365 1481). **Map Reference:** H10.

Rooms: 16. **Rates: $$$. Credit:** All. **Views:** Some rooms face Bondi Beach.

Located above Ravesi's restaurant, one of the area's favourites, are eleven rooms and five suites, all light and breezy, some with private terraces looking out over Sydney's most famous beach. Nearby are the many excellent restaurants and cafes of this active suburb, not to mention the beach.

Regents Court

18 Springfield Ave, Kings Cross (✆ 9358 1533; fax 9358 1833). **Map Reference:** F5.

Rooms: 30 studios. **Rates: $$$. Credit: Views:** Kings Cross, Potts Point.

Regents Court is a refurbished 1926 apartment building found in a leafy and quiet cul-de-sac and run by an extremely welcoming and hospitable family. Each studio has its own kitchen and a large bathroom, while a roof garden for the use of all guests is a considerable bonus. For an additional charge, guests can have a beautifully presented basket of breakfast provisions delivered with the morning paper. The owners will go to extreme lengths to make their patrons feel at home, even organising a lunch in the garden!

The Ritz Hotel

2 Oxford St, Woollahra (✆ 9331 2949; fax 9331 7657). **Map Reference:** H6.

Rooms: 7 rooms, 2 suites. **Rates: $$. Credit:** All. **Views:** Oxford Street or Woollahra.

Sitting on the corner of Jersey Road, the historic civic precinct of Paddington/Woollahra, and the quiet end of Oxford Street is the Art Deco Ritz Hotel, where seven rooms and two spacious corner suites, all decorated in Art Deco style and with balcony, await. The street level bar is very popular with the locals and hotel guests alike, while nearby are Centennial Park, all the cafes and shops of Oxford Street, and transport to the City and Bondi (ten minutes each).

The Savoy Hotel of Double Bay

41-45 Knox St, Double Bay (✆ 9326 1411; fax 9327 8464). **Map Reference:** F7.

Rooms: 34. **Rates: $$$. Credit:** All. **Views:** Double Bay streetscape.

This family run boutique hotel has quiet, comfortable rooms and suites, all with en suite and private facilities, television and air conditioning. Situated right in the middle of the Double Bay cafe and shopping precinct, it offers accommodation in a lovely residential area, full of charm and restaurants. From the front door, it is a two minute stroll from the Harbour and ferry jetty (ten minutes to the City), and five minutes by foot to Edgecliff train station.

Simpsons of Potts Point

8 Challis Ave, Potts Point (✆ 9356 2199; fax 9356 4476; Reservations: ✆ 008 090 600; fax 09-321 3271). **Map Reference:** E5.

Rooms: 14. **Rates: $$$$. NSWTC. Credit:** All.

Simpsons is located in a fully restored and refurbished, heritage listed 1892 mansion, offering elegance and charm in an old world setting. This is a luxurious boutique hotel in a leafy, quiet setting, featuring grand halls, stained glass, high ceilings and a conservatory. Close by are several of the city's best restaurants, and the City is only a five minute taxi ride away.

Sir Stamford Hotel

22 Knox St, Double Bay (✆ 9363 0100; fax 9327 3110). **Map Reference:** F7.

Rooms: 31 lofts; 32 Deluxe Queen & Parlour Queen rooms; 4 terrace suites; 4 Cosmo Executive suites; 1 Bellevue Suite. **Stars:** 4-41/2. **Rates: $$$$. NSWTC. Credit:** Amex BC D MC. **Views:** Double Bay rooftops and streetscape.

Here you will find all the exclusivity and luxury reminiscent of British private clubs. The rooms and suites are luxuriously fitted, some in New York loft style and some with four poster beds, but all exuding a characteristic European ambience. Some have glimpses over the roofs of the suburb to the Harbour while others offer views of the Double Bay streetscape. Facilities include a Roman style pool, spa and sauna, all of which are open twenty-four hours a day; a library with open fire and a cocktail lounge.

Trickett's Luxury Bed & Breakfast

270 Glebe Point Rd, Glebe (✆ 9552 1141; fax 9692 9462). **Map Reference:** F1.

Rooms: 7. **Rates: $$$. Credit:** none. **Views:** Leafy, heritage outlook.

If a home away from home in an historic mansion filled with antique fittings and furnishings and run by extremely friendly and welcoming owners, Trickett's is a very good choice. Comfortable and immaculately appointed lounges and a leafy outlook add to the considerable bonus of being in the middle of a residential area full of character, yet only ten minutes by bus or taxi from the City. Book early.

HOSTELS & BUDGET HOTELS

Victoria Street, Kings Cross is the city's backpacker epicentre where most budget travellers start looking for a bed. However, there are a number of other excellent budget and hostel options around Sydney. Almost none of the following will accept reservations, and 'check out or chuck out' time is usually around 9.30am, so this is the best time to start looking. Note that Australians may have difficulty getting a bed at some hostels, especially around Kings Cross, unless they can show their passport. Remember also that many of Sydney's pubs have inexpensive accommodation; these are listed in the chapter, Pubs.

CENTRE

Alfred Park Private Hotel

207 Cleveland St, City (✆ 9699 4031). **Map Reference:** H3.
Rooms: Dorms, doubles, singles and twins. **Rates:** $ (from $16; weekly rates available). **Credit:** V.
The Alfred Park offers friendly budget accommodation in an historic building, built in 1848 for a whaling captain and his fourteen children, and refurbished in 1993 to include a communal kitchen, sunroom, laundry, parking and thirty-five motel style rooms. Most have their own bathrooms, but all have television, refrigerator and bed linen. The hotel is kept very clean, and while close to transport, it is within reasonable walking distance of the City (south of Central Station).

EAST

Barncleuth House (The Pink House) Travellers Hostel

6 Barncleuth Sq, Kings Cross (✆ 9326 9675). **Map Reference:** F6.
Rooms: Doubles, twins and dorms. **Rates:** $ (from $14; weekly rates available). **Credit:** BC MC V.
Barncleuth House is a large Victorian mansion (around one hundred and forty years old) with leafy garden courtyards, open fires and modern bathroom and kitchen facilities, most recently refurbished between 1994 and 1995. Other facilities include televisions and videos, an outdoor barbecue, message, mail and fax services, and organised activities. A communal and friendly home-away-from-home atmosphere exists in this quiet location but just around the corner from all the action of Kings Cross. Good value food is also available.

Eva's Backpackers

6-8 Orwell St, Kings Cross (✆ 9358 2185). **Map Reference:** F5.
Rooms: 95 beds in dorms of 3-10 beds; doubles & twins. **Rates:** $ ($17-$40).
Credit: BC MC V.
Eva's is a luxurious, clean, family-run hostel offering good facilities. These include a large roof top garden (complete with barbecue and a great view), a fully equipped kitchen, laundry, booking service, safe, twenty-four hour access and fax. All linen is provided, and Eva's has a five star hostel rating from the NRMA.

Forbes Terrace

153 Forbes St, Woolloomooloo (✆ 9358 4327). **Map Reference:** E5.
Rooms: 80 beds in dorms of 4-6; 3 twins. **Rates:** $ ($17). **Credit:** None.
Forbes Terrace is found in a rambling, fully renovated terrace house, conveniently located between Kings Cross and the City. Facilities include a fully equipped kitchen, laundry, television and refridgerator in each room and twenty-four hour access. The hostel has a five star hostel rating from the NRMA.

Travellers' Rest

156 Victoria St, Kings Cross (✆ 9358 4606). **Map Reference:** F5.
Rooms: Dorms, singles, doubles and twins. **Rates:** $ (from $17; weekly rates available).
Credit: None.
This is one of the best run hostels amongst the Victoria Street cluster. The clean hostel offers rooms with televisions, refrigerators, free bed linen and a communal kitchen.

INNER WEST

Hereford Lodge YHA

51 Hereford St, Glebe (✆ 9660 5577). **Map Reference:** F1.
Beds: 2 & 6 bed dorms; single, double, triple and quad rooms. **Rates:** Dorms: $ (from $14); **Rooms: $$. Credit:** MC V.
Often cited as YHA's best Sydney hostel, Hereford Lodge offers the choice of small dorms or motel style rooms. All guests have the free use of a cafe, laundry, swimming pool and sauna, while the cinema, cafes and shops of this fascinating and leafy heritage-laden area are all at hand.

Sydney Glebe Point YHA

262-264 Glebe Point Rd, Glebe (✆ 9692 8418). **Map Reference:** F1.
Rooms: 2, 4 and 6 bed dorms. **Rates:** $ (from $14). **Credit:** BC MC V.
With small dorms and a leafy aspect, this is YHA's second best Sydney hostel. The office is open all day until 10pm.

Wattle House Hostel

44 Hereford St, Glebe (✆ 9692 0879). **Map Reference:** F1.

Rooms: 9 **Rooms:** 3 doubles/twins; 6 dorms. **Rates:** $ (from $18; weekly rates available). **Credit:** None.

This is a small, friendly, independent and well run hostel located in a charming, small house.

SOUTH EAST

Coogee Bay Backpackers

94 Beach St, Coogee (✆ 9315 8000). **Map Reference:** 3km south of H11.

Rooms: 160 beds in dorms of 4-8; 7 double rooms; 3 triple rooms. **Rates:** $ (from $16 in summer). **Credit:** None.

Located overlooking a cricket ground, only fifty metres from Coogee Beach and fifteen metres from McDonald's, back-packers will be forgiven for thinking they have found heaven at this hostel. Eighteen bathrooms, three kitchens and two television rooms add to the luxury.

FIVE STAR LUXURY HOTELS

ANA Hotel

176 Cumberland St, The Rocks (✆ 9250 6000; fax 9250 6250; reservations: 1800 801 080). **Map Reference:** D4.

Rooms: 390. **Rates: $$$$$. Credit:** All. **Views:** Darling Harbour, Harbour Bridge, Harbour, Opera House, City.

Located on the edge of The Rocks, the ANA is a grand hotel offering sweeping views of the Harbour Bridge and across Circular Quay to the Opera House. Enviable business facilities (including conference rooms and equipment) and a number of popular restaurants and bars, most notably the top floor Horizons Bar with floor to ceiling windows and breathtaking views, the ANA is full of action. A gym, indoor swimming pool and beauty services complete the package.

Observatory Hotel

89-113 Kent St, The Rocks (✆ 9256 2222; fax 9256 2233). **Map Reference:** D3.

Rooms: 96. **Rates: $$$$$. Credit: Views:** City, Western Harbour.

The Observatory is a very comfortable hotel, with plump, welcoming sofas strategically positioned amid warm lighting, a restaurant run by one of Sydney's most acclaimed chefs, and a magnificent indoor swimming pool domed by a celestial arrangement of stars echoing the hotel's location at the base of Observatory Hill. Other facilities include a fully equipped health club with spa, sauna, gym, float tanks and massages, and conference rooms.

Park Hyatt

7 Hickson Rd, The Rocks (✆ 9241 1234; fax 9252 2149). **Map Reference:** D4.

Rooms: 158 superior rooms and suites. **Rates: $$$$$. Credit:** All. **Views:** All rooms views of the Harbour and Opera House, most with private balconies.

The curvaceous, four storey high Park Hyatt hugs the Harbour shoreline opposite the Opera House and offers polished style and service in all respects. All rooms have stunning harbour views, and the hotel offers many peripheral services and facilities, including office services, fitness centre, sauna, roof terrace with pool and spa, several restaurants and bars.

Renaissance Sydney

30 Pitt St, City (✆ 9259 7000; reservations: 1800 222 431). **Map Reference:** D4.

Rooms:579 **Rates: $$$$$** (some **$$$$**). **Credit:** All. **Views:** City, Harbour, Harbour Bridge.

The Renaissance is located mid way between the finance precinct of the central business district and Circular Quay. With restaurants, bars, indoor and outdoor swimming pools, sauna and gym, this hotel offers luxury accommodation right in the middle of the city's action.

Regent Hotel

199 George St, City (✆ 9238 0000). **Map Reference:** D4.

Rooms: 600. **Rates: $$$$$. Credit:** All. **Views:** City, Harbour and Circular Quay.

Standing on the juncture between the city centre and The Rocks near Circular Quay, the Regent offers luxurious accommodation with fantastic views (depending on the room rate) with full facilities, including: health club, swimming pool, hair and beauty salons, and a number of lounges and restaurants.

Ritz Carlton Sydney

93 Macquarie St, City (✆ 9252 4600; fax 9252 4286). **Map Reference:** D4.

Rooms: 106. **Rates: $$$$$. Credit:** All. **Views:** Royal Botanic Gardens, Circular Quay, City depending on room type.

For evident opulence, the Ritz-Carlton is a knock out. Dripping with chandeliers, marble and dark, established club rooms and lounges, and located merely a short stroll from the Opera House, hotel guests can avail themselves of the swimming pool, fitness centre, or the bar and restaurant.

Sebel of Sydney

23 Elizabeth Bay Rd, Elizabeth Bay (✆ 9358 3244; Res: 1800 222 266). **Map Reference:** F6.

Rooms: 200 rooms and suites. **Rates: $$$$$. Credit:** All. **Views:**

The Sebel of Sydney is the well appointed and luxurious favoured haunt of rock stars and famous names from the arts, theatre and business. Overlooking tranquil Elizabeth Bay, facilities include a heated swimming pool, sundeck, sauna, gym, restaurant, function centre, complimentary parking, and a courtesy morning limousine to the City during the week.

Sheraton on the Park

161 Elizabeth St, City (✆ 9286 6000; fax 9286 66686; Res: ✆ 1800 073 535). **Map Reference:** F4. **Rooms:** 558 rooms & suites. **Rates:** **$$$$$**. **NSWTC**. **Credit:** All. **Views:** City, Hyde Park.

The Sheraton On The Park is a spacious, calm and eminently luxurious hotel which smoothly exudes established opulence. With full fitness facilities of a gym, pool, spa and sauna, comfortable, spacious rooms, several bars, lounges and restaurants, as well as a central city location, this is a great place to stay.

Sydney Marriott

36 College St, Sydney (✆ 9361 8400; fax 9361 8599; Res: ✆ 1800 02 5419). **Map Reference:** F4. **Rooms:** 198 rooms and suites. **Rates:** **$$$$**. **Credit:** All. **Views:** City, Hyde Park.

Located between the City and the vibrant Darlinghurst/Paddington entertainment and cafe district with a leafy outlook, some of the Sydney Marriott's rooms feature kitchens. Other facilities include pool, spa, sauna, gym, restaurant, bar, cafe, business centre, function room and complimentary parking.

SERVICED APARTMENTS

Serviced Apartments offer independent accommodation without the drawbacks of housekeeping. This is a popular option with visitors to Sydney, as the kitchens particularly allow guests to cook up fresh produce from the fish markets and be easily able to wash beachy clothes!

Medina Serviced Apartments

Central Bookings: (✆ free call 008 808 453).

Surry Hills: 359 Crown St (✆ 9360 6666, fax 9361 5965). **Map Reference:** G4. **Rooms:** 85 1 & 2 bedroom apartments. **Stars:** 5. **Rates:** **$$$$**. **Credit:** All. **Views:** Surry Hills streetscape.

Double Bay: 34 Ocean Ave (✆ 9361 9000; fax 9361 5965). **Map Reference:** F7. **Rooms:** 10 studios & 2 bedroom apartments. **Stars:** 4. **Rates:** **$$$$**. **Credit:** All. **Views:** Residential streetscape.

Paddington: 400 Glenmore Rd (✆ 9361 9000, fax 9332 3484). **Map Reference:** G6. **Rooms:** Studios, 1, 2 & 3 bedroom apartments. **Stars:** 4. **Rates:** **$$$**. **Credit:** All.

Elizabeth Bay: 68-70 Roslyn Gardens (✆ 9356 7400; fax 9357 2505). **Map Reference:** F6. **Rooms:** 58 studios. **Stars:** 3. **Rates:** **$$$**. **Credit:** All.

Also at Randwick: 63-65 St Marks Rd (✆ 9399 5144, fax 9398 4569) and Crows Nest: 167 Willoughby Rd (✆ 9430 1400).

The apartments of Medina on Crown are often referred to as being among Sydney's most luxurious and best equipped serviced apartments. This is hard to refute considering that each apartment is equipped with CD players, kitchens and balconies. Guests are also able to charge meals at nearby restaurants (of which there are many) back to their room. However, all of the Medina apartments (one, two and three bedrooms) offer comfortable accommodation in good areas.

Quay West

98 Gloucester St, City (✆ 9240 6000; fax 9240 6060). **Map Reference:** D4.

Rooms: 115: 1, 2 or 3 bedroom apartments. **Rates:** **$$$$$**. **Credit:** All. **Views:** Harbour or city.

Designed to provide a more independent alternative to five star hotel accommodation, each apartment features panoramic views of the Harbour, detailed furnishings, video, stereo, compact discs, a fully equipped kitchen, laundry and a big bathroom. Located at the junction of Circular Quay, the city centre and The Rocks, common facilities include a recreation deck and an amazing tiled, vaulted and pillared indoor pool looking directly onto the Harbour.

Savoy Serviced Apartments

Cnr King St & Kent St, City (✆ 9267 9211; fax 9262 2023). **Map Reference:** E4.

Rooms: 70 1 bedroom apartments. **Rates:** **$$$**. **Credit:** All. **Views:** City

These serviced apartment offer twin or double bedrooms, separate lounge/dining area, fully equipped kitchens and laundries.

The Stafford

75 Harrington St, The Rocks (✆ 9251 6711; fax 9251 3458). **Map Reference:** D4.

Rooms: 54 studios, 1 penthouse, 7 terrace houses. **Rates:** **$$$$** (weekly rates and longer term rates on application).

The Stafford is a varied collection of seven charming, fully restored and renovated two storey, one bedroom terrace houses (c.1870-1895), modern studios and one bedroom apartments in the heart of the historic Rocks district. Most apartments have balconies offering views across the Rocks rooftops to the Harbour, Circular Quay and the Opera House. The Stafford offers a great and extremely comfortable accommodation alternative. Facilities include security parking, sauna, spa, pool, gym, business facilities, fully equipped kitchens and a laundry.

The York

5 York St, City (✆ 9210 5000). **Map Reference:** E4. **Rooms:** 130. **Rates:** **$$$$**. **Credit:** All. **Views:** City and Darling Harbour.

The apartments in this twenty-eight storey building are all entitled to room service, porters, cleaning and laundry, and use of the restaurant, cocktail bar, pool, spa and sauna. Located in the heart of the City, the York is a convenient and comfortable establishment.

FOOD DIRECTORY

Following are the names only of restaurants and cafes included in the FOOD chapter, organised by cuisine. If you are looking for a particular type of food or eatery, whether it be a water view, a breakfast spot or Indian, use this directory. C, N, S, E and W denote City, North, South, East and West, and correspond with the listings in the Food chapter.

African
Fez (E)
Cafe Cairo (N)
Radio Cairo (N)

Australian
Edna's Table (C)
Kingsley's, City (C)
Riberries Taste Australia (E)

Bistro
Armstrong's (N)
Armstrong's At Manly (N)
Atlas Bar & Bistro (E)
Bistro Moncur, (E)
Dendy Bar & Bistro, City (C)
Fare Go Gourmet (N)
Macleay Street Bistro (E)
391 Restaurant (S)

Brasserie
Bayswater Brasserie, (E)
Mesclun Brasserie, (E)

Breakfasts & Brunches
Bathers Pavilion Refreshment Room (N)
Bayswater Brasserie (E)
Bill's (E)
Bistro Moncur (E)
Cafe Crown (E)
Cafe Niki (Cafes: E)
Centennial Park Cafe (Cafes: E)
Chester's Cafe in the Tin Shed(Cafes: W)
Dov (E)
Fez (E)
La Passion du Fruit (E)
Mohr Fish (E)
Ravesi's (E)
Sean's Panaroma (E)

Cafe
Bar Italia (W)
Bill's (E)
Black Wattle Canteen (W)
Brazil Cafe (N)
Cafe Crown (E)
Cafe Divino (E)
Cafe Niki (E)
Caffe Italia (W)
Centennial Park (E)
Dov (E)
Fez (E)
Golden Dog (E)
Jackie's (E)
La Passion du Fruit (E)
MCA (C)
Paradiso (C)
Picnic Cafe (E)
Rustic Cafe (E)
Sean's Panaroma (E)
Speedos (E)

Cambodian
Camira (W)

Chinese
Choyan (N)
East Ocean (C)
Emporer's Garden BBQ and Noodle (C)
Fu-Manchu (E)
Golden Century (C)
Regal (C)
Tang Dynasty (S)

Desserts
Bayswater Brasserie (E)
Little West (E)
Morgans (E)

European
Dov (E)

French
Bistro Moncur (E)
Claude's (E)
Merrony's (C)
Peninsula Bistro (W)
Tetsuya's (W)

Greek
Cosmos (E)
Niki (E)
Perama (S)

Indian
Cinema Cinema (N)
Flavour of India (E)
Oh! Calcutta! (E)

Italian
Buon Ricordo (E)
Castel Mola (W)
Frattini (W)
Gastronomia Chianti (E)
La Bussola (E)
Mario's (E)
Nielsen Park Kiosk (E)
Restaurant Manfredi (W)
Thirty Something (C)

Japanese
Edosei (E)
Haradokei (E)
Jiyu No Omise (W)
Tetsuya's (W)
Yutaka (E)

Kosher
Aviv (E)

Lebanese
Criterion (C)

Mediterranean
Fez (E)
Golden Dog (E)
Rustic Cafe (E)
The Pig and the Olive (E)

Modern Australian
Atlas (E)
Bathers Pavilion (N)
Bayswater Brasserie (E)
Bilson's (C)
Bistro Moncur (E)
Botanical Gardens (C)
Bouillon (C)
Brasserie Cassis (C)
Cafe Crown(E)
Cassis (C)
Catalina (E)
Centennial Park Cafe (E)
Cicada (E)
Clareville Kiosk (N)
Cosmos (E)
Darling Mills (W)
Fish Tank (W)
Golden Dog (E)
Gourmet Pizza Kitchen (N,E)
Le Kiosk (N)
Level 41 (C)
Macleay St Bistro (E)
MCA Cafe (C)
Merrony's (C)
Mesclun Brasserie (E)
Moran's (E)
Onzain (E)
Palisade (C)
Paramount (E)
Ravesi's (E)
Rockpool (C)
Sean's Panaroma (E)
Tabac (E)
Taylor Square Restaurant (E)
The Wharf Restaurant (C)

Noodles
Fu-Manchu (E)
Noodle King (E)
Wockpool (E)
Sailors Thai (C)

Pizza
The Edge (E)
Gourmet Pizza Kitchen (N,E)
La Bussola (E)
Pig and the Olive (N,E)
Thirty Something (E)

Pubs
For pubs with great food, see chapter, Pubs.

Seafood
Bilson's (C)
Catalina (E)
Circular Quay Oyster Bar (C)
Costi's Fish Cafe (E)
Doyles on the Beach (E)
Fishface (W)
Fish Tank (W)
Golden Century (C)
Mohr Fish (E)
The Pier (E)
Rockpool (C)
Sydney Cove Oyster Bar (C)
Sydney Fish Markets (C)

South West American
Rattlesnake Grill (N)
Yipiyiyo (E)

Spanish
Asturiana (C)

Thai
Darley St Thai (E)
Sailors Thai (C)
Thai Pothong (W)
T.T.T.E. Sarn (C)

Vegetarian
Lauries (E)
Metro (E)
Note: most Sydney restaurants and cafes have vegetarian dishes.

Vietnamese
Bach Dang (W)
Bay Tinh (S)

Water Views
Bather's Pavilion (N)
Bilson's (C)
Clareville Kiosk (N)
Catalina (E)
Doyles (E)
Level 41 (C)
MCA Cafe (C)
Sydney Cove Oyster Bar (C)
The Wharf Restaurant (C)

SUBURB BY SUBURB DIRECTORIES

Use these directories if you are in a particular part of town and want to find somewhere to eat or drink nearby. Detailed reviews can be found by cross-referencing to the relevant chapters.

BALMAIN

Cafes

Chester's Cafe in the Tin Shed
Pelican's Fine Foods

Food

Jiyu No Omise
Peninsula Bistro
Tetsuya's

Pubs

The Bridge
The Exchange (Safari Bar)
The London
Rose, Shamrock & Thistle (Three Weeds)
Sackville Hotel

Shopping

Balmain Markets
Darling Street (books, clothing, second hand wares)

BONDI BEACH

Cafes

Gusto Deli
Lamrock Cafe
Jackies
Sean's Panaroma
Speedos
Sports Bar

Food

Aviv
Gourmet Pizza Kitchen
Onzain
Ravesi's
Sean's Panaroma

Pubs & Bars

Hotel Bondi
Ravesi's Hotel

Shopping

Campbell Parade (clothing, swimwear)

CHINATOWN

Cafes

The Chinese Garden Tea House (See: Open Air Sydney: Parks & Gardens)

Food

BBQ King
Emperor's Garden BBQ and Noodle Shop
Golden Century Seafood
Happy Chef Phnom Penh Noodle
Jing May Noodle Restaurant
Marigold
Regal
Superbowl
TTTE Sarn

Chinese Herbalists

Win Duc Chinese Herbal Co
Wing Chung Herbs and Food

Shopping

Burlington (Chinese supermarket)
Yat San Vegetable & Grocery Shop (Chinese supermarket)

CITY

Cafes

Armani Express
Bar Cupola
Illy Cafe
Jackie's
Museum of Sydney Cafe
Old Sydney Coffee Shop
Paradiso
The Wharf

Food

Asturiana
Bennelong
Bilson's
Botanic Gardens Restaurant
Bouillon
Brasserie Cassis
Criterion
Dendy Bar & Bistro
Edna's Table
Kingsley's
Level 41
MCA Cafe
Merrony's
Museum of Sydney Cafe
Palisade
Rockpool
Sailors Thai
Sydney Cove Oyster Bar
Thirty Something
TTTE Sarn
The Wharf Restaurant

Pubs & Bars

The Australian
Horizon Bar
Lord Nelson Hotel

The Mercantile
The Orient
The Observer
The Palisade
Forbes Hotel
Marble Bar

Shopping
Chifley Plaza (clothing & accessories)
MLC Centre (clothing)
Queen Victoria Building (clothing & accessories)
The Rocks (clothing, crafts, souvenirs)
Skygarden (clothing & accessories)
Strand Arcade (clothing & accessories)

DARLINGHURST & EAST SYDNEY

Cafes
Bill's
Cafe Divino
Coluzzi Bar
Dov
Fez
Le Petit Creme
Little West

Food
Atlas Bar and Bistro
Balkan Seafood
Cosmos
Dov
Fez
Fishface
Fu-Manchu
La Bussola
Lauries
Mario's Restaurant
Metro
Oh! Calcutta!
Riberries
Tabac
Taylor Square Restaurant
The Edge

Pubs & Bars
The Albury
Burdekin (Dug Out Bar)
Court House Hotel
The Oxford (Gilligans)

Shopping
Oxford St (clothing)

GLEBE

Cafes
Blackwattle Canteen
Glebe Coffee Roaster
Kafenío
Well-Connected Cafe

Food
Darling Mills

Pubs & Bars
The Friend in Hand
The Nag's Head

Shopping
Glebe Markets
Glebe Point Rd (clothing, music)

KINGS CROSS & POTTS POINT

Cafes
Box
La Buvette
Hernandez

Food
Bayswater Brasserie
Cicada
Darley Street Thai
Edosei
Macleay St Bistro
Mesclun Brasserie
Moran's
Paramount
Pig and the Olive
Wockpool

Pubs & Bars
King's Cross Hotel

Shopping
Kings Cross market

PADDINGTON/WOOLLAHRA

Cafes
Centennial Park Cafe
The Chocolate Factory
Golden Dog
New Edition Tea Rooms

Food
Bistro Moncur
Buon Ricordo
Claude's
Golden Dog
Vamps

Pubs & Bars
The Bellevue
The Four in Hand
Glenmore Hotel
The Grand National
The London Tavern
The Royal
Paddington Inn
The Wollahra Hotel

Shopping
Glenmore Rd (clothing, art)
Oxford St (clothing)
Paddington Bazaar (market)
Queen St (antiques)

THE ROCKS

Cafes
La Renaissance Patisserie
MCA Cafe

Restaurants
Rockpool
Sailor's Thai
The Wharf Restaurant

Pubs & Bars
The Australian
The Glenmore Hotel
Lord Nelson Hotel
The Mercantile
The Orient
The Observer

SURRY HILLS

Cafes
Café Crown
Cafe Niki
La Passion du Fruit
Rustic Cafe

Food
Cafe Niki
Costi's Fish Cafe
Gastronomia Chianti
Mohr Fish
Rustic Cafe
Yipiyiyo

Pubs & Bars
The Dolphin
The Elephant's Foot
The Forresters
Strawberry Hills

Shopping
Crown St (clothing)
Oxford St (clothing)

INDEX

Author, Tessa Mountstephens

A NOTE ABOUT THE AUTHOR

Tessa Mountstephens has lived in Sydney for over twenty-five years, and graduated from the University of Sydney with a Bachelor of Arts and a Bachelor of Laws. While studying and travelling extensively overseas and throughout Australia, she found herself at the mercy of many inadequate guidebooks. Regularly advising and guiding overseas and interstate visitors around Sydney, she found that they were in a similar situation, and set about creating a guide which would reveal the vibrancy of the real, living city as the locals know and love it.

Acknowledgments

The author and publisher wish to acknowledge:

Bruce Baskerville, A Wander Around Old Newtown (South Sydney Heritage Society, 1995), a walk led by the South Sydney Heritage Society as part of Heritage Week. The society can be contacted at PO Box 2011 Strawberry Hills NSW 2012.

Paddington Walk: Department of Environment and Planning 1988 with permission from Department of Urban Affairs and Planning.

Thanks

The HARK! Publications think-tank is:
Author & Photographer: Tessa Mountstephens
Author of the architectural notes: Kate Mountstephens, B. Sc., B. Arch (Hons)
Business advisors: Robin and Tony Mountstephens
Co-ordination and organisation advisor: Eike Fietz
Golfing advisor: Tony Mountstephens
Legal advisor: John Wenden, JB Meagher & De Coek
Designer: Bradley Seymour
Publicity & Marketing: Katarina Vidovic

All enquiries should be sent to HARK! Publications PO Box 211 St Ives NSW 2075 Australia

Tessa would like to thank the energetic team who fearlessly read, criticised and shaped various aspects of the guide, its contents and its author, in particular: the eminently patient and logistically supportive Robin and Tony Mountstephens; the author of the architectural notes, Kate Mountstephens; Eike Fietz; Katarina Vidovic; Mary Pethard and Ian Parkin; Franco and Cristina Toller; John and Janice Wenden; David Moorhouse; Edward Hunter; Heinz Schweers; and Shirley Yeung, many of whom can now dine and relax in peace after acting as faithfully reviewing their leisure activities from 1994 to 1996 bite by bite and blow by blow. Thank you to Sue Wagner for her invaluable suggestions and advice. Thanks also to John Evernden at the Access Committee of Sydney City Council. The author would also like to thank the College of Law for convincing her of the right career path to follow, MQO, Mick Morris, Henri Cartier Bresson, Alfred Brendel, Jordi Savall, Placido Domingo, Giacomo Puccini and Franz Schubert.

Look out for future HARK! Publications.

Wet Days

What is there to do in Sydney when it's raining, or you just don't feel like being a tourist? Here are some suggestions.

Auction Houses

The most centrally located auction houses are Lawsons and Gavin Hardy. Here you can watch or take part in the cut and thrust of the sometimes ugly world of the auction, where a motley assortment of dodgy-looking ladies and gentlemen fight to the bitter end for anything from that must have five-piece bedroom suite to a collection of garden gnomes.

Lawsons

212 Cumberland St, St (✆ 9241 3411)

Gavin Hardy Auctions

57a Hereford St, Glebe (✆ 9552 2511).

For information and details of up-coming auctions, consult the Sydney Morning Herald's Saturday editions (See:Media).

Law Courts

There are several sets of law courts in central Sydney, and for real life theatre, they are hard to beat. In most, visitors may come and go as they please, but respect must be paid to the Magistrate or Justice presiding by making a small bow on entering and leaving the court, not talking and not eating. The courts sit all year except over Christmas and early January, and are open Monday to Friday, various hours.

The Supreme Court Of New South Wales

Queen's Square, City (✆ 9230 8111)

The information desk on the ground floor will advise which cases are being heard where, although be warned: spectators are more than likely to happen upon hard-to-decipher appeal cases here.

Downing Centre

Cnr Elizabeth St & Liverpool St, City (✆ 9287 7581)

The courts of the Downing Centre hear anything from fascinating criminal matters to simple traffic offences and bail applications, so this is the place to come for variety.

Parliament Of New South Wales

Parliament House, Macquarie St, City (✆ 9230 2111)

Open: Mon-Fri 9.30am-4.30pm. Parliament sits in three week blocks throughout the year.

At the parliament of New South Wales, visitors lucky enough to happen upon a session can listen to the politicians of this State arguing. The security personnel at the front desk will point you in the right direction.At other times, visitors are welcome to investigate the hallowed halls of one of Sydney's most historically important buildings. (See: Walks Around Sydney: Macquarie Street.

Libraries

Visit the State Library in Macqaurie Street and investigate the reading room, collections of newspapers and magazines, reference books, free movies and image banks. Other popular libraries around the city include the University Of Sydney's mighty Fisher Library, the largest book stack in the Southern Hemisphere.

Cafes

Do as the locals do: read a magazine or catch up on correspondence while listening to cool music, drinking coffee and eating cake in a cafe, such as Paddington's Chocolate Factory. For full details and more suggestions, **See:** Cafes.

Swimming

If it's wet anyway, why not go swimming. Any of the pools listed in the Sports chapter would do, but North Sydney Olympic Pool offers a view of the Harbour Bridge and Opera House.

Window Shopping

The arcades and inter-connecting shopping complexes of the City mean that pedestrians can do the rounds of Sydney's major retail precinct without getting wet. Paddington's bookshops and boutiques offer a long line of windows to admire (**See:** Shopping). Otherwise, extend the concept and take an aimless ride up a train line. Try the North Shore Line as far as Gordon, and discover suburban Sydney from inside a CityRail train (**See:** Sydney By Area and Transport).

University

A tour of the noble halls of the University Of Sydney offers a fascinating insight into one of Sydney's most important institutions (See:Tours). After discovering the secret passages of the Quadrangle and the treasures of the university's museums, visitors might like to eavesdrop on a lecture. Most are large enough to be completely anonymous.

Sporty Things

Embark upon one of the walking routes (See:Walks Around Sydney), go jogging, in-line skating or horse riding in Centennial Park - it looks great in the rain as long as a long raincoat and umbrella are close at hand. A coffee or a snack in the central cafes the perfect way to dry off. For the spectator sportspeaople among us, joining a Sportspace Tour at the SCG and Football Stadium might do the job (**See:**Tours Around Sydney).